Lecture Notes in Computer Science 8548

Commenced Publication in 1973
Founding and Former Series Editors:
Gerhard Goos, Juris Hartmanis, and Jan van Leeuwen

Klaus Miesenberger Deborah Fels
Dominique Archambault Petr Peňáz
Wolfgang Zagler (Eds.)

Computers Helping People with Special Needs

14th International Conference, ICCHP 2014
Paris, France, July 9-11, 2014
Proceedings, Part II

Volume Editors

Klaus Miesenberger
Johannes Kepler University, Linz, Austria
E-mail: klaus.miesenberger@jku.at

Deborah Fels
Ryerson University, Toronto, ON, Canada
E-mail: dfels@ryerson.ca

Dominique Archambault
Université Paris 8 Vincennes-Saint-Denis, France
E-mail: dominique.archambault@univ-paris8.fr

Petr Peňáz
Masaryk University, Brno, Czech Republic
E-mail: penaz@fi.muni.cz

Wolfgang Zagler
Vienna University of Technology, Austria
E-mail: zw@fortec.tuwien.ac.at

ISSN 0302-9743 e-ISSN 1611-3349
ISBN 978-3-319-08598-2 e-ISBN 978-3-319-08599-9
DOI 10.1007/978-3-319-08599-9
Springer Cham Heidelberg New York Dordrecht London

Library of Congress Control Number: 2014941710

LNCS Sublibrary: SL 3 – Information Systems and Application, incl. Internet/Web and HCI

Typesetting: Camera-ready by author, data conversion by Scientific Publishing Services, Chennai, India

Printed on acid-free paper

Springer is part of Springer Science+Business Media (www.springer.com)

Preface

Welcome to the ICCHP 2014 Proceedings!

Twenty-five years ago, after an intense state-of-the-art analysis, a group of computer science experts from the Austrian Computer Society, led by Prof. Roland Wagner and Prof. A Min Tjoa, started this conference. ICCHP is proud of this history and to this day it provides one of the few comprehensive and complete collections of scientific work in the field of assistive technologies (AT) and eAccessibility. All 19 volumes of past proceedings, covering more than 2,200 reviewed articles,[1] are a unique source for learning and understanding the theoretical, methodological, and pragmatic specializations of our field. This collection of work, with its unique user focus, offers a significant body of evidence for the enormous but often neglected impact on usability for all users regardless of their abilities.

In 2014, the proceedings of the 14th conference are delivered to you as a compendium of new and exciting scholarly and practical work going on in our field. The Call for Papers received 362 submissions. Each submission was carefully reviewed by at least three members of the international Program Committee, comprising 136 experts from all over the world listed in these proceedings. The panel of 18 conference chairs analyzed the review results and prepared the final decisions. Based on this intense and careful analysis, ICCHP 2014 accepted 132 submissions as full papers (36%) and 55 (15%) as short papers. As evidenced by these data, the proceedings and the conference are based on a highly competitive process guaranteeing the scientific quality.

As in the past, we welcomed over 500 participants from more than 50 countries in Paris at Université Paris 8 – Vincennes-St. Denis. The modern campus and, in particular, the team of researchers and teachers running a master's program in assistive technologies and the experienced team of service provision for students with disabilities at the university guaranteed an accessible, inclusive, and enjoyable event.

The program covered a broad spectrum of users of AT as well as domains where eAccessibility must be implemented. The concept of organizing "Special Thematic Sessions" again helped to structure the proceedings and the program in order to support a deep focus on highly desirable selected topics in the field as well as to bring new and interesting topics to the attention of the research community. One particular emphasis of this year's conference was on inclusive

[1] Due to the increasing interest in ICCHP, the five conferences published their proceedings in two volumes.

education and was based on the co-operation with Masaryk University Brno in organizing one track under the umbrella of "Universal Learning Design." The second focus was given to media accessibility (television, video, and animated content) using the unique occasion of co-locating the Media4D conference. The ICCHP Roland Wagner Award, the European finals of the SS12 Coding Competition, the Young Researchers Consortium, the ICCHP Summer University on Math and Science, and a series of parallel workshops and meetings again made ICCHP a unique meeting place for promoting assistive technologies and eAccessibility.

ICCHP 2014 was proud to once again be held – after 2010 and 2012 – under the patronage of the United Nations Educational, Scientific and Cultural Organization (UNESCO).

We thank all those who helped in putting together ICCHP and thereby supporting the AT field and a better quality of life for people with disabilities. Special thanks go to all our supporters and sponsors, displayed at: http://www.icchp.org/sponsors.

July 2014

Klaus Miesenberger
Deborah Fels
Dominique Archambault
Petr Peňáz
Wolfgang Zagler

Organization

ICCHP 2014 General Chair

Fels, Deborah	Ryerson University, Canada

Program Chairs

Fitzpatrick, D.	Dublin City University, Ireland
Manduchi, R.	University of California at Santa Cruz, USA
Ramesh S.K.	CSUN, USA
Watanabe, T.	University of Niigata, Japan
Weber, G.	Technische Universität Dresden, Germany

Program and Publishing Chairs

Archambault, D.	Université Paris 8, France
Miesenberger, K.	University of Linz, Austria
Peňáz, P.	Masaryk University Brno, Czech Republic
Zagler, W.	Vienna University of Technology, Austria

Young Researchers Consortium Chairs

Fels, D.	Ryerson-University, Canada
Fitzpatrick, D.	Dublin City University, Ireland
Gelderblom, G.-J.	Zuyd University, The Netherlands
Kobayashi, M.	Tsukuba University of Technology, Japan
Lam, S.	Project:Possibility, USA
Mihailidis, A.	University of Toronto, Canada
Morandell, M.	Austrian Institute of Technology, Austria
Pontelli, E.	New Mexico State University, USA
Prazak-Aram, B.	Austrian Institute of Technology, Austria
Weber, G.	Technische Universität Dresden, Germany
Zimmermann, G.	Stuttgart Media University, Germany

Workshop Program Chairs

Petz, A.	University of Linz, Austria
Pühretmair, F.	KI-I, Austria

International Program Committee

Abascal, J	Euskal Herriko Unibertsitatea, Spain
Abbott, C.	King's College London, UK
Abou-Zahra, S.	W3C Web Accessibility Initiative (WAI), Austria
Abu Doush, I.	Yarmouk University, Jordan
Abu-Ali, A.	Philadelphia University, Jordan
Andrich, R.	Polo Tecnologico Fondazione, Italy
Arató, A.	KFKI-RMKI, Hungary
Azevedo, L.	Instituto Superior Tecnico, Portugal
Banes	Qatar Assistive Technology Center, Qatar
Batusic, M.	Fabasoft, Austria
Bernareggi, C.	Università degli Studi di Milano, Italy
Bosse, I.	Technische Universität Dortmund, Germany
Bu, J.	Zhejiang University, China
Bühler, C.	TU Dortmund University, FTB, Germany
Chorbev, I.	Ss. Cyrill and Methodius University in Skopje, Macedonia
Christensen, L.B.	Sensus, Denmark
Chutimaskul, W.	University of Technology Thonburi, Thailand
Conway, V.	Edith Cowan University, Australia
Coughlan. J.	Smith-Kettlewell Eye Research Institute, USA
Craddock, G.	Centre for Excellence in Universal Design, Ireland
Crombie, D.	Utrecht School of the Arts, The Netherlands
Cudd, P.	University of Sheffield, UK
Cummins Prager, M.	California State University Northridge, USA
Darvishy, A.	Zürcher Hochschule für Angewandte Wissenschaften, Switzerland
Darzentas, J.	University of the Aegean, Greece
Debeljak, M.	University of Ljubljana, Slovenia
DeRuyter, F.	Duke University Medical Centre, USA
Diaz del Campo, R.	Antarq Tecnosoluciones, Mexico
Dupire, J.	CNAM, France
Emiliani, P.L.	Institute of Applied Physics "Nello Carrara", Italy
Engelen, J.	Katholieke Universiteit Leuven, Belgium
Galinski, C.	InfoTerm, Austria
Gardner, J.	Oregon State University, USA
Hanson, V.	University of Dundee, UK
Holzinger, A.	Medical University of Graz, Austria
Hoogerwerf, E.-J.	AIAS Bologna, Italy
Inoue, T.	National Rehabilitation Center for Persons with Disabilities, Japan

Iversen, C.M.	U.S. Department of State, USA
Jaworek, G.	Karlsruhe Institute of Technology, Germany
Jemni, M.	University of Tunis, Tunisia
Kalinnikova, L.	Pomor State University, Russia
Koronios, A.	University of South Australia, Australia
Kouropetroglou, C.	ALTEC, Greece
Kouroupetroglou, G.	University of Athens Greece
Kremser, W.	OCG, HSM Austria
Lauruska, V.	Siauliai University, Lithuania
Leahy, D.	Trinity College Dublin, Ireland
Leblois, A.	G3ict, USA
Lopez-Krahé, J.	Université Paris 8, France
Magnussen, M.	Stockholm University, Sweden
Matausch, K.	KI-I, Austria
Mathiassen, N.-E.	Statped, Norway
Mayer, C.	Austrian Institute of Technology, Austria
McDonagh, D.	University of Illinois at Urbana-Champaign, USA
McMullin, B.	Dublin City University, Ireland
Mohamad, Y.	Fraunhofer Institute, Germany
Muratet, M.	INS HEA, France
Normie, L.	GeronTech, Israel
Nussbaum, G.	KI-I, Austria
O Connor	NCBI Centre For Inclusive Technology, Ireland
Ohnabe, H.	Niigata University of Health and Welfare, Japan
Oku, H.	Kobe Gakuin University, Japan
Ono, T.	Tsukuba University of Technology, Japan
Paciello, M.	The Paciello Group, USA
Panek, P.	Vienna University of Technology, Austria
Petrie, H.	University of York, UK
Petz, A.	University of Linz, Austria
Rassmus-Groehn, K.	Lund University, Sweden
Rice, D.	National Disability Authority, Ireland
Sanchez, J.	University of Chile, Chile
Sax, C.	San Diego State University, USA
Sik Lányi, C.	University of Pannonia, Hungary
Simsik, D.	University of Kosice, Slovakia
Sloan, D.	The Paciello Group, UK
Snaprud, M.	University of Agder, Norway
Stephanidis, C.	University of Crete, FORTH-ICS, Greece
Stiefelhagen, R.	Karlsruhe Institute of Technology, Germany
Stoeger, B.	University of Linz, Austria
Suweda, O.	The Hyogo Institute of Assistive Technology, Japan

Svensson, H.	National Agency for Special Needs Education and Schools, Sweden
Takagi, H.	IBM, Japan
Takahashi, Y.	Toyo University, Japan
Tauber, M.	University of Paderborn, Germany
Teshima, Y.	Chiba Institute of Technology, Japan
Traunmüller, R.	University of Linz, Austria
Trehin, P.	World Autism Organization, France
Truck, I.	Université Paris 8, France
Uzan, G.	Université Paris 8, France
Velasco, C.A.	Fraunhofer Institute, Germany
Velleman, E.	Bartimeus, The Netherlands
Vigo, M.	University of Manchester, UK
Vigouroux, N.	IRIT Toulouse, France
Vlachogiannis, E.	Fraunhofer Institute, Germany
Votis, K.	CERTH/ITI, Greece
Wagner, G.	Upper Austria University of Applied Sciences, Austria
Weber, H.	ITA, University of Kaiserslautern, Germany
Weisman, J.	Rehab Technology Service, USA
Wöß, W.	University of Linz, Austria
Yamaguchi, K.	Nihon University, Japan
Yeliz Yesilada	Middle East Technical University, Cyprus
Zangla, K.	University of New Orleans, USA
Zetterstrom, E.	Qatar Assistive Technology Center, Qatar

Organizing Committee

Austrian Computer Society, Vienna, Austria
Göbl, R. (President)
Bieber, R. (CEO)
Kremser, W. (Working Group ICT with/for People with Disabilities)

Institute Integriert Studieren, Johannes Kepler University of Linz, Linz, Austria:
Feichtenschlager, P.
Heumader, P.
Koutny, R.
Miesenberger, K.
Murillo Morales, T.
Petz, A.
Pölzer, S.
Radu, N.
Schult, Ch.
Wagner R.

Masaryk University Brno, Brno, Czech Republic (ULD):
Peňáz, P.
Damm, Ch.

Université Paris 8 – Vincennes - St. Denis, Paris, France:
Archambault, D.
Dupire, J.
Muratet, M.
Parvanova, E.
Truck, I.
Uzan, G.

ICCHP Roland Wagner Award

We thank the Austrian Computer Society for announcing and sponsoring the Roland Wagner Award on Computers Helping People with Special Needs.

The Austrian Computer Society decided in September 2001 to endow this award in honor of Prof. Dr. Roland Wagner, the founder of ICCHP.

The Roland Wagner Award is a biannual award in the range of € 3,000. It is handed over at the occasion of ICCHP conferences.

Award Winners

- Award 0: Prof. Dr. Roland Wagner on the occasion of his 50th birthday, 2001
- Award 1: WAI-W3C, ICCHP 2002 in Linz
- Award 2: Paul Blenkhorn, University of Manchester, ICCHP 2004 in Paris
- Award 3: Larry Scadden, National Science Foundation, ICCHP 2006 in Linz
- Award 4: George Kersher, Daisy Consortium, ICCHP 2008 in Linz
- Award 5: ICCHP 2010 in Vienna
  - Harry Murphy, Founder, Former Director and Member Advisory Board of the Centre on Disabilities USA and
  - Joachim Klaus, Founder, Former Director of the Study Centre for Blind and Partially Sighted Students at the Karlsruhe Institute of Technology, Germany
- Award 6: The TRACE Centre of the University Wisconsin-Madison, ICCHP 2012 in Linz

Table of Contents – Part II

Tactile Graphics and Models for Blind People and Recognition of Shapes by Touch

Towards Automatically Generated Tactile Detail Maps by 3D Printers for Blind Persons 1
Timo Götzelmann and Aleksander Pavkovic

Opportunities and Limitations of Haptic Technologies for Non-visual Access to 2D and 3D Graphics 8
Helen Sullivan, Shrirang Sahasrabudhe, Jukka Liimatainen, and Markku Hakkinen

Do Blind Subjects Differ from Sighted Subjects When Exploring Virtual Tactile Maps? 12
Mariacarla Memeo, Claudio Campus, and Luca Brayda

Development of Synchronized CUI and GUI for Universal Design Tactile Graphics Production System BPLOT3 18
Mamoru Fujiyoshi, Akio Fujiyoshi, Akiko Osawa, Yusuke Kuroda, and Yuta Sasaki

Production of Accessible Tactile Graphics 26
Denise Prescher, Jens Bornschein, and Gerhard Weber

Edutactile - A Tool for Rapid Generation of Accurate Guideline-Compliant Tactile Graphics for Science and Mathematics 34
Mrinal Mech, Kunal Kwatra, Supriya Das, Piyush Chanana, Rohan Paul, and M. Balakrishnan

Mobility Support and Accessible Tourism

Tactile Map Automated Creation System Using OpenStreetMap 42
Tetsuya Watanabe, Toshimitsu Yamaguchi, Satoko Koda, and Kazunori Minatani

Narrative Map Augmentation with Automated Landmark Extraction and Path Inference 50
Vladimir Kulyukin and Thimma Reddy

The Mobile Travel Assistance System NAMO with Way-Finding Support in Public Transport Environments 54
Christian Bühler, Helmut Heck, Annika Nietzio, and Frank Reins

A Mobile Guidance Platform for Public Transportation 58
Reinhard Koutny, Peter Heumader, and Klaus Miesenberger

FB-Finger: Development of a Novel Electric Travel Aid with a Unique Haptic Interface 65
Kiyohide Ito, Yoshiharu Fujimoto, Ryoko Otsuki, Yuka Niiyama, Akihiro Masatani, Takanori Komatsu, Junichi Akita, Tetsuo Ono, and Makoto Okamoto

Open Accessibility Data Interlinking 73
Chaohai Ding, Mike Wald, and Gary Wills

Pre-journey Visualization of Travel Routes for the Blind on Refreshable Interactive Tactile Displays 81
Mihail Ivanchev, Francis Zinke, and Ulrike Lucke

Road Information Collection and Sharing System Based on Social Framework 89
Takatoshi Suenaga

Waypoint Validation Strategies in Assisted Navigation for Visually Impaired Pedestrian 92
Slim Kammoun, Marc J-M. Macé, and Christophe Jouffrais

ARGUS Autonomous Navigation System for People with Visual Impairments 100
Eduardo Carrasco, Estíbaliz Loyo, Oihana Otaegui, Claudia Fösleitner, Markus Dubielzig, Rafael Olmedo, Wolfgang Wasserburger, and John Spiller

A University Indoors Audio-Tactile Mobility Aid for Individuals with Blindness 108
Konstantinos Papadopoulos, Marialena Barouti, and Konstantinos Charitakis

An OpenStreetMap Editing Interface for Visually Impaired Users Based on Geo-semantic Information 116
Ahmed El-Safty, Bernhard Schmitz, and Thomas Ertl

Individualized Route Planning and Guidance Based on Map Content Transformations 120
Bernhard Schmitz and Thomas Ertl

Cognitive Evaluation of Haptic and Audio Feedback in Short Range Navigation Tasks 128
Manuel Martinez, Angela Constantinescu, Boris Schauerte, Daniel Koester, and Rainer Stiefelhagen

Smart and Assistive Environments: Ambient Assisted Living (AAL)

Unlocking Physical World Accessibility through ICT: A SWOT Analysis 136
Christophe Ponsard and Vincent Snoeck

Personalized Smart Environments to Increase Inclusion of People with Down's Syndrome: Results of the Requirement Analysis 144
Eva Schulze and Anna Zirk

ELDERS-UP!: Adaptive System for Enabling the Elderly Collaborative Knowledge Transference to Small Companies 148
Salvador Rivas Gil and Víctor Sánchez Martín

An Interactive Robotic System for Human Assistance in Domestic Environments 152
Manuel Vinagre, Joan Aranda, and Alicia Casals

RGB-D Video Monitoring System to Assess the Dementia Disease State Based on Recurrent Neural Networks with Parametric Bias Action Recognition and DAFS Index Evaluation 156
Sabrina Iarlori, Francesco Ferracuti, Andrea Giantomassi, and Sauro Longhi

Experiences and Challenges in Designing Non-traditional Interfaces to Enhance the Everyday Life of Children with Intellectual Disabilities 164
Janio Jadán-Guerrero and Luis A. Guerrero

Implementation of Applications in an Ambient Intelligence Environment: A Structured Approach 172
Laura Burzagli and Pier Luigi Emiliani

Text Entry for Accessible Computing

Applying Small-Keyboard Computer Control to the Real World 180
Torsten Felzer, I. Scott MacKenzie, and Stephan Rinderknecht

Design and Evaluation of Multi-function Scanning System: A Case Study 188
Frédéric Vella, Damien Sauzin, Frédéric Philippe Truillet, and Nadine Vigouroux

Semantic Keyboard: Fast Movements between Keys of a Soft Keyboard 195
Mathieu Raynal, I. Scott MacKenzie, and Bruno Merlin

The Application of Computerized Chinese Handwriting Assessment Tool to Children with Cerebral Palsy 203
Hui-Shan Lo, Chia-Ling Chen, Hsieh-Ching Chen, I-hsuan Shen, and Cecilia W.P. Li-Tzang

EyeSchool: An Educational Assistive Technology for People with Disabilities - Passing from Single Actors to Multiple-Actor Environment 210
Cristina Popescu, Nadine Vigouroux, Mathieu Muratet, Julie Guillot, Petra Vlad, Frédéric Vella, Jawad Hajjam, Sylvie Ervé, Nathalie Louis, Julie Brin, Joseph Colineau, Thierry Hobé, and Loïc Brimant

People with Motor and Mobility Disabilities: AT and Accessibility

Accessible 4D-Joystick for Remote Controlled Models 218
David Thaller, Gerhard Nussbaum, and Stefan Parker

Development of a Personal Mobility Vehicle to Improve the Quality of Life 226
Yoshiyuki Takahashi and Masamichi Miura

Automated Configuration of Applications for People with Specific Needs 234
Peter Heumader, Reinhard Koutny, Klaus Miesenberger, and Karl Kaser

Visualizing Motion History for Investigating the Voluntary Movement and Cognition of People with Severe and Multiple Disabilities 238
Mamoru Iwabuchi, Guang Yang, Kimihiko Taniguchi, Syoudai Sano, Takamitsu Aoki, and Kenryu Nakamura

A Virtual Reality Training System for Helping Disabled Children to Acquire Skills in Activities of Daily Living 244
Kup-Sze Choi and King-Hung Lo

The Possibilities of Kinect as an Access Device for People with Cerebral Palsy: A Preliminary Study 252
Isabel María Gómez, Alberto Jesús Molina, Rafael Cabrera, David Valenzuela, and Marcelo Garrido

Development of Sit-to-Stand Support System Using Ground Reaction Force 256
Hidetaka Ikeuchi, Masuji Nagatoshi, and Atuyoshi Miura

Assistive Technology: Service and Practice

A Critical Review of Eight Years of Research on Technologies for Disabled and Older People 260
Helen Petrie, Blaíthín Gallagher, and Jenny S. Darzentas

User Evaluation of Technology Enhanced Interaction Framework 267
Kewalin Angkananon, Mike Wald, and Lester Gilbert

A Unified Semantic Framework for Detailed Description of Assistive Technologies Based on the EASTIN Taxonomy 275
Nikolaos Kaklanis, Konstantinos Votis, Konstantinos Giannoutakis, Dimitrios Tzovaras, Valerio Gower, and Renzo Andrich

Results from Using Automatic Speech Recognition in Cleft Speech Therapy with Children 283
Zachary Rubin, Sri Kurniawan, and Travis Tollefson

Do-It-Yourself (DIY) Assistive Technology: A Communication Board Case Study 287
Foad Hamidi, Melanie Baljko, Toni Kunic, and Ray Feraday

A Decision-Tree Approach for the Applicability of the Accessibility Standard EN 301 549 295
Loïc Martínez-Normand and Michael Pluke

ADAPTAEMPLEO: Interactive Advisor to Adapt Workplaces for Persons with Disabilities and Promote Employment in the Retail Sector 303
Alberto Ferreras, Andrés Soler, Rakel Poveda, Alfonso Oltra, Carlos García, Purificación Castelló, Juan-Manuel Belda-Lois, and José Crespo

ICT-Based Learning Technologies for Disabled and Non-disabled People

ICT-Based Learning Technologies for Disabled and Non-disabled People: Introduction to the Special Thematic Session 307
Marion Hersh

The Development of Training Modules on ICT to Support Disabled Lifelong Learners 311
Simon Ball

Evaluating ICT Based Learning Technologies for Disabled People 315
Marion Hersh

Supporting Senior Citizen Using Tablet Computers 323
Ingo Dahn, Peter Ferdinand, and Pablo Lachmann

Development of Multimodal Textbooks with Invisible 2-Dimensional Codes for Students with Print Disabilities 331
Akio Fujiyoshi, Mamoru Fujiyoshi, Akiko Ohsawa, and Yuko Ota

Universal Learning Design: Methodology

Towards a Methodology for Curriculum Development within an Accessible Virtual Campus 338
Hector R. Amado-Salvatierra, Rocael Hernández, Antonio García-Cabot, Eva García-López, Concha Batanero, and Salvador Otón

The Use of Assistive Technologies as Learning Technologies to Facilitate Flexible Learning in Higher Education 342
Michael Goldrick, Tanja Stevns, and Lars Ballieu Christensen

The Literacy of Integrating Assistive Technology into Classroom Instruction for Special Education Teachers in Taiwan 350
Ming-Chung Chen, Chi Nung Chu, and Chien-Chuan Ko

University Examination System for Students with Visual Impairments 358
Konstantinos Papadopoulos, Zisis Simaioforidis, Konstantinos Charitakis, and Marialena Barouti

"Planet School": Blended Learning for Inclusive Classrooms 366
Ingo Karl Bosse

Universal Learning Design: Hearing Impaired and Deaf People

Ensuring Sustainable Development of Simultaneous Online Transcription Services for People with Hearing Impairment in the Czech Republic 374
Zdenek Bumbalek and Jan Zelenka

User Interface Design of Sound Tactile 382
Tatsuya Honda and Makoto Okamoto

Enhancing Storytelling Ability with Virtual Environment among Deaf and Hard-of-Hearing Children 386
Sigal Eden and Sara Ingber

Teaching Morse Language to a Deaf-Blind Person for Reading and Writing SMS on an Ordinary Vibrating Smartphone 393
Andras Arato, Norbert Markus, and Zoltan Juhasz

Urgent Communication Method for Deaf, Language Dysfunction and Foreigners 397
Naotsune Hosono, Hiromitsu Inoue, Miwa Nakanishi, and Yutaka Tomita

Building an Application for Learning the Finger Alphabet of Swiss German Sign Language through Use of the Kinect 404
Phuoc Loc Nguyen, Vivienne Falk, and Sarah Ebling

TerpTube: A Signed Language Mentoring Management System 408
Deborah I. Fels, Daniel Roush, Paul Church, Martin Gerdzhev, Tara Stevens, and Ellen Hibbard

Collaborative Gaze Cues and Replay for Deaf and Hard of Hearing Students 415
Raja Kushalnagar and Poorna Kushalnagar

Universal Learning Design: Sign Language in Education

Toward a Reversed Dictionary of French Sign Language (FSL) on the Web 423
Mohammed Zbakh, Zehira Haddad, and Jaime Lopez Krahe

A Novel Approach for Translating English Statements to American Sign Language Gloss 431
Achraf Othman and Mohamed Jemni

Sign Language Transcription, Recognition and Generation

Hand Location Classification from 3D Signing Virtual Avatars Using Neural Networks 439
Kabil Jaballah and Mohamed Jemni

Towards a Phonological Construction of Classifier Handshapes in 3D Sign Language 446
Kabil Jaballah and Mohamed Jemni

Efficient Tracking Method to Make a Real Time Sign Language Recognition System 454
Maher Jebali, Patrice Dalle, and Mohamed Jemni

A Virtual Signer to Interpret SignWriting 458
Yosra Bouzid and Mohamed Jemni

A Multi-layer Model for Sign Language's Non-Manual Gestures Generation 466
Oussama El Ghoul and Mohamed Jemni

SIGN^{MOTION}: An Innovative Creation and Annotation Platform for Sign Language 3D-Content Corpora Building Relying on Low Cost Motion Sensors ... 474
Mehrez Boulares and Mohamed Jemni

Gestures in Sign Language: Animation and Generation in Real-Time ... 482
Nour Ben Yahia and Mohamed Jemni

Universal Learning Design: Accessibility and AT

Improving Accessibility of Lectures for Deaf and Hard-of-Hearing Students Using a Speech Recognition System and a Real-Time Collaborative Editor ... 490
Benoît Lathière and Dominique Archambault

Examining the Characteristics of Deaf and Hard of Hearing Users of Social Networking Sites ... 498
Ines Kožuh, Manfred Hintermair, and Matjaž Debevc

A Smart-Phone Based System to Detect Warning Sound for Hearing Impaired People ... 506
Koichiro Takeuchi, Tetsuya Matsumoto, Yoshinori Takeuchi, Hiroaki Kudo, and Noboru Ohnishi

A Support System for Teaching Practical Skills to Students with Hearing Impairment - SynchroniZed TAbletop Projection System: SZTAP ... 512
Takuya Suzuki and Makoto Kobayashi

Differentiation, Individualisation and Influencing Factors in ICT Assisted Learning for People with Special Needs

Differentiation, Individualization and Influencing Factors in ICT Assisted Learning for People with Special Needs: Introduction to the Special Thematic Session ... 516
Andreja Istenic Starcic

Learning Environments – Not Just Smart for Some! ... 520
Andreja Istenic Starcic and Sharon Kerr

Different ICT Competency but Similar Pattern between Students with/without Learning Disabilities? - Results from Structural Equation Modeling Testing ... 528
Ming-Chung Chen, Chen-Ming Chen, Ya-Ping Wu, Chien-Chuan Ko, and Yao-Ming Yeh

The Application of Computer-Based Chinese Handwriting Assessment System to Children with Dysgraphia ... 532
Ting-Fang Wu, Guey-Shya Chen, and Hui-Shan Lo

Developing Accessible Teaching and Learning Materials within a User Centred Design Framework

Developing Accessible Teaching and Learning Materials within a User Centred Design Framework: Introduction to the Special Thematic Session ... 540
E.A. Draffan

eBooks, Accessibility and the Catalysts for Culture Change ... 543
E.A. Draffan, Alistair McNaught, and Abi James

Electronic Braille Blocks: A Tangible Interface-Based Application for Teaching Braille Letter Recognition to Very Young Blind Children ... 551
Rabia Jafri

Fostering Better Deaf/Hearing Communication through a Novel Mobile App for Fingerspelling ... 559
Jorge Andres Toro, John C. McDonald, and Rosalee Wolfe

Developing a New Framework for Evaluating Arabic Dyslexia Training Tools ... 565
Fadwa AlRowais, Mike Wald, and Gary Wills

A Fully Accessible Arabic Learning Platform for Assisting Children with Intellectual Challenges ... 569
Moutaz Saleh and Jihad Mohamad Aljaam

Using Mobile Technologies to Support Individuals with Special Needs in Educational Environments

Using Mobile Technologies to Support Individuals with Special Needs in Educational Environments: Introduction to the Special Thematic Session ... 577
Linda Chmiliar

Learning with the iPad in Early Childhood ... 579
Linda Chmiliar

The Influence of Age and Device Orientation on the Performance of Touch Gestures ... 583
Linda Wulf, Markus Garschall, Michael Klein, and Manfred Tscheligi

A Tablet-Based Approach to Facilitate the Viewing of Classroom Lecture by Low Vision Students ... 591
Stephanie Ludi, Michael Timbrook, and Piper Chester

The iPad as a Mobile Learning Tool for Post-secondary Students with Disabilities 597
Linda Chmiliar and Carrie Anton

Author Index 601

Table of Contents – Part I

Accessible Media

Accessible Media: Introduction to the Special Thematic Session 1
Deborah I. Fels

The Case of LIA – Libri Italiani Accessibili 4
Cristina Mussinelli

Semi-automatic DVS Authoring Method 8
Inseon Jang, ChungHyun Ahn, and Younseon Jang

Gaps between the Expectations of People with Hearing Impairment toward Subtitles and the Current Conditions for Subtitle Creation in Japan 13
Sawako Nakajima, Naoyuki Okochi, Kazutaka Mitobe, and Tetsujiro Yamagami

Empowerment by Digital Media of People with Disabilities: Three Dimensions of Support 17
Christian Bühler and Bastian Pelka

Tactile Captions: Augmenting Visual Captions 25
Raja Kushalnagar, Vignesh Ramachandran, and Tae Oh

Captioning System with Function of Inserting Mathematical Formula Images 33
Yoshinori Takeuchi, Yuji Sato, Kazuki Horiike, Daisuke Wakatsuki, Hiroki Minagawa, and Noboru Ohnishi

Synote Second Screening: Using Mobile Devices for Video Annotation and Control 41
Mike Wald, Yunjia Li, George Cockshull, David Hulme, Douglas Moore, Aidan Purdy-Say, and James Robinson

Digital Content and Media Accessibility

Digital Content and Media Accessibility: Introduction to the Special Thematic Session 45
David Crombie and Pierre Mersch

A Comparison of the Listening Speed of the Korean TTS for the Blind: Based on Their Screen Reader Experiences 49
Heeyeon Lee, Yujin Jang, and Ki-Hyung Hong

Dynamic Subtitle Authoring Method Based on Audio Analysis for the Hearing Impaired 53
Wootaek Lim, Inseon Jang, and Chunghyun Ahn

Communicating Text Structure to Blind People with Text-to-Speech 61
Laurent Sorin, Julie Lemarié, Nathalie Aussenac-Gilles, Mustapha Mojahid, and Bernard Oriola

TTS-Based DAISY Content Creation System: Implementation and Evaluation of DaisyRings™ 69
Kosei Fume, Yuka Kuroda, Taira Ashikawa, Yoshiaki Mizuoka, and Masahiro Morita

Patterns of Blind Users' Hand Movements: The Case of Typographic Signals of Documents Rendered by Eight-Dot and Six-Dot Braille Code 77
Vassilios Argyropoulos, Georgios Kouroupetroglou, Aineias Martos, Magda Nikolaraizi, and Sofia Chamonikolaou

Dialogue-Based Information Retrieval from Images 85
Pavel Hamřík, Ivan Kopeček, Radek Ošlejšek, and Jaromír Plhák

25 Years of the Web: Weaving Accessibility

Annotation Tool for the Smart Web Accessibility Platform 93
Sébastien Aupetit and Vincent Rouillé

Iberoamerican Observatory of Web Accessibility: A Benchmarking and Educative Tool 101
Carlos Benavidez, Claudia Cardoso, Jorge Fernandes, Emmanuelle Gutiérrez y Restrepo, Henry Gutiérrez, and Loïc Martínez-Normand

Checking Web Accessibility with the Content Accessibility Checker (CAC) 109
Eduard Klein, Anton Bolfing, and Markus Riesch

AdaptNow – A Revamped Look for the Web: An Online Web Enhancement Tool for the Elderly 113
Roberto Dias and Sergi Bermúdez i Badia

Accessibility of E-Commerce Websites for Vision-Impaired Persons 121
Roopa Bose and Helmut Jürgensen

jCAPTCHA: Accessible Human Validation 129
Matthew Davidson, Karen Renaud, and Shujun Li

Benefits and Challenges of Combining Automated and User Testing to Enhance e-Accessibility – The European Internet Inclusion Initiative ... 137
Mikael Snaprud, Kamyar Rasta, Kim Andreasson, and Annika Nietzio

Accessibility of MOOCs ... 141
Marco Bohnsack and Steffen Puhl

A First Look into MOOCs Accessibility: The Case of Coursera ... 145
Najd A. Al-Mouh, Atheer S. Al-Khalifa, and Hend S. Al-Khalifa

How to Increase Contrast Using Color Inversion ... 153
Josef Köble

Towards e-inclusion for People with Intellectual Disabilities

Easy to Surf - What Makes Websites Accessible to People with Intellectual and Learning Disabilities ... 157
Gabriela Antener, Anton Bolfing, and Stefania Calabrese

"Easy-to-Read on the Web": State of the Art and Needed Research ... 161
Klaus Miesenberger and Andrea Petz

Testing the Perceived Ease of Use in Social Media: Acceptance Testing for People with Intellectual and Cognitive Disabilities ... 169
Julia George, Nils Dietzsch, Michael Bier, Hannes Zirpel, Alexander Perl, and Susanne Robra-Bissantz

People with Learning Disabilities Using the iPad as a Communication Tool - Conditions and Impact with Regard to e-inclusion ... 177
Cordula Edler and Matthias Rath

The Impact of PDF/UA on Accessible PDF

Implementing PDF/UA in Microsoft Word - How Can PDF/UA Become an Everyday Part of Document Authoring? ... 181
Roberto Bianchetti, Samuel Hofer, and Markus Erle

PAVE: A Web Application to Identify and Correct Accessibility Problems in PDF Documents ... 185
Luchin Doblies, David Stolz, Alireza Darvishy, and Hans-Peter Hutter

Correcting "Last Mile" Errors - Quality Assurance of PDF/UA Documents Without Being a Developer ... 193
Roberto Bianchetti, Samuel Hofer, and Markus Erle

PDF Accessibility Checker (PAC 2): The First Tool to Test PDF Documents for PDF/UA Compliance 197
Andreas Uebelbacher, Roberto Bianchetti, and Markus Riesch

A Strategic Approach to Document Accessibility: Integrating PDF/UA into Your Electronic Content 202
Adam Spencer and Karen McCall

Accessibility of Non-verbal Communication

Accessibility of Non-verbal Communication: Introduction to the Special Thematic Session 205
Andreas Kunz and Klaus Miesenberger

Multimodal Fusion and Fission within W3C Standards for Nonverbal Communication with Blind Persons 209
Dirk Schnelle-Walka, Stefan Radomski, and Max Mühlhäuser

A Mind Map for Brainstorming Sessions with Blind and Sighted Persons 214
Dirk Schnelle-Walka, Ali Alavi, Patrick Ostie, Max Mühlhäuser, and Andreas Kunz

Presenting Non-verbal Communication to Blind Users in Brainstorming Sessions 220
Stephan Pölzer and Klaus Miesenberger

Towards an Information State Update Model Approach for Nonverbal Communication 226
Dirk Schnelle-Walka, Stefan Radomski, Stephan Radeck-Arneth, and Max Mühlhäuser

Virtual Braille-Keyboard in Co-located Meetings 231
Emre Zaim, Markus Gruber, Gottfried Gaisbauer, Peter Heumader, Stephan Pölzer, and Klaus Miesenberger

Accessibility of Brainstorming Sessions for Blind People 237
Andreas Kunz, Klaus Miesenberger, Max Mühlhäuser, Ali Alavi, Stephan Pölzer, Daniel Pöll, Peter Heumader, and Dirk Schnelle-Walka

Emotions for Accessibility (E4A)

Emotions for Accessibility: Introduction to the Special Thematic Session 245
Yehya Mohamad

Detection and Utilization of Emotional State for Disabled Users 248
Yehya Mohamad, Dirk T. Hettich, Elaina Bolinger, Niels Birbaumer, Wolfgang Rosenstiel, Martin Bogdan, and Tamara Matuz

Influence of Emotions on Web Usability for Users with Motor Disorders 256
José Laparra-Hernández, Juan-Manuel Belda-Lois, Álvaro Page, and Alberto Ferreras Remesal

User Participation in the Design of an Alternative Communication System for Children with Diskinetic Cerebral Palsy Including Emotion Management 260
Juan-Manuel Belda-Lois, Amparo López-Vicente, José Laparra-Herrero, Rakel Poveda-Puente, and Alberto Ferreras-Remesal

Games and Entertainment Software: Accessibility and Therapy

Digital Video Games for Older Adults with Cognitive Impairment 264
Arlene Astell, Norman Alm, Richard Dye, Gary Gowans, Philip Vaughan, and Maggie Ellis

"Gardener" Serious Game for Stroke Patients 272
Ágnes Nyéki, Veronika Szucs, Péter Csuti, Ferenc Szabó, and Cecilia Sik Lanyi

Towards an Interactive Leisure Activity for People with PIMD 276
Robby van Delden, Dennis Reidsma, Wietske van Oorsouw, Ronald Poppe, Peter van der Vos, Andries Lohmeijer, Petri Embregts, Vanessa Evers, and Dirk Heylen

Blind Bowling Support System Which Detects a Number of Remaining Pins and a Ball Trajectory 283
Makoto Kobayashi

Interacting Game and Haptic System Based on Point-Based Approach for Assisting Patients after Stroke 289
Mario Covarrubias, Alessandro Mansutti, Monica Bordegoni, and Umberto Cugini

Exploring the Usage of 3D Virtual Worlds and Kinect Interaction in Exergames with Elderly 297
Hugo Paredes, Fernando Cassola, Leonel Morgado, Fausto de Carvalho, Silvia Ala, Francisco Cardoso, Benjamim Fonseca, and Paulo Martins

Games for Wireless Cubes in Cognitive Enhancement Therapy 301
Krzysztof Dobosz, Magdalena Dobosz, Tomasz Depta, Tomasz Fiołka, and Marcin Wojaczek

Mobile Gamebook for Visually Impaired People 309
Krzysztof Dobosz, Jakub Ptak, Marcin Wojaczek, Tomasz Depta, and Tomasz Fiolka

Implementation and Take-up of eAccessibility

Implementation and Take-up of eAccessibility: Introduction to the Special Thematic Session 313
Helen Petrie

Accessibility and Inclusion Requirements for Future e-Identity Solutions 316
Trenton Schulz and Lothar Fritsch

Roadmap to eAccessibility 324
Andrea Petz and Klaus Miesenberger

Web Accessibility for Older Readers: Effects of Font Type and Font Size on Skim Reading Webpages in Thai 332
Sorachai Kamollimsakul, Helen Petrie, and Christopher Power

Self-Service Terminals for Older and Disabled Users: Attitudes of Key Stakeholders 340
Helen Petrie, Jenny S. Darzentas, and Christopher Power

Speaking the Language of Web Developers: Evaluation of a Web Accessibility Information Resource (WebAIR) 348
David Swallow, Christopher Power, Helen Petrie, Anna Bramwell-Dicks, Lucy Buykx, Carlos A. Velasco, Aidan Parr, and Joshue O Connor

Accessibility and Usability of Mobile Platforms for People with Disabilities and Elderly Persons

A Multimodal Tablet–Based Application for the Visually Impaired for Detecting and Recognizing Objects in a Home Environment 356
Rabia Jafri and Syed Abid Ali

Usage Situation Changes of Touchscreen Computers in Japanese Visually Impaired People: Questionnaire Surveys in 2011-2013 360
Takahiro Miura, Masatsugu Sakajiri, Haruo Matsuzaka, Murtada Eljailani, Kazuki Kudo, Naoya Kitamura, Junji Onishi, and Tsukasa Ono

Accessible Single Button Characteristics of Touchscreen Interfaces under Screen Readers in People with Visual Impairments 369
Takahiro Miura, Masatsugu Sakajiri, Murtada Eljailani, Haruo Matsuzaka, Junji Onishi, and Tsukasa Ono

Tablet-Based Braille Entry via a Framework Promoting Custom Finger Spacing 377
Stephanie Ludi, Michael Timbrook, and Piper Chester

Nonvisual Presentation, Navigation and Manipulation of Structured Documents on Mobile and Wearable Devices 383
Martin Lukas Dorigo, Bettina Harriehausen-Mühlbauer, Ingo Stengel, and Paul Dowland

Never too Old to Use a Tablet: Designing Tablet Applications for the Cognitively and Physically Impaired Elderly 391
Luuk Muskens, Rico van Lent, Alexander Vijfvinkel, Paul van Cann, and Suleman Shahid

Tablets in the Rehabilitation of Memory Impairment 399
Krzysztof Dobosz, Magdalena Dobosz, Tomasz Fiolka, Marcin Wojaczek, and Tomasz Depta

Portable and Mobile Platforms for People with Disabilities and Elderly Persons

Transit Information Access for Persons with Visual or Cognitive Impairments 403
German Flores, Benjamin Cizdziel, Roberto Manduchi, Katia Obraczka, Julie Do, Tyler Esser, and Sri Kurniawan

Indoor Navigation System for the Visually Impaired Using One Inertial Measurement Unit (IMU) and Barometer to Guide in the Subway Stations and Commercial Centers 411
Jesus Zegarra Flores and René Farcy

Communication System for Persons with Cerebral Palsy: In Situ Observation of Social Interaction Following Assisted Information Request.. 419
Yohan Guerrier, Janick Naveteur, Christophe Kolski, and Franck Poirier

Determining a Blind Pedestrian's Location and Orientation at Traffic Intersections 427
Giovanni Fusco, Huiying Shen, Vidya Murali, and James M. Coughlan

The Design and Evaluation of the Body Water Management System to Support the Independent Living of the Older Adult 433
Airi Tsuji, Naoki Yabuno, Noriaki Kuwahara, and Kazunari Morimoto

An Investigation into Incorporating Visual Information in Audio Processing 437
Ender Tekin, James M. Coughlan, and Helen J. Simon

Indoor Positioning for Visually Impaired People Based on Smartphones 441
Thomas Moder, Petra Hafner, and Manfred Wieser

People with Cognitive Disabilities: AT, ICT and AAC

Extended Scaffolding by Remote Collaborative Interaction to Support People with Dementia in Independent Living – A User Study 445
Henrike Gappa, Gabriele Nordbrock, Manuela Thelen, Jaroslav Pullmann, Yehya Mohamad, and Carlos A. Velasco

Effective Application of PALRO: A Humanoid Type Robot for People with Dementia 451
Kaoru Inoue, Naomi Sakuma, Maiko Okada, Chihiro Sasaki, Mio Nakamura, and Kazuyoshi Wada

The Feasibility and Efficacy of Technology-Based Support Groups among Family Caregivers of Persons with Dementia 455
Sara J. Czaja, Richard Schulz, Dolores Perdomo, and Sankaran N. Nair

Making Music Meaningful with Adaptive Immediate Feedback Drill for Teaching Children with Cognitive Impairment: A Dual Coding Strategy to Aural Skills 459
Yu Ting Huang and Chi Nung Chu

Evaluating New Interaction Paradigms in SEN Teaching: Defining the Experiment 463
Paloma Cantón, José L. Fuertes, Ángel L. González, and Loïc Martínez

How to Make Online Social Networks Accessible for Users with Intellectual Disability? 471
Carmit-Noa Shpigelman and Carol J. Gill

Autism: ICT and AT

Improving Social and Communication Skills of Adult Arabs with ASD through the Use of Social Media Technologies 478
Alaa Mashat, Mike Wald, and Sarah Parsons

The Role of User Emotional Attachment in Driving the Engagement of Children with Autism Spectrum Disorders (ASD) in Using a Smartphone App Designed to Develop Social and Life Skill Functioning 486
Joseph Mintz

Gamification for Low-Literates: Findings on Motivation, User Experience, and Study Design 494
Dylan Schouten, Isabel Pfab, Anita Cremers, Betsy van Dijk, and Mark Neerincx

Designing Tangible and Multitouch Games for Autistic Children 502
Weiqin Chen

You Talk! – YOU vs AUTISM 506
Alessandro Signore, Panagiota Balasi, and Tangming Yuan

A Game-Based Intervention for Improving the Communication Skills of Autistic Children in Pakistan 513
Muneeb Imtiaz Ahmad, Suleman Shahid, and Johannes S. Maganheim

Access to Mathematics, Science and Music

Access to Mathematics, Science and Music: Introduction to the Special Thematic Session 517
Arthur I. Karshmer

Intelligent Tutoring Math Platform Accessible for Visually Impaired People 519
Piotr Brzoza and Michał Maćkowski

Gesture-Based Browsing of Mathematics 525
Shereen El Bedewy, Klaus Miesenberger, and Bernhard Stöger

Towards the 8-Dot Nemeth Braille Code 533
Aineias Martos, Georgios Kouroupetroglou, Vassilis Argyropoulos, and Despina Deligiorgi

AudioFunctions: Eyes-Free Exploration of Mathematical Functions on Tablets 537
Marzia Taibbi, Cristian Bernareggi, Andrea Gerino, Dragan Ahmetovic, and Sergio Mascetti

Markdown – A Simple Syntax for Transcription of Accessible Study Materials 545
Jens Voegler, Jens Bornschein, and Gerhard Weber

Making Graph Theory Algorithms Accessible to Blind Students 549
Lukáš Másilko and Jiří Pecl

Braille Capability in Accessible e-Textbooks for Math and Science 557
Katsuhito Yamaguchi, Masakazu Suzuki, and Toshihiro Kanahori

MathMelodies: Inclusive Design of a Didactic Game to Practice Mathematics 564
Andrea Gerino, Nicolò Alabastro, Cristian Bernareggi, Dragan Ahmetovic, and Sergio Mascetti

An Interactive Workspace for Helping the Visually Impaired Learn Linear Algebra 572
Bassam Almasri, Islam Elkabani, and Rached Zantout

The LEAN Math Accessible MathML Editor 580
John A. Gardner

SVGPlott – Generating Adaptive and Accessible Audio-Tactile Function Graphs 588
Jens Bornschein, Denise Prescher, and Gerhard Weber

Free Tools to Help Blind People with Musical Learning 596
Nadine Jessel

The Development of a Music Presentation System by Two Vibrators ... 602
Nobuyuki Sasaki, Satoshi Ohtsuka, Kazuyoshi Ishii, and Tetsumi Harakawa

Multimodal Interface for Working with Algebra: Interaction between the Sighted and the Non Sighted 606
Silvia Fajardo-Flores and Dominique Archambault

Performance Metrics and Their Extraction Methods for Audio Rendered Mathematics 614
Hernisa Kacorri, Paraskevi Riga, and Georgios Kouroupetroglou

Blind and Visually Impaired People: AT, HCI and Accessibility

Developing Tactile Graphic Output Functions Necessitated in the Performance of Research Using Statistical Methods by Blind Persons ... 622
Kazunori Minatani

The Study of a New Actuator for a Two-Point Body-Braille System 630
Nobuyuki Sasaki, Kazuya Nakajima, Satoshi Ohtsuka, Kazuyoshi Ishii, and Tetsumi Harakawa

Design Guidelines of Tools for Facilitating Blind People to Independently Format Their Documents 634
Lourdes M. Morales, Sonia M. Arteaga, Peter Cottrell, and Sri Kurniawan

Contribution to the Automation of the Tactile Images Transcription Process 642
Yong Chen, Zehira Haddad, and Jaime Lopez Krahe

Dots and Letters: Accessible Braille-Based Text Input for Visually Impaired People on Mobile Touchscreen Devices 650
Elke Mattheiss, Georg Regal, Johann Schrammel, Markus Garschall, and Manfred Tscheligi

Real-Time Text Tracking for Text-to-Speech Translation Camera for the Blind 658
Hideaki Goto and Takuma Hoda

Towards Displaying Graphics on a Cheap, Large-Scale Braille Display 662
Elisabeth Wilhelm, Thorsten Schwarz, Gerhard Jaworek, Achim Voigt, and Bastian E. Rapp

Author Index 671

Towards Automatically Generated Tactile Detail Maps by 3D Printers for Blind Persons

Timo Götzelmann[1] and Aleksander Pavkovic[2]

[1] Department of Computer Science, Nuremberg Institute of Technology, Nuremberg, Germany
Timo.Goetzelmann@ohm-university.eu
[2] Bavarian Blind and Sight-Handicapped Organization, Munich, Germany

Abstract. This paper introduces an approach for the (semi)automatic generation of worldwide available, detailed tactile maps including buildings and blind-specific features based on recognized illustrators' guidelines and standards. These guidelines for tactile maps are investigated in order to define a formal rule set and to automatically filter map data accordingly. Using the rule set, our approach automatically abstracts map data in order to generate a 2.1D tactile model providing multiple height levels (layers) which can be printed by usual consumer 3D printers. Based on the popular OpenStreetMap map data, our automated approach allows to generate arbitrary detail maps blind persons individually interested in, without the need for manual adaption of the tactile map. Thus, this approach contributes to the goal to increase the autonomy of blind persons.

Keywords: Tactile Maps, Layering, 2.1D, Worldwide, Blind, Orientation, Accessibility, Haptic, Braille, 3D Printer, OpenStreetMap.

1 Introduction

Nowadays, there are several different kinds of tactile maps for blind persons. In the public, there are sophisticated realistic 3D models of local areas with or without textual annotations, abstracted maps at varied zoom levels, route plans for busses and underground trains as well as floor plans of buildings. Besides that, there are numerous tactile maps in form of books. All these local tactile maps share an elementary property: they are build (semi) manually. Illustrators and artists perform a laborious task to manually produce tactile maps which leads to qualitatively high results. However, this implies that they only exist for a limited number of places.

According to Espinosa et al. [1], tactile maps may contribute to the spatial understanding of blind users for unfamiliar urban environments, when they are able to carry the maps along with them. In their study, blind persons using detailed tactile maps performed significantly better in orientation tasks that those without tactile maps. In order to increase the informational autonomy of blind persons, it is desirable to allow to generate arbitrary tactile maps on the fly. Since 3D printers are currently developing in a very fast pace, in few years they will be a mass product which can be used by blind users to produce their individual tactile maps for improving their orientation.

K. Miesenberger et al. (Eds.): ICCHP 2014, Part II, LNCS 8548, pp. 1–7, 2014.

This paper introduces an approach for (semi) automatic generation of worldwide available, detailed tactile maps including buildings and blind-specific features based on recognized illustrators' guidelines and standards. It uses the free map data of the popular OpenStreetMap (OSM) project, which is a fast growing collaborative project [2] and has recently also been used for numerous scientific purposes (e.g., [3,4]). As initial step, the guidelines are transformed into formal rules. Using the online map corpus, filters are applied on user-selected segments of map data to conform to specific needs of blind persons. Next, the formalized rules are applied to the filtered map section in order to obtain an abstracted map. Finally, a 2.1D tactile model (according to the taxonomy of [5]) providing multiple height levels (layers) is generated which can be manufactured by usual consumer 3D printers.

This paper is structured as follows: Section 2 introduces the related work for this topic. Subsequently, Section 3 describes our approach and its prototypical implementation. Section 4 discusses our results and presents our ongoing and future work.

2 Related Work

A couple of decades ago, maps for the sighted were still produced manually by map illustrators. Their knowledge of visual reproduction of maps and their annotations was mainly spread by word of mouth or informal guidelines (e.g., [6]). With increasing graphics abilities and computational power of computers it was possible to apply formalized rule sets in order to automatically generate simple maps from a corpus of map data. Nowadays, even complex maps can be automatically produced by computers on the fly which is used every day by sighted users through popular web services such as Google maps, Yahoo maps etc. Conversely, for tactile maps this is not yet state of the art.

For creating tactile maps there are similarly informal guidelines. There are numerous books (e.g., [7,8]), conference publications (e.g., [9,10]) and webpages (e.g., [11,12]) on the generation of tactile graphics and maps and related production methods. Recently, the 900 series of the ISO standard 9241 have been released. The existing parts (see [13]) cover tactile and haptic interactions, however, up to now they do not specifically discuss the generation of tactile maps. Voigt&Martens [14] discuss the production and use of specified tactile 3D models. They mention a problem which is highly relevant to tactile maps: due to the limited production volumes of some consumer 3D printers, in some cases it might be necessary to subdivide the models in multiple parts before printing. They strongly agree that tactile models produced by 3D printers may contribute for the spatial understanding and orientation of blind users. Another publication [15] first introduces different ways for the production of tactile maps and compares three variants of a given model by user tests. The TMAP project [16] provided blind persons of free California maps containing exclusively streets as line drawings (greater zoom level) being partially labeled along the sides of the map, supported by auditive instructions. An approach for Japanese maps TMACS [17] generates maps at street zoom level (i.e., line-drawings) including landmark symbols labelled by keys and legend including an evaluation.

An interactive approach has been introduced by Wang et al. [18] which uses a popular web service MapQuest for obtaining route instructions and a corresponding map image of a given route. The map image is printed by a tactile printer (embosser) on swell paper and subsequently, placed it on a touchpad which is connected to a computer. By touching elements of the tactile map the user gets auditive route instructions. A similar approach by Sennette et al. [19] uses OSM map data. They manually edit a map section for adapting the map image to the needs of an embosser used to print the map representation on swell paper. For the joint use with portable devices, multimodal content is added.

None of these approaches processes international structural map data in order reduce the maps' complexity by abstraction for the automatic generation of tactile detail maps which can be printed by usual 3D printers. Since several years there is a promising open project called HaptoRender [20] which has similar intentions, however this project still is work in progress. Though, it already presents a manually constructed prototype of a tactile map generated by a 3D printer.

3 Approach

Beside map data for the generation of maps for sighted persons, the OpenStreetMap map corpus also comprises additional map features which can be important for blind people (e.g., accessible pedestrian signals). Using an existing interface of OpenStreetMap map corpus, map segments can be obtained for arbitrary geographic coordinates by a web interface. The retrieval results are stored in a readable XML format. Usual map renderers convert these XML data into bitmap images by using a defined rule set. In our case, we investigated illustrators' guidelines for tactile maps in order to define a specific rule set for blind persons (Section 3.1) and to filter map data for the needs of blind persons (Section 3.2). Section 3.3 describes the process of generating height map images and Section 3.4 the generation of printable 3D models.

3.1 Derivation of Formal Rules

The first step was to determine, which of the illustrators' guidelines can be used for defining a small set of formal rules to generate maps. There are three basic feature types for geographic objects: point-features which only consist of a single location (e.g., bus stops, traffic-lights), line-features consisting of a series of connected points (e.g., roads, rivers) and area-features which are a closed loop of connected points (e.g., places, buildings). An example for adapted guidelines for point features: maintain a minimum distance of 3mm between individual features (e.g., [11]). Some examples for line features: removal of short lines (e.g., [7]) and for area features: removal of small areas (e.g., [7]), difference in textures between areas (e.g., [12]).

Besides that, label placement is an important task. Our approach allows to generate multiple height levels for different map features, labels and symbols which helps to reduce clutter and confusion and allows blind users to understand tactile graphics more easily (see [8]). If possible, labels should be placed as close as possible to the named objects, only in case there is not enough space or too much clutter, keys and legend should be used instead (e.g., [6,7]).

3.2 Map Filtering

The map filtering process is crucial to reduce the map data to map features which are important for tactile maps. This comprises not only data which are important for visual maps (e.g., ways, roads, buildings), but particularly these which are interesting for blind persons (e.g., building entrances, accessible pedestrian signals, sidewalks, tactile pavings). We also implemented a method to optionally generate a list of keys and legends instead of extensive labels whereas a map scale complements the legend. A preprocessing step determined short line segments and small area features. Additionally, for complex line or area features simplification algorithms such as the Ramer-Douglas-Peucker algorithm were used in this step.

3.3 Map Abstraction and Rendering

To apply our rule set for the map abstraction, we decided to rely on an existing tool of an open project called Maperative. It allows to define formal rules in plain text and supports multiple output formats for the generated map image file. The resulting is a gray-scaled image file, which serves as height map in the succeeding step, i.e., the darker a pixel on the bitmap, the higher this location appears on the tactile map (see Figure 1). As can be seen, our rule set automatically renders map features such as areas, roads and buildings on different height levels. Labels are rendered in Braille letters, whereas a minimum size per letter can be ensured; the dots' height levels correspond to their objects. An optional scale helps blind persons to estimate distances. Additional blind specific attributes are automatically rendered as well, e.g., building entrances (see "x" of upper building in Figure 1).

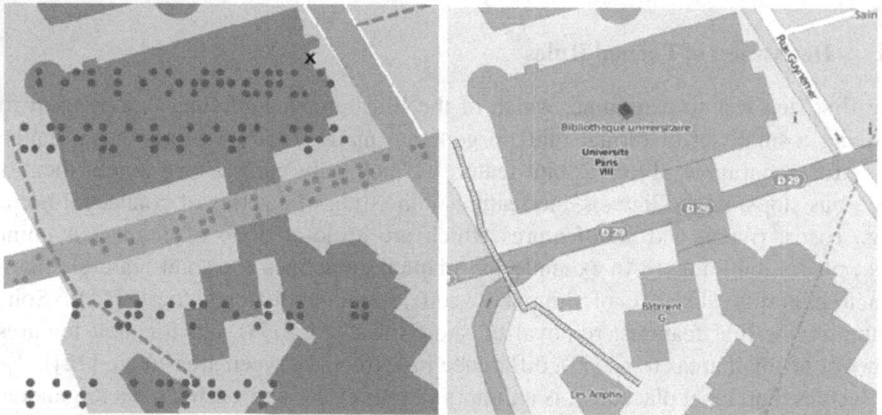

Fig. 1. Example of usual map rendering for the sighted (left), abstracted map rendering for the blind (right) serving as height map

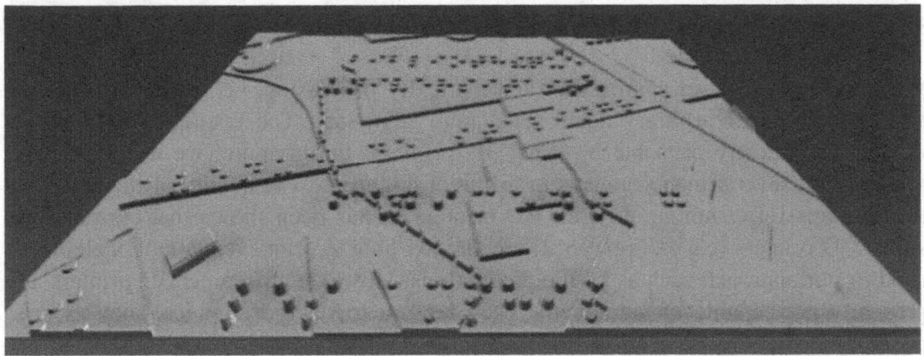

Fig. 2. Automatically generated 3D model in STL format

3.4 Generation of Printable 3D Models

The final step is to construct a geometric model which can be processed by standard 3D printers. Thus, a 3D mesh is generated (see Figure 2), whereas the coordinates of the mesh vertices are scaled to a pre-defined size of the resulting model. The image greyscale values serve as height map for the z displacement of the 3D mesh's vertices. In order to comply with the necessities of 3D printers, the resulting mesh is extended by a bottom layer in order to construct a valid STL model without holes. The resulting STL file format can be used with common 3D printers' software in order to generate hardware specific codes (so called G-codes) for 3D printers, i.e., to print these models. Depending on the hardware capabilities of the consumer 3D printer, several height levels can be realized. Figure 3 shows a sample printed tactile map of the size 10x7.5 cm produced by fused deposition modeling (FDM) using standard polylactide filament.

Fig. 3. 3D printed tactile map with multiple height levels

4 Discussion and Future Work

We introduced a novel approach of automatically processing, i.e., retrieval, filtering and abstraction of arbitrary detail level map segments. The resulting 2.1D tactile models are directly printable by usual 3D printers. Furthermore, we tested our approach with several map segments in different countries. The quality of the resulting tactile maps varies among different 3D printers. It has been shown that current consumer 3D printers (e.g., Ultimaker 2) are already able to print even complex elements used in our approach such as braille annotations. However, consumer 3D printers are presently not capable of reproducing each texture for tactile graphics, such as proposed by North American and Canadian Braille Authority (see [7], Appendix E).

Though, the autonomous process of printing a spatial model by a 3D printer by blind persons has not been in the scope of this paper. Our goal is obtaining a fully integrated process, where blind persons are able to generate each detail map segment they desire by our automated approach and to print the resulting model completely on their own. The task of developing an accessible user interface for 3D printers implies to carry out several user studies and is part of our future work.

The abstraction of the map data in our approach bases on recognized illustrators' guidelines for tactile maps. Without doubt, our results and possibly any computed maps will never be as good as manually crafted maps by illustrators. However, our automated approach allows to generate worldwide arbitrary detail maps, blind persons individually interested in, without the need for manual adaption of the map. Thus, this approach contributes to the goal to increase the autonomy of blind persons.

In order to refine the map abstraction used in our process, we are currently discussing with map illustration experts. Since this approach focuses on detail maps, we are exploring how tactile maps could be computed automatically for arbitrary zoom levels. Particularly, collaboration with other research groups exploring different zoom levels (e.g., [16,17]) could allow synergy effects.

References

1. Espinosa, M., Ungar, S., Ochaita, E., Blades, M., Spencer, C.: Comparing methods for introducing blind and visually impaired people to unfamiliar urban environments. Journal of Environmental Psychology 18, 277–287 (1998)
2. Haklay, M., Weber, P.: Openstreetmap: User-generated street maps. IEEE Pervasive Computing 7, 12–18 (2008)
3. Zook, M., Graham, M., Shelton, T., Gorman, S.: Volunteered Geographic Information and Crowdsourcing Disaster Relief: A Case Study of the Haitian Earthquake. World Medical & Health Policy 2, 7–33 (2010)
4. Latif, S., Islam, K.R., Khan, M.M.I., Ahmed, S.I.: OpenStreetMap for the disaster management in Bangladesh. In: IEEE Conference on Open Systems (ICOS), pp. 429–433. IEEE (2011)
5. Reichinger, A., Neumüller, M., Rist, F., Maierhofer, S., Purgathofer, W.: Computer-Aided Design of Tactile Models. In: Miesenberger, K., Karshmer, A., Penaz, P., Zagler, W. (eds.) ICCHP 2012, Part II. LNCS, vol. 7383, pp. 497–504. Springer, Heidelberg (2012)

6. Imhof, E.: Positioning Names on Maps. The American Cartographer 2, 128–144 (1975)
7. Guidelines and Standards for Tactile Graphics, Braille Authority of North America (2010)
8. Edman, P.K.: Tactile Graphics. American Foundation for the Blind, New York (1992)
9. Graf, C., Schmid, F.: From Visual Schematic to Tactile Schematic Maps. In: Workshop You Are Here 2: 2nd Workshop on Spatial Awareness and Geographic Knowledge Acquisition with Small Mobile Devices, pp. 15–28 (2010)
10. Zeng, L., Weber, G.: Accessible Maps for the Visually Impaired. In: IFIP INTERACT Workshop on Accessible Design in the Digital World, pp. 54–60 (2011)
11. Amick, N., Corcoran, J.: Guidelines for Design of Tactile Graphics. American Printing House for the Blind, http://www.aph.org/edresearch/guides.htm (accessed January 22, 2014)
12. Hasty, L.: Tactile Graphics: A How To Guide, http://www.tactilegraphics.org/index.html (accessed January 22, 2014)
13. van Erp, J.B.F., Kyung, K.-U., Kassner, S., Carter, J., Brewster, S., Weber, G., Andrew, I.: Setting the standards for haptic and tactile interactions: ISO's work. In: Kappers, A.M.L., van Erp, J.B.F., Bergmann Tiest, W.M., van der Helm, F.C.T. (eds.) EuroHaptics 2010, Part II. LNCS, vol. 6192, pp. 353–358. Springer, Heidelberg (2010)
14. Voigt, A., Martens, B.: Development of 3D tactile models for the partially sighted to facilitate spatial orientation. In: Proceedings of the 24th Conference on Education and Research in Computer Aided Architectural Design in Europe, pp. 366–370. CD-ROM (2006)
15. Vozenílek, V., Kozáková, M., Stávová, Z., Ludíková, L., Ruzivcková, V., Finková, D.: 3D Printing technology in tactile maps compiling. In: Proceedings of the XXIV International Cartographic Conference, pp. 1–10. CD-ROM (2009)
16. Miele, J.A., Landau, S., Gilden, D.: Talking TMAP: Automated generation of audio-tactile maps using Smith-Kettlewell's TMAP software. British Journal of Visual Impairment 24, 93–100 (2006)
17. Minatani, K., Watanabe, T., Yamaguchi, T., Watanabe, K., Akiyama, J., Miyagi, M., Oouchi, S.: Tactile map automated creation system to enhance the mobility of blind persons—its design concept and evaluation through experiment. In: Miesenberger, K., Klaus, J., Zagler, W., Karshmer, A. (eds.) ICCHP 2010, Part II. LNCS, vol. 6180, pp. 534–540. Springer, Heidelberg (2010)
18. Wang, Z., Li, N., Li, B.: Fast and independent access to map directions for people who are blind. Interacting with Computers 24, 91–106 (2012)
19. Senette, C., Buzzi, M.C., Buzzi, M., Leporini, B., Martusciello, L.: Enriching graphic maps to enable multimodal interaction by blind people. In: Stephanidis, C., Antona, M. (eds.) UAHCI 2013, Part I. LNCS, vol. 8009, pp. 576–583. Springer, Heidelberg (2013)
20. HaptoRender – OpenStreetMap Wiki, http://wiki.openstreetmap.org/wiki/HaptoRender (accessed January 22, 2014)

Opportunities and Limitations of Haptic Technologies for Non-visual Access to 2D and 3D Graphics

Helen Sullivan[1], Shrirang Sahasrabudhe[2], Jukka Liimatainen[3], and Markku Hakkinen[4]

[1] Rider University, Lawrenceville, New Jersey USA
hsullivan@rider.edu
[2] University of North Carolina, Greensboro, USA
s_sahasr@uncg.edu
[3] University of Jyvaskyla, Finland
jukka.t.liimatainen@gmail.com
[4] Educational Testing Service, Princeton, USA
mhakkinen@ets.org

Abstract. Existing and emerging haptic technologies offer methods for non-visually rendering and interacting with 2D and 3D graphical information. These technologies include force feedback devices, touch surfaces with vibro-tactile feedback, wearable vibrotactiles, and touch surfaces with electrostatic feedback. In this paper we will focus on approaches to non-visual access to 3D shapes. The interactive models focus on two approaches: simulation of 3D shape and perspective on a 2D touch surface; and interactive exploration of 3D shapes using physical motion in a virtual 3D space with either a force feedback controller or wearable haptics. The technologies will be reviewed along with suitability for their use by students with visual impairments. Methodology and results from an ongoing series of exploratory usability studies will be discussed. Benefits and limitations of the technologies and recommendations for further research will be presented.

Keywords: Tactiles, Haptics, non-Visual Displays, Tablets, STEM.

1 Introduction

Existing and emerging haptic technologies offer methods for non-visually render-ing and interacting with 2D and 3D graphical information. Research on haptics in fields such as robotics and telemedicine is significant, e.g. [1], and a growing body of research is focusing on how haptics can enhance access to information for people with visual disabilities. Some haptic interfaces can be complex mechanically, and expensive, which may limit application and use in educational settings. The complexity of some devices can pose further challenges in that implementing content is non-trivial and can require specialized skills. One promising development are haptic technologies that are incorporated in mainstream consumer products, thereby reducing cost and increasing availability. These technologies include force feedback devices, such as the Novint Falcon® game controller, and Android® tablets which incorporate

K. Miesenberger et al. (Eds.): ICCHP 2014, Part II, LNCS 8548, pp. 8–11, 2014.

vibrotactile feedback. Emerging developments in augmented reality, electrostatic feedback on touch surfaces, and low cost, wearable haptics offer further interesting possibilities. Our research focuses on how access to graphical information, specifically STEM content encountered by students with visual impairments, can be enhanced through use of haptic feedback on mainstream devices, and ideally, provide alternatives to physical tactiles. Though our initial work has focused on 2D shapes and graphics, we have recently begun exploring concepts for presenting 3D shapes on a 2D tablet surface [2]. When considering how to present 3D shapes non-visually, we can focus on two models: simulation of 3D shape and perspective on a 2D touch surface; and interactive exploration of 3D shapes using physical motion in a virtual 3D space with either a force feedback controller or wearable haptics. Before describing the two models, we will review current haptic technologies.

2 Haptic Technologies

Haptics is defined as relating to the sense of touch. In the context of human-computer interfaces, haptic feedback utilizes the sense of touch to convey information. The feedback may simulate contact with a virtual object, a physical action, such as pressing a key, or exploration of a virtual surface by simulating variations in texture. There are a number of technologies, both off the shelf and emerging from research labs. Of particular interest are those technologies either incorporated in, or planned for, mainstream consumer devices such as tablets.

2.1 Haptic Game Controllers

Game controllers, specifically, the Novint Falcon, provide a relatively low cost (USD 250) means to enable 3D exploration of information and environments. A number of studies [3,4,5,6] have evaluated the Falcon with students who have visual impairments and guidelines for haptic interfaces using a similar device have been developed [7]. The Falcon device can be envisioned as a 3D mouse, providing a means to explore a constrained virtual space, with force-feedback used to convey contact with objects or surfaces.

2.2 Vibrotactile Feedback on Tablets

The recent availability of low cost Android tablets with vibration-based haptics, or vibrotactile, has spawned a growing number of research efforts to explore its usability by people with visual impairments [8,9,10,11,12]. The research suggests that the built-in vibrotactile feedback has potential as a means of providing access to 2D graphics. Tablets supporting vibrotactile feedback utilize one or more vibration motors embedded within the device. One key limitation of current tablet-based haptic technologies is the lack of support for multi-touch interaction. Students with visual impairments are typically explore tactile diagrams with multiple fingers. In contrast, exploration of virtual tactiles on a vibrotactile tablet can only be explored with single finger.

2.3 Wearable Vibrotactile Feedback

Goncu and Marriott [8] have explored multi-touch haptics using specialized gloves with vibration motors mounted above the index finger on each hand. The current authors have developed prototype haptic "rings" that can be attached to the index fingers in a similar manner. The advantages of built in vibrotacile haptic technology in common off the shelf devices has clear economic benefits and technical simplicity when compared to the need for specialized, wearable technology that must be used in conjunction with a tablet. However, wearable haptics offer the advantage of multi-touch exploration. Further, if wearable haptics are combined with spatial movement sensing devices, such as Microsoft®, Kinect®. or LeapMotion®, the possibility exists for exploration of virtual objects in a constrained 3D space.

2.4 Electrostatic Feedback

Electrostatic feedback has been developed by Senseg® and Disney® Research. This technology applies an electrostatic field on the surface of a touch screen that can vary the perceived friction as a finger moves across the display. The result enables the creation of a "texture" effect, allowing the user to feel various surface features. Our initial investigations of this technology suggests that electrostatic haptics have unique capabilities in terms of conveying surface textures and is a good candidate for continued research.

3 Current Research: Two Models for 3D Haptic Presentation

Our initial success with 2D shapes evolved into an exploration of whether 3D shapes could also be rendered using the vibrotactile feedback approach [2]. If 2D geometric shapes could be recognized, could a third dimension be simulated using what we have termed audio and haptic perspective? In developing this approach, we examined raised-line 3D perspective images used in mathematics education and prototyped several approaches before deciding upon a method utilizing modulation of vibration, audio tone frequency and intensity to describe any point on a surface rendered in perspective. Feedback from prototype usage suggested enhancements including spoken cues for shape features such as edges or peaks. Electrostatic feedback will be evaluated during the coming year as an alternative to vibrotactile.

The next phase of the project is utilizing a low cost, prototype haptic stylus, which incorporates a piezo electric vibration motor, allowing exploration of a 3D object, both on the tablet display, as well as independent of the tablet using a virtual presentation space where the object is perceived to float in front of the user. In the latter approach, the spatial tracking of the stylus position is accomplished using a LeapMotion device. Vibration and audio cues, similar to those used in the 2D tablet approach, are presented as the stylus explores the 3D space containing the object. A demonstration video of the different approaches described is available: `http://www.talkinginterfaces.org/icchpdemo`.

References

1. Carignan, C.R., Krebs, H.I.: Telerehabilitation robotics: bright lights, big future? Journal of Rehabilitation Research and Development 43(5), 695 (2006)
2. Liimatainen, J., Sahasrabudhe, S., Hakkinen, M.T.: Access to 2D and 3D graphics using vibrotactile feedback and sonification. Presentation at the 29th International Conference on Technology and Disabilities (CSUN), San Diego, CA (2014)
3. Rassmus-Grohn, K., Magnusson, C., Eftring, H.: AHEAD-Audio-haptic drawing editor and explorer for education. In: HAVE 2007, IEEE International Workshop on Haptic Audio and Visual Environments and Games, pp. 62–66. IEEE (2007)
4. Magnusson, C., Gutierrez, T., Rassmus-Gröhn, K.: The ENABLED Editor and Viewer–simple tools for more accessible on line 3D models. In: 5th International Conference on Enactive Interfaces (2008)
5. White, G.R., Fitzpatrick, G., McAllister, G.: Toward accessible 3D virtual environments for the blind and visually impaired. In: Proceedings of the 3rd International Conference on Digital Interactive Media in Entertainment and Arts, pp. 134–141. ACM (September 2008)
6. Hansen, E., Rogat, A., Liu, L., Hakkinen, M.: Designing Accessible Science-based tasks. In: Paper Accepted for Presentation at the 29th International Conference on Technology and Disabilities, San Diego, CA (2014)
7. Sjöström, C.: Non-Visual Haptic Interaction Design (Doctoral dissertation, Phd thesis, Certec) (2002)
8. Goncu, C., Marriott, K.: GraVVITAS: Generic multi-touch presentation of accessible graphics. In: Campos, P., Graham, N., Jorge, J., Nunes, N., Palanque, P., Winckler, M. (eds.) INTERACT 2011, Part I. LNCS, vol. 6946, pp. 30–48. Springer, Heidelberg (2011)
9. Toennie, J.L., Burgner, J., Withrow, T.J., Webster III, R.J.: Toward Haptic/Aural Touchscreen Display of Graphical Mathematics for the Education of Blind Students. Paper Presented at the IEEE World Haptics Conference 2011, Istanbul, Turkey (2011)
10. Guidice, N.A., Palani, H., Brenner, E., Kramer, K.M.: Learning Non-Visual Graphical Information using a Touch-Baed Vibro-Audio Interface. Paper Presented at ASSETS 2012, Boulder, CO (2012)
11. Cayton-Hodges, G., Marquez, L., van Rijn, P., Keehner, M., Laitusis, C., Zapata-Rivera, D., Bauer, M., Hakkinen, M.T.: Technology Enhanced Assessments in Mathematics and Beyond: Strengths, Challenges, and Future Directions. In: Paper Presented at the Invitational Research Symposium on Technology Enhanced Assessments, Washingon, D.C May 7-8 (2012)
12. Häkkinen, M., Rice, J., Liimatainen, J., Supalo, C.: Tablet-based Haptic Interfaces for STEM content. In: Paper Presented at the 28th International Conference on Technology and Disabilities, San Diego, CA

Do Blind Subjects Differ from Sighted Subjects When Exploring Virtual Tactile Maps?

Mariacarla Memeo, Claudio Campus, and Luca Brayda

Robotics, Brain and Cognitive Sciences Dept.,
Fondazione Istituto Italiano di Tecnologia, Genoa, Italy
{mariacarla.memeo,claudio.campus,luca.brayda}@iit.it

Abstract. The access to graphical information is difficult for individuals who are blind or visually impaired. Taking advantage of the residual sensory abilities such as touch is one way to solve this issue. However, it is not yet clear if blind subjects perceive new tacto-spatial information in the same way that sighted people do. In this work we code the discovery of unknown tactile virtual objects in terms of subjective and behavioral variables, which result to be in-dependent on visual deprivation and dependent only on task difficulty. Our methodology can be employed in educational, orientation and mobility protocols.

Keywords: Blind, Visually Impaired, Haptic, Tactile, Cognition, Workload.

1 Introduction

A spatial representation (i.e. a mental map) comes from multiple sensory channels, which are sometimes restricted or unavailable. Congenitally blind people can build mental maps [1], yet through processes which may differ from sighted subjects, such as sensory substitution, i.e. the activation of the visual cortex during a non-visual task [2,3,4]. Then, the comparison between blind and sighted subjects can clarify the origin of spatial images [5]. Sensory substitution systems allow to assess the dependence of mental maps on sensory modalities and to use this knowledge to build effective interfaces. Learning maps is crucial to cope with mobility issues: prior knowledge of an unknown environment can modulate navigation in unknown environments [6]. Virtual maps allow tailoring information to specific user needs. Here we study two unsolved issues.

First, if it is possible to know why the construction of a map is a success or a failure. Simply asserting if a subject is able or not to build a map is not enough, as it does not allow to adopt tailored counter-measures. To solve this issue, one should target potential spatial abilities rather than just competence [7], meaning that the way subjects explore an unknown object may suggest something related to how difficult this task can be or even to reveal features linked to the success of the construction process. This can allow to code how people build mental maps.

K. Miesenberger et al. (Eds.): ICCHP 2014, Part II, LNCS 8548, pp. 12–17, 2014.

Second, whether or not blind and sighted subjects explore with similar strategies. It is not yet clear if spatial imagination of people with visual deprivation works similarly to that of sighted people [5]. This can clarify if early blind subjects as compared to late-blind or people who just lost their sight, should follow the same or different rehabilitation protocols.

2 Experimental Setup, Protocol and Statistical Analyses

Here we investigated the exploration of tactile maps provided through our TActile MOuse (TAMO) [8]. The TAMO is a mouse-shaped device providing haptic feedback corresponding to punctual heights of virtual objects; subjects attempted to self-develop exploration strategies and discovered three-dimensional information by proprioception and hand/arm motion.

Two groups of subjects were tested: 10 early blind volunteers (8 males and 2 females) with age 36±13 (range: 20-62 years) and 10 age- and sex-matched blindfolded sighted volunteers with age 36±12 (range: 20-60).

Subjects explored three virtual objects of increasing difficulty (Fig.1), with the TAMO. The aim was to allow construction of a cognitive map in a constrained amount of time: subjects explored each object ten times, each time for 10 s. Every trial started and stopped with two distinct sounds and was preceded and followed by 10 s of rest. A 2 min pause was induced in-between object explorations.

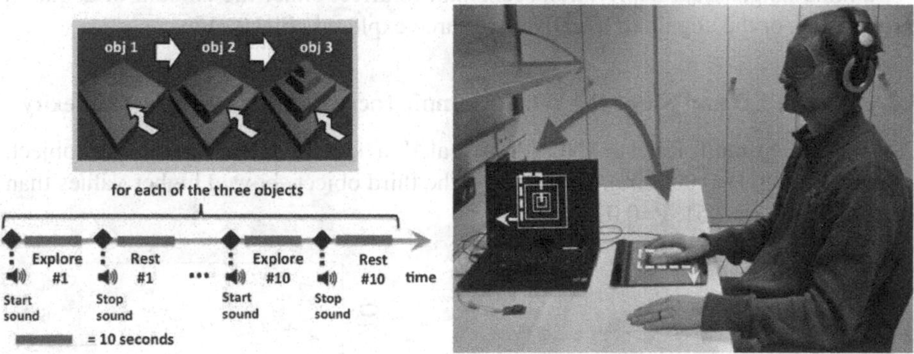

Fig. 1. Experimental protocol (left) and setup (right). The trajectory of the hand moving the TAMO is schematized with the dashed yellow arrow, while on the PC screen the top-view map (in this case of object 3) and the hand movement are shown.

R software was used for all the statistical analyses [9].

We considered two aspects characterizing explorations: the amount of information provided by the lever of the TAMO and subjects' cognitive load during the explorations.

Therefore, as a first dependent variable, we considered the Stimuli Rate (SR), an objective measure of acquisition rate of the haptic stimuli: for each object and subject, we counted the movements of the lever during the exploration, then dividing by the whole exploration time (equal to 100 s = 10 explorations × 10 s/exploration).

As a second dependent variable, we considered the Perceived Levels of Difficulty (PLD), a subjective measure resulting from the question: "Please rate the difficulty you perceived in constructing the map on a 1-10 scale (higher rates correspond to higher difficulties)". The question was asked after the ten explorations of each object were completed.

For both SR and PLD, we evaluated the effect of two factors: visual deprivation (distinguishing blind from blindfolded sighted subjects) and task complexity (distinguishing objects with an increasing number of levels): to this aim we performed analyses of variances (ANOVAs) followed by post-hoc t-tests. When normality assumption was violated (based on Shapiro-Wilk test), we replaced ANOVAs and t-tests with Kruskal-Wallis and Wilcoxon tests, respectively.

3 Results

3.1 Blind and Sighted Subjects Showed Globally Similar SR and PLD

Stimuli rates showed a non-normal distribution whether for blind, W=0.93 P=0.007 or for sighted subjects W=0.97 P=0.04. According to Kruskal-Wallis test, blind and sighted exhibited similar stimuli rates ($\chi^2(23)=25.11$, NS). Perceived levels of difficulties were non-normal for both groups, (W=0.897, P=0.006 for blind subjects; W=0.89, P=0.006 for sighted subjects). Blind and sighted subjects perceived similar difficulties while exploring ($\chi^2(8)=9.47$, NS).

Summarizing, visual deprivation seems not to affect either the amount of acquired information, or the cognitive load over the three explored objects (Fig. 2).

3.2 Both PLD and SR of the Whole Sample Increase with Object Complexity

Considering Stimuli Rates, ANOVA revealed a significant effect of the object, (F(2,38)=16.08, P=0.000008). At post-hoc, the third object showed higher values than the first one, t(2)=2.51, P=0.02.

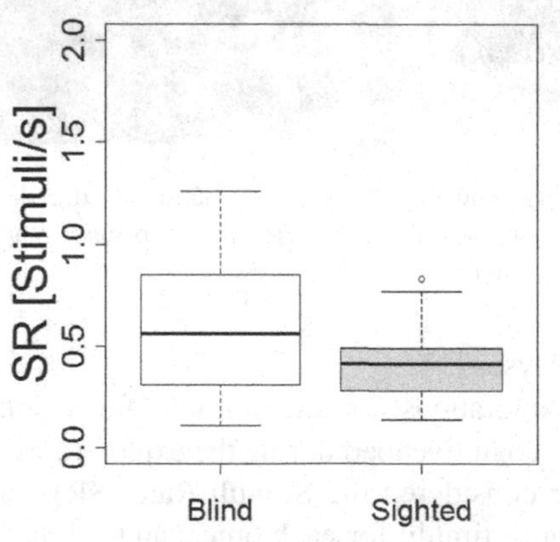

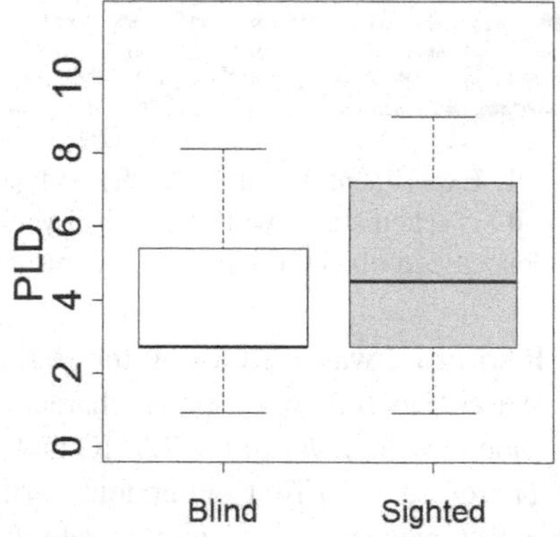

Fig. 2. Boxplot of SR and PLD, depending on the group. Boxplots show medians (continuous black lines), 25% and 75% quartiles (box limits) and whiskers embracing all the data set.

Considering Perceived Levels of Difficulty, normality assumption was violated for the first and the second object, respectively with W=0.80, P=0.001 and W=0.85, P=0.006. The Kruskal-Wallis test revealed a significant effect of the object on PLD, (χ^2(2)=28.1, P=0.0000008). Wilcoxon test revealed a significant increasing trend: the second object showed higher values compared to the first one (P=0.04), while the third object was higher compared to both the second (P=0.01) and the first one (P=0.0003).

Therefore, considering the whole sample, we observed a similar trend for SR and PLD: acquired amount of stimuli and cognitive load seem to similarly increase with object complexity.

3.3 PLD and SR Increase with Complexity also when Separating Groups

Blind Subjects. Analysis of variance showed a significant effect of object complexity on stimuli rates of blind subjects, F(2,18)=18.8, P=0.00004. At post hoc, SR for the third object resulted higher than for the first object, t(2)=2.28, P=0.04.

PLD of blind subjects was non-normally distributed for the first and the second object, respectively with W=0.78, P=0.008 and W=0.76, P=0.005. According to Kruskal-Wallis test, object had a significant effect on PLD, χ^2=12.51, P=0.002. In particular, an increasing trend was found from the first two objects to the last one, respectively with P=0.005 for the first and P=0.007 for the second object.

Sighted Subjects. Analysis of variance showed a trend effect of object complexity on stimuli rates of sighted subjects, F(2,18)=3.55, P=0.05. The trend was increasing with object complexity, due to higher values for the third compared to the first object, t(2)=2.26, P=0.02.

PLD of sighted subjects violated normality assumption for the first and the second object, respectively with W=0.82, P=0.03 and W=0.79, P=0.01. Kruskal-Wallis test revealed a significant effect of object, χ^2=6.71, P=0.03, with higher difficulties perceived while exploring the third compared with the first object (P=0.05).

Group Similarity Confirmed within each Object. For what concerns SR, t-tests performed separately for each object did not reveal any difference between blind and sighted subjects. A similar result was found considering PLD. In this case, normality assumption was violated for first object (W=0.78, P=0.008 for blind and W=0.84 and P=0.05 for sighted), therefore requiring Wilcoxon test.

Summarizing, considering both PLD and SR, blind and sighted subject showed similar patterns in function of object complexity. Moreover, no differences emerged even comparing the two groups separately considering each explored object (Fig. 3).

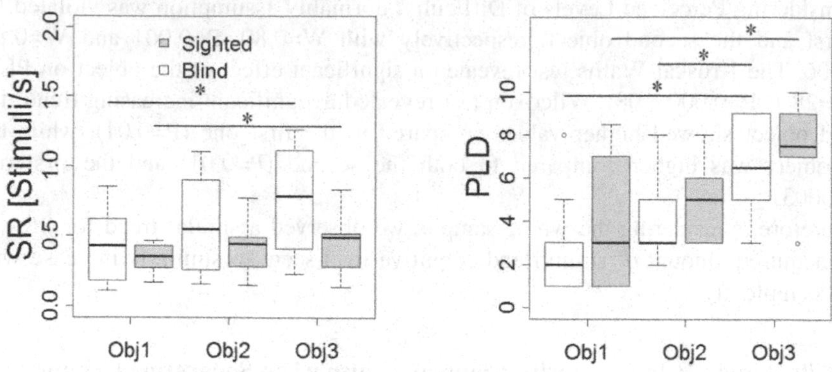

Fig. 3. Boxplot of SR and PLD, in function of the object for blind (white) and sighted subjects (grey). Stars and horizontal lines denote differences (*p<0.05).

4 Discussion

Our first main finding is that - for the whole sample - both the amount of acquired information and the subjective cognitive load increase with the complexity of the explored object and with similar trends. Second, we found this pattern also in each group, when independently considered. Finally, even separately considering single objects both blind and sighted subjects exhibit similar peculiarities. In a past study, comparing blind and sighted subjects in terms of strategies used and neurophysiological measurements linked to cognitive load, we found qualitative cues of spatial abilities independent on vision capabilities [10]: these hints are here confirmed with a quantitative analysis.

Measuring the amount of information acquisition and the cognitive load can highlight potential spatial abilities: in fact, the first can show if subjects are developing an exploration strategy or not, while the second can tell if the task is too difficult or, on the contrary, if complexity can be increased. In this way performance can be much better targeted and explained when coupled with the subjective and behavioral variables, something we already examined with sighted subjects only [8].

We considered also the possible influence of learning when exploring objects. Two issues could, possibly alter performance: first, the order in which objects were presented was not randomized, second, each object design is modular and progressive (each object geometrically includes the previous one). This could have in principle helped subjects deducing subsequent objects from previously explored structures. Had learning had an effect, cognitive load would have decreased from the first to the third object because of the augmented acquaintance. However this does not happen with our data: perceived difficulty showed the opposite trend, therefore the effect of learning, if present, appears to be qualitatively negligible.

We have shown that the amount of acquired information and the cognitive load can be modulated by means of three virtual objects of increasing complexity: we admit that the number of such objects is low, but here it appears sufficient for an adequate codification. In order to have more control on parameter variations, we used the number of virtual height levels as the variable linked to increasing difficulty. Other geometrical features such as shape, object location and size may be considered as linked to spatial complexity.

Based on our results we can claim that the construction of tactile virtual maps with the TAMO device is a process at least partially independent from visual deprivation. Therefore, the TAMO device seems to open similar encouraging prospects for the assimilation of mental maps, for individuals born blind, for visually impaired people and, especially, for blind de novo, that have not yet developed the peculiar spatial strategies of long-term blind subjects.

References

1. Picard, D., Lebaz, S.: Identifying raised-line drawings by touch: A hard but not impossible task. Journal of Visual Impairment & Blindness 106, 427–431 (2012)
2. Bach-y-Rita, P., Kercel, S.W.: Sensory Substitution and the Human-Machine Interface. Trends in Cognitive Sciences 7, 541–546 (2003)
3. James, T.W., et al.: Haptic study of three-dimensional objects acti-vates extrastriate visual areas. Neuropsychologia 40, 1706–1714 (2002)
4. Campus, C., et al.: Tactile exploration of virtual objects for blind and sighted people: the role of beta 1 EEG band in sensory substitution and supramodal mental mapping. Journal of Neurophysiology 107, 2713–2729 (2012)
5. Struiksma, M.E., Noordzij, M.L., Postma, A.: What is the link be-tween language and spatial images? Behavioral and neural findings in blind and sighted individuals. Acta Psychologica 132, 145–156 (2009)
6. Lahav, O., Mioduser, D.: Construction of cognitive maps of un-known spaces using a multi-sensory virtual environment for people who are blind. Comput. Hum. Behav. 24, 1139–1155 (2008)
7. Ungar, S.: Cognitive Mapping without Visual Experience. Cognitive Mapping: Past, Present, and Future 4 (2000)
8. Brayda, L., Campus, C., Gori, M.: Predicting successful tactile mapping of virtual objects. IEEE Transaction on Haptics 6 (2013)
9. R Core Team. R: A language and environment for statistical computing. R Foundation for Statistical Computing, Vienna, Austria (2013), http://www.R-project.org/
10. Brayda, L., et al.: An Investigation of Search Behaviour in a Tactile Exploration Task for Sighted and Non-Sighted Adults. In: Proc. Extended Abstracts on Human Factors in Computing Systems (2011)

Development of Synchronized CUI and GUI for Universal Design Tactile Graphics Production System BPLOT3

Mamoru Fujiyoshi[1], Akio Fujiyoshi[2], Akiko Osawa[1], Yusuke Kuroda[3], and Yuta Sasaki[3]

[1] National Center for University Entrance Examinations, Meguro, Tokyo
{fujiyosi,ohsawa}@rd.dnc.ac.jp
[2] Ibaraki University, Hitachi, Ibaraki
fujiyosi@mx.ibaraki.ac.jp
[3] University of Electro-Communications, Chofu, Tokyo
{koktoh96,misurneo}@gmail.com

Abstract. Synchronized CUI and GUI are developed for the universal design tactile graphics production system BPLOT3. BPLOT is the first tactile graphics production system for the blind that enables the blind to produce tactile graphics by themselves. With the new synchronized CUI and GUI of BPLOT3, the blind and the sighted can collaboratively produce tactile graphics. Proofreading of tactile graphics by a blind person is necessary in order to produce elaborate tactile graphics which can be used in textbooks or questions of entrance examinations. Because a blind person can modify tactile graphics by himself with BPLOT3, it will be a powerful tool.

Keywords: Blind, Tactile Graphics, Universal Design, User Interface.

1 Introduction

In this paper, we introduce synchronized CUI and GUI newly developed for universal design tactile graphics production system BPLOT3. BPLOT is the first tactile graphics production system for the blind that enables the blind to produce tactile graphics by themselves [1,2]. BPLOT produces tactile graphics from a source text file written in our specially designed plotter control language for BPLOT. Because a source file for BPLOT is a text file, it is editable with any text editors by any person who has learned the plotter control language. Therefore, BPLOT enables not only the sighted but also the blind to produce tactile graphics by themselves. Since BPLOT can be used only with CUI (Character User Interface) and is not WYSIWYG (What You See Is What You Get), the development of GUI (Graphical User Interface) was requested. In 2007, GUI for BPLOT was developed, and BPLOT2 was introduced [1]. With GUI, the usability of BPLOT2 for the sighted was significantly improved because a sighted user does not need a detailed knowledge of the plotter control language. This time,

K. Miesenberger et al. (Eds.): ICCHP 2014, Part II, LNCS 8548, pp. 18–25, 2014.

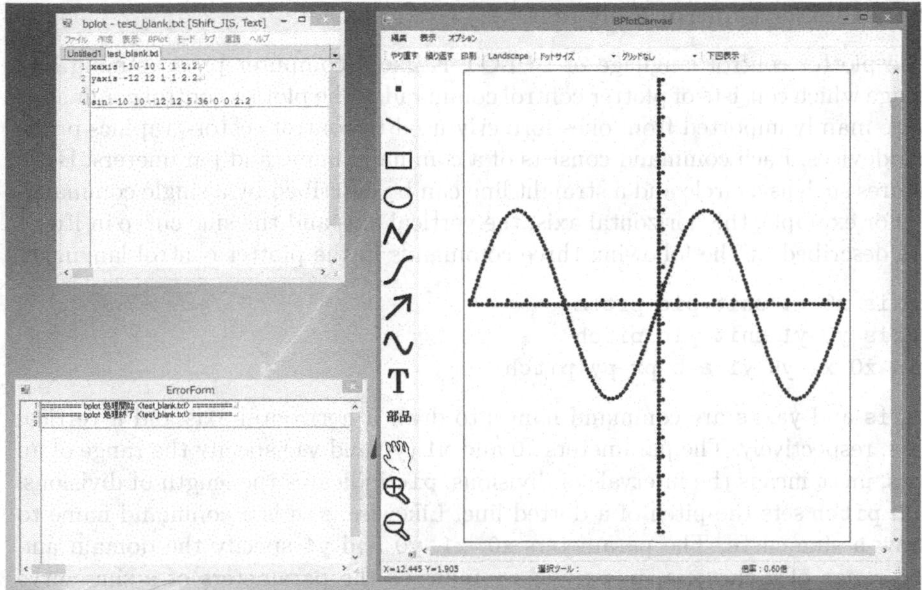

Fig. 1. Synchronized CUI and GUI of BPLOT3

a synchronized mechanism between CUI and GUI was developed, and we introduce BPLOT3 (Fig. 1). With the new synchronized CUI and GUI of BPLOT3, the blind and the sighted can collaboratively produce tactile graphics.

Tactile graphics design applications such as BES [3] and EDEL-plus [4] have sophisticated GUI and enable the sighted to produce tactile graphics easily. However, because of the necessity for mouse operations, the blind cannot use these applications by themselves. Tiger Software Suite [5] can create tactile graphics by translating graphics on computer screen into tactile graphics automatically. Both the blind and the sighted can use it. However, it is not enough for the blind to produce elaborate tactile graphics for figures in textbooks or questions of entrance examinations.

Some other new features are also implemented in BPLOT3.

2 Outline of BPLOT3

2.1 The System

BPLOT3 runs on Microsoft Windows XP, Vista, 7 or 8. It works with the braille printer ESA721 or ESA600G (JTR Corporation). In order to obtain tactile graphics of high quality, we chose ESA721 and ESA600G. They are braille graphic printers that can produce tactile graphics with very high resolution: 73 dpi (dot/inch) for ESA721 and 100 dip for ESA600G. The resolution of ordinary braille printers is only about 20 dpi. The main program of BPLOT3 is written in C++, and the user interface part is written in C#.

2.2 Plotter Control Language

The plotter control language of BPLOT is like a computer programming language which consists of plotter control commands. The plotter control commands were mainly imported from ones formerly used to control vector-graphics printing devices. Each command consists of a command name and parameters. Basic figures such as a circle and a straight line can be described by a single command.

For example, the horizontal axis, the vertical axis and the sine curve in Fig. 1 are described by the following three commands in the plotter control language.

```
xaxis x0 x1 unit pic pitch
yaxis y0 y1 unit pic pitch
sin x0 x1 y0 y1 a b px py pitch
```

`xaxis` and `yaxis` are command names to draw a horizontal axis and a vertical axis, respectively. The parameters `x0` and `x1` (`y0` and `y1`) specify the range of an axis, `unit` means the intervals of divisions, `pic` indicates the length of divisions, and `pitch` sets the pitch of a dotted line. Likewise, `sin` is a command name to draw a sine curve. The parameters `x0`, `x1`, `y0` and `y1` specify the domain and the range of a curve, `a`, `b`, `px` and `py` indicate the parameters of a sine curve $y = a\sin(b(x - px)) + py$, and `pitch` sets the pitch of a dotted line.

We can magnify and reduce the output tactile graphics with the same sense of touch because dotted lines are drawn with the same pitch. The pitch a dotted line is specified in the parameter of a command.

The detail of the plotter control language is described in [1].

2.3 New Features of BPLOT3

Synchronized CUI and GUI. The new synchronized CUI and GUI of BPLOT3 enables the collaboration between the blind and the sighted in production of tactile graphics. A screen shot of the synchronized CUI and GUI is shown in Fig. 1. On the desktop, there are a text editor window, a canvas window and a message window. When a user edits a text, the change will be reflected on the canvas window. Similarly, when graphics on the canvas window is manipulated, the result will be reflected on the text editor window.

Tablet Input for the Blind. BPLOT3 supports tablet input for the blind. When a tablet device is connected to a PC, we can draw a picture directly on the canvas window of BPLOT3. See Fig. 2. This feature is very important for the blind. By typing a shortcut key on the keyboard instead of clicking an icon on the canvas window, a blind user can change the drawing method. When the tablet is touched with a stylus pen, coordinates are inputted, and both the canvas window and the text editor window reflect the input. With this feature, a blind user can input a picture by tracing a draft version of tactile graphics on the tablet. A sample of a traced picture inputted by a blind user is shown in Fig. 3. The character 'i' consists of connected straight line segments, while the other characters are drawn as connected spline curves.

Fig. 2. Tablet Input for the Blind

Presenting a Draft Picture as a Background Picture. On the canvas window, a draft picture can be presented as a background picture. A sighted user can easily trace the draft picture. A draft picture can be made with a digital camera or an image scanner.

This function enables the digitization of a large amount of tactile graphics produced in the past. These digitized tactile graphics can be modified and reused.

3 Practical Evaluation

3.1 Usability Check by a Blind Person

In order to check whether BPLOT3 can easily be used by the blind, we asked a blind person to use BPLOT3. This person is an instructor working for a sales and support company of computers and software for the blind. The followings are the results:

1. BPLOT3 can be installed on Windows 7 by the blind person by himself with some screen readers on Windows.
2. Text commands can be inputted on the text editor window.
3. Text files can be loaded to the text editor window, and the contents can be read easily.
4. Tactile graphics can be printed out with a braille printer.
5. Online help can be used. However, the person pointed out that a manual is desired in addition to online help.

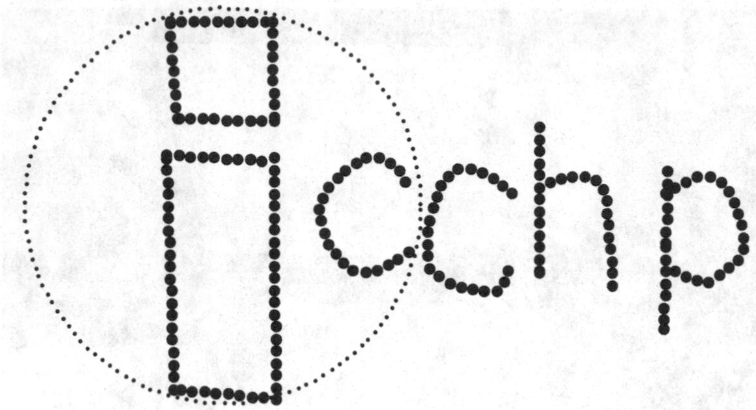

Fig. 3. A Sample of Traced Picture

3.2 Production of Tactile Graphics with the Tablet Input Function for the Blind

The usability of the table input function for the blind was checked by producing tactile graphics of the logo of ICCHP shown in Fig. 3. The followings are the steps to produce tactile graphics with this function.

1. Make a draft version of tactile graphics using heat sensitive capsule paper (PIAF).
2. Place the draft on a tablet device connected to a PC. See Fig. 2.
3. Type a shortcut key on the keyboard to select a drawing method and trace the draft by touching some points with a stylus pen. To trace the character 'i', "connected straight line segments" was selected as a drawing method and corners of the rectangles were touched. To indicate the last point of a figure, it was double-tapped. To trace the other characters, "connected spline curves" was selected as a drawing method and some points on the characters were sequentially touched.
4. Modify tactile graphics on the text editor window. The circle enclosing the character 'i' was first traced as connected spline curves, and then it was replaced by a circle drawing command after calculating the radius and the coordinates of the center.

3.3 Example of Practical Use

It was evidentially proved that only blind persons can produce tactile graphics of a one-year amount of the graphs and figures in the questions of the National Center Test for University Admissions of all subjects (mathematics, English language, Japanese language, physics, chemistry, biology, earth science, world history, Japanese history, geography, contemporary sociology, and politics and economy).

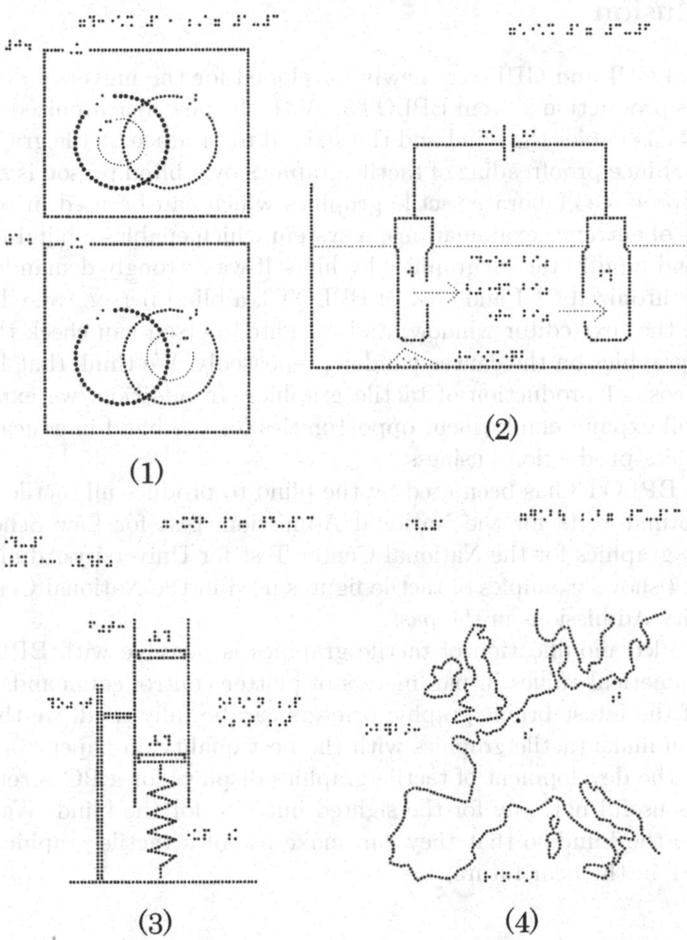

Fig. 4. (1) Venn Diagrams in Mathematics, (2) Electrolysis in Chemistry, (3) A Cylinder and Pistons with a Spring in Physics, and (4) A Map of Europe in World History

First, a draft version of tactile graphics of original figures was made using heat sensitive capsule paper by a sighted person. From the draft version, a blind person produced tactile figures with BPLOT3. The tactile graphics were proofread by a pair of another blind person and a sighted person. In accordance with the result of proofreading, the blind person modified the tactile figures. This proofreading and modification process was continued three times with different pairs of proofreaders.

Some examples of tactile figures used in the National Center Test for University Admissions are shown in Fig. 4.

4 Conclusion

Synchronized CUI and GUI were newly developed for the universal design tactile graphics production system BPLOT3. With the new synchronized CUI and GUI, BPLOT3 enables the blind and the sighted to produce tactile graphics collaboratively. Since proofreading of tactile graphics by a blind person is necessary in order to produce elaborate tactile graphics which can be used in textbooks or questions of entrance examinations, a system which enables a blind person to proofread and modify tactile graphics by himself was strongly demanded. With the new synchronized CUI and GUI of BPLOT3, a blind person can edit tactile graphics on the text editor window, and a sighted person can check the modified tactile graphics on the canvas window, repeatedly. We think that BPLOT3 reduce the cost of production of tactile graphics. In addition, we expect that BPLOT3 will expand employment opportunities for the blind in education and tactile graphics production business.

Actually, BPLOT3 has been used by the blind to produce all tactile graphics of braille format tests for the National Admission Test for Law Schools and some tactile graphics for the National Center Test for University Admissions in Japan. Fig. 4 shows examples of tactile figures used in the National Center Test for University Admissions in the past.

Since detailed modification of tactile graphics is possible with BPLOT3 by adjusting numerical values in parameters of plotter control commands and the functions of the latest braille graphic printers can be fully used, we think that BPLOT3 can make tactile graphics with the best quality on paper.

Recently, the development of tactile graphics displays for a PC is remarkable [6,7]. GUI is useful not only for the sighted but also for the blind. We want to offer GUI to the blind so that they can make use of a tactile graphics display with BPLOT in the near future.

References

1. Fujiyoshi, M., Fujiyoshi, A., Ohtake, N., Yamaguchi, K., Teshima, Y.: The development of a universal design tactile graphics production system BPLOT2. In: Miesenberger, K., Klaus, J., Zagler, W.L., Karshmer, A.I. (eds.) ICCHP 2008. LNCS, vol. 5105, pp. 938–945. Springer, Heidelberg (2008)
2. Fujiyoshi, M., Kaneko, T., Fujiyoshi, A., Oouchi, S., Yamazawa, K., Ikegami, Y., Watanabe, Y., Teshima, Y.: Development of Tactile Graphics Production Software for Three-Dimensional Projections. In: Miesenberger, K., Klaus, J., Zagler, W., Karshmer, A. (eds.) ICCHP 2010, Part II. LNCS, vol. 6180, pp. 541–547. Springer, Heidelberg (2010)
3. BES, `http://www.ttools.co.jp/product/eyes/BES/` (in Japanese)
4. EDEL-plus, `http://www7a.biglobe.ne.jp/~EDEL-plus/` (in Japanese)

5. Tiger Software Suite, VIEWPLUS, `http://www.viewplus.com/products/software/braille-translator/`
6. Nishi, A., Fukuda, R.: Graphic Editor for Visually Impaired Users. In: Miesenberger, K., Klaus, J., Zagler, W.L., Karshmer, A.I. (eds.) ICCHP 2006. LNCS, vol. 4061, pp. 1139–1146. Springer, Heidelberg (2006)
7. Völkel, T., Weber, G., Baumann, U.: Tactile Graphics revised: The novel BrailleDis 9000 Pin-Matrix Device with Multitouch Input. In: Miesenberger, K., Klaus, J., Zagler, W.L., Karshmer, A.I. (eds.) ICCHP 2008. LNCS, vol. 5105, pp. 835–842. Springer, Heidelberg (2008)

Production of Accessible Tactile Graphics

Denise Prescher, Jens Bornschein, and Gerhard Weber

Technische Universität Dresden, Institut für Angewandte Informatik, Dresden, Germany
{denise.prescher,jens.bornschein,gerhard.weber}@tu-dresden.de

Abstract. To allow blind and visually impaired users participation in learning visualized concepts and ideas it is important to provide them not only with text but also with graphics. As the effort and expertise needed for manually transcribing graphics is time-consuming we need a better understanding of the decision-making process leading to the support of alternative descriptions and materials for tactile exploration. We performed two surveys, the first one on current practices used for the production of accessible graphics in Germany, the second one on user experiences in exploring and constructing tactile graphics. As result we have defined some requirements for enhancing the production of accessible tactile graphics by a software tool that not only supports the creation of image masters and descriptions, but also includes blind users in the editing process.

Keywords: Tactile Graphics, Image Descriptions, Textbook Production, Accessible Distribution, Transcription Process, Survey, Visually Impaired Users.

1 Introduction

The development of new tactile displays may improve availability of graphics in textbooks. Several new technologies are able to present graphical information by actuating taxels[1] against the skin and in particular finger tips. Researchers have proposed for example TeslaTouch, MEMS (micro-electro-mechanical systems) devices, hydrogels, lateral skin deformation, force feedback and pin-based piezo-electric displays. The HyperBraille display [1] has demonstrated a working area of 120 by 60 pins allowing interactive exploration of diagrams at various scales by supporting zooming and panning while presenting both Braille and tactile graphics.

However, production of accessible graphics in textbooks is to be supported by alternative descriptions according to Web Content Accessibility Guidelines (WCAG 2.0). Various guidelines exist for expressing alternative contents, but when it comes to textbooks and its graphics, alternative descriptions can become complex and the text requires some structuring in order to generate a readable text. For some kind of graphics alternative descriptions are hard to develop, in particular maps and diagrams showing graphical notations, such as electrical circuit or UML diagrams, etc. For such diagrams tactile graphics together with an appropriate legend or audio-haptic ap-

[1] Taxels can be static or dynamically changing pins, reliefs made out of polymers etc.

K. Miesenberger et al. (Eds.): ICCHP 2014, Part II, LNCS 8548, pp. 26–33, 2014.

proaches can be more suitable. In particular merging verbal descriptions and tactile drawings simplify the need to develop verbalizations. The transcription process requires design of spoken feedback together with the design of a tactile layout.

Currently there is no single approach for supporting all of above approaches. As the effort and expertise needed for manually transcribing graphics is time-consuming [2] we need a better understanding of the decision-making process leading to the support of alternative descriptions, printed tactile graphics as well as reading graphics on interactive tactile displays. In the following we describe current practices used for the production of accessible graphics in Germany. As a result we define some requirements and give a short roadmap for our Tangram project which should enhance the production of tactile graphics.

2 Supporting Tactile Graphics Production

Some studies on translating text and graphics into Braille report about work practices and training of transcribers in the United States [3,4]. Such analyses are important for developing new efficient tools, such as Tactile Graphics Assistant (TGA), that should enhance and accelerate the process of transcribing graphics. In contrast to the participants in the survey of Ladner et al. [3] we have focused not on individual experts, but on institutions which are not tactile graphics specialists. Typically, regular employees, such as teachers or scientific assistants, perform the transcription of text and graphics[2].

Therefore, we considered to perform our own studies to find particular needs of that group of transcribers preparing tactile graphics for people with visual impairments. Besides, we want to involve blind and visually impaired people to esti-mate the quality of the resulting graphic. Therefore we conducted two surveys, both were organized in an accessible online questionnaire in German language.

2.1 Survey on the Production of Tactile Graphics

The first survey addresses institutions preparing textbooks and graphics for use by blind and visually impaired people. The objective of this survey is to provide an insight into current processes and methods used to transcribe graphics in tactile or textual versions. For this purpose, the questionnaire consists of 29 questions regarding the institution and its target group, the production of textbooks, personal/time resources, kinds of graphics and production methods, document formats, hard- and software, quality management, re-use of results, storage as well as basic experiences and expectations of a future software tool supporting the production of tactile graphics and descriptions.

In total, 27 different institutions of German-speaking countries have participated in the survey (see Fig. 1). Most of them produce graphics for Braille readers and also for large print users. Only one library does not conduct any graphic production and therefore is not included in the following.

---

2 As a result of our survey, we found that only in 4 of 21 cases qualified specialists do the image description and in 6 of 19 cases tactile graphics are produced by qualified persons.

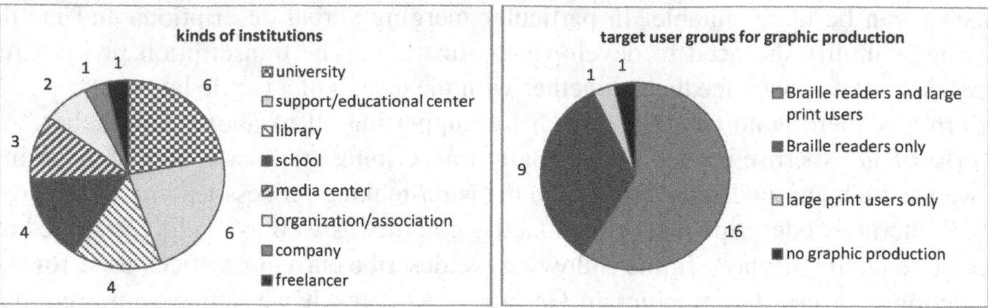

Fig. 1. Institutions (left) and target user groups for graphic production (right)

In general, the process for preparing textbooks can be divided into eight steps: organizational research, digitalization of the source file, adaption of the text in an accessible version, conversion into Braille or audio version, test printing, quality check, distribution and archival storage. In most cases (73%), the adaptation of graphics is done in parallel to the text. As the production of tactile graphics is very time consuming (on average about 1 to 2 hours per graphic is reported), not every institution deals with all of the graphics in a textbook. Sometimes only very relevant graphics are converted in an accessible version. Thereby, the source files are mostly PDF files (21 of 22 institutions), scans (13 of 22) or word documents (11 of 22).

69% of the institutions produce tactile graphics as well as image descriptions, but there is usually no fixed order for their creation (12 of 18). Of the remaining institutions four do only image descriptions, three produce tactile images without description and one institution only produces material for large print readers. Frequently reported factors for the decision if a graphic will be provided as a tactile version or only as a textual description, are as follows: insufficiency of description (6 of 20 institutions), user request/need (6 of 20), relevance/importance (5 of 20), complexity (4 of 20), cost/time effort (3 of 20) as well as suitability for tactile presentation (3 of 20).

For the production of tactile graphics, most institutions use microcapsule paper, Braille embossers or the vacuum-forming method (see Fig. 2). Collages and 3D mod-els are not so popular until now, because of the much worse possibilities of duplication. Each institution uses an average of four different software tools during the pro-duction of accessible graphics. Two of them use even ten different tools. Often, MS Word was mentioned to be used for image description and Corel Draw for image pre-processing and mastering tactile graphics. Overall, the responses are very heterogeneous (see Fig. 3).

Most of the institutions (23 of 25) have some kind of quality assurance. 21 of 23 institutions let check their results by blind or visually impaired people. But only 10 of them perform a full evaluation, while the others do a random checking. It is also common to do a revision after user feedback (17 of 23) and to apply some kind of guidelines (16 of 23). Predefined construction kits are rarely used (2 of 23), but 20 of 22 institutions sometimes do some kind of re-use (see Fig. 4). We conclude, for enabling a consistent and time-saving production of tactile graphics re-use is very important. Therefore, while many tools are in use, independently from specific editing tools a new type of support is needed for editors allowing re-use across a variety of technical approaches for delivering tactile graphics.

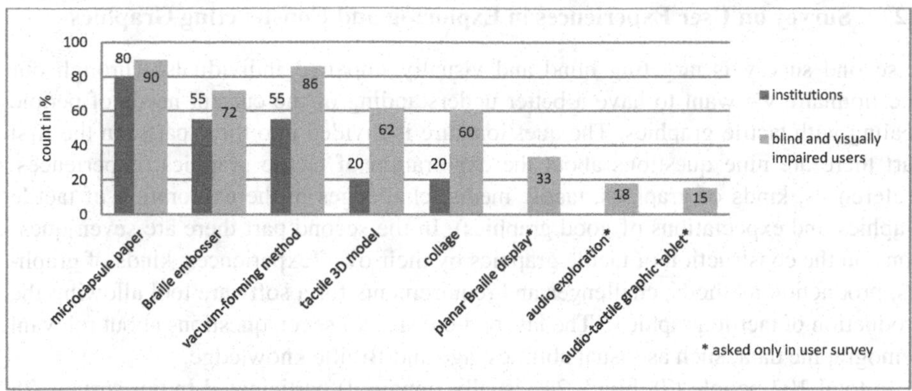

Fig. 2. Tactile media used by institutions for graphic production (n = 20) and familiarity by blind and visually impaired users (n = 78)

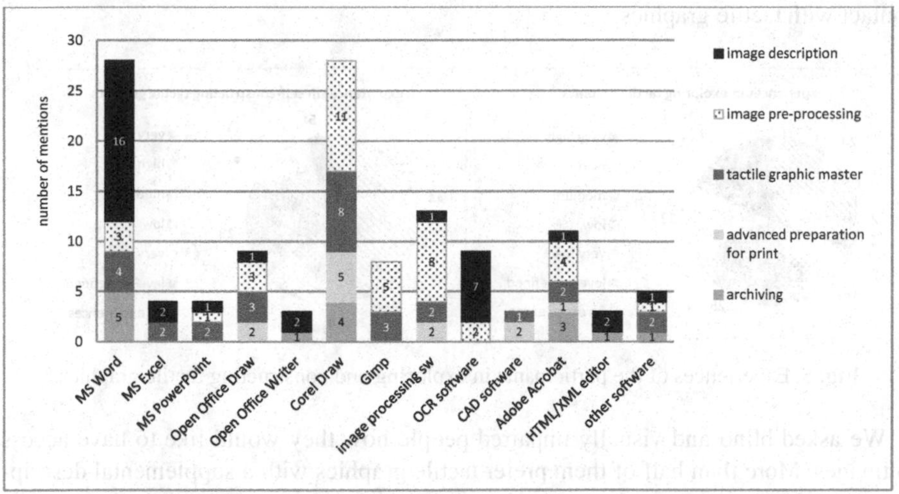

Fig. 3. Software used during the different steps of graphics production

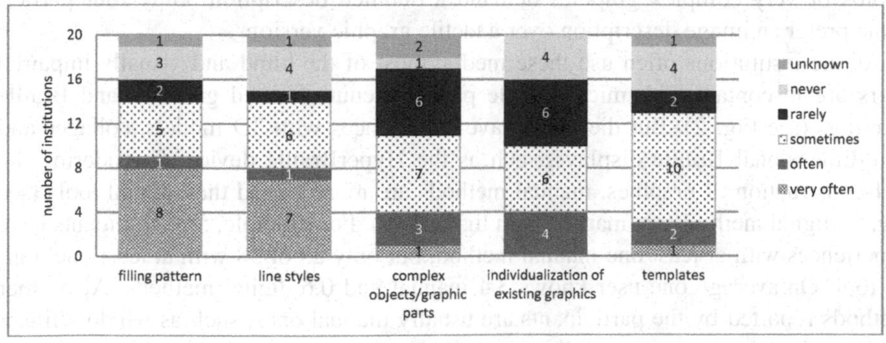

Fig. 4. Types of re-use applied by institutions during the graphics production

2.2 Survey on User Experiences in Exploring and Constructing Graphics

A second survey is targeting blind and visually impaired individuals. Through our questionnaire we want to have a better understanding of the current needs of people dealing with tactile graphics. The questionnaire is divided into three parts: In the first part there are nine questions about the exploration of tactile graphics (experiences, preferences, kinds of graphics, tactile media, challenges in the exploration of tactile graphics and expectations of good graphics). In the second part there are seven questions on the construction of tactile graphics by their own (experiences, kinds of graphics, production methods, challenges and requirements for a software tool allowing the production of tactile graphics). The last part consists of seven questions about relevant demographic data, such as visual abilities, age and Braille knowledge.

In total 102 people (78 blind, 24 visually impaired) participated in our survey. 78 of them have experiences with exploration (64 blind, 14 visually impaired, see Fig. 5 left) and 58 with self-construction of tactile graphics (52 blind, 6 visually impaired, see Fig. 5 right). Most of the participants without any experiences would like to get in contact with tactile graphics.

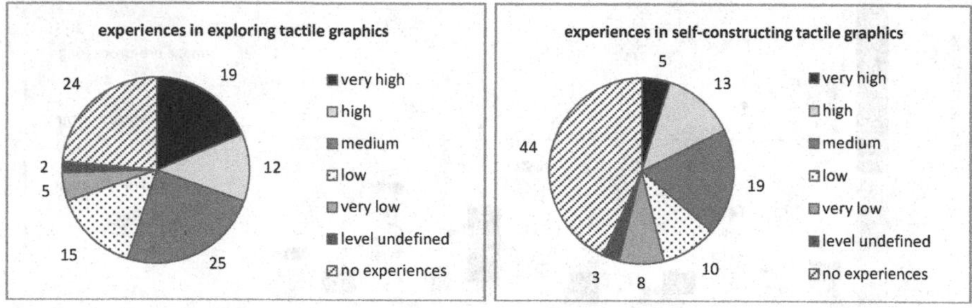

Fig. 5. Experiences of the participants in exploring and constructing tactile graphics

We asked blind and visually impaired people how they would like to have access to images. More than half of them prefer tactile graphics with a supplemental description (41 of 78). 26 respondents mentioned that it depends on type and usage of the image. For example maps and diagrams should be available in a tactile version, while photos or very complex graphics demand a detailed description. Only four participants prefer an image description over a tactile graphic version.

As the institutions often use these media, most of the blind and visually impaired users are in contact with microcapsule paper, vacuum-formed graphics and Braille printings (see Fig. 2). But they also have experiences with 3D models, collages and two-dimensional Braille displays, such as the HyperBraille device. Considering the self-construction of graphics, manual methods are more spread than digital tools (see Fig. 6, digital methods are marked with light color). For example, 55 participants have experiences with at least one manual method, but only 23 of 58 with at least one digital tool. On average one user knows 3.4 manual and 0.6 digital methods. Also other methods reported by the participants are usually manual ones, such as window/finger colors, collages or geometry toolkits.

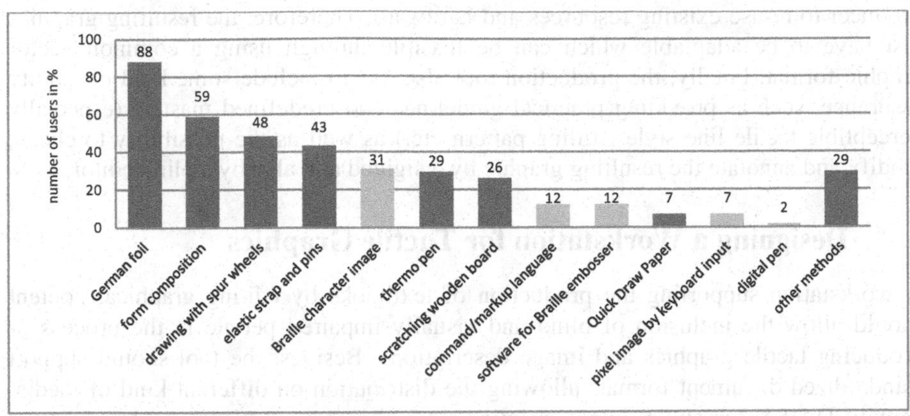

Fig. 6. Methods for constructing tactile graphics used by the participants (n = 58)

Difficulties encountered in exploring and creating tactile graphics is very revealing. The results of our survey related to the difficulties are shown in Fig. 7. Overloading tactile graphics with too much information is a major problem. In constructing their own graphics, blind users especially criticize the limited possibilities of error correction, which is due to the fact that they use manual methods in the most cases.

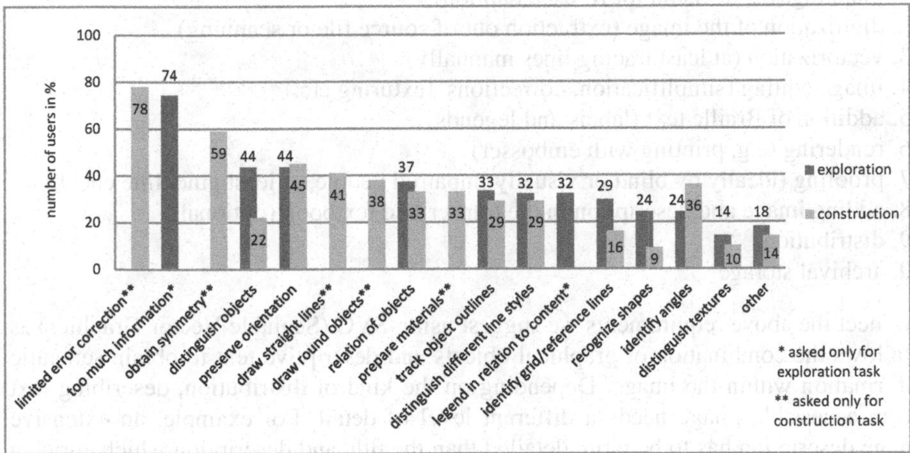

Fig. 7. Difficulties in exploring (n = 78) and constructing (n = 58) tactile graphics reported by blind and visually impaired users (multiple answers were possible)

2.3 Requirements for a Tool Enhancing the Production of Tactile Graphics

Based on the results of the two surveys, we can define the following requirements. As the combination of tactile graphic and description is very important for the comprehensibility of an image, a production tool should include a link between these two parts. Furthermore, different distribution channels should be handled allowing the producer to re-use existing resources and hardware. Therefore, the resulting graphics just have to be adaptable which can be feasible through using a common vector graphic format. Finally, the production tool also has to include some kind of quality assurance, such as providing practical guidelines and predefined masters (especially perceptible tactile line styles, filling pattern etc.) as well as the possibility to check, modify and annotate the resulting graphic by a sighted and also by a blind editor.

3 Designing a Workstation for Tactile Graphics

A workstation supporting the production of textbooks by editing graphical content should allow the inclusion of blind and visually impaired people in the process of producing tactile graphics and image descriptions. Besides, the tool should support standardized document formats allowing the distribution on different kind of media, namely DAISY for audio output, printing on embossers or microcapsule paper for tactile output, HyperReader fullscreen [1] or other tactile displays as well as IVEO system or Talking Tactile Tablet for audio-tactile output.

In order to provide an effective integration into existing workflows, a tactile graphics workstation should support common tasks an editor has to complete while producing appropriate tactile graphics. Our findings based on the responses in our survey are very similar to the observations of work practices of Ladner et al. [3]. All in all, we have identified the following ten subtasks:

1. planning (i.a. decision for re-use/adaption)
2. digitization of the image (extraction out of source file or scanning)
3. vectorization (at least tracing lines manually)
4. image editing (simplification, corrections, texturing etc.)
5. addition of Braille text (labels and legends)
6. rendering (e.g. printing with embosser)
7. proofing (ideally by blind or visually impaired people, at least guideline check)
8. adding image and description in the transcribed textbook (optional)
9. distribution
10. archival storage

To meet the above requirements we suggest using SVG (Scalable Vector Graphics) as it allows the combination of graphical objects and descriptive text to obtain semantic information within the image. Depending on the kind of distribution, describing text of an accessible image needs a different level of detail. For example, an extensive image description has to be more detailed than the title and description which enrich a tactile image for exploring on an audio-tactile device such as the IVEO system. Already in that system, SVG is a vital approach to publish mainstream graphics while being accessible to blind and visually impaired users [5].

Another requirement which has to be considered is the customizability of produced tactile graphics - not only for different distribution media, but also for diverse user needs. For that purpose, the Access2Graphics project dynamically generates SVG graphics depending on user profiles within a server-based approach[3]. Another strategy can be the adaption of the output of SVG by Cascading Style Sheets (CSS), which is

3 Access2Graphics project, see `http://a2g.faw.uni-linz.ac.at/`

very common for XML-based formats. For example, we use CSS for adapting tactile function graphs to different output media [6]. This also enables the user to customize a graphic to his specific needs or preferences after delivering without the need of any special application.

4 Conclusion and Outlook

Overall the surveys show that blind and visually impaired people are very interested in dealing with tactile graphics, but there are many difficulties, if the tactile material is not well prepared. Typically, institutions have no specialist producing tactile graphics, even if there are exceptions such as the National Centre for Tactile Diagrams in the UK. For this reason the integration of blind users into the production process can be very helpful, in which planar tactile displays, such as the HyperBraille device, can provide new opportunities.

Within the Tangram project we want to enhance the time-consuming production of tactile graphic materials by a software tool that not only supports the creation of image masters and descriptions, but also includes blind users in the editing process. First requirements were collected by conducting two surveys on the target groups, namely tactile graphic editors and users with visual impairment. In the following steps we want to identify guidelines and basic graphic primitives (e.g. lines and filling patterns) which can be applied by non-experts to produce accessible tactile graphics and descriptions.

Acknowledgements. We thank all participants of our surveys. The Tangram project is sponsored by the Federal Ministry of Labour and Social Affairs (BMAS) under the grant number R/FO125423.

References

1. Prescher, D., Weber, G., Spindler, M.: A tactile windowing system for blind users. In: ASSETS 2010, pp. 91–98 (2010)
2. Motti, L.G., Burger, D.: Adapting Diagrams for DAISY Books. In: Proc. DAISY, Leipzig (2009)
3. Ladner, R.E., Ivory, M.Y., Rao, R., Burgstahler, S., Comden, D., Hahn, S., Renzelmann, M., Krisnandi, S., Ramasamy, M., Slabosky, B., Martin, A., Lacenski, A., Olsen, S., Groce, D.: Automating Tactile Graphics Translation. In: ASSETS 2005 (2005)
4. Corn, A.L., Wall, R.S.: Training and Availability of Braille Transcribers in the United States. Journal of Visual Impairment & Blindness, 223–232 (April 2002)
5. Gardner, J., Bulatov, V., Kelly, R.: Making journals accessible to the visually impaired: the future is near. Learned Publishing: Journal of the Association of Learned and Professional Society Publishers 22(4) (2009)
6. Bornschein, J., Prescher, D., Weber, G.: SVGPlott - Generating Adaptive and Accessible Audio-tactile Function Graphs. In: This Proceedings

Edutactile - A Tool for Rapid Generation of Accurate Guideline-Compliant Tactile Graphics for Science and Mathematics

Mrinal Mech, Kunal Kwatra, Supriya Das, Piyush Chanana, Rohan Paul, and M. Balakrishnan

Assistive Technologies Group, Indian Institute of Technology Delhi, India
{cs5090246,ird10432,mbala}@cse.iitd.ernet.in
http://assistech.iitd.ernet.in

Abstract. In this paper the authors have presented the design and implementation of Edutactile, a cross-platform software which automates the process of creation of tactile diagrams. Edutactile provides for automated application of guidelines or presets as well as Braille translation and thus abstracts away the production related issues. This relieves special educators for the visually challenged from having to learn the workings of the graphics editing software (Photoshop, CorelDraw) which are currently being used to produced tactile graphics and instead focus on the content of the diagram.

Keywords: Visually Challenged Students, Tactile Graphics, Mathematical and Scientific Diagrams, Special Educators.

1 Introduction

According to WHO about 39 million people are estimated to be blind worldwide, 90% of whom live in the developing world. Out of these, 2 million are children under the age of 15 years [1]. Teaching and learning of science and mathematics is particularly challenging due to the graphical and diagrammatic content (chemical equations, mathematical graphs etc). Increasingly, embossed tactile representations are playing a significant role in assisting special educators in conveying concepts for diagram comprehension and practice.

Tactile representation requires certain guidelines to be followed for comprehension and perceptibility of the diagrams. These guidelines (BANA[1], RNIB[2]) recommend/constrain the use of line types, line thicknesses and texture types.

Former, existing software solutions are general purpose graphics software (CorelDraw, Adobe Photoshop). They have a high learning curve and are more sophisticated than what's required. Furthermore these software are proprietary with high licensing costs and are tied to a specific output method or product like braille embossing, thermoforming or swell. Additionally, current solutions

[1] http://www.brailleauthority.org
[2] http://www.rnib.org.uk

K. Miesenberger et al. (Eds.): ICCHP 2014, Part II, LNCS 8548, pp. 34–41, 2014.

mostly cater to a specific category of diagram and do not holistically address the needs of a typical special educator.

Hence, there is a need for a software that relieves the special educators from the workload of conforming to guidelines, braille labelling and layouts for production and hence allows them to concentrate on the quality and the expression of the diagram.

This paper presents the design and implementation of Edutactile, a cross-platform Java-based software which facilitates the creation of tactile graphics specialised for scientific and mathematical content. It automatically handles layout and formatting thus relieving special educators and enabling them to concentrate on the content of the diagrams. During the development, feedback was taken from special educators as well as visually impaired students. Initial feedback has been positive regarding both the software as well as the quality of diagrams produced using it.

2 Related Work

There are commercially available software like TactileView [2] , TGD-Pro [3] etc aimed at the creation of tactile graphics but limitations arise due to their generic nature with them being tied to a specific output method. Further drawbacks include their proprietary nature and a high learning curve. R.E. Ladner et. al. [4] from the University of Washington present a system for automation of the graphics creation process. Drawbacks arise as this system only converts pre-existing printed images and does not generate new tactile diagrams. This does not guarantee the accuracy of many of the diagrams, as the original images might have errors.

3 System

3.1 Software Design Aspects

Edutactile is built on a Java framework with the front-end GUI being implemented using Java Swing and images being rendered using the Java class Graphics2D. Tactile diagrams are input/generated in the .svg (Scalable Vector Graphic) format. Input .svg files are preprocessed by first parsing them using SVGSalamander[3] and then by converting them to a table-like *Shape* data structure. Braille translation (in multiple languages) is done by an open source braille translator BrailleTrans [4].

Focus groups were formed during the design and development process of the system. Constant feedback was taken from users and special educators throughout to know their needs. Keeping these specifications in mind, three modules have been incorporated into the system.

[3] `https://svgsalamander.java.net/`

[4] `http://alasdairking.me.uk/brailletrans/`

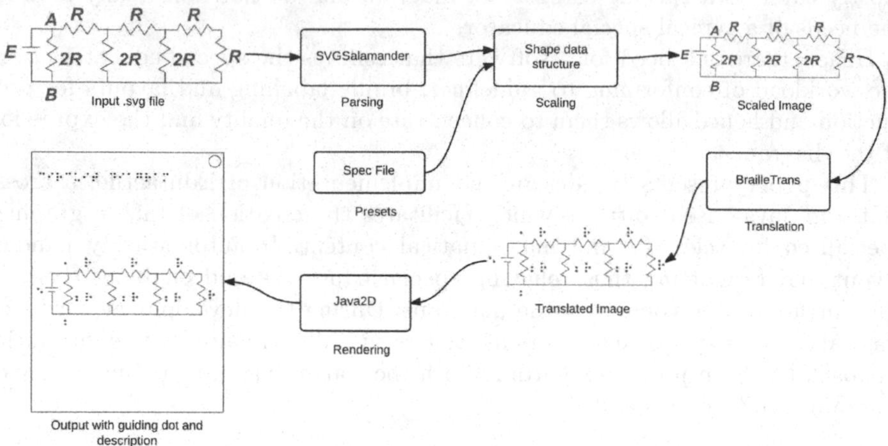

Fig. 1. Process of conversion for a standard image into a tactile graphic suited for a production method and conforming to guidelines

1. **Image Converter Module** - Automates the translation of a standard textbook figure into a tactile version conforming to guidelines with descriptions and accessible labeling
2. **Chemical Equations Module** - Generates chemical equations with the help of a drag and drop library of commonly used chemical symbols
3. **Mathematical Functions Module** - Provides entry, parsing and plotting of complex mathematical functions

3.2 Image Converter Module

The image converter module takes as input a basic .svg figure and applies guidelines as well as does transformations like scaling, spatial decluttering, occlusion removal, braille conversion, changing edge thicknesses/textures, marking and positioning to create a better diagram. The system allows for specifications for guidelines. Specification files can be imported and applied to a class of diagrams. Furthermore, the special educator can add annotations.

The input .svg file is parsed and the component shapes (embedded in XML tags) are converted into a *Shape* data structure which is a table where each entry corresponds to a particular shape and it's attributes (radius, length, breadth etc).

Scaling is done by finding the bounding boxes for all the shapes (done with the help of the *Shape* data structure) in the image. Then a maximal bounding box is found whose dimensions are compared with the page dimensions after which appropriate scaling is applied.

To facilitate the changing of line thicknesses, shapes are decomposed into their constituent lines/arcs via modifying their entries in the *Shape* data structure. The entry corresponding to the shape being decomposed is replaced by entries

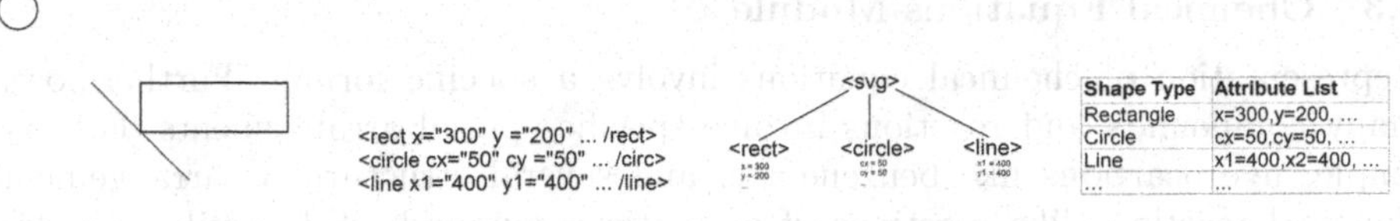

Fig. 2. Parsing of an input .svg file

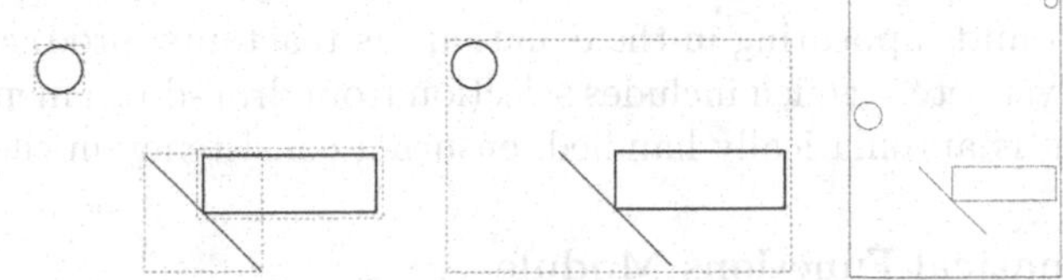

Fig. 3. Scaling of image

corresponding to it's constituent parts. This enables a user to click and change the thickness/nature of a particular line/arc.

Textures can be changed via the click of a mouse button. To simplify this process the regions bounded by the various components of the image are calculated. The system also warns a user if adjacent textures are too similar.

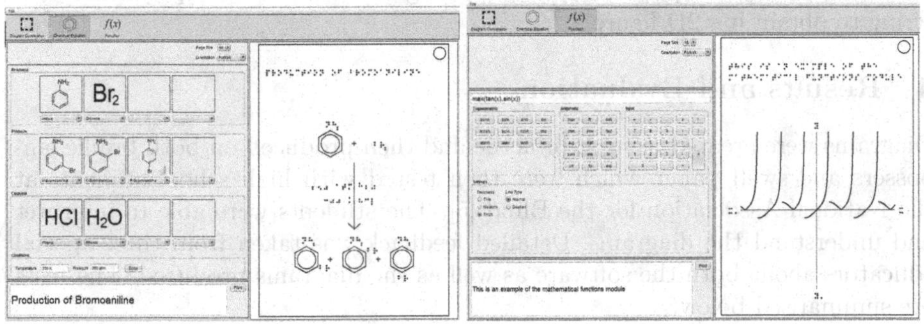

Fig. 4. GUI for chemical equations and mathematical functions modules. The chemical equation shown is the production of bromoaniline. The mathematical function shown is the *maximum* of $sin(x)$ and $tan(x)$.

3.3 Chemical Equations Module

Representation of chemical equations involve a specific format. Furthermore, many compounds and reactions involve specific spatial arrangements. For example, hydrocarbons like benzene etc. and several structural re-arrangement chemical reactions like reactions of aromatic compounds. Edutactile provides for creation of tactile versions of such chemical equations. During the creation and edition many operations can be performed, promoting insertion, deletion, modification and movement of chemical symbols. Concurrently with entering chemical compounds appearing in the equations as reactants, products, precipitates and catalysts etc. - which includes selection from drop-down menus - layout and positioning is automatically handled, ensuring consistency in the diagram.

3.4 Mathematical Functions Module

Graphs of mathematical functions are a key diagrammatic component of imparting mathematical education. A variety of functions exist which are difficult to graph manually. Edutactile provides for interpolation based plotting of 1D mathematical functions. The software supports polynomial, logarithmic, trigonometric, exponential and statistical functions as well as any combination of them either by mathematical operators (addition, subtraction etc) or by function composition. The mathematical function plotting module takes the expression as an input that is parsed (with the help of a open source parser Math Expression String Parser[5]) and then point wise interpolated to yield the function graph. Different line types and labelings are also added. Since this module has no visual component as input, a visually challenged student may input a function string to obtain it's 2D figure.

4 Results and Evaluation

Diagrams were created using Edutactile and then produced on both braille embossers and swell paper which were then tested with high school students at the National Association for the Blind [5]. The students were able to interpret and understand the diagrams. Detailed feedback was taken from three special educators about both the software as well as the diagrams produced. The tests are summarised below.

4.1 User Evaluation on Software

The three special educators were asked to rate the software on various criteria on a 5 point Likert scale (with 1 being the lowest possible score and 5 being a perfect score). Furthermore, they also assigned scores to the perceived diagram quality and output interpretability by students. The scores are summarised below.

Feedback from the special educators was positive, as can be seen in the universally high ratings. They stressed on the need for such a tool, especially in the context of teaching blind children in India.

[5] `http://sourceforge.net/projects/expression-tree/`

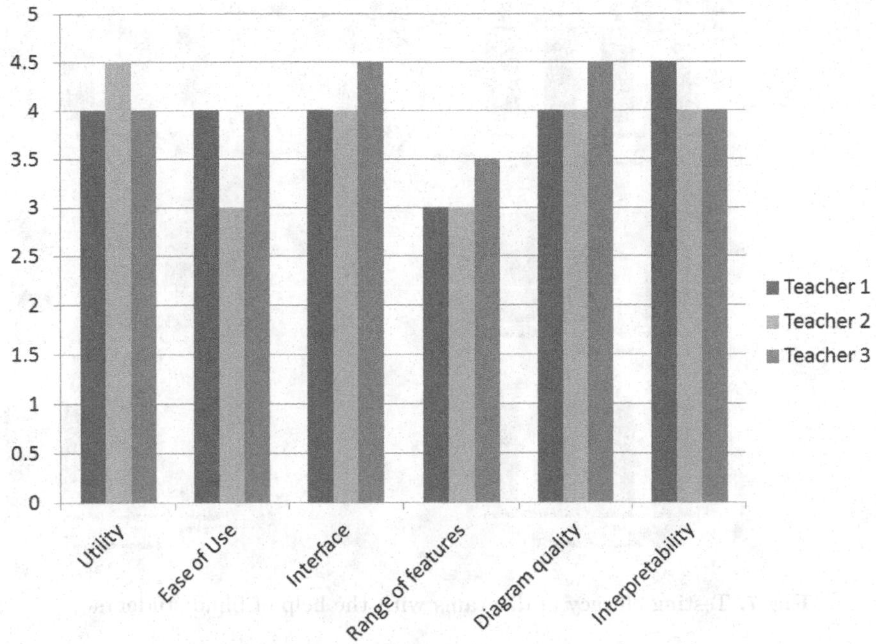

Fig. 5. Ratings by special educators

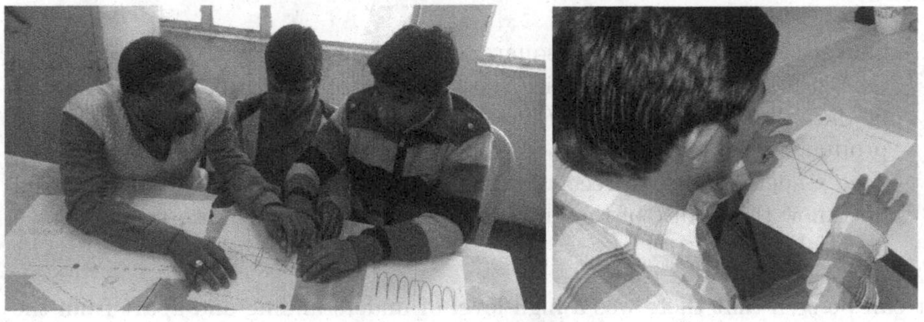

Fig. 6. Output tactile diagrams being tested by high-school students and special educators at the National Association for the Blind, New Delhi

4.2 User Evaluation on Diagrams

To gauge the effectiveness of the diagrams produced, a set of six diagrams was given to three students and they were asked to interpret what the diagrams meant. The results are summarised below.

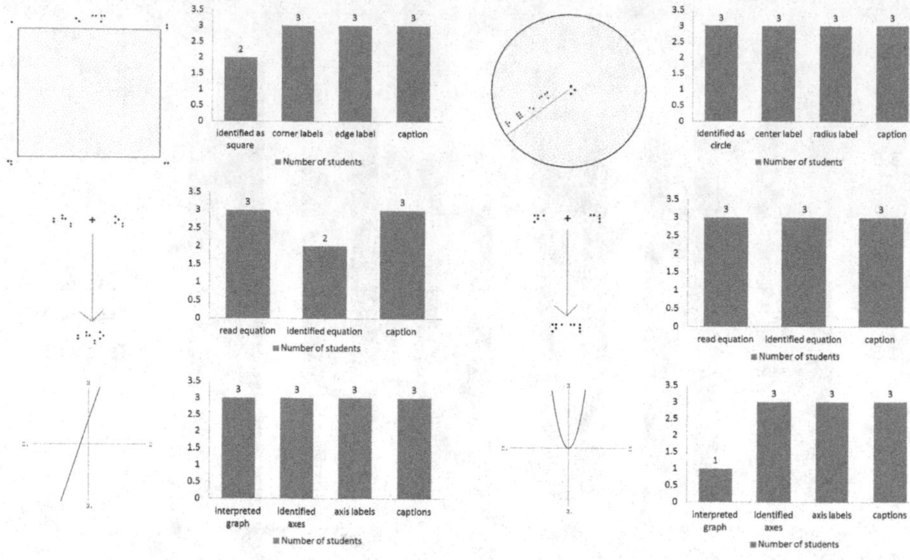

Fig. 7. Testing efficacy of diagrams with the help of blind students

Almost all elements of all the images were located, identified and interpreted by the students. In four instances a student failed to interpret a particular element.

- One student interpreted the square as a rectangle.
- One student couldn't recognize the equation of the formation of water as he didn't know the equation (although he could tell what the reactants and products were).
- Two students failed to recognize the graph of $y = x^2$ as both of them did not know the nature of the graph for that function. One interpreted it as a parabola.

It can be seen that there was a high level of understanding and apart from the first case any mistakes in interpretation were due to the lack of knowledge of the student rather than the quality of the diagram.

5 Conclusion and Future Work

In this paper, we have presented the design and development for an open source cross-platform system which amelerioates challenges faced by special educators. Hence, making it easier for special educators to focus on the quality and content of the diagrams. The system provides a low barrier to entry as it uses simple mouse actions for interaction. Feedback has been very positive from special educators and end-users during preliminary feedback. In future, we plan to improve the accessibility and diagram generation directly for end-users. Also addition of newer functionalities is planned, e.g., conversion of printed images into tactile drawings. A beta version has been released online [6] which is updated regularly. Both the source code and an executable is available.

References

1. http://www.who.int/mediacentre/factsheets/fs282/en/1
2. Tactile View, http://www.tactileview.com
3. TGD-Pro, http://www.duxburysystems.com/tgd.asp?choice=pro
4. Ladner, R.E., Ivory, M.Y., Rao, R., Burgstahler, S., Comden, D., Hahn, S., et al.: Automating tactile graphics translation. In: The 7th International ACM SIGACCESS Conference on Computers and Accessibility (ASSETS), Baltimore, USA, pp. 181–184. IEEE Press, New York (2001)
5. National Association for the Blind, http://www.nabindia.org

[6] https://github.com/assistech-iitd/Edutactile

Tactile Map Automated Creation System Using OpenStreetMap

Tetsuya Watanabe[1], Toshimitsu Yamaguchi[2], Satoko Koda[2], and Kazunori Minatani[3]

[1] University of Niigata, Faculty of Engineering, Niigata, Japan
[2] Graduate School of University of Niigata, Niigata, Japan
[3] National Center for University Entrance Examinations, Meguro-ku, Tokyo, Japan
{t2.nabe,t.yamaguchi}@eng.niigata-u.ac.jp, minatani@dnc.ac.jp

Abstract. We have developed a Web-based tactile map automated creation system *tmacs*. Users simply type in an address or the name of a building and the system instantly creates an image of a tactile map, which is then printed on capsule paper and raised up by a heater. This time we modified this system to deal with OpenStreetMap (OSM). The advantage of using OSM data is that *tmacs* becomes to be able to create tactile maps of any location in the world and include information which is useful for blind people such as tactile paving. Another feature of the new system is that sighted users can change the point and scale of a tactile map in the same way as a regular Google Map. We are exploring the possibility of increasing the number of countries whose tactile maps can be created with *tmacs*.

Keywords: Blind People, Tactile Map, Tactile Perception, OpenStreetMap, Automated Creation.

1 Introduction

Tactile maps are useful in providing prior knowledge for blind persons on unfamiliar locations of mobility training, business travelling, shopping, and leisure travelling [1]. Here, a tactile map refers to a sheet of a map or a set of maps, which are portable and have an advantage of being explored at home elaborately beforehand. The biggest problem with tactile maps is that creating them requires a lot of time and effort as map data in general is complex and they should be designed to be readable by touch [2].

In order to alleviate this problem, we have developed a tactile map automated creation system called tmacs that is available on the Web and has been in use since 2010 [3]. Users simply type in an address or the name of a building and the system instantly creates an image of a tactile map. This image is then printed on capsule paper and raised up by a heater. A tactile map of any location in Japan can be created in about a minute. This system can also create embossed maps.

Currently, tmacs uses only commercially available geographical data of Japan. If the system could deal with OpenStreetMap (OSM) data, which covers the entire globe, it could create tactile maps of any location in the world in a very short period of time. This is what we plan to achieve.

K. Miesenberger et al. (Eds.): ICCHP 2014, Part II, LNCS 8548, pp. 42–49, 2014.

2 Related Work

The pioneering work in this field was the tactile map automated production (TMAP) system developed at the Smith-Kettlewell Eye Institute in 2004 [4]. This system uses topologically integrated geographic encoding and referencing (TIGER) data to create tactile maps of any location in the U.S. on both embossed and capsule papers. The TMAP system motivated us to develop a comparable system for producing tactile maps in Japan.

Geospatial Information Authority of Japan also developed a tactile map image creation system and opened it for testing in 2006 [5]. However, this GUI system requires mouse operation and cannot be used by blind people. Therefore, we developed tmacs most of whose operations are done automatically and designed in accordance with Web accessibility so that blind people can make tactile maps by themselves.

A project to create tactile maps by referencing OSM data was started by Lulu-An in April 2009 [6]. In the framework of the HaptoRender project, several maps have been made of copper, plastic sheets, and other materials. However, automated creation is still in the conceptual phase as far as can be seen on the Wiki Web site.

Various other researchers have also used OSM data for their own research purposes [7],[8].

3 Use of OSM Data

3.1 OpenStreetMap

OpenStreetMap is a collaborative project to create a free editable map of the world [9]. There are three key advantages of using OSM data:

1. Information that is useful for blind and visually impaired persons can be registered in the map and later expressed on tactile maps.
2. OSM data covers the globe (as far as contributors strive).
3. OSM data can be used for free.

3.2 Conversion of OSM Data to GIS Database

We downloaded XML files of OSM data and converted them into database tables using a utility program, osm2pgsql, and inserted into a GIS database. A database management system called PostgreSQL was used along with PostGIS to deal with the GIS data. In converting and using OSM data, there were two technical problems to be solved.

First, the default osm2pgsql style file does not include tags for tactile paving, signals with sound, and obstacles. As these pieces of information are useful for blind people, we modified the style file so as to include tags for them.

Second, the osm2pgsql program defines GIS data in SRID: 900913. So we modified the mapfile we use in the map rendering to be able to refer to SRID: 900913 using EPSG coding.

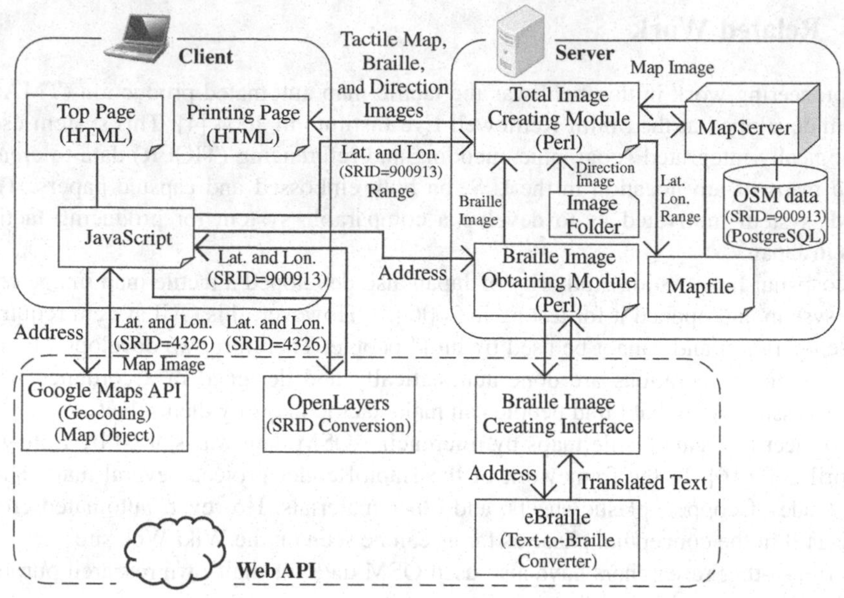

Fig. 1. System configuration of *tmacs* for OSM

4 Flow of System Operation

Figure 1 shows the system configuration of tmacs for OSM. This figure is helpful for understanding steps (1) to (4) of the system operation flow below.

(1) Figure 2 shows the top page of the developed Web application system. This page has two textboxes, three buttons, and a map. Users type the address or building name around which they want to create a tactile map into the relevant textbox and press the “Search” button. The address and/or building name is then geocoded using the Google Maps API. If a geocoding error occurs or the building name has two or more candidate addresses, a dialog box appears and asks the user to respond.

When the geocoding is finished, the map is moved to the geocoded point. The range of this map becomes that of the tactile map to be produced. Sighted users can change the point and scale of the map by operating it in the same way as a regular Google Map.

(2) Text for the address or building name is sent to a text-to-Braille converting server, eBraille [10], and the server returns the converted text. Using this text and Braille Font [11], Braille Image Creating Interface creates a Braille image that is readable by touch.

(3) When the “Output” button is pressed, the longitudes and latitudes of the edges of the map are obtained and converted from SRID:4326 to SRID:900913 by using OpenLayers, an open source JavaScript library. These locational data are added to the mapfile, in which the rendering attributes of roads, railways, and other objects are

defined. This mapfile is read by an open source map rendering software, "MapServer," to render the map.

(4) Total Image Creating Module integrates the images of the map, Braille, and the direction symbol into one tactile map for printing. This map is displayed in a new window. Users print this map image on capsule paper and heat it for the map image to be raised (Fig. 3).

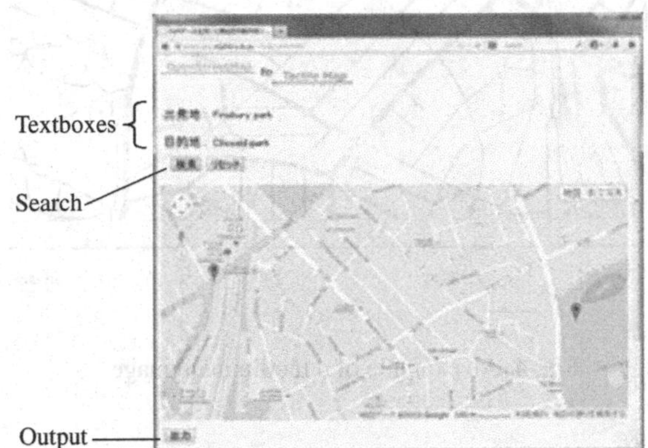

Fig. 2. Top page of *tmacs* for OSM

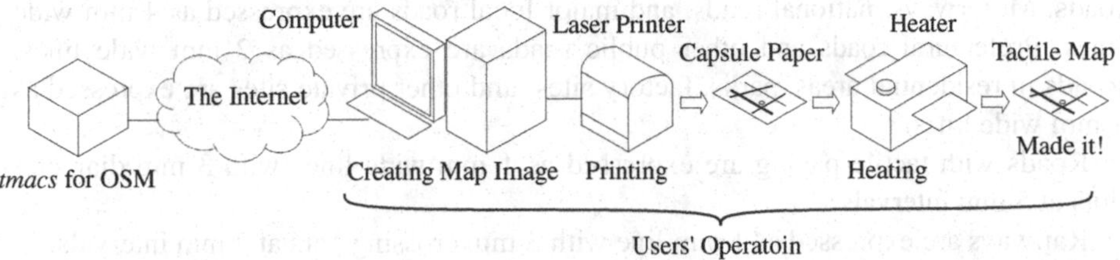

Fig. 3. Use of *tmacs* for OSM

5 Tactile Map Image

An example of a tactile map located in London, U.K. is shown in Figure 4. Tactile maps created by tmacs include roads, railways, rivers, stations, water areas, traffic signals, obstacles, and starting and goal points. The attributes of these tactile line, area, and point symbols are determined based on several previously established tactile graphics guidelines [12]–[17] as well as the results of our own tactile perception experiments [18]–[21]. The specifications of these symbols are elaborated below and their images are shown in Table 1.

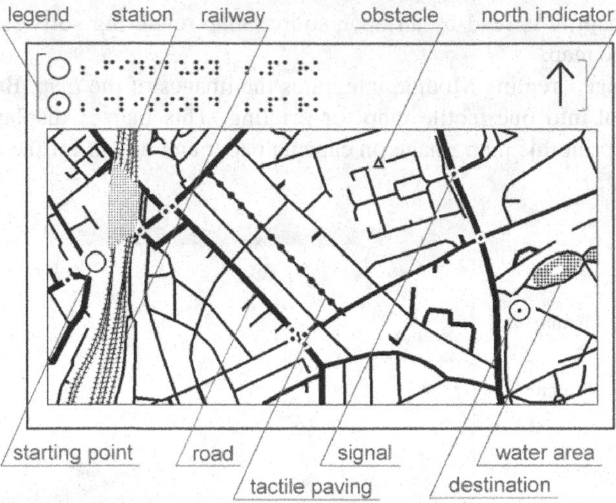

Fig. 4. An example of a tactile map image

5.1 Line Symbols

Roads are expressed as lines with three different widths according to the types of the roads. Motorways, national roads, and major local roads are expressed as 4 mm wide lines. Prefectural roads and other public roads are expressed as 2 mm wide lines. Roads in residential areas, parks, factory sites, and other private sites are expressed as 1 mm wide lines.

Roads with tactile paving are expressed as 1 mm wide lines with 3 mm diameter dots at 5 mm intervals.

Railways are expressed as 1 mm line with 3 mm crossing bars at 2 mm intervals.

Rivers are expressed as 0.7 mm wide double lines with 0.5 mm spacing.

5.2 Area Symbols

Water areas and stations are expressed as different dot matrices. Water areas use 1.5 mm diameter dots at 2.7 mm intervals and stations use 0.8 mm diameter dots and 1.3 mm intervals.

5.3 Point Symbols

Traffic signals are expressed as 2 mm diameter dots.

Obstacles to pedestrians such as road construction sites are expressed as regular triangles with 4 mm sides.

The starting and goal points are expressed as 9 mm diameter circles of 0.7 mm wide lines. The goal point has a 1.0 mm diameter dot in the center of the circle.

When point symbols are placed on other symbols, about 2.5 mm space are left around them for point symbols to be discerned easily by touch.

Table 1. Tactile symbol images

Types of symbols	Objects	Images (Not actual size)
Line	Road	
	Road with tactile paving	
	Railway	
	River	
Area	Water area	
	Station	
Point	Traffic signal	
	Obstacle	
	Starting and goal points	

6 Conclusion and Future Work

We modified our tactile map automated creation system, tmacs, to deal with OSM data. Up to now, we confirmed that tactile maps in the U.K. are available using our system.

Future work on tmacs for OSM is as follows.

(1) Rendering wide rivers and seas

As OSM data does not include polygons for wide rivers and seas but outlines of lands, the current tmacs for OSM cannot render them. Therefore, it is required to specify the water area from these outline data and render them as tactile area symbols.

(2) Regular spacing of dots and crossing bars on line symbols

Some railways and roads with tactile paving have irregular spaces of dots and crossing bars. The reason for this is that these line symbols are composed of a series of line data although human users see them as one line. We have to devise ideas to address this problem.

(3) Change of line widths of roads with tactile paving

Line width of roads with tactile paving should be changed according to the types of roads.

(4) Appropriate rendering according to the range of a map

The objects to be rendered on tactile maps and their attributes should be appropriately selected according to the range of the map. For example, when a wide area is chosen for a tactile map, only main roads such as national roads are to be rendered with fine lines and other local roads should be eliminated because too many objects on a map make it hard to be understood by touch.

(5) Expression of arbitrary routes

If the system has a function of expressing arbitrary routes such as walking logs, recommended routes, and escaping routes, on the map, tactile maps become more useful for blind people.

(6) Localizing the system

Increasing the number of countries whose tactile maps can be created with tmacs for OSM is our chief purpose.

References

1. Ungar, S., Blades, M., Spencer, C.: The role of tactile maps in mobility training. British J. of Visual Impairment 11(3), 59–61 (1993)
2. Jehoel, S., McCallum, D., Rowell, J., Ungar, S.: An empirical approach on the design of tactile maps and diagrams: the cognitive tactualisation approach. British J. of Visual Impairment 24(2), 67–75 (2006)
3. Watanabe, T., et al.: Development and evaluation of a tactile map automated creation system accessible to blind persons. IEICE Trans. D J 94-D(10), 1652–1663 (2011)
4. Miele, J.A., Gilden, D.B.: Tactile map automated production (TMAP): Using GIS data to generate braille maps. In: Proc. CSUN Int. Conf. on Technology and Persons with Disabilities, LA, CA, USA (2004)
5. Geospatial Information Authority of Japan, http://tenpuchizu.gsi.go.jp/shokuchizu/index.html
6. HaptoRender, http://wiki.openstreetmap.org/wiki/HaptoRender
7. Zeng, L., Weber, G.: Audio-haptic browser for a geographical information system. In: Miesenberger, K., Klaus, J., Zagler, W., Karshmer, A. (eds.) ICCHP 2010, Part II. LNCS, vol. 6180, pp. 466–473. Springer, Heidelberg (2010)
8. Kurata, T., et al.: Development of a smartphone-based talking navigation system and tactile trajectory creation system to support walking training. In: Proc. 39th Sensory Substitution System, pp. 23–26 (2013)
9. OpenStreetMap, http://en.wikipedia.org/wiki/OpenStreetMap
10. eBraille - Japanese-into-Braille Translating Server, http://ebraille.med.kobe-u.ac.jp/
11. Nippon Lighthouse, Braille Font for Printing, http://www.eonet.ne.jp/~tecti/tecti/br-font.html
12. Eriksson, Y., Strucel, M.: A guide to the production of tactile graphics on swellpaper, AB PP Print, Stockholm (1995)
13. Eriksson, Y., Gunnar, J., Strucel, M.: Tactile maps - Guidelines for the production of maps for the visually impaired. The Swedish Library of Talking Books and Braille, Enskede (2003)
14. American Printing House, APH Guidelines for Design of Tactile Graphics (March 2010), http://www.aph.org/edresearch/guides.htm
15. The N.S.W. Tactual and Bold Print Mapping Committee: A guide for the production of tactual and bold print maps, 3rd edn., Sydney (2006)

16. Japan Committee of Social Welfare Facilities for the Blind: Handbook for producing pedestrian tactile maps, Tokyo, 1984
17. Japan Braille Library: An introduction to tactile graphics for braille transcribing, 2nd edn., Tokyo (1988)
18. Watanabe, K., et al.: Development of an embossed map automated creation system and evaluation of the legibility of the maps produced. IEICE Trans. D J95-D(4), 948–959 (2012)
19. Ishibashi, K., et al.: Easy detectable symbol's size in tactile maps: A study with persons familiar and unfamiliar with braille. Japanese J. Visual Rehabilitation 2(1), 1–10 (2013)
20. Watanabe, T., et al.: Evaluation of the legibility of tactile maps made of capsule paper. IEICE Trans. D J96-D(4), 1075–1078 (2013)
21. Watanabe, T., et al.: Discriminability of dot patterns embossed by the tactile map automated creation system. IEICE Trans. D J96-D(11), 2737–2745 (2013)

Narrative Map Augmentation with Automated Landmark Extraction and Path Inference

Vladimir Kulyukin and Thimma Reddy

Computer Science Assistive Technology Laboratory, Department of Computer Science, Utah State University, Logan, UT, USA

Abstract. Various technologies, including GPS, Wi-Fi localization, and infrared beacons, have been proposed to increase travel independence for visually impaired (VI) and blind travelers. Such systems take readings from sensors, localize those readings on a map, and instruct VI travelers where to move next. Unfortunately, sensor readings can be noisy or absent, which decreases the traveler's situational awareness. However, localization technologies can be augmented with solutions that put the traveler's cognition to use. One such solution is narrative maps, i.e., verbal descriptions of environments produced by O&M professionals for blind travelers. The production of narrative maps is costly, because O&M professionals must travel to designated environments and describe large numbers of routes. Complete narrative coverage may not be feasible due to the sheer size of many environments. But, the quality of produced narrative maps can be improved by automated landmark extraction and path inference. In this paper, an algorithm is proposed that uses scalable natural language processing (NLP) techniques to extract landmarks and their connectivity from verbal route descriptions. Extracted landmarks can be subsequently annotated with sensor readings, used to find new routes, or track the traveler's progress on different routes.

1 Introduction

Various technologies, including GPS, Wi-Fi localization, and infrared beacons [1], to name just a few, have been proposed to increase travel independence for visually impaired (VI) and blind travelers. Such systems take readings from sensors, localize those readings on a map, and instruct the traveler where to move next. Unfortunately, sensor readings can be noisy, absent, or no longer representative of the traveler's location [2], which decreases the traveler's situational awareness and makes it harder for the traveler to use her cognitive abilities en route. Many VI and blind people receive extensive O&M training. During training, these individuals learn how to navigate indoor and outdoor environments, follow sidewalks, detect obstacles and landmarks, and cross streets [3]. They master techniques to remain oriented as they move inside buildings or on sidewalks and streets. Many individuals improve their O&M skills through independent traveling experiences. Gaunet & Briffault [4] showed that blind travelers can follow verbal directions outdoors. Nicholson & Kulyukin [2] investigated the utility of verbal instructions indoors in a longitudinal study of blind

K. Miesenberger et al. (Eds.): ICCHP 2014, Part II, LNCS 8548, pp. 50–53, 2014.

shopping in supermarkets and showed that independent blind travelers can navigate modern supermarkets given adequate route descriptions.

Indoor and outdoor localization technologies can be augmented to better utilize the traveler's cognition. One approach to maximizing the traveler's cognitive and physical skills is *narrative maps* (www.clickandgomaps.com), i.e., verbal, egocentric or allocentric, descriptions of specific environments. Narrative maps are written by O&M professionals to take advantage of perceptual abilities of blind travelers, i.e., transitions from carpet to tile, obstacle detection, localization, shorelining, contextual cues for orientation and re-orientation, etc. The production of narrative maps requires the expertise of O&M professionals who must travel to designated environments and describe large numbers of routes. Complete route coverage is rarely feasible due to the sheer complexity of many environments. However, existing narrative maps can be augmented by automated landmark extraction and path inference. In this paper, we propose an algorithm that uses scalable natural language processing (NLP) to extract landmarks and their connectivity from verbal route descriptions. Extracted landmarks can be subsequently annotated with sensor readings (e.g., Wi-Fi clusters or digital compass readings), used to find new routes, or track the traveler's progress en route.

The paper is organized as follows. In Section 3, we outline the algorithm. In Section 4, we present the experiments with the algorithm and discuss the results.

2 Landmark Extraction and Path Inference Algorithm

The conceptual basis of our algorithm is Kuipers' Spatial Semantic Hierarchy (SSH) [6], a hybrid knowledge representation framework for spatial cognition. In our previous study [2], the SSH was shown to be appropriate for the communication of verbal routes to blind supermarket shoppers. The SSH represents environments in terms of four levels: sensory, causal, topological, and metric. Of specific relevance to this paper is the topological level of the SSH that describes the environment as maps of places, paths, regions, and their connectivity and containment.

> There are 2 doors to Caribbean Ballroom 6. From the door along the inner hallway which also has Boca rooms 1 through 4, exit room 6, walk 3 steps and turn right. Continuing straight, you reach a large perpendicular hallway in 40 feet. In another 35 feet, you reach the center of the Caribbean foyer, and the main automatic building doors are on the left side.

Fig. 1. Partial route description from Caribbean Ballroom 6 to Caribbean foyer at Caribe Royale Convention Center Orlando from www.clickandgomaps.com

The input of our algorithms is verbal route descriptions, one of which is shown in Fig. 1. The descriptions are split into sentences and the sentences are tokenized. The tokenized sentences are tagged with parts of speech (POS) and parsed to identify noun phrases (NPs) and verb phrases (VPs). We have used the Stanford Parser (nlp.stanford.edu) for both POS tagging and parsing. Fig. 2 shows a parse tree with POS tags for the sentence "Grand Sierra Ballroom foyer begins 75 feet ahead as the carpet changes to tile." Landmarks are extracted by finding NP nodes from parse trees and applying regular expressions to the corresponding text segments. Each landmark receives a unique ID and is saved in an SQL database. VP nodes from parse trees and regular expressions are used to extract actions and their parameters as well as landmark connectivity information. For example, from the sub-tree (VP (VB walk) (NP (CD 3) (NNS steps))), the algorithm extracts the action WALK that can be parameterized by the unit STEP quantified by numeral 3. If at least one action is detected between two landmarks, the landmarks are considered connected in a directed graph that represents the connectivity of the environment. If it cannot be determined which landmarks are connected by an extracted action, two virtual landmarks are generated and stored in the database. New paths are inferred from landmark nodes and action edges by finding landmarks common to a pair of routes, as shown in Fig. 3. The reader may consult [5] for more details.

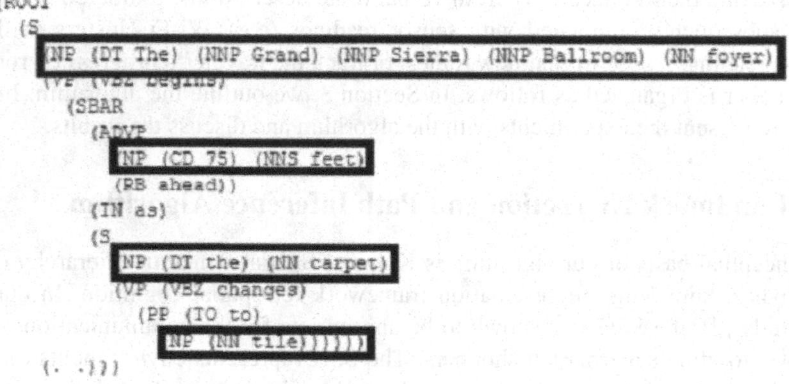

Fig. 2. Results of POS Tagging and Parsing

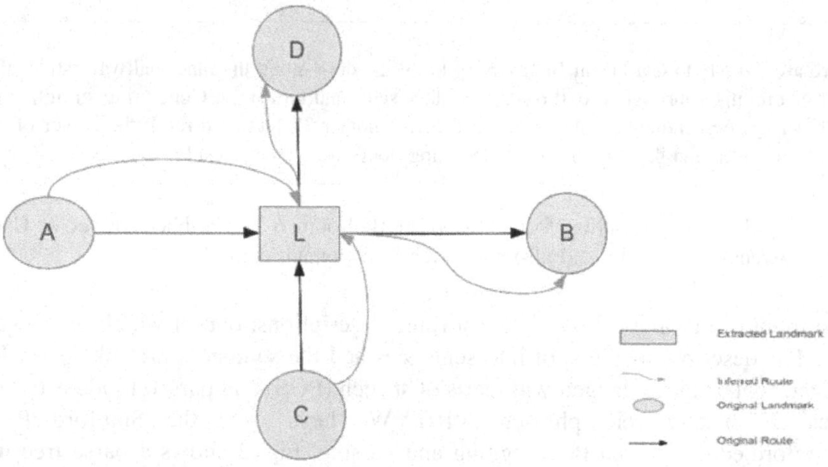

Fig. 3. Path Inference

3 Experiments

The algorithm is implemented in Java and tested on 272 verbal route directions for Caribe Royale Convention Center Orlando from www.clickandgomaps.com. The algorithm extracted 421 landmarks and 884 action edges. Of 421 landmarks, 361 (86%) were true positives and 60 (14%) were false positives. Of 884 actions, 873 (98%) were true positives and 11 (2%) false positives. The algorithm also inferred 2,210 new paths.

References

1. Goldsmith, A.: Wireless Communications. Cambridge Press (2005)
2. Nicholson, J., Kulyukin, V., Coster, D.: ShopTalk: Independent Blind Shopping Through Verbal Route Directions and Barcode Scans. The Open Rehabilitation Journal 2, 11–23 (2009)
3. Golledge, R.G., Klatzky, R.L., Loomis, J.M.: Cognitive Mapping and Wayfinding by Adults without Vision. In: Portugali, J. (ed.) The Construction of Cognitive Maps. Kluwer Academic Publishers, Dordrecht (1996)
4. Gaunet, F.: Verbal Guidance Rules for a Localized Wayfinding and Intended for Blind Pedestrians in Urban Areas. Universal Access in the Information Society 4(4), 338–353 (2006)
5. Kulyukin, V., Nicholson, J.: Toward Blind Travel Support through Verbal Route Directions: A Path Inference Algorithm for Inferring New Route Descriptions from Existing Route Directions. The Open Rehabilitation Journal 5, 22–40 (2012)
6. Kuipers, B.: The Spatial Semantic Hierarchy. Artificial Intelligence 119, 191–233 (2000)

The Mobile Travel Assistance System NAMO with Way-Finding Support in Public Transport Environments

Christian Bühler, Helmut Heck, Annika Nietzio, and Frank Reins

Forschungsinstitut Technologie und Behinderung (FTB) der Evangelischen Stiftung Volmarstein, Germany
namo@ftb-esv.de
www.ftb-esv.de

Abstract. Many older people rely on public transport to maintain their personal mobility and thus quality of life. However, problems may arise in unfamiliar environments or during unexpected events. Especially when changing trains in complex stations, many people experience orientation problems or feel insecure and overwhelmed. The *namo* travel assistant combines technical and human support during the journey. The users can choose the presentation of the information which suits them most: The application offers photos with directional arrows, station plans with marked paths, and contact to a service hotline to get direct support. In this way, *namo* helps maintain personal mobility in old age while offering an increased sense of security.

1 Introduction

Independent living and personal mobility are key factors for quality of life of older people. To maintain their mobility as long as possible seniors may need assistance. While previous generations often preferred human support, an increasing number of seniors has more technical knowledge and is willing to use technical support such as a mobile travel assistant application on a smartphone.

The project *Seamless barrier-free information and mobility chains for older people (namo)* is developing a mobile travel assistant. The *namo* application can be used to plan the journey and it can provide up-to-date information and active support during the trip. Besides information on foot paths and public transport connections, the system also helps in difficult situations, e.g. when changing the trains or in case of delays.

The *namo* system does not rely on technical components alone. Human assistance is part of the system as well. Users can contact service suppliers, service hotlines, and family members. Additionally, an emergency call function to contact police or medical aid will be provided.

This paper presents the results of the requirement analysis that was conducted with focus groups and user tests under realistic conditions. We also show how the requirements are addressed by the *namo* application and how the way-finding support will be implemented.

K. Miesenberger et al. (Eds.): ICCHP 2014, Part II, LNCS 8548, pp. 54–57, 2014.

2 Travel Information Systems and Navigation Support

Initially, information systems developed to support people with disabilities and older people in public transport focused on extended functionality for planning a trip. The *BAIM* project [1] supports people with disabilities in planning barrier-free journeys by public transport. The *BAIMplus* project [2] integrates real-time data and improved usability for seniors. The latest developments add additional functionality that supports users during the trip, such as navigation support for blind users in *m4guide*, or intermodal travelling in urban or rural areas. The new systems also integrate information from several transport systems, so that the user can plan a trip "from door to door", i.e. using a combination of private and public transport. Mobile devices and the integration of real-time and situation-based information offer further opportunities for assistance during the journey.

Research concerning the orientation and navigation capability of older people shows that the cognitive capabilities decrease with increasing age [5], especially for tasks requiring good memory and abstract thinking. Older people have more problems in transferring information from maps to real environments. Although they recognise characteristic objects or features along the route as well as younger people, they exhibit greater difficulty selecting the relevant ones [6]. The *HaptiMap* project [4] has summarised the aspects that need to be taken into account when designing maps for older people [3].

3 Methodological Approach and Requirement Analysis

The *namo* project explores possibilities for mobile assistance for older travellers that have a realistic chance of being implemented and sustained in the real world of public transport. Therefore, the technical development is based on existing information systems. The IT service provider of the *Rhine/Main Regional Transport Association (RMV)* is participating in the project so that the project can use real world data to test and evaluate the prototype system.

The application runs on commonly available smartphones, which already include useful sensors and technology such as cellular network, GPS, WLAN, and NFC reader. It will apply only such features or functions for orientation and way-finding that do not require modification of the environment or infrastructure. The system can refer to existing signage or location signals but does not distribute new visual markers or radio labels.

3.1 User Participation

Older users participate in all phases of the *namo* application development. During the user requirement analysis, the problems and practical difficulties of using public transport were analysed together with the seniors. A group of seniors was invited to try out different travel information systems on a smartphone and to comment on their preferences regarding user interaction and presentation of information. In a subsequent test phase various options for orientation and way-finding support were designed. These options were tested and compared by older users under realistic conditions.

The analysis of common problems faced by older people using public transport showed that many people experience orientation problems or feel overwhelmed, especially when changing vehicles in complex environments. The negative effects on the travellers include overload of information by numerous signs and messages, orientation difficulties in unknown environments, time pressure and stress caused by noisy environments and unfavourable lighting conditions.

The combination of these conditions and the possibly reduced sensory and motor capabilities of older persons require special solutions not only for the presentation of information and user interaction but also for the appropriate selection of the information provided by the application. The application is designed to take the strengths and experiences of seniors into account.

4 *namo* Concept of Orientation Support

The *namo* system computes optimal paths taking into account the user's security and mobility preferences. The concept for orientation and way-finding support regards the user as an integral part of the *namo* system. Several layers of assistance help the user to overcome potential problems during the trip.

Pre-trip information: Photos enhanced with navigation information help the user prepare for the trip. They can take a "virtual tour" of critical locations to familiarise themselves with the route and thus gain confidence.

Time-related on-trip information: The *namo* application alerts the users to exit or change vehicles right on time.

Orientation-related on-trip information: On footpaths inside station buildings, users get orientation clues consisting of photos and textual descriptions. By combining photos with additional information (directional arrows and textual explanations), the users' attention is directed towards the most relevant orientation features.

Location-based on-trip information: The *namo* application can indicate the user's current location, given that a GPS or other positioning signal is available. If the user leaves the planned path, the system can compute a new route. Inside buildings, the user can scan QR-codes or NFC-tags.

Accompanying service: If part of the journey would be too difficult without human help, users can book a free accompanying service via the application.

Service hotline: If the technical orientation support of *namo* is not sufficient, the user can call a service hotline of the public transport provider via the *namo* application to get individual human assistance. The *namo* system can provide current GPS data and data of the planned journey as additional background information for the service hotline operator.

Family contact: The users can also send information about their journey to friends and relatives, or contact them directly should problems arise.

5 Conclusion and Planned Activities

The user test of *namo's* orientation support functionality was conducted with twelve participants who used the test system under realistic conditions. After the participants had had the opportunity to get used to the smartphones, initial reservations were quickly overcome. In general, the seniors perceived the system as helpful, highlighting the usefulness in unknown environments. Both ways of presentation – the abstract map view and the realistic presentation with photos – achieved comparable acceptance rates, showing that seniors are not a uniform group but have individual preferences. Therefore both views will be implemented in the system. Moreover, the user test revealed a number of improvement suggestions that will be taken into account in the further development. Key factors are the quality of information and the approach to selective presentation (so that only the important items are shown).

In the next project phase the *namo* system will be equipped with more data on the environment, including footpaths and Points of Interest, as well as public transport information from the metropolitan area of Frankfurt, where the field test is taking place. In the final project phase a sustainable exploitation concept will be developed.

Acknowledgements. The *namo* project is co-funded by the German Federal Ministry of Education and Research under the grant reference no. 16SV5683. The authors are responsible for the content of this publication. The partners in the *namo* consortium are Rhein-Main-Verkehrsverbund Servicegesellschaft mbH, HaCon mbH, IVU Traffic Technologies AG, Evangelische Stiftung Volmarstein, TU Dortmund Fachgebiet Verkehrswesen und Verkehrsplanung, Forschungsgesellschaft für Gerontologie, ivm GmbH, Stiftung Gesundheit Fördergemeinschaft.

References

1. Bühler, C., Heck, H., Becker, J.: How to Inform People with Reduced Mobility about Public Transport. In: Miesenberger, K., Klaus, J., Zagler, W.L., Karshmer, A.I. (eds.) ICCHP 2008. LNCS, vol. 5105, pp. 973–980. Springer, Heidelberg (2008)
2. Bühler, C., Heck, H., Radek, C., Wallbruch, R., Becker, J., Bohner-Degrell, C.: User Feed-Back in the Development of an Information System for Public Transport. In: Miesenberger, K., Klaus, J., Zagler, W., Karshmer, A. (eds.) ICCHP 2010, Part 1. LNCS, vol. 6179, pp. 273–279. Springer, Heidelberg (2010)
3. Kovanen, J., Oksanen, J., Sarjakoski, L., Sarjakoski, T.: Simple Maps –A Concept of Plain Cartography within a Mobile Context for Elderly Users. In: Proceedings of the GIS Research UK 20th Annual Conference (2012)
4. Magnusson, C., Rassmus-Gröhn, K., Deaner, E.: HaptiMap – User requirements and design guidelines for map applications (2012)
5. Schönfeld, R.: Alters- und Geschlechtsdifferenzen in der Raumkognition. Ph.D. thesis, Otto-von-Guericke-Universität Madgeburg (2008)
6. Wilkniss, S.M., Jones, M., Korol, D., Gold, P., Manning, C.: Age-Related Differences in an Ecologically Based Study of Route Learning. Psychology and Aging 12(2), 372–375 (1997)

A Mobile Guidance Platform for Public Transportation

Reinhard Koutny, Peter Heumader, and Klaus Miesenberger

Johannes-Kepler Universität- University of Linz, Institute Integriert Studieren, Linz, Austria
{reinhard.koutny,peter.heumader,klaus.miesenberger}@jku.at

Abstract. This paper presents an approach which allows people with disabilities to use public transportation more effectively in supporting them throughout the whole journey. Besides the common feature set, like offering time table information and planning trips consisting of multiple rides it additionally includes information when to get on or off a vehicle and performs route re-planning in the case of unexpected events like delays. Moreover, it provides information particularly important for people with disabilities, like wheelchair users or blind persons. Depending on the user profile, information regarding the accessibility of vehicles and also routing information for footpaths are delivered in real-time, which is especially important at major transfer points like railway stations where routes tailored to the user's capabilities are provided. As it cannot be guaranteed that every footpath and every obstacle is charted and up-to-date, users can improve routing information on their own in a crowd sourcing based approach.

Keywords: Public Transport, Assistive Technology, Navigation, Blind Person, Wheelchair User.

1 Introduction

People with disabilities mostly rely on means of public transportation to independently travel, however, to many of them, public transportation raises difficulties. Blind people do need to know the route by heart and run into troubles if unexpected events occur. Wheelchair users require the knowledge that the whole route, normally including multiple pedestrian sections, is barrier-free. VIATOR (lat. „traveler“) is a system for active travel assistance for mobile devices like smartphones or tablets for users of means of public transportation, with special but not sole focus on people with disabilities. Compared to frequently used and commonly accepted mobile applications considering the topic of public transportation which show time tables and the like, this approach goes beyond existing ones in multiple areas and provides more extensive support for the traveler throughout the whole journey. The user interface, the concept of operations and the information provided, is optimized to support manifold target groups including blind or visually impaired persons and wheelchair users. As this platform employs a location-based service which allows storage, retrieval and notifications considering the position of the mobile device, it can provide up-to-date context-aware information during the journey. For it, up-to-date travel information of

K. Miesenberger et al. (Eds.): ICCHP 2014, Part II, LNCS 8548, pp. 58–64, 2014.

multiple public transportation companies is combined offering guidance covering a great deal of Austria's public transportation system. Besides, it reacts to unexpected events which require adjustment, like recalculations of routes and automatic suggestions of alternatives.

2 State of the Art

These days, numerous applications for mobile devices exist which intend to support public transportation or mobility in general. However, most of them only partly cover the whole journey from door to door using public means of transportation. Applications in this area usually offer timetable information; more advanced ones allow the calculation of a sequence of different means of public transportation. Most of them do not deal with pedestrian sections adequately, though, which are at least as important as the actual bus trip, especially for people not familiar with the area. Another issue, which is barely dealt with, is accessibility. People with disabilities, like blind or visually impaired people and wheelchair users do have different demands on an application like this. Blind people need a user interface which allows them to interact and navigate with the application via their screenreader, like Talkback[1] or VoiceOver[2]. In addition, they also require context and location based information, like when to get on or off the bus. Wheelchair users need additional information regarding accessibility at stops, railway stations, bus terminals and pedestrian sections at transfer points in general.
In terms of support throughout the whole trip, hardly any solution exists so far. Mostly, public transportation companies offer their customers services and smartphone apps mainly displaying time schedules and allowing basic planning of connections for trips involving multiple means of public transportation. However, they are usually restricted to basic functionality, not or hardly considering accessibility and support for people with disabilities and are mostly limited to their own fleet.

Applications which can be used in Austria are amongst others SCOTTY[3] and NEXTSTOP[4]. For both products, smartphone application for the major platform, Android and iPhone, are available. Both combine multiple public transportation companies, however not all major public transportation service providers of all Austrian states are included and accessibility is not considered adequately. Besides, both solutions are mainly focused to deliver the right time tables.

MobileCity, the developer of NEXTSTOP offers timetables, bus schedule calculations for many Austrian public transportation companies and even rudimentary pedestrian navigation to bus stops, which makes it a positive exception. However, accessibility is lacking and real time vehicle localization and notifications, when to enter or leave a vehicle, are missing.

TransitTimes+[5] provides a similar feature set mostly for cities in the USA. Rudimentary accessibility information for wheelchair users is already integrated like if stops are accessible or not. However, explicit features to support blind people or wheelchair users throughout the whole journey are not integrated. Real-time vehicle localization and accurate notifications, when to enter or leave a vehicle, are missing too.

Besides, there are research projects addressing the issues people with disabilities are facing when using means of public transportation. One of the issues are that blind persons, waiting at a stop for the vehicle to arrive, need either to identify the right vehicle and entrance or signal their want to enter it.

NAVCOM [5] deals with this requirement and proposes a WIFI-based solution which establishes communication between the vehicle and the blind traveler and guides him or her to the right entrance. Another key issue which still remains to be unsolved in many cases is indoor navigation at transfer points, which was focused in the project ways4all. RFID tags were used for tactile paving to perform indoor positioning [6].

More generic approaches offer location-based information to people with limited mobility, in the case of Wheelmap [7] to wheelchair users. They try to overcome the existing lack of information which decreases the mobility in addition to the actual sensory, physical or cognitive impairment. Wheelmap offers a platform and client applications for various platforms to look up and annotate accessible public places like cinemas, bar and supermarkets. This supports mobility inasmuch as it allows wheelchair users to avoid inaccessible places.

3 Conceptual Solution

VIATOR relies on a location- and context-based service called, Digital Graffiti [8], which logically links textual as well as multimedia information to any location. Every item is virtually surrounded by areas defining when client devices get informed about its existence and when additional data like multimedia content gets transferred automatically. Outdoors GPS positioning is used and indoors Wi-Fi-positioning. The platform also offers to define actions in the event of a client device comes into reach of an executable item.

Using Digital Graffiti as basis, places and objects, their locations and important information can be described and made accessible to client devices. Therefore, places like bus stops and railway stations, but also moving vehicles and accessibility related infrastructure like tactile paving or wheelchair ramps can be charted, holding the necessary information for travel guidance.

Through the so called Common Transportation Interface partner public transportation companies, namely ÖBB[1] (Austrian Federal Railway Company), OÖVG[2] (Upper Austrian Transportation Organization) and Linz AG[3] respectively Linz Linien[4], the public transport division of Linz AG (a local transportation company in Linz, Austria), needed to provide live data of time tables, delays, geographic locations of vehicles and so forth. As Digital Graffiti allow holding executable content, this mechanism can be employed to perform routing and time schedule calculation. This is used to keep track of the time schedule of the complete mobility chain, including

[1] http://www.oebb.at/

[2] http://www.ooevv.at/

[3] www.linzag.at

[4] http://www.linzag.at/portal/portal/linzag/linzag/linzlinien

connecting buses, trams and trains. Therefore, VIATOR can react to delays and cancellations and automatically adapts the route and suggests appropriate alternatives. CEIT Alanova provides pedestrian route calculations for disabled persons. Even though not all information regarding objects, places, routes and infrastructure in general is charted from the beginning, a crowd sourcing based approach provides an interface for every user to enhance and update missing or incorrect information. This could be an elevator which is out of order for two weeks or a temporarily moved bus stop.

4 Prototype

The conceptual solution was implemented prototypically by the University of Linz at the department of Business Informatics – Software Engineering in cooperation with the Institute Integrated Study, using JBoss[5] AS7 Java Enterprise Application for the server components while the mobile client application is based on Android. The user interface is especially designed to support assistive technology for people with disabilities like blind or visually impaired users. Therefore, informal user evaluations and early integration of target groups, including wheel chair users and blind users assured an accessible user interface supporting and optimized for the Android[6] screenreader Talkback [2].

Besides, generic user profiles allowed an easy way for users starting the prototype the first time to adapt the behavior to their needs. For example the profile "wheelchair user" considered longer durations for pedestrian sections and barrier-free routes avoiding stairs and escalator.

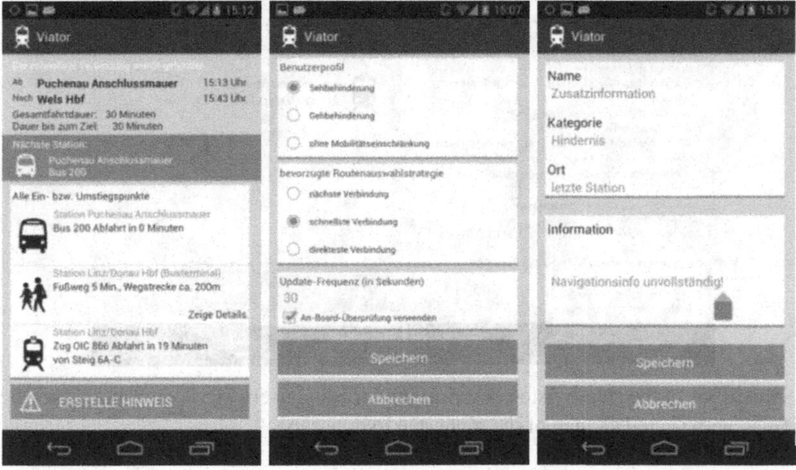

Fig. 1. Screenshot of route overview (a), screenshot of user profile (b), screenshot of self-created content (c)

---

[5] http://www.jboss.org

[6] http://www.android.com/

After the initial selection of the generic user profile at the first start, the user is only requested to enter the travel destination or select one of a list of suggested locations. The route (see Fig.1a) is calculated according to the preferences of the generic user profile, the custom preferences (see Fig.1b), the user can set in addition, and the user's current location. In addition to key travel information like the next transfer point, the travel destination, the estimated duration and time of arrival, the user interface shows a list of the following travel sections. If the user decides to start the journey, the system will suggest routes to the user for pedestrian sections to and between stops, if the necessary information is available. In case of a blind user, the description which are supposed to guide him or her between to stop look like those at Fig.2a. Even though it does not look very appealing, it is optimized to meet requirements deriving from users of screenreaders, like blind users. If adequate information for guidance is not available, the user can add descriptions (see Fig.1c) which are available afterward for other users traveling in the same area. The system is active throughout the whole journey and reacts to unexpected events, like delays and cancellations. In that case, the user gets informed and the route is automatically recalculated (see Fig.2b). Besides that, the system informs the user when the vehicle arrives, when to get on it, and when to get off.

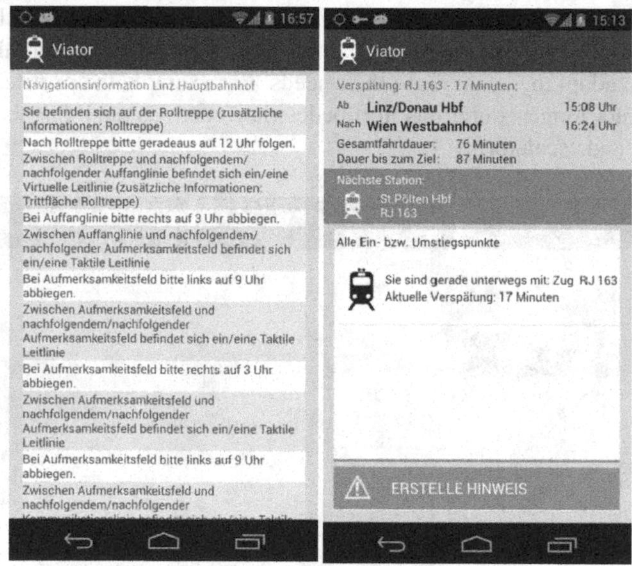

Fig. 2. Screenshot of the step-by-step descriptions for blind users (a), Screenshot of notification indicating an unexpected change of the route due to delay (b)

Informal tests with the prototype with both blind persons and wheelchair users confirmed the benefit for both target groups. However, these tests also revealed weaknesses during pedestrian sections, especially indoors, where on the one hand specific navigation hints and therefore precise positioning is necessary, which is so far still an unsolved issue for many cases. On the other hand, routes are more complicated and often differ between the target groups.

5 Further Work

Experiences gained in this and other projects have shown that there exists a gap at pedestrian sections in the so called mobility chain. This is the sequence of actions and paths a traveler needs to accomplish to get from the start to the travel destination. This includes footpaths for example from home to the next bus stop, the actually bus ride, the footpath at the transfer point and so on. It also includes footpath which are not necessarily important to get from point A to point B using public transportation, but need to be managed anyway. For example a traveler who does not own an annual ticket needs to buy a ticket before entering a train to avoid additional fees for buying during the ride. Especially at pedestrian sections, most difficulties occur. The traveler might need to buy a ticket. He or she needs to figure out when and where the connecting bus or train leaves. The traveler needs to identify the right vehicle if, for instance, several buses share the same bus stop. The traveler also needs to get the right directions at, sometime rather huge and confusing, transfer points, like main railway station of bigger cities. This is particularly important for people who suffer from limited mobility due to difficulties in orientation and navigation. This group includes, blind persons, people suffering low vision, learning disabilities and people who are not familiar with the local language like tourists or persons with migration background. VIATOR already partly tackled the issue of making footpaths accessible; however it is still lacking an adequate solution, also as it focused on a narrower target group. A follow-up project is running, called PONS (lat. bridge), which aims at bridging this gap. The project consortium of PONS has realized that the gap in the mobility chain at pedestrian sections originates from deficiencies regarding (1) provision of information, (2) orientation and (3) provision of services for users of public transportation. The focus of research lies in dealing with these deficiencies.

1. The lack of (1) provision of information is dealt with, by the definition and development of new information and maneuver elements for pedestrian navigation, and inclusion into map systems. Therefore, map annotations which are relevant are going to be determined in cooperation with several end user organizations representing the majority of the focused target group, including blind and visually impaired persons, persons with cognitive disabilities and elderly people. As the annotation of new location-based information is of utmost importance an easy to use editor operable by all focused target groups will be developed to enrich map data of known and established open source/crowd sourcing map systems.
2. The lack in (2) orientation is handled by employing dead reckoning and inertial navigation in combination with traditional indoor positioning approaches to provide a more precise, robust and cost-efficient method for indoor positioning. As infrastructure-based indoor positioning is usually quite costly due to either expensive hardware or high personnel costs to install the infrastructure, this combined approach should solve these issues and provide a real-world solution. An issue which should be solved in addition is that for example in subway station special fire regulations need to be considered and applied, which prevents the extensive employment of infrastructure in these areas.

3. The lack of (3) provision of services will be tackled by the development of new interaction paradigms which aim at reducing the effort to use services related to traveling. Exemplary, new concepts for intermodal contact-free ticketing will be developed. Beneath a framework, based on the crowd-sourcing idea, shall provide tools to enable users and external developers to deliver additional content, enhance existing content and solutions, and even develop new services based upon this framework.

References

1. Google Inc., TalkBack (2014), https://play.google.com/store/apps/details?id=com.google.android.marvin.talkback
2. Apple Inc., VoiceOver for iOS (2014), http://www.apple.com/de/accessibility/ios/voiceover/
3. OEBB, Scotty (2014), http://www.oebb.at/de/Reiseplanung/Fahrplanauskunft/Mobile_Dienste/SCOTTY_mobil/index.jsp
4. Fahrplanauskunft und Routenplaner - nextstop.at, MobileCity (2014), http://www.nextstop.at
5. Zervaas Enterprises, TransitTimes+ Trip Planner (2014), http://transittimesapp.com/
6. Bischof, W., Krajnc, E., Dornhofer, M., Ulm, M.: NAVCOM — WLAN Communication Between Public Transport Vehicles and Smart Phones to Support Visually Impaired and Blind People. In: Miesenberger, K., Karshmer, A., Penaz, P., Zagler, W. (eds.) ICCHP 2012, Part II. LNCS, vol. 7383, pp. 91–98. Springer, Heidelberg (2012), http://dx.doi.org/10.1007/978-3-642-31534-3_14
7. Kiers, M., Bischof, W., Krajnc, E., Dornhofer, M.: ways4all – Indoor Navigation without absolute Coordinates for the Visually Impaired and Blind People. In: FHK Conference 2011, Vienna (2011)
8. Wheelmap.org (2014), http://wheelmap.org/en/
9. Narzt, W., Pomberger, G.: Digital Graffiti - A Smart Information and Collaboration System. In: International Conference on Electronic Engineering and Computer Science (2013)

FB-Finger: Development of a Novel Electric Travel Aid with a Unique Haptic Interface

Kiyohide Ito[1], Yoshiharu Fujimoto[1], Ryoko Otsuki[1],
Yuka Niiyama[1], Akihiro Masatani[2], Takanori Komatsu[3],
Junichi Akita[4], Tetsuo Ono[5], and Makoto Okamoto[1]

[1] Department of Media Architecture, Future University Hakodate, Hakodate, Japan
{itokiyo,g2112008,g2114024,maq}@fun.ac.jp, fujimonia@gmail.com
[2] Graduate School of Electrical and Computer Engineering,
Kanazawa University, Kanazawa, Japan
masatani@ifdl.jp
[3] Faculty of Textile Science and Technology, Shinshu University, Ueda, Japan
tkomat@shinshu-u.ac.jp
[4] School of Electrical and Computer Engineering, Kanazawa University, Kanazawa, Japan
akita@is.t.kanazawa-u.ac.jp
[5] Graduate School of Information Science and Technology,
Hokkaido University, Sapporo, Japan
tono@complex.ist.hokudai.ac.jp

Abstract. We developed a unique haptic interface, the "FB-Finger," which enables users to detect the distance to an object. When a user holds the FB-Finger and places his/her forefinger on a link, the finger bends or extends depending on the link's angular motion (which corresponds to the metric distance between the user and the object). We expected the FB-Finger to provide more accurate distance estimation than similar commercial electric travel aids. To test this hypothesis, we conducted psychological experiments with blindfolded sighted participants who were asked to make distance estimations in conditions using three different devices. Results revealed that the FB-Finger allowed participants to make more accurate judgments compared to the other devices. These findings suggest that using the FB-Finger provides significant potential for ETA application among visually impaired individuals.

Keywords: Haptic Interface, Electric Travel Aid, Perception.

1 Introduction

Numerous devices, referred to as electric travel aids (ETAs), have been introduced to assist locomotion in individuals with blindness. In order to ensure locomotion safety, ETAs have incorporated functions that obtain information regarding orientation. For example, ETA sensors determine a user's location, the direction in which the user moves, and the distance of nearby objects.

K. Miesenberger et al. (Eds.): ICCHP 2014, Part II, LNCS 8548, pp. 65–72, 2014.

However, visually impaired individuals have difficulty handling such ETAs skillfully. The main reason is that these individuals need to exert substantial effort learning to use these devices. For instance, associating haptic (vibratory intensity and frequency) or auditory (sound intensity and frequency) output variables with the distance or direction of surrounding objects is challenging. To address this problem, our pervious study proposed a novel and intuitive haptic interface to assist walking among visually impaired individuals. This interface, depicted in Figure 1, was termed the CyARM [1]. The CyARM has been shown to be effective in detecting obstacles during locomotion. [2]

Additionally, our previous study indicated that sighted individuals who were blindfolded could recognize the size and shape of objects by using the CyARM [3]. The CyARM was quite effective in enabling participants to explore obstacles and specify distances to those objects without excessive effort for training.

However, the CyARM is impractical for daily use among the visually impaired for two reasons. For one, the CyARM is too large. Secondly, the CyARM constrains a user's arm and trunk movement due to the device's mechanics. Since the CyARM is not portable, we developed a novel and easy-to-handle device for intuitively exploring an environment. Below, we discuss the outline of this device, which we termed the "FB-Finger," and demonstrate the usefulness of this device based on results from two separate experiments.

Fig. 1. Representation of the CyARM

2 Outline of the FB-Finger

We designed the FB-Finger in order to address user interface problems encountered with the CyARM. The FB-Finger is expected to enable users to intuitively obtain spatial information, such as the direction and distance, to an object.

Figure 2 depicts how to operate the FB-Finger. Users hold the FB-Finger and place their forefinger on the link. The finger bends or extends depending on the link's angular motion. The angle changes from 0 to 70 degrees in correspondence with the metric distance between a user and an object. The FB-Finger can provide users with distance information since the extent that the user bends his/her forefinger is directly associated with the link's movement. The link's angle increases when the distance between the FB-Finger and an object decreases (e.g., when an object approaches), whereas it decreases when the distance increases.

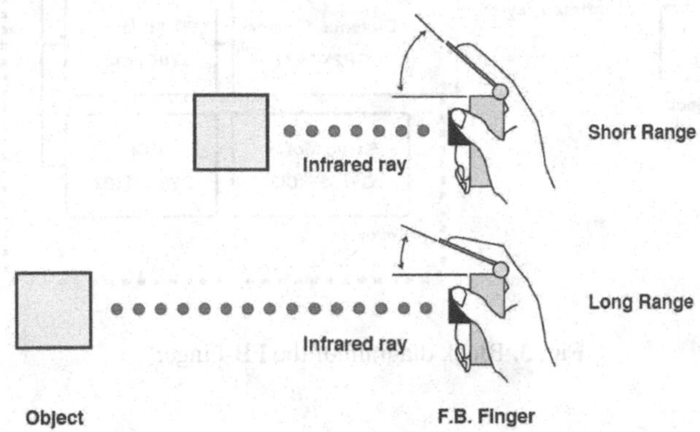

Fig. 2. Operation of the FB-Finger

3 Hardware Configuration

The hardware specifications of the prototype FB-Finger are as follows: weight, 60 g; height, 7.5 cm; width, 4.5 cm; and depth, 3.5 cm. The hardware architecture of the prototype FB-Finger is shown in Figure 3. The developed FB-Finger consists of three functional blocks—a controller, sensor, and actuator units—that are connected to a common communication channel. Each unit has a microcontroller (MCU, Cypress CY8C21123). The sensor unit has a position-sensitive device, a (PSD)-type distance sensor, that radiates infrared rays toward an object; this device detects the reflection position of the received rays by using a PSD that implements a trigonometric distance measurement technique. The microcontroller on the sensor unit calculates the distance from the FB-Finger to the object. The actuator unit has a servo motor equipped with a 55-mm-long lever to form a 1-DOF (one-degree-of-freedom) link. The microcontroller on the actuator unit controls the servo motor according to received angular information. The controller unit periodically requests distance information from the sensor unit, converts the measured distance to angular information, and transmits this information to the actuator unit; this chain of operations forms the sensor-actuator system.

The prototype FB-Finger can install two different distance ranges of sensor units: short-range and the long-range sensors. For the short-range sensor, the distance measured varies from 0.3 to 1.4 m, while for the long-range sensor the distance measured varies from 0.1 to 2.8 m. The link angle changes from 70 to 0 degrees for both sensors.

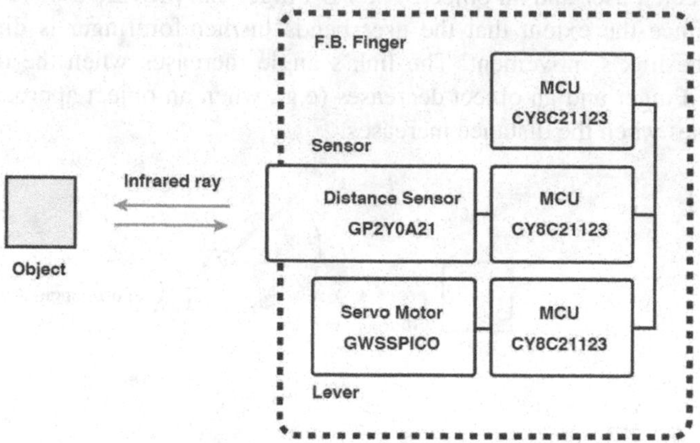

Fig. 3. Block diagram of the FB-Finger

4 Experiment 1: Relationship between Perceived and Actual Distance

4.1 Purpose

The first step in evaluating the effectiveness of the FB-Finger included an experiment conducted to reveal the correlation between the actual and perceived distance to an object in the different distance sensors conditions.

4.2 Method

Participants. Eight sighted adults served as participants.

Object for Stimuli. A piece of cardboard adhered to a whiteboard (1.6 m × 1.0 m × 0.02 m) was used as the object. We used a standard stimulus and five test stimuli for the trials.

Experimental Conditions. The short distance range sensor (hereafter, "short condition") and the long distance range sensor (hereafter, "long condition") were set. In the short condition, the object was presented at a distance of 0.4 m from an FB-Finger device fixed on a table ("standard stimulus") or at one of five positions ranging between 0.4 and 1.2 m from the table ("test stimuli"). The distance between each pair of adjacent test stimuli was 0.2 m. In the long condition, the object was presented at a distance of 1.0 m from an FB-Finger ("standard stimulus") or at one of five positions ranging between 1.0 and 2.6 m from the device ("test stimuli"). The distance between each pair of adjacent test stimuli was 0.4 m.

Procedure. Figure 4 shows the experimental setup. All participants put on noise-canceling headphones with blindfolds so that auditory and visual cues could not be used. During each trial, participants were asked to use the FB-Finger to detect the distance to a stimulus that was presented for three seconds. Initially, the standard stimulus was presented, after which one of the five test stimuli was randomly presented. A magnitude estimation method was used to estimate the distance to the presented stimulus. For this method, a participant was asked to report the magnitude of a stimulus that corresponded to some proportion of the standard. The participant estimated his/her subjective experience by assigning numbers to the stimuli that reflected the judged magnitudes of his/her experiences. During magnitude estimation, each stimulus was assigned a number that reflected its distance as a proportion to the standard. The standard stimulus was set at "100." If a test stimulus was subjectively twice as far as the standard, a participant was required to assign it a magnitude of "200." Under each sensor range condition, every participant performed six trials for each of the five stimuli.

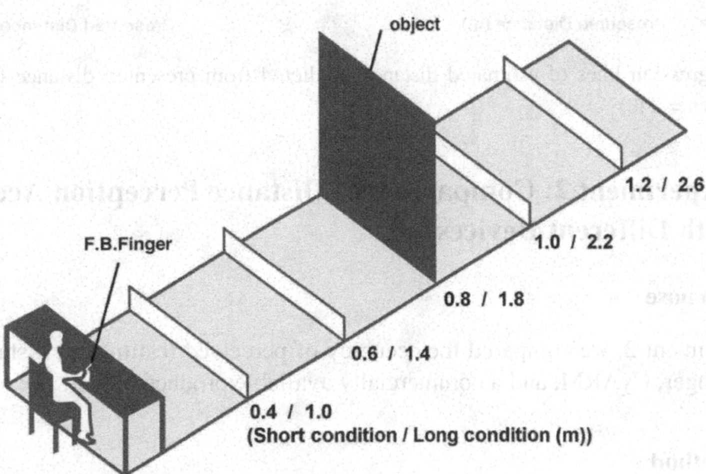

Fig. 4. Experimental setup

4.3 Results and Discussion

For each condition, a Pearson's product-moment correlation coefficient (r) between the presented distance (i.e., the stimulus actually presented) and the estimated distance was computed. The correlation values were 0.94 for the short condition and 0.95 for the long condition. There was no significant difference between these values. Thus, regardless of sensor distance range (short condition or long condition), distance estimation of the object was strongly correlated with the actual distance. This result suggests that users can detect both near and far distances using both sensors.

We also conducted a linear regression analysis on estimated magnitude against the actual distance and computed a coefficient of determination (r^2). Figure 5 depicts regression lines for each sensor range condition ($r^2 = 0.88$ for the short condition and $r^2 = 0.90$ for the long condition, respectively). Results revealed rather high r^2 values for both conditions. This suggests that estimated distance was linearly predicted from actual distance, further indicating that users could perceive distance with high accuracy.

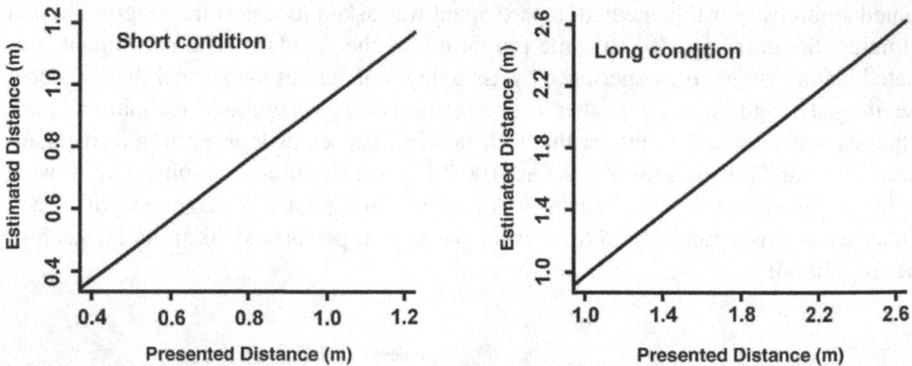

Fig. 5. Regression lines of estimated distance predicted from presented distance for the two conditions (n = 240)

5 Experiment 2: Comparison of Distance Perception Accuracy with Different Devices

5.1 Purpose

For Experiment 2, we compared the accuracy of perceived (estimated) distance using the FB-Finger, CyARM, and a commercially available product.

5.2 Method

Device Conditions. The three types of ETA devices were used. These included the FB-Finger, CyARM, and a Vibratory device. The FB-Finger and CyARM were our original developed devices. The Vibratory device was a commercial product, the size of which was similar to the FB-Finger. This device had a haptic interface that transformed measured distances into vibratory signals.

Participants. 24 sighted individuals wearing blindfolds and noise-canceling headphones participated. Eight participants were randomly assigned to each device condition.

Object for Stimuli. We used the same object as Experiment 1.

Procedure. Most procedures (experimental setup, magnitude estimation method, and total trials for each participant) were the same as in Experiment 1 except that the standard stimulus was set as 1.0 m, and the five test stimuli varied from 1.0 to 2.6 m.

5.3 Results and Discussion

As in Experiment 1, Pearson's product moment correlation coefficients (*r*s) were computed for all three device conditions. Correlation values for the FB-Finger, CyARM, and Vibratory device were 0.95, 0.84, and 0.85, respectively. Thus, the association between estimated and actual distance appeared to be higher for the FB-Finger relative to the other two devices.

Regression analyses for each device condition resulted in mean r^2 values of 0.90 for the FB-Finger, 0.72 for the CyARM, and 0.72 for the Vibratory device (Figure 6). A one-way analysis of variance was conducted with device condition (FB-Finger, CyARM, and Vibratory device) as a between-subjects factor. The main effect of device condition was significant ($f(2, 21) = 3.73, p < 0.05$). Multiple comparison tests between the three device conditions showed significant differences between FB-Finger and the CyARM ($p < 0.05$) and between the FB-Finger and the Vibratory device ($p < 0.05$). There was no significant difference between CyARM and Vibratory device.

These results suggest that FB-Finger gives users two advantages not found in the other devices. First, estimated distance better corresponds with actual distance. Second, FB-Finger allows users to more accurately detect distance to an object.

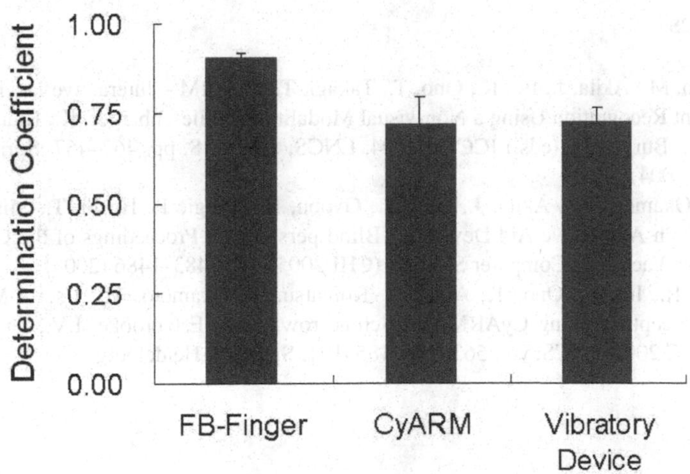

Fig. 5. Mean Determination Coefficients for the three device conditions

6 Conclusion

We originally developed CyARM as an ETA device assuming that visually impaired individuals could use it intuitively. However, given the cumbersome nature of CyARM, we developed a new type of ETA: FB-Finger. Two experiments were conducted to evaluate the usefulness of this new device. Results showed that highest distance accuracy was obtained with FB-Finger as compared to a commercial product and CyARM. These findings suggest that FB-Finger has the potential for being a useful travel aid while also serving to enhance the quality of daily life among visually impaired individuals.

It is remarkable that FB-Finger enabled blindfolded, sighted participants to judge accurately the distance to an object even though these individuals had little experience with haptic exploration. Taking into account that visually impaired individuals have keen haptic perception skills, it is conceivable that results from the present study provide promising applications of FB-Finger among this population.

FB-Finger is a novel alternative device that should be rather useful as a travel/exploration aid. However, future studies will need to include visually impaired participants to more fully determine the efficacy of this device.

Acknowledgments. The authors wish to extend our special thanks to those who volunteered to participate in our study. We are also grateful to Miho Takahashi and Yasuko Nagasaki for their help. This work was supported by JSPS KAKENHI Grant Number 25282004.

References

1. Okamoto, M., Akita, J., Ito, K., Ono, T., Takagi, T.: CyARM – Interactive Device for Environment Recognition Using a Non-visual Modality. In: Miesenberger, K., Klaus, J., Zagler, W.L., Burger, D. (eds.) ICCHP 2004. LNCS, vol. 3118, pp. 462–467. Springer, Heidelberg (2004)
2. Ito, K., Okamoto, M., Akita, J., Ono, T., Gyobu, I., Takagi, T., Hoshi, T., Mishima, Y.: CyARM: an Alternative Aid Device for Blind persons. In: Proceedings of the Conference on Human Factors in Computer Systems (CHI 2005), pp. 1483–1486 (2005)
3. Mizuno, R., Ito, K., Ono, T., Akita, J., Komatsu, T., Okamoto, M.: User's Motion for Shape Perception Using CyARM. In: Schmorrow, D.D., Estabrooke, I.V., Grootjen, M. (eds.) FAC 2009. LNCS, vol. 5638, pp. 185–191. Springer, Heidelberg (2009)

Open Accessibility Data Interlinking

Chaohai Ding, Mike Wald, and Gary Wills

Web and Internet Science Group, ECS, University of Southampton, Southampton, UK
{cd8e10,mw,gbw}@ecs.soton.ac.uk

Abstract. This paper presents the research of using Linked Open Data to enhance accessibility data for accessible travelling. Open accessibility data is the data related to the accessibility issues associated with geographical data, which could benefit people with disabilities and their special needs. With the aim of addressing the gap between users' special needs and data, this paper presents the results of a survey of open accessibility data retrieved from four different sources in the UK. An ontology based data integration approach is proposed to interlink these datasets together to generate a linked open accessibility repository, which also links to other resources on the Linked Data Cloud. As a result, this research would not only enrich the open accessibility data, but also contribute to a novel framework to address accessibility information barriers by establishing a linked data repository for publishing, linking and consuming the open accessibility data.

Keywords: Linked Data, Open Accessibility Data, Information Retrieval, Data Interlinking.

1 Introduction

Accessible tourism is listed as a significant research topic proposed by the European Commission because of the difficulties faced by people with disabilities [6]. Due to the complex conditions of travelling, to address the discordance between the expectation of people with disabilities and transport patterns would be a significant challenge [4]. There have been several research projects proposed for improving accessibility for people with special needs or disabilities [1], [5], [7]. According to the literature review [3], there have been some problems identified in these projects, such as accesibility data isolated from different systems, missing accessibility related information or difficulties for fetching useful content. Another issue is that most current standards for accessibility metadata research are focussed on the user interface or Web content rather than the guidelines for publishing the accessibility metadata to describe facilities in the real world, such as buildings, train stations or restaurants. The motivation of this research is to address the information barriers between users' needs and accessible facilities or places by integrating heterogeneous accessibility related resources and then applying the Linked Data principles to establish a linked open accessibility data repository. This paper firstly presents the survey of four different accessibility related datasets and then demonstrates the approaches and challenges for

K. Miesenberger et al. (Eds.): ICCHP 2014, Part II, LNCS 8548, pp. 73–80, 2014.

mapping and interlinking these datasets. Finally, this paper indicates the opportunities and potential benefits of publishing and consuming open accessibility data.

2 Open Accessibility Data

Open accessibility data is the data related to the accessibility issues and associated with geographic data, such as step-free access, accessible entrances, accessible toilets, accessible parking, large print or systems to aid hearing. Accessibility data also refers to the data that benefits people with special needs, such as baby change facilities, staff help, carrying large luggage or travelling with a baby pushchair. This section presents a brief summary of open accessibility data within the UK based on the datasets retrieved from four different sources, namely Wheelmap[1], Factual[2], Step-free Access Guide Feed (London Tube)[3], and National Rail[4].

Wheelmap is a crowdsourcing-based online map service to provide information about wheelchair accessible places around world. It is based on Open Street Map (OSM)[5] project and the nodes are the most primitive geographic entities in OSM using WGS84 reference system to represent geographic information. Based on the dataset extracted from Wheelmap on 29/11/2013, there are 421666 nodes within UK and 1.11% places are annotated as wheelchair accessible, while 0.24% nodes are not wheelchair accessible. 0.21% places have limited wheelchair accessibility and there are 98.44% entities without the wheelchair accessible information.

Factual is a location platform that provides over 65 million local businesses and points of interest in 50 countries. The only UK based accessibility related dataset is the Restaurants-UK dataset. There are 210613 restaurant entities in the dataset provided by the Factual Team on 10/01/2014, 8904 restaurants are annotated as wheelchair accessible while 1786 entities are indicated as not accessible. However, there are 94.92% restaurants that are unknown for this attribute.

Transport for London (TfL) provides a series of Open Data for developers, which includes the step free tube guide data, station facilities and some real time data. The step-free tube guide data contains the step-free access information of London tube, DLR and Overground stations. According to the data we downloaded on 10/01/2014, there are 362 tube station entities and approximately 50% stations are annotated as either wheelchair accessible or not, while the rest of the entities are unknown. There is an accessible interchanges attribute, which presents the accessible metadata for interchanging to other public patterns.

UK national railway stations accessibility data was crawled from the national rail website on 14/01/2014 and we converted the extracted data into the JSON format. There are 2601 railway stations data associated with accessibility information, such as

---

[1] http://wheelmap.org/en/

[2] http://www.factual.com/

[3] http://www.tfl.gov.uk/syndication/feeds/step-free-tube-guide.xml

[4] http://www.nationalrail.co.uk/

[5] http://www.openstreetmap.org

ramps for train access, step free access, accessible toilets, accessible ticket machines and accessible car parking. There are also some attributes for people with special needs, such as toilets, car park and baby changing facilities. Most attributes are annotated with metadata and the percentage of entities without annotation is just 1%. But for some attributes, such as baby changing, accessible toilets, accessible payphones and accessible ticket machines, there are more than 50% entities annotated as unknown.

According to the brief survey of open accessibility data presented in the previous section, there are some accessibility related datasets available online, which refer to the real world locations. These accessibility datasets are from multiple heterogeneous sources, and currently there is no standard guideline for specifying the attributes to annotate the accessibility metadata for public places or facilities. Crowdsourcing is not enough for obtaining open accessibility data due to the different data schemas or data quality cross the different systems or applications. Therefore, in order to fulfil the missing information and improve the quality for accessibility related data, we applied the Semantic Web technologies and Linked Data principles to map and interlink these datasets as a public Linked Data repository for accessibility metadata research, such as the research of accessibility metadata schema for publishing accessible place information or the research of guidelines to add accessibility metadata for existing buildings or facilities resources on the Web.

3 Accessibility Data Interlinking

As a core data layer of the Semantic Web, Linked Data exposes the advanced characteristics for knowledge sharing, such as human and machine readable data, well-structured data, standard data format, ontology-based reasoning and domain specified [2]. Ontology is the formal, explicit specification of a shared conceptualization. There are three different ways to integrate data based on ontology, namely the single ontology approach, multiple ontologies approach and hybrid approach. However, a single ontology approach would face the problems of the mappings between low dimensional entities (only one wheelchair accessible attribute) and high dimensional entities (multiple attributes stands for wheelchair accessible). The mappings between the multiple ontologies are still a challenging issue, which is a research area involved a large number of research efforts. According to the fact of multiple heterogeneous schemas among the datasets, we proposed two different ontology driven approaches to integrate the datasets.

The first approach is a hybrid approach, which is to design an individual ontology for each dataset to represent the entities based on its own schema and some existing ontologies, namely the accessible tube stations ontology, the wheelmap ontology, accessible restaurants ontology and accessible train stations ontology. Then we design a top-level ontology to define the basic accessibility terms in the accessible buildings domain, which could reduce the difficulties for multiple ontologies mapping. However, building specific ontologies for each dataset is difficult and not scalable for future integration. For example, Figure 1 presents the ontology graph for the data schema extracted from Wheelmap. If the data provider changes the data schema into another different structure, then the ontology needs to be redesigned. There is also another issue due to the fact that the ontology should be the formal, explicit specification of a shared conceptualization rather than the specific data schema in different applications.

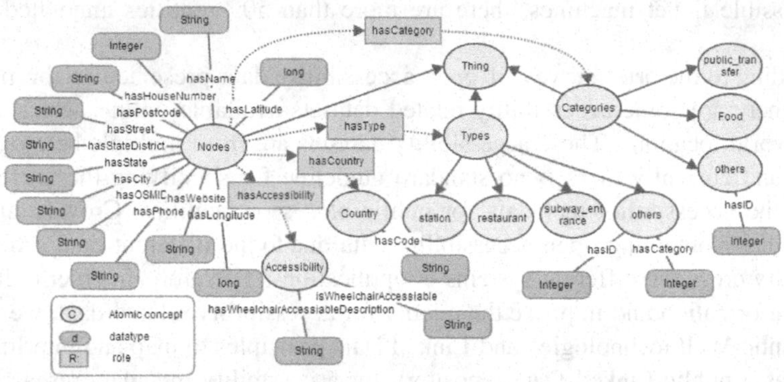

Fig. 1. Ontology Graph in Wheelmap

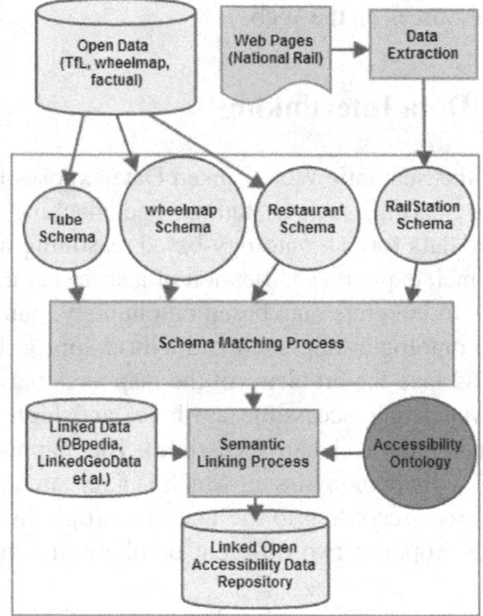

Fig. 2. Architecture of Mapping and Interlinking Open Accessibility Data

The second approach is the single ontology approach, which is the approach applied in this paper. Figure 2 presents the architecture of mapping and interlinking open accessibility data. Due to the problem of mappings between low dimensional properties and high dimensional properties in ontology reasoning, we firstly developed a basic schema of matching rules to map the same entities in different datasets by observing the data schemas in different datasets. Figure 3 demonstrates the example of two equivalent entities in both wheelmap and National Rail datasets. There are some basic properties to describe the place information, such as name, geographic data, phone, address. For accessibility related properties, there is only one property called Accessibility with wheelchair and the description for wheelchair accessible. By contrast, National Rail provides more than 50 properties to describe the accessibility issues. Another problem is the rules for entity mapping. As indicated in Figure 3, the name of train station in National Rail is London Euston Rail Station compared with Euston in wheel map. The latitude and longitude of the entity in two datasets are also slight different.

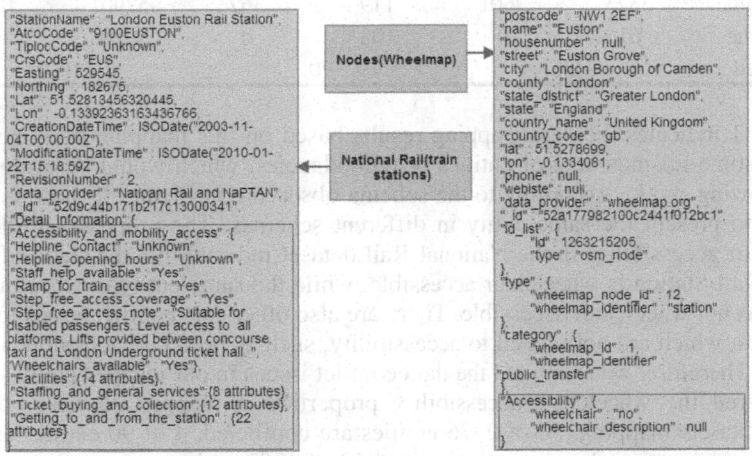

Fig. 3. Same Entities in Wheelmap and National Rail Datasets

Due to the fact that there is geographical data available for each entity in these four datasets, therefore, we develop a simple mapping rule including geographic distance matching, entity name matching and other information matching, such as address, postcode, phone number and other specified identifiers. The Mapping Rules for each entity is described as follows:

- **Step one**, the Entity Type Matching: there are 12 primary categories and 130 different types of places in wheelmap dataset, such as train station, tube station, platform and restaurants. Therefore, it is easier to map other datasets to wheelmap datasets based on the entity categories and types.
- **Step two**, the Name Similarity Matching: this step is mainly for both entities with name. If not, then go to step three. In this step, it applied the Regular Expression Matching and Jaro-Winkler Distance algorithm to get the name similarity score between two entities.
- **Step three**, Geographic Distance: calculating the geographic distance based on latitude and longitude for each entity.
- **Step four**, Additional Information Matching: matching any additional information available for both entities, such as telephone, postcode, website or identifiers.

- **Final Step**: based on the scores calculated in previous matching steps, we defined the candidate matched entities should be satisfied with following criteria: Geo Distance<=200 and Name Similarity Score>=0.85 (if there is name similarity score). If there is more than one pair of entities in the candidate list, the entities with smallest geo distance would be matched.

Table 1. Entities Mapping between Wheelmap and Other Datasets

	Train Wheelmap	Train Stations	Tube Wheelmap	Tube Stations	Food Wheelmap	Factual restaurant
Total	3384	2601	222	362	56970	10629
With Name	3323	2601	119	362	52901	10629
No Name	61	0	103	0	4071	0
Mapped	2438		90		1907	

Table 1 indicates the data mapping results based on this mapping rule. However, there is some mismatching of entities or redundancies, which would be evaluated in the following work. According to the schema observing in Figure 3, there is a data conflict to present the same entity in different schemas. The properties to describe wheelchair accessibility in the National Rail dataset indicate that the station London Euston Rail Station is wheelchair accessible, while the same entity in wheelmap displays it as not wheelchair accessible. There are also other data conflict issues for other properties, which are not related to accessibility, such as postcode, telephone or even address. Therefore, we examined the data conflict issues in our mapped entities. Table 2 compared the wheelchair accessibility properties in mapped entities. For train station datasets mapping, 50 of 2436 entities are conflicted. 4 of 90 entities are conflicted in tube station datasets mapping and 52 of 1907 entities are conflicted in restaurant datasets mapping. However, there is large amount of accessibility data enrichment archived during this datasets mapping. For instance, there are 2225 train stations, 26 tube stations and 1794 restaurants with wheelchair accessibility data mapped to the same entities in wheelmap dataset.

Table 2. Open Accessibility Data Mapping

ItemA	ItemB	No.	ItemA	ItemB	No.	ItemA	ItemB	No.
Train wheelmap	Train Station	2436	Tube wheelmap	Tube Station	90	Food Wheelmap	Factual restaurant	1907
Null	No	1068	Null	No	12	Null	Yes	1794
Null	Yes	1157	Null	Yes	14	Yes	Yes	61
Null	Null	27	Null	Null	39	No	Yes	23
Yes	No	25	Yes	No	1	Limited	Yes	29
Yes	Yes	85	Yes	Yes	3			
Yes	Null	3	Yes	Null	0			
No	No	46	No	No	3			
No	Yes	4	No	Yes	1			
No	Null	0	No	Null	14			
Limited	No	10	Limited	No	1			
Limited	Yes	11	Limited	Yes	1			
Limited	Null	0	Limited	Null	0			

Then we designed the ontology related to the place accessibility called Place Access Ontology[6] to describe the basic concepts and semantic relationships for different places. The place class in Place Access Ontology mainly refers to the place class in Schema Ontology[7]. There are 50 different categories and 120 types in schema ontology and there are some existing properties to describe the place class, such as name, geo (latitude and longitude), address, telephone or the url to present the place on the Web. There is no existing ontology to describe the accessibility facilities for the buildings or places. Therefore, we need to construct the accessibility related classes for facilities, such as Braille, LargePrint, SignLanguage, AutomaticDoor, HearingSystem, HelpPoints, Lift, AccessibleParking, AccessibleToliets, StepFree and AccessibleChangingRoom as well as some object properties and data properties to define the relationships, constraints and reasoning rules. As described in Figure 4, we stored all extracted data in MongoDB, a NoSQL document-based database and dumped the database into JSON-LD[8], a W3C standard format for Linked Data by annotating the semantic metadata to each entity in the database with Place Access Ontology. Based on the entities mapped in previous sections, we used equivalent assertions (owl:sameAs) to interlink the same entity from different data sources. By applying named entities recognition, the entities in linked open accessibility repository could also be linked to other resources in the Linked Data Cloud, such as DBpedia, Freebase and LinkedGeoData.

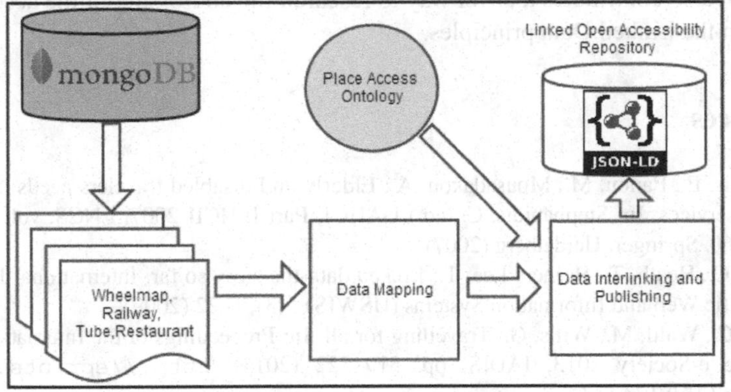

Fig. 4. Mapping and Interlinking Process

However, there are still several problems and challenges exposed in this experiment. The first problem is to improve the mapping rules for the same entity from different datasets. The second problem is to address the data conflict for the accessibility properties. Another problem is mappings between low dimensional properties and high dimensional properties based on ontology reasoning and inference rules. The

---

6 Available on: `http://waisvm-cd8e10.ecs.soton.ac.uk/2014/2/ontology/placeaccess.owl`

7 `http://schema.org/docs/schemaorg.owl`

8 `http://www.w3.org/TR/json-ld/`

question is how to determine the place object is accessible based on its accessibility level of several facilities available on the Web. All these problems will be our future research work.

4 Conclusion

Although crowdsourcing is a powerful approach to fetch millions of data entities, it is still difficult to obtain the accessibility data with good quality, compared with the accessibility data published by government. Therefore, we proposed the approach to map and interlink different accessibility related datasets into a public Linked Open Data repository. According to the demonstration of the mapping and linking results in previous sections, this approach could enrich the metadata and improve the data quality related to accessibility issues. There are also some problems and challenges proposed for this linking approach. The next step of this research is the evaluation of mapping methods and results as well as the test based on the linked open accessibility data repository. Based on this research, researchers could evaluate the accessibility level of different areas while developers could use the service to produce more accessible applications or contribute to the repository. Users could get more useful accessibility related information based on their special needs. As a consequence, this research would not only propose a method to improve and enrich the open accessibility data, but also contributes a novel way to research the addressing of the accessibility issues with the Linked Data principles.

References

1. Bekiaris, E., Panou, M., Mousadakou, A.: Elderly and disabled travelers needs in infomobility services. In: Stephanidis, C. (ed.) UAHCI, Part I, HCII 2007. LNCS, vol. 4554, pp. 853–860. Springer, Heidelberg (2007)
2. Bizer, C., Heath, T., Berners-Lee, T.: Linked data-the story so far. International Journal on Semantic Web and Information Systems (IJSWIS) 5(3), 1–22 (2009)
3. Ding, C., Wald, M., Wills, G.: Travelling for all. In: Proceedings of the International Conference e-Society 2013, IADIS, pp. 519–522 (2013), `http://eprints.soton.ac.uk/350984/`
4. Packer, T.L., McKercher, B., Yau, M.K.: Understanding the complex interplay between tourism, disability and environmental contexts. Disability and Rehabilitation 29(4), 281–292 (2007), doi:10.1080/09638280600756331
5. Vanderheiden, G.C.: Using Distributed Processing to Create More Powerful, Flexible and User Matched Accessibility Services. In: Stephanidis, C. (ed.) UAHCI 2009, Part II. LNCS, vol. 5615, pp. 438–444. Springer, Heidelberg (2009)
6. Westcott, J.: Improving information on accessible tourism for disabled people. Office for Official Publications of the European Communities (2004)
7. Wiethoff, M., Sommer, S.M., Valjakka, S., Van Isacker, K., Kehagias, D., Bekiaris, E.: Specification of information needs for the development of a mobile communication platform to support mobility of people with functional limitations. In: Stephanidis, C. (ed.) UAHCI 2007 (Part II). LNCS, vol. 4555, pp. 595–604. Springer, Heidelberg (2007)

Pre-journey Visualization of Travel Routes for the Blind on Refreshable Interactive Tactile Displays

Mihail Ivanchev, Francis Zinke, and Ulrike Lucke

Department of Computer Science, University of Potsdam, Potsdam, Germany
{mihail.ivanchev,francis.zinke,ulrike.lucke}@uni-potsdam.de

Abstract. In this paper we report on our continuing research of an audio-tactile system for visualizing travel routes on modern interactive refreshable tactile displays for blind users. The system is especially well suited for pre-journey route learning. Similar to systems for sighted users, e. g. online map services like Google Maps, we utilize an audio-tactile interactive map based on a concept from third-party research work and freely available geographic data. The system was implemented as a prototype for a touch-sensitive tactile display. Our main research interest is to explore audio-tactile concepts for displaying routes on a slippy map. We therefore developed a catalogue of ideas currently featuring tactile textures and indications for the route's course, waypoint symbols, audio indications etc. We summarize the results of an initial user test which indicates that the route visualization with our set of strategies is feasible and justifies further research.

Keywords: GIS, Accessible Geographic Routes, Visually Impaired, Blind.

1 Introduction

The wide availability of general-purpose geographical maps and route visualization tools on modern personal computers simplifies a lot of everyday tasks for the sighted user. The user is able to collect information on nearly all traveling aspects of an upcoming journey by simply accessing a web map service like Google Maps. Having effective tools for learning, a route prior to a journey is crucial for every traveler. Our work provides an easily operable tool for blind users to learn routes similar to the conventional usage of interactive maps.

Learning a route from a proper graphical representation is usually more efficient than studying a textual description [1]. A common way to visualize a route is to plot it onto a general-purpose geographical map by marking objects along its course. The route is often represented as a sequence of straight lines connecting waypoints. Highly interactive map visualizations on computers referred to as slippy maps simplify the learning even further. Routes can be automatically generated and visualized on top of a slippy map. Moreover, the user can generate a route by freely positioning waypoints. Focusing, zooming and receiving additional information on points of interest (POI) are available functions.

K. Miesenberger et al. (Eds.): ICCHP 2014, Part II, LNCS 8548, pp. 81–88, 2014.

Plotting routes on tactile maps has been a subject of research since at least 1980 [2]. Swell paper and tactile plots are static print-outs and thus bound to significant production costs and handling inconvenience compared to the actual state of the art. Human interface devices (HID) as the Talking Tactile Tablet bridge between tactile maps and computer technology. Thus, they enable interactive exploration of maps by blind users. Refreshable interactive tactile displays offer dynamic maps with no additional cost because their tactile surface is freely reconfigurable. The tactile display, referred to as BrailleDis, developed in the research project HyperBraille[1] , has a resolution of 120×60 dots and features multi-touch sensitivity.

In this paper, we report on our research on audio-tactile concepts for plotting travel routes in a slippy map for refreshable tactile displays. We begin by describing the design of the slippy map we use for our conceptual research and the implementation of a functional prototype for the touch-sensitive BrailleDis. We then elaborate on the different concepts for displaying routes with the slippy map and summarize the outcome of an explorative user test of the route visualization configurations. The computation of accessible routes is beyond the scope of our work.

2 Slippy Maps on Refreshable Tactile Displays

Slippy maps leverage the capabilities of modern computer hardware to provide a highly dynamic and productive environment for working with map data. Since slippy maps greatly simplify the access to geographical information, they are currently found across a wide number of application types. It is natural to assume that visually impaired users could also benefit from the convenience of such interfaces.

A thorough overview on the current research is provided by Senette et.al. in their survey [3]. A slippy map interface for tactile displays was pioneered by Zeng and Weber [4]. They also designed a tactile map concept including a special symbol set which takes into account the low device resolution. The interface supports nearly all features of slippy maps for sighted users: dynamic map generation with layering, panning, zooming and searching to name a few. [5] added a community approach to make accessible maps available, and performed a formative evaluation of their work with positive results. Another system was suggested by Schmitz and Ertl [6].

A useful function often found in slippy maps is the ability to visualize travel routes by selecting checkpoints on the map and providing secondary options such as the desired mode of travel or time constraints. The service calculates and highlights a suitable route, e.g. by indicating the course with straight lines of a single color.

Showing travel routes on refreshable tactile displays is an unaddressed research problem. Therefore, we suggest a catalogue of audio-tactile concepts for the visualization of routes on this device class. For the reasons described above, all our ideas are embedded in the context of an audio-tactile slippy map. Thus, we strive to provide the visually impaired user with an experience as close as possible to that of a sighted user working with a slippy map in order to learn a travel route.

---

[1] Developed in the HyperBraille project (BMWi grant 01MT07004) `http://www.hyperbraille.de/`

To test our ideas in practice, we implemented a functional prototype of a slippy map for the BrailleDis. Our system uses the tactile map concept of [4], but we simplified it reducing the symbols in the prototype. Paths are rendered as straight lines of one pin thickness, and points of interest are represented using the house symbol. All depicted points of interest in the prototype are buildings.

In order to use existing and standardized technologies for processing geographical data and to be able to experiment with different route visualization techniques in an efficient manner, we based our system on a client-server architecture with standard geo-information services. The server manages a source of geographical data, renders the tactile maps and computes the requested travel routes. The client manages the refreshable tactile display, handles the user interactions, provides the audio-tactile slippy map interface, requests tactile maps, synthesizes audio notifications etc. With this setup, changes in the route visualization strategy require no reconfiguration of the client application. Instead, the client polls the available concepts from the server and the user just chooses an interaction mechanism.

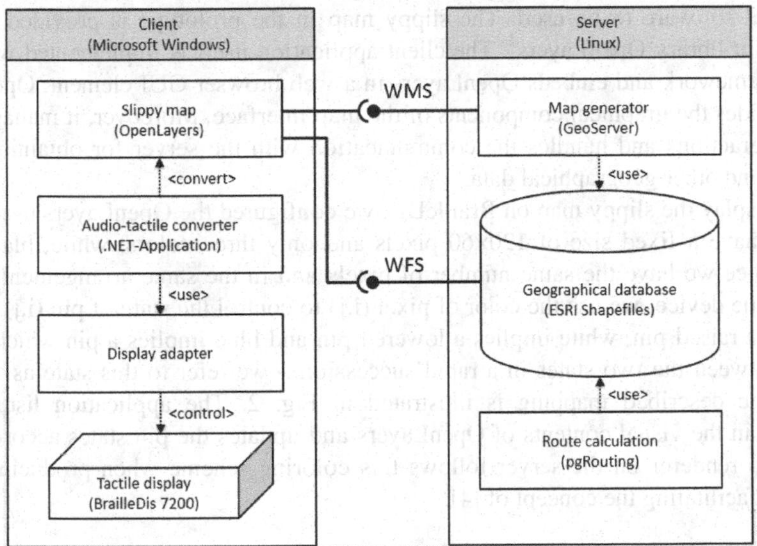

Fig. 1. Software architecture of the slippy map and the translator to the tactile display

This architectural approach (Fig. 1) guarantees high performance and technological independence. It is meaningful to assume that the server is a resourceful system. Thus, the maximum time for an update following a user interaction is roughly equal to the time required to send the server request and receive the response. The technological freedom is guaranteed on the conceptual level, because the architecture makes use of standardized web interfaces for the exchange of geographical data instead of proprietary software tools. These interfaces are already implemented by a large body of existing applications.

The functions on the server are provided by an instance of GeoServer[2] , a widely used application for processing geographical data. GeoServer supports numerous data formats and is highly interoperable with many other data processing technologies through means of standardized interfaces. It also features an elaborate and highly configurable map renderer in which the map structure and design can be described using a standardized domain-specific language.

As a source of geographical information we used a regional extract of the OpenStreetMap[3] database for the German capital city Berlin from an online archive in the format ESRI Shapefile. Also, instead of implementing a route planning service, we pre-calculated three routes in Berlin and stored them on the server for the evalua-tion. The routes are not necessarily accessible for handicapped persons. The server is responsible for highlighting the route on the produced map images using the same map renderer.

The client application is based on the idea that a conventional graphical slippy map interface can be automatically converted to a tactile representation for the target device. This simplifies the development to a great extent, because it allows existing graphical software to be used. The slippy map in the prototype is provided by the JavaScript library OpenLayers[4]. The client application itself is implemented with the .NET framework and embeds OpenLayers in a web browser GUI element. OpenLayers provides the graphical components of the map interface. Moreover, it manages the user interactions and handles the communication with the server for obtaining map images and other geographical data.

To display the slippy map on BrailleDis, we configured the OpenLayers user interface to have a fixed size of 120×60 pixels and only three colors: white, black and blue. Since we have the same number of pixels and in the same arrangement as the pins of the device, we use the color of pixel (i,j) to control the state of pin (i,j). Black implies a raised pin, white implies a lowered pin and blue implies a pin which alternates between the two states in a rapid succession – we refer to this state as "blinking". The described mapping is illustrated in Fig. 2. The application listens for changes in the visual contents of OpenLayers and updates the pin states accordingly. The map renderer on the server follows this coloring scheme when producing map images, facilitating the concept of [4].

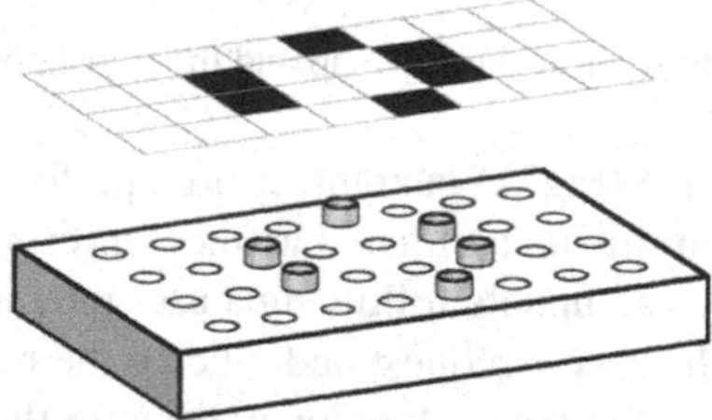

Fig. 2. The mapping between the pixels of the slippy map and the pins of the device

2 http://geoserver.org/

3 http://www.openstreetmap.org/

4 http://openlayers.org/

Due to this mapping, the tactile map exactly resembles the visual representation of the GUI of interactive map environments for sighted users as shown in Fig. 3. A route is highlighted in the map image by coloring every third pixel blue along its course. In the tactile representation, this results in every third pin blinking.

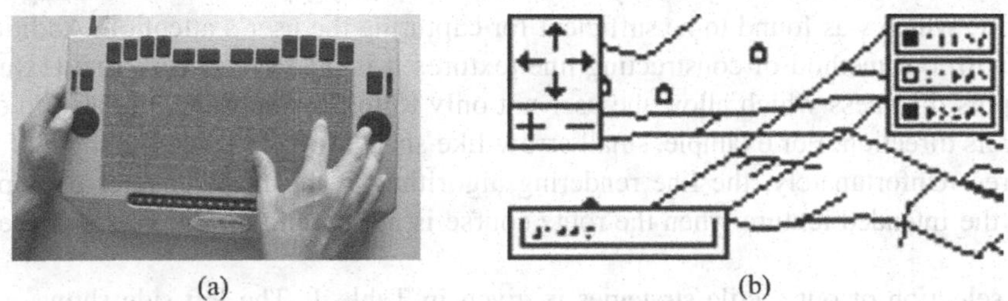

(a) (b)

Fig. 3. Slippy map with a route (a) on BrailleDis and (b) with the adapted OpenLayers GUI

The user can touch any point on the map and receives spoken information about the geographical objects in the vicinity of the touched point. The text is synthesized from server-provided data using the standard speech synthesis tools of the operating system. Every interaction of the user with the slippy map is acknowledged by an audible indication. Text is shown in 6-dot Braille code using the standard text display mechanisms of the operating system. For this purpose, a pixel-perfect TTF font was crafted. The BrailleDis hardware buttons are mapped to keyboard keys, and surface touches are translated to mouse clicks. Thus, the user has different means of controlling the map interface and cycling through the route visualization concepts.

3 Route Visualization Concepts

Our main research focus is to explore different audio-tactile concepts for visualizing routes in the map interface described. We developed a catalogue of ideas divided into the following categories: (1) tactile line textures for the route's course, (2) tactile symbols for the route's waypoints, (3) tactile indications of the route's direction and (4) audio indications. Additionally, we analyzed measures for improving the usability of the slippy map regarding the route visualization. The catalogue considers the advanced features of BrailleDis: the blinking mode of the pins and the multi-touch sensitivity of the surface. One of our goals was to analyze the importance of these features for the user experience.

To systematize the conceptual work we established intuitive guidelines characterizing the ideas, for example: (A) the route is the most important object in the map interface, (B) the user should be able to locate the route in a simple and quick manner and (C) the user should be able to confidently follow the route with his hands. An important design factor influencing our decisions is the implementation complexity of the concept in the described slippy map system.

Similar to systems for sighted users, we highlight the route's course with straight line segments textured with a tactile pattern. The largest part of our research effort so far is concerned with the study of different tactile textures for the route's course. We considered textures of up to three pins thickness. All suggested textures can be implemented by stacking dashed lines of variable thickness, dash length and dash spacing on top of each other. This approach is particularly easy to implement using our setup. The tactile textures partially make use of blinking pins with a blinking rate of 3 s-1, which was found to be sufficient for capturing the user's attention. Additionally, with our method of constructing line textures it is possible to construct textures of 3 pins thickness which allow the user not only to follow the route, but also to discover its direction. For example, small arrow-like shapes are embedded in some of the textures. Unfortunately, the line rendering algorithm of the map renderer used perturbs the intended texture when the route course is not parallel to the x-axis or the y-axis.

A selection of our tactile strategies is given in Table 1. The left side shows a 15 pins long cutout of a fully horizontal route passing from the left to right. This is the intended pattern of the texture without rendering artifacts. Filled black dots are raised pins, unfilled black dots are lowered pins, gray dots are blinking pins, and unfilled gray dots are pins which are not part of the texture and whose state is thus unaffected by the texture. The first two textures are identical except that the permanently lowered pins in the first are turned into blinking pins in the second. By making this change throughout the catalogue we analyze the significance of the blinking mode for the discoverability of the route. The given texture of 3 pins thickness consists of visually clearly distinguishable arrow symbols which are 2 pins apart pointing in the direction of the route. Our intention is to enable the user to recognize the direction of the route from the orientation of the arrows.

Table 1. Selected tactile line textures for visualizing the course of the route

Pattern	Description
○○○○○○○○○○○○○○○ ●●○●●○●●○●●○●●○ ○○○○○○○○○○○○○○○	1 pin thickness: 2 raised pins followed by 1 lowered pin.
○○○○○○○○○○○○○○○ ●●◍●●◍●●◍●●◍●●◍ ○○○○○○○○○○○○○○○	1 pin thickness: 2 raised pins followed by 1 blinking pin.
○○○○○○○○○○○○○○○ ●◍●◍●◍●◍●◍●◍●◍● ◍●◍●◍●◍●◍●◍●◍●◍ ○○○○○○○○○○○○○○○	2 pin route thickness: diagonally stippled pins, thickness and stroke length of 1 pin, raised and blinking pins.
○○○○○○○○○○○○○○○ ●●○●●●○●●●○●●●○ ●●●○●●●○●●●○●●● ●●○●●●○●●●○●●●○ ○○○○○○○○○○○○○○○	3 pin route thickness: stippled pins with arrows pointing in the route direction.

For the end point markers we adapted the symbols suggested in [7] using a resolution of 11×11 pins. For the interior waypoints on the BrailleDis we designed custom symbols with a size of 7×7 pins. Blinking pins are used for half of the interior way-point symbols. No blinking pins are used for the end point markers. Our design decisions were mainly guided by the requirement that waypoint symbols should be discoverable through a quick scanning motion across the tactile surface. Thus, we assumed that the waypoint markers should be significantly larger than the rest of the map symbols.

Aside from suggesting tactile textures and waypoint symbols, we examined several possibilities how the user could learn the direction of the route's course with a minimal effort. This is important, because otherwise the blind user has to tediously trace the whole route in order to discover its direction. Should the end points not be visible in the map region currently displayed, the task becomes even more complicated. An immediate solution is to make sure that the end points are always visible on the map. This could be achieved either by rendering them at their true locations when they lie inside the map region or at the intersections of the route with the map borders.

Another approach to indicate the direction of the route is to send a wave or an impulse along the route using blinking pins. At regular intervals, all pins of the route would be lowered and then they would begin to assume their original state one by one in the direction of the route. However, caution should be exercised not to confuse the user.

Both described strategies are ineffective when the route contains loops. Therefore, a third approach is to let the user blend in the segments of the route one after another using an additional control mechanism.

Additional information about the route can sometimes be recognized more efficiently via audio than via touch. For instance, if a sound is played as soon as the user touches a waypoint symbol, the user would know immediately the type of the object. We distinguish two types of audio indicators: earcons and speech. Earcons are quite suitable for marking waypoints as already pointed out. Furthermore, the direction of the route can simply be transmitted as a tone whose pitch rises with a decreasing according with the distance to the destination. This would also render the task of discovering and following the route trivial.

4 Evaluation and Conclusion

We conducted a pilot study with a female blind expert-user in order to assess the implemented concepts, to identify additional important design factors and to collect suggestions on how to improve and extend the concept catalogue. The evaluation was a cognitive walkthrough applying the thinking aloud method.

The subject stated that the blinking pins render the task of locating and tracing the route largely trivial. They allowed her to follow the route using both hands simultaneously. The user deemed the other factors of the tactile texture to be much more insignificant. Blinking pins are necessary for the waypoint symbols as well. Whether this is true when earcons are used still needs to be evaluated. We observed that the mechanical sound of blinking pins is a useful indication of the route's location. We assume that an experienced user would also be able to tell by the sound where exactly the route is located. The potential of this effect is yet to be studied.

Moreover, the subject provided interesting insights regarding the rendering of lines on the intersections with roads and paths. Overall, the subject was able to find and trace the route reliably with some concepts and unable to do with other implementations. This could be interpreted as a confirmation that the route visualization is indeed practically useful and justifies further research on such concepts. This qualitative analysis provided the necessary basis for later quantitative reviews.

The developed prototype enables visually impaired users to easily explore a route on OpenStreetMap. Different tactile and audio visualization concepts were tested with promising results. The web-based implementation with high performance offers technology-independent enhancements.

In the future, the route should automatically adjust to user-specific needs. Additionally, the delivered map information could be enriched with relevant accessibility details like from the "AccessibleMap Project" [8]. Distinctive properties of the route, e.g. cobblestones or remarkable ambient noise, could be delivered through auditory feedback, which could improve the recall of the route.

References

1. Meneghetti, C., Borella, E., Grasso, I., De Beni, R.: Learning a route using a map and/or description in young and older adults. Journal of Cognitive Psychology 24(2), 165–178 (2012)
2. Easton, R.D., Bentzen, B.L.: Perception of tactile route configurations by blind and sighted observers. Journal of Visual Impairment and Blindness 74, 254–265 (1980)
3. Senette, C., Buzzi, M.C., Buzzi, M., Leporini, B., Martusciello, L.: Enriching Graphic Maps to Enable Multimodal Interaction by Blind People. In: Stephanidis, C., Antona, M. (eds.) UAHCI 2013, Part I. LNCS, vol. 8009, pp. 576–583. Springer, Heidelberg (2013)
4. Zeng, L., Weber, G.: Audio-Haptic Browser for a Geographical Information System. In: Miesenberger, K., Klaus, J., Zagler, W., Karshmer, A. (eds.) ICCHP 2010, Part II. LNCS, vol. 6180, pp. 466–473. Springer, Heidelberg (2010)
5. Zeng, L., Weber, G.: ATMap: Annotated Tactile Maps for the Visually Impaired. In: Esposito, A., Esposito, A.M., Vinciarelli, A., Hoffmann, R., Müller, V.C. (eds.) Cognitive Behavioural Systems 2011. LNCS, vol. 7403, pp. 290–298. Springer, Heidelberg (2012)
6. Schmitz, B., Ertl, T.: Interactively Displaying Maps on a Tactile Graphics Display. In: SKALID 2012, Germany, p. 13 (2012)
7. Paladugu, D.A., Wang, Z., Li, B.: On presenting audio-tactile maps to visually impaired users for getting directions. In: Proceedings of CHI, pp. 3955–3960. ACM Press, Atlanta (2010)
8. Klaus, H., Marano, D., Neuschmid, J., Schrenk, M., Wasserburger, W.: AccessibleMap - Web-Based City Maps for Blind and Visually Impaired. In: Miesenberger, K., Karshmer, A., Penaz, P., Zagler, W. (eds.) ICCHP 2012, Part II. LNCS, vol. 7383, pp. 536–543. Springer, Heidelberg (2012)

Road Information Collection and Sharing System Based on Social Framework

Takatoshi Suenaga

Sendai National College of Technology, Aoba-ku, Sendai, Miyagi 989-3128, Japan
sue@sendai-nct.ac.jp

Abstract. Walking is an important factor in good health, and people derive many benefits from travelling by foot. However, walking entails risks such as traffic accidents and falls. If people recognize specific risks before walking, then they may avoid such accidents. This paper proposes a road information collection and sharing tool for the public. The proposed system stores passive risks from the properties of the landscape and active risks identified by people. Moreover, it realizes an easy way to access such risk information. When people know and avoid these risks, they will be able to walk safely.

Keywords: Road Information, Landscape Gradient, Word of Mouth, Social Framework, Walking Support.

1 Introduction

Walking is important for good health. Not only does it benefit one's body, but it facilitates interactions with friends, shopping, and sightseeing. However, some people lose their ability to walk owing to traffic accidents or other injuries. Some accidents are caused because of uneven landscapes such as steep hills and places with poor visibility. Recognizing such risks prior to walking can help avoid potential accidents. These risks can be classified into passive and active risks. A passive risk is related to the gradient information of the route. For example, elderly people whose muscles have declined with age and who have lived in the same neighborhood since childhood may confidently walk down a potentially uneven road because they are in familiar surroundings. Such road conditions are considered as passive risks for the walker. In contrast, active risks are mainly related to automobile traffic.

The objective of this research is to develop a road information sharing system for residents to reduce active and passive risks. When a resident knows about such passive risks, they can choose safer routes.

2 Social Framework

Our proposed system handles place-oriented information, and therefore, requires significant support from the residents. The system collects information from residents

K. Miesenberger et al. (Eds.): ICCHP 2014, Part II, LNCS 8548, pp. 89–91, 2014.

and allows them to share it with each other. This type of system architecture is called a "Social Framework," in which an android smartphone is used to collect road information. The proposed system consists of a "Crawler Device" and a "Mobile Data Viewer."

2.1 Crawler Device

The crawler device is made of a rollator equipped with a smartphone. The crawler is used to objectively collect road gradient information over a large area. The smartphone is mounted on the dolly, which holds the phone parallel to the surface of the road. A data-collection application running on the smartphone polls global positioning system (GPS) information. In general, the accuracy of GPS is more than 5 m; however, for certain coordinates, poor satellite visibility can cause the GPS accuracy to drop to 20 m. While moving the crawler, if the GPS detects a change of position, the application obtains the gradient from the 3D-axis accelerator sensor.

After collecting data about active and passive risks, the data is stored on a database server, and then, the keyhole markup language (KML) data is generated for Google Maps. Each data point is displayed using a colored marker using the Google Maps application programming interface (API). Google Maps is a map service compatible with many devices, which enables people to view map information on a smartphone or computer.

2.2 Mobile Data Viewer

As previously mentioned, people can view road information on a smartphone or computer. However, such equipment may not be user-friendly for the very young or elderly people. In this research, the author developed a special mobile data viewer for such people. The mobile data viewer consists of a microcomputer board, 3G-network module, and an LCD display module (Fig. 1 left). When the viewer device queries the database server for the current location (latitude and longitude), the viewer receives landscape gradient information for the current area (Fig. 1 right). In this case, each square's color (red, yellow, green, etc.) corresponds to a landscape gradient. No operation is required to obtain such information, which makes it ideal for children and the elderly.

Fig. 1. Mobile data viewer

3 Field Experiments

The proposed system was evaluated by conducting field experiments in the Nakayama area. Fig.2 shows the results of our previous experiments [2]. Different colored markers indicate the gradient of the road used in the test. The colors of the markers indicate mild shifts in the landscape gradient. The mobile data viewer successfully obtained the same information shown in fig.2.

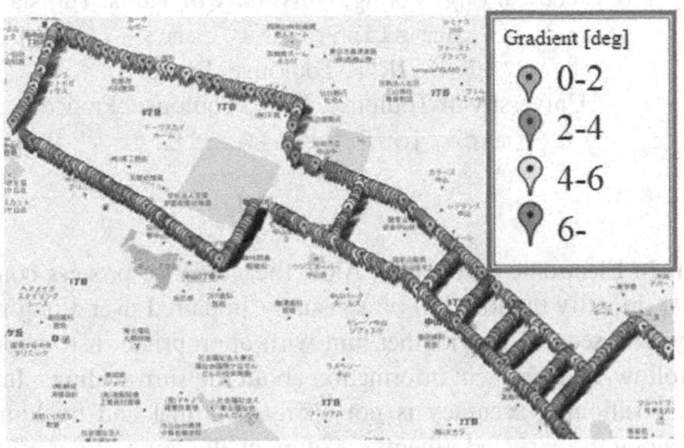

Fig. 2. Field experiment results

4 Conclusion

This paper proposed a road information collection and sharing system. A field experiment was conducted to demonstrate the collection and display of passive risk data. When more information about the Nakayama area is collected using the proposed system, residents can then better understand the properties of the landscape and minimize passive risks.

Acknowledgment. This work was supported by JSPS KAKENHI, Grant-in-Aid for Challenging Exploratory Research Number 23650359 and 25560293.

References

1. Area Information about NAKAYAMA - Japanese (2013), `http://www.city.sendai.jp/katsudo/__icsFiles/afieldfile/2013/02/25/A-16.pdf`
2. Suenaga, T.: Road Information Collecting and Sharing System. In: Proceedings of the The 35th Annual International Conference of the IEEE Engineering in Medicine and Biology Society (IEEE EMBC 2013). IEEE (2013)

Waypoint Validation Strategies in Assisted Navigation for Visually Impaired Pedestrian

Slim Kammoun[1], Marc J-M. Macé[2,3], and Christophe Jouffrais[2,3]

[1] Research Laboratory of Technologies of Information and Communication & Electrical Engineering, University of Tunis, Tunisia
kammslim@gmail.com
[2] CNRS, IRIT, Toulouse, France
[3] University of Toulouse, IRIT, Toulouse, France
{mace,jouffrais}@irit.fr

Abstract. In Electronic Orientation Aids, the guidance process consists in two steps: first, identify the location of a visually impaired user along the expected trajectory, and second, provide her/him with appropriate instructions on directions to follow, and pertinent information about the surroundings. In urban environment, positioning accuracy is not always optimal and tracking the user's progress along the expected itinerary is often challenging. We present three new waypoint-based validation strategies to track the user's location despite low positioning accuracy. These strategies are evaluated within SIMU4NAV, a multimodal virtual environment subserving the design of Electronic Orientation Aids for visually impaired people. Results show that the proposed strategies are more robust to positioning inaccuracies, and hence more efficient to guide users.

Keywords: Assisted Navigation, Guidance, Virtual Environment, Assistive Technology, Wayfinding.

1 Introduction

One of the main consequences of visual impairment is a reduced autonomy in terms of mobility and orientation. Electronic Orientation Aids (EOAs) have been proposed to compensate for wayfinding issues, and help visually impaired people in their daily travels. EOAs provide users with directions along planned itineraries, and also include landmark indications and spatial descriptions [1] . Hence, EOAs are essential devices which, in conjunction with traditional mobility aids, such as the long cane or guide-dog, improve wayfinding autonomy of blind people.

EOAs are usually based on 3 essential components: 1) A positioning system (e.g. GPS); 2) A Geographical Information System (GIS) that includes both a digitized map and software designed to calculate routes and extract environmental features; 3) A User Interface that relies on non-visual (i.e. auditory or tactile) interaction. In addition to these three components, an EOA contains a central processing unit that performs all the computation (user tracking & guidance; space description…) and ensures efficient communication between the components.

K. Miesenberger et al. (Eds.): ICCHP 2014, Part II, LNCS 8548, pp. 92–99, 2014.

The guidance process in an EOA consists first in identifying the location of a visually impaired user relatively to the expected itinerary (tracking), and then provides her/him with appropriate direction instructions (guidance, which may be enhanced with space description). Obviously, a precise estimation of the user's position during tracking is essential in order to provide an accurate guidance. For instance, it may be impossible, and somehow dangerous, to guide a blind user towards a pedestrian crossing when positioning is inaccurate. In real conditions, positioning accuracy is rarely better than 10 to 50 meters in urban environments due to atmospheric effects, signal strength, and multipath interference. It is then necessary to take into account positioning accuracy and the specificity of visually impaired pedestrian locomotion [2]when designing an EOA tracking function. Methods for improving positioning accuracy have been proposed using Inertial Measurement Unit through dead reckoning algorithms [3], DGPS [1] or embedded vision [4], but results are not widely convincing due to the complexity of heterogeneous data fusion, partial availability of DGPS ground stations signal, and the numerous issues related to embedded vision systems. A second approach to compensate for inaccurate positioning is based on the adaptation of tracking and guidance in order to increase their robustness to positioning inaccuracies. In this paper, we focus on how to improve the pedestrian user tracking algorithm.

2 Pedestrian Tracking in Assisted Navigation

In the context of assisted navigation, a selected route can be presented as a list of geolocated waypoints [5]. Between two successive waypoints, a straight section (line) is defined. The guidance process then consists in providing users with appropriate directional instructions to reach the upcoming waypoints. Obviously, tracking is critical to estimate the distance between user's position and planned itinerary. In current systems, two different tracking methods are used. The first one consists in tracking the user within a corridor. The notion of "corridoring" has been introduced within the Personal Guidance System proposed by [6] . Essentially, a corridor of an arbitrary width (e.g. 3 m) is defined around the selected route. As long as the traveler keeps walking within the defined corridor, there is no interruption in the guidance process and planned directional instructions are provided. When substantial veering occurs, the traveler walks out of the corridor boundaries, and a warning message is played. The traveler is then reoriented toward the corridor. This strategy is very conservative. Indeed, with the "corridoring", a user is not allowed to deviate from the planned itinerary, which may give rise to conflicts with mobility skills or previous knowledge of the environment. For instance, a user may prefer to cross a street where he believes it is safer or more appropriate according to mobility rules learned during orientation and mobility training. In that case, the "corridoring" method will constantly display warning messages and dramatically increase distraction and stress.

To overcome these limitations, waypoint-based tracking has been proposed and used in several devices such as[7] and [8]. User tracking with waypoints consists in determining the location of the user relative to predefined itinerary points. In this case, the user is free to select the most appropriate trajectory toward the next waypoint. However, empirical observations show that the strategy most commonly used in EOAs (called "capture radius", see [8]) frequently leads to guidance issues due to positioning inaccuracy. In the current study we designed different waypoint-based tracking strategies aimed to minimize these issues. In the next sections, we first present the capture radius strategy, and then introduce three new waypoint validation strategies. We finally show that time and distance spent on-route are minimized with the designed validation strategies.

3 Waypoint Validation Strategies

Each waypoint in an itinerary is specified with geographical coordinates. The system defines a "capture radius" around each waypoint to validate them as the user passes by (see Fig.1). This capture radius allows some flexibility: the user doesn't need to be exactly on the waypoint to validate it. With this strategy, the waypoints are also validated despite the inevitable global positioning inaccuracy. The length of the radius is carefully selected so that the user is considered as "close enough" to the waypoint to be validated. If the capture radius is too small, the user might consistently miss the waypoint. If the radius is too large, the user may consider that he has reached the waypoint too early, which could lead to erroneous guidance and poor direction choices. An optimal capture radius would keep the person close to the intended path while still allowing some flexibility. An experimental study has been performed in a virtual environment by [8], which concludes that a capture radius of approximately 1.5m is optimal. However, in real situation where positioning is rarely more accurate than 5-10m, a capture radius of 1.5m is definitely too precise and a larger value is more appropriate.

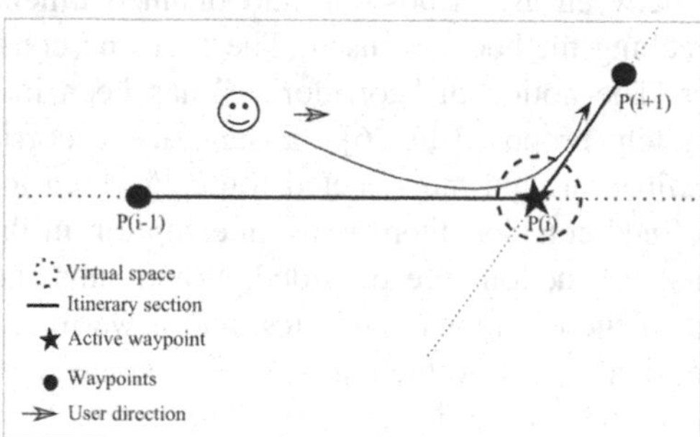

Fig. 1. Capture radius strategy [8]. The waypoint is considered as validated when the pedestrian crosses the virtual circle. The "active" waypoint is the waypoint that the user must currently reach.

In the current study, we designed alternative waypoint validation strategies that are more flexible and robust than the capture radius strategy. The first one is called Distance to Sections (D2S) and is presented in Fig.2. In this strategy, a waypoint is reached when the distance to the next section of the itinerary (d2) is smaller than the distance to the current section (d1). d1 and d2 are computed as presented in Fig.2.

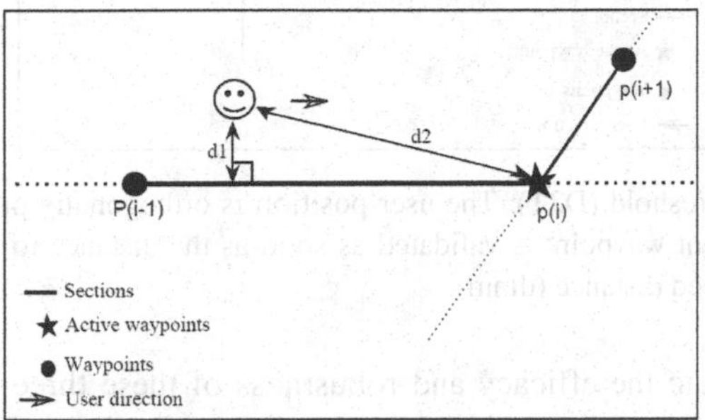

Fig. 2. Distance to Sections strategy (D2S). d1 is the shortest distance between the user position estimate and the current section. d2 is the distance between the user position estimate and the current waypoint. The current waypoint is validated as soon as d2 is smaller than d1.

The second strategy is called Distance to Lines (D2L). This strategy is an alternative to the previous one where the different sections of the itinerary are virtually extended with "lines". A waypoint is reached when the distance to the next line (d2) is smaller than the distance to the current line (d1) as presented in Fig.3.

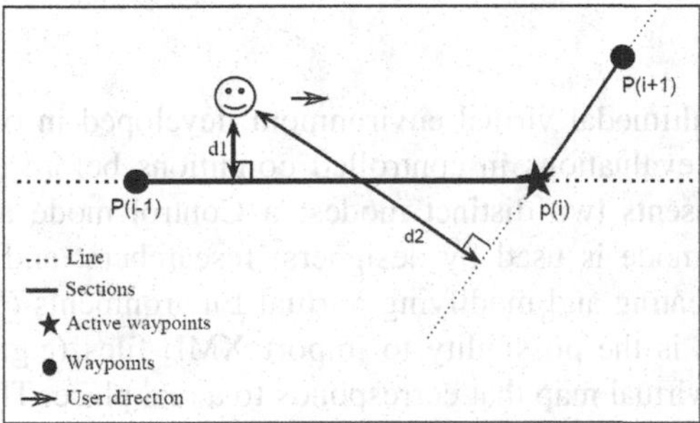

Fig. 3. Distance to Line strategy (D2L). d1 is the shortest distance between the user position estimate and the current section. d2 is the shortest distance between the user position estimate and the next line. The current waypoint is validated as soon as d2 is smaller than d1.

In the third strategy, called Distance to Threshold (D2T), the user position is orthogonally projected onto the current section. The waypoint is validated when the distance between the projected point and the current waypoint is smaller than a predefined threshold (see Fig.4).

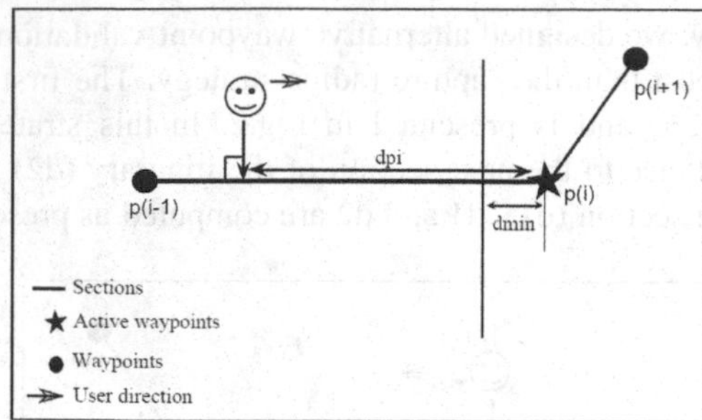

Fig. 4. Distance to Threshold (D2T). The user position is orthogonally projected onto the current section. The current waypoint is validated as soon as the distance to the waypoint (dpi) is smaller than a predefined distance (dmin).

In order to evaluate the efficacy and robustness of these three new strategies, we performed an experiment in a virtual environment. In the following section, we present the protocol and discuss the results.

4 Evaluation of the Waypoint Validation Strategies

The evaluation has been performed within SIMU4NAV [9], a multimodal virtual environment subserving the design of Electronic Orientation Aids for the Blind and developed in the context of the NAVIG project [5]

4.1 SIMU4NAV

SIMU4NAV is a multimodal virtual environment developed in order to assist EOA designer to perform evaluations in controlled conditions before onsite implementation. The device presents two distinct modes: a Control mode and an Exploration mode. The Control mode is used by designers, researchers, and O&M instructors. This mode allows creating and modifying Virtual Environments (VE). A key feature of the Control mode is the possibility to import XML files (e.g. from Open Street Map) to create a 3D virtual map that corresponds to a real place. This makes it easy to import maps of real neighborhoods or cities. Another function allows manual or automatic selection of starting and destination points, as well as paths between them. The Control mode also includes a feedback editor to assign arbitrary tactile and/or auditory feedback to any event in the VE. The Evaluation mode allows researchers to record the events and user's behavior, with a function to replay all of them later. More precisely, the system records, in a text file, all the information concerning the interactions (keystrokes, joystick, audio, haptic stimuli), as well as the avatar's position, orientation and speed.

Two empirical observations were also modelled in SIMU4NAV. First, in a real environment, a blind pedestrian who intends to move along a straight path typically deviates about 10% to the right or to the left. An adjustable drift has been added to the avatar's displacement to simulate this behavior. Second, EOAs usually rely on GNSS positioning which accuracy may vary depending on environment. A random positioning error – within adjustable range – was added to the position of the avatar in the VE to account for GNSS error.

The visual output of the VE - for the experimenter only - displays different textures applied to the surfaces (building, etc.) or the objects (e.g. tar texture for roads) encountered in the VE. The platform was implemented in C++ and the rendering was performed with OGRE 3D engine.

4.2 Protocol

For the current study, we designed a guidance task within a fictional virtual environment. Four pre-defined routes were generated within SIMU4NAV. Each route was 225 m long and composed by the same number of turns (1* 0° (no turn), 1*30°, 2*60°, 2*90°, 2*120° and 1*150°) and sections (lengths: 1*40 m, 5*25m and 4*15m). Routes were randomly generated to ensure that learning could not affect the results. Each validation strategy was randomly assigned to one route.

Sixteen blindfolded subjects gave their written informed consent to participate in this study. They were aged between 22 and 48 (mean: 28.7 years). They were seated in front of a keyboard and equipped with headphone. They were able to move within the VE using keyboard arrows. During a session, each blindfolded subject followed a total of 4 routes, each one with a different waypoint validation strategy. Users were guided with a virtual 3D sound that was placed over the waypoint to reach. When the current waypoint was validated, the next one was indicated. All subjects' trajectories were logged in a text file and then analyzed. Fig. 5 illustrates the travel of one subject with the capture radius strategy.

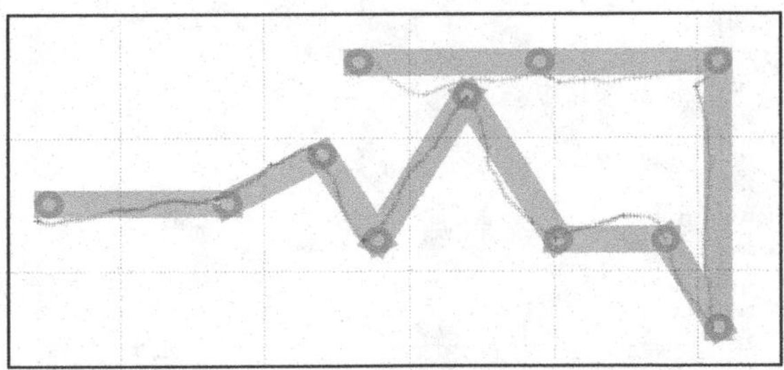

Fig. 5. Example of itinerary and journey performed with the capture radius validation strategy. Green circles present the capture radius around the waypoints. Blue segments are sections between waypoints. User position is represented with successive crosses (color is shifted towards red with increasing locomotion speed).

4.3 Results

As presented in figure 6, the average distance traveled (16 subjects) was significantly different across the four validation strategies (Anova: $F(3, 56)=5.87$, $p<0.001$). A

Fisher LSD post-hoc test showed that the capture radius strategy induced significantly longer path compared to the three other strategies (see Fig.6). However, there was no significant difference between the three new strategies.

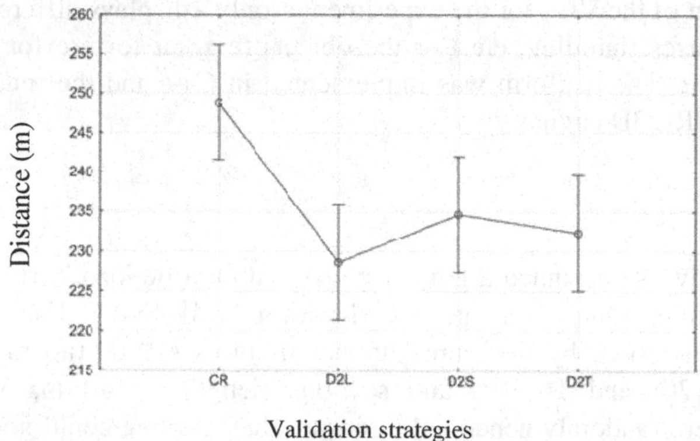

Fig. 6. Average (16 subjects) total distance across the different validation strategies. The total distance is significantly higher for the capture radius strategy than for the three other.

We also noticed that the average time to complete the journey was significantly different depending on the strategy used (Anova: F(3, 56)=8.93, p<0.0001). The Fisher LSD post-hoc test showed that the capture radius strategy induced significantly longer travel times compared to the three other strategies (see Fig.7).

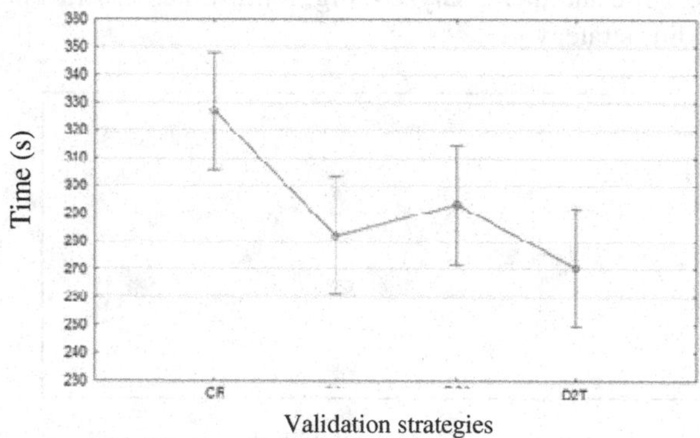

Fig. 7. Average (16 subjects) duration of travel across the different waypoint-validation strategies. Travel duration is significantly higher for the capture radius strategy than for the three other.

5 Conclusions and Discussion

The results presented here show that it is possible to significantly decrease travel time and travel distance when the waypoint validation strategy used in an EOA is improved. According to Golledge [10], the distance is the first criteria considered by the visually impaired people when choosing a path, and then time spent on route. As we have shown here, when the behavior of the blind pedestrian (angular drift) and the error in positioning are considered -which was not the case in [10]-, the "capture radius" strategy is clearly not optimal. The three alternative strategies proposed here are more efficient and more robust to positioning inaccuracies and would probably provide better guidance in EOAs.

We think that the proposed strategies are more flexible than 'capture radius' because they put less constraints on the mobility of blind users. Indeed, waypoint validation is less conservative, and the guided pedestrian is able to make his own choices without being forced to go through specific places (virtual circle). In addition, we eliminate the tricky issue of choosing the correct capture radius value.

Obviously, we need to confirm these results with blind users guided by an EOA in real conditions (e.g. with the NAVIG system [5]). Additional evaluation could also be performed in different mobility situations; the most important point would be to check that using the guide-dog or the long cane does not make any difference. We would then be able to define which specific strategy to use among the three new ones according to the circumstances. A dynamic switch between strategies depending on the situation and positioning uncertainty could also be an elegant solution.

References

1. Loomis, J.M., Golledge, R.G., Klatzky, R.L., Speigle, J.M., Tietz, J.: Personal guidance system for the visually impaired. In: First Annual ACM Conference on Assistive Technologies - Assets 1994, pp. 85–91. ACM Press, New York (1994)
2. Brabyn, J.A.: New developments in mobility and orientation aids for the blind. IEEE Trans. Biomed. Eng. 29, 285–289 (1982)
3. Nam, Y.: Map-based Indoor People Localization using an Inertial Measurement Unit. J. Inf. Sci. Eng. 1248, 1233–1248 (2011)
4. Brilhault, A., Kammoun, S., Gutierrez, O., Truillet, P., Jouffrais, C.: Fusion of Artificial Vision and GPS to Improve Blind Pedestrian Positioning. In: International Conference on New Technologies, Mobility and Security (NTMS 2011), pp. 1–5. IEEE (2011)
5. Katz, B.F.G., Kammoun, S., Parseihian, G., Gutierrez, O., Brilhault, A., Auvray, M., Truillet, P., Thorpe, S., Jouffrais, C.: NAVIG: Augmented reality guidance system for the visually impaired. Virtual Real. J. 16, 253–269 (2012)
6. Golledge, R.G., Klatzky, R.L., Loomis, J.M., Speigle, J.M., Tietz, J.: A geographical information system for a GPS based personal guidance system. Int. J. Geogr. Inf. Sci. 12, 727–749 (1998)
7. Heuten, W., Henze, N., Boll, S., Pielot, M.: Tactile wayfinder: A non-visual support system for wayfinding. In: Proceedings of the 5th Nordic Conference on Human-Computer Interaction: Building Bridges, pp. 172–181. ACM Press, New York (2008)
8. Walker, B., Lindsay, J.: Navigation performance with a virtual auditory display: Effects of beacon sound, capture radius, and practice. J. Hum. Factors 48, 265–278 (2006)
9. Kammoun, S., Macé, M.J.-M., Jouffrais, C.: Multimodal Virtual Environment Subserving the Design of Electronic Orientation Aids for the Blind. In: Proceedings of the 2012 ACM Symposium on Virtual Reality Software and Technology, pp. 189–190. ACM Press (2012)
10. Golledge, R.: Path selection and route preference in human navigation: A progress report (1995)

ARGUS Autonomous Navigation System for People with Visual Impairments

Eduardo Carrasco[1], Estíbaliz Loyo[1], Oihana Otaegui[1], Claudia Fösleitner[2], Markus Dubielzig[3], Rafael Olmedo[4], Wolfgang Wasserburger[5], and John Spiller[6]

[1] Vicomtech-IK4, Donostia-San Sebastián, Spain
{ecarrasco,eloyo,ootaegui}@vicomtech.org
[2] TeleConsult Austria, Graz, Austria
claudia.foesleitner@tca.at
[3] Siemens AG, Paderborn, Germany
markus.dubielzig@siemens.com
[4] OK-Systems, Madrid, Spain
rafael@ok-systems.com
[5] CEIT Alanova, Schwechat, Austria
w.wasserburger@ceit.at
[6] The 425 Company Ltd, Hambledon, UK
john.spiller@the425company.co.uk

Abstract. This work addresses the challenge of designing an effective, reliable and affordable autonomous navigation system for blind and visually impaired people which also covers journey planning and post journey activities (such as recommendations and experiences sharing) . The main contribution focuses on the integration of accurate real-time user positioning data with binaural 3D audio based guiding techniques on mobile devices and a web services delivering platform. The aim is to produce an autonomous navigation system that can be used to guide targeted users along pre-defined tracks and that can be used also before and after the journey to carry out several related tasks such as journey planning, training and sharing of experiences. A preliminary prototype of this concept has been built and tested with 4 end users in both rural and urban environments, obtaining encouraging results.

Keywords: Blind Navigation, Binaural Audio Guidance, Global Navigation Satellite Systems (GNSS), Inertial Navigation Systems (INS), Assistive Technology.

1 Introduction

The population of blind and visually impaired in Europe is estimated over 30 million. On average, 1 in 30 Europeans experience sight loss. Furthermore, sight loss is closely related to old age in Europe, where age-related eye conditions are its most common cause, resulting in 1 in 3 senior citizens over 65 experiencing it. [1].

K. Miesenberger et al. (Eds.): ICCHP 2014, Part II, LNCS 8548, pp. 100–107, 2014.

Being able to navigate autonomously is one of the most relevant needs for blind people. Research on autonomous navigation systems which use spatialised audio (also known as binaural audio) information [2] for guiding blind people has been carried out since 1985 [3]. Recently, it has been discovered that spatialised audio instructions are faster to interpret, more accurate and more reliable than instructions given in natural language. Also spatialised audio perception is less affected by increased cognitive load on users than language information [4].

In parallel, relevant progress is being carried out regarding satellite positioning technology. The European Geostationary Navigation Overlay Service (EGNOS), which is essentially Europe's precursor to the GALILEO system, is currently providing a terrestrial commercial data service named EDAS (EGNOS Data Access Service). It offers GPS data correction for providing increased positioning accuracy and integrity [5].

Besides, significant industrial activity has been carried out in order to provide useful navigation support systems for blind people. It's worth noticing that eAdept [6,7] has succeeded in validating a complete navigation support platform in the city of Stockholm. Furthermore, commercial products like Kapten by Kapsys [8] or Trecker Breeze by Humaware [9] have successfully reached the market. Nevertheless, they don't provide yet binaural audio guidance support in order to safely and thoroughly meet the navigation needs of the blind users. To overcome current systems' limitations research is still ongoing [10,11].

2 The ARGUS Autonomous Navigation Concept

ARGUS FP7 project [12] proposes an innovative system for the safe and autonomous navigation of blind and partially sighted people based on binaural audio guidance, which also covers pre-journey activities for journey planning and post-journey activities including sharing experiences and recommendations.

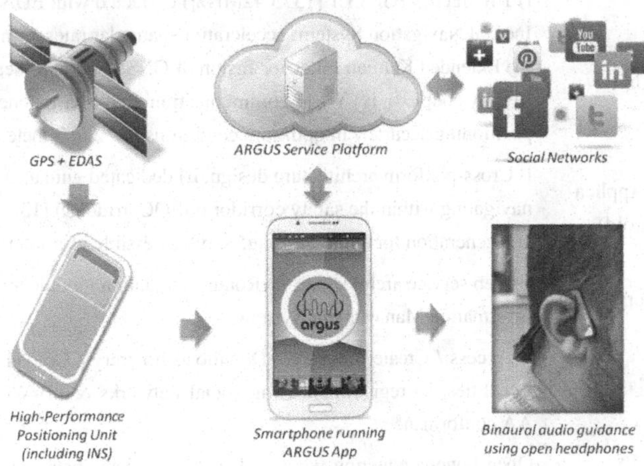

Fig. 1. ARGUS autonomous navigation support system concept

The ARGUS autonomous navigation concept is explained next. Firstly, an ARGUS Website is provided to perform the journey planning activities. The ARGUS Web User Interface is hosted in the ARGUS Service Platform. Secondly, by means of the ARGUS App running in an Android Smartphone with Internet connection, the planned routes can be downloaded from the Web Service Platform. Then, once on the route, the external High-Performance Positioning Unit (HPPU) corrects the GPS signals with EDAS data for obtaining accurate user positions and, using an Inertial Navigation System (INS), the user's heading is also calculated. Additionally, dead reckoning is implemented in the HPPU in order to support the user in areas with limited satellite coverage. The HPPU continuously transfers the updated user position and heading in real time to the Smartphone. Then, the Smartphone uses a navigation algorithm that compares the actual current user position and heading with the route to follow, and computes the binaural acoustic cues that will be transmitted in order to guide the user through the planned route. Bone conduction open headsets will be used in order to allow the user to hear surrounding sounds. Finally, the ARGUS Website is available after the journey for sharing recommendations, points of interests or performed tracks with friends or relatives through current mainstream social networks.

3 Methodology

3.1 Prototype

A user centric approach has been followed during the whole design and technical development process of the ARGUS prototype in which the end users and accessibility experts have been intensively involved. Table 1 shows the main technical features.

Table 1. Technical specifications of the integrated ARGUS prototype

#	Module	Technical specifications
1	High-Performance Positioning Unit	i) 1 frequency (GPS L1 [1575.42MHz]) corrected with EDAS data, ii) Inertial Navigation System: accelerations, angular rates & magnetometer, iii) Extended Kalman Filter for fusion of GNSS and INS measurements (tightly coupled), iv) Wi-Fi communication with smartphone, & v) total positioning accuracy in optimum conditions of 2 to 3 meters, at 4 Hz.
2	Smartphone Application (for Android)	i) Cross-platform architecture design, ii) dedicated guidance algorithm for navigating within the safety corridor (GEOCorridor®) [13], iii) binaural cue generation for audio guiding, & iv) accessible user interface.
3	Service Platform	i) Web service architecture, ii) Route Calculation module, & iii) Multilayer Information Management System.
4	User Website	i) Access / Create Itinerary / Download itinerary / Upload itinerary functionalities, ii) registration using social networks & iii) WCAG 2.0 Level AA conformance
5	Headphones.	Open bone-conducting wireless headphones have been integrated to meet users' needs on comfort and safety (AfterShokz®).

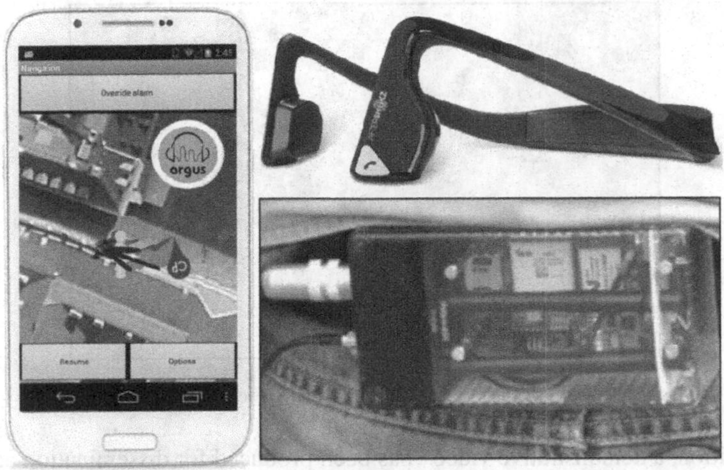

Fig. 2. Pictures of the portable components of the ARGUS prototype: Smartphone running ARGUS App, wireless open headphones and High-Performance Positioning Unit

3.2 User Tests

Small scale tests with 4 end users have been carried out in order to assess the performance of the ARGUS autonomous navigation prototype and gather initial users' opinions. Table 2 summarizes the main specifications of these tests.

Table 2. Description of the main specifications of the user tests

#	Specification	Description
1	Testing sites	User tests took place in October 2013, in Soest (Germany). Two routes were defined: i) urban route in the city centre, & ii) suburban route in a public park.
2	User recruitment	4 end users were recruited. Age, technical skills, gender and visual impairment were balanced : i) 2 users < 30 years old, ii) 2 users were technically skilled, iii) 1 woman, & iv) 2 blind people & 2 partially sighted
3	User training	The training covered 4 main stages: i) ARGUS web user interface, ii) gesture training for Android devices, iii) ARGUS App handling, & iv) ARGUS binaural guidance
4	User Tests	Users were requested to perform a set of tasks related to: i) journey planning, ii) binaural navigation, & iii) experience sharing after the journey.
5	User feedback retrieval	All users were interviewed on a one-by-one basis after each task. 2 dedicated questionnaires (Likert 1-5 scale based) were developed, i) one for the pre and post journey activities evaluation, and ii) one for the evaluation of the binaural guided navigation.
6	Privacy	Users signed an informed consent document & the user tests were video recorded.

Fig. 3. Photographs taken during the user tests

In addition, a demonstrative video[1] has been produced for dissemination activities.

4 Main Results

4.1 Analysis of Users' Tracks

First of all, the accuracy of the routes provided by the ARGUS Service Platform was assessed. Both urban and suburban routes were first automatically computed and downloaded from the ARGUS Service Platform, and then compared to the real track performed by a sighted expert person. The results obtained show a deviation less than 1 meter for both scenarios.

Next, users performed 6 tracks, 4 in the urban scenario and the other 2 in the suburban scenario. Corresponding data has been collected: i) GNSS reception: the numbers of satellites in view, Dilution of Precision (DOP) and Horizontal Dilution of Precision (HDOP) values, ii) User track: distances from resulting tracks to the ideal path and distances to the safety corridor (GEOCorridor®) have been computed, and iii) Heading instructions & user reaction: real heading instructions transmitted to the users during the journey and the real track performed by them have been compared.

Graphical and numerical analysis have been carried out on the previous data. Results obtained show that all users achieved to follow the routes. Next table shows the distances to the ideal path.

Table 3. Numerical analysis of distances to ideal track on urban and suburban routes

User	Scenario	Maximum(m)	Average(m)	Stdev(m)
U1	Urban	9,37	6,32	2,51
U2	Urban	13,66	6,86	3,33
U3	Urban	11,76	6,4	2,94
U4	Urban	4,69	1,54	1,37
U1	Suburban	6,68	0,9	1,53
U2	Suburban	6,19	2,6	1,51

1 http://youtu.be/IskZZ58Ih50

The analysis shows that average distances to the ideal path for suburban tracks take really low values (<3m), due to the good coverage of these areas. However, this data is less encouraging for the urban scenarios where user positioning is worse. Besides, results show that in most of the cases spatial sound perception was clearly perceived and followed by the users.

Fig. 4. User track and heading instructions analysis of urban and suburban scenarios

4.2 Analysis of Users' Feedback

Pre and Post-journey Activities Evaluation. Users were requested to perform a set of pre and post-journey activities by means of the ARGUS Website. The results obtained by means of the questionnaire con-firmed that the specific requirements of all test users in terms of accessibility were met. Besides, all users were able to accomplish all proposed tasks successfully. Next picture shows the answers that were collected.

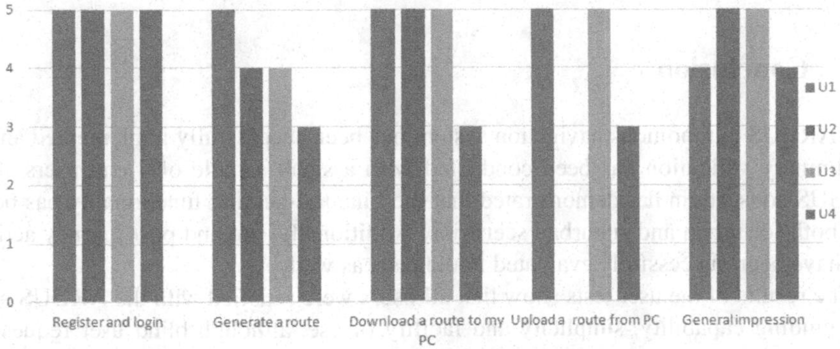

Fig. 5. Results to the questionnaire regarding pre and post journey activities

Binaural Guided Navigation Evaluation. Users were asked to navigate an urban and suburban route using the ARGUS sys-tem (Figure 2). All users were able to use it properly. All assistive technologies re-quested by the users such as the screen reader Talkback, Zoom and speech control capabilities of the used Android OS were fully supported. Additional equipment like external keyboards, headphones and Braille-devices were also used. Results to the questionnaire are shown in the next picture.

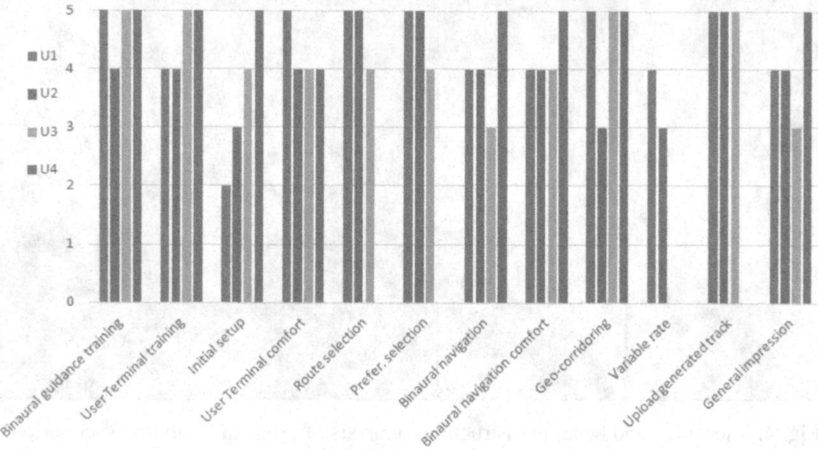

Fig. 6. Results to the questionnaire regarding binaural guided navigation

With regards to the outdoor navigation performance, users reported at the personal interviews conducted after each test that the current version of the ARGUS system worked already excellent for partially sighted users on both urban and suburban scenarios. Additionally, blind users reported that the system worked excellent for them in the suburban scenario, but that was not still reliable enough for them in the urban scenario, because blind users require higher accuracy of the system for safe navigation in the urban scenario. Besides, users reported that the training session on binaural guiding principles previous to the tests was relevant for them.

5 Conclusion

The ARGUS autonomous navigation system has been successfully implemented and a preliminary validation has been conducted with a small sample of 4 end users. The ARGUS consortium has demonstrated that the binaural guiding functionality has been met both for urban and suburban scenarios. Additionally, pre and post journey activities have been successfully evaluated in the tests as well.

The results of the user tests show that all users were satisfied with the ARGUS system guiding capability, simplicity and facility of use, although blind user requested more accuracy in the urban scenario to fully meet their safety needs. Additionally, users stated that a short training session on binaural guiding principles previous to the guiding process is needed in order to use the system correctly.

The data analysis of the tracks performed after the tests confirmed that the system is suitable for partially sighted people in both urban and suburban scenarios, but it does not provide yet accuracy enough in order to meet the needs of blind people in urban environments.

In this sense, the positioning accuracy of the system in urban areas will be improved for example by adding GLONASS to increase the number of satellites in view. Adaptive navigation algorithms may be also needed to meet the differences between urban and suburban scenarios.

Finally, the outcomes of these tests have been very encouraging. Currently the prototype is being updated and the full validation of the system at a larger scale will be carried out during 2014.

References

1. European Blind Union. Key facts and figures concerning blindness and sight loss, http://www.euroblind.org/resources/information/nr/215 (last accessed on June 12, 2013)
2. Blauert, J.: Spatial hearing: the psychophysics of human sound localization. MIT Press, Cambridge (1983)
3. Loomis, J.M.: Digital map and navigation system for the visually impaired. Unpublished paper, Department of Psychology, University of California, Santa Barbara (July 25, 1985), http://www.geog.ucsb.edu/pgs/papers/loomis_1985.pdf
4. Giudice, N.A., et al.: Environmental Learning without Vision: Effects of Cognitive Load on Interface Design. In: Proceedings of the 9th International Conference on Low Vision 2008, Montreal, Quebec, Canada (2008)
5. EDAS - EGNOS Data Access Service, http://www.gsa.europa.eu/egnos/edas
6. e-Adept project. Electronic Assistance for Disabled and Elderly Pedestrians and Travellers, http://www.eadept.se/ (last accessed on June 12, 2013)
7. Jonsson, A., et al.: Urban guidance for the blind and visually impaired – pedestrian route planning and navigation using a mobile handset. In: Challenges and Achievements in E-business and E-work, eChallenges. IOS Press, Amsterdam (2007)
8. Kapten Mobility. Kapsys, http://www.kapsys.com (last accessed on June 12, 2013)
9. Breeze, T.: Humanware, https://www.humanware.com/en-united_kingdom/products/blindness/talking_gps/trekker_breeze
10. Carrasco, E., et al.: Autonomous Navigation based on Binaural Guidance for People with Visual Impairment. Assistive Technology: From Research to Practice. IOS Press (2013)
11. Koutny, R., Miesenberger, K.: Virtual mobility trainer for Visually impaired People. Assistive Technology: From Research to Practice. IOS Press (2013)
12. ARGUS FP7 project: http://www.projectargus.eu/ (last access on June 12, 2013)
13. Otaegui, O., et al.: ARGUS Assisting Personal Guidance System for People with Visual Impairment. In: Proceedings of the 26th International Technical Meeting of The Satellite Division of the Institute of Navigation (ION GNSS+ 2013), pp. 2276–2283 (2013)

A University Indoors Audio-Tactile Mobility Aid for Individuals with Blindness

Konstantinos Papadopoulos, Marialena Barouti, and Konstantinos Charitakis

University of Macedonia, Thessaloniki, Greece

kpapado@uom.gr, {kcharitakis, ekpmet129}@uom.edu.gr

Abstract. This article presents the development of an Audio-Tactile aid in order to facilitate and enhance the spatial knowledge as well as the independent and safe movement of individuals with blindness in the University of Macedonia indoors. Moreover the developed aid provides information that helps blind individuals to obtain a cognitive image of the university indoors, plan routes they wish to track and easily identify specific locations and services. The implementation procedure of the Audio-Tactile navigation system included the following steps: 1) development of digital maps that include specific spatial information for people with blindness, 2) production of tactile maps 3) research on the readability of the tactile maps by blind individuals and development of revised tactile maps, 4) development of Audio-Tactile maps and their connection with touchpad devices, and 5) a study to derive the most appropriate locations where 10 touchpads will be installed in the university indoors.

Keywords: Mobility, Visual Impairments, Audio-Tactile System.

1 Introduction

Students with visual impairments are less likely to complete their studies in comparison to their sighted colleagues [1]. There are several factors that inhibit the representation of individuals with disabilities in higher education [2]. Such factors include difficulties relating to physical access, low expectations and poor levels of awareness. Independent and safe mobility is vital for individuals with visual impairments, and inevitably the issue of mobility around the university campus has been stressed as a significant barrier for studying in higher education [1].

Individuals with blindness are facing significant difficulties during their orientation and mobility in space, as they do not have access to all spatial information that will enable them to move successfully and safely. The majority of the researchers that examined spatial performance of individuals with visual impairments and sighted individuals came to the conclusion that visual experience influences decisively spatial behavior [3,4]. Moreover, blindness has a negative impact on the development of blind people's spatial skills [5,6].

Individuals with blindness are unable to collect the external visual stimuli from the environment or to use conventional maps [7]. The difficulties are more acute when

K. Miesenberger et al. (Eds.): ICCHP 2014, Part II, LNCS 8548, pp. 108–115, 2014.

the movement takes place in new environments or in environments with complex structure. Beyond the fact that there is always the possibility of injury due to the existence of various obstacles in the path of motion, the identification of the location of specific information is particularly problematic, especially when referring to an environment with a great abundance of important locations. Such an environment is that of the indoors of University of Macedonia where several academic departments and administrative services are located in the same single building.

This article presents an application in which audio, tactile, and Audio-Tactile information will be available in combination in order to facilitate and enhance the cognitive maps as well as the independent and safe movement of individuals with visual impairments in the indoors of the University of Macedonia. Moreover, the goals of the project are the provision of information that helps blind individuals to obtain a cognitive image of the university indoors, to plan routes they wish to track and easily identify specific locations and services.

For individuals with visual impairments, the sense of touch is considered as a basic modality for acquiring and selecting spatial information [8]. The importance of the tactile aids as tools that provide spatial information is widely acknowledged [9]. Tactile maps can provide individuals with visual impairments with knowledge about immediate and distant places and also contribute to successful wayfinding [10].

The great benefits of tactile maps are also emphasized by the results of studies in which tactile maps have been found to be more helpful for cognitive mapping of spaces by individuals with visual impairments in comparison to direct experience [11]. The contribution of tactile maps in formatting new cognitive maps or in reforming the existing ones is very important. Tactile maps can also be an extremely effective tool for representing spatial information for the orientation and mobility (O&M) of individuals with visual impairments [12]. Individuals with visual impairments can obtain information about the spatial relationships between places and locations from a tactile map faster than they will by direct experience with the environment, if they understand scale and can translate distances on a map into distances in the environment [13]. Espinosa and Ochaita [14] estimated the effects of three instructional methods - direct experience, cartographic representation and verbal description - on the spatial knowledge of 30 adults who were blind. According to the results, the participants' practical spatial knowledge was better when they learned the route with a tactile map than with either of the two other conditions.

One other primary category of orientation aids is verbal aids. Verbal aids are spoken or written descriptions of spatial layout or ways to travel within the environment [15]. Verbal aids can include detailed information about landmarks, suggestions for the use of specific techniques for specific travel situations, historical routes to be travelled, and cultural and aesthetic information for particular environments. One great advantage of verbal aids is that they can include much more information on these issues in comparison to tactile maps. Furthermore, verbal aids do not require braille skills nor sufficient remaining vision to read print [15].

Despite the advantages of tactile maps, numerous limitations have been mentioned [16]. Many individuals with visual impairments have difficulty in accomplishing the task of reading the tactile map [17]. In general, individuals with visual impairments read a tactile map slower and understand it less than sighted people who see a visual print of the same map [17]. Recognition through touch is not direct, as in the case of sight. First, we see the whole, and then we observe its parts. However, in the sense of touch, the construction of the whole is a mental process that takes place after the perception of the parts [18]. Jacobson [16] mentions the low fingertip resolution compared to eye's, the problems that cartographers are facing when rendering visual maps, such as simplification, generalisation, classification and symbolization of information included, extended use of Blaille labeling and the use of separate legends, as limitations of the tactile maps. Besides, not every visually impaired person can read Braille.

Multimodal interactive maps undoubtedly represent a solution to overcome these problems [19]. The benefits of tactile maps have been combined in previous studies with those of the verbal aids through the use of technological devices, such as the touchpad (Touch-Tablet) [20]. Touchpad offers at the same time access to the benefits of tactile maps and verbal aids. The implementation of multisensory environments on the field of maps' construction for individuals with blindness can be of great significance, particularly in the field of construction of Orientation and Mobility (O&M) aids. In the case of Audio-Tactile maps, in addition to tactile symbols and braille labels, audio and Audio-Tactile symbols (e.g. a tactile symbol that when a user touches it, he/she can hear additional information like names, descriptions etc.) are used as well. That means that a considerable piece of information is presented in auditory modality.

2 The Audio-Tactile System

The implementation of the Audio-Tactile navigation system included the following steps: 1) development of digital maps, on which specific spatial information for people with visual impairments was added, 2) production of tactile maps 3) research on the readability of the tactile maps by blind individuals and development of revised tactile maps, 4) installation of digital maps on special touchpads and addition of audio/verbal information, and 5) study to derive the most appropriate locations where 10 audio tactile devices will be installed in the indoors of University of Macedonia.

Special techniques of digital tactile cartography were applied for the development of the tactile maps. Initially, the basic cartographic background was created, i.e. digital maps of the indoors of the University through a process of converting raster to vector, which was implemented on screen digitizing of the floor plans of the University. Then, the following steps took place: 1) a detailed recording and mapping of the changes that have occurred from the date when the building was delivered for use onwards and are not depicted in the floor plans of the building. This was implemented with On-site inspection of the premises and labeling changes 3) a detailed recording and mapping of specific information for individuals with blindness not mapped in the derived plans (e.g. obstacles and information that are useful to a blind person) 4) generalization of cartographic elements (point, linear, areal symbols and labels) so as to be recognizable by touch - not all information collected were depicted on maps since the large amount of information may affect negatively the readability of the tactile map (the choice was based on the importance of each information) 5) the development of tactile symbols (points, linear, and areal) using appropriate haptic variables (shape, size, texture, value, orientation and rise) that are used for converting the optical language to haptic, and 6) printing of maps in tactile form - the Stereo-Copying process was used with microcapsule paper. A total of 10 tactile maps of university indoors were produced, in order to be placed at the respective locations in the indoors of the university.

The readability of the produced tactile maps was tested in a study with 10 blind participants aged from 20 to 35 years old. Nine of them were braille readers while six of them were students or graduates of the University of Macedonia. The participants were not experienced readers of tactile maps.

The aim of the study was to evaluate the symbols of the map in order to select the most appropriate ones. The study evaluated the time of symbol recognition, the number of symbols identified, the possible confusion between symbols and the preference of individuals with blindness to specific symbols regarding their suitability. During the test procedure two maps were used. The two maps depicted the ground floor and the first floor of the University of Macedonia building respectively. The duration of the test procedure was 90 minutes on average and the participants were tested individually. The evaluation process included the following stages: 1) matching between tactile symbols and information. Specifically the participants touched one by one the tactile symbols included on map key and then the researcher informed them about the information that was represented by each one of the tactile symbols 2) searching of each tactile symbol on the tactile map and recording of the correct and false answers as well as the time of detection, 3) evaluation of the suitability of each symbol based on a 5-point Likert scale ("Not suitable at all" to "Perfectly suitable"), 4) detection of lecture rooms and academic staff offices and recording of correct and false answers as well as the time of detection, 5) independent scanning on the map and identification of the represented information, and 6) feedback from participants on the improvement of the symbols.

The research revealed a number of key findings, which were then used to revise the tactile maps. In particular, after analyzing the responses of subjects tested, major changes to the maps were made, such as: 1) replacement of symbols, 2) greater differentiation of the thickness of linear symbols 3) enlargement of symbols and increase of the distance between them for better tactile effect and 4) erasure of information/details.

In the next phase the digital tactile maps were installed on the touchpads and all audio information was added to them. The software application Iveo Creator pro 2.0 together with the device touchpad, was used to develop the Audio-Tactile map. Both of them are products of "ViewPlus® Technologies" company. The Iveo Creator pro 2.0 is a WYSIWYG editor [21] and has the potential to create and/or edit any type of image format. The files produced by the software are saved in Scalable Vector Graphics (SVG) format. The touchpad device is a pointing device consisting of spe-cialized surface that can translate the motion and position of a user's fingers to a relative position on the computer screen and has the potential to offer tactile, kinaesthetic and auditory information [22].

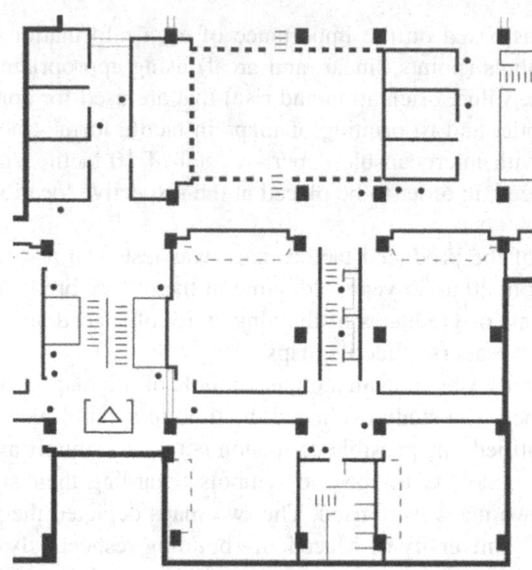

Fig. 1. Tactile map of part of university building with lecture theaters, lecture rooms and offices

Audio information consist of: descriptions of routes to and from specific locations of the university (such as the library, restaurant, information desk, elevator to each floor), lecture classrooms and theaters, changes of the material of the walking surface producing different sounds on white cane, pillars, benches, tactile cues, ramps, garbage bins, fire extinguishers, furniture, photo copying machines, poster boards, glass windows, counters, etc. The creation of the verbal descriptions of lecture classrooms and lecture theaters as well as of walking routes are based on existing theoretical data regarding the orientation and mobility of blind individuals and the creation of cognitive maps through verbal descriptions.

It was decided that the verbal descriptions should be adapted to the way with which individuals with visual impairments are coding their surroundings preferably by serial encoding and not encoding in the bird's eye form. In order to decide the final form of verbal description of the indoors and lecture rooms of the University of Macedonia, three types of verbal descriptions were produced: 1) a general description with basic elements of the respective space, 2) a more detailed description and 3) a very detailed description of the respective space. Then, the verbal descriptions were tested by 10 blind individuals aged from 21 to 47 years old. Seven of the participants were students or graduates of the University of Macedonia. The opinion of individuals who were not students of the university was also taken into consideration since it is important that the descriptions of the indoors of the university can be used by visitors and individuals who are not familiar with the university buildings. The participants were asked to evaluate each one of the three above mentioned types of descriptions, for three different types of rooms respectively. A large lecture theater, a medium sized lecture theater and a small lecture room (9 verbal description files in total).

All descriptions were converted from text files to audio format files (.mp3) using a Text-to-Speech software. The participants were then asked to listen to the three different audio files for each one of the three selected spaces and choose which one of them they thought it is more helpful for them for spatial understanding. Moreover the participants were asked to justify their choice, report any corrections, enhancements or suggestions that they consider necessary in order to be applied to the verbal descriptions of all the university buildings. The main changes pointed out concerned: a) the order of space information presented. The most frequent order of information occurred was: a general description of the hall, location of the entrance, of lecturer's desk, of the walkways between the students' seats, of pillars, of student seats, b) the number and type of detailed information of space to be included in the descriptions. Their suggestions were used in order to create the final verbal descriptions integrated on the audio tactile maps.

It was decided that the 10 touchpad devices will be installed in the indoors of the University of Macedonia as follows: 2 on the ground floor, 2 on the first floor, 3 on the second floor where most of the lecture theaters and lecture rooms are located and 1 on each one of the 3 sections of the university building (each section has 3-4 floors where the offices of the academic staff and some laboratories are located). A study was held in order to determine the optimal locations for the installation of 10 touchpad devices in the indoors of the university of Macedonia. Five blind students and graduates of the university participated in the study. The preferences of the blind students as well as the necessity of minimum additional building constructions were taken into consideration in order to determine the final locations. In particular the following process was followed: 1) the university's technical department was asked to indicate suggested locations within the university premises that would allow easy access to power supply for the audio tactile devices and that would not hinder students' mobility, 2) feedback from participants regarding the number of locations at each floor, their indoors movement and suggestions for the optimal location for installing the touchpad devices, and 4) evaluation of the locations indicated by the technical department in step 1.

The audio tactile navigation system provides information related to the location of important university services such as the administration offices of each academic department, offices of academic staff, lecture classrooms and lecture theaters, the ceremony hall, the library, the computer laboratories, the restaurant, the information desk, toilets, canteen, etc. It also provides information that helps the mobility of students with visual impairment such as elevators, stairs, main entrances and exits, emergency exits, ramps, changes on the walking surface that produce different sounds on the white cane as well as the location of "dangerous spots" such as class windows, steep slopes, low and high obstacles, railings etc.

3 Conclusion

Such an application could help individuals with visual impairments to familiarize themselves with unknown areas, to learn routes on these areas and to be aware of the important spatial features. This implication is of great importance since individuals with visual impairments do not often travel independently and when they do so they prefer to travel in familiar areas and follow familiar routes. Regarding familiar areas, the combined use of tactile maps and verbal aids as suggested in this study, could help individuals with visual impairments to update their cognitive maps and learn new routes before deciding to navigate within these areas.

The Audio-Tactile system provides solutions on the difficulties individuals with visual impairments are facing during their indoors movement within the university, providing access to spatial information allowing them safe and independent movement. Another important advantage offered by the construction of digital Audio-Tactile maps is the fact that it allows easy updating of the maps and the information they contain, if new information or changes in the indoors of the University occur.

The project will benefit students and graduates with blindness, but also a large number of individuals with visual impairments who are visiting daily the University of Macedonia and use the provided university services.

Future research should examine the contribution of Audio-Tactile maps for the development of cognitive maps and their update. Moreover, the choice of tactile, audio and Audio-Tactile symbols that are suitable for different types (mobility maps, thematic maps, maps of indoor places, etc) of Audio-Tactile maps should be considered.

Acknowledgements. The work presented in this paper was supported by the Operational Programme for Information Society (OPIS, see `www.digitalplan.gov.gr`) of the Greek Ministry of Economy & Finance, as part of the project titled "Support Services for Individuals and Students with Disabilities at the University of Macedonia". The opinions expressed in this paper do not necessarily reflect views of the OPIS.

References

1. Richardson, J.T., Roy, A.W.N.: The representation and attainment of students with a visual impairment in higher education. The British Journal of Visual Impairment 20(1), 37–48 (2002)
2. Priestley, M.: Introduction: The global context of disability. In: Priestley, M. (ed.) Disability and the Life Course: Global Perspectives, pp. 3–14. Cambridge University Press, Cambridge (2001)
3. Papadopoulos, K., Koustriava, E., Kartasidou, L.: The impact of residual vision in spatial skills of individuals with visual impairments. Journal of Special Education 45(2), 118–127 (2011)
4. Papadopoulos, K., Koustriava, E.: The Impact of Vision in Spatial Coding. Research in Developmental Disabilities 32(6), 2084–2091 (2011)
5. Koustriava, E., Papadopoulos, K.: Mental Rotation Ability of Individuals with Visual Impairments. Journal of Visual Impairment and Blindness 104(9), 570–574 (2010)
6. Koustriava, E., Papadopoulos, K.: Are there relationships among different spatial skills of individuals with blindness? Research in Developmental Disabilities 33(6), 2164–2176 (2012)

7. Papadopoulos, K.S., Karanikolas, N.: Tactile maps provide location-based services for individuals with visual impairments. Journal of Location Based Services 3, 150–164 (2009)
8. Papadopoulos, K.S.: Automatic transcription of tactile maps. Journal of Visual Impairment and Blindness 99(4), 242–245 (2005)
9. Papadopoulos, K., Livieratos, E., Boutoura, C.: A large scale city atlas for the blind. In: Proc. 20th International Cartographic Conference of ICA, Beijing, China (2001)
10. Passini, R., Dupré, A., Langlois, C.: Spatial mobility of the visually handicapped active person: a descriptive study. Journal of Visual Impairment and Blindness 80(8), 904–907 (1986)
11. Caddeo, P., Fornara, F., Nenci, A., Piroddi, A.: Wayfinding tasks in visually impaired people: The role of tactile maps. Cognitive Processing 7, 168–169 (2006)
12. Lawrence, M.M., Lobben, A.K.: The Design of Tactile Thematic Symbols. Journal of Visual Impairment & Blindness 105(10), 681–691 (2011)
13. Ungar, S., Blades, M., Spencer, C., Morsley, K.: Can visually impaired children use tactile maps to estimate directions? Journal of Visual Impairment & Blindness 88, 221–233 (1994)
14. Espinosa, M.A., Ochaita, E.: Using tactile maps to improve the practical spatial knowledge of adults who are blind. Journal of Visual Impairment & Blindness 92(5), 338–345 (1998)
15. Bentzen, B.L.: Orientation Aids. In: Blasch, B.B., Wiener, W.R., Welsh, R.L. (eds.) Foundations of Orientation and Mobility, 2nd edn., pp. 291–355. AFB Press, New York (1997)
16. Jacobson, R.D.: Navigating maps with little or no sight: An audio-tactile approach. In: Proc. Workshop on Content Visualization and Intermedia Representations, Montréal, Canada, pp. 95–102 (1998)
17. Harder, A., Michel, R.: The target-route map: evaluating its usability for visually impaired persons. Journal of Visual Impairment & Blindness 96(10), 711–723 (2002)
18. Revesz, G.: The psychology and art of the blind. Longmans Green, London (1950)
19. Brock, A., Truillet, P., Oriola, B., Picard, D., Jouffrais, C.: Design and User Satisfaction of Interactive Maps for Visually Impaired People. In: Miesenberger, K., Karshmer, A., Penaz, P., Zagler, W. (eds.) ICCHP 2012, Part II. LNCS, vol. 7383, pp. 544–551. Springer, Heidelberg (2012)
20. Holmes, E., Jansson, G.: A touch tablet enhanced with synthetic speech as a display for visually impaired people's reading of virtual maps. In: Proc. CSUN 12th Annual Conference on Technology for People with Disabilities, California State University, Northridge (1997)
21. Kanahori, T., Naka, M., Suzuki, M.: Braille-Embedded Tactile Graphics Editor with Infty System. In: Miesenberger, K., Klaus, J., Zagler, W.L., Karshmer, A.I. (eds.) ICCHP 2008. LNCS, vol. 5105, pp. 919–925. Springer, Heidelberg (2008)
22. Jansson, G., Juhasz, I.: The reading of virtual maps without vision. In: Proc. XXIII International Cartographic Conference, Moskow, Russia, August 4-10, Available on Conference CD (2007)

An OpenStreetMap Editing Interface for Visually Impaired Users Based on Geo-semantic Information

Ahmed El-Safty[1], Bernhard Schmitz[2], and Thomas Ertl[2]

[1] German University of Cairo, Cairo, Egypt
Ahmed.Abdel-Ghany@student.guc.edu.eg

[2] Institute for Visualization and Interactive Systems (VIS), University of Stuttgart, Stuttgart, Germany
{Bernhard.Schmitz,Thomas.Ertl}@vis.uni-stuttgart.de

Abstract. We present a system for editing OpenStreetMap data, which is based on the idea that common-sense preconceptions about the world can be encoded semantically and thus used in conjunction with preexisting data about an area to predict probable changes. The system can thus reduce the number of OpenStreetMap tags from which the user can choose.

Keywords: OpenStreetMap, Semantic Web, User Interface.

1 Introduction

Building an open-source world map was one of the main reasons OpenStreetMap (OSM) was founded. Over 1.4 million contributors participate in editing the world map collaboratively [6]. It has been shown that navigational information created by blind people is better suited to help other blind people navigate than information created by sighted people [4]. We assume that this would also be true with information committed to OpenStreetMap, i. e. that navigation and information systems for blind users would profit from data created by blind contributors. Unfortunately, until now there is little support for blind and visually impaired users to mingle into the OSM community. The goal of our project is to create an assistive OSM editing application that allows them to create information on-site, i. e. a mobile application that allows quickly adding new information at the user's current position.

OpenStreetMap's data format, consisting of nodes, ways and relations that are tagged with key-value pairs in order to denote their meaning, creates a difficulty for blind users: Either the user would need to remember a plethora of key-value pairs and enter them by hand, or he would need to scroll through exceedingly long lists of pre-created keys and values. Our approach aims to create a recommendation system for tags that makes those lists manageable for the user by reducing and sorting them according to semantic information about the data of the surrounding area that models common-sense preconceptions about the world, e. g. a ticket machine will always be near a station or a platform.

K. Miesenberger et al. (Eds.): ICCHP 2014, Part II, LNCS 8548, pp. 116–119, 2014.

2 Related Work

Noppens et al. [5] implemented a mobile application for semantic-based mobile service discovery. His aim was to create a flexible graph-based representation that allows OWL ontology browsing. Becker and Bizer [3] developed a mobile application, which presents nearby locations from DBPedia on a map and allows the user to browse information on these locations and related entities by following the data links in the semantic data set. Auer et al. [1] presented an open source framework, that permits the OpenStreetMap data to be translated and imported to an Open Linked Data repository in RDF. Consequently, users were able to use the SPARQL RDF query language at a public endpoint on the Web, in order to retrieve geodata of a particular region. Ballatore et al. [2] have developed an OSM Wiki Crawler, that extracts a semantic network from the OSM wiki website in the form of an RDF graph. Moreover, co-citation algorithms were used to find similarities in a graph of inter-linked objects, based on the intuition that similar objects are referenced together.

3 Design

As we mentioned in Section 1, our goal is a system that allows editing OpenStreetMap while being at a specific position. For this work, we assumed that the mobile platform (i. e. the smartphone) would provide accurate positioning data. This is not yet always correct, but we expect the position data to become more accurate with the advancement of technology.

Our current design is based on two relatively simple tasks: Editing existing nodes in OpenStreetMap and adding new nodes. First, the user is presented with a list of nodes in the immediately surrounding area. He can then select a node to edit, or choose to add a new node. If he decides to edit a node, he is presented with the node's list of current tags, where he can delete tags, edit them or add new tags.

When editing an existing node, the recommendations are based on the tags that are already existing for the node. When editing a tag, the system recommends tag values based on the tag's key. When creating a new node, the tags of the relevant enclosing polygon are used to create the recommendations. This could, for example, be a railway platform or a building. Determining the relevant enclosing polygon is not trivial. The current solution is to use the smallest enclosing polygon. However, there are cases in which several enclosing polygons, e. g. overlapping building polygons, can contain relevant tags. Using the tags from all enclosing polygons is not a viable option either, as there can be enclosing polygons which are relatively irrelevant, e. g. municipal boundaries.

Based on those tags a SPARQL query is sent to the underlying RDF in order to retrieve tags that are related to the already existing tags. Those related tags are then sorted according to the number of occurences, i. e. a tag that is related to several already existing tags is rated higher, creating a list of recommendations in order of relation to the existing tags. Another possibility is to query for the n-th

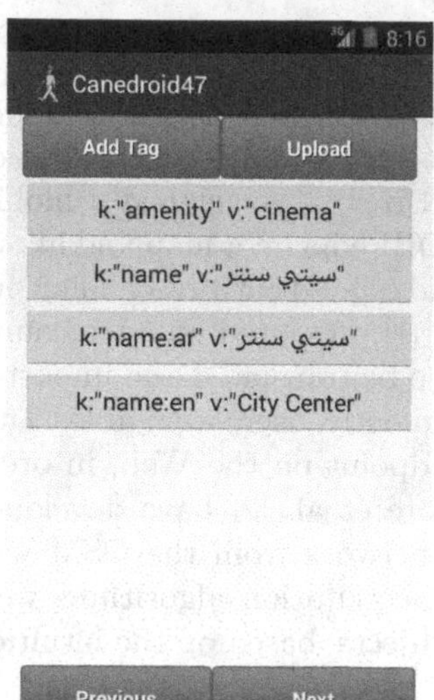

Suggestions by People	Recommendations by System
	leisure
name (5)	name
website	website
phone (2)	phone
	contact
drive_in (2)	drive_in
	wheelchair
building	building
vending_machine	
opening_hours	
address	

Fig. 1. Screenshot of the application at the cinema in Cairo, Egypt (left), and the possible tags for this node, sorted according to the recommendation of the system (right). Numbers in parentheses show how many people suggested a specific tag.

level of relation, i. e. tags that are related to the related tags, which can be used if very few tags are related to the already existing tags. We first used the RDF file created by Ballatore et al.'s wiki crawler [2]. However, because the RDF is created automatically, the similarities between tags are often inconsistent. Additionally, the RDF is lacking negative relations, i. e. a relation that implies that those tags should not occur together in reality. For further testing purposes we used a small RDF file created manually that also included negative relations. These negative relations are used to remove tags from the recommendation list. These negative relations are especially useful if querying deeper than the first level of relations, as the number of resulting tags grows quickly.

4 Evaluation

In order to evaluate the recommendation system, we asked six people (two female, four male) for information that they would expect or like to add at a cinema. The answers were mapped onto OpenStreetMap tags. For three suggestions (popcorn, price and category) we could not find a an adequate mapping. The recommendation system was then used at a cinema in Cairo, Egypt. For this test a pruned version of Ballatore et al.'s RDF was used, querying only one level of relation, i. e. directly related tags.

Figure 1 shows the aggregation of all the tags that could be mapped from suggestions of the participants, and the recommendations for tags by the system. If one were to consider the aggregation as a ground truth, precision and recall for tags regarding the cinema would both be about 0.6.

5 Future Work

Currently, two main aspects of future work remain: Firstly, the user interface of our current implementation needs additional work. As we concentrated on the recommendation system, the user interface displays the relevant tags and is also accessible via a text to speech engine, but it is still rudimentary and can be improved with further testing. Secondly, the semantic network needs some work. While the RDF of Ballatore et al. has some problems due to its being created automatically, our own test RDF is not large enough for a real-world application. Therefore a full RDF network should be created for final use in the application, with proportionate and logical relations, possibly even in a combination of automatic and manual creation.

Additionally, our system currently only uses the specific nodes, that are being edited, or enclosing polygons. Nearby nodes, ways and relations in a radius around the user could be used as further input of the recommendation system. Furthermore, the user could be notified if his modifications already exist in nearby nodes. This could help to avoid redundancies and help to keep the OpenStreetMap database free from clutter.

Acknowledgements. This work was funded by the Deutsche Forschungsgemeinschaft (DFG).

References

1. Auer, S., Lehmann, J., Hellmann, S.: LinkedGeoData: Adding a spatial dimension to the web of data. In: Bernstein, A., Karger, D.R., Heath, T., Feigenbaum, L., Maynard, D., Motta, E., Thirunarayan, K. (eds.) ISWC 2009. LNCS, vol. 5823, pp. 731–746. Springer, Heidelberg (2009)
2. Ballatore, A., Bertolotto, M., Wilson, D.C.: Geographic knowledge extraction and semantic similarity in openstreetmap. Knowledge and Information Systems, 1–21 (2012)
3. Becker, C., Bizer, C.: Exploring the geospatial semantic web with dbpedia mobile. Web Semantics: Science, Services and Agents on the World Wide Web 7(4), 278–286 (2009), http://www.websemanticsjournal.org/index.php/ps/article/view/266
4. Bradley, N.A., Dunlop, M.D.: An experimental investigation into wayfinding directions for visually impaired people. Personal and Ubiquitous Computing 9(6), 395–403 (2005), http://www.springerlink.com/content/h611644756666775/
5. Noppens, O., Luther, M., Liebig, T., Wagner, M., Paolucci, M.: Ontology-supported preference handling for mobile music selection. In: Proceedings of the Multidisciplinary Workshop on Advances in Preference Handling, Citeseer, Riva del Garda (2006)
6. OSM: Openstreetmap stats (January 2014), http://wiki.openstreetmap.org/wiki/Stats

Individualized Route Planning and Guidance Based on Map Content Transformations

Bernhard Schmitz and Thomas Ertl

Institute for Visualization and Interactive Systems, University of Stuttgart, Stuttgart, Germany
{Bernhard.Schmitz,Thomas.Ertl}@vis.uni-stuttgart.de

Abstract. We have created a system of rule-based map content transformations that allows to create maps that are better fit for specific purposes and user groups than the base material. In this paper we demonstrate the application of the map content transformations in route planning and route guidance of a navigation system for specific user groups. We show that it is possible to create maps that are better suited to these tasks than the material on which they are based.

Keywords: Map Content Transformations, OpenStreetMap.

1 Introduction

People with disabilities can profit from navigation systems that are tailored to their needs. OpenStreetMap contains data that is explicitly intended for such cases. As anyone can add data to the OpenStreetMap database, disabled users can share information that is specifically relevant for their community. There are already several projects that provide navigation for specific user groups, for example an OpenStreetMap-based routing interface for wheelchair users [3], or navigation systems and maps for blind users [1,2] However, all of those projects use algorithms that are specifically tailored for their specific user group. Furthermore, none use all the data that is available in OpenStreetMap, and the routing that is available works only on street level, i. e. it does not take into account the existence or absence of sidewalks, the locations of pedestrian crossings, and similar data.

In [4] we have presented a system of map content transformations that allows to transform maps according to specific rules with the goal of producing maps that are better suited for a specific task. We also showed that with those map content transformations it is possible to produce maps that are better suited for presentation to blind users than the original, unchanged maps.

In this paper, we show that map content transformations can also be used to create individualized route graphs. By combining data that is implicitly present in the base data with user specific requirements encoded into the transformation rules, those new route graphs can be much more suited to a specific task, e. g. guiding a pedestrian with a specific disability, than the base data they are derived from.

K. Miesenberger et al. (Eds.): ICCHP 2014, Part II, LNCS 8548, pp. 120–127, 2014.

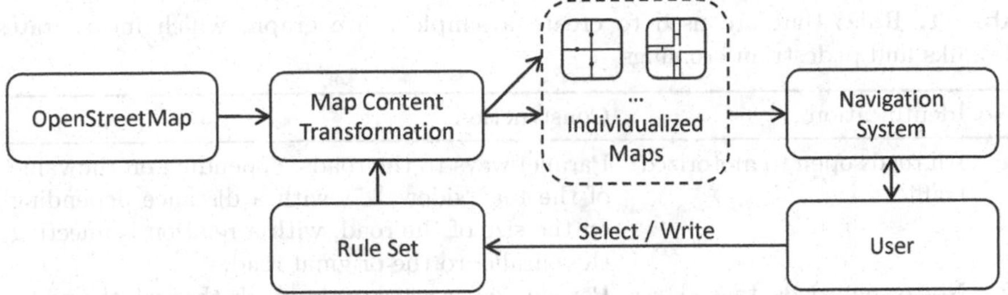

Fig. 1. Schematic showing how map content transformations interact with OpenStreetMap and a navigation system

2 System Architecture

The general idea of map content transformations is that everybody uses the same base data, in our case OpenStreetMap. This data is then transformed by the map content transformation into a personalized map, based on the specific requirements of the user group. Figure 1 shows a schematic of the use of map content transformations in a navigation system. The map content transformations are realized in an independent module that gets OpenStreetMap data as an input, and outputs the transformed map in the same data format. This was a conscious decision that demonstrates that map content transformations are not tied to a specific system: They could even be made to run on the server side, which would allow for caching of transformed maps that are used often.

Map content transformation can be used with any navigation system that can parse OpenStreetMap data. However, in order to benefit from the flexibility of map content transformations, it is necessary to keep the navigation algorithm as generic as possible and rely on the transformation to provide the individualization. In the following sections, we will therefore separate between the general explanation of the map content transformations, and the decisions that are specific to our implementation of the navigation system, which reflect the goal of staying generic, but could still differ in other navigation systems.

3 Creation of Route Graphs with Map Content Transformations

OpenStreetMap's data format consists of three kinds of entities: nodes, ways and relations. All three of them can be tagged with an arbitrary number of key-value pairs. It is important to note that nodes and ways are not equivalent to the vertices and edges of a graph, as ways can span several nodes, but graph edges are by definition the connection of two vertices. However, when using OpenStreetMap in routing algorithms, the data can easily be used as a graph by dividing the ways at each node. As our map content transformations intentionally use the OpenStreetMap data format as output, they do not create edges and

Table 1. Rules that are used to create a simple route graph, which incorporates sidewalks and pedestrian crossings

No.	Identification	Construction
1	All roads open to motorized traffic.	Parallel ways to the roads, depending on the value of the tag "sidewalk", with a distance depending on the size of the road, with a relation connecting the parallel to the original road.
2	Nodes on roads tagged as pedestrian crossings.	Perpendicular ways to the roads through the node, length a little longer than twice the distance used in Rule 1, plus relation connecting it to the road.
3	Intersections of roads.	Perpendiculars similar to Rule 2, on each road near the intersection.
4	Intersections of roads, with relations to the sidewalks created in Rule 1.	Topologically connect the correct sidewalks of roads which are directly adjacent in the intersection.
5	Perpendicular ways created in Rule 2 and 3 with parallels created in Rule 1.	Topologically connect the perpendiculars (crossings) with the parallels (sidewalks).
6	Ways created in Rule 1, 2, and 3.	Crop the protruding parts, i. e. parts that are not connected to anything else.
7	Nodes on houses near streets that have the same name as the addr:street tag of the house.	A node on the sidewalk of the street, at the position where the perpendicular to the street through the node on the house intersects the sidewalk.

vertices, but simply new OpenStreetMap data, according to the rules created by the writer of the transformation.

Map content transformations consist of an arbitrary number of rules written in XML format that can change and create tags, geometry and topology in OpenStreetMap, based on the already existing data. Each rule consists of two parts, an identification and a construction. The identification describes certain "situations", i. e. specific combinations of objects. These combinations of objects include the tags of the object, as well as their spatial relationship (e. g. "a building near a street") and their topological relationship (e. g. "a traffic light on a street"). The construction describes how the new geometry and topology is to be created in relation to those objects that have been identified. It is applied to each situation on a given map that fulfills the conditions described in the identification part of the rule. Additionally, rules can be applied to geometry that has been created by other rules, making it possible to create a new map step-by-step. Among other things these rules can be used to create explicit representations of information that is only implicitly present in the original data.

A typical example of data that is only implicitly present are sidewalks. These can either be presumed to exist in areas where they are not tagged, or are explicitly tagged with the key "sidewalk" in conjunction with the value "left", "right"

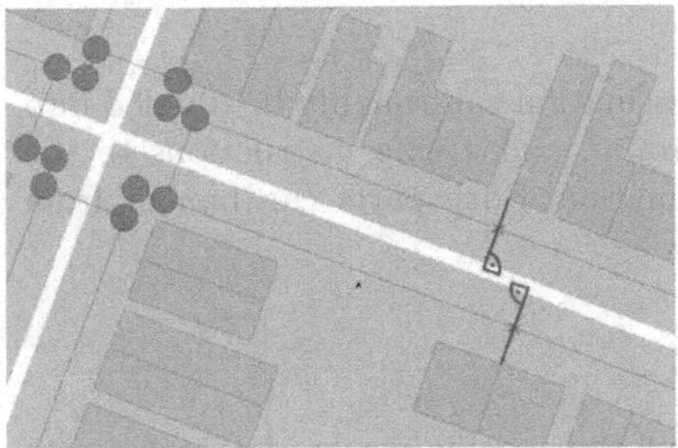

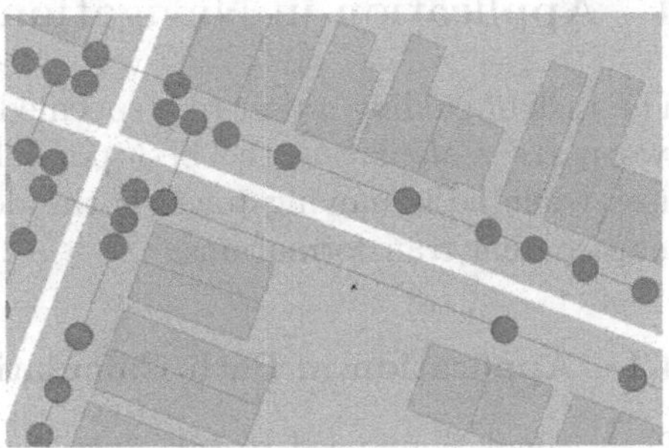

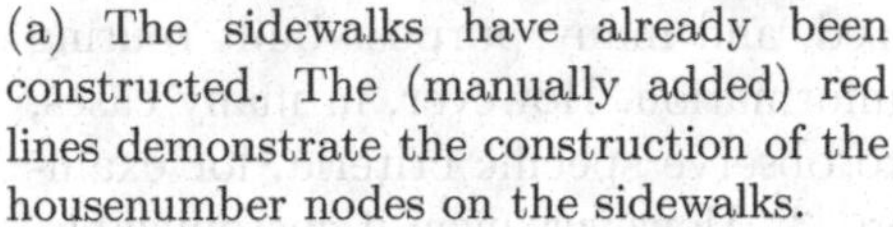

(a) The sidewalks have already been constructed. The (manually added) red lines demonstrate the construction of the housenumber nodes on the sidewalks.

(b) All houses are now represented with nodes on the sidewalk and can be selected as destinations

Fig. 2. Construction of a route graph with house numbers. Perpendiculars to the street that go through a node on the building's outline (preferrably the tagged entrance) are intersected with the sidewalk (a). The intersection points are added as new nodes and thus become possible destinations in the route graph (b).

or "both". Additionally, there are tags that denote the existence of pedestrian crossings at specific nodes on streets. However, this information will not be used by normal routing algorithms because in the topology of the original data, there is only a single line denoting the street.

By applying the rules shown in Table 1, it is possible to create a route graph that treats both sidewalks independently as parallels to streets and creates connections between them where appropriate. The rules shown in the table have been simplified in order to transport the general idea and reduce repetitiveness. A real transformation needs additional rules, e. g. to connect footways with the sidewalks. Figure 2a shows the result of the transformation. The background shows the original OpenStreetMap data, the route graph created by the transformation is shown in blue. The route graph has a topology that differs from the topology of the streets, but it is still based on the original layout.

Another example of a useful map content transformation in the creation of route graphs are house numbers. The addresses of houses are stored as tags in the building outline. However, there is no representation in the data of the connection between buildings and street they belong to; the only association between the two is the name of the street and its counterpart in the building address. Therefore a standard route finding algorithm based on OpenStreetMap cannot guide a user to a specific house number. A transformation rule that maps a node on the building onto the sidewalks (Rule 7 in Table 1) makes it possible that any standard route finding algorithm can guide the user to a position on the sidewalk in front of the specific building. The screenshot in Figure 2b shows the result of the transformation: Every house now has its specific node on the sidewalk; and each node can be used as a possible destination.

4 Application in Navigation

The task of guiding a user to a specified destination can roughly be divided into two parts: Calculating the best possible route, and giving instructions to the user while he is moving towards the destination. Both parts can benefit from map content transformations.

4.1 Application in Path Calculation

Path calculations need to take into account the specific needs and preferences of the user. This has been widely recognized, and many purpose-built routing algorithms take into account this sort of information. However, in many cases, the routing algorithm itself is optimized to observe specific criteria, for example the slope in routing for wheelchair users [3]. However, even if customizable, this approach still presupposes that the developer of the algorithm knows something about those criteria and allows for their inclusion and customization in the algorithm.

By employing map content transformations, it becomes possible to use any shortest path algorithm based on a specific data format and map the criteria onto that data format. Any criteria that the author of the algorithm does not foresee can later be transformed into that data format by the transformation.

In our implementation, we use a simple shortest path algorithm working on edge weights. The shortest path algorithm accepts both weights given as absolutes and as multipliers. Values given as multipliers are multiplied with the distance between the vertices. If no weight is given, the distance between the vertices is calculated. It is thus upon the writer of the map content transformation to ensure that the route graph reflects the needs and preferences of the user.

Coming back to the example from Table 1, as none of the created ways have a weight, the distances between the nodes is used as an edge weight. Figure 3a shows a route calculated based on that transformation. It can be used for a user who is comfortable with crossing a street without a zebra crossing or a pedestrian light, because the transformation included implicit crossings near intersections. For other user, who prefer using explicit crossings, these implicit crossings should be given a higher distance multiplier. Figure 3b shows the resulting route if the multiplier given to the perpendiculars created in Rule 2 in Table 1 is lower than the one given to the perpendiculars create in Rule 3. This route, while slightly longer, guides the user across a pedestrian traffic light to cross the street.

In addition to that, our implementation supports so-called meta-nodes. These are sets of nodes connected through a relation that can have a specific name. Meta-nodes can serve as a destination, and the user will always be guided to the nearest node of the meta-node. This makes it possible to create fuzzy destinations, such as intersections, and the routing will stop as soon as the destination is reached, without unnecessary further guiding steps, e. g. across a street.

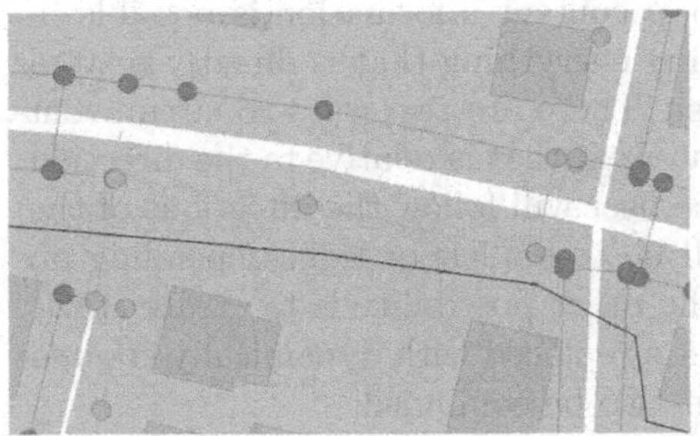

(a) The shortest way includes crossing a street at an intersection without pedestrian crossings

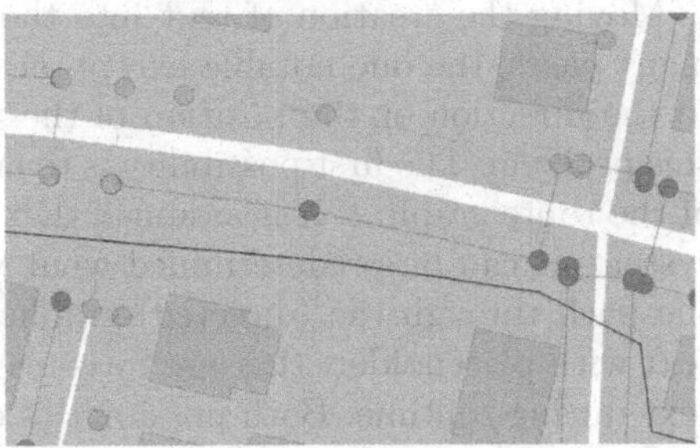

(b) Setting appropriate multipliers will make the route planning select a way that is a little longer, but uses a pedestrian crossing

Fig. 3. Comparison of two routes with the same start and destination. Both routes were calculated by a simple A*-Algorithm. The route graph for (a) is based on nothing but distance between nodes. The route graph for (b) was created by a transformation with a penalty factor on crossings that are not explicitly represented in OpenStreetMap.

4.2 Application in Route Guidance

After the route has been calculated, the user needs to be guided to the destination. This can be accomplished by different modalities, again depending on the specific needs of the user. However, natural language descriptions will most likely play a role in these modalities. Even if the main mode of route guidance is another one, e. g. vibration or sound based, text output can be helpful.

Two kinds of text output can be distinguished in navigation systems: Static text and dynamic text. Static text is stored in the map, whereas dynamic text is created on-the fly during the navigation itself and in most cases depends on the direction or position of the user. The normal approach is to combine those two kinds of texts, e. g. the sentence "Turn right into St. Denys Road" contains a directional hint that is created relative to the user's direction, and the name of a street that is statically stored in the map.

Naturally, map content transformations can only influence static text in maps. However, specifically adapted static text can already be beneficial, and in addition it is possible to move some of the text creation that would normally be dynamic into the map content transformation. As an example, a navigation system for blind users might dynamically create text to describe whether a pedestrian traffic light has an acoustic guidance system, depending on the tag in OpenStreetMap. Moving this text creation into the map content transformation by creating a generalized tag key for such information and having its value filled by the transformation has the advantage that even information that was not foreseen when the navigation system was implemented can be used with a suitable transformation.

Moving the creation of text into the map content information is possible in many cases, the one notable exception being everything that is directly related to the direction or the position of the user. There are two ways to circumvent this problem: The first possibility is to create text that is relative to the direction of the route graph. If it is assumed that the user will follow the directions of the system, it can be predetermined what will be to his left or right depending on the path through the (directed) graph. The other possibility is to create static text with placeholders that are by convention replaced with dynamically created text during runtime. Both possibilities can also be combined.

Our implementation of the navigation system employs the first possibility, but adds dynamically created directional text. It can therefore not be considered as the only way to handle this, but it can serve as a demonstration of the usefulness of map content transformations in route guidance.

Obviously, the descriptive texts need to be stored in tags as values to specific keys recognized by the navigation system. One approach would be to store the texts in the nodes. However, the problem with this approach is that it is completely direction agnostic, i. e. a text that is stored in a node cannot differ depending on where the user should go after he reaches that node. Another possibility is storing the descriptive text in the ways. Unfortunately, as was explained in Section 3, OpenStreetMap's data format does not match exactly on a graph structure. As a consequence, when storing texts in a way, it is not clear when the text should be output to the user.

Because of these difficulties, our implementation leaves as much possibilities to the writer of the transformation as possible. It allows for direction agnostic texts in nodes as well as texts in ways. Text that is stored in ways is used at every node contained by the way. This can be used, if there is a need to repeatedly output the same text. Otherwise, the writer of the transformation should ensure that the result is sensible, e. g. by making sure that each way consists of only two nodes. Additionally, texts can be stored in relations that connect a way with a specific node, thus avoiding the problem of the ambiguity when storing the text directly in a way. For ways and relations, there need to be different texts when a user starts at the beginning of the edge and when he arrives at its end. Additionally, both of these should also be available as reversed versions, as OpenStreetMap's ways are inherently directed, and the text that is output should differ according to the direction of the user.

Thus, our implementation outputs all texts to a user once he arrives at a node as follows:

1. Output value of key `arrivetext` of the way that that was active before the user reached the node or of the relation that connects that way with the current node.
2. Output value of key `arrivetext` of node.
3. Output dynamically created directional hint, depending on current direction of user and next node.
4. Output value of key `starttext` of node.
5. Output value of key `starttext` of way connecting current node with next node, or of the relation that connects that way with current node.

If the direction of the user in the route graph is the opposite of the inherent direction of the OpenStreetMap way, the value of the key `starttext_reverse` or `arrivetext_reverse` is read out resp. for ways and relations.

In the example, the rules that create new nodes (i. e. Rule 4, 5, and 7 in Table 1) need to be adapted: The names of the streets and, for Rule 7, the housenumbers are stored in a variable and inserted at the appropriate place into a text describing the situation fitting to the rule. It thus becomes possible to create output like "Turn right. Then use the pedestrian light to cross St. Denys Road.", "Turn half left. The street ends here, but a footway continues." or "You arrive at Intersection North Road St. Denys Road. Turn right. You will then have to cross North Road without a pedestrian crossing".

5 Conclusions

We have shown that map content transformations can be used to create route graphs that include additional information such as sidewalks and pedestrian crossings, and can individualize both path calculation and route guidance. The transformations are already implemented as part of our navigation system. This paper concentrated on the map content transformations, and therefore does intentionally not include a user study, as it would mainly evaluate the navigation system itself. Nevertheless, future work should include a large-scale test of the combination in order to optimize the interaction of both and to find out what kind of transformations should exactly be used for which specific user group.

Acknowledgements. This work was funded by the Deutsche Forschungsgemeinschaft (DFG).

References

1. Kammoun, S., Macé, M.J.-M., Oriola, B., Jouffrais, C.: Towards a geographic information system facilitating navigation of visually impaired users. In: Miesenberger, K., Karshmer, A., Penaz, P., Zagler, W. (eds.) ICCHP 2012, Part II. LNCS, vol. 7383, pp. 521–528. Springer, Heidelberg (2012)
2. Klaus, H., Marano, D., Neuschmid, J., Schrenk, M., Wasserburger, W.: AccessibleMap. In: Miesenberger, K., Karshmer, A., Penaz, P., Zagler, W. (eds.) ICCHP 2012, Part II. LNCS, vol. 7383, pp. 536–543. Springer, Heidelberg (2012)
3. Müller, A., Neis, P., Auer, M., Zipf, A.: Ein routenplaner für rollstuhlfahrer auf der basis von openstreetmap-daten - konzeption, realisierung und perspektiven. In: Angewandte Geoinformatik 2010 – 22. AGIT-Symposium (2010)
4. Schmitz, B., Ertl, T.: Creating task-specific maps with map content transformations. In: Proceedings of the 1st ACM SIGSPATIAL International Workshop on MapInteraction, MapInteract 2013, pp. 84–90. ACM, New York (2013)

Cognitive Evaluation of Haptic and Audio Feedback in Short Range Navigation Tasks

Manuel Martinez[1], Angela Constantinescu[2], Boris Schauerte[1], Daniel Koester[1], and Rainer Stiefelhagen[1,2]

[1] Karlsruhe Institute of Technology Institute for Anthropomatics and Robotics, cv:hci lab, Karlsruhe, Germany
[2] Study Center for the Visually Impaired Students, Karlsruhe, Germany
{manuel.martinez,angela.constantinescu,boris.schauerte, daniel.koester,rainer.stiefelhagen}@kit.edu

Abstract. Assistive navigation systems for the blind commonly use speech to convey directions to their users. However, this is problematic for short range navigation systems that need to provide fine but diligent guidance in order to avoid obstacles. For this task, we have compared haptic and audio feedback systems under the NASA-TLX protocol to analyze the additional cognitive load that they place on users. Both systems are able to guide the users through a test obstacle course. However, for white cane users, auditory feedback results in a 22 times higher cognitive load than haptic feedback. This discrepancy in cognitive load was not found on blindfolded users, thus we argue against evaluating navigation systems solely with blindfolded users.

Keywords: Sonification, Haptics, Navigation, Assistive System, Blind.

1 Introduction

Visually impaired people face a wide amount of challenges when navigating outdoors without the assistance of a sighted person. Current standards suggest to walk only through predefined and previously known routes, while using a white cane for short range obstacle avoidance. Although guide dogs are a popular alternative, their availability is limited, and their costs very high. Recently, the widespread use of mobile phones with GPS has been a revolution in the field, allowing blind people to reach new places and thus providing an increased feeling of freedom. But the white cane is still necessary, as there are some problems that GPS-based systems cannot solve such as detection of obstacles in real time, finding crosswalks, etc.

Several systems have attempted to replace or enhance the white cane (*e.g.* [1, 2, 3, 4]). However the perception challenges of those systems have overshadowed the task of conveying real time obstacle information to the visually impaired users. Most GPS systems use speech to convey directions to the user, but this approach is not valid for real-time tasks, thus more fundamental audio and haptic interfaces are required.

K. Miesenberger et al. (Eds.): ICCHP 2014, Part II, LNCS 8548, pp. 128–135, 2014.

In this work, we have performed an in-depth analysis for the task of conveying short range navigation information to the blind user. In particular, we compared haptic against audio interfaces on a similar navigation scenario.
Performing a fair comparison between haptic and audio modalities is complex due to the large variety of possible interfaces. In our lab we have developed several interfaces for a wide variety of tasks, so we chose our *state-of-the-art* audio and haptic interfaces as representatives of their respective modalities.
Our audio based system used open headphones to pulse 20ms beeps at 800Hz. While the haptic system used a versatile bluetooth module to drive two linear vibration motors in 25ms pulses at 190Hz.

In our preliminary tests, we found that two of the most common objective metrics used to evaluate the performance of user interfaces (speed and success rate) were of little use for this task. Particularly, on object finding tasks, users spent more time on a task when they enjoyed the interface, therefore a quick success does not necessarily imply a better interface. Success rate was also not relevant, as if the users are focused enough, they were able to achieve their goal using almost any kind of feedback. Therefore we based our evaluation on the well known NASA-TLX protocol that rates the perceived workload of each modality.
The NASA-TLX (Task Load indeX) protocol is a subjective test developed by the Human Performance Group at NASA. It measures the perceived workload of a task over six categories: Mental Demands, Physical Demands, Temporal Demands, Own Performance, Effort and Frustration, and also weights the relevance of each category.

Our results suggest that blind participants strongly favor haptics over audio. White cane users were accustomed to perceive short range navigation information from the haptic channel, and therefore found the system intuitive to use. On the other hand, they use the auditory channel for other tasks (i.e. orientation, communication, alerts), and its use for navigation was linked to an increase in stress.

Blindfolded people however, reacted differently. People used to navigate with their eyes slightly favored the audio interface and found the haptic interface confusing.
These results are important as, in studies researching interfaces for blind persons, blindfolded people are usually used as proxies for visually impaired people in order to have a significant amount of participants. Our results stresses the importance of having visually impaired users in the loop while researching user interfaces for the blind, instead of relying only on blindfolded people.

Furthermore, we suggest that cognitive evaluation of navigation systems can reveal important cues that are not evident under objective measures such as speed or success rate.

2 Related Work

Short range navigation for the visually impaired has received a lot of attention both in indoor and outdoor scenarios [1, 2, 3, 4, 5, 6, 7, 8].

Fig. 1. 20m x 5m obstacle course used in our experiments. Eight chairs were used as obstacles. Each chair was labeled with an orange paper, as we simulated the obstacle detection part of the experiment using a wearable, camera based, color recognition system. Three obstacle configurations were used: one for the preliminary exploration, one for the audio round, and one for the haptic round.

The problem is divided into two major components: perceiving the spatial information and conveying directions to the user. The perception problem was traditionally approached using ultrasonic distance sensors [1], [3], [4], however several computer vision systems are being currently researched [2], [5], [7], as they have the potential of providing better guidance from a richer representation of the environment.

Conversely, a wide variety of methodologies are used to convey directions to the user. Sonification systems are common in spatial localization tasks (*e.g.* [9]) and have been used for short range navigation [3].
Haptic actuators are very popular, however ultracane [1] places them on the handle of their smart cane while Cardin et al. [4] place them on their vest. Belts, gloves and bracelets are other common placement options, but there is no clear winner.

Some user interfaces have been designed specifically for navigation tasks: GuideCane [3] pulls your hand towards the right direction while the tactile map presented by Velazquez et Al. [2] conveys directions using a 8x8 binary dot matrix.

3 Experimental Setup

3.1 Test Methodology

The evaluation was performed outdoors albeit on a quiet neighborhood. We set up an obstacle course of 20 meters length and 5 meters width. The obstacles were represented by eight chairs and labeled in orange. Fig. 1.

The test started with a briefing where users were allowed to familiarize themselves with the maze and the test (blind users used their white cane to explore the maze).

Then the audio system was introduced, the obstacles were rearranged, and the users traveled several times through the maze until they were familiarized with the system. At that point, the experience was evaluated using the NASA-TLX protocol, and their opinions were also registered. The haptic test followed similarly.

One hour was required per person, in order to allow enough time to familiarize with the interfaces and adjust them perfectly to their needs. None of the users had previously evaluated any of our systems.

3.2 Object Detection System

To localize the obstacles, we labeled them using orange papers and detected them using our color recognition software from camera glasses.

This color recognition software is an evolved subset of our object localization system [9]. The original system beeped every time a frame was processed (*i.e.* between 1 and 10 times per second depending on the mode of operation). Users were satisfied with the system, but claimed that lag on the feedback made the usage of the system in dynamic tasks difficult.

We upgraded the system with a simpler and faster image processing algorithm. It allows 30Hz performance while achieving a very small delay between the video input and its derived audio output (between 5ms and 20ms). Increased speed introduced a small detriment of precision and a small increment of false detection ratio, but our users preferred the faster feedback.

However, during the test, there were a few occasions were the color recognition software could not be used, and a Wizard-of-Oz approach was used instead. In those cases the test operator manually signaled the obstacles using bluetooth from an Android device.

3.3 Audio Feedback System

Our audio feedback system was developed originally in 2011 together with our object localization software [9]. The original system beeped every time a frame was processed, mapping the horizontal coordinate to sound panorama (left-right) and the vertical coordinate to pitch.

The system was upgraded to reduce the lag between the capture of the image and the signal of the information. This fast feedback allowed us to drop the vertical axis mapping, as users found that performing a beam scan with the camera was faster than processing the frequency information. Unexpectedly, we found that most test users were able to identify up to four items when sonifying them all simultaneously if they were focused enough.

To further diminish the latency, we use a very lightweight interface based on OpenAL [12]. Each time a frame is processed, the information about the color blobs, their size, and a confidence value between 0 and 1 is mapped into

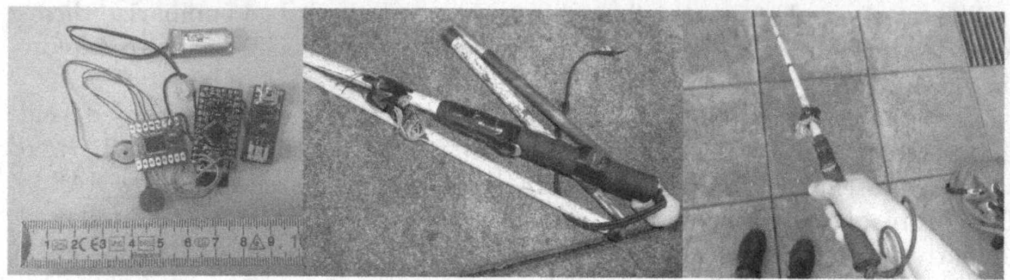

Fig. 2. Left: our haptic module with a battery, arduino processor, bluetooth communication, charger, motor driver, and two lentil linear vibration motors. Total weight: 16g. Center and right: haptic module installed on a white cane with the motors attached to the handle of the cane. The placement of the motors was customizable to each user.

audio. All detected blobs are sonified simultaneously. The frequency was fixed to 800Hz and the pulse duration to 20ms. The volume is mapped to the product of selection confidence and its area (bigger and clearer color areas are stronger). Although the camera has a field of view of approximately 60°, the output sound is mapped between -90°and 90°(*i.e.* the angle is 3x magnified).

The current evaluation achieved very positive results from our blind colleagues, who are accustomed to test our systems.

In the navigation scenario, most users found that the simultaneous sonification of multiple obstacles was confusing, therefore the camera was worn pointing to the ground, resulting in only one obstacle usually being inside the field of view.

3.4 Haptic Feedback System

To develop and evaluate haptic systems, we designed a tiny module capable of driving a wide array of different vibration motors (see Fig. 2).

Each module is managed by an arduino processor, includes a battery, a bluetooth communication module, and a motor driver capable of driving two motors. It weights 16g.

Bluetooth connectivity allows us to control the vibration modality either from a laptop or an android phone and interfaces easily with our computer vision systems. Each module can control up to two vibration motors independently, but there is no limit on the number of modules that can be controlled simultaneously.

We have been using this platform since 2012 to evaluate a variety of haptic configurations which involved placing the motors on gloves, belts and white cane handles. Although we tested several different vibration configurations, for this evaluation we fixed the frequency to 190Hz and the pulse duration to 25ms.

The placement configuration we evaluated in this paper was the most promising one: placing two motors on the handle of a white cane. We used linear haptic motors which provided finer tuning and faster response time than conventional eccentric-weight based motors. Vibration bursts were used to signal obstacles, with one motor signaling left, the second motor signaling right. Simultaneous vibration of both motors signaled front. Only one obstacle was signaled at a time.

The haptic system required more customization than the audio system. Some users were not able to distinguish between left and right, in those cases both motors were activated only when their path was blocked by an obstacle.

4 Evaluation

4.1 NASA Task Load indeX

The NASA TLX [10] protocol was developed in 1986 at the Human Performance Center at NASA to evaluate the sources of workload of a particular task. This protocol has become a widely accepted tool used to evaluate cognitive aspects in a multidimensional way.

The six dimensions measured are: Mental Demands, Physical Demands, Temporal Demands, Own Performance, Effort and Frustration. Three of them relate to the demands imposed on the subject (Mental, Physical and Temporal demands), while the other three evaluate the interaction of the subject with the task (Effort, Frustration and Performance).

The test is meant to be straightforward to apply. It consists of two steps. First, the 15 possible pairwise comparisons between the six dimensions are presented, and the subject selects the member of each pair that contributed more to the workload of that task. The number of times that a dimension has been selected establishes the relevance of each dimension (0-5). The second step is to obtain numerical ratings (between 0 and 100) for each dimension that reflect the magnitude of that factor in a given task. The final workload value for each category is the product between the rating and the dimension.

The maximum value for a single category is 500 (100 rating $*$ 5 relevance), but the maximum value for the overall workload is 1500, as the sum of all relevance values is 15. Therefore, by dividing the sum of all workload values by 15, we obtain the percentage of total workload.

In our case we administered the paper and pencil version [11].

4.2 Results

Due to the extensive test procedure, only six persons with different levels of visual impairment were evaluated. Half of them were white cane users while the other half took the test blindfolded.

Results on the blindfolded group showed an overall cognitive workload ratio of 32.6% for the audio system against a 56.6% ratio for the haptic system. However on the blind group, the cognitive workload of the audio was of 74.7% against a mere 3.3% of the haptic system. For the complete results see Fig. 3.

In general, the physical demand was the lightest of the six categories evaluated by the NASA-TLX test, followed closely by the performance category. This is because both systems were able to adequately guide the users through the obstacle course and were qualified as useful for the task.

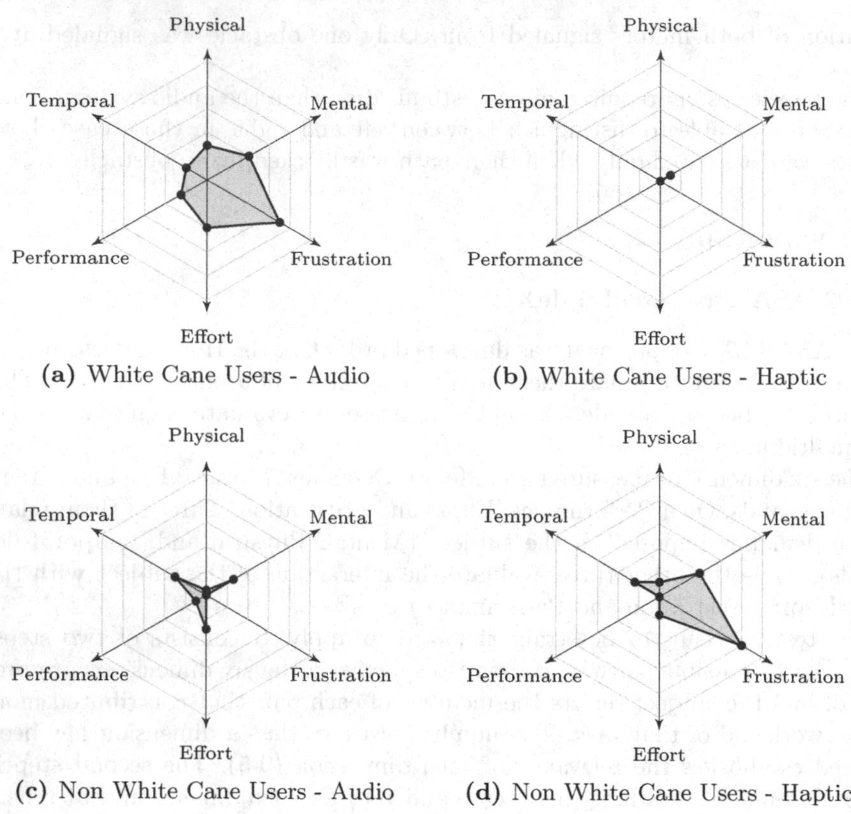

Fig. 3. NASA Task Load indeX: Sources of workload for our short range navigation experiment. The workload of the audio system was 74.7% on white cane users, 23.3% of which came from their own frustration while only 6.6% came from their performance. The workload of the haptic system was of 3.3%. On blindfolded users the results were inverted. The workload of the audio system was 32.6% with no frustration, while the workload of the haptic system was 56% of which 26% came from frustration.

In the open questionnaire that was taken after the test, blindfolded users reflected on how the haptic system felt more limited than the audio system, as it was more difficult to discern between left and right signals. On the other hand, white cane users were not comfortable using audio as a feedback, since the auditory channel usually needs to be used for safety purposes (such as detecting cars, other people, and generally making sense of the environment).

5 Conclusions

We have evaluated two *state-of-the-art* interfaces for blind users for the task of obstacle avoidance in short range navigation systems, one based on audio and the other on haptic feedback. Although both systems were qualified as satisfactory by the users, the cognitive load of the audio system was rated by the blind users more than 22 times higher than the load of the haptic based system. This is because haptics are very intuitive for white cane users while the auditory channel is being used much more for other important tasks. This bias was not present when both systems were evaluated by blindfolded users. Those results suggest that the common practice of using blindfolded test users to evaluate user interfaces for the blind should be avoided in short range navigation tasks.

Acknowledgements. This research has been partially funded by Google through a Google Faculty Research Award.

References

1. http://www.ultracane.com/
2. Velazquez, et al.: Coding the environment in tactile maps for real-time Guidance of the Visually Impaired In: MHS 2006 (2006)
3. Shoval, S., et al.: Navbelt and the guide-cane[obstacle avoidance systems for the blind and visually impaired] In: RAM 2003 (2003)
4. Cardin, S., et al.: Wearable obstacle detection system for visually impaired people In: VRHTPDO 2005 (2005)
5. Koester, D., et al.: Accessible Section Detection for Visual Guidance In: MAP4VIP 2013 (2013)
6. Chen, D., et al.: An infrastructure-free indoor navigation system for blind people In: IRA 2012 (2012)
7. Le, M.C., et al.: Pedestrian lane detection for the visually impaired In: DICTA 2012 (2012)
8. Martinez, J.M.S., et al.: Stereo-based aerial obstacle detection for the visually impaired In: WVAVI 2008 (2008)
9. Schauerte, B., Martinez, M., Constantinescu, A., Stiefelhagen, R.: An assistive vision system for the blind that helps find lost things. In: Miesenberger, K., Karshmer, A., Penaz, P., Zagler, W. (eds.) ICCHP 2012, Part II. LNCS, vol. 7383, pp. 566–572. Springer, Heidelberg (2012)
10. Hart, et al.: Development of NASA-TLX: Results of empirical and theoretical research In: HMW 1988 (1988)
11. http://humansystems.arc.nasa.gov/groups/TLX/downloads/TLXScale.pdf
12. http://kcat.strangesoft.net/openal.html

Unlocking Physical World Accessibility through ICT: A SWOT Analysis

Christophe Ponsard[1] and Vincent Snoeck[2]

[1] CETIC Research Center, Charleroi, Belgium
cp@cetic.be

[2] GAMAH Association for Better Accessibility, Namur, Belgium
vincent.snoeck@gamah.be

Abstract. Despite progress in awareness and increasing electronic availability of accessibility information, getting a clear picture of physical accessibility of an infrastructure or journey remains an uncertain task. Over the past few years, a number of emerging technologies have gained maturity and adoption. Some examples are smartphones, open data, social networks, and routing engines. They are also triggering societal shifts about the way people interact together through technology. The purpose of this paper is to analyse how these technologies can positively or negatively impact the evolution of physical accessibility by using a SWOT (Strengths-Weaknesses-Opportunities-Threats) approach.

1 Introduction

Accessibility of physical infrastructures or while travelling is a concern for an estimated 30 percent of the population and potentially for anyone at some point of life, especially when aging. While new buildings, roads, vehicles have to comply with stronger accessibility requirements, perfect accessibility cannot realistically be reached. Hence, the accessibility characteristics of many places will still require to be assessed, documented and published. Information and Communication Technologies (ICT) are already supporting all those processes by easing the data collection (e.g. using tablets), their processing according to specific criteria (now standardised under ISO21542 [12]) and their publication typically through online searchable databases.

However the ICT domain is evolving at a fast pace and a number of maturing technologies can help in bringing dramatic enhancements to the way accessibility information is produced and made available, in terms of quantity, quality, rate, etc. As illustrative scenario, we can think about a person in wheelchair who wants to attend a live concert. The event accessibility can be checked against agreed requirements and confirmed online in a matter of hours. People can then be guaranteed of a good experience and start planning their trip through public transportation, possibly requesting assistance (e.g. for getting on/off a train). When travelling using his smartphone, a person can be warned of possible delays in order to anticipate changes. To reach the event site from the train station,

K. Miesenberger et al. (Eds.): ICCHP 2014, Part II, LNCS 8548, pp. 136–143, 2014.

he/she can use his/her smartphone GPS to follow an accessible route specifically computed for a wheelchair profile.

A good starting point to identify new enabling technologies is the Gartner Hype Cycle for Emerging Technologies [6]. This report is updated yearly and the 2013 hype cycle is depicted in figure 1. A key characteristic is the evolving relationship between human and machines especially from an accessibility point of view: machines better at understanding humans in their environment (location intelligence), smarter machines (big data, analytics), machines augmenting human capabilities (wearable interfaces, augmented reality).

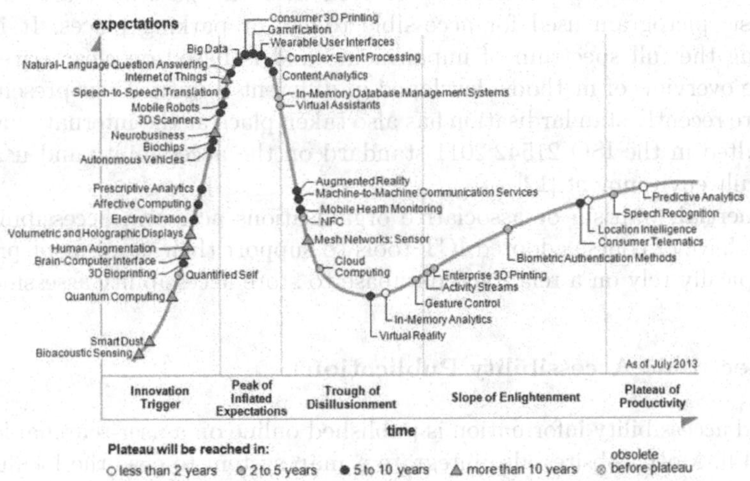

Fig. 1. Gartner Hype Cycle 2013

As the impact can be both positive and negative, this paper presents an objective methodology based on a SWOT (Strengths-Weaknesses-Opportunities-Threats) approach. In our specific case, strengths and weaknesses (internal factors) will relate to the current ICT capabilities while opportunities and threats (external factors) will be referring to technologies in adoption phase among those presented in figure 1. Those aspects will be developed in section 2, 3, 4, and 5 respectively.

- **Strengths**. Achievements/capabilities of current ICT in supporting physical accessibility.
- **Weaknesses**. Challenges of current ICT in supporting accessibility.
- **Opportunities**. New possibilities enabled by maturing technologies, illustrated by some early adopters.
- **Threats**. New barriers possibly raised by those new technologies with a discussion on how to address them.

The purpose of a SWOT is to guide a strategic decision process. In our context, we believe it is important to share our analysis so that other can take informed decision in their own adoption process of some of the mentioned technologies. In the final section, we also recapitulate our vision about accessibility.

2 Strengths - ICT Achievements w.r.t. Accessibility

2.1 ICT Supported Assessment Methods

Accessibility methods have strongly evolved over the past 20 years, starting from basic pictogram used for accessible toilets or parking places. It is now embracing the full spectrum of impairments and is based on clear criteria. A complete overview of methods developed in different countries was presented in [19]. More recently standardisation has also taken place at the international level and resulted in the ISO 21542:2011 standard on the accessibility and usability of the built environment [12].

Commercial, tourism or associative organisations active in accessibility assessment have of course adopted ICT tools to support their assessment process. They typically rely on a relational database to store accessibility assessment.

2.2 Electronic Accessibility Publication

Validated accessibility information is published online on a user-searchable website [1],[14]. Most websites also integrate a map system to ease the localisation and travel planning [5],[8],[22]. The following figure illustrates a typical map integration.

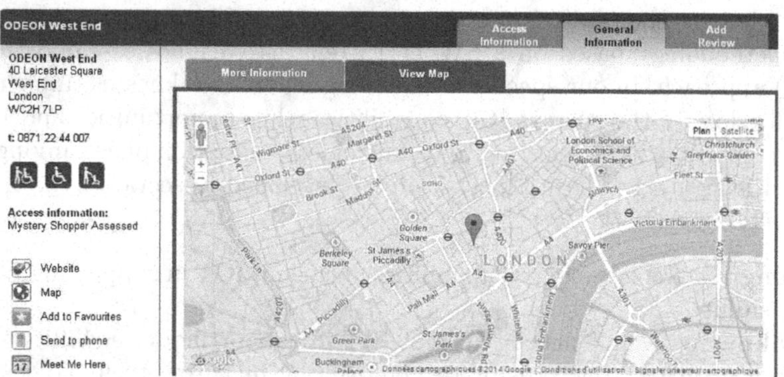

Fig. 2. Inclusive London Website

2.3 Mobile Devices

Mobile devices are largely adopted by mobility impaired people as they enable specific assistance for example location-based navigation, identification of nearby services and money recognition for blind users [2]. Accessibility assessors can also benefits of tablets to conduct electronic survey which can directly feed an accessibility database.

3 Weaknesses - Current ICT Limitations

3.1 Close Databases and Lack of Interoperability

Most accessibility databases are managed under closed form. They do not provide any possibility to be queried by other applications (except through web-scraping) which could enlarge the diffusion scope and enable other usage of the information. Some organisations may be afraid of losing the control over their data while for others technical expertise or the infrastructure might be the blocking factor.

Note that in the scenario of open databases, there is also a need to combine data from different sources. Those sources are also likely to originate from different methods because the alignment on common standard is not yet a reality and will probably never be fully achieved.

3.2 Routing Limitations

Current routing engines are only starting to provide a good support for computing accurate pedestrian route but still lack support for specific impairments like wheelchairs. The main reason is the lack of availability of impairment related geographic information such as slopes (requiring elevation information) or specific signaling equipment (e.g. for blind people).

4 Opportunities - New ICT-related Enablers

4.1 Social Networks

Social networks are now largely adopted and have enabled new forms of collaboration, also in the area of accessibility information gathering.

This can take different forms. Basic collaboration can be achieved by keeping a controlled website and just gathering feedback through a review feature (e.g. Inclusive London [5]). On the other extreme, Wheelmap is a pure collaborative project based on the combined input of the community members [22]. Another approach is to try to combine inputs from different information owners like the French jaccede.com [13] (see figure 3). Each alternatives has different specific threats related to community adoption, data quantity and data quality as discussed in the dedicated section.

Fig. 3. Jaccede.com

A specific instrument that can be associated with social networks is the *Hackaton*. The purpose of such an event is to put together community members having programming skills to trigger a new development during a short-time and intensive effort. In addition to producing prototypes that can later evolve and be adopted (or not), it also enables community members to get closer to each other. An example of this is the French #Hackcess [21] targeting the accessibility of train stations. In preparation to this effort, contributors from OpenStreetMap were asked to enrich accessibility information related in and around train stations. Based on the gathered information, a specific routing engine called NO WAY was prototyped to take into account a wheelchair type of profile, as show in figure 4.

Fig. 4. Pedestrian vs wheelchair itinerary near a railway station

4.2 Open (Linked) Data

Open Data is a recent trend based on the natural idea that public information should be free to use, reuse and redistribute [16]. Some example of such information are public sector data from government (e.g. statistics about population, mobility, energy, etc.). Data can also originate from a collective effort (e.g. OpenStreetMap [17]).

Accessibility information should of course be open data and nowadays different cities are releasing such data. Having a larger diffusion will not only help more people and in a better way but will also put more pressure for improvement. Several cities (like Brussels and Vancouver) have started to publish localisation information of disability parking. The city of London has produced a linked-data driven mobile web application providing dynamic searches for accessible underground stations. The relevant data is collected from different data sets that are mashed-up within a user-friendly mobile web interface [15].

4.3 Ontologies and Semantic Techniques

In tight relation with Open Data, ontologies and semantic techniques are enablers for easing the open exchange of information. Ontologies provide the way to capture the meaning of data over a given domain based on specific standards (like OWL and RDF). Semantic web techniques can then process and reason on those data and event put them in relation across different domains.

Related to disability, there are a few ontologies available such as for the International Classification of Functioning, Disability and Health [23], published by the BioPortal [3]. Regarding physical accessibility, only a preliminary ontology was proposed by [9]. The followed approach refines qualitative accessibility objectives into quantitative metrics. It is quite similar to our previous work [19], although it is based on semantic web technologies rather than goal-oriented techniques.

4.4 Smart Routing Engines

Efficient Open Source routing engines coupled with open data have been developed over the past few years [7][18]. They have enabled experiments with other transportation modalities. There are a few on-going initiatives building on top of those tools such as the already mentioned NO WAY proof-of-concept (targeting railways stations) and a wheelchairs specific portal specific for Germany [20].

5 Threats - New ICT-Related Barriers

5.1 Mobile Devices eAccessibility

The use of smartphones among impaired people requires specific adaptations to be available on those devices (like screen readers, and button-based interface rather than tactile for blind people). Recent version of smartphone operating systems provide the same level of accessibility option as computers (control over font size, contrast, availability of text-to-speech, etc.). In addition, specific apps are also available to further enhance the experience and the power of device processing is also not a bottleneck.

5.2 Quality of Community Gathered Data

Relying on a community to gather data raises the issue of data quality. Possible issues are subjective or partial data (e.g. a wheelchair user will probably not report possible issues affecting a blind user). However even such data remains useful as the confidence will increase with the number of contributors for a specific infrastructure. To cope with this, confidence information can be made visible (number of contributors, experience of contributor, voting system). Some form of complementary assessment and review by experts can also be used.

Another point is that the accessibility will evolve over time. It is rather a long term process, however it is useful to capture some temporal information so it is possible to have an idea of the freshness of a contribution. In addition, some feedback may also identify and manage temporary accessibility problem.

5.3 Managing the Community and the Contributors

Data will only be collected if the people believe in the system and are encouraged to contribute. This starts with basic things such as providing a good usability of the website, giving feedback about the contribution, stating the objectives and reporting about global progress. With this respect, social science come into play and beyond the pure aspect of securing enough resources to collect enough data, the project is also a mean to raise social awareness about accessibility [11].

In addition to this, contributors should also not feel that their privacy is exposed. The case of accessibility is sensible because people have often a specific profile which can reveal information about themselves. A social study showed that such issues are managed through some form of negotiation taking place within the system but also through external channels, and that the system must be open to the result of this negotiation [10].

6 Conclusion and Perspectives

In this paper, we have proposed a SWOT analysis of physical accessibility based on maturing technologies identified from the Gartner Hype Cycle. In our evaluation process, we discovered that those technologies could be adopted either in a rather conservative way (i.e. keeping the information under strict control) or in a totally open and innovative way (i.e. gathering data through multiple sources and relying on a community to make them open and available to all kinds of usage). The latter approach is more promising but also yields the danger of lack of information quality and trustability. Successful approaches will probably adopt some intermediary path. Nevertheless, a driving keyword should be the openness of the data, formats, code and more generally the mind of the involved people.

We have performed this analysis in the context of our regional accessibility roadmap and we are in the process of implementing it within the access-i initiative [4]. We also believe that this work can help other organisations or communities in their own decision process related to the adoption of emerging ICT technologies for enhancing physical accessibility.

Acknowledgements. This work was financially supported by the Walloon Region through the QualIHM project (convention nr 1217570).

References

1. Acces City: Website, `http://www.anlh.be/accescity`
2. AppsGoneFree: Apps For Blind And Visually Impaired, `http://appadvice.com/applists/show/apps-for-the-visually-impaired`
3. BioPortal: ICF Ontology, `http://bioportal.bioontology.org/ontologies/1411`
4. CAWAB: Website, `http://www.access-i.be`
5. Direct Enquiries: Inclusive London, `http://inclusivelondon.com`
6. Gartner: Gartner's 2013 hype cycle for emerging technologies (July 2013), `http://www.gartner.com/newsroom/id/2575515`
7. GraphHopper: Road Routing in Java with OpenStreetMaps, `http://graphhopper.org`
8. HandiStrict: Accessibility for all, everywhere, in one clic, `http://handistrict.com` (in french)
9. Hjelseth, E.: Experiences on converting interpretative regulations into computable rules. In: CIB W078 Conference (October 2012)
10. Holone, H., Herstad, J.: Negotiating privacy boundaries in social applications for accessibility mapping. In: Proc. of the 6th Nordic Conference on Human-Computer Interaction: Extending Boundaries. ACM, New York (2010)
11. Holone, H., Herstad, J.: Social software for accessibility mapping: challenges and opportunities. In: The International Conference on Universal Technologies, Unitech 2010 (May 2010)
12. ISO: ISO21542:2011 - Building construction Accessibility and usability of the built environment (2011)
13. Jaccede.com: Pour une cité accessible, `http://www.jaccede.com`
14. Kéroul: Website, `http://www.keroul.qc.ca`
15. Li, Y., Draffan, E., Glaser, H., Millard, I., Newman, R., Wald, M., Wills, G., White, M.: Railgb: using open accessibility data to help people with disabilities. In: International Semantic Web Conference 2012 (November 2012)
16. Open Knowledge Foundation: Open Definition, `http://opendefinition.org`
17. OpenStreeMap: Collaborative mapping project, `http://www.openstreetmap.org`
18. OSRM Community: Open Source Routing Machine, `http://project-osrm.org`
19. Ponsard, C., Snoeck, V.: Objective Accessibility Assessment of Public Infrastructures. In: Miesenberger, K., Klaus, J., Zagler, W.L., Karshmer, A.I. (eds.) ICCHP 2006. LNCS, vol. 4061, pp. 314–321. Springer, Heidelberg (2006)
20. Rollstuhlrouting: Route Planning without Barriers - Germany-wide, `http://www.rollstuhlrouting.de` (in German)
21. SNCF (French Railways): #Hackcess Accessibility Hackaton (November 2013), `http://data.sncf.com/news/laureats-hackathon-hackcess`
22. Wheelmap Community: Collaborative website about wheelchair accessibility, `http://wheelmap.org/en`
23. World Health Organisation: International Classification of Functioning, Disability and Health, `www.who.int/icidh`

Personalized Smart Environments to Increase Inclusion of People with Down's Syndrome

Results of the Requirement Analysis

Eva Schulze and Anna Zirk

Berlin Institute for Social Research, Berlin, Germany
{e.schulze,a.zirk}@bis-berlin.de

Abstract. POSEIDON aims at developing a tablet app for people with Down's Syndrome (DS) to become more independent and integrated. It follows an user-centered approach by involving primary (people with DS) and secondary users (parents, carers etc.). In order to assess the needs and requirements as well as the usage of technology of people with DS an online survey was conducted. Results indicate that a majority of them use tablets in their daily life. Most of the carers agree that technical assistants can help to overcome daily challenges and that there is a need for support in the fields of communication, socializing and school/work/learning. Important features and design aspects were mentioned.

Keywords: Down's Syndrome, Smart environment, Inclusion, Requirements.

1 Introduction

DS affects a substantial number of European citizens: one of 700-800 newborns having this condition [1]. Most of the people with DS experience low integration within society. But new opportunities for their integration in mainstream education and work provided numerous cases where levels of achievement exceeded the (limiting) expectations e.g. [2]. Contrary to common belief, there is considerable variety between individuals with DS (e.g. [3]). POSEIDON (PersOnalized Smart Environments to Increase Inclusion of people with DOwn's syNdrome) aims to develop a technological infrastructure which can foster a growing number of services to help people with DS.

2 State of the Art

Many research approaches address the aim to support people with cognitive disabilities to overcome challenges in specific areas (e.g. [4]). Just a few of them are directly addressing the needs of people with DS [5]). Most of them concentrate on using computers [6] or e-learning tools [7]. Computer devices are of great importance for people with DS as 80 % of them already start using computers by the age of six years [6]. People with DS mainly use computers for learning activities or for entertainment [6]. It can be taken for granted, that despite cognitive disabilities, people with DS have

K. Miesenberger et al. (Eds.): ICCHP 2014, Part II, LNCS 8548, pp. 144–147, 2014.

great affinity for technology. For that reason, technology should not exclusively be seen as a learning aid or for entertainment but as a possibility to enhance the independence, safety and mobility of people with DS. So the main aim of POSEIDON is to develop a useable tablet app to empower people with DS to manage everyday day life challenges more easy and to become a vital part of society.

Right from the beginning of the project it was specified which features and functions in general should be provided by POSEIDON. Nevertheless it was necessary to find out to what extend people with DS are used to technology, in which areas they need support and which features and design aspects are important.

3 Methods

The questionnaire on the requirements of people with DS is addressed to people who take care of them. It includes 174 items organized in about 35 questions (only the main results will be presented). The questionnaire focuses on topics like the usage of technology, help needed in using technology, integration of people with DS, helpfulness of assistive technologies and important features and design aspects an assistive technology should provide. Anonymity according scientific standards was guaranteed. Answering the questionnaire took about half an hour. Overall, a total of 397 carers from the three participating countries (Germany, United Kingdom and Norway) took part in this survey in order to provide information about the person they take care of. From this follows that 397 people with DS (57.5% female; 42.5% male) were described within this survey. 65.2 % of them are 18 years and younger. About 85 % are living with their parents.

4 Results

Results indicate that a majority of people with DS uses modern information technologies: tablet 71.2 %; Smartphone 60.8 %. Most easy seem to be the use of tablets (only 42.6 % need help using them) while 65.6 % of people with DS need to be assisted when using a Smartphone. Modern assistive technology is regarded as helpful by their carers to overcome challenges in daily life (57.7%). Social integration varies highly between work/school and leisure time. 44.8 % are described as well integrated at school or work but only 23.3 % seem to be well integrated in leisure time. Most important seems to be support in the fields of communicating, socializing and school/work/learning. More than 50% of participants consider these aspects as very important. 75% of the carers indicate that checking that the person they care for has reached a destination as well as locating the person would be very helpful features for them.

Concerning the usability and design especially the motivating and fun aspects are stressed (67.1% and 61.7% considered them as very important).Very important are also an adaptability to individual needs (62.5%), the avoidance of a need for fast reactions (58.1%), and the aspect that the device should be robust (57.8%).

5 Discussion

Results indicate that information technologies are of great importance for people with DS as more than 70 % of them use tablets. This seems to be an important prerequisite since POSEIDON will be offered as a tablet app. Furthermore results show that more than 40 % need help using apps on tablets which indicates that there seems to be a need for an easy to use software for people with DS. Most of the carers of people with DS share the opinion that assistive technologies can help to overcome daily challenges which might result in an increase of integration. Especially in three areas there seems to be a need for support: communicating, socializing and school/work/learning. POSEIDON tries to address the area of communication by providing easy to use communicating channels, features like multimodal input and output, speech recording and auto complete suggestions. These features hopefully enhance communication activities not only between people with DS and their carers but also with friends, peer group members etc. Socializing will be supported by making travelling more easy and safer by providing easy understandable maps, a help button in case someone gets lost, the opportunity to locate the person with DS and a message function for carers when the respective person has reached his or her destination. These functions should enable people with DS to travel more independently and by that help to establish and maintain friendships more easily. School/work/learning will be supported by calendar and reminder functions. People with DS should be enabled to manage their daily activities alone by reminding them of which day is, what their appointments are, what duties they have (school/work) and therefore what clothes they have to wear (e.g. working clothes) and what equipment they need. To meet these requirements it is also necessary to consider usability and design aspects rated as important by the carers. Therefore POSEIDON tries to address fun and motivating aspects by implementing e.g. entertainment functions like a music player. Furthermore POSEIDON will be adaptable to individual needs and avoid need for fast reactions.

6 Impact

Including persons with DS in the information society improves their independence and abilities for education and work. This represents a significant economic and social benefit to the community. POSEIDON will not only improve quality of life for people with DS but also create new business opportunities, include more members of society in ICT and contribute to the creation of standards which can help to promote inclusion.

7 Conclusions and Planned Activities

The analysis of the requirements of people with DS emphasizes the need for support in communicating, socializing and school/work/learning. Since a majority of people with DS seems to have a high affinity for technology, it can be assumed that a tech-nical assistant customized to meet the respective requirements can help to overcome daily challenges. To make help needed less necessary, especially while using tablets, POSEIDON should provide an easy to use interface and consider the mentioned as-pects

The described requirement analysis serves as the basis for the development of a first prototype. In all participating countries field usability tests and user focused workshops will be conducted. The results will shape the development of this prototype which finally should be launched to the market.

Acknowledgements. Project Partners: Karde AS (N), Tellu AS (N), Norsk Netverk for Down Syndrom (N), Middlesex University (GB), Down's Syndrome Association (GB), Fraunhofer Institut für Graphische Datenverarbeitung (D), Berliner Institut für Sozialforschung GmbH (D), Arbeitskreis Down-Syndrom e.V. (D), Funka Nu AB (S).

Funded by the European Union.

References

1. Schaner-Wolles, C.: Sprachentwicklung bei geistiger Retardierung: Williams-Beuren-Syndrom und Down-Syndrom. In: Grimm, H. (ed.) Sprachentwicklung. Enzyklopädie der Psychologie, Goettingen, Hogrefe, vol. C III 3, pp. 663–685 (2000)
2. Pablo Pineda: http://en.wikipedia.org/wiki/Pablo_Pineda
3. Lazar, J., Kumin, L., Feng, J.H.: Understanding the Computer Skills of Adult Expert Users with Down Syndrome: An Exploratory Study. In: The Proceedings of the 13th International ACM SIGACCESS Conference on Computers and Accessibility, New York, pp. 51–58 (2011)
4. Dawe, M.: Understanding Mobile Phone Requirements for Young Adults with Cognitive Disabilities. In: Proceedings of the 9th International ACM SIGACCESS Conference on Computers and Accessibility, New York, pp. 179–186 (2007)
5. Seale, J.K., Pockney, R.: The use of the Personal Home Page by adults with Down's syndrome as a tool for managing identity and friendship. British Journal of Learning Disabilities 30(4), 142–148 (2002)
6. Feng, J., Lazar, J., Kumin, L., Ozok, A.: Computer Usage by Young Individuals with Down Syndrome: An Exploratory Study. In: Proceedings of the 10th International ACM SIGACCESS Conference on Computers and Accessibility, New York, pp. 35–42 (2008)
7. Kirijian, A., Myers, M., Charland, S.: Web fun central: online learning tools for individuals with Down syndrome. In: Lazar, J. (ed.) Universal Usability: Designing Information Systems for Diverse User Population, pp. 195–230. John Wiley & Sons, Chichester (2007)

ELDERS-UP!
Adaptive System for Enabling the Elderly Collaborative Knowledge Transference to Small Companies

Salvador Rivas Gil and Víctor Sánchez Martín

Ingeniería y Soluciones Informáticas del Sur, SL (ISOIN), Seville, Spain
{salvador.rivas,vsanchez}@isoin.es

Abstract. Elderly are sometimes set apart in some situations due to the fact that they are considered less efficient and productive, for example, in the work environment. For many elderly, their jobs represent the way of feeling useful for themselves and the society and also for having goals which keeps them motivated. Although our current society is led by productivity and efficiency both in professional and personal scenarios, today, information is the key for efficiency; those who are able to manage the information are the ones that survive the daily rush without sinking in it.

Keywords: Elders, Adaptive User Interface, Engagement, Motivation, Cognitive Conditions.

1 Introduction

The main idea behind Elders-Up! project is to bring the valuable experience of elderly to start-ups and small companies, addressing intergenerational knowledge transfer to use skills and competencies based on experience.

The special Eurobarometer on Active Ageing showed that the 41% of people aged 55 and over tend to be keener on working beyond the age at which they are entitled to a pension, in contrast to younger respondents (ranging from 30% to 33%) [1]

The Elders-Up! project will build an ICT-based ecosystem for collaboration on which these two groups are the main actors, thus strengthening the European experts workforce and maintaining their productivity and usefulness to the society.

2 Elders Up! System

The heart of Elders-Up! system will be its end user interface. This interface and a set of sensors (e.g. touchscreen, webcam, microphone and others) will serve to gather information about the way the end users interact with the system. One of the biggest innovations of Elders-Up! project will be the possibility to extract data from these common sensors which are currently available in many devices, i.e. tablets or SmartTVs, and to get useful information about the cognitive abilities and engagement

K. Miesenberger et al. (Eds.): ICCHP 2014, Part II, LNCS 8548, pp. 148–151, 2014.

level of the end user. These parameters and many other (e.g. self-reports) will be the inputs for the user state analysis which will decide the best configuration of the Elders-Up! interface for adapting to the end user cognitive abilities and to motivate the user in collaboration.

The main innovation of the Elders-Up! system is that will monitor the end user state through its interaction with the collaborative Elders-Up! workspace in order to:

- Adapt the interface and content of the workspace to the cognitive conditions of the user applying the necessary changes to provide them an easy interaction and usage.
- Engage and motivate the elderly in optimal collaboration in the work team for a prolonged period of time.
- Protect the elderly from fail into apathy and frailty after their retirement by providing them means to keep their minds active and to transfer their valuable knowledge.

2.1 Technology Methodology

Skills Matching Service. A prerequisite for the development of techniques to match the skills required by the small companies with the skills reported by the elderly end-users is the development of an ontology for semantically describing the elderly end-users skills. The concepts from this ontology will be used to semantically annotate the end-user skills stored in the Users Skills Knowledge base and will drive/guide the construction of the semantic requests for skills of the small companies through the Semantic Request for Skills Construction Interface.

The Elders-Up! Skills Matching Service will provide two main functionalities: (i) discovery of skills and (ii) the multidisciplinary elderly workforce construction. Discovery of skills functionality is achieved by searching the Users Skills Knowledge Base to identify elderly end-users that have registered skills that semantically match the ones required by the small companies. A multidisciplinary elderly workforce will be constructed when there are several skills required by a company for implementing a specific activity and during the discovery of skills phase more than one elderly end-user matching the required skills was selected.

Sensors and Self-report Data Gathering. The merely interaction of a user with a device as a tablet, a laptop or a SmartTV could provide valuable inputs for gathering information about him. Elders-Up! project will gather information about the end user cognitive limitations and the levels of motivation, through two main pillars: i) the sensors data collector (SDC), and ii) the subjective self-reporting collector (SRC).

The Sensor Data Collector (SDC) will act as the coordinating master of the sensors available in the devices. The sensing components considered in the SDC will be the touchscreen, the microphone (voice recognition) and any other available. The SDC architecture will specify a model-driven data acquisition, whereby multiple components involved in the process of capturing information collect and report their measurements. It will be considered the scalability of the architecture for including more sensors as the accelerometers of a tablet or a remote control (smartTV).

The self-report collector (SRC) will gather subjective information from the users when working with the Elders-Up! system. The advantages of self-report are that it gives the person's own perspective, and that there is no other way to access the person's own experience, so self-reporting methods will be a clear input of the end user levels of motivation and levels of engagement. Self-reports are considered complementary to the sensor-data, and together the two data sources form a more complete picture of the situation. The SRC includes mechanisms to assess changes in self-reported parameters in time, which in turn enables the adaptation decision-maker service to adapt the motivational mechanisms used for the individual user.

The Data Manager (DM) will be the upper layer module which will merge both kind of data and provide inputs for the Adaptation decision-maker.

Adaptation Decision-maker Service. The goal of this service is to automatically decide and select the best configuration for presenting the information to the elderly by using the Elders-Up! system. This service will take as input data regarding the interaction of the elderly end-users with the Elders-Up! system, and will optimize user engagement in time by rewarding the user for contributions and by inviting the user to continue using the system. This service is described on figure 1

The potential configurations of the Elders-Up! system on which the Adaptation Decision-maker Service may decide will be exposed as a set of atomic services part of the Elders-Up! Collaborative & Adaptive workspace. These services will provide functionalities of an automatic and adaptive change of screen feature (i.e. font size, style, items organisation on the screen, etc.) and also alternative controls (voice control). In this context, the main objective of the Adaptation Decision-maker Service is to seamless and automatic compose the atomic services provided by the Collaborative & Adaptive Workspace so that the visual elements of the Elders-Up! system are displayed according to the elder end-user cognitive capabilities and its level of engagement. The atomic services composition solution space will be modelled by means of Enhanced Planning Graph (EPG)[2].

Collaborative and Adaptive Workspace. The Elders-Up! Workspace will be an interface fully customizable either visually and with additional functionalities.

2.2 Impact on Quality of Life

About one third of retirees have difficulties adjusting to some aspects of retirement, social status loss; have a higher risk of isolation and depression. Engaging in productive activities is associated with favourable outcomes from health and well-being of older adults. The eco-system of collaborations between SMEs and seniors proposed by Elders-Up! will be highly valuable for elderly end users but also to broader society. Overall, Elders Up! system will contribute to maintain a professional status, improve social networks while enhancing competitiveness of business customers.

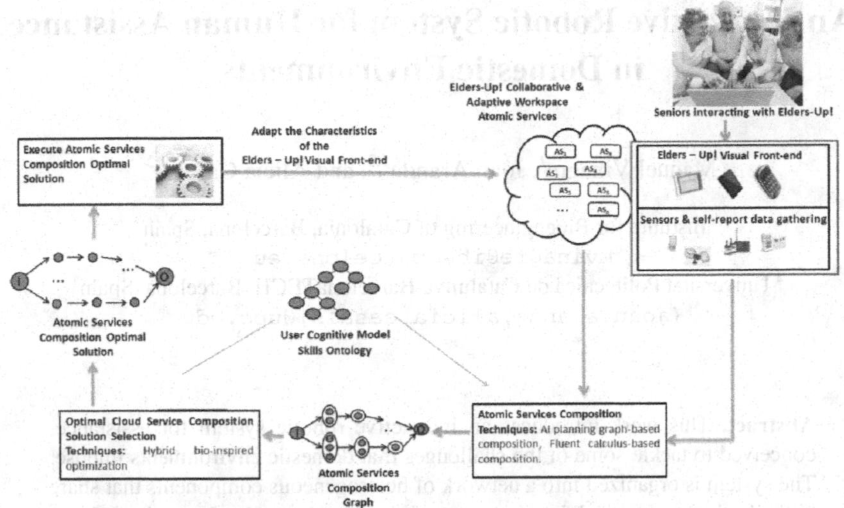

Fig. 1. The Elders-Up! Cognitive Adaptive Decision-maker Service

The elderly could be set apart in work situations due to the fact that they are considered less efficient and productive, and finally leading to a forced retirement even before the national retirement age. About one third of retirees have difficulties adjusting to some aspects of retirement. In fact, after retirement some older persons face social status loss; have a higher risk of isolation and depression. For many elderly, their jobs represent the way of feeling useful for themselves and the society. Furthermore, the fact of for having goals keeps them motivated and the social life that is related to the people that are work mates is beneficial.

Elders-Up! project aims to create impact on the elderly community and provide them with the means of being part again of a work team, having team mates and demonstrating their valuable experience to the society. The eco-system of collaborations between SMEs and seniors proposed by Elders-Up! will be highly valuable for elderly end users but also to broader society. Overall, Elders Up! system will contribute to maintain a professional status, improve social networks while enhancing competitiveness of business customers.

References

1. Active Ageing - Special Eurobarometer 378 / Wave EB76.2 – TNS opinion & social, `http://ec.europa.eu/public_opinion/archives/ebs/ebs_378_en.pdf`
2. Pop, C.B., Chifu, V.R., Salomie, I., Dinsoreanu, M.: Optimal Web Service Composition Method based on an Enhanced Planning Graph and Using an Immune-inspired Algorithm. In: Proceedings of the IEEE 5th International Conference on Intelligent Computer Communication and Processing (ICCP), pp. 291–298. IEEE (2009) ISBN: 978-1-4244-5007-7

An Interactive Robotic System for Human Assistance in Domestic Environments

Manuel Vinagre[1], Joan Aranda[1,2], and Alicia Casals[1,2]

[1] Institute for Bioengineering of Catalonia, Barcelona, Spain
mvinagre@ibecbarcelona.eu
[2] Universitat Politècnica de Catalunya-BarcelonaTECH, Barcelona, Spain
{joan.aranda,alicia.casals}@upc.edu

Abstract. This work introduces an interactive robotic system for assistance, conceived to tackle some of the challenges that domestic environments impose. The system is organized into a network of heterogeneous components that share both physical and logical functions to perform complex tasks. It consists of several robots for object manipulation, an advanced vision system that supplies in-formation about objects in the scene and human activity, and a spatial augmented reality interface that constitutes a comfortable means for interacting with the system. A first analysis based on users' experiences confirms the importance of having a friendly user interface. The inclusion of context awareness from visual perception enriches this interface allowing the robotic system to become a flexible and proactive assistant.

Keywords: Robot Assistance, Human-Robot Interaction, Accessibility, Ambient Intelligence, Activity Recognition.

1 Introduction

Robotic assistance in domestic environments imposes special requirements due to the need to adapt to a great diversity of users and to a wide variety of situations. In these environments, robots have to face many unexpected situations related to daily life activity, since humans do not follow standard labours or strict action rules. Thus, assumptions on human behaviour or sequence of activities cannot be easily specified, as it happens in industrial applications where its structured environment allows a previous planning and thus, predefined actions can be programmed.

This work presents an interactive robotic system for human assistance, conceived to tackle some of the challenges that appear in domestic environments. Its implementation is focused on the concept of system's functionality in a bottom-up design. Our robotic system is organized into a network of components that share physical and logical functions to perform complex tasks. Several robots (two arms Baxter, Cartesian robot and Mico arm) are used for manipulation, a vision system provides information about objects and user activity and an augmented reality interface facilitates a comfortable interaction with the system.

K. Miesenberger et al. (Eds.): ICCHP 2014, Part II, LNCS 8548, pp. 152–155, 2014.

2 State of Art

Current robotic technologies for assistance to elder and disabled, mostly rely on distributed networks of different agents (robots, environmental sensors, interfaces, etc.) which provide flexible and effective systems in real environments.

The PEIS project [2] combines the field of autonomous robots and ambient intelligence into a new concept of ecology of networked physically embedded intelligent systems. The RoboCare project [3] addresses the particular goal of creating a multi-agent system for the elderly in domestic environments.

Several advances in hardware and software middleware's have contributed to design and improve new distributed assistive systems. The recent Robot-Era project [4] aims to design, implement and validate a set of robotic services for elderly user-needs, facing new challenges on robotics, ambient intelligence and robot architectures.

Our interactive robotic system for human assistance presented in [1] has been improved by the integration of new features based on the ROS middleware and its associated packages. Specifically, the MoveIt package [5] facilitates the generation of an updated representation of the user's surroundings for collision avoidance. Additionally, RGB-D cameras allow us improving the perception and therefore the interaction of the system with people and the environment.

3 Methodology

To achieve a high level of functionality, the proposed system integrates three main modules: perception, reasoning and execution (Fig. 1). From them, our system can achieve context awareness, intelligent behaviour and natural interaction.

The perception module senses the user's environment. This module is composed of two types of components, depending on their sensing function: user's context components (as action recognition) and scenario's context components (as objects location and identification).

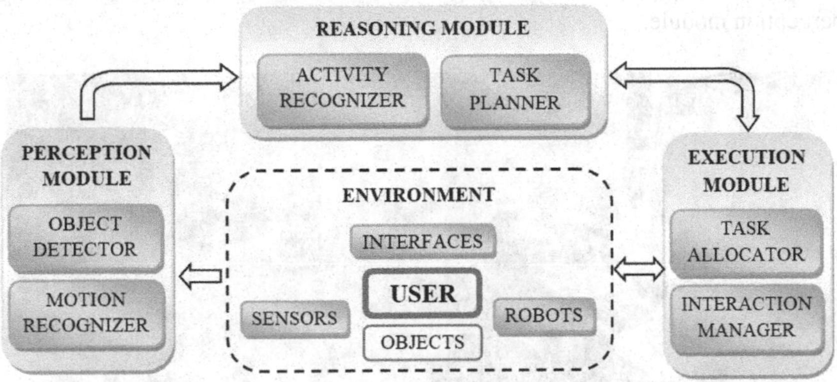

Fig. 1. Main modules of the robotic system

The performance of the perception module plays a major role in the overall success of the system. It aims to obtain reliable perception information, maintaining the coherence between the perceived objects and user, the robots in the scene and the modelled environment (Fig. 2).

The integration of novel RGB-D cameras allows us to guarantee safety, usability and interactivity of the whole system, achieving the following objectives:

- Detection of the presence of humans in the environment.
- Localization and tracking of objects among a known set of objects.
- Maintenance of the coherence between the real environment and its representation.
- Interpretation of human motion and intention, thus allowing users to interact with the system through gestures or just their natural activity.

The reasoning module assists the user by providing the system with intelligent behaviour, by means of two components which share information from the context and from prior knowledge. The first recognizes user's activity from a given set of possible activities and a sequence of observed actions [6]. The second plans a sequence of assistive actions for the given activity. The result of this planning process is fundamental to perform a proactive assistance, sharing the same user's goal or intention. In this way, the system can suggest coordinated or complementary actions to assist the user's activity.

Finally, the execution module generates assistance actions in a coordinated way. With this goal, the execution module takes into account the possible planning for assistance provided by the reasoning module and user's decisions. At the coordination stage, the robot proposes a way to carry out tasks, but should wait for its validation from the user. For a successful execution of human-robot shared activity, the two teammates must communicate each other their own intention in order to coordinate the actions addressed to execute the shared plan.

The allocation of system tasks is performed by selecting the most suitable robot (performance, location, safety…). The safety strategy relies in the MoveIt package [5]. Robots can generate and execute motion plans by accessing to a real-time 3D representation of the environment using data fused from the constant monitoring of the perception module.

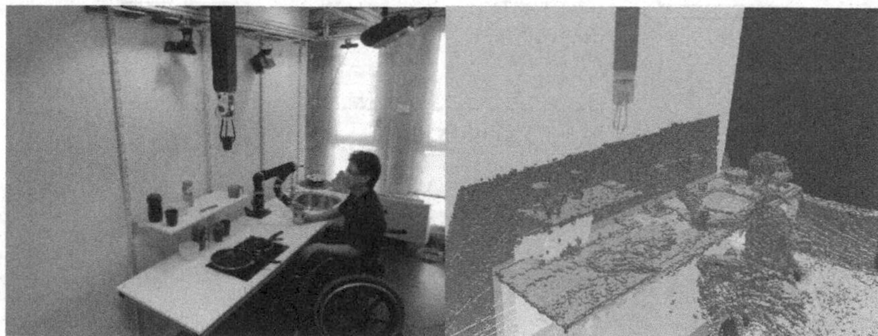

Fig. 2. (Left): Real scene. (Right): 3D representation and real-time vision data fusion.

4 Evaluation and Preliminary Results

An application framework has been developed in order to analyze the usability of the system. We have tested the performance of a simple kitchen activity consisting in preparing a cup of coffee with milk. This activity has been executed by different users and we have collected their opinion about the interaction experience through a questionnaire, estimating factors such as intuitiveness and satisfaction. Additional objective information has been collected online from the human-system interaction, such as users' responses when required for assistance from the system, and degree of agreement.

Preliminary results from user's experiences shows a proper usability level and easy-to-use system via our intuitive advanced user interface that actively supports users in their interaction with the robotic system. The way the information is presented to the user is a key issue, and thus is treated as a significant part of this work.

On the other hand, these results depict the importance of the availability of context awareness from an accurate and real-time environment representation. The inclusion of context awareness from visual perception enriches the system allowing it to become a flexible and proactive assistant and furthermore, be able to face some unexpected situations.

Acknowledgments. This work has been done under the project IPRES, DPI2011-29660-C04-01 of the Spanish National Research Program, with partial FEDER funds. It has also been partially founded by Fundació La Caixa, inside the Recercaixa 2012 research program, P6-L13-AL.INHAND.

References

1. Aranda, J., Vinagre, M., Martín, E.X., Casamitjana, M., Casals, A.: Friendly Human-Machine Interaction in an Adapted Robotized Kitchen. In: Miesenberger, K., Klaus, J., Zagler, W., Karshmer, A. (eds.) ICCHP 2010, Part 1. LNCS, vol. 6179, pp. 312–319. Springer, Heidelberg (2010)
2. Saffiotti, A., Broxvall, M., Gritti, M., LeBlanc, K., Lundh, R., Rashid, J., Seo, B.S., Cho, Y.J.: The PEIS-Ecology Project: vision and results. In: Proc. of the IEEE/RSJ Int. Conf. on Intelligent Robots and Systems (IROS), Nice, France (September 2008)
3. Bahadori, S., Cesta, A., Grisetti, G., Iocchi, L., Leone, R., Nardi, D., Oddi, A., Pecora, F., Rasconi, R.: RoboCare: an Integrated Robotic System for the Domestic Care of the Elderly. In: Proceedings of Workshop on Ambient Intelligence AI*IA-2003, Pisa, Italy (2003)
4. Robot-Era project (2014), `http://www.robot-ra.eu/robotera/`
5. Chitta, S., Sucan, I., Cousins, S.: MoveIt! [ROS Topics]. IEEE Robotics & Automation Magazine 19(1), 18–19 (2012)
6. Vinagre, M., Aranda, J., Casals, A.: Human Motion Recognition from 3D Pose Information – TRISAREA: A new Pose-Based Feature. In: Proc. of the 10th Int. Conf. on Informatics in Control, Automation and Robotics(ICINCO), Reykjavik, Iceland (July 2013)

RGB-D Video Monitoring System to Assess the Dementia Disease State Based on Recurrent Neural Networks with Parametric Bias Action Recognition and DAFS Index Evaluation

Sabrina Iarlori, Francesco Ferracuti, Andrea Giantomassi, and Sauro Longhi

Dipartimento di Ingegneria dell'Informazione Università Politecnica delle Marche, via Brecce Bianche, 60131 Ancona, Italy
a.giantomassi@univpm.it

Abstract. Within 2050, demographic changes, due to the significant increase of elderly, will represent one of the most important aspect for social assistance and healthcare institutions, particularly in European Union. Great attention is given to dementia diseases with over 35 million people worldwide who live in this condition, affected by cognitive impairment, frailty and social exclusion with considerable negative consequences for their independence. Preference will be given to intervention with high impact on the quality of life of the individual associated with a socio-economic burden, also for people who care for them. The main challenge comes from the social objective of assisting and keeping elderly people in their familiar home surrounding or to enable them to "aging in place".

1 Introduction

Research shows that most people, currently living with dementia, have not received a formal diagnosis, considering that only 20-50% of dementia cases are recognized and documented [6]. Early therapeutic interventions can be incisive in improving cognitive function and delaying institutionalization, it allows timely access to information and opens a pathway to effective intervention and care, since the start of the disease course.

For this reason, information and communication technologies (ICT), imagine and video processing techniques are of interest and may overcome the limitations in reducing the inter/intra-rather variability due to human interpretation. By these methods patients' actions in real life situations are captured.

Dementia is diagnosed when progressive cognitive decline occurs and has noticeable impacts upon a person's ability to carry out everyday activities. As indicated by National Institute on Aging Alzheimer's Association (NIA-AA), people with Mild Cognitive Impairment (MCI) present mild problems performing complex tasks. Formal neuropsychological testing may be able to detect impairments relative to memory and other cognitive functions, or to that the person has performed in the previous test. Rating scales are diffused diagnostic

K. Miesenberger et al. (Eds.): ICCHP 2014, Part II, LNCS 8548, pp. 156–163, 2014.

tools for dementia, monitoring symptoms as well as the evaluation of treatment effects. Instruments for this scope are questionnaires self-reported and based on performance assessment. Limitations about these tests regard accuracy, reproducibility and objectivity drop.

A high quality dementia diagnosis requires even more costs for an early intervention so the idea is that of using a computer-based vision system able to monitor and diagnose the stage of advancing illness in dementia patients. The system is designed to observe elderly people during activity of daily living, chosen among those present in the functional domain of Direct Assessment of Functional Status (DAFS) index in order to detect anomalies during the performance [13].

1.1 State of the Art

In order to capture the behavioral, functioning and cognitive disturbances in dementia disease, ICT are of interest. In [10] and [11] a Video Monitoring System (VMS) is developed, to help in evaluation of Instrumental Action of Daily Living (IADL) index in dementia and in MCI. Feasible studies of VMS methods are conducted in well defined scenarios, where the activities proposed by a tester observation are monitored by the video system.

About cognitive impairments and neurologic conditions, in [7] a new approach to monitor the effect of cognitive exercise interventions is tested. The continuity and frequency of measurements over times provide clinicians new abilities to detect cognitive problems early and to have timely feedback in treatment interventions, in order to avoid a cognitive assessment infrequently achieved and the visit to a clinician's office. Many AD patients consider the current neuropsychological tests very onerous especially as their cognitive functions decline. In [5] the system is able to recognize problems indicative of dementia or some other activities that would not be expected by normal individuals. Disease monitoring could also warn if behavior is indicative of disease progression and can be used to detect household maintenance such as running faucets and showers, or monitor household appliances as blocked or overflowing toilets.

Different works about monitoring systems have been realized in order to assess properly the subject's performance or assist him in accomplishing tasks. In [1] a system based on computer vision and Support Vector Machines (SVMs) is proposed to estimate the patients' behavioral profile. Another approach, proposed in [14], focuses on recognizing activities of daily living by developing skeleton structure-motion using 3D information by RGB-D cameras. Computer vision systems are a solution to help people to reduce invasivity of body worn sensors and allow a continuous monitoring control, avoiding loss of information and without any interference in daily life activities [9].

2 Proposed Methodology

The index, chosen to discriminate the presence of dementia, the DAFS index, comprises 7 items that investigate both functional and cognitive aspects, treated separately [13]. The DAFS observes the patient behavior during daily activity tasks, performed during the clinical test and is able to discriminate people affected by dementia. If the action is correctly done the score is 1, otherwise 0.

The proposed contribution consists of a computer vision system able to diagnose the stage of illness, by DAFS index, in patients affected by MCI, observing actions present in the DAFS test and detecting anomalies during the performance, in order to assign a score if the action is correct or not. In the context of Ambient Assisted Living (AAL), the system monitors people in home environment during daily personal care activities. The proposed technology consists of a low cost RGB-D camera and a computer. The system acquires camera frames and applies motion preprocessing algorithms in order to reduce data size and extract the subject motion informations.

2.1 Developed Algorithm

The preprocessing step consists of computing Motion History Image (MHI) and extracts characteristic motion features [3]. MHI represents how the elements of an image sequence are moving. It is a cumulative gray scale image, incorporating the spatial as well as the temporal information, related to the action.

MHI represents the location, the shape, and the movement direction of an action in a picture sequence and is defined as:

$$H_\tau(x,y,t) = \begin{cases} 255 & \text{if } D(x,y,t) \geq \tau \\ max(0, H_\tau(x,y,t-1) - \sigma) & \text{otherwise,} \end{cases} \tag{1}$$

where $D(x,y,t) = \|I(x,y,t) - I(x,y,t-1)\|, I(x,y,t)$ denotes the pixel with coordinates x and y at time t of image I, τ is the sensitivity threshold of the pixels variation between two consecutive frames, σ is the motion history decay constant. Once the MHI is computed, a down-sampling of the video frames is performed and a bounding box on the user is evaluated in order to discard all non-useful information. Inside the bounding box, the Pyramid Histograms of Orientation Gradients (PHOG) algorithm is applied over each image. PHOG is a method to represent the local shapes by a histogram of edge orientations within an image subregion quantized into K bins, where each bin in the histogram describes the number of edges that have orientations within a certain angular range [4]. The contribution of each edge is weighted according to its magnitude. In detail magnitude $m(x,y,t)$ and orientation $\theta(x,y,t)$ of the gradient of each pixel (x,y) at time t within the bounding box is computed as:

$$\begin{aligned} m(x,y,t) &= \sqrt{g_x(x,y,t)^2 + g_y(x,y,t)^2} \\ \theta(x,y,t) &= \arctan \tfrac{g_x(x,y,t)}{g_y(x,y,t)}, \end{aligned} \tag{2}$$

where $g_x(x,y,t)$ and $g_y(x,y,t)$ are the image gradients along the x and y frame directions. Each gradient orientation is quantized into K bins. In each cell of each level, gradients over all the pixels are concatenated to form a local K bins histogram. As a result, a Region Of Interest (ROI) at level l is represented. All cells at different pyramid levels are combined to form a final PHOG histogram with dimension $d = K \sum_{l=0}^{L-1} 4^l$ to represent the whole ROI.

The histogram, of each video frame, represents the features extracted from the PHOG algorithm and is processed by the neural network classifier. A Recurrent Neural Network with Parametric Bias (RNNPB) is applied to these features to learn movements connected with a specific action and recognizes human activities by parametric bias that work like mirror neurons. Finally the recognized actions are classified to verify the sequences and assess the accuracy of the whole. In this way the subject index is updated and reports are sent to doctors.

Authors have developed the procedure and have realized a laboratory bench tester, where tests are made on 10 actors (6 males and 4 females), in order to collect preliminary results and validate the proposed methodology. RNNPB and the whole algorithms must be trained initially on the subject, at this stage the methodology learns the subject movements and the characteristic features. Once the procedure is trained, then the system starts the subject monitoring. A flow chart of the whole developed procedure, described by different steps, is shown in Fig. 1 and summarized below:

```
for all video frames, If the patient is in the bathroom:
- acquire RGBD frame, preprocess RGB and Depth flows;
- compute MHI from RGB video and down-sampling;
- compute bounding box around the user;
- motion features extraction by PHOG algorithm;
- process motion features by RNNPB and compute the action label;
- the RNNPB output is stored.
Classify the stored sequence and assign DAFS score.
```

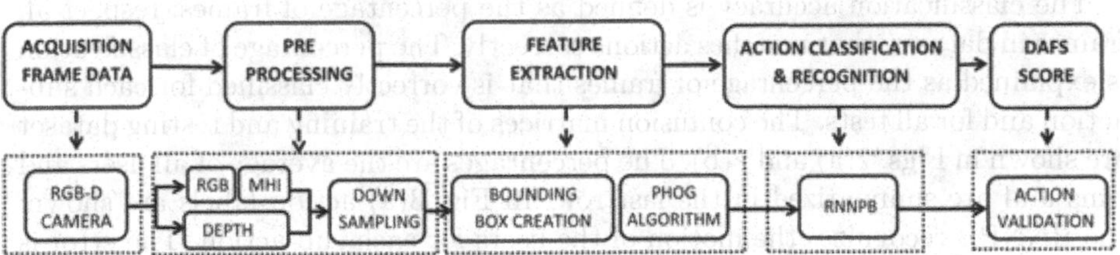

Fig. 1. Flow chart of the developed procedure for the recognition of human daily living activities

The classification is performed by the PBs combination while the RNN prediction error is evaluated to verify that the RNNPB performance does not degrade.

3 Results

Results regard grooming hair by a hairbrush, brushing teeth and washing hands actions. Experiments prove that the proposed computer vision system can learn

Table 1. Sub-Action PB labels and descriptions

Lab.	Sub-Actions	Lab.	Sub-Actions
1	Washing hands	5	Unscrew the toothpaste cap
2	Take/putting away things	6	Brushing teeth
3	Grooming hair	7	Putting the soap on the hands
4	Open/closing the faucet	8	Putting the toothpaste on the toothbrush

and recognize complex human activities and evaluates DAFS score about personal care. The experimentation consists of making actions like "grooming hair", "washing teeth" and "washing hands" by ten actors who have realized the actions of DAFS test. For each person, each sub-action runs 5 times for the training phase, and for the testing phase the action is repeated 3 times. The described actions do not consider all possible movements that are performed during their execution. Then, in this work a set of so called sub-actions are considered, in order to better perform the classification, and then the sequences of sub-action, classified by the RNNPB, are evaluated and matched with the defined DAFS actions. Thus 8 groups are defined, as described in Tab. 1. It can be noted that some sub-actions are grouped due to their similarities.

The considered RNNPB has 50 neurons for each layer, the number of PBs is 6, the learning rate ϵ is set to 0.1, the momentum η is 0, δ is 10 and ζ varies linearly from 1 to 0.99 as learning proceeded [12]. The RNNPB is trained with 2000 epochs. The performance reached a Mean Square Error (MSE) of $2.5 \cdot 10^{-04}$ at the last epoch.

The classification accuracy is defined as the percentage of frames, respect all frames in dataset, that matches actions correctly. The percentage of classification is explained as the percentage of frames that is correctly classified for each sub-action and for all tests. The confusion matrices of the training and testing dataset are shown in Figs. 2(a) and 2(b). The percentages are the average of all users and runs and are summarized in the last row. In Fig. 3(a) action labels are shown: the RNNPB recognizes the motion of the users for each sub-action. The error is localized during the sub-action change, because the neural network needs some frames to adapt the PBs and recognizes the sub-action.

The grooming hair activity is composed by a sequence of three sub-actions: the user takes the comb, grooms hair and puts away the comb. Fig. 3(a) shows the sub-action labels recognized by the RNNPB during the described activity. The classification accuracy for "grooming hair" activity is 90.91%. In this case, as shown in Fig. 3(a), if the user performs the correct sequence then the DAFS index is set to 1.

The second test shows the brushing teeth activity that is composed by a sequence of nine sub-actions: the user takes the toothpaste, removes the cap of toothpaste, takes the toothbrush, puts the toothpaste on the toothbrush, puts away the toothpaste, opens the faucet, brushes the teeth, closes the faucet

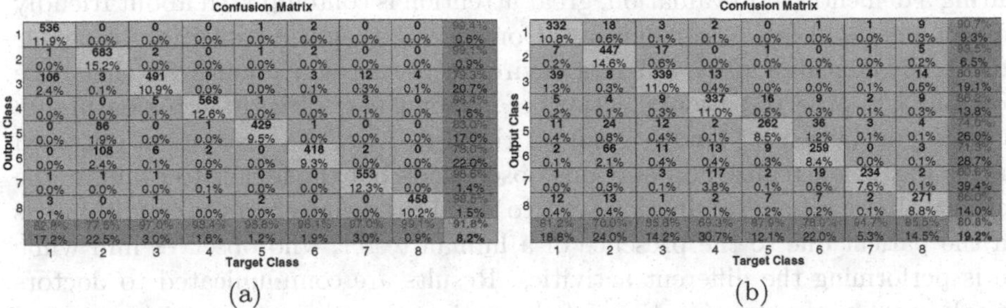

Fig. 2. Confusion matrices; a) training dataset; b) testing dataset

and puts away the toothbrush. Fig. 3(b) shows the action labels recognized by the neural network during the brushing teeth activity, as described above. The classification accuracy for this activity is 80.15%. In this case, as shown in figure, the user performs the correct sequence and the DAFS index is set to 1.

The last test shows the washing hands activity that is composed by a sequence of six sub-actions: the user takes the soap, puts the soap on the hands, puts away the soap, opens the faucet, washes the hands and closes the faucet. Fig. 3(c) shows the action labels recognized by the neural network during the washing hands activity, as described above. The classification accuracy for this activity is 88.20%. In this case, as shown in figure, the user performs the correct sequence and the DAFS index is set to 1.

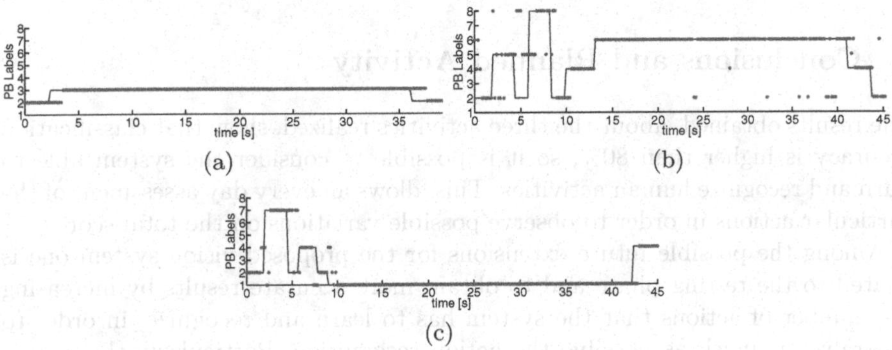

Fig. 3. Sub-Action labels recognized by the RNNPB in the case of correct sequence performed by the user; a) grooming hair action; b) brushing teeth action; c) the washing hands action

4 Practical Impact and Contributions

The practical impact believed about the application of the video monitoring system regards the introduction of an early diagnosis of dementia state, without negative effect on the patients. Among different factors that can affect patients during a dementia test evaluation, great attention is contemplated about friendly environment and self ease condition. Considering that the transition of people affected by dementia into a different environment can be traumatic for them, the possibility to observe patient's actions of personal care directly in his bathroom is an important aspect for the result of the test. Also, the assessment obtained in this way is not realized on only one observation but the idea is to evaluate the activity after a set of examination tests to avoid clustering errors or conditionings on the patient due to the presence of a human tester, who observes him while he is performing the different activities. Results are communicated to doctors to take note of the deteriorations of the patient dementia stage, with practical advantages to take note of the evolving condition.

In this context, it is very important to work especially respecting the patient privacy right [2]. The target of this research is represented by aging people affected by Alzheimer at the early stage and the scenario, focused for the monitoring actions proposed, regards only the sink space in order to limit the intrusion in the user bathroom. On the base of the compromised decision making level of the patient, an informed consent will be required to him or his legally authorized representative, providing written information about the study aim, procedure, scheduled period of monitoring and people who can access to video recorded and processed by the system [8]. It is possible to distinguish two information levels: one more sensitive, represented by the clip recorded, and one less sensitive connected with an information computed from it. Authors use only second level access to video information and only doctors and caregivers can access to the video.

5 Conclusions and Planned Activity

The results obtained, about the three activities realized, show that classification accuracy is higher than 80%, so it is possible to consider the system able to learn and recognize human activities. This allows an every day assessment of the particular actions in order to observe possible variations on the total score.

Among the possible future extensions for the proposed vision system one is related to the testing phase and to obtain more accurate results by increasing the number of actions that the system has to learn and recognize, in order to generalize as much as possible the action recognition. Particularly the goal is to implement also all the other actions present in the personal care item of DAFS index. Another future research is to investigate the possibility of using the activities recognition algorithm in other care and health contexts.

Another purpose concerns the involvement of people with dementia in testing stage and the goal is to verify how this index, which is periodically evaluated, can be used by medical staff for dementia's assessment.

References

1. Avgerinakis, K., Briassouli, A., Kompatsiaris, I.: Video monitoring for activities of daily living recognition. In: AAL Forum, Eidhoven, pp. 24–27 (September 2012)
2. Bharucha, A.J., London, A.J., Barnard, D., Wactlar, H., Dew, M.A., Reynolds, C.F.: Ethical considerations in the conduct of electronic surveillance research. The Journal of Law, Medicine & Ethics 34(3), 611–619 (2006)
3. Bobick, A., Davis, J.: The recognition of human movement using temporal templates. IEEE Transactions on Pattern Analysis and Machine Intelligence 23(3), 257–267 (2001)
4. Bosch, A., Zisserman, A., Munoz, X.: Representing shape with a spatial pyramid kernel. In: Proceedings of the 6th ACM International Conference on Image and Video Retrieval, pp. 401–408. ACM (2007)
5. Dishman, E., Carrillo, M.C.: Perspective on everyday technologies for alzheimer's care: Research findings, directions, and challenges. Alzheimer's & Dementia 3(3), 227–234 (2007), `http://www.sciencedirect.com/science/article/pii/S1552526007004827`
6. EU: The benefits of early diagnosis and intervention (2011), `http://ec.europa.eu/health-eu/my_health/elderly/index_en.htm`
7. Jimison, J., McKanna, J., Ambert, K., Hagler, S., Hatt, W., Pavel, M.: Models of cognitive performance based on home monitoring data. In: 2010 Annual International Conference of the IEEE Engineering in Medicine and Biology Society (EMBC), pp. 5234–5237 (August 2010)
8. Kenner, A.M.: Securing the elderly body: Dementia, surveillance, and the politics of "aging in place". Surveillance & Society 5(3), 252–269 (2008)
9. Mégret, R., Dovgalecs, V., Wannous, H., Karaman, S., Benois-Pineau, J., El Khoury, E., Pinquier, J., Joly, P., André-Obrecht, R., Gaëstel, Y., Dartigues, J.: The immed project: wearable video monitoring of people with age dementia. In: Proc. of the Int. Conf. on Multimedia, MM 2010, pp. 1299–1302 (2010)
10. Romdhane, R., Mulin, E., Derreumeaux, A., Zouba, N., Piano, J., Lee, L., Leroi, I., Mallea, P., David, R., Thonnat, M., Bremond, F., Robert, P.: Automatic video monitoring system for assessment of alzheimers disease symptoms. The Journal of Nutrition, Health & Aging 16(3), 213–218 (2012)
11. Sacco, G., Joumier, V., Darmon, N., Dechamps, A., Derreumaux, A., Lee, J.H., Piano, J., Bordone, N., Konig, A., Teboul, B., et al.: Detection of activities of daily living impairment in alzheimer's disease and mild cognitive impairment using information and communication technology. Clinical Interv. in Aging 7, 539 (2012)
12. Tani, J., Ito, M., Sugita, Y.: Self-organization of distributedly represented multiple behavior schemata in a mirror system: reviews of robot experiments using rnnpb. Neural Networks 17(8-9), 1273–1290 (2004)
13. Zanetti, O., Frisoni, G., Rozzini, L., Bianchetti, A., Trabucchi, M.: Validity of direct assessment of functional status as a tool for measuring alzheimer's disease severity. Age and Ageing 27(5), 615–622 (1998)
14. Zhang, C., Tian, Y.: Rgb-d camera-based daily living activity recognition. Journal of Computer Vision and Image Processing 2(4) (2012)

Experiences and Challenges in Designing Non-traditional Interfaces to Enhance the Everyday Life of Children with Intellectual Disabilities

Janio Jadán-Guerrero[1,3] and Luis A. Guerrero[1,2]

[1] Doctoral Program in Computer Science, Universidad de Costa Rica
[2] Centro de Investigaciones en Tecnologías de la Información y Comunicación, CITIC, San José, Costa Rica
[3] Universidad Tecnológica Indoamérica, Av. Machala y Sabanilla, Quito, Ecuador
janio.jadan@ucr.ac.cr, luis.guerrero@ecci.ucr.ac.cr

Abstract. Some experiences regarding children with disabilities carried out in Ecuador, Costa Rica and Spain have contributed to realize the importance of reading in order to enhance their daily life activities, independence and social integration. This article describes a qualitative study to understand general issues related to the design of non-traditional technologies for children with intellectual disabilities. A methodological approach is described and explained through the results of exploratory surveys and interviews. According to the information obtained from experts and the method of literacy acquisition proposed by Troncoso and Del Cerro, the design of a smart kit using non-traditional user interfaces is presented. A preliminary evaluation of the first prototype is described. The paper concludes by reflecting upon the importance of literacy acquisition and the challenges to design non-traditional interfaces to support learning of children with intellectual disabilities. The development of the phase two of the prototype and empirical evaluation is part of the future work.

Keywords: Non-Traditional User Interfaces, Human-Computer Interaction, Literacy Acquisition, Children with Intellectual Disabilities, Daily Life Activities.

1 Introduction

Computer technologies have become an integral part of our society. Laptops, tablets, smartphones, game consoles and other non-traditional devices are changing our habits [2]. Adults and children interact with these technologies is some daily activities as communication, education or entertainment [11]. It is very gratifying that many of these technologies can also help people with special needs [1,2,7,13,14,18]. However there are new challenges and opportunities in the design of interaction paradigms for these technologies. The pervasiveness and portability of emerging devices and computing systems allow the users to benefit from assistive technologies all day [14,18]. In this context, the article describes the background and some experiences carried out

K. Miesenberger et al. (Eds.): ICCHP 2014, Part II, LNCS 8548, pp. 164–171, 2014.

in Ecuador, Costa Rica and Spain to find valuable insights related to the literacy acquisition [17], supported by emerging technologies for children with intellectual disabilities.

The methodology section describes the various instruments utilized to gather data of experts. Psychologists, pedagogues and teachers were interviewed in order to analyze the importance of literacy acquisition for children with intellectual disabilities [16], [19], and how it would help to enhance daily life activities, independence and social integration. The information obtained to apply exploratory surveys and interviews are detailed in the section of discussion and results. As result of these experiences the design of the first prototype of a modular smart kit and a preliminary evaluation are described. Finally, the conclusions and future work are described in the last section of the paper.

2 Background and Related Work

The motivation behind the design of computer technologies for children with special education needs (SEN) came from an experience of one of the authors in Ecuador, in which the research team of Universidad Tecnológica Indoamérica designed three prototypes: AINIDIU (Intelligent agent for children with visual impairment) that has the ability to interact with a blind child through a voice synthesizer and screen reader to enhance the interaction with computers; HELPMI (Tool that emulates a language through Pictograms), which is an application for mobile devices to help children with language impairments to communicate with others; and CANDI (Support centre for different children), which is a web platform that allows the diffusion of technological innovations and services to parents of the SEN children [7]. These researches enabled the University to sign a cooperation agreement among Vice President of the Republic of Ecuador and The National Federation of Blind in Ecuador (FENCE). In this cooperation process the AINIDIU software was evaluated and selected to be installed in approximately 1000 laptops donated by the program Manuela Espejo Solidarity Mission. All the laptops were distributed to visually impaired children of 22 provinces of Ecuador. In this experience of technological transfer both educators and students of the Universidad Indoamérica were responsible to train children in the use of technologies [8].

This rewarding experience of working with people committed to change the life of children with disabilities has allowed new opportunities and challenges. Authors are still studying about the design and implementation of non-traditional interfaces [9] for children with intellectual disabilities. This research is actually supported by Centro de Investigaciones en Tecnologías de la Información y Comunicación (CITIC) of Universidad de Costa Rica and Centro de Investigación, Innovación y Desarrollo (CIID) of Universidad Indoamérica from Ecuador.

The research highlights the importance of designing non-traditional user interfaces, in which computers, mobiles devices and tangible objects could be interconnected to create enjoyable, interesting interactions for boost children motivation and to promote learning by sceneries of the real life [3], [18]. Recent developments in technology are providing new opportunities for Human-Computer Interaction (HCI) techniques [9,10]. Areas like Ambient intelligence (AmI), Natural User Interfaces (NUI) or tangible user interface (TUI) have significantly developments in recent years in the educational scope. They offer new ways to overcome specific problems associated with people with disabilities [1,2,3,4,5], [14,15], [18]. It is due to the type of interaction that is highly motivating enabling positive outcomes in users especially when they are children who require a personalized education [17], [19].

In brief, the design of non-traditional user interfaces offer an opportunity to let children with intellectual disabilities learn how to read and write, in order they overcome real life problems. However, literacy acquisition is a process that requires input from caregivers, teachers as well as therapists. The study aims to identify the most important inputs necessary to design new non-traditional user interfaces.

3 Methodology

The methodological approach is based on a qualitative study for collecting data from experts. The study was designed in three phases. In Phase 1 some non-structured interviews and one exploratory survey were undertaken to explore the method for literacy acquisition used by experts. In Phase 2 a structured interview was developed in order to obtain information about the features of the method for children with intellectual disabilities. In Phase 3 a semi-structured interview was developed to determine the activities and resources the method applies. All of these instruments aimed to know the importance of literacy acquisition for children with intellectual disabilities and how literacy acquisition could enhance daily life activities, independence and social integration. From the HCI perspective this exploratory study helps to identify specific situations, problems and needs of the experts in the educational field [10]. The experts were recruited from three countries: Ecuador, Costa Rica and Spain. This group of experts was composed of psychologists, pedagogues and educators who work with children with intellectual disabilities.

The procedure was done during three months. At the first Phase the interviewer - one of the authors of this article - conducted some non-structured interviews in Costa Rica. Professionals at Instituto de Investigación en Educación (INIE) and educators of Universidad de Costa Rica mentioned the Global Method for literacy acquisition and a method developed in Spain for children with Down syndrome –Troncoso and Del Cerro [17]. According to the opinion of educators the last method is little known in Costa Rica. In order to investigate whether this method is applied in Ecuador, the interviewer traveled to Quito and applied an exploratory survey at Fundación Virgen de las Mercedes (FUVIME). Ten teachers of special education volunteered to participate in the process. The method used by them was the Global Method.

While reviewing the literature, we saw the method Troncoso and Del Cerro has been designed especially for children with Down syndrome and it has been successfully apply in other countries like Spain and Chile. In order to know more about this method, at the Phase 2 the interviewer requested an appointment with the creator of the method. He traveled to Santander in Spain to visit the Fundación Iberoamericana

Down21, in which he conducted a structured interview. The author of the method explained in detail the different activities, resources and experiences applied in children with Down syndrome for more than ten years in Spain.

The goal of the Phase 3 was to determine how the method and technology were applied by pedagogues. In this context, the interviewer traveled to Valencia in Spain to visit the Fundación ASINDOWN. A semi-structured interview was applied. The interviewer had the opportunity to visit the Fundación ONCE in Madrid, in which a non-structured interview was conducted to identify technology for people with disabilities. Finally, a non-structured interview was conducted to the head of FutureLab-ISSI from Polytechnic University of Valencia in order to know about the experiences of applying HCI techniques with people with disabilities.

4 Discussion and Results

After the data collection process was complete, the surveys were coded and all interviews were transcribed and analyzed using content analysis procedures to identify the perceptions of the experts [10].

The surveys were structured in four sections. The first one identified the demographic data of educators and children with intellectual disabilities. Section 2 focused to identify the most important abilities before literacy acquisition. The 80% of the interviewed people said they highlight memory, association, selection and discrimination skills and the other 20% said that behavior and control are important. In Section 3 they mentioned some methods for literacy acquisition: Global method, use of symbols, pictograms and the traditional method. On the other hand, 70% of them coincide that technology enables children with intellectual disabilities to participate fully in all aspects of their daily life (home, school, and community) and 30% were indifferent to it. In Section 4, 60% said that the literacy acquisition is important for children lives.

The interviews were codified selecting recurring topics and summarizing the thoughts of the experts for each one. Table 1 summarizes this information.

Table 1. Results of content analysis procedures in the interviews of experts

Professional	List of terms of relevance
Educators	Inclusion, technology for classroom, tools, support, easy to use, behavior, communication.
Pedagogues	Tangible, imaginary, abstract, positive effects on teaching and learning skills.
Psychologists	Love, stimulus, feedback, motivation, patience, evaluation, enjoyable, dynamic sceneries, attention.
Method 'author	Memory, selection, association, discrimination, skills, literacy acquisition, independence, social inclusion, daily life activities, encouragement.
Computer Researchers	Feasibility, usability, HCI, user experience, technology for educators and caregivers, empirical evaluation.

The most important terms collected from experts show the aspects more important for each group. In addition, all of them coincide that literacy acquisition can help to the process of social inclusion. The author of the method said that the final goal to literacy acquisition is secondary respect to the process inside it. It is possible that not everyone overcome to read. However, the activities help to enhance their learning about the real word. We analyzed the different perceptions of the experts from their professional perspective.

The information obtained from an interdisciplinary group of experts opens the possibility to design new technologies for specific problems, particularly in Latin American where educational and technological resources for children with disabilities are few. This rewarding experience of researching the problems of children with intellectual disabilities and professionals committed to change the life of these children, has allowed opening new opportunities and challenges to design technologies to enhance their everyday life activities.

5 Prototype

From the specifications obtained from the literature review and the exploratory study we propose the design of a prototype based on non-traditional user interfaces. This prototype consists on a modular smart kit to support literacy acquisition for children with intellectual disabilities. The development was designed in two phases. Phase 1 focuses in the design of the technological architecture, in which the educational resources are structured as standard learning objects [13]. The idea for developing a client-server Web framework is to share the material designed for the research team or educators in the future. According to the cognitive conditions of a child with intellectual disabilities [16] and learning theories [19] developed for educators the process of teaching and learning must be adapted for each child. In this sense, educators use cards or sheets with illustrations related to the environment of each child. Educators configure a series of steps, in which each step includes a set of structured activities. The design of the first prototype try to encapsulate these features and the specifications of the method Troncoso and Del Cerro, in order to promote the development of language and reading skills. Regarding technological aspects, the first version of the prototype will be designed for computers, the second one for tablets and the third one for systems with non-traditional user interfaces. Each design considers the support of experts to obtain interfaces that are easy to configure for non-technical users. Figure 1 shows the proposed architecture accessible for educators for creating resources with traditional interfaces and for teaching with traditional or non-traditional interfaces.

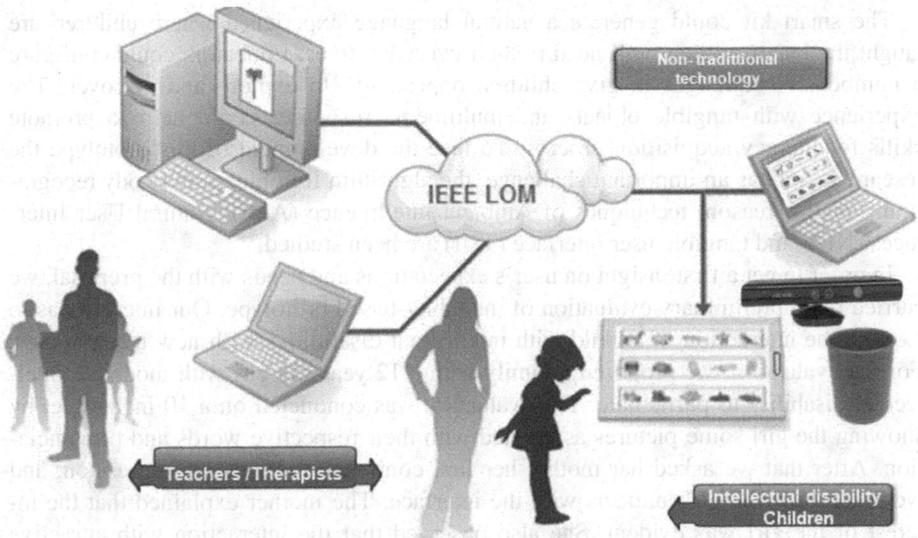

Fig. 1. Proposed architecture of the prototype

The Phase 2 focuses in the design of a new prototype with non-traditional user interfaces. This prototype aims to take advantage of new technologies -tablets, smart phones, videogames and other digital age tools. According to Prensky theory [12], children have the ability to interact with technology in a natural way. The prototype considers this theory and the activities of the method Troncoso and Del Cerro. The main idea is to develop a modular smart kit as learning tool with objects and situations of the real life. Figure 2 shows the idea of scenery in which children interact with tangible objects and non-traditional technologies for literacy acquisition.

Fig. 2. Sample of Smart Kit's scenarios designed with Microsoft Kinect [6] and tablets

The smart kit could generate a natural language experience where children are taught the language they will need in their everyday lives. Educators could configure a number of challenges to give children opportunity to explore and discover. The experience with tangible objects and multimedia resources could help to promote skills for literacy acquisition process. To face the development of this prototype the research team has an important challenge: the algorithm for objects and body recognition. For this reason, techniques of Ambient intelligence (AmI), Natural User Interfaces (NUI) and tangible user interface (TUI) are been studied.

In order to get a first insight on user's expectations and needs with the proposal, we carried out a preliminary evaluation of the tablet-based prototype. Our interest was to explore the interaction of a child with intellectual disabilities with new technologies. For the evaluation, we proposed a family with a 12 year-old girl with moderate intellectual disability to participate. The evaluation was conducted on a 10 inch tablet by showing the girl some pictures associated with their respective words and pronunciation. After that we asked her mother her first comment and general impression, and we asked how the girl interacts with the interface. The mother explained that the interest of the girl was evident. She also observed that the interaction with attractive illustrations and sounds made an enjoyable time. This first assessment encourages us to continue with the challenge to design novel technologies adapted to the needs of Costa Rica and Ecuador.

6 Conclusion and Future Work

In this paper we have described experiences that motivated the use of non-traditional user interfaces, especially focused on literacy acquisition. We collected the opinion of some professional about the importance of literacy acquisition and how it can benefit the daily life activities of children with intellectual disabilities. We proposed the design of a modular smart kit with non-traditional interfaces to help the work of educators. Our future work will focus on the development of the Phase 2 of the prototype and the empirical evaluation. We aim to assure that these interfaces comply with real world user needs, specially the children with intellectual disability, that makes it worth the effort.

Acknowledgements. This research would not have been possible without the valuable collaboration of institutions through their openness and collaboration. This project has received support from SENESCYT (Secretaría Nacional de Educación Superior, Ciencia y Tecnología) and Universidad Tecnológica Indoamérica of Ecuador. We also acknowledge support from CITIC (Centro de Investigación en Tecnologías de la Información y la Comunicación) of Universidad de Costa Rica.

References

1. Rahman, A., Qamar, A.M., Ahmed, M., Rahman, A., Basalamah, S.: Multimedia interactive therapy environment for children having physical disabilities. In: Proceedings of the 3rd ACM Conference on International Conference on Multimedia Retrieval (2013)

2. Drigas, A.S., Ioannidou, R.-E.: ICTs in special education: A review. In: Lytras, M.D., Da Ruan, Tennyson, R.D., Ordonez De Pablos, P., García Peñalvo, F.J., Rusu, L. (eds.) WSKS 2011. CCIS, vol. 278, pp. 357–364. Springer, Heidelberg (2013)
3. Xavier, C., Gerardo, H., Javier, S., Javier, P., Lorena, T., Ángel, F., Jordan, R., Luis, R., Carlos, P., Blanca, V.: Pictogram Room. Videojuegos educativos diseñados para trabajar áreas claves del desarrollo de personas con autismo. Grupo de autismo y dificultades de aprendizaje, Spain (2012)
4. Chang, Y.-J., Chou, L.-D., Wang, F.T.-Y., Chen, S.-F.: A kinect-based vocational task prompting system for individuals with cognitive impairments. Personal and Ubiquitous Computing 17(2), 351–358 (2011)
5. Dave, A., Bhumkar, Y., Abraham, A., Sugandhi, R.: Project MUDRA: Personalization of Computers using Natural Interface. International Journal of Computer Applications 54(17), 42–46 (2012)
6. Justina, H.-M.: The Potential of Kinect in Education. International Journal of Information and Education Technology 1(5) (December 2011)
7. Janio, J.: AINIDIU, CANDI, HELPMI: ICTs of a personal experience. In: 2012 Workshop on Engineering Applications (WEA), pp. 1–7 (2012)
8. Janio, J.: AINIDIU: An experience among university, organizations and government. In: 2013 XXXIX Latin American Computing Conference (CLEI), pp. 1–8 (2013)
9. Philip, K.: HCI Beyond the GUI: Design for Haptic, Speech, Olfactory, and Other Nontraditional Interfaces. Morgan Kaufmann Publishers Inc., CA (2008)
10. Lazer, J., Fenq, J.H., Hochheiser, H.: Research Methods in Human-Computer Interaction. Wiley (2010)
11. Mäkelä, S., Bednarik, R., Tukiainen, M.: Evaluating user experience of autistic children through video observation. In: CHI 2013 Extended Abstracts on Human Factors in Computing Systems on - CHI EA 2013, Finland, p. 463 (2013)
12. Marc, P.: Digital Natives, Digital Immigrants, vol. 9(5). MCB University Press (2001)
13. Sampson, D.G., Zervas, P., Chloros, G.: ASK-LOM-AT 2.0: A Web-Based Tool for Educational Metadata Authoring of Open Educational Resources. In: 2011 IEEE International Conference on Technology for Education (T4E), pp.76–80, 14–16 (2011)
14. Shih-Ching, Y., Wu-Yuin, H., Tzu-Chuan, H., Wen-Kang, L., Yu-Tsung, C., Yen-Po, H.: A Study for the Application of Body Sensing in Assisted Rehabilitation Training. In: 2012 International Symposium on Computer, Consumer and Control (IS3C), pp. 922–925 (2012)
15. Soltani, F., Eskandari, F., Golestan, S.: Developing a Gesture-Based Game for Deaf/Mute People Using Microsoft Kinect. In: Sixth International Conference on Complex, Intelligent, and Software Intensive Systems, Iran, pp. 491–495 (2012)
16. Sternberg, R.: Cognitive Psychology. Wadsworth, Cengage Learning, pp. 269–275 (2009)
17. María, T., Mercedes, D.C.: Síndrome de Down: lectura y escritura, Fundación Iberoamericana Down21, Satander-España (2009)
18. Tse, E., Marentette, L., Ishtiaque, A., Thayer, A., et al.: Educational interfaces, software, and technology. In: Proceedings of the 2012 ACM Annual Conference Extended Abstracts on Human Factors in Computing Systems Extended Abstracts, CHI EA 2012, p. 2691 (2012)
19. Vigotsky, L., Leontiev, A., Luria, A.: Psychology and Pedagogy, 3rd edn., pp. 81–90. Akal Ediciones Sa (2007)

Implementation of Applications in an Ambient Intelligence Environment: A Structured Approach

Laura Burzagli and Pier Luigi Emiliani

IFAC NCR, Institute for Applied Physics "Nello Carrara", National Research Council of Italy
{l.burzagli,p.l.emiliani}@ifac.cnr.it

Abstract. Based on the work in the FOOD project, an approach for the design of an intelligent environment and the development of applications to favour independent living is presented. Starting from the definition of activities to be carried out in the different living environments, the approach is based on the formalization of information relevant to describe functionalities, technology and users and the presence of "intelligence" for adapting the functionalities and their interfaces to individual users.

Keywords: Ambient Intelligence, ICT Applications, Artificial Intelligence, Natural Interfaces.

1 Introduction

Recently, interest has grown in the emergence of the Information Society as an ambient intelligence (AmI) environment, both with reference to specific user groups (see for example, the AAL programme dealing with older people) and to society in general (see, for example, the different SmartCities initiatives).

In AAL, the FOOD[1] Project (Framework for Optimizing the prOcess of FeeDing), under the responsibility of the Italian Company Indesit, has developed a kitchen environment with interconnected appliances, an Internet link and services and applications dealing with all aspects of feeding (e.g. from accessing databases of recipes and getting ingredients for cooking to socialising around food topics with friends).

The FOOD kitchen and related services/applications are now in a pilot phase in apartments of older people in Italy, The Netherlands and Rumania. Not only interaction with the new technology is considered, but also the relevance of all functionalities made available to allow a correct performance of activities related to feeding is under test. Activity and results are reported elsewhere [1]. In this paper, FOOD is used from one side as a source of practical and concrete examples to support the discussion and from the other as a source of remaining problems to be considered in future developments.

In fact, the FOOD project, as many successful developments, has contributed to point out limitations of the present approach to the development of intelligent

---

[1] http://www.food-aal.eu

K. Miesenberger et al. (Eds.): ICCHP 2014, Part II, LNCS 8548, pp. 172–179, 2014.

environments, particularly for groups of people with activity limitations (sometimes partial and/or potential as in the case of older people). Some of these limitations and a possible structured way out of them are presented in the paper in order to contribute to the discussion about future activities.

2 Critical Points of the Present Approach

The developments in the FOOD project clearly show some critical aspects shared by most of the activities aimed to favour an independent life of people in the AmI environment.

First, it evident that so far most emphasis has been on problems related to safety, security and health care, because, as prerequisites to independent life, people need to live in a secure environment and be in good health. A lot of technology has been developed for these applications (e.g. sensors, remote control services, eHealth services) and its deployment started in many countries. It is now time to take also care of well-being of people in their living environments, aiming to grant them comfort, entertainment, possibilities of social contact. Old people, particularly if they have some activity limitation, are normally perceived as a problem that can be solved, sometimes with use of technological support, by granting them a safe and secure living environment. Their right of having a pleasant life is often overlooked.

Then, the starting point of developments is technology driven and directly aimed to serve well-defined groups of people. When a new technology is made available, for example Ambient Intelligence, the problems of a group or several groups of people with activity limitations are considered. They are normally expressed in questions as, for example, the following: how can people, who are blind or have a (minor) decrease of ability to see as many older people, be included in a smart house? How can they use the available technology? Can they take advantage of this technology? Alternatively, attempts are made to use the new technology to support explicitly specific groups of users. For example, the GPS is made available and investigations are started about how this technology can be used to allow navigation of blind people or to track the position of older people who could get lost. These approaches should be revised. The starting point in the deployment of new technology leading to set up intelligent environments should be the identification of activities relevant to allow people (all people) to live an independent and satisfactory life in these environments (e.g. the kitchen). Then, the technology for implementing the functionalities (for example, access to recipes) necessary for supporting the activities to be carried out (e.g. feeding) should be carefully selected, deployed and interconnected considering as many user groups can be reasonably served (Design for All). Finally, when necessary, i.e. when obstacles are present, different possible technological supports should be examined, choosing the ones that maximise advantages (e.g. reduction of cost, number of people who can use it). Obviously, if the chosen technological solutions are not suitable for some user group, special adaptations could be looked for (based on assistive technology), taking into account that different people may be in the same environment and the needs, requirements and preferences of all of them should accommodated as much as reasonably possible.

Finally, in many cases, accessibility to ICT and human computer interaction (not human environment interaction) aspects are the focus of activity. Obviously, they represent one basic element, but the concern about them may have a limiting effect on the functionalities to be considered as part of the applications to be implemented. Only functionalities that can easily be made available through the planned interface are considered, without an analysis of other different modalities, often available, for a more appropriate implementation of the environment and its related applications.

As an example, in the FOOD project two interaction options have been considered from the very beginning. The first is distributed and based on the interfaces of the single appliances. The second is aimed to allow the control of the entire kitchen and the connection with the outside world. It is based on a tablet using the Android operating system. In this case, interaction with the environment is taken back to the normal model of an interaction with a computer (windows, menus, etc.), using the accessibility supports offered by the operating system itself or available in the Google Play market[2].

3 A Structured Design Approach

The above outlined features of the present activity for setting up an intelligent environment, even if far from a complete analysis of the related problems, are sufficient to show that this is fragmented (with reference to different users), technology driven (both from the perspective of functionalities to be made available and of the offered interactions), and biased by stereotypes of human computer interaction. Moreover, resources are often wasted in rediscovering problems and possible solutions.

Even if it is obviously difficult to influence the development of basic technology, its integration in complex environments should be organised in a structured procedure (Fig.1), starting from the identification of activities that people need to perform in them. Then, the environments should be implemented in a way that allows them to favour the performance of these activities and to evolve according to the varying user needs and the availability of new technology.

3.1 Identification of Activities

Very often, the identification of requested activities is made on an ad hoc way, for example with interviews with end users, often in an inadequate number. In fact, knowledge about activities to be carried out in order to live independently and their connection with necessary abilities has been widely collected and made available in a structured form in the WHO ICF document [2]. This classification can be used as it is or expanded if necessary. WHO ICF is a widely accepted document, produced through the agreement of people around the world. It is well structured and, therefore, usable in mechanised procedures.

[2] https://play.google.com/store

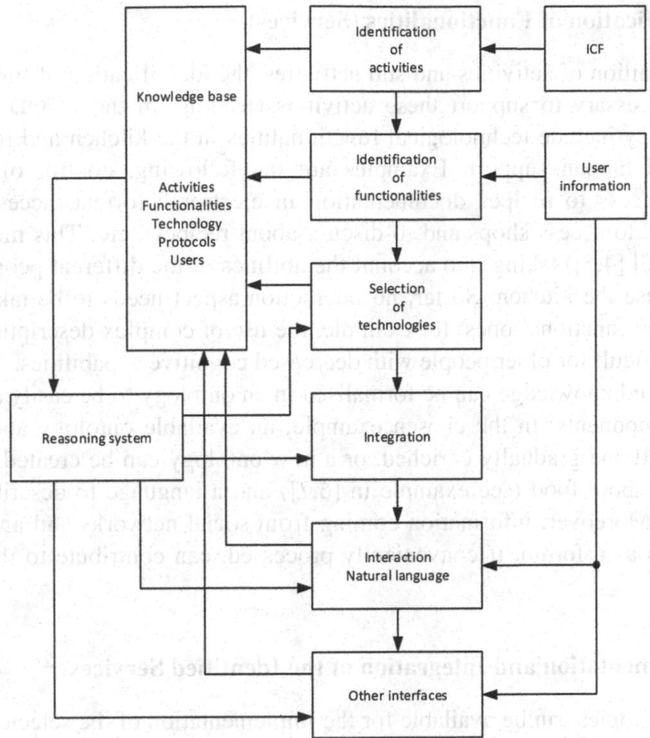

Fig. 1. The structured approach

This does not mean that user research is not useful, but, as all research activities, it should be carried out to generate new knowledge and not to rediscover what is already known. For example, it is not very fruitful to run user research activities related to the kitchen environment to discover that for feeding people need to be supported in the following activities: (1) getting the food (e.g. selecting and paying for it remotely); (2) being informed about how to use and cook it (e.g. access to recipes); (3) cooking it without spoiling it and running the danger of burning themselves. Much of this information is already available in the WHO ICF document (chp.6 - Domestic life), which is structured and thought in terms of its possible expansions [3]. Obviously, persons could have different preferences about how these activities should be organised and carried out and a lot of user research activity is necessary to set up and feed the user models necessary to reason about their requirements and preferences. Moreover, users' evaluation and testing still are essential phases in the process leading to the implementation of services/applications. If users are not obliged to rediscover available knowledge, they can spend more effort in helping designers in the most critical part of the proposed approach, i.e. in the production of relevant new knowledge.

3.2 Identification of Functionalities (Services)

After the definition of activities and sub activities, the identification of functionalities (services), necessary to support these activities (feeding, in the FOOD project), is necessary. They include technological functionalities in the kitchen and remote technological and human support. Examples are the following: control of the single appliances, access to recipes documentation in electronic format, access to social networks (e.g. to access shops and to discuss about recipes), etc. This must be done (Design for All [4,5]) taking into account the abilities of the different people who are supposed to use the kitchen. So far, no interaction aspect needs to be taken into account, but only functional ones: for example, the use of complex descriptions of recipes can be difficult for older people with decreased cognitive capabilities.

The produced knowledge can be formalised in an ontology to be easily available to reasoning components. In the chosen example, an available ontology about feeding can be adopted and gradually enriched, or a new ontology can be created. A number of ontologies about food (see example in [6,7]) and a language to describe food [8] are available Moreover, information coming from social networks and any other application such as a forum, if conveniently processed, can contribute to the ontology construction.

3.3 Implementation and Integration of the Identified Services

Several technologies can be available for the implementation of the selected functionalities. The features of the technologies must be described in a formalised way together with the communication protocols and added to the knowledge base available for the design and implementation of the entire system.

After a careful selection, they need to be integrated. This must be carried out with a holistic approach, i.e. taking into account all the different aspects:

- Activities to be carried out
- Functionalities to be made available
- Available technology
- Users and their abilities (including their possibly conflicting needs).

If at the end of the procedure problems still exist for some groups of people, then solutions can be looked for, considering:

- The possibility of using additional technology for adaptation
- The possibility of offering the same functionality in different form.

It is important to observe that at this point the discussion is still at the level of functionalities. For example, the problem is not to adapt a telephone to be usable if hands are busy for a different purpose (e.g. washing vegetables), but to grant people the corresponding functionality, i.e. remote communication by voice. This can be offered, for example, using the microphone of the tablet and the loudspeaker of the television set.

3.4 Implementation of the (Natural) Interaction

From the interaction perspective, it is important to observe that in complex situations as the ones emerging in ambient intelligence environments, interaction cannot only be analysed from the perspective of being able to access the available interface. A real exchange of information between people and the system, which must be able to assist the users, learn from their behaviour, test the validity of its assumptions and react to explicit requests, must be established.

In any environment (e.g. the kitchen), two interfaces are normally available: the interface of the single intelligent objects (e.g. the home appliances) and the interface of the entire system (e.g. a tablet). They can be adapted to the needs of different users, with and without activity limitations.

However in all documents about intelligent environments (see e.g. [9]), reference is made to a not-defined natural interface. Apparently, a natural interface is any interface that a person perceives as natural. People are normally used to exchange information through face-to-face conversation in natural language. Natural language is the "natural" interface between them. Therefore, the interaction between the environment and people living in them could be probably based on a dialogue in natural language. Interfaces based on windows, menus, command lines are only a poor way out of the real problem, due to limitations of the present technology. However, trends of developments in information technology and artificial intelligence (see, for example, the SIRI applications by Apple [http://www.apple.com/ios/siri/] and the Watson project by IBM [http://www-03.ibm.com/innovation/us/watson/) show real possibilities of a successful evolution in this direction.

It is true that speech interaction with machines has had many difficulties in becoming widespread. For example, cars have been equipped with voice recognisers for opening the doors without using a key. The approach has not been very successful. Apparently, people were not comfortable in being observed while speaking to their car. However, when people are alone in their environment there is not probably any sociological reason why they should be more comfortable in getting a glass of water from the fridge, if they are not able to open it for physical problems, using an adapted tablet than telling the fridge "I am thirsty". The intelligent environment should not be seen as a "big brother" controlling and judging the person, but as a friendly set of functionalities controlled by the user. Moreover, it is presently very common, going around in the street, to see people who are apparently speaking to the open space, when they are using a mobile telephone set with a headphone. Attitudes of people are changing very fast.

Obviously, also a communication in natural language may create interaction problems to some groups of people with activity limitations. They must be identified and formalised, and the reasoning system is supposed to introduce the necessary adaptations as a function of the user and the carried out activity.

3.5 Alternative Interactions

Apparently, natural language interaction is considered a promising and viable possibility, where industry is heavily investing. In the meantime, it will be necessary to work with suboptimal solutions, as the ones considered in the FOOD project.

Problems potentially caused by these interactions must be carefully analysed and formalised to allow a control of the corresponding interfaces by the reasoning system.

4 The Working Environment

After the implementation, the intelligent environment must be able to deliver adapted functionalities according to the information available at login, the interconnected technology, the activities to be carried out and the abilities of the users.

In addition, it must be able to evolve in order:

- To accommodate, when necessary, new activities and functionalities
- To be able to adapt to new users or to the possibly changing abilities of the users (also in real time)
- To incorporate developments of the available technology and new technology
- To accommodate suitable interfaces and possible changes in them.

It may seem a tautology, but this means that in order to develop intelligent environments, "intelligence" is necessary[10,11]. Presently, this is mainly assumed to mean that there are computers in the environment. However, the main difference between a caregiver and the environment in supporting people is that the caregiver has a brain, i.e. s/he is able to reason about user needs, while the environment is not able to reason at all in most of the presented smart environment. Instead, it should be able to do it. How and to what extent this is possible or will be possible is under discussion, but the system should be able to continue to run according to the block diagram in Fig. 1.

It is clear that, taking into account the preceding observation, the most important block in the diagram is the reasoning system that, in this case, is not the designer but an artificial intelligent inference machine, working on the knowledge available (e.g. as ontologies) in a database. This is the reason why the need of formalising the knowledge in a machine-readable form has been particularly emphasised during the discussion of the design and implementation phase.

In principle, the system should be able to acquire automatically and formalise additional information about activities (e.g. modification of ICF), functionalities, available technology and its communication and interaction protocols, interaction options and, most important, user needs, requirements and preferences. If this is not yet possible, the knowledge base should be structured to be open to explicit addition of Information.

5 Conclusions

Ambient intelligence is offering interesting new possibilities to allow a comfortable life for all citizens and support for independent life of people with activity limitations.

Artificial and collective intelligence can favour the use of procedures for eliciting information from users about their way of using facilities in the environment and their requirements and preferences. This information can be formalised in ontologies describing different levels of activities leading to the implementation of living environments, usable by a reasoning system to match the features of the environment to the needs of all users.

References

1. Allen, J., Boffi, L., Burzagli, L., Ciampolini, P., De Munari, I., Emiliani, P.L.: FOOD: Discovering Techno-Social Scenarios for Networked Kitchen Systems. In: Encarnação, P., Azevedo, L., Gelderblom, G.J. (eds.) Assistive Technology: From Research to Practice: AAATE 2013, vol. 33, pp. 1143–1148. IOS Press (2013)
2. WHO International Classification of Functioning, Disability and Health (ICF), World Health Organization, Genève (2001)
3. List of Official ICF Updates, `http://www.who.int/classifications/icfupdates/en/`
4. Emiliani, P. L., Burzagli, L., Billi, M., Gabbanini, F., Palchetti, E.: Report on the impact of technological developments on eAccessibility, DfA@eInclusion Project, D2.1 (2008), `http://www.dfaei.org`
5. Emiliani, P. L., Aalykke, S., Antona, M., Burzagli, L., Gabbanini, F., Klironomos, I.: Document on necessary research activities related to DfA, DfA@eInclusion Project, D2.6 (2009), `http://www.dfaei.org`
6. Kehagias, D., Kontotasiou, D., Mouratidis, G., Nikolaou, T., Papadimitriou, I.: Ontologies, typologies, models and management tools, OASIS, Project D1.1.1 (2008)
7. Snae, C., Brückner, M.: FOODS: A Food-Oriented Ontology-Driven System. In: Second IEEE International Conference on Digital Ecosystems and Technologies Proceedings, pp. 168–176 (2008)
8. LanguaL™ - the International Framework for Food Description (2012) , `http://www.langual.org/Default.asp`
9. Ducatel, K., Bogdanowicz, M., Scapolo, F., Leijten, J., Burgelman, J. C.: Scenarios for ambient intelligence in 2010. Technical report, Information Society Technologies Programme of the European Union Commission (IST) (2001)
10. Ramos, C., Augusto, J.C., Shapiro, D.: Ambient Intelligence-the Next Step for Artificial Intelligence. IEEE Intelligence Systems 23, 15–18 (2008)
11. Weber, W., Rabaey, J.M., Aarts, E.: Ambient Intelligence. Springer, Heidelberg (2005)

Applying Small-Keyboard Computer Control to the Real World

Torsten Felzer[1], I. Scott MacKenzie[2], and Stephan Rinderknecht[1]

[1] Institute for Mechatronic Systems,
Technische Universität Darmstadt, Darmstadt, Germany
{felzer,rinderknecht}@ims.tu-darmstadt.de
[2] Dept. of Electrical Engineering and Computer Science,
York University, Toronto, Canada M3J 1P3
mack@cse.yorku.ca

Abstract. This paper presents a usability study for text entry with a new version of the assistive keyboard replacement *OnScreenDualScribe*. Over five sessions (approximately 1 hr/session), three able-bodied novice participants achieved an entry rate of 13.9 wpm. In a case study, one disabled expert achieved an entry rate of 6.6 wpm. The main aspects of the software are described and differences to the ancestor *DualScribe* are highlighted. Finally, the potential impact of the system for persons with neuromuscular diseases – a user group it particularly accommodates – is elaborated.

Keywords: Human-computer Interaction, Assistive Technology, Word Prediction, Ambiguous Keyboards, Neuromuscular Diseases, Keyboard Replacement, Mouse Alternative, Combined Input Device.

1 Introduction

OSDS (or *OnScreenDualScribe*) is a tool that replaces the standard PC input devices (i.e., a full-size keyboard and a mouse) with a single, compact device, while allowing efficient interaction. It consists of a numeric keypad and software translating physical keystrokes into virtual events directed at the currently active window.

Prospective users of *OSDS* are persons who are either unable or unwilling to employ standard input devices for controlling a computer. The former group particularly includes users with a neuromuscular disease, while the latter refers to mobile users or users operating an entertainment-centered PC. In both situations, it is important to replace the large keyboard with a small, albeit usable, alternative. For able-bodied users, this admittedly often involves touch-based devices, but those are unsuitable for many disabled users due to the absence of haptic feedback.

The input device for which *OSDS* is designed, called *DualPad*, has been subject to considerable development. It started as a game controller, evolved into a special-purpose keyboard, and ended up as an off-the-shelf numeric keypad with

K. Miesenberger et al. (Eds.): ICCHP 2014, Part II, LNCS 8548, pp. 180–187, 2014.

stickers attached to the keys. It is ideal for persons with a neuromuscular disease who often have specific problems using a full-size keyboard without holding on to anything. The *DualPad* is gripped firmly with every key reachable using the thumbs. Repositioning the hands is never necessary.

After considering the different research areas in the development of *OSDS*, the tool is briefly described, focusing on the new features. The section that follows introduces a usability study evaluating the text entry capabilities of the newest software version. Results are presented for three able-bodied participants and for the first author (as a disabled, but experienced supplement) transcribing more than 500 phrases (each between 20 and 40 characters long). A summary and a look to future work conclude the paper.

2 Related Work

Related work in association with the *OSDS* input technique involves several areas of human-computer interaction. One is *two-thumb text entry*, which refers to the way an input device is operated. Various realizations exist, for example split keyboards for touch-based applications [1] or mini-QWERTY keyboards, realized either as physical devices or as a soft keyboard on a touchscreen [2,3]. As mini-QWERTY keyboards generally contain a similar number of keys as a full-size keyboard, except with smaller keys, even physical realizations are not suitable for users with reduced fine-motor control.

Since *OSDS* is not limited to text entry, but offers emulation of pointing operations as well, a second related area is *combined input devices*: Every smart phone is an example. However, smart phones (and tablets) are touch-oriented and not suitable for every user. Of course, there are examples that add haptic feedback to a touchscreen using transparent tangible objects [4], but whether those solutions can effectively mimic a physical keyboard is unclear.

Another related area deals with the question of how to implement a *keyboard-driven mouse replacement*. A simple way is to assign keys to moving a mouse pointer in cardinal directions and other keys to the emulation of clicks at the current pointer position [5]. It will become clear below that this is not the only solution.

In addition, *OSDS*, is designed for *real-world applications*. For example, editing is not restricted to deletion of the character entered last (as for most proof-of-concept implementations, e.g., [6]), but cursor operations as well as copy, cut, and paste are supported. *OSDS* is not only a helpful assistant for text entry, it also offers mouse control. Single left clicks, double clicks, right clicks, and dragging operations are all supported (see also [7]).

3 System Description

The first author has the progressive neuromuscular disease Friedreich's Ataxia [8]. He developed *OSDS*, as an extension to *DualScribe* [9], with the objective to regain productivity lost due to the progression of his disease. The main extension

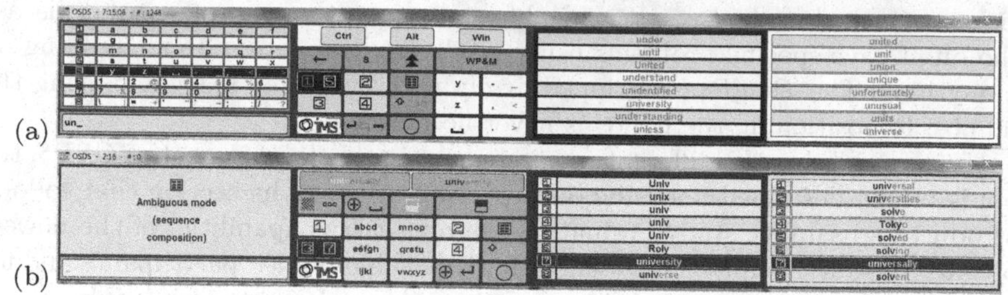

Fig. 1. Text entry in *OSDS*: (a) *dual mode* with (from left to right) character matrix, *DualPad* avatar, top-ranked completion candidates (#1 – #8), candidates ranked #9 – #16; (b) in *ambiguous mode*, the *DualPad* avatar illustrates a slightly modified key layout

is that *OSDS* behaves similarly to an onscreen keyboard, working as a mediator between the user and the active application.

Unlike its ancestor, *OSDS* does not rely on a dedicated editor window: It does not even require input focus. Instead, it intercepts the input signals before they reach the window in focus (which may belong to, for example, an email client) and generates new, virtual input events that are sent to the window. In doing so, the tool seamlessly interfaces with any existing application on the user's computer. This means that users of *OSDS* have full access to the editing functionality offered by other programs (without being restricted to a single proprietary editor).

All computing tasks a user may encounter are grouped into a dozen modes, all offered by the current software. The *DualPad* key triggering an action depends on the current mode. However, the program window shows an avatar of the *DualPad* which reveals the valid key associations.

The major goal in devising the tool was to replace the regular keyboard with a smaller alternative while optimizing for text entry. The text entry component, which shares basic ideas with the older version, comprises two different input methods.

In *dual mode* (fig. 1a), printable characters are arranged in a rectangular matrix, with corresponding keys emulated by selecting the coordinates of the characters. While entering a prefix, the software looks for completions in an internal dictionary and suggests selectable candidates.

Ambiguous mode works like T9 (known from the numeric keypad of mobile phones) with six ambiguous keys. The candidate lists suggest matches of the entered key sequence using the same dictionary (fig. 1b depicts the situation after entry of four letters).

Even though *DualScribe* caters to a proprietary editor window, the first author began to use it in practice, copying the entered texts and pasting them into other edit controls. However, this was almost as cumbersome as the regular keyboard, since using a pointing device for starting or activating other programs still required constant repositioning of the hands. Therefore, it was decided to include an internal mouse mode in the next version [10].

Initially [11], mouse control was realized in the form of a keyboard mouse, but since keyboard mice require pressing or releasing keys at exact points in time, this solution was far from optimal: Many persons with neuromuscular diseases have difficulties with temporal synchronization because they have a longer reaction time.

As an alternative, the newest version of *OSDS* implements a mouse mode that is not time-critical. Target acquisition is done in a stepwise fashion by recursively selecting tiles and sub-tiles on the screen, terminating with a click (of any type) at the target position.

In addition, *OSDS* offers a huge number of small (and some not-so-small) features, for example (to name a few), the operating system's task switcher can be called quickly, the program window may be hidden while the tool works in the background, the language environment can be switched at runtime, and typematic delay and repeat rate can be configured for ease of use. It is this kind of miscellaneous functionality that turns a promising idea into a practical input device replacement.

4 Evaluation

Our initial evaluation of *OnScreenDualScribe (OSDS)* 2.0 is now described. The evaluation focused on the *dual mode* text entry method depicted in fig. 1a. The evaluation involved 15 hours of testing with able-bodied users. Instead of testing 15 participants, one hour each, 3 participants were tested over 5 one-hour sessions each. Thus, patterns of learning should emerge. After presenting the initial evaluation, a case study with a member of the target user community is described.

4.1 Participants

The participants were members of the local community at the second author's university. There were two males, one female, with a mean age of 21.0 years (*SD* = 1.4). All are regular users of computers reporting usage of 4.3 hours per day. None had prior experience with *OSDS*.

4.2 Apparatus

The *DualPad* hardware consisted of a Perrix numeric keypad (`www.perix.com`) with keytop labels affixed for operation with the *OSDS* software (see fig. 2a). The keypad is connected via a USB cable to a host desktop computer running *Windows 7*.

There were two components to the software. The *OSDS* software captured the input signals and preprocessed them according to the current mode (i.e., *dual mode* text entry). *OSDS* presents a UI showing the current mode (see fig. 1a). Most characters require two keystrokes. A keystroke with the left thumb selects a group of characters. This is followed by a keystroke with the right

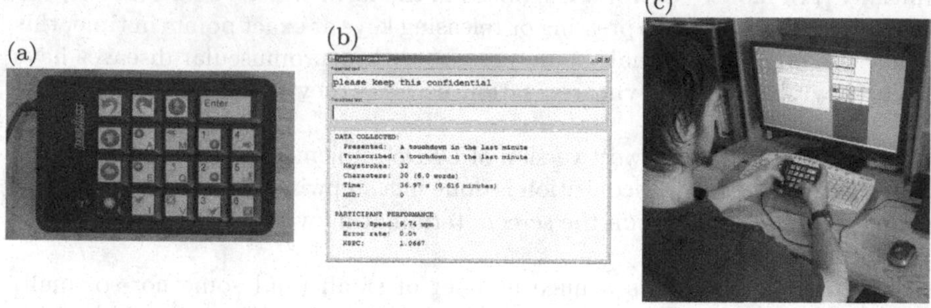

Fig. 2. Usability study: (a) Perrix numeric keypad with keytop labels for *OSDS*; (b) *Typing Test Experiment* evaluation software; (c) a participant entering text using *OSDS* and *Typing Test Experiment*

thumb to select the character within the group and transfer the character to the application in focus. As entry proceeds, up to 16 candidate words are presented in the bottom half of the UI (see right two images in fig. 1a). If the desired word appears, early word selection is possible with two key presses: "WP+M" on the right thumb (see second image of fig. 1a) followed by a left-thumb key press to select the word.

The evaluation software was *Typing Test Experiment*, a general-purpose text entry evaluation tool written in Java[1] ([12], p. 317). The tool randomly selects a phrase of text from a set and presents it in a text field. The user enters the phrase using the current text entry method (in this case, *OSDS* in *dual mode*). The transcribed phrase appears in a separate text field. When the user presses ENTER, the results appear in a static textbox and a new phrase is presented for entry. An example is shown in fig. 2b. Keystroke data, timestamp data, and summary statistics are also written to a disk file for follow-up analyses.

4.3 Procedure and Design

After a brief introduction and demonstration, testing began. Each session (aka "day") consisted of 3 practice blocks following by 10 data-collection blocks. Each block consisted of three phrases of entry. There were five sessions scheduled on consecutive days (or sometimes with one or two intervening days). Fig. 2c shows a participant entering phrases.

4.4 Results and Discussion

The grand mean for entry speed was 10.9 wpm, ranging from 7.1 wpm in session 1 to 13.9 wpm in session 5 (see fig. 3a). The grand mean for character-level error rates was 3.2% (see fig. 3b).

[1] The software is freely available as a download at `http://www.yorku.ca/mack/HCIbook/`.

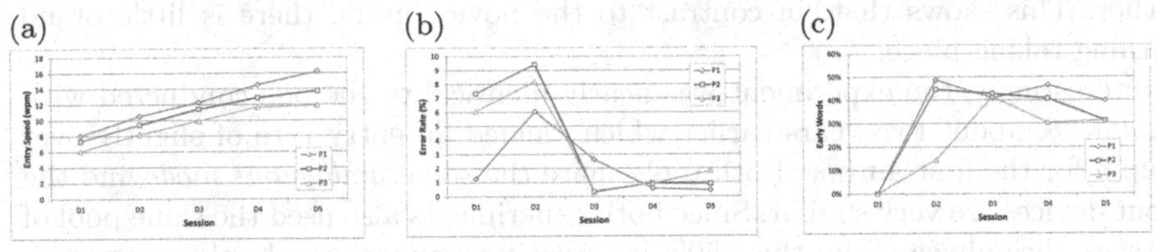

Fig. 3. Results for (a) entry speed, (b) error rates, and (c) early word selections

The unusual pattern for error rates is likely due to basic learning in session 1, learning to use early word selection in session 2, and the acquisition of skill in sessions 3, 4, and 5.

As noted, participants did not use early word selection until the second session. The percentage of words selected early is shown in fig. 3c. With practice, participants settled in to a routine whereby 30–40% of the words are selected early.

The results of the initial evaluation provide a general validation for text entry using *OSDS* in *dual mode*. We now describe a case study with a member of the target user community.

4.5 Case Study

The first author (who has Friedreich's Ataxia) entered text using *OSDS* in *ambiguous mode* along with *Typing Test Experiment*. Entry was performed in one day with a total of 75 phrases, presented in 15 blocks with 5 phrases each. The overall mean entry speed was 6.6 wpm (fig. 4) The mean error rate (not shown) was 0.5%.

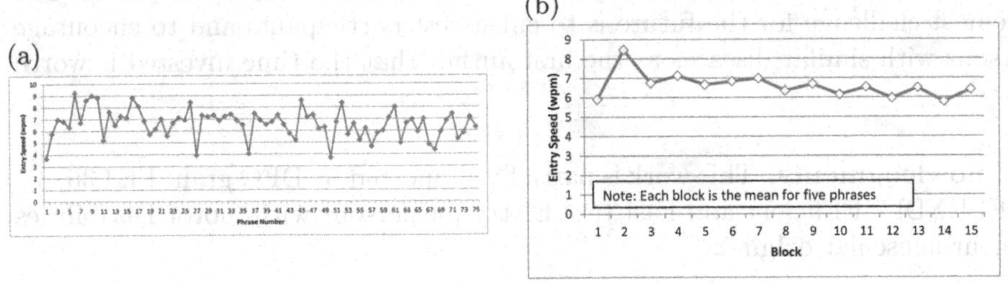

Fig. 4. Entry speed by the participant in the case study: (a) all 75 phrases; (b) 15 blocks with 5 phrases each

Fig. 4a might give the impression that the entry rate is very jittery, erratically jumping between a low of 3.7 wpm and a high of 9.2 wpm. However, as seen in fig. 4b, the average entry rate is rather constant – only block 2 is a (statistical)

outlier. This shows that, in contrast to the novice users, there is little or no learning taking place.

Interestingly, the experiment was nearly identical to the one conducted with *DualScribe* about two years earlier which yielded an entry rate of slightly over 4 wpm for the first author. Both tools share the same *ambiguous mode* and the input devices are very similar. Since both experiments also used the same pool of phrases, the only cause for the >50% increase in entry rate can be the experience gained in the intervening time.

Furthermore, the preparation of this paper represents an intrinsic demonstration of the usability of the system, since the first author has written large parts by himself: As a consequence of generally using little else to control a computer, he employed *OSDS* for nearly all tasks during composition. The only exception were two keystrokes on the snapshot key[2] to produce figs. 1a and 1b. Therefore, it is clear that the tool can effectively be used in practice – the first author can use it, so others should be able to as well.

5 Conclusion

This paper presented a computer control method to replace standard input devices with a single device and new software to achieve a compact and powerful input system that is well-suited for persons with certain disabilities. The most important property of the software, called *OSDS*, is its suitability for practical broad-based use instead of being restricted to particular computing tasks.

The system is in daily use by the first author who has Friedreich's Ataxia and growing motor problems since late childhood. His experience shows that it is truly life-changing. Use of a regular keyboard (which had required ever-increasing physical effort) for general tasks, and text entry in particular, became slower and slower. For entry speed, *OSDS* has turned back the clock by about ten years; the effort is gone almost completely.

However as the tool is quite complex, novice users require considerable practice (up to several months) before they are able to make full use of its power. The foremost challenge for the future is to enlist test participants and to encourage persons with similar diseases as the first author that the time invested is worth it.

Acknowledgments. This work is partially supported by DFG grant FE 936/6-1 "EFFENDI – EFficient and Fast text ENtry for persons with motor Disabilities of neuromuscular orIgin".

References

1. Oulasvirta, A., Reichel, A., Li, W., Zhang, Y., Bachynskyi, M., Vertanen, K., Kristensson, P.O.: Improving two-thumb text entry on touchscreen devices. In: Proc. CHI 2013, pp. 2765–2774. ACM (2013)

[2] Of course, *OSDS* offers a mode to emulate the snapshot key, but when the tool is in other modes, striking that key on a regular keyboard cannot be avoided.

2. MacKenzie, I.S., Soukoreff, R.W.: A model of two-thumb text entry. In: Proc. Graphics Interface 2002, pp. 117–124. Canadian Information Processing Society (2002)
3. Clarkson, E., Lyons, K., Clawson, J., Starner, T.: Revisiting and validating a model of two-thumb text entry. In: Proc. CHI 2007, pp. 163–166. ACM (2007)
4. Weiss, M., Wagner, J., Jansen, Y., Jennings, R., Khoshabeh, R., Hollan, J.D., Borchers, J.: SLAP widgets: Bridging the gap between virtual and physical controls on tabletops. In: Proc. CHI 2009, pp. 481–490. ACM (2009)
5. RH Designs: Mouse Emulator, `http://rhdesigns.browseto.org/mouseemulator.html` (accessed on January 17, 2014)
6. Felzer, T., Strah, B., Nordmann, R.: Automatic and self-paced scanning for alternative text entry. In: Proc. IASTED Telehealth/AT 2008, pp. 1–6 (2008)
7. Jansen, A., Findlater, L., Wobbrock, J.O.: From the lab to the world: Lessons from extending a pointing technique for real-world use. In: Ext. Abstracts CHI, pp. 1867–1872. ACM Press (2011)
8. Delatycki, M., Williamson, R., Forrest, S.: Friedreich Ataxia: An overview. Journal of Medical Genetics 37(1), 1–8 (2000)
9. Felzer, T., MacKenzie, I.S., Rinderknecht, S.: DualScribe: A keyboard replacement for those with Friedreich's Ataxia and related diseases. In: Miesenberger, K., Karshmer, A., Penaz, P., Zagler, W. (eds.) ICCHP 2012, Part II. LNCS, vol. 7383, pp. 431–438. Springer, Heidelberg (2012)
10. Felzer, T., Rinderknecht, S.: Mouse mode of OnScreenDualScribe: Three types of keyboard-driven mouse replacement. In: CHI EA 2013, pp. 1593–1598. ACM Press (2013)
11. Felzer, T., MacKenzie, I.S., Rinderknecht, S.: OnScreenDualScribe: A computer operation tool for users with a neuromuscular disease. In: Stephanidis, C., Antona, M. (eds.) UAHCI/HCII 2013, Part I. LNCS, vol. 8009, pp. 474–483. Springer, Heidelberg (2013)
12. MacKenzie, I.S.: Human-computer interaction: An empirical research perspective. Elsevier (2013)

Design and Evaluation of Multi-function Scanning System: A Case Study

Frédéric Vella, Damien Sauzin, Frédéric Philippe Truillet, and Nadine Vigouroux

IRIT, CNRS 5505, Université Paul Sabatier, Toulouse, France
{vella,sauzin,truillet,vigouroux}@irit.fr

Abstract. We present in this paper an assistive technology of communication and command for quadriplegics. To carry out this assistive technology, a user centered design approach with the patient, his occupational therapists and his family was conducted. Various iterative versions of the prototype have been defined by means of the SOKEYTO platform to meet the needs and the abilities of the quadriplegic person. Options carried out and consecutive choice will be reported as well the difficulties to implement. The assistive technology was used by one quadriplegic person. A qualitative evaluation is also reported.

Keywords: Quadriplegic People, Scanning, User Centered Design, Communication, Environment Control.

1 Introduction

"In memory of Matthieu"

Developing scanning-based assistive systems for quadriplegic people is not a new issue. Several studies have proposed a model of man-machine interaction applied to the scanning based communication devices to adapt the scanning time based on an analysis of the data recorded in "log files" of the EDitH use [1]. Steriadis and Constantinou [8] have developed the "Autonomia" application to assist a quadriplegic person in using an ordinary personal computer. Autonomia was designed to be used through mouse and keyboard simulation through the use of specially designed "wifsids" (Widgets For Single switch Input Devices) for four frames (Cursor frame, Virtual keyboard frame, Console frame and Macros frame). Additional functionalities are also possible like dial-up connections, phones calls, etc. These solutions aim to reduce as soon as possible the expense of the cognitive load [3]. Hurst and Tobias [4] illustrates that it is possible to custom-build Assistive Technology (AT) and argues why empowering users to make their own AT can improve the adoption process. Boujrad et al. [5] have developed a participatory approach with patients and therapists to design a human computer interface for quadriplegic. Even though some work has been done, there are still needs for asking accessibility solutions for disabled people in Ambient Intelligence environments and with cheap available technologies.

Consider the case study of Matthieu. He was living in a rehabilitation center near Paris. He was a quadriplegic person without spoken communication. Matthieu had

K. Miesenberger et al. (Eds.): ICCHP 2014, Part II, LNCS 8548, pp. 188–194, 2014.

visual deficiency. He communicated with his family and his caregivers through his thumb movement. Matthieu only answered by two consecutive movements which mean "yes" (See Fig. 1 a). In this context, the dialog between Matthieu and his human environment -family and caregivers- was long, poor and difficult even if some facial expressions report Matthieu's intention. The learning to understand Matthieu was long time consuming.

The therapist team is heavily workloaded. In consequence Matthieu wished to be more independent and more autonomic to choose his leisure time - free to select himself the music played, the movie watched on the Web, the TV channel or the radio. He liked also to express his needs or feels as "I am cold", "I am not installed in my chair", "I want to change room", etc. to anyone.

To meet the needs of Matthieu, a user centered approach was lead including the therapist team, his father, his brother and a team specialized in the design of assistive technologies. After some observations the de-sign team has decided to design a virtual keyboard with scanning controlled by a switch connected to the input/output of a Arduino Uno box (http://www.arduino.cc).

The needs of Matthieu meet the two key issues suggested in [6] to be of primary importance, regarding the efficiency of the scan: (a) locating the target item; and (b) getting to the target item and selecting it. The first issue is affected by the appearance of the scan-items (e.g. dimensions, color, boldness, transparency etc.) while the second issue deals with the method of scan and the optimal arrangement of the items. The Information Communication Technology -Internet on TV, Ambient Intelligence, etc.- raise again needs to news services. There are technologies available at low cost.

This paper will describe how the SOKEYTO platform permits to design the Matthieu's scanning system taking into account both the issues of the user centered design step and first end-user trials. Then quantitative result about utility, utility and user satisfaction will be discussed.

2 Architecture of the Matthieu's Scanning System

The designed assistive technology (AT) consists of Matthieu's scanning system, a switch (See Fig. 1 b) and an Arduino box (See Fig. 1 c).

The SOftware KEYboard Toolkit (SOKEYTO v2) [7] has been used to design Matthieu's scanning system. This platform enables to design virtual keyboards for communication, environment control command, computer application like Internet or audio message linked to a key. This platform also permits to choose the type of interaction -pointing, scanning and its settings -and offer highly reconfigurable options to adapt the scanning system to the abilities of the user. All these functionalities have been used. Pictogram characteristics can be edited: color, pictogram representation, form, text and/or audio description and size as recommended by [6]. The Matthieu's scanning system exchanges with others Windows applications -like the SAPI5 component to control the Text-To-Speech (TTS) Synthesis- and the Arduino electronics prototyping platform through the through the Ivy middleware [9]. Ivy is language-independent and allows to prototype rapidly and easily multimodal systems by exchanging text messages.

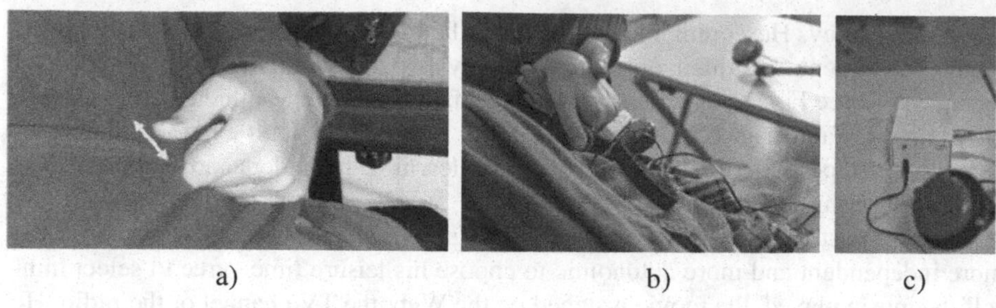

a) b) c)

Fig. 1. a) Matthieu's thumb movement, b) Matthieu's switch position, c) Switch on/off

3 Arduino Uno Box

The hardware part is composed of an Arduino Uno board. This board embeds a switch in order to simulate mouse clicks and two leds. The first one stands for click feedback. The second one is an InfraRed (IR) emitter to control home automation or other stuff (like control TV, radio ...). Once a double click is received from the switch, the Arduino Uno board sends data to the PC in order to control the scanning system. Finally, the board is able to receive and send IR commands from the PC (several protocols are implemented such as NEC, Sony, RC5 and raw mode). We made the choice of a low cost technology to design our scanning system. The price is around fifty Euros.

4 User Centered Design Method

The characteristics (pictographic representation, interaction techniques, and sound feedback) have been iteratively defined with close collaboration with the therapists and the family.

We conducted a participatory design process [9,10] during six months with Matthieu. Many adaptations of the design cycle were necessary. Matthieu was personally involved to implement the "Do-It-Yourself Assistive Technology" [4]. Hence, we have proposed an approach based on high-fidelity iterative prototypes allowing both to test the design of the Matthieu's AT and to identify the interaction capabilities and needs. To maximize experience feedbacks with a minimal cost implementation, we initially used technologies "off the shelf" in particular for the hardware part. This step was very important in the definition and the criticality of the offered services.

4.1 Pictograms

The Matthieu's scanning system consists of 51 metaphoric pictograms. There are structured into two levels. Eight pictograms compose the first level (See Fig. 2 a) corresponding to TV channel, Internet movie, leisure and game, music, communication, phone call, and environment control. The stop pictogram interrupts the scanning.

The other 43 pictogram corresponds to an action (for instance, selecting a pictogram to play a message). The left arrow pictogram (See Fig. 2 c) represents the backward to the first level of the scanning system. The current pictogram size is width = 132 pixels and height = 132 pixels. The visual pictogram accessibility is modifiable by adjusting the size. It is wide because the patient is visually impaired: consequently he has also difficulty focusing his eyes on the screen.

4.2 Validation Command

A switch is hooked on the thumb's Matthieu. Tests with a single pressure on the switch were conducted without success. In consequence, we have defined the double pressure on the switch as the validation click (400 ms). This double pressure is chosen to keep the current principle of communication (two movements of thumb to say "yes").

4.3 Scanning Strategy

The scanning is firstly performed row by row; when a row is selected, the scanning is then performed column by column. The columns are scanned only once: this option is defined to avoid cognitive overload.

The Fig. 2 a and Fig. 2 b show the visual feedback implemented. The current row scanning is identified by a red border around all pictograms (See Fig. 2 a). The current column scanning is marked by a red border around the item (See Fig. 2 b). The scanning returns in row mode if there is no selected column during a first row scanning or if a column has been selected. This setting was specific for Matthieu to minimize the number of validation in the case he does a row error. The Fig. 2 c illustrates the pictograms of the communication theme.

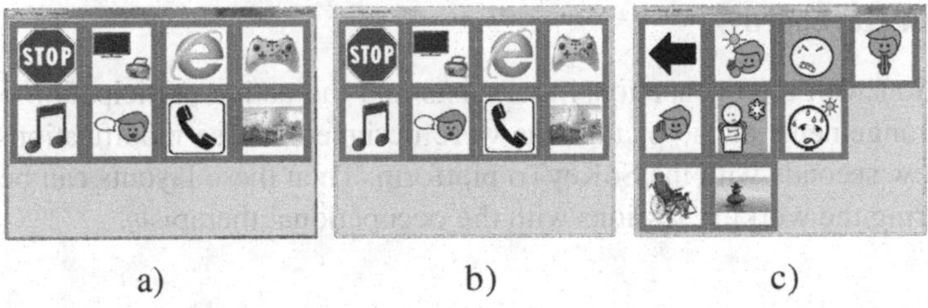

Fig. 2. a) First level, row mode, b) First level, column mode, c) Second level Communication Menu

Different scanning options were available to adapt the scanning to Matthieu's abilities:

- The scanning rate;
- The automatic interruption scanning option; this option is useful when a windows application is running on the screen to avoid disturbance (from instance, sound from the scanning and sound from the movie);

- The keyboard transparency: when this option is true, the keyboard disappears when a windows application is running; the keyboard appears again when the user clicks somewhere in the scanning system area.

4.4 Vocal Feedback

An oral message description is associated to each pictogram; this message could be easily modified with the SOKEYTO environment

5 Trial Effects on the Iterative Design

5.1 Vocal Feedback

Several options of pictogram reading were specially defined to address Matthieu's needs. This setting was designed to allow Matthieu to acquire the mental representation of the interactive system layout. The TTS plays all the messages of a row of pictograms. Then if a row is selected, the TTS plays pictogram per pictogram. If Matthieu selects the pictogram the TTS repeat it as a vocal validation feedback.

5.2 Invisible Scanning System

For instance, the validation of an Internet movie automatically generates an interruption of the scanning system. This option allows the movie in full screen and put the scanning system transparent. This option is essential to avoid disturbances between the TTS sound and the movie sound.

5.3 Layout Keyboard

In collaboration with the occupational therapists and the active participation of Matthieu new arrangements of the pictograms were designed. These modifications could be made in few seconds with the SoKeyTo platform. Then these layouts can be tested right now during the working sessions with the occupational therapists.

6 Post Questionnaire about Matthieu Interactive System

The Matthieu's system was used during two months. During these two months a lot of redesigns have made to meet the needs and the abilities of Matthieu. Three persons have answered to the questionnaire (see Table 1): Matthieu and two members of his family who taught him the use of the system.

Table 1. Answers of post questionnaire

Criteria	Scale	Comments
Utility	Quite useful	Scanning adjustments were needed as well as the timer of the double click validation
Transparency	Quite useful	Allows watching movies in full screen and the Matthieu's interactive system disappears
Vocal restitution	Significant	Matthieu listened more than he watched the screen (partially visually impairment and head position)
Ease of memorization	Neutral	Need more time to learn the layout due to visual difficulties
Pictograms	Strongly affordance	This feature was highly-appreciated to define several semantic blocks of keys.

Matthieu and his family have strongly appreciated the possibility of quickly adapting the interactive system. This design has demonstrated the needs to have good representation of pictograms. The vocal restitution of the pictogram made easier the training of the Matthieu interactive system.

7 Discussion and Conclusion

The iterative design cycle has to be adapted for our study. We had to make very many cycles between a state of the prototype and a test phase. The trials have often been partial. They often concern one dimension of the interaction: feedback, scanning, pictogram arrangement and representation, double click definition, … because only one scanning system setting is unsuitable for the end-user. These fine settings have needed a close collaboration between the designers and the therapist team to schedule the design and test priorities. These difficulties must be considered within the deployment of a user centered method and the Do-It-Yourself Assistive Technology [4].

Our user centered approach will be deployed in order to be tested in the framework of the design of assistive technologies for Locked-In-Syndrome subjects.

References

1. Ghedira, S., Pino, P., Bourhis, G.: Conception and experimentation of a communication device with adaptive scanning. ACM Trans. Access. Comput. 1(3), Article 14 (2009)
2. Steriadis, C.E., Constantinou, P.: Designing Human-Computer Interfaces for Quadriplegic People. ACM Transactions on Computer-Human Interaction 10(2), 87–118 (2003)
3. Niemeijer, D.: In memoriam of Bérard, C.: Striving for effort reduction through on-screen keyboard word prediction. In: Assistive Technology: from Virtuality to Reality - 8th European Conference for the Advancement of Assistive Technology in Europe (AAATE 2005), Lille, France (2005)
4. Hurst, A., Tobias, J.: Empowering Individuals with Do-It-Yourself Assistive Technology. In: ACM SIGCHI Conf. on Computers and Accessibility (ASSETS 2011), pp. 11–18. ACM, New York (2011)
5. Boujrad, A., Jouffrais, C., Truillet, P., Marque, P.: Conception d'un outil de contrôle et de communication pour personnes tétraplégiques. In: IHM 2010, Luxembourg, pp. 117–120 (2010)
6. Shein, F.: A prototype expert system for the design of a visual keyboard. In: Proceedings of the Third International Conference on Rehabilitation Engineering, Montreal, pp. 382–383 (1988)
7. Sauzin, D., Vella, F., Vigouroux, N.: SOKEYTO v2: a toolkit for designing and evaluating virtual keyboards (poster). In: European Conference for the Advancement of Assistive Technology in Europe (AAATE 2013), Vilamoura, Portugal, vol. 33, pp. 939–945. IOS Press (2013)
8. Buisson, M., Bustico, A., Chatty, S., Colon, F.-R., Jestin, Y., Maury, S., Martz, C., Truillet, P.: Ivy: Un bus logiciel au service du développement de prototypes de systèmes interactifs. In: Interaction Homme-Machine (IHM 2002), Poitiers, pp. 223–226. ACM Press (2002)
9. ISO/TR 16982:2002 Ergonomics of Human-System Interaction – Usability Methods Supporting Human-Centred Design, Switzerland (2002)
10. Mackay, W.E.: Educating Multi-Disciplinary Design Teams. In: Proc. of Tales of the Disappearing Computer, Santorini, Greece, pp. 105–118 (2003)

Semantic Keyboard: Fast Movements between Keys of a Soft Keyboard

Mathieu Raynal[1], I. Scott MacKenzie[2], and Bruno Merlin[3]

[1] IRIT – ELIPSE Team, University of Toulouse, Toulouse, France
mathieu.raynal@irit.fr
[2] Department of Electrical Engineering & Computer Science, York University, Toronto, Canada
mack@cse.yorku.ca
[3] Universidade Federal do Pará, Cametá, Brasil
brunomerlin@ufpa.br

Abstract. In this paper we describe Semantic Keyboard: a soft keyboard augmented by semantic pointing. The cursor crosses faster over keys containing low-probability letters (considering the prefix already entered). This optimization reduces the movement of the pointer by 60%, and increases the text entry speed by 13.5% after the first character in a word. Accuracy is equivalent to a regular soft keyboard.

Keywords: Soft Keyboard, Text Entry, Character Prediction.

1 Introduction

Highly used since the emergence of mobile phones with touch screens, soft keyboards were originally designed to enable people with motor disabilities to access computers. The basic soft keyboard imitates a physical keyboard. Motor-disabled people use it with an adapted pointing device. However, the use of a single pointer slows text input. In addition, repetitive movements between keys tire the user quickly.

To solve these problems, several solutions have been explored. Many take advantage of letter co-occurrence (aka digram) statistics in the language. They typically lead to a static or dynamic reorganization of the keyboard or other improvements considering co-occurrence. A well known technique is to provide a completion list [2],[7] to reduce the number of actions to input a word. However, every solution is a compromise: New layouts are hard to learn; dynamic changes increase cognitive load and completion lists are often used inefficiently.

Our goal is to dynamically exploit language statistics to improve typing performance without adding visual changes that disturb the user. The aim is to reduce key pointing time while maintaining the accuracy of pointing. Our system is useful when using a soft keyboard with any device that manipulates a pointer on the screen. Consequently, our main end users are motor-impaired persons. In this report, we present our system and an initial evaluation with able-bodied users which confirms our hypothesis. A use-case with end users is ongoing; those results will be presented in a final report.

K. Miesenberger et al. (Eds.): ICCHP 2014, Part II, LNCS 8548, pp. 195–202, 2014.

2 Use of Character Prediction Systems

Entering text with a standard soft keyboard through a single pointing device corresponds to pointing to keys one by one. The task can be modeled by Fitts' law [4]. Toward this, two solutions are possible to increase text input speed: reducing the distance between the keys or expanding the keys.

The first solution involves switching the layout to reduce the distance between the most frequent co-occurrences [6],[9],[13]. However, a new letter arrangement imposes a learning period which often discourages the user. Therefore, this solution is rarely used.

Also, while this solution works well for common co-occurrences, it is less effective for infrequent co-occurrences. To improve optimization whatever the input letter, it is important use a dynamic prediction system. In 80% of cases, the desired letter is among the four most probable to be typed [10]. This statistic increases as the length of the prefix increases: Likely letters are more numerous and therefore more predictable. Two strategies simplify pointing for the most probable letters. The first is to dynamically change the letter arrangement (key position) and size during input [1],[8]. The second is to introduce additional keys near the pointer [10] that contain the most likely letters.

However, these solutions have limits: Dynamic changes in the layout induce a cognitive cost. It is tiring for the user and it adversely impacts performance. So, in the end, input speed is not improved with these keyboards. Similarly, when new GUI elements appear, visual scanning time increases and text input speed is reduced.

Consequently, to benefit from prediction without changing the appearance of the standard keyboard, we propose to dynamically modify the pointer speed according to the probability of typing the crossed-over keys.

3 Semantic Keyboard

3.1 Principle

Our Semantic Keyboard is based on the paradigm of semantic pointing [3]: that is, separating the visual space and motor space. The interface retains the same visual appearance. However, every object occupies a different area in the motor space. The size of the area depends on the object's importance in the interaction context. In our Semantic Keyboard, visual space is the soft keyboard and motor space is represented through the pointing device. Keys bearing letters with low probability get less emphasis in the motor space: The pointer will quickly cross over them. Conversely, keys bearing letters with high probability get more emphasis in the motor space: The cursor dwells longer.

Specifically, the idea is to accelerate the cursor when it passes over keys displaying letters with low probability and, reciprocally, to lower the cursor velocity when passing over keys containing letters with high probability. Thus, the user should more quickly access letters of interest while still maintaining the possibility of inputting other letters. But, at the same time, the visual aspect of the keyboard remains unchanged.

3.2 Implementation

Our Semantic Keyboard uses a character prediction system based on a lexical tree [2]. When the user enters a prefix, the prediction system classifies letters by their probability of occurrence and then associates an enlargement coefficient with each key. With the enlargement coefficient, the pointer will accelerate or slow down.

Each key K_i has a coefficient C_i between 1 and N. N is the maximum value of acceleration. C_i is calculated from the character frequency F_i of the key K_i. The character frequency F_i is calculated from the prefix already entered:

$$C_i = F_i \times N \text{ and } \sum_{i=1}^{NB} F_i = 1, \text{with } NB \text{ the number of keys} \quad (1)$$

When the pointer passes over the keyboard, it may cross neighboring keys with different probabilities. To avoid dramatic speed variations, the acceleration coefficient applied to the pointer depends on the position of the pointer on the key. If the pointer is close to another key, the coefficient is calculated according to the coefficient of the closest keys and the distance separating the center of neighboring keys and the pointer. D_i is the distance between the pointer position and the center of the nearest key. W_i is the size of the key:

$$C = \begin{cases} C_i & \text{if } D_i < MAX \\ \frac{\sum_{j=1}^{NB\_Keys} D_j \times C_j}{\sum_{j=1}^{NB\_Keys} D_j} & \end{cases} \quad (2)$$

NB_Keys is the number of the nearest keys included in the calculation and MAX the maximum distance from the center of the key on which the coefficient remains unchanged. After this maximum distance, the coefficient is weighted by the coefficients of nearby keys.

Thanks to this coefficient, the pointer position is:

$$P = P_{old} + ((P_{new} - P_{old}) \times C \times Speed) \quad (3)$$

P_{old} is the old pointer position and P_{new} is the new one before the addition of the acceleration.

After each character input, the probabilities of character occurrence are recalculated and keys are resized (in the motor space).

4 Method

4.1 Hypothesis

To test our Semantic Keyboard, we conducted an experiment comparing the Semantic Keyboard with a typical AZERTY keyboard. The two main hypotheses were that semantic pointing would decrease the distance travelled by the cursor of the pointing device and lightly improve user performance. We define performance as text input speed and accuracy.

4.2 Participants

Twelve able-bodied participants, two females and ten males, took part in the experiment. They ranged in age from 21 to 44 ($mean = 28.6, SD = 6.15$). All were volunteers, right-handers, and computer specialists. All participants were regular users of desktop computers and were acquainted with pointing devices.

4.3 Apparatus

The experiment was conducted using a Dell laptop with 2.5 GHz speed and the Microsoft Windows 7 operating system. Participants interacted with the soft keyboard through a mouse. Keyboard layouts were restricted to the 26 characters of the Latin alphabet and the space bar. The soft keyboard was developed in Java SE 6.

4.4 Procedure

Participants entered 21 sentences with the both keyboards. They were instructed to enter the sentences as quickly as possible. The sentence to copy was presented on a line, and the text input by the participant appeared on the line below. Text entry errors were not displayed on the screen. Instead, there was visual and auditory feedback signaling the error. The cursor did not move until the participant entered the correct character. At the end of each sentence, participants hit the Space bar. After the experiment, participants were asked to complete a questionnaire soliciting demographic information and impressions on the both keyboards.

4.5 Design

A repeated-measures design was used. There was a single factor, keyboard, with two levels: AZERTY and Semantic Keyboard. Participants were randomly assigned to two groups of six. In the first group, participants began with the AZERTY keyboard and ended with the Semantic Keyboard. The order was counterbalanced by groups. For each keyboard, participants entered 21 sentences. The sentences were chosen randomly from a set of 50.

The sentences contained common words and were statistically representative of the participants' language, which was French (respecting the frequency of bigrams and trigrams). The dependant variables were the distance travelled by the cursor, text entry speed, and accuracy.

5 Results and Discussion

A statistical analysis showed that the order in which the exercises were performed had no impact on the results ($F_{1,10} = 0.059$, $p = .81$). Thus, counterbalancing had the desired effect.

5.1 Distance

The distance covered by the pointer in the motor space (in pixels) was computed for both keyboards. The results show that distance was 60% less with the Semantic Keyboard than with the AZERTY keyboard. The mean distance covered by the pointer to point to a key was 225 pixels with AZERTY compared to 90 pixels with the Semantic Keyboard. The difference was statistically significant ($F_{1,10} = 2721.5$, $p < .001$).

5.2 Entry Speed

Entry speed was computed two ways. First, we computed the text entry speed per sentence. This was calculated by dividing the length of the sentence (including the space character between words and at the end of a sentence) by the time (in seconds) to enter this sentence. Finally, this speed in characters per second (cps) is multiplied by sixty and divided by five to obtain the speed in words per minute (wpm) [12].

The input speed was almost equivalent for the two keyboards: 10.30 wpm versus 10.43 wpm ($F_{1,10} = 0.223$, $p = .65$). Interviews with participants after the experiment helped to identify potential issues: Several participants described being confused by the Semantic Keyboard at the beginning of words. Indeed, the prediction system predicts the probability of each character after a prefix is already entered. Thus, for the first character, Semantic keyboard offers no acceleration factor, which bothered some participants.

To verify this, entry speed was recalculated taking into account only the words. Entry time was calculated between the first character of the word and pressing the Space bar at the end of the word. The number of characters here is the length of the word. With this method of calculation, the entry speed was 13.10 wpm for the Semantic keyboard. This is 14% higher than the rate of 11.54 for the AZERTY keyboard. The difference was statistically significant ($F_{1,10} = 21.12$, $p = .005$).

The average word entry speed shows that Semantic Keyboard works well when the system predicted the most likely characters. Figure 1 shows the entry speed by sentence. The effect of the Semantic Keyboard is immediate. The Semantic Keyboard does not require learning, even if the improvement grows lightly during the first sentences.

5.3 Accuracy

During entry, when the current character differed from the expected character, an error was recorded. The error rate was obtained by dividing the number of errors by the number of characters. The number of errors was computed using the MSD method [5],[11]. The error rate was 1.3% for the Semantic Keyboard and 0.95% with the AZERTY keyboard. This difference was not significant ($F_{1,10} = 4.204$, $p = .065$). Overall, error rates were below 3% which is generally acceptable for text input.

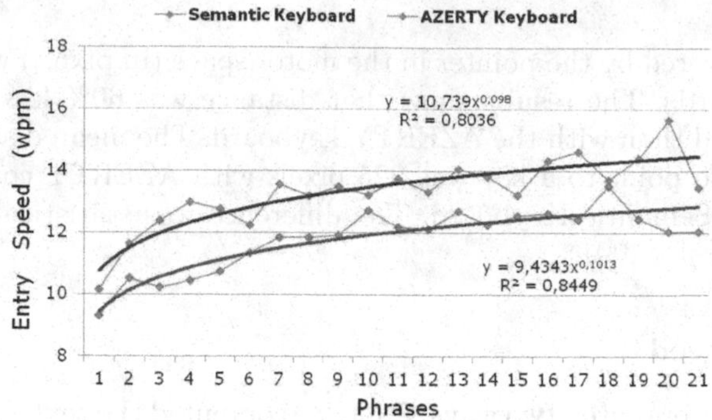

Fig. 1. Entry speed by keyboard and phrases

5.4 User Satisfaction

Responses were rated on a 7-point Likert scale, with 1 the least favorable response and 7 most favorable. The questionnaire solicited responses about comfort, fatigue, effort, accuracy and speed perception for the both keyboard (see Fig. 2).

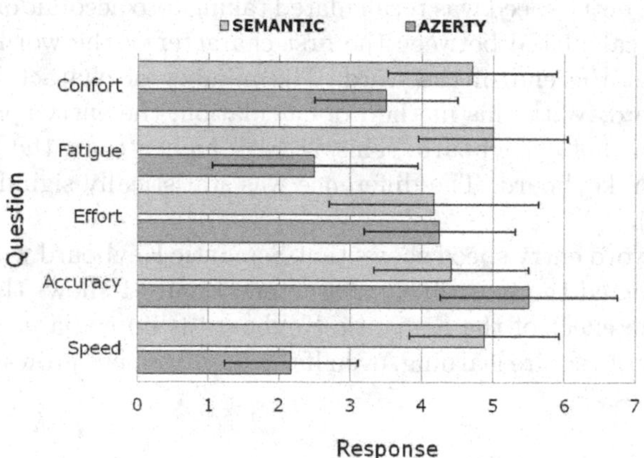

Fig. 2. Results of the questionnaire. A response of 7 is most-favorable, and 1 least-favorable.

The opinion of participants corroborates the quantitative results. We observed the following: On the one hand, the Semantic Keyboard is faster than the AZERTY keyboard. On the other hand, the AZERTY keyboard is more accurate than the Semantic Keyboard. Another important finding is that participants rated the Semantic Keyboard less tiring than the AZERTY keyboard ("Fatigue" in Fig. 2). This information is important because motor-impaired users, who are often forced to use a soft keyboard, often suffer from fatigue during text input.

6 Case Study with Motor-Disabled Person

To verify the relevance of these initial results for the target population, we conducted a case study with a motor disabled person suffering from muscular dystrophy. The subject conducted the same experiment as the able-bodied participants but with fewer phrases to copy because of anticipated fatigue.

We draw two conclusions from the case study: First, the participant had more difficulty to handle the mouse pointer. As a result, he traveled more distance with the mouse pointer to type a word: With AZERTY keyboard, the movement distance was 35% less for able-bodied persons than the motor-disabled person (225 pixels versus 346). Therefore, he entered text slower than the able-bodied participants (6.58 wpm versus 11.54 wpm).

The other important observation is that the results obtained in the first experiment were confirmed in the case study. Indeed, the distance travelled by the pointer decreases 30% using Semantic Keyboard (244 pixels). This decrease causes an increase of the text input speed of 15%. The speed with the Semantic Keyboard was 7.59 wpm and with the regular keyboard 6.58 wpm.

7 Conclusion

The Semantic Keyboard presents a technique that uses character prediction to alter the cursor speed without changing the appearance of the keyboard. It has the advantage of character prediction without disturbing the user. The technique reduces the distance covered by the cursor but does not reduce the input time. In an experiment, the entry speed was about 14% higher after the first character in a word for the Semantic Keyboard compared to an AZERTY keyboard.

The experiment showed that the semantic pointing could work well in concert with a robust character prediction system. Since the Semantic Keyboard can be effective for text input, we expect to improve the prediction system so it can also be used at the beginning of the word. As well, the system should consider accents and punctuation in order to offer a comprehensive keyboard suitable for everyday tasks.

References

1. Aulagner, G., François, R., Martin, B., Michel, D., Raynal, M.: Floodkey: Increasing software keyboard keys by reducing needless ones without occultation. In: Proc. ACS 2010, pp. 412–417. WSEAS (2010)
2. Badr, G., Raynal, M.: Evaluation of wordTree system with motor disabled users. In: Miesenberger, K., Klaus, J., Zagler, W., Karshmer, A. (eds.) ICCHP 2010, Part II. LNCS, vol. 6180, pp. 104–111. Springer, Heidelberg (2010)

3. Blanch, R., Guiard, Y., Beaudouin-Lafon, M.: Semantic pointing: Improving target acquisition with control-display ratio adaptation. In: Proc. CHI 2004, pp. 519–526. ACM (2004)
4. Fitts, P.M.: The information capacity of the human motor system in controlling the amplitude of movement. Journal of Experimental Psychology 74, 381–391 (1954)
5. Levenshtein, V.: Binary codes capable of correcting deletions, insertions and reversals. Soviet Physics Doklady 10, 707 (1966)
6. MacKenzie, I.S., Zhang, S.X.: The design and evaluation of a high-performance soft keyboard. In: Proc. CHI 1999, pp. 25–31. ACM (1999)
7. Masui, T.: An efficient text input method for pen-based computers. In: Proc. CHI 1998, pp. 328–335. ACM (1998)
8. Merlin, B., Raynal, M.: Evaluation of SpreadKey system with motor impaired users. In: Miesenberger, K., Klaus, J., Zagler, W., Karshmer, A. (eds.) ICCHP 2010, Part II. LNCS, vol. 6180, pp. 112–119. Springer, Heidelberg (2010)
9. Raynal, M., Vigouroux, N.: Genetic algorithm to generate optimized soft keyboard. In: Extended Abstracts Proc. CHI 2005, pp. 1729–1732. ACM (2005)
10. Raynal, M., Vigouroux, N.: KeyGlasses: Semi-transparent keys to optimize text input on virtual keyboard. In: Proc. AAATE 2005, pp. 713–717. IOS Press (2005)
11. Soukoreff, R.W., MacKenzie, I.S.: Measuring errors in text entry tasks: An application of the Levenshtein string distance statistic. In: Extended Abstracts Proc. CHI 2001, pp. 319–320. ACM (2001)
12. Yamada, H.: A historical study of typewriters and typing methods, from the position of planning Japanese parallels. Journal of Information Processing 2, 175–202 (1980)
13. Zhai, S., Hunter, M., Smith, B.A.: The Metropolis keyboard: An exploration of quantitative techniques for virtual keyboard design. In: Proc. UIST 2000, pp. 119–128. ACM (2000)

The Application of Computerized Chinese Handwriting Assessment Tool to Children with Cerebral Palsy

Hui-Shan Lo[1], Chia-Ling Chen[2], Hsieh-Ching Chen[3], I-hsuan Shen[4], and Cecilia W.P. Li-Tzang[5]

[1] Department of Special Education, National Taiwan Normal University, Taipei, Taiwan
80209003e@ntnu.edu.tw

[2] Department of Physical Medicine and Rehabilitation, Chang Gung Memorial Hospital, Taoyuan County, Taiwan
clingchen@gmail.com

[3] Department of Industrial Engineering and Management, National Taipei University of Technology, Taipei, Taiwan
imhcchen@ntut.edu.tw

[4] Graduate Institute and Department of Occupational Therapy, Chang Gung University, Kwei-Shan Tao-Yuan, Taiwan
shenih@mail.cgu.edu.tw

[5] Department of Rehabilitation Sciences, The Hong Kong Polytechnic University Hung Hom, Kowloon, Hong Kong SAR, China
Cecilia.Li@inet.polyu.edu.hk

Abstract. The purpose of this research is to assess Chinese handwriting skills of children with cerebral palsy (CP) by computerized tool. This tool can provide immediate information about children's handwriting process and products. The parameters of process record the spatial and temporal characteristics of handwriting, which including the total writing time, on-paper time, in-air time, the ratio, and writing speed. The parameter of production is accuracy of handwriting. 14 children with CP and 13 typically developing children participated in this study. The results indicated that children with CP had significantly lower accuracy rate in Chinese handwriting. In addition, children with CP also demonstrated longer on-paper time and in-air time in writing Chinese. Further studies will focus on identifying clinical factors which result in the handwriting difficulties of children with CP.

Keywords: Cerebral palsy, Handwriting.

1 Introduction

Cerebral palsy (CP) describes a group of disorders of the development of movement and posture, causing activity limitation, that are attributed to non-progressive disturbances that occurred in the developing fetal or infant brain [1]. Spastic CP is the most common type, accounting for 70% to 85% of all CP cases [2]. Spastic CP is further classified into diplegic, hemiplegic, quadriplegic, and monoplegic subtypes based on

K. Miesenberger et al. (Eds.): ICCHP 2014, Part II, LNCS 8548, pp. 203–209, 2014.

the topographic distribution of the affected areas of the body [2]. The motor disorders of CP are often accompanied by disturbances of sensation, perception, cognition, communication, and behavior, by epilepsy, and by secondary musculoskeletal problems [3]. Furthermore, the accompanied disturbances in children with CP further influence handwriting functions of the affected child.

Handwriting is an important occupational activity for children. Children spend up 31%~60% of total school time on fine motor activities, of which 85% is paper-and-pencil tasks [4]. Handwriting proficiency is an essential activity required for children's success and participation in school, which enables the expression, recording, and transmission of ideas of students throughout their educational career [5].

Children with CP who have good function on upper extremity are generally expected to learn to write alongside their peers. A previous study indicated that parents and teacher report 69-75% of children with CP have handwriting problems [6]. Greatest difficulty was reported with the ability to write from dictation, or to maintain neatness over long periods of time or at speed [6]. Previous studies on handwriting in children have been performed more frequently on healthy children, but studies of CP children with handwriting problems are limited and few studies examine handwriting problems in detail.

Many computer-assisted handwriting assessment systems have been developed [7] [8]. The computerized handwriting assessment system provides objective temporal and spatial measures of handwriting performance, and the kinematic analysis of writing provides the description of the characteristics of handwriting [9,10,11,12]. However, there are few studies to investigate the effectiveness of computerized handwriting evaluation tool applied in children with CP. The aims of this study were to compare handwriting performance in children with CP and children without CP by computerized tool.

2 Experiment Method

2.1 Participants

The study recruited 14 children with CP (6 male, 8 female) and 13 typically developing children of similar age (7 male, 6 female). They were grade 2 and grade 3. The children with CP were recruited from a general hospital in Taoyuan County in Taiwan, and the typically developed children were recruited from elementary school in the same area. Table 1 demonstrates the demographic data of children with and without CP. Among all participants, 11 children were diagnosed with diplegia type and 3 were diagnosed with hemiplegia type. The severity of the gross motor disturbance in CP was classified by using the Gross Motor Function Classification System (GMFCS) [13]. The gross motor function of children with CP were categorized as GMFCS level I (n=8), II (n=6) and III (n=1). The severity of the upper extremity disturbance in CP was classified using Manual Ability Classification System (MACS) [14]. The function of upper extremity to writing of children with CP were categorized MACS level I (n=9) and II (n=5), which can manipulate most activities independently.

Table 1. Demographic data of children with and without CP

	CP (N=14)	without CP (N=13)
Gender: male	6(42.9%)	7 (53.7%)
Writing hand: right hand	9(64.3%)	13(100%)
CP type		
Hemiplegic	8(57.1%)	
Diplegic	3(42.9%)	
GMFCS Level		
Level I	8(57.1%)	
Level II	6(42.8%)	
Level III	1(0.1%)	
MACS Level		
Level I	9(64.3%)	
Level II	5(35.7%)	

2.2 Instrument

In this study, we used the Chinese Handwriting Assessment Tool (CHAT), which be developed by the research team of the Hong Kong Polytechnic University [15]. The CHAT evaluates both the speed and the legibility in terms of sharpness, tidiness, stroke sequence, missing strokes, extra strokes, handwriting speed, in-air time and ground time during writing.

It consisted of a digitized writing board (WACOM Intuos4 digitizer) to be used with a ball pen, which can capture the handwriting data such as sequence of strokes and pressure exerted on the writing board while a user is writing on the grid paper. The template of CHAT consisted of 90 common Chinese characters. The characters were based on structural forms and stroke units. All the structural forms in Chinese characters were included in the 90 characters. The 90 characters were displayed in 9 columns of 10 characters. The display sequence of the columns was randomized each time when the system was operated [15].

2.3 Procedure

Each participant was assessed individually in a quiet evaluation room. The participants were instructed to copy the displayed characters with a pen on a piece of paper with a 9X10 grid pasted on the writing board of the CHAT system. Each grid size is 1.5cm X 1.5cm. The participants were asked to copy according the sequence of target characters shown on the computer screen. The participants copied the text on the test sheet and were told to write in their most nature manner instead of their fastest speed. In addition, they were asked not to correct their writing as soon as they wrote.

2.4 Measurement Parameters

In this study, we measure six parameters to assess students' handwriting process and products. The parameters of handwriting process include the total time of writing, on-paper time, in-air time, the ratio, and the speed. The total time, in-air time and on-paper time, were recorded in second. The parameter of final writing product is accuracy. Accuracy is percentage of correctly written characters in 90 characters.

The definitions of above parameters are:

- Accuracy: number of correctly written characters/ 90 characters
- Writing speed: the number of character/ minute
- Total writing time: the length of time from the first character to the last character
- On-paper time: the length of time when the pen touches tablet
- In-air time: the total writing time minus on-paper time
- Ratio: the ratio of in-air time/ on-paper time

3 Result

Table 2 demonstrates the differences between the two groups in copying Chinese characters. Children with CP demonstrated significantly lower accuracy rate than children without CP. In the study, children without CP could copy the target characters almost correctly (99.4%), but the children with CP only have 97.4% correct rate. The common errors include adding or missing a stroke, or wrong radical of the Chinese.

Table 2 also demonstrated that the children spend more on-paper time, in-air time and total writing time than children without CP. The children wrote less character in one minute than children without CP. The results of this study showed that there was no significant difference in ratio between children with and without CP.

Table 2. The Chinese handwriting performance of children with CP and without CP

	CP(N=14) (mean±S.D.)	without CP(N=13) (mean±S.D.)	*p*
Accuracy (%)	97.4±1.9	99.4%±0.7	0.002**
Writing speed (character/min)	5.7±2.9	7.9±2.0	0.032*
Total writing time (sec)	1144.7±420.2	722.1±172.1	0.002**
On-paper time (sec)	329.9±118.5	242.4±66.1	0.03*
In-air time (sec)	814.9±331.3	479.7±125.1	0.002**
ratio	2.6±0.89	2.0±0.42	0.07

* p<.05; ** p<.01

The handwriting products of children with CP and without CP were respectively shown in figure 1 and figure 2. The children with CP had demonstrated worse accuracy and poor legibility than children without CP. In the handwriting sample of children with CP, there were more characters out of the grid, and the legibility were poor than children with-out CP.

Fig. 1. Handwriting product of children with CP

Fig. 2. Handwriting product of children without CP

4 Discussion

In summary, the major difference between two groups was found in accuracy, writing speed, total writing time, on-paper time and in-air time. Compared with previous research, that children with CP wrote significantly less accurate and spent more writing time than their peers was also shown in Li-Tsang's study [15]. The reason may due to that the children with CP had poor visual perceptual skills, poor motor control and visual-motor integration skills which result in writing slowly and incorrectly [16] [17].

According to the study result, the children with CP had slower writing speed than children without CP. The result differed from the Bumin & Kavak's research [18], but similar to Li-Tsang's study. According to Bumin & Kavak's research [18], the writing rate of children with hemipleagia was not significant lower than their peers. The reason may result from the different writing task. In Bumin & Kavak's study, the children were asked to copy English word in 2.5 minutes [18]. However, in our study, the children were asked to write 90 Chinese characters continuously and recorded the total time of writing whole 90 Chinese characters. Because of the muscle strength and endurance of children with CP were poor, we can found the children with CP maintain writing speed at the beginning, but write slower and slower over time.

According to the study result, the children with CP did not have grater ratio than children without CP. The result is different form Li-Tsang's study [15]. In Li-Tsang's study, the subjects with physical disabilities had grater ratio than the typical subjects in writing task. The reason may result from the different diagnosis of participants. In Li-Tsang's study [15], most of subjects were musculoskeletal problems and vascular diseases, whose upper extremity function were not poor than typical students. The students with physical disabilities may did not need to spend more on-paper time when copying target characters. However, in our study, children with CP not only spent more in-air time but also spent more on-paper time in copying target characters. The results indicated that the children with CP may need to spend the same effort to control motor of hand and to processing the visual cues.

Children with CP who have good function on upper extremity are generally expected to learn to write alongside their peers. Nevertheless, children with CP are not only had motor impairment but also had deficits of sensation, perception and cognition. The computerized tool was able to record the real time handwriting performance of pupil with and without writing difficulties. The tool provided the temporal and spatial characteristics of children's handwriting for assisting teachers identify children's writing problems. Further studies will focus on identifying clinical factors which result in the handwriting difficulties of children with CP.

References

1. Bax, M.C., Flodmark, O., Tydeman, C.: Definition and classification of cerebral palsy. From syndrome toward disease. Dev. Med. Child. Neurol. Suppl. 109, 39–41 (2007)

2. Jones, M.W., Morgan, E., Shelton, J.E., Thorogood, C.: Cerebral palsy: introduction and diagnosis (part I). J. Pediatr. Health Care 21(3), 146–152 (2007)
3. Rosenbloom, L.: Definition and classification of cerebral palsy. Definition, classification, and the clinician. Dev. Med. Child Neurol. Suppl. 109, 43 (2007)
4. McHale, K., Cermak, S.A.: Fine motor activities in elementary school: preliminary findings and provisional implications for children with fine motor problems. Am. J. Occup. Ther. 46(10), 898–903 (1992)
5. Engel-Yeger, B., Nagauker-Yanuv, L., Rosenblum, S.: Handwriting performance, self-reports, and perceived self-efficacy among children with dysgraphia. Am. J. Occup. Ther. 63(2), 182–192 (2009)
6. DuBois, L., Klemm, A., Murchland, S., Ozols, A.: Handwriting of children who have hemiplegia: A profile of abilities in children aged 8-13 years from a parent and teacher survey. Australian Occupational Therapy Journal 51(2), 89–98 (2004)
7. Rosenblum, S., Chevion, D., Weiss, P.L.: Using data visualization and signal processing to characterize the handwriting process. Pediatr Rehabil 9(4), 404–417 (2006)
8. Rosenblum, S., Dvorkin, A.Y., Weiss, P.L.: Automatic segmentation as a tool for examining the handwriting process of children with dysgraphic and proficient handwriting. Hum. Mov. Sci. 25(4-5), 608–621 (2006)
9. Khalid, P.I., Yunus, J., Adnan, R.: Extraction of dynamic features from hand drawn data for the identification of children with handwriting difficulty. Res. Dev. Disabil. (2009)
10. Rosenblum, S., Parush, S., Weiss, P.L.: Computerized temporal handwriting characteristics of proficient and non-proficient handwriters. Am. J. Occup. Ther. 57(2), 129–138 (2003)
11. Rosenblum, S., Parush, S., Weiss, P.L.: The In Air phenomenon: Temporal and spatial correlates of the handwriting process. Percept. Mot. Skills 96(3 pt 1), 933–954 (2003)
12. Lam, S.S.T., Au, R.K.C., Leung, H.W.H., Li-Tsang, C.W.P.: Chinese handwriting performance of primary school children with dyslexia. Research in Development disabilities 32, 1745–1756 (2011)
13. Palisano, R., Rosenbaum, P., Walter, S., Russell, D., Wood, E., Galuppi, B.: Development and reliability of a system to classify gross motor function in children with cerebral palsy. Dev. Med. Child. Neurol. 39, 214–223 (1997)
14. Eliasson, A.C., Krumlinde-Sundholm, L., Rosblad, B., Beckung, E., Arner, M., Ohrvall, A.M., Rosenbaum, P.: The Manual Ability Classification System (MACS) for children with cerebral palsy: scale development and evidence of validity and reliability. Dev. Med. Child. Neurol. 48(7), 549–554 (2006)
15. Li-Tsang, C.W.P., Au, R.K.C., Chan, M.H.Y., Chan, L.W.L., Lau, G.M.T., Lo, T.K., Leung, H.W.H.: Handwriting characteristics among secondary students with and without physical disabilities: A study with a computerized tool. Research in Development Disabilities 32(1), 207–216 (2010)
16. Tseng, M.H., Cermak, S.H.: The influence of ergonomic factors and perceptual-motor abilities on handwriting performance. American Journal of Occupational Therapy 47, 919–926 (1993)
17. Tseng, M.H., Chow, S.M.K.: Perceptual-motor function of schoolage children with slow handwriting speed. American Journal of Occupational Therapy 54, 83–88 (2000)
18. Bumin, G., Kavak, S.T.: An investigation of the factors affecting handwriting skill in children with hemiplegic cerebral palsy. Disabil. Rehabil. 32(8), 692–703 (2010)

EyeSchool: An Educational Assistive Technology for People with Disabilities - Passing from Single Actors to Multiple-Actor Environment

Cristina Popescu[1], Nadine Vigouroux[2], Mathieu Muratet[1], Julie Guillot[1], Petra Vlad[1], Frédéric Vella[2], Jawad Hajjam[3], Sylvie Ervé[3], Nathalie Louis[3], Julie Brin[3], Joseph Colineau[4], Thierry Hobé[5], and Loïc Brimant[5]

[1] Grhapes (EA 7287) - INS HEA, 58-60 Avenue des Landes, 92150 Suresnes, France
[2] IRIT - Université Paul Sabatier, 118 route de Narbonne, 31062 Toulouse Cedex 9, France
[3] CENTICH, 51 rue du Vallon, 49000 Angers, France
[4] Thales Research and Technology, Campus Polytechnique, 1 Avenue Augustin Fresnel, 91767 Palaiseau Cedex, France
[5] Synerlog, 9 rue René Hersen, 49240 Avrille, France

Abstract. Since 2005, public policy in France has strongly been encouraging young people with disabilities inclusion within the regular school system. This has found a direct application through technical innovation, intended to help students being more independent within their learning activities. In this context, the purpose of this paper is to underline the manner in which using assistive information and communication technologies may improve the inclusive education for people with disabilities. The case study we present underlines the complexity of the social world into which the use of a precise assistive tool takes it place.

Keywords: Educational Assistive Technology, Notes-taking Tool, Inclusion, Multiple-actor Environment.

1 Introduction

Since 2005, public policy in France has strongly been encouraging young people with disabilities inclusion within the regular school system. This has addressed some new challenges for the "field" actors, as well as transformation within teaching practices. A human support is often needed in order to assist the student. In the same time, the different actors raised questions about the manner in which the educational content management should be improved. A direct application was then found through technical innovation, intended to help students being more independent within their learning activities.

Nonetheless, the paradigm of an average student as the final user of assistive technologies could hardly apply in this case, as students with disabilities have different kind of needs from the non-disabled but also between themselves. Specialised computer programs were for instance developed in order to be used by

K. Miesenberger et al. (Eds.): ICCHP 2014, Part II, LNCS 8548, pp. 210–217, 2014.

specific categories of people: *for people with visual impairments*: Zoomtext, Dolphin, Speakback, Wordread, Zoom-Ex, etc.; and *for people with learning difficulties* ScreenRuler, Medialexie, Speakback, Wordread, Cordial, Antidote, Skippy, etc.

Literature about the manner in which students with disabilities, and in general, people with disabilities are using assistive or "adapted" new technologies also tends to cluster around specific impairments, as visual [1],[4], hearing [7], physical or cognitive ones [3]. We use the term "adapted technologies" in order to designate the mainstream technologies whose uses were adapted to the needs of people with disabilities, for instance the general environment of Windows requiring special settings for people with visual impairments, etc.

Moreover, technologies and more precisely computer programs designed for education could be divided into the pedagogical ones - in general, teachers design exercises for their students, for instance "Langagiciel", "Genex" software, etc. and those encouraging the autonomy of their users - the students choose how to use and organise their contents, for instance the orDYScan ou AUSY projects.

In this context, the purpose of this presentation is to underline the manner in which using assistive information and communication technologies may improve the inclusive education for people with disabilities. We will therefore present a recently device developed for students with visual and hearing impairments and also with dyslexia, dyspraxia and dysphasia. It is also intended to encourage the autonomy of its users. The case study we present below underlines the complexity of the social world into which the use of this precise assistive tool takes it place.

2 Description of EyeSchool Project

The Eyeschool[1] projet is supported by the French Department of Education and is funded by "Fonds national pour la société numérique". This project started in December 2012 with a two years duration. It includes four partners: CENTICH, a specialised centre for technologies for ageing people and for people with disabilities; Thales Group, a major electronic systems company; INS HEA, a specialised institute for the education of people with disabilities and Synerlog, a small company offering digital services.

As mentioned before, the project aims to test a digital notes-taking tool within a large population. It therefore means to encourage the participation of students with disabilities within their education environment. In this way, they may become more autonomous actors within their own notes-writing actions. Four French regions participate to the project. For each of them, one hundred students are expected to test the device during a school year period.

EyeSchool device is intended for three kinds of impairments at once: visual and hearing impairments and "dys" (dyslexia, developmental dyspraxia and dysphasia). All levels of education are covered: primary and secondary school as well as higher education. And these criteria may determine a universal device for people

[1] `http://www.eyeschool.fr/` accessed April 3, 2014.

with different kind of needs, but this will also bring challenges into its making and testing process.

3 The Integrated-Package Description

The EyeSchool package consists of hardware and software components. On the one hand, the hardware part counts on a computer, a webcam and a scanner. This is the main configuration as intended for a large number of users. But there are some other possible combinations like: a computer and an interactive whiteboard or a computer and a MimioCapture device.

On the other hand, the software solution offers multiple functionalities. The final user has the liberty to use them all or online a selection of them. An advanced setting system allows keeping inside the main interface only those functionalities one may consider interesting for him or her personal work.

Therefore, the EyeSchool main functionalities are the following ones: *customising user interface*: font size, colours, zoom, text-to-speech voice (used by people with visual impairments, dyslexia, dyspraxia and dysphasia) etc.; *saving and modifying the blackboard image*: contrast and luminosity level, zoom, colours filter, predefined colour options, etc.; *scanning documents* as image or as text with the help of an OCR software; *editing and annotating* text documents; *adding notes* to previously-saved images; *help in organising contents* (images, text documents and notes).

Even if for an experimental reason a specific webcam and portable scanner models were chosen, the software component is generally compatible with all TWAIN devices. SAPI compatibility is also available. Moreover, any video source recognised by Windows also works with EyeSchool image capturing software (Portanum).

In its present configuration, EyeSchool is first of all a mobile tool, less heavy and from an initial point of view, easier to be used or modified if one may compare it to other similar solutions. The fact of including different software tools (OCR, capturing and modifying images) in one single interface may bring a significant gaining in time. The note-taking system allows an easier classification of the documents.

EyeSchool was developed in order to respond to a mobility need, a relatively light system, easy to take into the classroom and that does not occupy too much place inside the school bag or on the table during school classes. The system was also initially designed in order to take less space on computers memory, as well as to have a low cost.

EyeSchool was build on the basis of an older free software for people with partial visual impairments, Portanum. This computer program allows saving images taken by a camera, modifying and adapting them to ones specific needs. There was nonetheless a less developed function from the notes taking point of view. EyeSchool were then designed in order to simplify this process. The scanner and OCR solutions appeared too. So from software initially intended for people with partial visual impairments, it could become a possible solution for other kind of specific needs. The fact of capturing the image of a blackboard seemed to be useful for people with dyslexia, especially when there were complex formulas or long texts. Having the possibility to quickly register this kind of contents might be for instance an opportunity for people with hearing impairments to concentrate on what it is transmitted by a sign language interpreter.

In the end, these entire hypotheses needed to be tested in a real situation. A large experimentation was designed and applied in four French regions.

4 Description of the Initial Protocol

An initial step-by-step action description of experimental actions was initially included within the project. The four participant regions were thus expected to follow it alike. To sum up, the protocol included three main phases. *The first one* was intended to last three months. It concerned the recruitment of students and their pedagogical and computer science referees. Their identification was imagined in a double way: through social health-care centres and public national education institutions, as well as Universities. Disability-specialised officials were expected to define the list of students and to inform the participant institutions.

Afterwards, *a second phase* as designed by the project was about organising regional meetings in order to present the project and train referees to install and to use EyeSchool device. These were considered as one-time events, lasting no longer than a half day.

Lastly, *the third phase* scheduled a one-time information meeting with public national educational institutions. The disability-specialised officials were expected to organise these meetings at the regional level.

Even if this protocol took into account some broad categories of actors, it tended to minimalize their diversity. Later on, we could see how same category actors behaved differently even if they were initially considered as similar. In the same time, some other participants like the students were not clearly defined as deciding actors within their recruitment.

We have chosen to detail the components of this step-by-step initial procedure in order to compare them to how testing was effectively done. One may consider this as unimportant in relationship with a computer program test, but we can discover that modification in actions determine for instance transformations in duration of use and therefore on the responses a participant might give about his of her use of the technical solution. Or how agenda unavailability might decide on the manner in which some people integrate or not the testing process.

5 A Need to Observe the "Social World"

Studies about assistive technologies for people with disabilities are mainly oriented towards technology assessment and/or laboratory trials in order to measure their utility and usability. They take into account the final users, the people with disabilities, but they give small details on the manner in which these individuals were found and how the people surrounding them may participate to the relationship they build with the assistive technologies. There are only few studies that focus on the manner in which these technologies are used in a "social" environment. And this could be mainly due to the complexity of the social world. If we take into account the actors involved in the EyeSchool deployment, we will see how they have different forms of expertise. Unexpected interactions and configurations can therefore occur between these same actors who do not hesitate to build their own "world". Especially when studying the use of a new assistive technology appears inside a network of some already existing relationships between school, child-care and family actors. And we will also see that this kind of elements cannot be anticipated or formalised in advance. Defining the studys fieldwork will thus become a complex activity.

Three different conceptions were therefore identified within our study of the impact of technology on education for people with disabilities: technology assessment, laboratory trials and social observations. Firstly, the technology assessment concerns the reliability of the device and of the software. Secondly, the laboratory observations are based on the interaction between the students and the object. And thirdly, the social observations add the family, therapists and education system including teachers and computer experts to the previous model.

We can finally associate this modelling to the actor-network theory. Michel Callon and Bruno Latour [2] developed it within the social sciences in order to explain for instance how innovations emerge. Therefore, the actors, as they are understood by this theory could be both human and non-human. When describing a network, it is important to underline the different relationships established between all the participants. Hélène Mialet [6] translated this theory within a new research she made on Stephen Hawkings public figure construction. She therefore shows how behind this unique person there is an entire network of actors (students, administrative assistants, nurses, a special computer, a special artificial voice, etc.) who are almost invisible. All of these will help us to better understand the position of the Student within our project and of the actors surrounding him.

6 Methodology

In order to better understand the previously described processes, as well as variations and similarities we could initially notice from one region to another and even inside a confined geographic area, we will focus our study on a ***practice analysis***. That means we will focus on the analysis of those *ensembles of patterned activities* [5] we could identify within our work. Camis *et al.* [5] describe practices as particular ways in which the human being organises his or her activities: "[...] *we define "practices" as the ensembles of patterned activities - the "modes of working and doing,"* [...] *by which human beings confront and structure the situated tasks with which they are engaged.*"

Subsequently, we will draw upon our own experience inside the project, as well as on documents exchanged between the different actors: meetings schedule;

paper and electronic lists of students, tables of equipment and referees; Observation diaries of the experimenters.

We therefore combine and compare data gathered in this manner. Additional piece of information came from official websites or literature about the organisation of the educational system in France with a special point of view on inclusion for young people with disabilities.

7 Work and Results

Almost ten months after the beginning of the project, approximately 300 students were identified within the four regions. There are big variations, from 25 to 103 students per geographical area.

Students present different levels of implication: from the ones already using the device, to the ones who might be interested in doing this. If the initial inclusion criteria of students were strict, during the process of deployment they became more lax. For instance, besides the three categories of impairments addressed in the beginning, new requests were added for upper-limb motor impairments and other kinds of learning disabilities. Concerning the level of education, new categories were also included, for instance the lifelong learning training. Criteria concerning the level of computer expertise gradually opened themselves too.

A modification of the initial schedule was also observed. For instance, the first and the third phase sometimes mixed themselves. We can also have the case in which the third phase was not really implemented because of the length of the two previous ones, and also because there were school representatives who become direct referees for the student testing the device. The different participation of child-care actors and teachers influence the manner in which the technical object is used. The results are still processed, but the pedagogical part is not very visible for the moment. Moreover, if we look at the important number of meetings already organised during a short period of time (less than 6 month), we can say that the project, as well as the technical solution need to be introduced to their users. They need to learn how to use it, how to get used to it in order to deliver it around them, to the students "recruited" for the project.

The first observations of figure 1 show that even if we can identify a same category of actors, their actions are not the same through the different regions or academies. Each actor has its own demands and needs and this influences the general organisation of the experiment. In the same time, two big categories of actors accompany the young people within their learning process. They meet and interact in various ways, often they know each other, but sometimes they meet for the first time due to the need to work together in order to open the access of the students to the assistive technology. On the one hand, we can find the child-care professionals, on the other the public education representatives.

Child-care professionals are in general working in specialised centres, but there are also those belonging to private practices. An important number of centres appears in those regions were the number of participants students are higher. These actors accept very often to install the software on students computers,

Table 1. Comparing the four regions

	Region 1	Region 2	Region 3	Region 4
Number of academies	3	1	1	1
Child-care centres	11	4	9	3
Public Education support	medium	medium	high	high
Number of presentation meetings with referees	14 2-10 ref.	1 25 ref.	9 3-15 ref.	3 5-20 ref.
Number of training meetings with referees	11 3-10 ref.	2 8-20 ref.	6 5-15 ref.	6 2-20 ref.
Number of presentation meetings with teaching establishments	Indirect + email	Together with the child-care centres	Together with the child-care centres	-
University students	23	9	1	19
Total students	103	25	83	85

but there are some exceptions too, when there are no IT professionals among them. An important part of them are speech therapists, orthoptists, child psychologists, or occupational therapists, but this last category often assists the technical learning process. As said before they meet the professionals from public education during the project. They can participate to the same meetings, or work with the same children.

Education professionals intervene less during the technical process. There are of course exceptions, especially when the child-care professionals do not assume this task. They are very diverse too, from inspectors to specialised teachers. The IT professionals often have an "expert" eye on the device, comparing it to similar solutions. Moreover, teachers and school officials participate to the identification of those young people who might be interested by the device. As mentioned before, their teaching role is less visible, but their one relationship to new technologies is important in how the novelty is received when the student is encouraged (or not) to use it.

Families also appear in relation with this testing process. They have to give their consent for their young children participation, but in the same time, some of them ask for supplementary information or insist on this participation seen as a way of making easier the manner in which they assist their children.

8 Conclusion and Planned Activities

Our paper underlines the main steps of our fieldwork, as well as its similarities and differences from the initial protocol. Is also calls attention on the fact that unexpected transformations can have an important impact on the resources and time allocated for the deployment.

Some other actors than students look to be important during the technology learning and inclusion within school processes, even if their figure will not initially appear. We could therefore identify the role of some professionals like the occupational therapists within the health-care centres or the computer technicians within the EyeSchool system-installing phase.

This presentation emphasises how the experiment might not be neutral. Sometimes it can influence the general environment of the participating actors. By testing a technical tool, it might also arise additional questions, as in our case, questions about pedagogical practices or organisational ones. For instance, we can easily include in this last category those questions about providing computers for young people with disabilities who do not have one.

Finally, a more detailed phase of evaluation is planned to take place at the end of the school year. This is different from the testing process we have just described, as it looks at the answers the concerned actors give and less at their configuration and past history. A quantitative research was therefore designed. It uses as main tools a questionnaire for students, their families and the professionals that work with them, as well as the analysis of logs we could received after the period of test.

References

1. Ando, B., Baglio, S., La Malfa, S., Marletta, V.: Innovative Smart Sensing Solutions for the Visually Impaired. In: Pereira, J. (ed.) Handbook of Research on Personal Autonomy Technologies and Disability Informatics, ch. 5, pp. 60–74 (2010)
2. Callon, M., Latour, B.: Unscrewing the Big Leviathans. How Do Actors Macrostructure Reality. In: Knorr, K., Cicourel, A. (eds.) Advances in Social Theory and Methodology: Toward an Integration of Micro and Macro Sociologies, London, Routledge (1981)
3. Draffan, E.A., Evans, D.G., Blenkhorn, P.: Use of assistive technology by students with dyslexia in post-secondary education. In Disability and Rehabilitation: Assistive Technology 2(2), 105–116 (2007)
4. Lopez-Krahe, J.: Introduction to Assistive Technology for the Blind. The European Journal for the Informatics Professional 8(2), 4–9 (2007)
5. Camis, C., Gross, N., Lamont, M.: Social Knowledge in the Making. University of Chicago Press (2011)
6. Mialet, H.: Hawking incorporated: Stephen Hawking and the Anthropology of the Knowing Subject. The University of Chicago Press (2012)
7. Rekkedal, A.M.: Assistive Hearing Technologies Among Students With Hearing Impairment: Factors That Promote Satisfaction. Journal of Deaf Studies and Deaf Education 17(4), 499–517 (2012)

Accessible 4D-Joystick for Remote Controlled Models

David Thaller, Gerhard Nussbaum, and Stefan Parker

Competence Network Information Technology to Support the Integration of People with Disabilities (KI-I), Linz, Austria
{dt,gn,sp}@ki-i.at

Abstract. Presently there are hardly any toys available which can be used by children, adolescents and adults with severe physical disabilities. A very interesting group of non-trivial toys are remote controlled (RC) models because the remotes can be easily substituted with custom ones. Since RC models need very accurate commands with very low latency in several channels concurrently, the remote for usage by people with severe physical disabilities must implement several requirements. This paper describes and discusses the prototype of a mouth operated joystick accessible for people with severe physical disabilities to accurately control RC model helicopters, multicopters, airplanes, boats or cars.

Keywords: Joystick, Assistive Technology, RC models, Non-Trivial Toys.

1 Introduction

Playing with toys is much more than amusement and the right to play is specified in the "Convention on the Rights of the Child" [1] by the United Nations.

Additionally studies by Keith Sawyer [2] from the Washington University state that toys are very important for the physical and cognitive development of children and young adults. Playing with other children fosters social skills and can be used to teach children important things for their lives. All these benefits are hardly accessible for people with severe physical disabilities or only via custom made adaptions. The goal of this work was to create an input device which is useful to control complex remote controlled (RC) toys without using ones hands.

The category of remote controlled toys was chosen because only the remote control has to be changed and no adaptions or modifications have to be done with the actual toy. This has the advantage of not losing warranty of the device and that people can buy off the shelf toys to play with.

2 Related Work

In the past different researchers tried to create accessible interfaces for toys. One group of the Archimedes project [3] from the University of Hawaii adapted existing toys to suit the needs of children. They used standard toys and adapted the user

K. Miesenberger et al. (Eds.): ICCHP 2014, Part II, LNCS 8548, pp. 218–225, 2014.

interface to make them accessible. Furthermore the group created learning material and held courses to teach students and concerned parents how to modify toys. The problem with this approach is that it is not possible to buy toys in normal shops and use them directly. Every supported toy had to be adapted before it was usable for a child with disabilities.

Cole Galloway et. al. from the University of Delaware [4] adapted small motor driven toy cars to be accessible for children with physical and mental disabilities by substituting the driving wheel with a single switch. While the switch is pressed the car starts to drive in a circle.

The above projects are/were quite successful and helped children with physical disabilities to get access to toys. The only downside is that most of the adapted toys were for children under the age of six. This is because all of the above mentioned projects supported switches or joysticks as a user input modality which doesn't allow the control of more complex games or toys, e.g. flying an RC helicopter model.

A more advanced control interface for the quadcopter AR-drone was developed by Karl LaFleur et al. [5] from the University of Minnesota. This flying drone can be controlled via WIFI signals. Therefore the remote control can be implemented on a standard computer sending TCP packets. As control input they used motor imagery EEG BCI. Their test proved the possibility to fully control the drone in 3D space with the system. The problem of using a BCI system is reaction speed. When flying a pitch controlled RC helicopter the user needs a fast and responsive system to hold the helicopter steady in the air which is currently impossible to achieve with a BCI system.

The KI-I [6] development team did some experiments with the RC coaxial-helicopter Syma S107 [7]. As input devices the joystick of the power wheelchair control PG Drives R-net [8] (usable as Bluetooth mouse) and a modified OpenEEG [9] to gather muscle signals were used. To gather the signals of the input devices and to process them the open source software AsTeRICS [10] was used in combination with an Arduino based IR-sender to control the Syma S107 helicopter. Due to the fact that AsTeRICS already contains lots of signal processing plugins specialized and optimized to the needs of people with physical disabilities, the prototyping was fast and effective. The construction plans and the software of the first prototype were released under the GPL license for free on the project webpage [11]. This setup worked quite well since the Syma S107 is very easy to fly and just needs three command channels. The results of further experiments showed that this approach is not feasible to control more complex and professional RC models.

3 Implementation

3.1 4D-Joystick

The prototype of the 4D-Joystick, see Fig. 1, was developed for and with a user with severe physical disabilities (tetraplegia) who is only able to move his head and to raise his left forearm. The arm could only be used to trigger a switch but not to control complex systems. Therefore the possibilities with available chin and mouth controls were evaluated.

The problem was that most RC-models like helicopters or airplanes need at least four accurate input modalities to control all possible movements and throttle of the vehicle. On the market there are no suitable joysticks for people with severe physical disabilities available and therefore a new type of joystick was developed.

Fig. 1. The 4D-Joystick used to control RC models

The 4D-Joystick allows to control up to six channels (input modalities) concurrently: channel 1 by moving the joystick up and down, channel 2 by moving the joystick to the left and the right, channel 3 by moving the joystick forwards and backwards, channel 4 by sip/puff and channels 5 and 6 by binary sensors like push buttons (see Fig. 2).

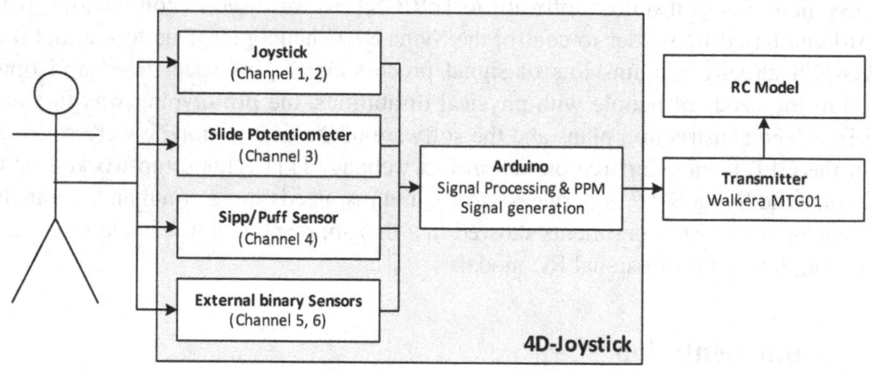

Fig. 2. Schema of the 4D-Joystick

The development was based on the concept of participatory design – the target user himself was one of the inventors, developers and authors of this paper. With the help of his assistant Sabina Wiesinger the target user created a very rudimentary prototype of the 4D-Joystick as feasibility study. For implementing the logic the open source software AsTeRICS was used. After successful tests the idea and a list of features and requirements were discussed in the development team including the target user. After every milestone of the development process the prototype was tested by the target user.

The joystick mounted on the laser-cut transparent Acrylglas is a standard replacement joystick for remote control transmitters, bought from an RC model supplier. The Acrylglas was used as mounting material because the user can look through the plates and therefore does not lose much of his field of view.

Instead of the original joystick control stick a biocompatible mouth piece was attached via a cardan joint which allows very precise movements (<1mm) of the joystick while the mouthpiece stays in an optimal position in the mouth of the user. Inside the mouthpiece there is a hole leading from the front side to a pneumatic connector located at the right side of the mouthpiece to which a sip and puff sensor (Freescale MPXV7007DP [12]) can be connected with a pipe. This allows the user to sip/puff at through mouthpiece while controlling the x, y and z axis. The whole joystick itself is mounted on a base plate by a HIWIN Linear Guideway MGN9 [13] on which the joystick can be moved forward and backwards. To gather the values from the z axis a slide potentiometer (ALPS 402127 [14]) is used.

The sensor values are read and processed by an Arduino Uno board [15] and encoded into Pulse-Pause-Modulated (PPM) frames [16], which are then sent to the actual RC transmitter. Pulse-Pause-Modulation is a well standardized and documented protocol to talk between all major brands of RC model transmitters and allows the control of boats, cars, helicopters, multicopters, airplanes and many other toys that can be interfaced with remote controlled receiver technology. As transmitter for the prototype the Walkera deVention Magic Cube MTC-01 [17] is used.

3.2 Configuration Software and Firmware

The joystick allows to create and to store up to six different profiles for RC models which can be edited and stored on the joystick using a PC configuration program or the touchscreen at the right side of the 4D Joystick. The PC software communicates with the Joystick via USB and lets the user's assistant set, load and store parameters for all channels of an RC model. The user interface is shown in Fig. 3.

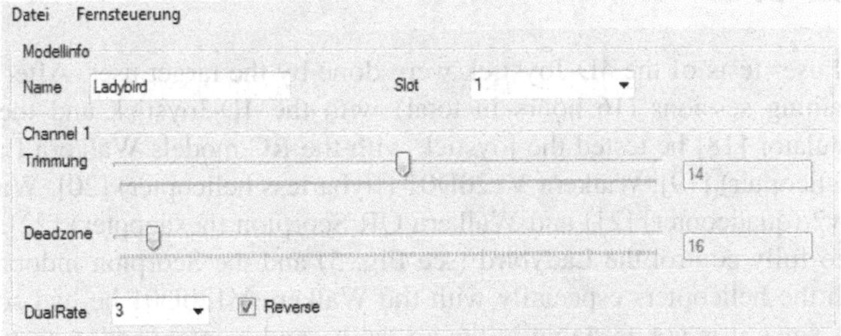

Fig. 3. User interface of the PC-Configuration Tool

The firmware supports inverting and trimming of each channel to compensate mechanically caused drifts of an RC model. Additionally two methods were implemented for adapting the behaviour of the joystick to requirements of people with physical disabilities. The first method is to limit a channel to a maximum value (e.g. half throttle) and interpolate this smaller range to the same joystick movement. This allows a much smoother control of a channel and the possibility to oversteer an RC model decreases drastically. The only downside when limiting the value too much is that the RC model cannot do fast movements anymore. To support users with a tremor or who cannot move the stick very accurately, a dead zone can be set for each channel, which filters control inputs around the centre of a channel.

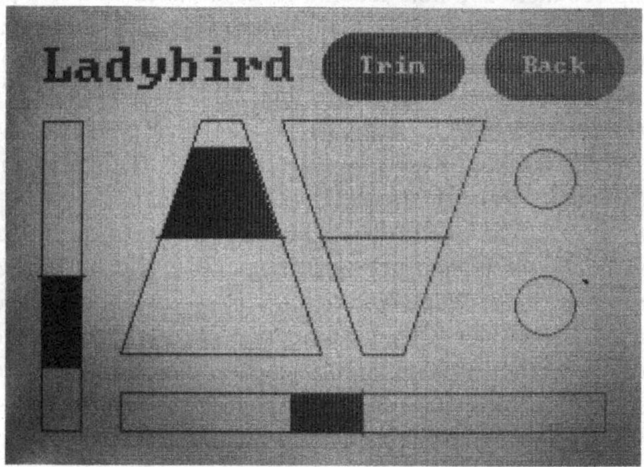

Fig. 4. Screenshot of the 4D-Joystick User Interface

For first impressions on how accurate the user can move the stick the touchscreen can display graphical feedback for each channel in real-time, which visualises the set parameters and how they affect the actual output signals. This helps to optimise the control input for different user requirements, see Fig. 4.

4 User Tests

The initial user tests of the 4D-Joystick were done by the target user. After eight extensive training sessions (16 hours in total) with the 4D-Joystick and the Phoenix Flight Simulator [18] he tested the joystick with the RC models Walkera Lama 400d (coaxial helicopter) [19], Walkera V120D01 (flybarless helicopter) [20], Walkera QR Ladybird v2 (quadcopter) [21] and Walkera QR Scorpion (hexacopter) [22]. The user was able to fully control the Ladybird (see Fig. 5) and the Scorpion indoor and outdoor. With the helicopters especially with the Walkera V120D01 he had some more difficulties since it is not as stable in the air as the multicopters and even more difficult to control. But the learning curve to get used to the 4D-Joystick inputs was very flat because the user already utilizes a joystick with his chin to steer his power wheelchair. In the meantime flying RC models became a hobby of this user.

Fig. 5. User controlling the Walkera QR Ladybird v2 quadcopter

Flying the RC models needs lots of concentration and is quite demanding since at least four channels have to be controlled at all times by either precise movements or by keeping them very stable.. By flying the RC models the user experienced an intensive training of his three-dimensional perception and also his fine motor skills of his head movements.

The only problem with the current prototype for the user was that he could not set the input parameters independently and always needed an assistant when he started with a new RC model.

After these first successful tests the authors plan to extend these tests with other users with (severe) motor disabilities who have a very good control of their head movement.

5 Conclusion and Future Work

The 4D-Joystick is a new type of Assistive Technology. The functional prototype of the 4D-Joystick is fully working and in use by the person it was developed for and with. The 4D-Joystick allows users to control up to six channels smoothly with an analogue to digital converter resolution of 10 bit for every sensor. The only problem of the test user was that he could not set the parameters for the 4D-Joystick without an assistant. Therefore a new configuration mode will be implemented in the next version of the 4D-Joystick's firmware which allows the configuration of the 4D-Joystick behaviour using predefined control input patterns using only the x, y and z axis and the sip and puff sensor. It is also planned to implement a new configuration parameter which maps the control inputs of the joystick to the output signal in an exponential way. Therefore the controls around the centre will be very smooth, but on the outlines the full steering control can still be reached. Another useful feature of the next version will be the functionality to individually rearrange the mapping of the 4D-Joystick input functions (x, y and z axis, sip and puff sensor, external binary sensors) to the different channels of an RC model which increases the flexibility of the 4D-Joystick to suit the users' needs.

After the next release in-deep user tests are planned with several other persons with severe motor disabilities to get more feedback about the system. Additionally the authors will organize flying events for and with them, to gain a user group which constantly gives feedback about the 4D-Joystick. Furthermore the impact on the three-dimensional perception of the users will be evaluated.

There are also ideas to explore new application domains for the 4D-Joystick like input for the computer, video games or environment controls. For this work a USB implementation of the HID protocol will be implemented on the already integrated microcontroller which now handles the USB configuration of the 4D Joystick.

References

1. United Nations: Convention on the Rights of the Child. Human Rights, ch. IV, New York (1989)
2. Schoenherr, N.: Finding educational toys is not hard; key is keeping child's age in mind, Washington University (2006), `http://news.wustl.edu/news/Pages/12032.aspx` (retrieved January 19, 2014)
3. Scott, N., Gabrielli, S.: ARCHIMEDES Hawaii - Ideal Access Technology for Lifelong Learning in the Pacific Rim. In: CSUN Conference Proceedings, San Diego (2004)
4. Huang, H.-H., Galloway, J.C.: Modified ride-on toy cars for early power mobility: a technical report. Pediatric Physical Therapy 24(2), 149–154 (2012)
5. LaFleur, K., Cassady, K., Doud, A., Shades, K., Rogin, E., He, B.: Quadcopter control in three-dimensional space using a noninvasive motor imagery-based brain–computer. Journal of Neural Engineering 10/4, 046003 (2013)
6. KI-I: `http://www.ki-i.at/` (retrieved March 23, 2014)
7. Syma Toys: Syma S107G, `http://www.symatoys.com/product/show/1874.html` (retrieved March 23, 2014)
8. PG Drives Technology: R-net, `http://www.pgdt.com/Products/R-net.aspx` (retrieved March 23, 2014)
9. The OpenEEG Project: OpenEEG, `http://openeeg.sourceforge.net/doc/` (retrieved March 23, 2014)
10. Nussbaum, G., Veigl, C., Acedo, J., Barton, Z., Diaz, U., Drajsajtl, T., Garcia, A., Kakousis, K., Miesenberger, K., Papadopoulos, G.A., Paspallis, N., Pecyna, K., Soria-Frisch, A., Weiss, C.: AsTeRICS - Towards a Rapid Integration Construction Set for Assistive Technologies. In: AAATE Conference 2011, Maastricht, The Netherlands (2011)
11. KI-I: Helicopter controlled with muscle signals - Construction plans and documentation, `http://www.ki-i.at/helicopter/` (retrieved March 23, 2014)
12. Freescale: MPXV7007DP -7 to 7kPa, 5.0V, Differential and Gauge Pressure Sensor, `http://www.freescale.com/webapp/sps/site/prod_summary.jsp?code=MPXV7007DP` (retrieved March 21, 2014)
13. HIWIN: Linear Guideway MG Series, `http://www.hiwin.com/html/lg/mg.html` (retrieved March 21, 2014)

14. ALPS Electric Co. Ltd.: RS6011DY6 10K Slide Potentiometer, http://www.alps.com (retrieved March 21, 2004)
15. Arduino: Arduino Uno, http://arduino.cc/en/Main/ArduinoBoardUno#.Uywds4XRous (retrieved March 21, 2014)
16. The Model Electronics Company: How It Works – The PPM Radio Control System, M.E.C. Technical Note, Issue 1.1 (2007)
17. Walkera: WalkeradeVention Magic Cube MTC-01 2.4 GHz radio transmitter, http://walkera.com/en/showgoods.php?id=446 (retrieved March 23, 2014)
18. Runtime Games Ltd.: Phoenix R/C 5 Professional Radio Control Flight Simulation, http://www.phoenix-sim.com (retrieved March 21, 2014)
19. Walkerasite: Walkera Lama 400 EC135 (same technical base as Lama 400D), http://www.walkerasite.com/walkera_lama_400_ec135.html (retrieved March 23, 2014)
20. WOW Hobbies: Walkera V120D01, http://www.wowhobbies.com/walkera-v120d01-helicopter.aspx (retrieved March 21, 2014)
21. Walkera: QR Ladybird v2, http://walkera.com/en/showgoods.php?id=467 (retrieved January 19, 2014)
22. Walkera: QR Scorpion, http://walkera.com/en/showgoods.php?id=466 (retrieved January 19, 2014)

Development of a Personal Mobility Vehicle to Improve the Quality of Life

Yoshiyuki Takahashi and Masamichi Miura

Toyo University, Department of Human Environment Design,
Faculty of Human Life Design, Oka 48-1, Asaka-shi, Saitama, 351-8510 Japan
y-takahashi@toyo.jp

Abstract. In today's aging society, the importance of assistance for the people with limited mobility is acknowledged. Therefore, the personal mobility vehicle (PMV) for the people with limited mobility is proposed in this paper. Proposed PMV is propelled by kicking motion with power assisted wheels. It aims to assist short distance transportation in urban area e.g. moving from a home to a train station. By using a folding mechanism, it will be possible to carry the vehicle on public transportations and this will help to extend the area of the user's activities. In this paper, the overview of our developed PMV and the results of preliminary experiments are introduced.

Keywords: Personal Mobility, Limited Mobility, Transportation.

1 Introduction

'Transportation' is not only moving a person to a destination, but also one of the fundamental activities of the human life. It is for leading an independent life and participating in the social activities as an active member of society.

In Japan, after the 'Transportation Accessibility Improvement Law' was enforced, lots of barriers of transportation were solved. However, still many people suffering from limited mobility exist. For example, walking is a burden for some elderly persons due to reducing muscle strength and pain on the back and lower limbs. If limited mobility people could stretch the range of transportation by using their own physical function even just a little, transportation will contribute to their health.

Therefore, we propose a new mobility, the personal mobility vehicle (PMV) for the people with limited mobility. Proposed PMV is propelled by kicking off the ground and power-assisted wheels. It aims to support short distance transportation in urban area e.g. moving from a home to a train station. By using a folding mechanism, it will be possible to carry the vehicle on public transportations and will help to extend the area of the user's activities. That is for improving the quality of life.

2 Related Researches

Devices to assist the transportation already exist and many researches are ongoing. Wheel chairs and electrical scooters are widely used. In recent years, new generation

K. Miesenberger et al. (Eds.): ICCHP 2014, Part II, LNCS 8548, pp. 226–233, 2014.

personal mobility vehicles are being developed. Toyota motor company developed several personal mobility vehicles, e.g. i-REAL [1]. i-REAL is a three wheeled robotic vehicle for individuals and it is designed for the daily travel. Seated driver controls the vehicle by a controller set on the armrest. Segway [2] and winglet [3] are other types of PMV. The user stands up on the devices and by shifting her/his center of gravity can control the direction and speed. Honda Motor Company developed UNI-CAB [4] that is also a robotic transporter and it has similar control strategy as to Segway. The user sits on the seat and by changing her/his posture can control the vehicle.

Sitting and moving device is suited for limited mobility user however, if the user still has a motor function, using this device may reduce her/his motor function. On the other hand, controlling vehicle motion by changing posture is difficult for elderly and people with disabilities. Therefore, it is required a device which allows to train or maintain user's motor function and also can be easy to control, ensuring safety.

3 Concepts of Design

Concepts of design and feature points of developed PMV are as follows,

(1) Seamless Mobility

Portable PMV carriable on to the public transportation will enable to combine different mode of transportation e.g. moving by a PMV, get on a train and changing to another train. It assists the walking and extends the range of transportation (Fig. 1).

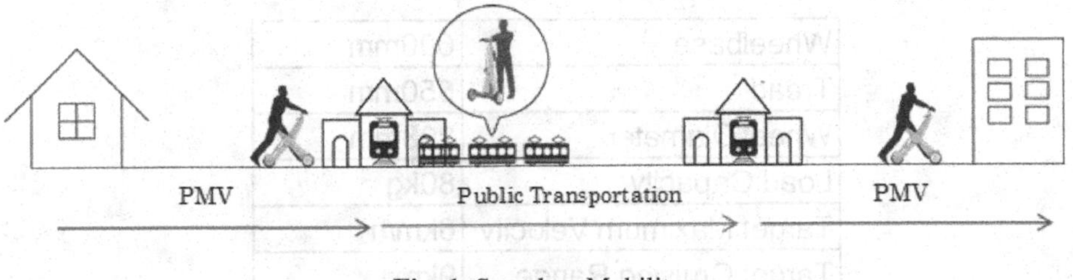

Fig. 1. Seamless Mobility

(2) Moving mean Exercising

Electric wheelchair and cart are fully motorized and the user does not need to move using its own lower limb. On the other hand, to move ahead a PMV, the user needs to kick on the ground. Then, the electrical motor will assist the gliding on the ground. Moving the body will reduce the risk of disuse syndrome and keep the motor functions (Fig. 2 (a)).

(3) Moving with Stability

Three wheels (two in front, one in rear) layout is enabled to stand by itself and ensure a stable running (Fig. 2 (b)). Diameter of the wheels is 200mm in order to get over the road gap. Maximum velocity is up to 6 km/h, according to the maximum velocity for a motor wheel chair. To bring it on to the public transportation, lightweight body and folding mechanism are equipped (Fig. 2 (c)).

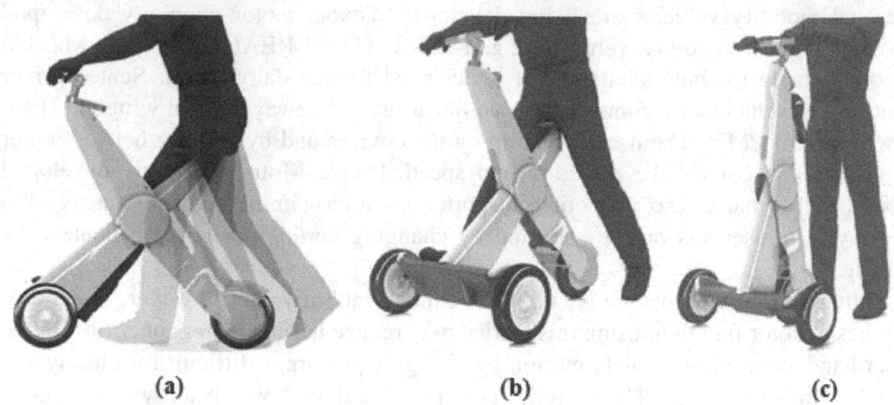

Fig. 2. Features of PMV; Exercise, Stable Running and Folding Mechanism

4 System Overview

According to the concepts of design, PMV has been developed. Specifications are shown in Table. 1 and external view is shown in Fig. 3. The size is decided in way to ensure the necessary space to move the legs. The tread is to be able to pass through the ticket gate of the train station.

Table 1. Specifications of PMV

Wheelbase	600mm
Tread	550mm
Wheel Diameter	203mm
Load Capacity	80kg
Target Maximum Velocity	6km/h
Target Cruising Range	9km
Steering	Drive-by-Wire
Minimum Turning Radius	1230mm

PMV is propelled by kicking off the ground and power-assisted by the motor on the rear wheel. Power assist system consists of a servo motor, a rotary encoder, a micro controller and a motor driver. System diagram is shown in Fig. 4. Fig. 5 shows the rear wheel assembly. Fig. 6 shows the flowchart of the power assist system. Rotary encoder is attached on the rear wheel and measures the wheel rotation. If angular acceleration of the rear wheel excess the threshold, micro controller estimate that the user kicked off the ground. Therefore, the servo motor starts to rotate and assist the rotation of the rear wheel to reduce the deceleration.

Fig. 3. External view of PMV

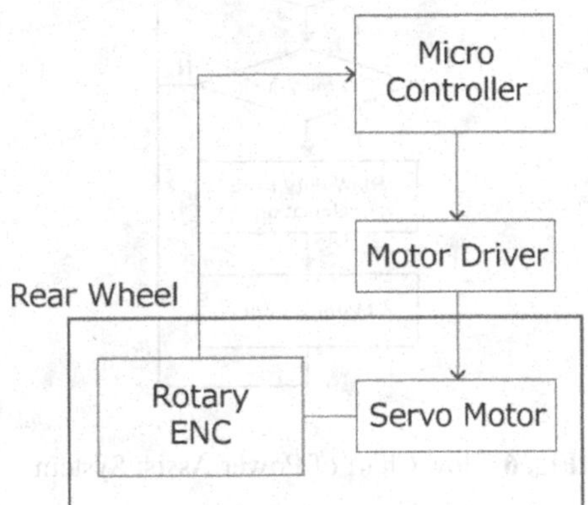

Fig. 4. System Diagram of PMV

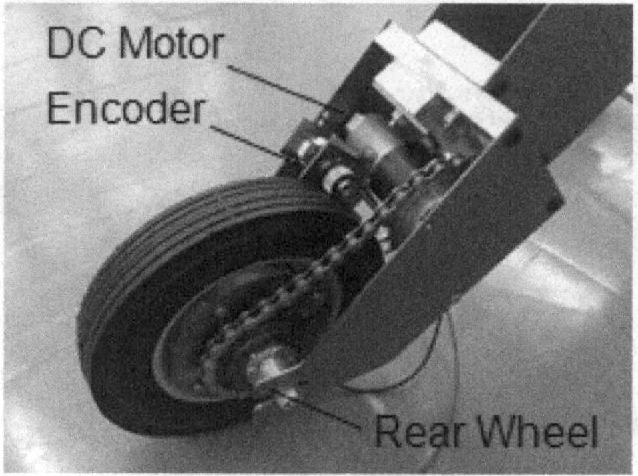

Fig. 5. Rear Wheel Assembly

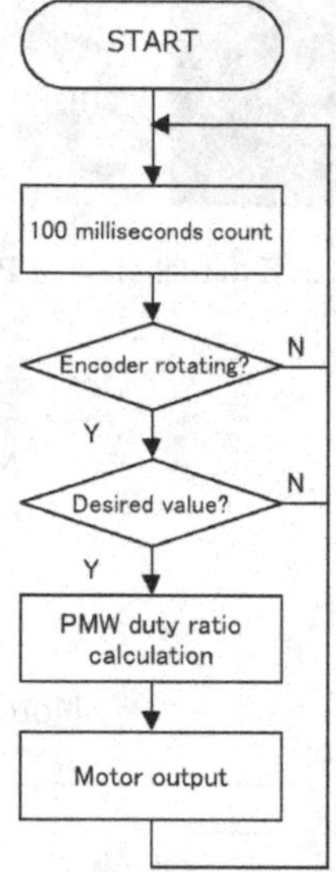

Fig. 6. Flow Chart of Power Assist System

5 Experiments and Results

Preliminary experiments were carried out to confirm the functions of the PMV. Two young participants (age 24 female and male), three elderly participants (age 60 female and age 72 male) were enrolled in the experiments. Fig. 7 shows the scene of experiments.

Experiments with young participants were done on indoor flat floor. They kicked off the ground only once as much as they can. Fig. 8 shows the comparison of the gliding distance between without assistance and with assistance. The gliding distance was from 2.3m to 2.53m (average 2.45m) without assistance and the gliding distance was from 2.83m to 3.25m (average 3m) with assistance. When using power assist function, the gliding distance was stretched 18.3%. In case of five times kicking off the ground in a row, the gliding distance was 8.28m without assistance and 10.3m with assistance. The distance was 24% stretched.

Experiments with elderly participants were also done. They rode PMV freely and post riding interview were carried out. Fig. 9 shows the typical velocity profile and Fig.10 shows the distance profile. In this case, the average of maximum speed was 1.19 m/s (non-assisted) and 1.36m/s (assisted). The gliding distance was 2.23 m (non-assisted) and 2.6 m (assisted). 17% stretched.

Fig. 7. Scene of the Experiment with Elderly Participant

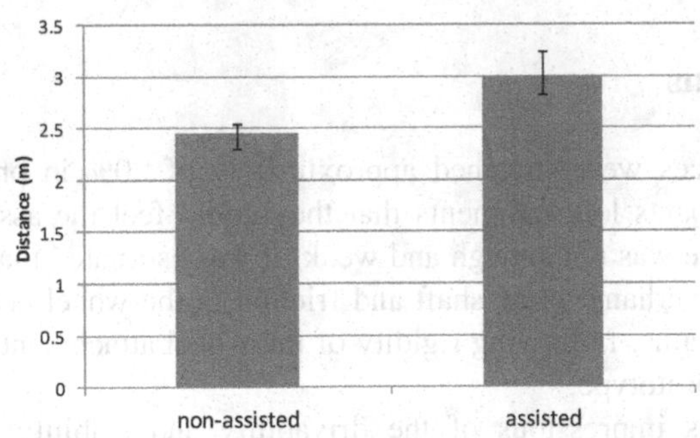

Fig. 8. Comparison of the Gliding Distance between without Assistance and with Assistance

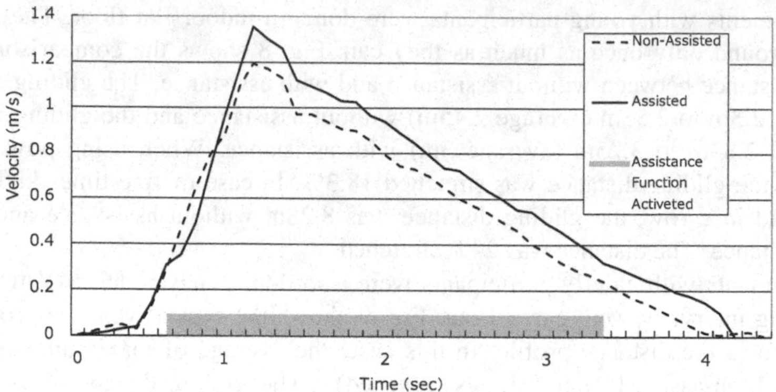

Fig. 9. Typical Velocity Profile of Elderly Participant

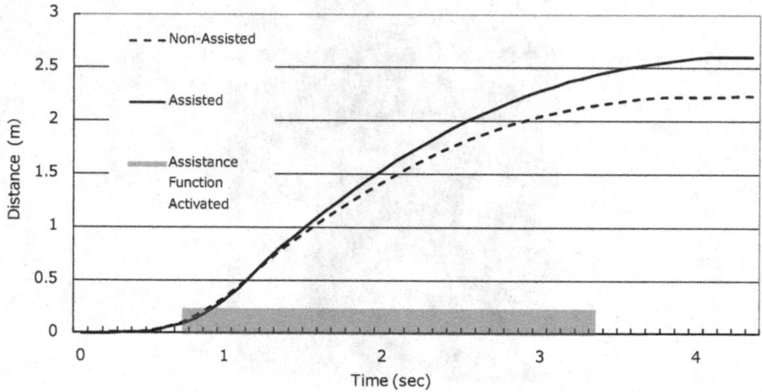

Fig. 10. Typical Distance Profile of Elderly Participant

6 Discussions

The gliding distances were stretched approximately of 20% in preliminary experiments. The participants left comments that they could feel the assistance force, but also assistance force was not enough and weak. It was estimated that the front wheels are attached with overhang to the shaft and friction in the wheel bearings was higher than the designed value. Improving rigidity of the wheel attachment is required in the design of the next prototype.

The participant's impressions of the drivability and stability were as follows, "Force feedback on the steering was weak", "Running fast and turn was difficult". Steer-by-wire system is equipped in this system. Spring force of the spring to re-center the steering bar should be strong and stable. Positive impressions are as follows, "Feet could contact to the ground and felt it safe", "There is a footrest and kicking off the ground alternately. Therefore, propel the PMV long time".

Other impressions are as follows, "It was good exercise and move", "Seat was hard and small", "It could be difficult to ride putting skirt on". Currently, a bicycle seat is used. Appropriate seat is required for easy to kicking off the ground and PMV body shape should be re-designed for easy to ride for the people who wear the skirt on.

In this experiment, folding was not evaluated. PMV can fold however, it is still not compact. Portability of the PMV will be discussed in the design of next prototype.

7 Conclusions

A new mobility, the personal mobility vehicle (PMV) for people with limited mobility has been developed. The developed PMV could propel by kicking off the ground and power-assisted wheels. It aimed to support short distance transportation in the urban area. By using a folding mechanism, it will be possible to take the vehicle on to public transportations and will help to extend the area of the user's activities. In the next step, experiments with higher number of elderly persons in the real field should be carried out. It will be necessary to evaluate the safety, usability and durability of the system.

References

1. TOYOTA (i-REAL), http://www.toyota-global.com/innovation/personal_mobility/
2. Segway, http://www.segway.com/
3. TOYOTA(winglet), http://www.toyota.com.hk/innovation/personal_mobility/winglet.aspx
4. Honda (UNI-CUB), http://world.honda.com/UNI-CUB/

Automated Configuration of Applications for People with Specific Needs

Peter Heumader[1], Reinhard Koutny[1], Klaus Miesenberger[1], and Karl Kaser[2]

[1] University of Linz, Institut Integriert Studieren, Austria
{peter.heumader,reinhard,koutny,klaus.miesenberger}@jku.at
[2] LIFETool, Linz, Austria
karl.kaser.@lifetool.at

Abstract. This paper presents an approach to store user settings and abilities in a user profile that can be used to automatically adjust the settings of applications on mobile or desktop devices for people with special needs. The user profile and the settings are determined automatically with a wizard like application or manually with a carer and are dispatched to other devices with the use of cloud services. By this users with special needs will be able to operate new applications without the need of a carer setting up the application for them.

1 Introduction

A major concern for carers of people with physical and cognitive disabilities is the adjustment of applications for the target group. Due to their impairments, they interact in their own specific way or with a special input device with the application. As the target group is usually not able to setup the application by itself, a carer is needed. This setup process has to be done for every application and for every device the user wants to operate. On shared computers, things get even worse because every time the user changes, the setup process has to be repeated.

In this paper we present an approach that counteracts this drawback. We determine the settings of a user automatically with a game-like wizard or with the help of a carer and save those settings in a user profile. This profile is then distributed over cloud services to every other application based on our framework, even if the user owns multiple devices. As a result the settings only need be configured once for each user.

2 State of the Art

Intense research has shown that up to date there are hardly any related projects in this field that store information about the user's capabilities and preferred input methods in the profile. The Capcom Project aimed to offer adaptive user interfaces for people with cognitive disabilities. Depending on the user's needs, the user interface changes in terms of difficulty and complexity of language, colour, icons etc. These preferences

K. Miesenberger et al. (Eds.): ICCHP 2014, Part II, LNCS 8548, pp. 234–237, 2014.

are also determined by a game-like wizard and stored in a profile. The Capcom approach however only deals with the presentation of information and how to adjust it to people with cognitive disabilities in contrary to our approach where we consider necessary adaptations of the relevant parameter for interaction [3].

Cloud4All also aims at creating a profile describing the user and his or her capabilities which is used to determine fitting applications in terms of necessary accessibility and context of use. According to the user's preferences both the user interface and the content get adapted including augmentation of the level of accessibility through special web services and cloud based assistive technology [4].

3 Concept

The concept had its origins in a research project called Assistive Technology Laboratory (ATLab) which focuses on the development of a software framework for NUI-based tablet apps and desktop applications that allows rapid creation of accessible games. The framework features the easy integration of new hardware(e.g., IntegraMouse, external switch buttons) and offers alternative interaction methods for applications based upon the framework, namely touch-input, mouse, keyboard, switches, eye-tracking, gestures and touch-scanning, which is similar to switch access scanning but uses a touch screen instead.

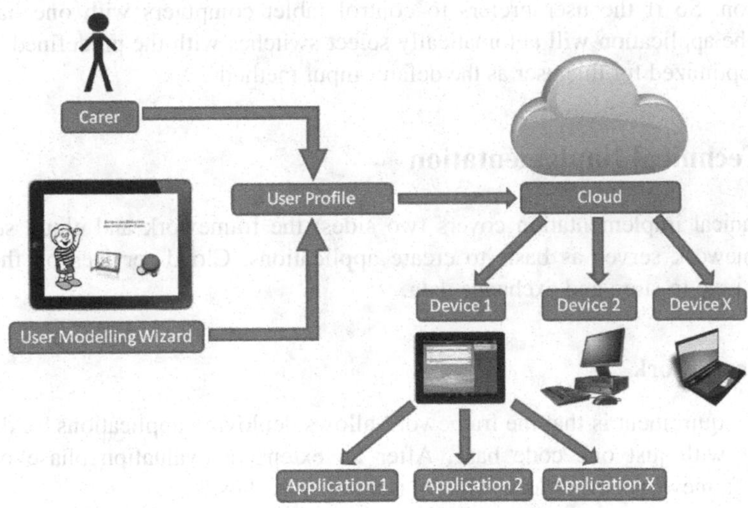

Fig. 1. Concept Overview

Out of this project we saw the need for an easier way to configure apps for people with special needs. Depending on the user's disabilities, users have different capabilities to interact with an application. While people with spastic tetraplegia might be able to operate a tablet device with touch input - people with paraplegia are unable to do so. They have different ways of controlling applications like switch access scanning or eye-tracking. In our approach we determine the user's abilities for each of these input methods. We defined several features for each input method that describe the user's capabilities in handling an input method. An example for a feature used would be the user's ability to reach every region of the screen of a tablet device. The screen is divided into several regions and for each region it is determined whether the user is able to touch the region. If he is able to touch the region, it is also saved whether the user had problems like shivering through a tremor when touching the region. Features like this are defined for each of the framework's currently supported input methods (touch-input, mouse, keyboard, switches, eye-tracking and touch-scanning).

As seen in Figure 1, the concrete values of these features are either determined by a carer or automatically generated by an avatar based wizard without the need of interference by the consultant. It is designed as a little game with an avatar that guides the user through different screens. In each screen the user has to perform a specific task, by which the features are unobtrusively filled with values.

As soon as features are detected they are stored in the user profile which is uploaded to our cloud service. Whenever the user starts an application that is based on the ATLab-Framework and an internet connection is available, the user profile is downloaded. Depending on the device (tablet pc, desktop, laptop) the user is currently using and the input devices (hardware switch, mouse, touch) that are currently plugged in, the preferred way of interaction for the user is automatically set up by the application. So if the user prefers to control tablet computers with one hardware switch, the application will automatically select switches with the predefined settings that are optimized for this user as the default input method.

4 Technical Implementation

The technical implementation covers two sides: the framework and cloud services. The framework serves as basis to create applications. Cloud services on the other hand are used to store and exchange data.

4.1 Framework

One key requirement is that the framework allows deploying applications on different platforms with just one code base. After an extensive evaluation phase of cross platform frameworks the Adobe AIR [6] runtime was chosen.

Its components are based on Robotlegs [1] and Apache Flex [2]. Robotlegs is a framework that provides tools to ease communication tasks within the application, structuring the project and managing dependency injection. Flex SDK is an open source framework for creation of web apps that run on Adobe AIR[5]. This environment allows rapid deployment of applications that can be operated by everyone and that run on the most popular mobile devices and desktop systems.

4.2 Cloud Services

As for technology used, the cloud service is based on Windows Azure[6], which is one of the major cloud computing platforms and infrastructures, developed by Microsoft, through a globally distributed network of Microsoft-managed data centres. This cloud service uses WCF and is based on SOAP. Since sensitive data will be transferred using the cloud service, communication is established through HTTPS. From the point of view of the cloud side, the service is stateless, meaning that there is basically no login-process. Every request carries its own user credentials for authentication and authorization which are stored in the SOAP header encrypted through HTTPS as well. However, applications can still support user logins at the application start-up and store the credentials temporarily and locally which can be added to every request.

5 Current Status and Further Work

Currently the framework and the basis for the cloud services have been implemented. Also a prototypic implementation of the wizard has been implemented and already tested. However, the automatic synchronization between user profiles and applications is still work in progress and will need some time until the implementation is finished. Another long term goal is the automated adaption of the user settings based on user input. At this, the system would monitor all input of the user. If the system recognizes that the user fails to activate a control like a button multiple times, the system will change the settings of the input device or even the size and position of the control so that the user is able to activate the control.

References

1. Robotlegs: Robotlegs AS3 Micro Architecture (2013), `http://www.robotlegs.org/`
2. Apache: Flex (2013), `http://flex.apache.org/`
3. Petz, A., Radu, N., Lassnig, M.: CAPKOM – innovative graphical user interface supporting people with cognitive disabilities. In: Miesenberger, K., Karshmer, A., Penaz, P., Zagler, W. (eds.) ICCHP 2012, Part II. LNCS, vol. 7383, pp. 377–384. Springer, Heidelberg (2012)
4. Vanderheiden, G.C., Treviranus, J., Gemou, M., Bekiaris, E., Markus, K., Clark, C., Basman, A.: The evolving global public inclusive infrastructure (GPII). In: Stephanidis, C., Antona, M. (eds.) UAHCI 2013, Part I. LNCS, vol. 8009, pp. 107–116. Springer, Heidelberg (2013)
5. Wikipedia: Adobe Integraded Runtime (2014), `http://en.wikipedia.org/wiki/Adobe_Integrated_Runtime`
6. Microsoft: Windows Azure (2014), `http://www.windowsazure.com/de-de/`

Visualizing Motion History for Investigating the Voluntary Movement and Cognition of People with Severe and Multiple Disabilities

Mamoru Iwabuchi[1], Guang Yang[1], Kimihiko Taniguchi[2], Syoudai Sano[2], Takamitsu Aoki[3], and Kenryu Nakamura[1]

[1] Research Center for Advanced Science and Technology, University of Tokyo, Tokyo, Japan
{mamoru,yang,kenryu}@bfp.rcast.u-tokyo.ac.jp
[2] Takamatsu Special Education School, Kagawa, Japan
hamuossan8603@river.ocn.ne.jp, s_sanocch@ybb.ne.jp
[3] Inariyama Special Education School, Nagano, Japan
aokitaka@mac.com

Abstract. Two case studies were conducted with two children with severe physical and cognitive disabilities in this research, and a computer-vision based technique called Motion History was applied to visualize their movement. By changing the conditions of intervention to the children, the Motion History successfully helped to find their voluntary movement and effective stimuli that attracted their attention. It was concluded that finding the changes of movement is very important for extracting voluntary movement and Motion History is suitable for that purpose. This gives us a greater possibility of evidence-based interaction with people with severe and multiple disabilities.

Keywords: Motion History, Voluntary Movement, Cognition, Severe and Multiple Disabilities, OAK.

1 Introduction

Medical advancement helps more and more new bone babies, who could not sur-vive in the past, to survive in recent years. Hence supporting people with severe and multiple disabilities is becoming increasingly needed and important. However, it is still very difficult to have good support and interaction in an effective way particularly when their disabilities are very severe and there are little or involuntary responses.

Out team has developed a computer vision-based noncontact switch software called OAK (Observation and Access with Kinect) for people with severe and multiple disabilities [1,2]. The software uses Microsoft Kinect for Windows to observe the motion of the user. One of unprecedented features of OAK is Motion History which visualizes the history of movement [1], [3]. Technically, Motion History is created based on the frequency of the brightness change, which corresponds to the motion of the user, in each pixel of the captured video. OAK counts the number

K. Miesenberger et al. (Eds.): ICCHP 2014, Part II, LNCS 8548, pp. 238–243, 2014.

of the brightness change and present it in a heat map format with a six-color scale (purple, blue, green, yellow, orange, and red). The redder the color of a pixel is in the Motion History, the greater the movement was at the point during the observation. Selecting the most active region of the Motion History allows the user to create a sensitive switch to activate [4]. Motion History can also provide helpful information about the cognitive state of the user by comparing the data of the situations before/after an effective interaction.

In this paper, two case studies are described, where Motion History was applied to improve the understandings of the conditions of two children with severe physical and cognitive disabilities and to find a good approach to supporting them.

2 Case Study A: Understanding Voluntary Movement

In the first case, Motion History was used to distinguish voluntary movement of a twelve year old male child with intellectual disability and profound paralysis due to cerebral hypoxia at birth.

2.1 Background

The boy had only subtle movement and what his voluntary movement was unclear. He was non-speaking and had no distinctive response associated to any specific situation. Teachers at the special school tried to read his intention by checking the increase/decrease of the muscle tone, eyes' movement, and possible change of facial expressions. It was said that the boy seemed uneasy when his classroom teacher was not with him, and had relaxed look with the teacher. However, this was only a subjective interpretation of the teacher. Moreover, it was unknown how much and often the change occurred.

2.2 Method

In order to understand the boy's voluntary movement, an experimental session was conducted once for two weeks. Each session took about an hour. There were two conditions for the boy (1) with and (2) without the teacher. The conditions repeated reciprocally and the Motion History of the boy was recorded for every 5-10 seconds. The difference of the Motion History of the two conditions was investigated.

2.3 Results and Discussion

Figure 1 shows the transition of the Motion History of the boy. Both Fig. 1(a) and 1(c) are taken from the condition with the teacher, and 1(b) without the teacher. The teacher standing next to the boy told him she was going out of the room at the timing between Fig. 1(a) and 1(b). The teacher came back and spoke to the boy between Fig. 1(b) and 1(c).

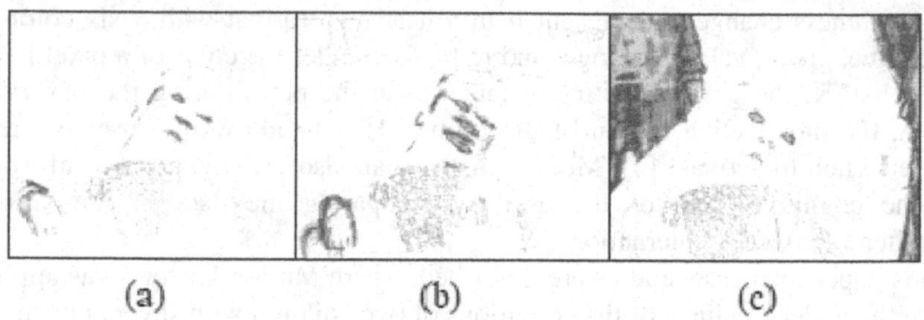

Fig. 1. Motion History of the boy in the session. His classroom teacher stood by him in (a) and (c). The teacher was not with him in (b).

The Motion History tells that the boy did not move very much, but blinked and slightly shook his head when the teacher stood by him in Fig. 1(a). When the teacher went out of the room, the boy shook head more as shown in Fig. 1(b). The boy stopped shaking his head when the teacher came back to him in Fig. 1(c). His blinking was solely observed in the last picture.

The Motion History showed the boy's voluntary movement of shaking his head according to the teacher's attendance, although no evidence could be seen about his uneasiness or relaxed mood here.

Conventional observation, such as just watching the person or a recorded video of them, may overlook occurring subtle change as this, whereas Motion History keeps the transition in an integrated image that makes it much easier to find the movement.

This finding led further investigation, which is currently conducted, to try to figure out what attracts the boy's head movement by comparing several other conditions, e.g. with/without voice, musical sound, and light.

3 Case Study B: Effective Interaction Based on Motion History

In the second case, Motion History was used to distinguish voluntary movement of an eleven year old male child with cerebral palsy and intellectual disability who was non-speaking.

3.1 Background

No substantial success was made in communicating with the boy until this case study. It was thought that the boy enjoyed self-stimuli and often shook his body and touched his lips. His classroom teacher hoped to find a way to turn his attention from the self-stimuli to interaction with others.

3.2 Method

In order to understand the boy's voluntary movement, an experimental session was conducted once for two weeks. Each session took about an hour. The boy's Motion

History and video were taken under conditions of several different stimuli. The Motion History was recorded for every 5-10 seconds. The Motion History of these conditions were compared to investigate the change of the boy.

3.3 Results and Discussion

Figure 2 shows the Motion History recorded under four conditions in the first week session with the boy. The boy sat on the wheelchair. Five images taken from the beginning of the observation are shown for each condition here. There was no intervention in the condition of Fig. 2(a). A cover was put over his eyes in Fig. 2(b), and a massager was put behind his back in Fig. 2(c). No intervention applied again in Fig. 2(d). The four conditions were applied in this order.

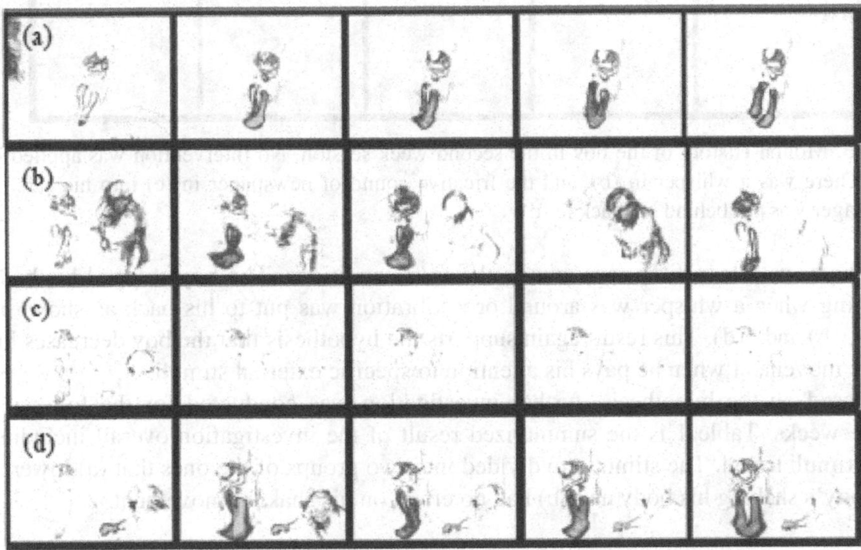

Fig. 2. Motion History of the boy in the first week session. No intervention was applied in (a) and (d). A cover was put over his eyes in (b). A massager was put behind his back in (c).

White images tell us that the boy did not move. The result here led a hypothesis that the boy stopped shaking his body when his attention was paid to a specific stimulus from outside. The stimulus that stopped his body was the vibration to his back as shown in Fig. 2(c) in the first week session.

In the second week session, other stimuli were tested in order to confirm the hypothesis from the first week. Figure 3 shows the Motion History recorded in the second week session. The boy was lying on a mattress on the floor. No intervention was applied in the condition of Fig. 3(a). There was a whisper and the fricative sound of newspaper into his ears in Fig. 3(b) and 3(c), respectively. A massager was put behind his back in Fig. 3(d).

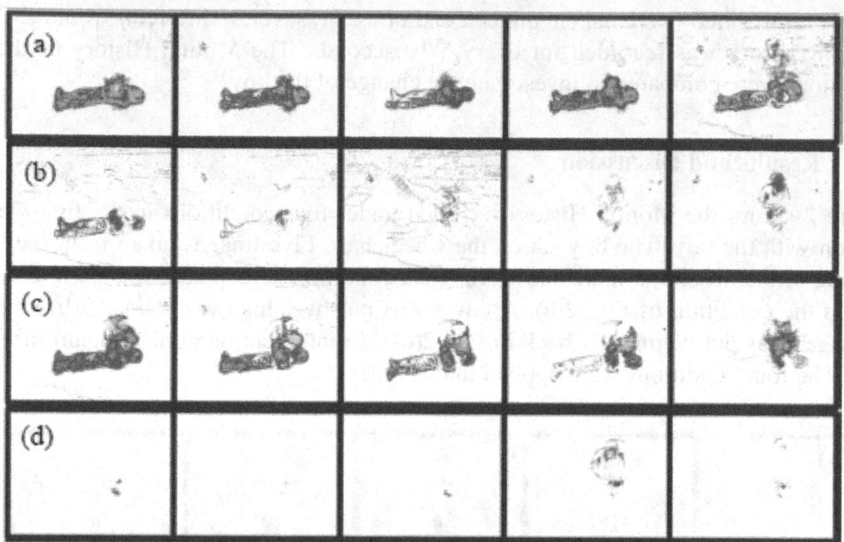

Fig. 3. Motion History of the boy in the second week session. No intervention was applied in (a). There was a whisper in (b), and the fricative sound of newspaper in (c) into his ears. A massager was put behind his back in (d).

There was clear difference among the four conditions. The boy stopped his body shaking when a whisper was around or a vibration was put to his back as shown in Fig. 3(b) and 3(d). This result again supports the hypothesis that the boy decreases his body movement when he pays his attention to specific external stimuli.

Based on the hypothesis, further investigation was conducted for the following three weeks. Table 1 is the summarized result of the investigation overall including the stimuli tested. The stimuli are divided into two groups of the ones that (a) lowered the boy's shaking his body and (b) had no effect on his shaking movement.

Table 1. Tested stimuli in the sessions

(a) **Stimuli that lowered the boy's shaking his body**	(b) **Stimuli that had no effect on the boy's movement**
Massager behind his back	Blinking light
Whisper into his ear	Fricative sound of newspaper
iPad screen to touch & get a sound feedback	iPad screen to see
Small drum sound	Large drum sound
Tapping on the palm of his left hand	Tapping on his foot

Motion History helped to visualize voluntary movement here, and this was possible by paying attention to the stop/decrease of the boy's movement. The stop/decrease of the movement are easily ignored in observation compared with positive transition of movement. In fact, the comments on the boy's everyday reaction collected from his classroom teachers were all about increased/initiated movements, such as that the boy opened his mouth when fed and smiled when bouncing on a trampoline. Motion History is good at finding the stop/decrease of the movement, and this can be a key to extract voluntary component from the person's movement.

His teachers started using the evidence found through the sessions. The stimuli in the group of Table 1(a) were expected to create a better interaction with the boy and his voluntary movement. For example, a new activity that uses his left hand with touching the iPad screen seems to work for him to search the screen himself. Another new approach is tapping on his left palm followed by whispering a message instead of just telling it aloud.

4 Conclusions

This study used a computer-vision based technique called Motion History that visualizes the history of movement of the user. Motion History successfully helped to investigate voluntary movement and cognition of children with severe and multiple disabilities in the two case studies. In the first case, it helped to find the boy's voluntary movement of shaking his head according to his teacher's attendance. In the second case, it revealed several effective stimuli that attracted the boy's attention. Both findings were not recognized among their teachers before the study.

As the results of the case studies, it was found that the observation using Motion History has the following characteristics as its strength compared with conventional observation, such as just watching the person or a recorded video of them. Motion History transforms transitions of the user's movement for a certain period of time into a single image, and therefore, it makes a comparison easier to find the changes under different conditions. This gives us a greater possibility of evidence-based interaction with people with severe and multiple disabilities.

Acknowledgement. This study was partly funded by the research grants from the Ministry of Health, Labour and Welfare of Japan (Shogaisha Taisaku Sougo Kenkyu Jigyo) and Microsoft Japan Co., Ltd. The authors would like to show their sincere gratitude to them.

References

1. Yang, G., Iwabuchi, M., Nakamura, K., Sano, S., Taniguchi, K., Aoki, T.: Observation and potential exploration for people with severe disabilities using vision technology. In: Proceedings of Human Interface Symposium 2013, pp. 107–110 (2013)
2. Assist-I. Observation and Access with Kinect (2014), http://www.assist-i.net/at/en/
3. Bobick, A.F., Davis, J.W.: The Recognition of Human Movement Using Temporal Templates. IEEE Transactions on Pattern Analysis and Machine Intelligence 23(3), 257–267 (2001)
4. Yang, G., Iwabuchi, M., Nakamura, K.: Automatic convenient switch fitting based on motion history for people with physical disabilities. Correspondences on Human Interface 15(11), 5–6 (2013)

A Virtual Reality Training System for Helping Disabled Children to Acquire Skills in Activities of Daily Living

Kup-Sze Choi[1] and King-Hung Lo[2]

[1] Centre for Smart Health, School of Nursing, The Hong Kong Polytechnic University, Hung Hom, Kowloon, Hong Kong

[2] Occupational Therapy Department, Hong Kong Red Cross Princess Alexandra School, Kwun Tong, Kowloon, Hong Kong

kschoi@ieee.org

Abstract. Deficiency of hand function presents difficulty to disabled people in various activities of daily living. While rehabilitation training in occupational therapy is helpful for them to cope with their deficiency, the paper presents a virtual realty based system in attempt to provide an alternative approach to complement the conventional methods. The system simulates tasks of daily living in virtual environments and produces real-time interactive graphics and forces to enable trainees to practise the skills in cyberspace. Currently, three tasks are simulated, namely, door opening, water pouring and meat cutting. Visual, audio and haptic cues are produced as guidance in response to user's actions. The performance of the users is recorded automatically on the fly with quantifiable metrics to enable objective analysis of the learning progress. Findings from initial trials with disabled children show that they found it very interesting to use the system and could adapt to the virtual training environment for practicing the tasks. Further study will be conducted to improve system usability and to evaluate the training effectiveness.

Keywords: Virtual reality, activities of daily living, haptic device, force feedback, occupational therapy.

1 Introduction

Deficiencies in hand dexterity present challenges to disabled children in performing various activities of daily living (ADLs). The impairment does not only affect their self-care abilities but could also lead to low self-esteem and other psychological impacts. Special schools for the physically disabled have been providing special education and rehabilitation services to the students. In ADL training, occupational therapists strive to improve the students' self-care abilities and maximize their level of independence.

Conventional ADL training is conducted in real or physically simulated environments through various training modalities [1], including behavioural approach for skill acquisition, neuro-developmental approach, conductive education, constrain-induced movement therapy and biofeedback. However, the training is associated with

K. Miesenberger et al. (Eds.): ICCHP 2014, Part II, LNCS 8548, pp. 244–251, 2014.

potential issues concerning safety, logistics, efficiency and cost. Besides, the approaches are not readily customizable for people with different levels of disability, where therapists are required to focus on meeting specific training needs rather than teaching technical strategies [2].

In this regard, we propose to use virtual reality (VR) technology and haptic user interface to complement conventional ADL training, so as to improve the teaching and learning of self-care skills. By leveraging these technologies, ADL training can be conducted in computer-simulated environments which can offer various advantages [3], e.g. flexible and realistic settings in virtual environment, customizability, quantitative assessment, safe training on risk-prone skills and repetitive training.

2 Related Work

The burgeoning VR technologies has found many practical applications in rehabilitation [4, 5]. The applications include hand rehabilitation after stroke [6, 7] and brain lesions [8], manual dexterity assessment [9, 10] and hand-eye coordination training [11], where haptic devices are used to enable users to make use of the sense of touch in the therapy. While providing feedback forces in real time, the haptic devices also make possible real-time quantitative measurement of position and orientation during rehabilitative training [7], [9], [12], thus allowing objective performance evaluation of kinematic and dynamic motor abilities [9], [13].

Nevertheless, VR training systems specifically developed for ADL are relatively scarce, particularly with the use of haptic technology. An early work on VR ADL training is the Virtual Life Skills project, which developed a virtual city involving a house, cafe and transport system [14, 15]. Therapists used the system to teach children with learning difficulty the use of public toilet, for example. An immersive virtual kitchen was also proposed for people with traumatic brain injury (TBI) to learn meal preparation tasks [16]. VR training system simulating a real supermarket was developed to allow patients with TBI to practise the shopping tasks [3], such as exploring the virtual supermarket and picking up goods. However, these applications focused on the training of cognitive abilities. Users only made use of non-intuitive input devices like joystick or mouse as user interface, making it impractical to train the actual manual skills involved. A more recent work employed touch-screen monitor to create a virtual environment simulating the operation of an automated teller machine to train and assess persons with brain injury [17]. Furthermore, with haptic devices, computer-generated force feedback is introduced to provide interactive haptic guidance in handwriting training for children with cerebral palsy [18-21].

3 The Virtual Training System

3.1 System Framework

Given the variety of tasks in ADL training, the design of the proposed VR system adopts a modular design approach where individual training tasks are simulated and developed as separate software modules that can be "plugged" into the system to "play" the specific training task. The hardware components of this system include a computer with keyboard and mouse, an LCD monitor, speakers and most importantly a pair of haptic devices. The software components include a simulation engine, a model database and a user performance database. The system framework is shown schematically in Fig. 1.

With the haptic devices, user can manoeuvre virtual objects with the pen-like stylus while feeling the computer-generated feedback forces in real time through the handle. Furthermore, the pen-like handle is detachable and can be replaced by customized handles mimicking real objects involved in ADLs, e.g. key, jar or knife.

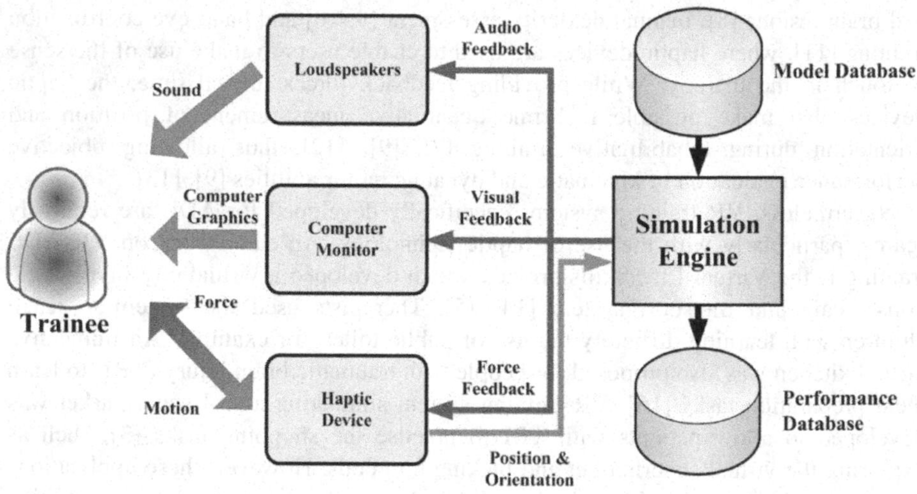

Fig. 1. The system framework

The simulation engine models the interactions between the virtual objects according to the user's input through the haptic device. Based on the input, the engine computes and generates real-time responses in the form of visual, audio and force feedback that are presented to the user via computer monitor, loudspeaker, and the haptic device respectively. In the prototype system, three task modules are developed for the training, namely, Task 1: door opening, Task 2: water pouring, and Task 3: meat cutting. Tasks 1 and 2 involve one-hand operation, while Task 3 requires bimanual coordination.

3.2 User Interface

The proposed system has been implemented with a desktop computer with Intel Core 2 Duo E8500 3.17GHz CPU, 4 GB RAM, and Nvidia GeForce GTX650 display card. The haptic devices employed are the Phantom® Omni® manufactured by the SensAble Technologies Incorporated. The device has 6 degrees-of-freedom input (position and orientation) and 3 degrees-of-freedom output (feedback force). 3D printing technology is adopted to fabricate a key (for Task 1), a jar (for Task 2), a piece of luncheon meat and the handle of a knife (for Task 3), as shown in Fig. 2. These 3D-printed "handles" are attachable to the haptic devices, by which the user can interactively manoeuvre the corresponding virtual objects being rendered visually on the computer monitor.

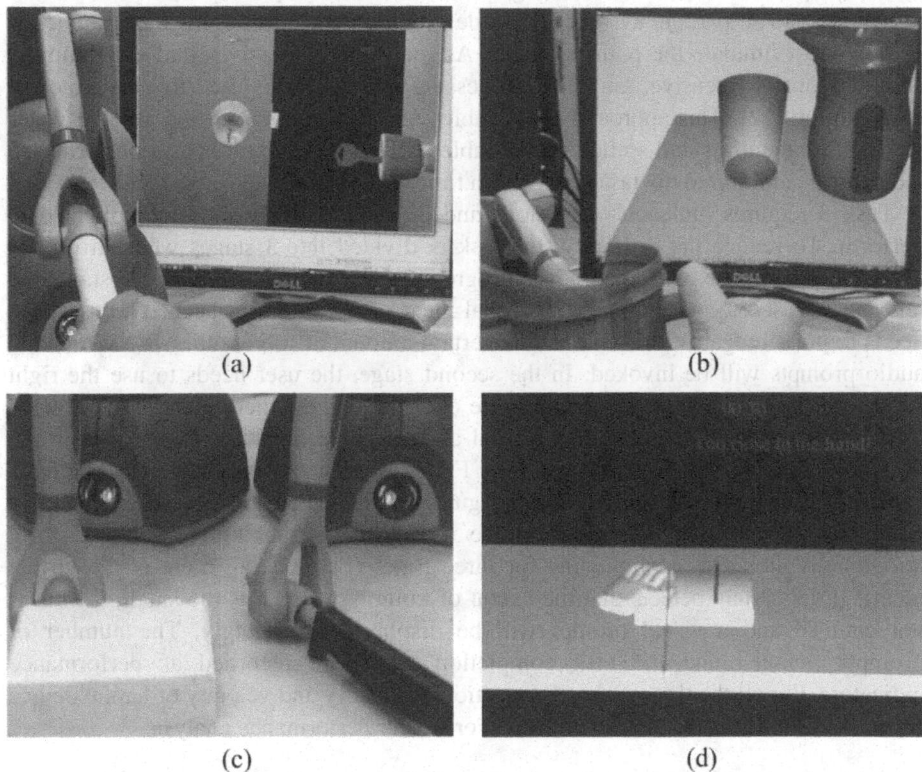

Fig. 2. Haptic-enabled VR simulation of three training tasks: (a) inserting a key into the key hole; (b) pouring water into a glass; (c) 3D-printed "handles" for the meat-cutting tasks, with the white block on the left as the "meat" and the black handle on the right as the knife; (d) visual prompt (top right on the screen) is invoked when the knife (yellow) is too close to the left hand, while a cut should be made along the guideline (red).

3.3 Training Task Simulation

For Task 1, front view and side view of the scene are provided to assist user to determine the relative position of the keyhole and the key in order to facilitate key insertion. Collision detection and response are performed so that user can feel the resistive forces (as haptic cues) when the key is in contact with the door or the door knob. The task is completed after the key is inserted into the key hole and the user turns the key by 90 degrees. Sound clips are also played when the turning of the inserted key is made. The task completion time and the number of collisions are recorded for performance evaluation.

For Task 2, the user holds the handle of the 3D-printed jar to control the position and orientation of the jar and to fill the glass with water. Different audio cues are played when water is poured into the glass and mistakenly spilled on the table surface respectively. The particle system technique commonly used in computer graphics is employed to simulate the pouring water. As real-time interactive fluid simulation is computationally intensive, graphical processing unit (GPU) is used to accelerate the computation [22]. This approach also enables the measurement of the amount water poured into the glass and spilled on the table surface, which serves as a performance indicator in addition to the task completion time.

Task 3 requires bimanual operations and is thus relatively more complicated to perform. To reduce the difficulty, the task is divided into 3 stages where a user is required to complete one stage before progressing into the next. In the first stage, the left hand is used to put the piece of virtual meat on the table surface. The user also needs to press it against the table with a certain amount of force; otherwise visual and audio prompts will be invoked. In the second stage, the user needs to use the right hand to move the edge of the virtual knife over the region where a cut is to be made (highlighted with a red guideline). Visual and audio prompts are invoked when the knife is too close to the left hand (see Fig. 2(d)). In the last stage, the knife is constrained to be moved only along the guideline indicated in the second stage. To complete the task, the user needs move (slide) the virtual knife back and forth horizontally along the straight line for three times (i.e., making a cut at the virtual meat). If the system detects that the extent of knife movement is too small, the cut is not counted and a visual prompt will be displayed accordingly. The number of prompts invoked and the task completion times are recorded as performance indicators. For all the three tasks, the position, trajectory and velocity of haptic device stylus, as well as the contact forces are recorded for performance analysis.

4 Trials

Preliminary trials had been conducted to collect user feedback on the prototype system. Students and occupational therapists of a special school were invited to participate in the trials (see Fig. 3). While some effort was required for the disabled students to adapt to the virtual environments and to develop an association between the input interface (the 3D-printed handles) and the objects in the virtual environment,

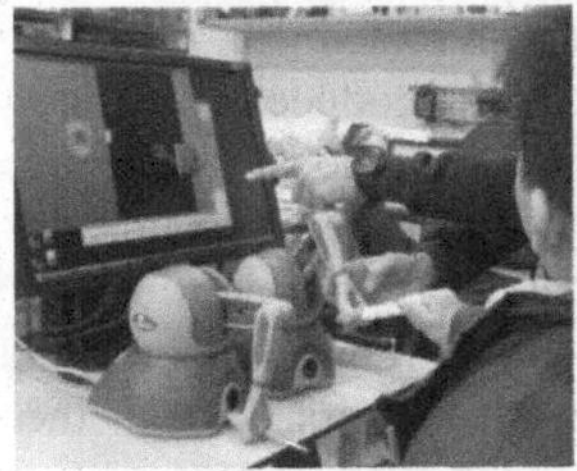
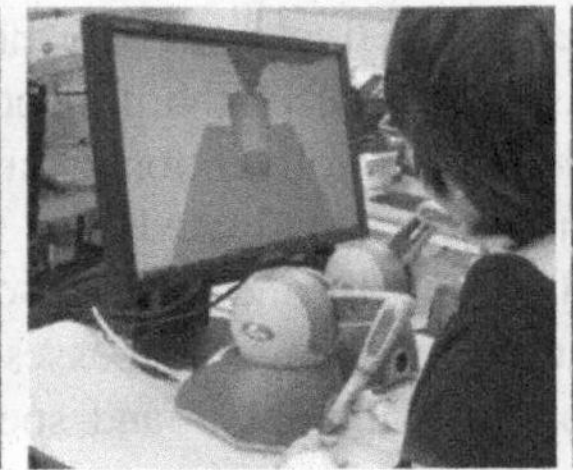
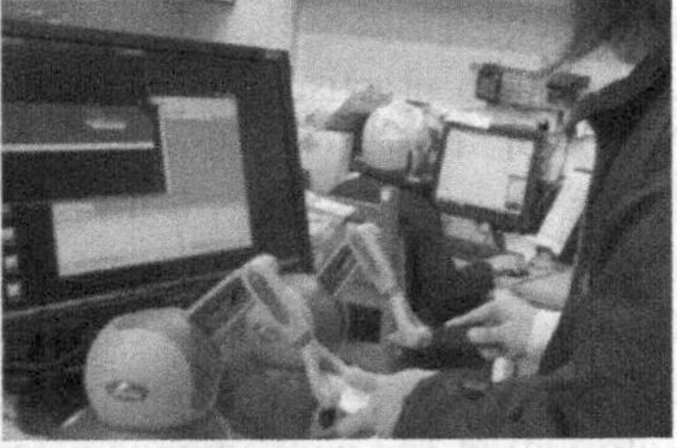

Fig. 3. Preliminary field trials of the virtual ADL training system

they found it very interesting to use the VR system to learn ADL skills. The computer-game-like setting is a motivation to the students. Observations from the trials also suggest that the system is suitable for students of mild to moderate disability.

5 Discussion

Initial feedback and comments on the proposed VR ADL training system from the occupational therapists and the students are quite positive. While the bimanual operations in Task 3 is relatively difficult, the children were found to be able to adapt to the virtual environments developed for simulating the single-handed tasks Task 1 and Task 2. The children demonstrated the ability to correct their hand movement based on the visual feedback displayed on the screen and the force feedback they perceived via the haptic device, thereby successfully inserting the virtual key into the key hole and pouring water into the virtual glass.

A comprehensive study is being planned to investigate the feasibility of the proposed training system. The purpose of the study is to (1) evaluate the training effectiveness of the system, particularly the effectiveness of the transfer of the skills learned from the virtual world into reality, (2) determine the usability of the system, (3) identify the user groups that can be most benefited from the system, and (4) identify practical issues and rooms for further enhancement in order to make it practical for use as a routine training exercise. A pre-post test design will be adopted where subjects with various degrees of impairment are invited to practise with the VR system repeatedly. Their virtual learning performance will be measured and recorded to analyse the training progress. Before and after the virtual training, the subjects are also required to perform the three ADL in real environments, where their performance will be video-taped and assessed by occupational therapists. The results will be used to determine the training effectiveness of the proposed system.

6 Conclusion

The project is an example of interdisciplinary effort to meet special education needs, demonstrating the synergy of occupation therapy and information technology to benefit disabled children. Through innovative use of VR technology and haptic user interface, a safe, flexible and cost-effective environment is created for disabled children to practise various ADLs. The goal of the project is to produce a practical VR ADL training system to complement conventional training methods. There are few training systems of this kind. It is anticipated that the proposed system can improve the learning curve of self-care skills and raise the children's self-confidence. In addition, as the system can be used for therapy and assessment, it has the potential to reduce the workload of occupational therapists and special teachers through the automation and convenience offered.

Acknowledgement. This work is supported in part by the Quality Education Fund of the Education Bureau of the Hong Kong SAR (Project No. 2011/0162) and the General Research Fund of the Hong Kong Research Grants Council (Project No. PolyU 5134/12E).

References

1. Activities of Daily Living Training Manual for Stroke: Application of Motor Relearning and Neuro-Developmental Treatment Approach. Hong Kong Occupational Therapy Association, Hong Kong (2006)
2. Guidetti, S., Tham, K.: Therapeutic Strategies Used by Occupational Therapists in Self-Care Training: A Qualitative Study. Occupational Therapy International 9(4), 257–276 (2002)
3. Lee, J., Ku, J., Cho, W., Hahn, W., et al.: A Virtual Reality System for the Assessment and Rehabilitation of the Activities of Daily Living. Cyberpsychology & Behavior 6(4), 383–388 (2003)
4. Burdea, G.C.: Virtual Rehabilitation - Benefits and Challenges. Methods of Information in Medicine 42(5), 519–523 (2003)
5. Holden, M.K.: Virtual Environments for Motor Rehabilitation: Review. Cyberpsychology and Behavior 8(3), 187–211 (2005)
6. Merians, A., Jack, D., Boian, R.: Virtual Reality-Augmented Rehabilitation for Patients Following Stroke. Phys. Ther. 82, 898–915 (2002)
7. Broeren, J., Rydmark, M., Katharina, S.: Virtual Reality and Haptics as a Training Device for Movement Rehabilitation after Stroke: A Single-Case Study. Arch. Phys. Med. Rehabil. 85, 1247–1250 (2004)
8. Piron, L., Cenni, F., Tonin, P., Dam, M.: Virtual Reality as an Assessment Tool for Arm Motor Deficits after Brain Lesions. In: Stud. Health Technol. Inform., pp. 386–392 (2001)
9. Bardorfer, A., Munih, M., Zupan, A., Primozic, A.: Upper Limb Motion Analysis Using Haptic Interface. IEEE/ASME Transactions on Mechatronics 6(3), 253–260 (2001)
10. Pernalete, N., Wentao, Y., Dubey, R., Moreno, W.: Development of a Robotic Haptic Interface to Assist the Performance of Vocational Tasks by People with Disabilities. In: Proceedings of the IEEE International Conference on Robotics and Automation, ICRA 2002, pp. 1269–1274 (2002)
11. Arsenault, R., Ware, C.: Eye-Hand Co-Ordination with Force Feedback. In: Proceedings of the SIGCHI Conference on Human Factors In Computing Systems. ACM, The Hague (2000)

12. Broeren, J., Bjorkdahl, A., Pascher, R., Rydmark, M.: Virtual Reality and Haptics as an Assessment Device in the Postacute Phase after Stroke. Cyberpsychol. Behav. 5, 207–211 (2002)
13. Prisco, G.M., Avizzano, C.A., Calcara, M., Ciancio, S., et al.: A Virtual Environment with Haptic Feedback for the Treatment of Motor Dexterity Disabilities. In: Proceedings of the 1998 IEEE International Conference on Robotics and Automation, vol. 4, pp. 3721–3726 (1998)
14. Cobb, S.V.G., Neale, H.R., Reynolds, H.: Evaluation of Virtual Learning Environments. In: The 2nd Euro. Conf. Disability, Virtual Reality & Assoc. Tech (ECDVRAT), Skövde, Sweden (1998)
15. Brown, D., Neale, H., Cobb, S., Reynolds, H.: Deveopment and Evaluation of the Virtual City. The International Journal of Virtual Reality 3(4), 27–38 (1998)
16. Zhang, L., Abreu, B.C., Seale, G.S., Masel, B., et al.: A Virtual Reality Environment for Evaluation of a Daily Living Skill in Brain Injury Rehabilitation: Reliability and Validity. Arch. Phys. Med. Rehabil. 84, 1118–1124 (2003)
17. Fong, K.N., Chow, K.Y., Chan, B.C., Lam, K.C., et al.: Usability of a Virtual Reality Environment Simulating an Automated Teller Machine for Assessing and Training Persons with Acquired Brain Injury. Journal of Neuro Engineering and Rehabilitation 7(19) (2010)
18. Choi, K.S.: Learning Handwriting with Interactive Assistive Forces. In: The 5th International Convention in Rehabilitation Engineering and Assistive Technology (i-CREATe 2011), Bangkok, Thailand (2011)
19. Choi, K.S.: A Virtual Training System for Children with Upper Extremity Disability. Cyber Therapy & Rehabilitation (4), 15–16 (2011)
20. Choi, K.-S., Chow, C.-M., Lo, K.-H.: A Rehabilitation Method with Visual and Haptic Guidance for Children with Upper Extremity Disability. In: Miesenberger, K., Klaus, J., Zagler, W., Karshmer, A. (eds.) ICCHP 2010, Part II. LNCS, vol. 6180, pp. 77–84. Springer, Heidelberg (2010)
21. Choi, K.S., Lo, K.H.: A Hand Rehabilitation System with Force Feedback for Children with Cerebral Palsy: Two Case Studies. Disability and Rehabilitation 33(17-18), 1704–1714 (2011)
22. Nguyen, H. (ed.): GPU Gems 3. Addison-Wes., Upper Saddle River (2008)

The Possibilities of Kinect as an Access Device for People with Cerebral Palsy
A Preliminary Study

Isabel María Gómez[1], Alberto Jesús Molina[1], Rafael Cabrera[1], David Valenzuela[2], and Marcelo Garrido[1]

[1] Electronic Technology Department, Universidad de Sevilla, Spain
{igomez,almolina}@us.es,
rcabrera@dte.us.es
[2] ASPACE, Sevilla, Spain
TSASPACEV@telefonica.net

Abstract. Cerebral palsy (CP) is a general term for a group of permanent, non-progressive movement disorders that cause physical disability in development, mainly in the areas of body movement but it might also affect intellectual capabilities. Among all this diversity of profiles, we find that, for some of them, access to a computer application is almost impossible in spite of the great variety of commercial devices based of different technologies. Kinect might be a viable possibility in order to facilitate access to games and computer applications that help users improve their skills or communication.

Keywords: Access Device, Kinect, Cerebral Palsy, Middleware Software.

1 Introduction

The use of Kinect in the case of CP can be found mainly in the area of rehabilitation. In [1] a preliminary study to evaluate the usefulness of games based on Kinect is done. In [2] participants played 4 video games and a quantitative evaluation of its potential for physical activity promotion and rehabilitation is explained. In [3] games are specifically designed to promote physical rehabilitation and include information of progress for the therapist. In [4] a specific application called Move it to improve it (Mitii) was used to determine if 20 weeks of intensive training can improve upper-limb activity (unimanual and bimanual), occupational performance and cognitive skills in children and adolescents with CP compared to standard care. In [5] the work is focused on how to design the game in order to be both fun and efficient in terms of motor skills development or attitude change, emphasizing the adaptation to physical skill a motivating social participation.

Furthermore Kinect can be used as an access device based in gestures that allows the control of computer applications in general. There are several tools that translate gestures into mouse or keyboard events which allow the use of applications that can be controlled by such events. Two of them are based exclusively in hands:

K. Miesenberger et al. (Eds.): ICCHP 2014, Part II, LNCS 8548, pp. 252–255, 2014.

Tip-TepMouse [6] and Winect[7]. In [8] the Flexible Action and Articulated Skeleton Toolkit (FAAST), a middleware software framework for integrating full-body interaction with virtual environments, video games, and other user interfaces is described. A case study is presented that is made up of in improving accessibility for people with mobility difficulties. However some problems are encountered such as tool configuration and gesture recognition.

2 Methodology Used

In this paper four applications have been tested. Three of them are described in [6,7,8]. They are available for free download. The fourth one is of our own design. This tool is called KIVIAD (Kinect Virtual Access Device). The advantage of KIVIAD is that it has been designed to deal with specific necessities that have been observed during several training sessions in ASPACE (Association of people with cerebral palsy of Seville). With this tool we have two kinds of control: one of them is with a precise gesture and the other one generates the event choosing any voluntary movement, eliminating the need to maintain the same position and repeat the same pattern of movement. The event is generated based only in the velocity of movement.

2.1 Subjects

We have conducted the experiment using two groups of users:

- Healthy people. Three individuals aged between 29 and 47, two males and one female tested the software.
- Adults with cerebral palsy. Five users, two males and three females were chosen. The trials were carried out in a daycare center of ASPACE. The users had different profiles. Two of them could not speak and used a notebook of pictograms to communicate. Subjects were asked which body movement they had more control over. Three subjects selected head movement, one selected their left hand and finally the last selected their right hand.

2.2 Tests Description

The tests designed had to be established in accordance with the tools under evaluation. Tip-Tep and Winect translate specific hand gestures to a mouse event (including click and displacement). With these tools gestures cannot be configured. In FAAST any kind of gesture can be chosen and translates them into all kinds of events (mouse and keyboard). To do the configuration, this tool has a series of menus. KIVIAD has a different orientation in its design, being designed for people with mobility problems, works alone in discrete mode. This means this tool translates between gestures and mouse click or keyboard key_press but not in cursor mouse movements. So, two kinds of tests have been considered:

- The test in continuous mode, Tip_Tep, Winect and FAAST have been used. An activity that requires cursor movement and mouse clicks is proposed. The cursor began in the central point of the screen. Users must do the following action in a computer: open Virtual keyboard (VK); open Web Browser; write bbc and press INTRO in the browser bar using VK; displace mouse cursor to the first link and select it; then scroll the selected web page for its reading. In order to do these actions, we need two gestures that are different depending on the tool used. Time spent in performing each task and mistakes were measured. Users answered a small test related with tools usability.
- Test in discrete mode. In this case activity only requires a mouse click. A communication application based on pictograms has been used for tests. This tool works by scanning, this being controlled by the mouse click. Users must transmit three ideas built by pictograms. The application is prepared to receive clicks only and does not work properly if cursor movement is transmitted. So in this test only FAAST and KIVIAD were used because both of them can be configured to transmit only the click. It is very important to determine the gesture to be used for the event generation corresponding to this click, especially with subjects with cerebral palsy. It is not possible to ask for a specific gesture, since they do not have control over the movement. The only way to widen the user profile and that they work comfortably is to base the movement on speed without restriction of direction and ask them to choose the right hand, left hand or the head. If no errors are made, the time required to transmit each idea depends on the position of the icons on panels so, only errors were measured. An error was made when the icon is not selected when the scanning reaches it. False clicks can also take place when the skeleton is not tracked properly.

KIVIAD and FAAST are different in their configuration. KIVIAD is especially designed for people with disabilities and FAAST has a broader spectrum. For this reason, KIVIAD design has not considered a great variety of input gestures and neither a wide variety of output events. It is not necessary more because this is not used in the environment of its use. Furthermore, events are generated in a lower level than in FAAST. There are some kind of software that cannot operate with events in the upper level, in fact some games designed for the same people where XNA Game Studio has been used cannot be controlled using FAAST but work properly with KIVIAD. It was considered important to obtain point of view of therapist about usability of these tools.

2.3 Method

Healthy subjects did both tests, continuous and discrete. Three sessions with each tool were held for each of them. In this form, the experience acquired can be evaluat-ed. Users with cerebral palsy only did the test in discrete mode. Three sessions were held with each user and the therapist. Continuous mode was discarded after talking to the therapist and noted that it was not possible for users to have the required accuracy in the movements.

3 Results

In continuous mode Tip-Tep presented the best results(less time, less errors and the best answer in usability). In discrete mode, KIVIAD and FAAST were functionality equivalent. But KIVIAD is more intuitive and presented better configuration.

4 Conclusions

In cerebral palsy is more common to consider Kinect as a tool for supporting rehabilitation therapies. There are very few studies which have considered it as an access device.

Besides testing Kinect applications for CP users, this work also aims to conduct an assessment of this system as an access device itself and remark what this technology may contribute with respect to other established solutions. Special emphasis has been taken into account in those cases where appropriate solutions for computer access have not been found yet.

The proposed of Kinect as access device raises questions because users must perform control actions with nothing tangible and without seeing his image. However users that did the trials have gotten the operation of the device and have managed to complete the tasks that were established.

References

1. Luna-Oliva, L., et al.: Kinect Xbox 360 as a therapeutic modality for children with cerebral palsy in a school environment: A preliminary study. Neuro Rehabilitation 33(4), 513–521 (2013), doi:10.3233/NRE-131001
2. Howcroft, J., et al.: Active Video Game Play in Children With Cerebral Palsy: Potential for Physical Activity Promotion and Rehabilitation Therapies. Archives of Physical Medicine and Rehabilitation 93(8), 1448–1456 (2012)
3. Roy, A.K., Soni, Y., Dubey, S.: Enhancing Effectiveness of Motor Rehabilitation Using Kinect Motion Sensing Technology. In: Global Humanitarian Technology Conference: South Asia Satellite (GHTC-SAS). IEEE (2013)
4. Boyd, R.N., et al.: Move it to improve it (Mitii): study protocol of a randomised controlled trial of a novel web-based multimodal training program for children and adolescents with cerebral palsy bmjopen-2013-002853 (2013)
5. de Greef, K., van der Spek, E.D., Bekker, T.: Designing Kinect games to train motor skills for mixed ability players. In: Games for Health: Proceedings of the 3rd European Conference on Gaming and Playful Interaction in Health Care, pp. 978–973. Springer Fachmedien Wiesbaden (2013) ISBN: 978-3-658-02896-1
6. `http://tiptep.com/index.php/products`
7. `http://xorastudios.com/portfolio/winect`
8. Suma, E., Krum, D., Lange, B., Koenig, S., Rizzo, A., Bolas, M.: Adapting user interfaces for gestural interaction with the flexible action and articulated skeleton toolkit. Computers & Graphics 37(3), 193–201 (2013)

Development of Sit-to-Stand Support System Using Ground Reaction Force

Hidetaka Ikeuchi, Masuji Nagatoshi, and Atuyoshi Miura

Oita University, Faculty of Engineering, Oita, Japan
{hikeuchi,nagatosi,miuraa}@oita-u.ac.jp

Abstract. This paper shows our developing sit-to-stand support system using ground reaction force to operate device. Computer system control sit-to-support mechanism automatically by information of the user ground reaction force (GRF). The user of this device don't need to operate the switch or button. This paper shows first prototype device and describe about device control rule, experiment results and the found problems of control, at first. Secondly, to solve these problems, experiment device for second prototype design is shown, and experiment method is described. Finally, preliminary results are shown in these experiments.

Keywords: Sit-to-stand Support, Grand Reaction Force, Human Motion Analysis.

1 Introduction

Sit-to-Stand movement is difficult for elder or patient with enfeebled lower limb function, however, it is necessary to their daily activity. There are assist chair using gas cylinder [1], stand assist toilet [2] seat and so on, as sit-to-stand helping device in Japan. Support power of these device is constant and they needs user operation using switch or button.

Our sit-to-stand support device is controlled by user's ground reaction force. The computer installed in our system estimate whether user will sit or stand using information of ground reaction force, and our device is able to assist according to user's limb power. Although the user have to put power into their limb to sit-to-stand, it is expected that this device play a role of rehabilitation device.

2 First Prototype and Control Method

2.1 Overview of First Prototype

Fig.1, left, shows control flow in our system. The user's GRF increases in standup phase. This increment is sensed by GRF Sensor and the computer drives air cylinder. The bar of device is actuated by air cylinder and the bar lifts user's body. On other hand, the air cylinder compressed according that GFR decreases in sitting. The

K. Miesenberger et al. (Eds.): ICCHP 2014, Part II, LNCS 8548, pp. 256–259, 2014.

support of body by the bar was adopted in first prototype because the user might feel secure. The Wii Balance BoardTM that is manufactured by Nintendo is used as GRF Sensor since low cost and using only vertical component of GRF. WiimoteLib[3] was used to read GRF data from The Wii Balance Board. Control program was made using Microsoft Visual Studio 2010.

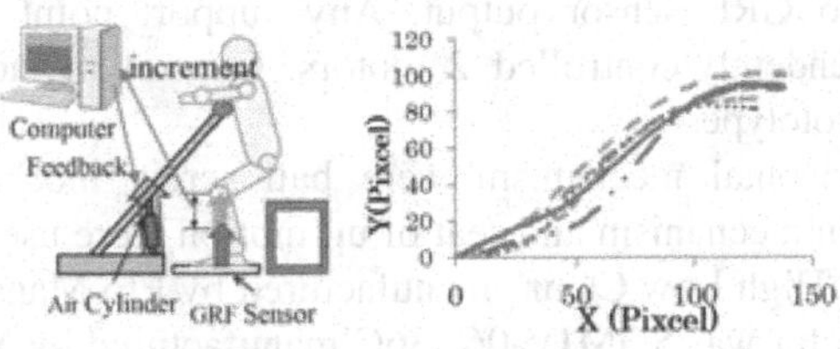

Fig. 1. Left: Control flow in stand up phase. Right: Hip Trajectories.

2.2 Control Method

If user want to standup, GRF increase. On other hand, when user sit, GRF de-crease. So judgment of sitting or standing is determined by differential value of GRF. Actually, deferential value dF is calculated from moving average of GRF is used to remove high frequency component. If $dF > \alpha$ then up command is send to actuator. If $dF < \beta$ then down command is send. Where α and β are each defined thresholds of up and down command. And then, when GRF is larger than 80% of subject's weight or smaller than 30% of subject's weight, that is, user is completely standing or sitting, the computer send up or down command regardless of dF.

2.3 Hip Trajectory in Sit-to-Stand

This prototype was tested by normal subject that was 76kgw and male. Basic function actuated without faults. However, when subject held the bar hardly and push his body against the bar, device didn't work enough. If subject hold the bar hardly, GRF is decreased in standing up phase. So control system send down command, therefore, motions of device and subject are difference. We thought body support by the bar was problem. And then, we considered modifying support method to support at the hip.

Sagittal trajectory of hip in sit-to-stand of normal subject are measured to get ideal support trajectory. Subjects with markers setting at hip, shoulder, knee and ankle stand up from sitting. This motion was recorded by video camera from the side. Subjects were 5 person from 22 to 23 years old. Their upper limbs were crossed and they stand with both feet together. Video images were processed to 2 dimension coordinate value by FrameDIAS II manufactured by DKH Co. Ltd.

Results are shown in Fig.1, right. It found that hip trajectory was forward tilting S curve. However, results of Bando et al.[4] were different. Because the device in reference [4] was passive actuated system, easy comparison wasn't preferred. But this difference suggests to need more consideration.

3 Experiment Device for Analysis of Support Trajectory

3.1 Overview of Device

We produced experiment device for analysis of support trajectory in our proposed device shown Fig.2. This device had 2 degree freedom of X and Y, and actuated 2 motors according to GRF sensor output. Any support point trajectory could be produced by independently-controlled 2 motors. Control method and GRF sensor were same to first prototype.

Vertical and horizontal mechanism were ball screw mechanisms actuated by electric motors. Main mechanism and seat of up motion were used a part of produced sit-to-stand device ("High Low Chair" manufactured by Eto Manufacturing Co. Ltd.). Vertical direction motor was SGMJV-06A36C manufactured by YASKAWA Electric Corp. and horizontal direction motor was SGMJV-02A3A6C manufactured by YASKAWA Electric Corp. Control program was made using Microsoft Visual Studio Express 2013.

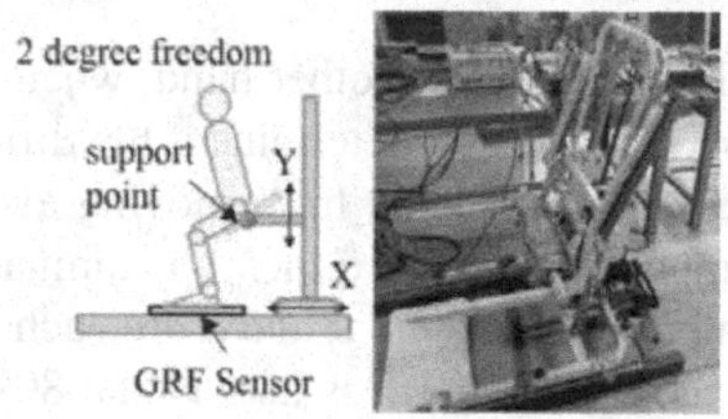

Fig. 2. Experiment device for standup analysis

3.2 Candidate Trajectories

5 Candidate trajectories are planned. Trajectory A is straight line from sitting hip point to standing hip point. Trajectory B is fitted curve to average result of our sit-to-stand experiment. Trajectory C is symmetrical curve of B about A. Trajectory D is a part of convex upward arc of radius 600mm passing sitting point and standing point. Trajectory E is is symmetrical curve of D about A.

3.3 Preliminary Experiments and Results

Preliminary experiments for adjustment of control parameter (α, β) and assessment of trajectories were conducted. Subjects were 4 person who were 22 or 23 old normal male. One subject could not stand smoothly because his body size was larger.

Trajectories assessment experiments using remaining three subject were conducted. Experiments were normal situation (Normal exp.) and wearing elder person simulated brace "Urasimataro"[5] (Elder exp.). "Urasimataro" were developed by WAC (Wonderful Aging Club, Japan). Each subject tested two trajectories which selected randomly and answered better trajectory in one set. Experiments were conducted ten set on each subject, so each subject tested all combination of trajectories. Assessment method was pair comparison method [6].

In normal exp., trajectory D got most high score. And the rest was the order of A, B, E and C. In elder exp., best trajectories ware A and E that were same score. And the rest was the order of D and B, C (same score). In these experiments, the results were inaccurate because number of subject was low. But it was interesting that trajectory A was better and B or C were low score.

In addition, one subject in normal situation was measured muscle potential of lower limb. Muscle potential in using our device is lower than no using device.

4 Conclusion

We are developing sit-to-stand support system using GRF. First prototype was produced and simple control rule using differential value of GRF were proposed. To solve the problem of First prototype, we consider next version system with hip support method. Experiment device to determine best support trajectory was produced. 5 candidate trajectories is planned. Preliminary experiments in normal and simulated elder were conducted.

Further actions is following,

- More accurate assessment using human subject
- Determining of best support trajectory
- Design and produce of second prototype
- Assessment of second prototype using normal or disable subject
- Considering of practical realization

Acknowledgement. This work was supported by JSPS KAKENHI Grant Number 24500651.

References

1. TS-101G/S, TAKANO HEART WORKS, http://www.takano-hw.com/ (Japanese)
2. EWC140N at el., TOTO ltd., http://www.toto.co.jp (Japanese)
3. WiimoteLib 1.7, http://brianpeek.com/page/wiimotelib
4. Bando, N., et al.: Development of assist machine for the motion of standing up using human's upperarm power (II) –Relation between orbit of movement on seat and feelings (2007), http://www.life.rd.pref.gifu.lg.jp (Research Reports of the Gifu Prefectural Research Institute for Human Life Technology) (Japanese)
5. Urasimataro, Wonderful Aging Club (public interest incorporated association), http://www.wac.or.jp/ (Japanese)
6. Ishii, G.: Jikken keikakuhou no kiso (basic of design of experiments). Saiensu'sha Co., Ltd. Publishers, Tokyo (1972) (Japanese)

A Critical Review of Eight Years of Research on Technologies for Disabled and Older People

Helen Petrie[1], Blaíthín Gallagher[1], and Jenny S. Darzentas[2]

[1] University of York, United Kingdom
{helen.petrie,blaithin.gallagher}@york.ac.uk
[2] University of the Aegean, Greece
jennyd@aegean.gr

Abstract. This paper presents the initial results of a critical review of recent research on new and emerging technologies designed for older people and people with disabilities. The review covers research published between 2005 and 2012 in a range of international peer-reviewed journals and conferences, in the areas of technology, human-computer interaction, disability, assistive technologies and gerontology. On the basis of this review of research, we are exploring what issues for disabled and older people are being addressed by researchers and developers, whether the research is motivated by user needs, the methodologies used, and outcomes achieved.

Keywords: Older Users, Disabled Users, Assistive Technology, New Technology, Methods for Working with Disabled and Older Users.

1 Introduction

In the past 25 years there has been an increasing emphasis on using technology to support disabled and older people. In Europe, this work received a particular boost from the European Union's TIDE (Technology Initiative for Disabled and Elderly People) Programme in the early 1990s [1, 2, 3] and from continued funding from a range of European initiatives. A number of reviews have been undertaken of technological developments for older people [4, 5], but these have been from a North American viewpoint. We have not been able to find a comprehensive review of research for disabled and older people from a European perspective in recent years, so decided it would be useful to the community of researchers to undertake such a review.

2 Method

2.1 Conference Proceedings and Journals Included in the Review

We selected a number of quality conference proceedings and journals, based on their Impact Factor [6] and rankings by the Australian Research Council's ranking of journals and conferences [7]. We selected mainstream journals and conferences in the

K. Miesenberger et al. (Eds.): ICCHP 2014, Part II, LNCS 8548, pp. 260–266, 2014.

area of human factors, ergonomics and human computer interaction, as well as specialist journals and conferences on aging, disability and technology. Within a pool of possible conference proceedings and journals, a random selection was made. The journals and conferences in the final selection are listed in Table 1.

Table 1. Conference Proceedings and Journals included in the review

Mainstream Conference Proceedings and Journals	
Conference Proceedings	ACM Conference on Human Factors in Computing Systems (CHI) British Computer Society Interaction Specialist Group Conference (BCS HCI) IFIP TC 13 Conference on Human-Computer Interaction (INTERACT) Nordic Conference on Human-Computer Interaction
Journals	ACM Transactions on Computer-Human Interaction Behaviour and Information Technology Human Computer Interaction Human Factors International Journal of Human-Computer Studies
Specialist Conference Proceedings and Journals	
Conference Proceedings	ACM Conference on Computers and Accessibility (ASSETS) International Conference on Computers Helping People with Special Needs (ICCHP)
Journals	ACM Transactions on Accessible Computing Gerontechnology Educational Gerontology Technology and Disability Universal Access to the Information Society

For the mainstream conference proceedings and journals, papers were included in the review if disabled or older people were mentioned as a target user group in the title, abstract or key words. A list of the relevant terms covering disabled and older people that were considered is available at www.yorkhci.org/criticalreview/. The only exceptions were papers that mentioned "sign language" (which often did not mention the fact that Deaf people are the target user group) and papers about "web accessibility" (which often do not mention the various target user groups).

For the specialist journal that is not specifically about technology (Educational Gerontology), papers were included in the review if a technology related topic was mentioned in the title, abstract or key words. A list of the relevant terms is also available at www.york.ac.org/criticalreview/.

3 Results

5653 papers have been scanned for the review, 3823 from the mainstream conference proceedings and journals and 1830 from the specialist conference proceedings and journals. Of the papers reviewed from the mainstream outlets, 249 relate to older or disabled people and 1373 papers from the specialist outlets. Thus 3.4% of all papers in the mainstream outlets and 75.0% of all papers in the specialist outlets reviewed so far are about technology for disabled and older people. Table 2 shows the breakdown of papers analysed thus far into the different target user groups. Research about technology for older people account for the largest group of papers, in both mainstream and specialist outlets, with approximately 35% of papers. Research about technology for people with visual disabilities accounts for the next largest group of papers, with approximately 25% of papers. Whereas research about

Table 2. Breakdown of papers in mainstream and specialist outlets by target user group

User Group	Mainstream outlets % (N)	Specialist outlets %(N)	Total % (N)
People with Visual Disability	23.0 (57)	25.9 (152)	25.1 (209)
People with Hearing Disability	5.0 (12)	7.5 (44)	6.7 (56)
People with Cognitive Disability	10.8 (25)	9.7 (57)	9.8 (82)
People with Physical Disability	6.5 (17)	9.4 (55)	8.6 (72)
Older people	46.8 (117)	30.4 (179)	35.5 (296)
Papers covering more than one disability (and/or older people)	6.5 (17)	15.5 (91)	12.9 (108)
Other stakeholders (e.g. carers, web developers, IT professionals)	1.6 (4)	0.9 (7)	1.3 (11)
Total	249	585	834

technology for people with hearing disabilities only accounts for about 7% of papers, although there are many more people with hearing disabilities than visual disabilities. The category "other stakeholders" refers to the fact that there is some research about how to support other stakeholders associated with older and disabled people, such as carers and also how to educate and inform particular group of stakeholders, such as web developers, about people with disabilities and older people.

Table 3. Breakdown of papers by issue addressed

Issue	Mainstream outlets % (N)	Specialist outlets % (N)	Total % (N)
Mobility and wayfinding (e.g. indoor, outdoor navigation)	8.3 (22)	1.0 (1)	6.4 (23)
Access to and use of information (e.g. search, graphics, maps, mathematics, music)	8.3 (22)	16.5 (16)	10.4 (38)
Communication and social interaction (e.g. encouraging socializing, supporting communication, collaboration)	13.2 (35)	5.2 (5)	11.0 (40)
Interacting with/using technology (e.g. input/output, interaction techniques)	20.8 (55)	8.2 (8)	17.4 (63)
Attitudes to / experience with technology	4.2 (11)	13.4 (13)	6.7 (24)
Education	4.5 (12)	13.4 (13)	6.9 (25)
The web (e.g. use, assessing accessibility, teaching developers about web accessibility)	12.8 (34)	25.8 (25)	16.3 (59)
Tasks of daily life (e.g. memory support, home monitoring, cooking, banking, exercise, games)	16.2 (43)	7.2 (7)	13.8 (50)
Methods for working with disabled/older people	11.7 (31)	9.3 (3)	11.0 (40)
Total	265	97	362

The papers have also been categorized into the following main types:

- Development of new technologies/systems to support disabled or older people
- Understanding how people with disabilities or older people use technology, their attitudes towards technology
- Standards, guidelines and best practice for the development of technology for people with disabilities and older people, also research on how best to educate developers
- Methods for conducting research with disabled and older people

Table 4. Breakdown of papers by country of researchers

Country	% (N) of papers
Germany	13.0 (58)
USA	11.6 (52)
Japan	10.5 (47)
Austria	10.1 (45)
Spain	6.5 (29)
UK	5.8 (26)
France	4.7 (21)
Italy	4.7 (21)
Canada	2.7 (12)
Czech Republic	2.5 (11)
Belgium	2.2 (10)
Ireland	2.2 (10)
Others	23.5 (105)
Total	100.0 (447)

Finally, papers have been categorized into the issue of importance for disabled and/or older people. Table 3 shows the breakdown of papers analysed thus far into the nine major categories. Methods for conducting research with disabled and older people is considered an issue of importance as well as a type of paper, so is included in this table. Research is quite evenly distributed between the issues, with six issues (interacting with/using technology, web accessibility, tasks of daily living, access to and use of information, communication and social interaction, methods for working with disabled/older people) having between 10% and 17% of the papers. The most frequently researched issue is interacting with/using technology, but it is only slightly more frequent than web accessibility.

Table 5. Breakdown of papers by transnational collaboration type

Type of collaboration	% (N) of papers
Intra-EU	6.4 (26)
EU – Non-EU	2.5 (10)
Non-EU – Non-EU	0.5 (2)
Single country	90.6 (366)
Total	100.0 (404)

Table 4 shows the breakdown of papers by country of the researchers involved. Thus far, researchers from 42 countries have been tabulated. The 12 countries listed in Table 4 show the countries with most researchers publishing in these outlets on technology for disabled and older people, and account for 76.5% of all the researchers. Table 5 shows the types of collaborations represented in the papers. 9.4% of papers have researchers from more than one country. Only 6.4% of papers are collaborations between EU countries[1], which is surprising, given the considerable European funding that has been provided in this area in the past 20 years. A further 2.5% of papers were collaborations between EU and non-EU countries, for example a collaboration between Germany and Japan. Finally, 0.5% of papers were collaborations between non-EU countries, for example a collaboration between Canada and the USA.

4 Discussion and Conclusions

Technology has the potential to have important impact on the lives disabled and older people, supporting their activities and participation in society, improving functioning and access to services. Our review explores research on technologies for disabled and older people in the last seven years to investigate to what progress has been made in this area. The review has turned out to be a far greater enterprise than we originally anticipated, and many more detailed analyses need to be undertaken. We will be investigated to what extent potential users' needs are taken into account in the research, how users are involved in the research, the ethics of research and what gaps exist in the portfolio of research.

Acknowledgements. This research programme has received funding from the European Union Seventh Framework Programme FP7 Marie Curie Intra-European Fellowship Scheme under grant agreement n° PIEF-GA-2011-303184.

[1] For this analysis we used the EU27 countries.

References

1. Ballabio, E., Placencia-Porrero, I., Puig de la Bellacasa, R. (eds.): Rehabilitation technology: strategies for the European Union. IOS Press, Amsterdam (1993)
2. Placencia-Porrero, I., Puig de la Bellacasa, R. (eds.): The European context for assistive technology. IOS Press, Amsterdam (1995)
3. Placencia-Porrero, I., Ballabio, E. (eds.): Improving the quality of life for the European citizen. IOS Press, Amsterdam (1998)
4. Czaja, S.: Human factors research needs for an aging population. National Academy Press (1990)
5. Rogers, W.A., Stronge, A.J., Fisk, A.D.: Technology and aging. Reviews of Human Factors and Ergonomics 1(1), 130–171 (2005)
6. Reuters, T.: The Thomson Reuters Impact Factor (2013), http://thomsonreuters.com/products_services/science/free/essays/impact_factor/
7. Australian Research Council. Excellence in research for Australia (2010), http://www.arc.gov.au/era/era_2010/era_2010.htm

User Evaluation of Technology Enhanced Interaction Framework

Kewalin Angkananon, Mike Wald, and Lester Gilbert

Electronic and Computer Science (ECS), University of Southampton, UK
{ka3e10,mw,lg3}@ecs.soton.ac.uk

Abstract. This paper focuses on user evaluation of the Technology Enhanced Interaction Framework (TEIF). Questionnaire results from participants using or reviewing the TEIF method to evaluate requirements and design technology solutions for problems involving interactions with hearing impaired people showed that they thought it helped them more than the Other methods and that it would also help them to gather requirements and to design technology solutions for all disabled people if information about other disabilities than hearing impairment was provided. The objective results from the experimental tasks will be analysed to investigate how the participants performed on the requirements evaluation and solutions evaluation tasks with the TEIF method and the other preferred method. These results will be compared with the participants' questionnaire answers which reflected what they thought about the TEIF method. Future work includes extending the Method and Technology Suggestions Table to include information about other disabilities than just hearing impairment.

Keywords: Framework, Interaction, Evaluation, Accessibility, Hearing Impairments.

1 Introduction

Researchers have been concerned with how to use technology to support communication between people and improve interactions between people, technology and objects [1,2,3,4,5,6,7]. For example, artefact-mediated-communication has been used to sup-port cooperative work [2,3], [7,8], a mobile digital guidebook has been used to enhance visitors' interaction with physical objects in museums [6], [9] and mobile devices have been used as mediators for the interaction with a physical object using QR codes, RFID tags and NFC tags [5], [10]. Many publications and projects in human computer interaction (HCI) focus on using technologies as a tool to enhance experiences: in the same place but at a different time (e.g. using systems for supporting group learning such as notice boards, questions and answers, electronic debates and collaborative learning [10]); in a different place but at the same time (e.g. using a Synchronous Communication Tool such as video conferencing, instant messaging and online chats to interact with learners to improve their communication with the Instructor [11]); and in a different place at a different time (e.g. using

K. Miesenberger et al. (Eds.): ICCHP 2014, Part II, LNCS 8548, pp. 267–274, 2014.

blended learning, students can access e-learning in order to learn in a different place at a different time [12]). There has, however, been no framework that has helped technology designers to consider all of the possible interactions that occur at the same time and in the same place although there have been projects concerned with how to use technology to support some of these interactions.

2 The Technology Enhanced Interaction Framework (TEIF)

The TEIF was adapted from Dix's [13] and Gaines's [14] Frameworks with the aim of supporting designers evaluating and designing technology enhanced interactions involving disabled and non-disabled people. There are seven main components in the TEIF. A person has a role when communicating with others. Roles normally come in pairs such as speaker and audience. People have abilities and disabilities which can affect their use of technology or understanding of language and which can lead to communication breakdown. The components "Object" and "Technology" are used in order to extend Dix's framework to show any type of interaction. Objects are defined as having three sub-components: dimensions, properties, and content. Technology has a cost and can be electronic or non-electronic, online or off-line, and mobile or non-mobile. Furthermore, it may or may not have stored content and may additionally have an interface and be an application or provide a service. Interactions and communication are classified into three groups:

- Direct communication: P-P - people in one way or two way communication with people.
- Direct Interaction: P-T - people can control technology and may also use it to store or retrieve information; P-O -People can control objects and retrieve information from objects.
- Technology Mediated Interaction: P-T-P - technology can mediate communication between people; P-T-O - people can control objects with technology and may also be enabled to use objects to store and retrieve information.

Time and Place can be same or different. Context can include location, signal quality, background noise, and weather conditions. The role played by the interactions and communication may be classified into one of six interaction layers, adapted from Gaines [14]. The TEIF was successfully validated and reviewed by two groups of the experts: designer experts and accessibility experts. The designer experts focused on the main and sub-components while accessibility experts focused on checking the accessibility aspects. The results of this validation and review have been reported elsewhere [15].

3 Technology Enhanced Interaction Framework Method

The TEIF method aims to help designer in two stages of software developing life cycle: (a) gathering and evaluating requirements, (b) designing and evaluating technology solutions to situations, particularly when disabled people are involved by helping designers think about the user requirements, designing interactions to meet these requirements and the criteria related to the requirements to evaluate the interactions. The TEIF method does not replace other methods of identifying requirements but supports them by providing examples of requirement-questions and answers. Then, the process links the answers to technology suggestions which lead to the design and evaluation stages. In order to explain how the TEIF method works, the start of an example scenario that only involves hearing impairment and the TEIF steps will be presented as follows:

"Suchat Trapsin allocated some parts of his house to become the Shadow Puppets Museum, in Thailand. There are exhibits of shadow puppets inside the museum, but there is no information provided in text format …"

Designers analyse their scenario and answer the multiple-choice questions [16] to elicit requirements based on the scenario. One example questions is:

What "types" of speech did the presenter use?

- prepared or rehearsed speech (a)
- spontaneous speech (b)

The answers will suggest relevant technologies with the help of the technology suggestions Table (a small part of which is shown in Table 1) which contains descriptions with indications by ticks and crosses of whether they meet the requirements based upon an analysis of answers to the requirement questions. An online version uses tooltips to display the explanations for the ticks or crosses.

Table 1. Technology Suggestion Table

Technology suggestions	Descriptions	6b speaker speaks Thai	7b audience speak Thai	9a hearing impaired	11a people-people	11b people - objects	12a online technology	13a mobile devices	14a pre-prepared speech	17a noise	18a low cost solution
Flashing light	A flashing light alert gets attention of hearing impaired people. Normally used for room lighting only off-line. High cost wireless systems are becoming available.	✓	✓	✓	✓	✗	✗	✗	✗	✓	✓
Speech recognition	Speech recognition helps clarify using words but sometimes make errors. Number of errors will increase depending on noise. Speak recognition works best if the microphone is close to user: http://www.w3.org/TR/UNDERSTANDING-WCAG20/media-equiv-real-time-captions.html	✗	✗	✓	✓	✗	✓	✓	✓	✗	✓

4 Experiment Pilot Studies

Three software engineers conducted face to face interviews with the researcher playing the role of the client in order to investigate whether the engineers could gather and identify requirements in this "realistic" way. They found this task very difficult as they had not had experience of interviewing before. The researcher therefore decided on a different approach using a written document explaining the scenario for a task of evaluating requirements. The researcher developed and piloted two styles of presenting the scenario information: a "report" and an "interview transcript" as research [17] has found that using an interview transcript with direct speech was more realistic and engaging than a descriptive document using indirect speech. The start of the transcript is:

"Interviewer: Could you please tell me about your recent visitor?

Suchat: "Chuty is a very successful Thai businesswoman in her 30s who has lived in Thailand all her life and only speaks Thai. She became hearing impaired in her twenties and depends completely on her hearing aids and lip-reading. She speaks clearly and I had no problem understanding her".

The interview transcript was chosen to be used in the experiment as eight out of twelve participants preferred the interview transcript style to the report style. Six participants were asked to pilot the Evaluate Requirements Task which involved evaluating the best 10 requirements from 27 provided for a technology solution to the disability related problems they identified from the interview transcript. Modifications based on the feedback were clearer explanations, re-ordering the position in the list, and adding one more requirement to the list. To pilot the whole experiment eight software engineers at the university, both English native speakers and non-native speakers, were mixed equally between two groups and four participants were asked to use the TEIF method while the other four were asked to use their preferred other methods. The process for the pilot study was that the individual participant sat down with the researcher and applied the TEIF method steps to complete the Evaluate Requirements Task and then the Evaluate Technology Solutions Task (Evaluating three solutions for each of 10 requirements by rating between 0 and 10) and finally answer a questionnaire. Participants were asked to do the tasks independently and the researcher only intervened to explain an instruction if a participant found it unclear. Improvements as a result of the pilot study included: providing a glossary to clarify words some non-native English speakers did not understand (e.g. shadow puppet, spontaneous speech); shortening and modifying the transcript to make it more realistic and more difficult to identify the requirements; instructions, requirements and transcript were made clearer to understand.

5 Experimental Design

The TEIF method was designed to help improve a designer's awareness of interaction issues involving disabled people and their understanding of how environment context affects the accessibility of interactions and to provide a technology suggestions table to help with designing technology solutions. The purpose of this experiment was to evaluate the TEIF method by asking participants questions about the materials presented. Participants took between one hour and one hour and a half to complete the experiment. Thirty-six experienced software engineers were divided into two equal independent groups of eighteen participants with four English native speakers and fourteen non-native English speakers in each group (section 6.1). One group of the participant used the TEIF method to complete the Evaluate Requirements Task and the Evaluate Technology Solutions Task (section 6.2) while the second group of participants used their preferred other methods to complete the Evaluate Requirements Task and the Evaluate Technology Solutions Task and were then shown the TEIF method. Both groups of participants were asked questions to check whether the TEIF method helped in these ways (section 6.3).

6 Questionnaire Results and Analysis

As the Evaluate Requirement Task only involved evaluating requirements and the Evaluate Technology Solutions Task only involved evaluating designs the questionnaires asked the participants' opinion about whether the TEIF method would help them in gathering requirements and designing technology solutions when hearing impaired people or people with other disabilities were involved.

6.1 Participants' Profile

An independent sample t-test shows that there was no significant difference for participants in the two groups in the experience of designing software (4.89 years for TEIF method group and 4.19 years for the Other method group) or designing technology solutions for disabled people (22% for the TEIF method group, 17% for the Other method group).

6.2 Questions Asked to the TEIF Method Group Only

The participants from the TEIF method group were asked to complete the questions related to the TEIF Method they used for the experiment. One sample t-tests on questionnaire results using a five point Likert scale where 5 meant they "strongly agreed" showed each mean rating for answers was a significantly difference greater than 3 with $p < .001$ and that:

- participants thought the TEIF method helped in Evaluate Requirements Task to evaluate requirements for technology solutions to problems involving interaction with hearing-impaired people better than the Other methods (mean = 4.5).
- participants thought the TEIF method helped in the Evaluate Technology Solutions Task to evaluate technology solutions for problems involving interaction with hearing-impaired people better than the Other methods (mean = 4.3).

- participants thought that the TEIF method helped improve awareness of interaction issues involving hearing impaired people (mean = 4.4).
- participants thought that the TEIF method helped improve understanding of how environment context affects interaction when hearing impaired people are involved (mean = 4.4).
- participants thought that the Technology Suggestions Table helped identify technology solutions to issues involving hearing impaired people (mean = 4.4).

6.3 Questions Asked to Both Groups

The participants from both method groups were asked to completed the questions about their opinion in:

- gathering requirements to interaction problems involving hearing impaired people
- designing technology solutions to interaction problems involving hearing impaired people.
- using the whole TEIF method (both the evaluate requirements task and evaluate technology solutions task) would be needed for designing technology solutions.
- gathering requirements to interaction problems involving other disabilities.
- designing technology solutions to interaction problems involving other disabilities.

The one sample t-test was used to test whether the mean ratings were significantly greater than 3. There was a significant difference of mean ratings was greater than 3 with $p < .001$ and that:

- participants thought that the TEIF method would be helpful in gathering requirements for technology solutions to interaction problems involving hearing impaired people (mean = 4.5).
- participants thought that the TEIF method would be helpful in designing technology solutions to interaction problems involving hearing impaired people (mean = 4.4).
- participants thought that the whole TEIF method would be needed for designing technology solutions (mean = 4.6).
- participants thought that the TEIF method could help in gathering requirements to interaction problems involving a wider range of disabilities than just hearing impairment (mean = 4.5).
- participants thought that the TEIF method could help in designing technology solutions to interaction problems involving a wider range of disabilities than just hearing impairment (mean = 4.3).

The independent sample t-test statistic was used to test whether and how the TEIF method helped in gathering requirements, designing technology solutions and with other disabilities where 5 meant they strongly agreed. The results show that there was no significant difference of mean ratings between the two methods:

- participants in both groups thought that the TEIF method would be helpful to gathering requirements for technology solutions to interaction problems involving hearing impaired people (TEIF mean = 4.6, Other mean = 4.5).
- participants in both groups thought that the TEIF method would be helpful in designing technology solutions to interaction problems involving hearing impaired people (TEIF mean = 4.3, Other Mean = 4.4).
- participants in both groups thought that the whole TEIF method would be needed for designing technology solutions (TEIF mean = 4.6, Other mean = 4.5).
- participants in both groups thought that the TEIF method could help in gathering requirements to interaction problems involving a wider range of disabilities than just hearing impairment (TEIF mean = 4.5, Other mean = 4.4).
- participants in both groups thought that the TEIF method could help in designing technology solutions to interaction problems involving a wider range of disabilities than just hearing impairment (TEIF mean = 4.2, Other mean = 4.3).

7 Conclusion and Future Work

Questionnaire results from participants using or reviewing the TEIF method to evaluate requirements and design solutions for problems involving interactions with hearing impaired people showed that they thought it helped them more than the Other methods and that it would also help them to gather requirements and to design solutions for all disabled people if information about other disabilities than hearing impairment was provided. The objective results from the experimental tasks will be analyzed to investigate how the participants performed on the requirements evaluation and solutions evaluation tasks with the TEIF method and the other preferred method. These results will be compared with the participants' questionnaire answers which reflected what they thought about the TEIF method. Future work includes extending the method and technology suggestions table to include information about other disabilities than just hearing impairment.

References

1. Berne, E.: Games People Play – The Basic Hand Book of Transactional Analysis. Ballantine Books, New York (1964)
2. Dix, A.: Challenges for Cooperative Work on the Web: An Analytical Approach. Journal of Computer Supported Cooperative Work (CSCW) 6(2), 135–156 (1997)
3. Dix, A., Finlay, J., Abowd, D.G., Beale, R.: Human-Computer Interaction, Harlow, England. Pearson/Prentice-Hall, New York (2004)
4. Laurillard, D.: Rethinking University Teaching: a framework for the effective use of educational technology. Routledge, London (1993)
5. Rukzio, E., Broll, G., Wetzstein, S.: The Physical Mobile Interaction Framework (PMIF). Technical Report LMU-MI-2008-2, University of Munich, Munich, Germany (2008)
6. Sung, Y.-T., Chang, K.-E., Hou, H.-T., Chen, P.-F.: Designing an electronic guidebook for learning engagement in a museum of history. Computers in Human Behavior 26(1), 74–83 (2010)

7. Vyas, D., Dix, A., Nijholt, A.: Role of Artefacts in Mediated Communication. In: CHI 2008. ACM SIGCHI, Florence (2008)
8. Dix, A.: Cooperation without (reliable) communication: Interfaces for mobile applications. Distributed Systems Engineering 2(3), 171 (1995)
9. Broll, G., Siorpaes, S., Rukzio, E., Paolucci, M., Hamard, J., Wagner, M., et al. (eds.): Supporting Mobile Service Usage through Physical Mobile Interaction. In: Fifth Annual IEEE International Conference on Pervasive Computing and Communications, PerCom 2007, March 19-23 (2007)
10. Lee, D.S., Armitage, S., Groves, P., Stephens, C.: Systems for supporting group learning (2009)
11. Wang, S.-K.: The Effects of a Synchronous Communication Tool (Yahoo Messenger) on Online Lerners' Sense of Community and their Multimedia Authoring Skills. Journal of Interactive Online Learning 7(1) (2008)
12. Klink, M.: The use of interaction methods in a blended learning environment. In: Educational Science and Technology 2006. University of Twente (2006)
13. Dix, A.J.: Computer supported cooperative work - a framework. In: Rosenburg, D., Hutchison, C. (eds.) Design Issues in CSCW, pp. 23–37. Springer (1994)
14. Gaines, B.R.: A conceptual framework for person-computer interaction in complex systems. IEEE Transactions on Systems, Man and Cybernetics 18, 532–541 (1988)
15. Angkananon, K., Wald, M., Gilbert, L.: Findings of Expert Validation and Review of the Technology Enhanced Interaction Framework. In: 12th International Conference on Software Engineering Research and Practice, SERP 2013 (2013)
16. Angkananon, K., Wald, M., Gilbert, L.: Applying Technology Enhanced Interaction Framework to Accessible Mobile Learning. In: 5th International Conference on Software Development and Technologies for Enhancing Accessibility and Fighting Info-exclusion, DSAI 2013 (2013), Procedia-Computer Science Journal 2013
17. Yao, B.: Mental simulations in comprehension of direct versus indirect speech quotations. PhD thesis, University of Glasgow (2011), `http://theses.gla.ac.uk/3067`

A Unified Semantic Framework for Detailed Description of Assistive Technologies Based on the EASTIN Taxonomy

Nikolaos Kaklanis[1], Konstantinos Votis[1], Konstantinos Giannoutakis[1], Dimitrios Tzovaras[1], Valerio Gower[2], and Renzo Andrich[2]

[1] Information Technologies Institute, Centre for Research and Technology Hellas, Thessaloniki, Greece

{nkak,kvotis,kgiannou,Dimitrios.Tzovaras}@iti.gr

[2] CITT, Fondazione Don Carlo Gnocchi Onlus, Milano, Italy

{vgower,randrich}@dongnocchi.it

Abstract. This paper presents a unified semantic framework that can used by vendors/service providers that would like to semantically describe their assistive technologies according to the categorization proposed by the ISO 9999 standard as well as the EASTIN taxonomy. The framework is based on an approach towards a unified semantic description of assistive technologies by combining information coming from different sources. The wealth of information of the EASTIN network, the biggest and most comprehensive information service on assistive technology serving older and disabled people, is currently exploited by the proposed framework in a unified way. The proposed framework offers an easy mechanism for including a new assistive technology in the whole Cloud4all/GPII infrastructure.

Keywords: Semantic Alignment, Ontology, Assistive Technologies, Application Classification.

1 Introduction

Assistive Technologies (ATs) play an increasingly central role in equalising opportunities for people with functional limitations in all aspects of life. The great importance of providing accurate and detailed information about the characteristics and limitations of ATs to all the stakeholders involved in the AT service delivery systems has been recognized as a key issue by several European studies [6,7], [15].

Ontologies can play a very crucial role in describing various types of assistive technologies. However, a typical problem that often appears in ontology-based systems includes the lack of interoperability between other similar systems or even sub-components of the same framework, due to different representations of identical terms. Ontology alignment in the sense of identifying relations between individual elements of multiple ontologies is a necessary precondition to establish interoperability between agents or services using different individual ontologies [8].

K. Miesenberger et al. (Eds.): ICCHP 2014, Part II, LNCS 8548, pp. 275–282, 2014.

Moreover, the semantic alignment enables the searching or browsing of the knowledge represented in numerous sources in a transparent way for the end-users.

Even if many approaches have been proposed for describing the existing ATs [3,4], [16], there is a need for a unified framework that will combine information coming from different sources and will also enable the classification of the most common assistive technologies (both software and hardware) according to well-known accessibility standards as well as the description of all the supported adjustments/settings and their alignment with similar settings of other technologies. Thus, in the current work, our main purpose is to present the Semantic Alignment Tool, a tool developed within the premises of the Cloud4all FP7 EC project that fulfils the aforementioned requirements.

2 Related Work

There are several efforts towards the direction of defining ontological concepts and architectures for the semantic representation of assistive technologies within the area of e-Inclusion and personalized interfaces. For example, besides user modelling, the ontologies developed in ACCESSIBLE [19] and AEGIS[1] FP7 projects incorporate the semantic description of solutions, applications and user interaction terms targeting users with functional limitations. Also the INREDIS Knowledge Base [14], stores all the ontologies that collect formal descriptions of the elements in the INREDIS domain (e.g. users, AS, devices, software requirements, etc.) and its instances.

The use of metadata and meta-reasoning was proposed by Castro et al. [5] to address the design challenges encountered when building an ontology repository for an application framework devoted to ATs that can be browsed and queried in a highly heterogeneous and expressive way. They analyzed how metadata can be used in the context of open repositories of ontologies, and how it can and needs to be extended in various ways. More specifically, they studied a redesign of the Ontology Metadata Vocabulary (OMV) [10] by restructuring and enriching it with the ABC ontology [12] and domain-specific categories for assistive technologies.

An effort to use semantic web technologies for providing a generic solution for integrating the assistive technology, the web, and the signs and symbol language used traditionally by people with communication problems for text interpretation has been also launched by the WWAAC EU project. More specifically, the Concept Coding Framework (CCF) [13] was defined as a means to break down the isolation and barriers between different augmentative and alternative communication (AAC) symbol vocabularies by defining an open technology for connecting these vocabularies to other vocabularies and to standard lexical resources. The CCF included a plain concepts list called Concept Code Definitions, the Base Reference Ontology (concepts mapped from WordNet to used symbols) and the Complementary Reference Ontology specifying missing concepts.

---

[1] `http://www.aegis-project.eu/index.php?Itemid=65`

The present paper goes one step beyond the state of the art by presenting a unified framework for describing ATs that combines information coming from different sources and also enables their classification according to well-known accessibility standards. Moreover, it enables the description of all the supported adjustments/settings and their alignment with similar settings of other technologies.

3 The Semantic Alignment Tool

The Semantic Alignment Tool (SAT)[2] aims mainly at providing a common interface to all interested vendors, providers, etc., that intend to include their applications/solutions in the Cloud4all/GPII infrastructure [17,18]. More specifically, they can add/modify the description of their applications/solutions as well as align their application-specific settings with similar settings of other ATs (Fig. 1). This information, which includes general descriptions and metadata, is then stored in the solutions ontology [11], whose terms are classified according to the ISO 9999 standard. When entering information regarding a solution through the SAT tool, information about the specific solution can be also retrieved automatically from the EASTIN databases [1] using a set of web-services [9] and it is combined with the information entered manually by the vendor.

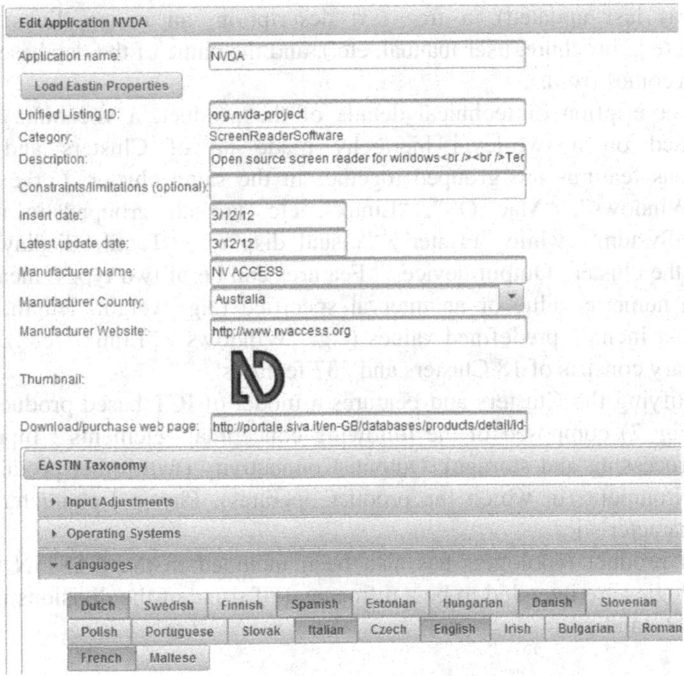

Fig. 1. Entering description of an AT through the SAT tool

[2] The SAT tool is available at: `http://160.40.50.183:8080/`

The European Assistive Technology Information Network (EASTIN) is an association including the organizations responsible for the major European AT information systems. The EASTIN website[3] aggregates the information of 8 national databases (in Denmark, United Kingdom, The Netherlands, Germany, Italy, France, Belgium and Spain), and currently includes descriptions of about 70.000 products available on the European market produced/distributed by about 10.000 companies (manufacturers/suppliers, retailers). The data retrieved from the EASTIN databases are structured according to the EASTIN taxonomy, a dataset for standardizing the description of ICT-based AT products that has been developed within the European Thematic Network on Assistive Information and Communication Technologies (ETNA) [2].

4 The EASTIN Taxonomy

The EASTIN taxonomy is made up of two parts: a basic dataset and a vocabulary for the description of technical details.

The basic dataset represents the minimum set of information needed to uniquely identify an assistive product and understand what kind of product it is. Basic dataset includes: the product name, manufacturer information, the product typology, information on update dates (when the record has been added to the database and when it was last updated), a free text description, an image, links to further information (e.g. brochure, user manual, etc.), and the name of the database where the information comes from.

For the description of technical details of the product, a vocabulary has been created based on a two-level hierarchy made up of Clusters and Features. Homogeneous features are grouped together in the same cluster. For example the features "Windows", "Mac OS", "Linux", etc. are all grouped in the cluster "Operating System", while "Printer", "Visual display", "Tactile display", etc. are grouped in the cluster "Output devices". Features can be of two types: measures, that can have a numeric value or an interval specified (e.g. weight, length, etc.), and attributes that include predefined values (e.g. "Windows", "Linux", etc.). Currently the vocabulary consists of 18 Clusters and 237 features.

For identifying the Clusters and Features a model of ICT based product has been used (see Fig. 2) composed of the following conceptual "elements": Input, Central Unit (for processing and storage), Output, Connectivity (with other products or services), Environment (in which the product operates), Physical characteristics, and Software characteristics.

A list of product typologies has also been included in the EASTIN taxonomy. Those typologies are intended to be a refinement of some of the divisions included in the ISO 9999 standard.

[3] http://www.eastin.eu

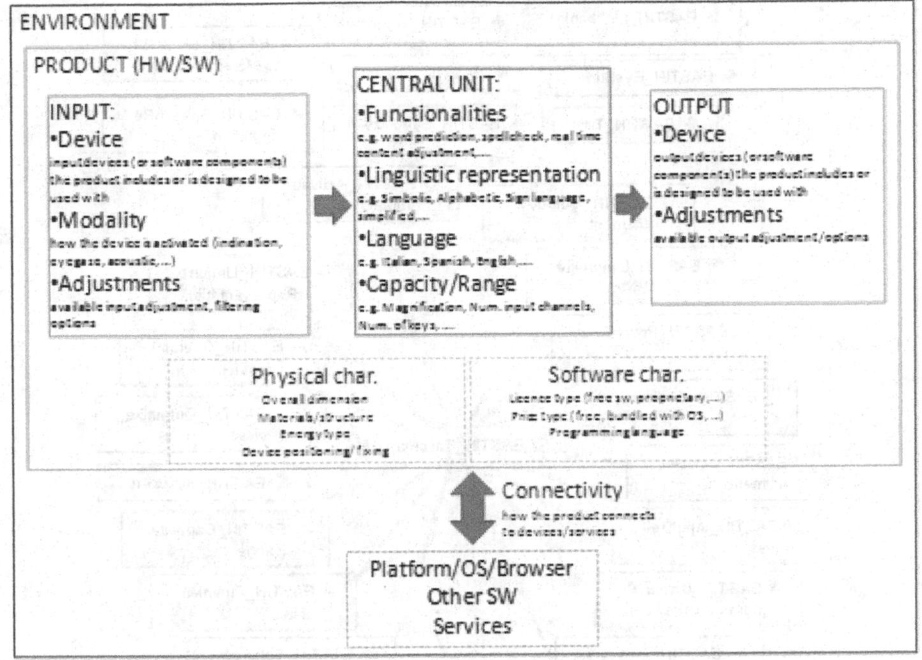

Fig. 2. Model of ICT-based AT product used for the EASTIN taxonomy

The items of the vocabulary have also been put in relation with the divisions (i.e. the product typologies) identified by the ISO 9999 standard. A matrix has been created to indicate for which product typologies a specific item of the vocabulary is relevant, and what is the level of relevance (on a 1-100% scale). For instance, the item "Linux (Operating Systems)" has 70% "relevance" for the ISO division "22.36.03 Key-boards" and 100% relevance for the ISO division "22.36.18 Input software". This "relevance ranking" allows presenting, in a data entry form, the vocabulary items ordered by relevance with respect to the specific product category, thus facilitating the data entry process.

As the information coming from the EASTIN databases, by using the SAT tool, is finally stored in the solutions ontology, corresponding classes and properties have been added in the solutions ontology. Fig. 3 presents the classes of the solutions ontol-ogy corresponding to the clusters of the EASTIN taxonomy.

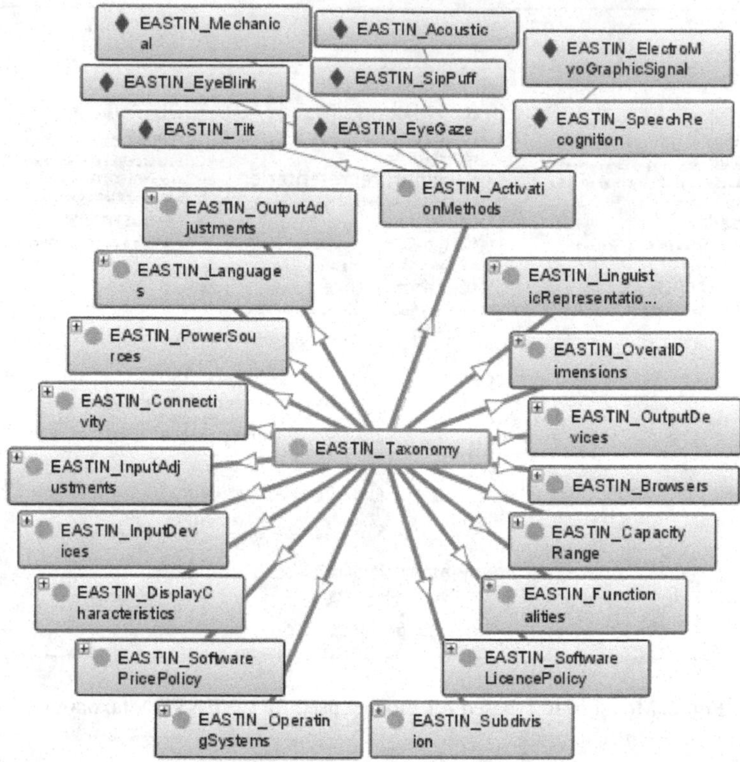

Fig. 3. Solutions ontology – Classes describing the EASTIN taxonomy

4.1 Taxonomy Management Tools

The EASTIN taxonomy is intended to be a dynamically changing vocabulary. As the market of AT evolves, new items will in fact be needed for appropriately describing the new products. For managing the EASTIN taxonomy two tools are available. The first, integrated into the EASTIN system, allows the administrators of the EASTIN portal to enter, edit, or delete items of the taxonomy, to manage the "relevance ranking" of the items with respect to product typologies, and to localize the items into the different languages (and cultures) supported by the EASTIN portal (currently 31).

The second tool, integrated into the SAT, allows AT manufacturers or resellers to propose new items to be added to the taxonomy vocabulary. By using this new functionality of the SAT tool, AT manufacturers (or resellers) will be able to suggest new items for the vocabulary while they are entering information about their product. The tool allows the manufacturer to propose new product Typologies, new Features, and new Clusters (i.e. a group of features) for describing their product. When a new term is proposed, the tool searches within the taxonomy and returns a list of existing vocabulary items that are possibly similar to the one proposed (in a "did you mean" like fashion), in order to help the manufacturer in appropriately using the existing taxonomy items.

A restricted area has been created for taxonomy administrators where all the submitted proposals are reported. Within such area of the SAT tool, taxonomy administrators are able to accept, modify or reject proposals.

5 Conclusions

The SAT can be considered as a novel tool that can used by vendors/service providers that would like to semantically describe their ATs according to the categorization proposed by the ISO 9999 standard as well as the EASTIN taxonomy. The tool is based on an approach towards a unified semantic description of ATs by combining information coming from different sources. The wealth of information of the EASTIN network, the biggest and most comprehensive information service on assistive technology serving older and disabled people, is currently exploited by the SAT tool in a unified way. The SAT tool offers an easy mechanism for including a new solution/application in the whole Cloud4all/GPII infrastructure. Future work may include the extension of the SAT tool in order to communicate with other external databases / ontologies describing various types of ATs.

Acknowledgements. This work is supported by the EU co-funded project Cloud4all (FP7 – 289016).

References

1. Andrich, R.: Towards a global information network: the European Assistive Technology Information Network and the World Alliance of AT Information Providers. In: Gelderblom, G.J., Soede, M., Adriaens, L., Miesenberger, K. (eds.) Everyday Technology for Independence and Care, pp. 190–197. IosPress, Amsterdam (2011)
2. Andrich, R., Gower, V., Vincenti, S.: Information Needs Related to ICT-Based Assistive Solutions. In: Miesenberger, K., Karshmer, A., Penaz, P., Zagler, W. (eds.) ICCHP 2012, Part I. LNCS, vol. 7382, pp. 207–214. Springer, Heidelberg (2012)
3. ATIS4all Thematic Network on ATs (2014), http://www.atis4all.eu
4. Bitelli, C., Hoogerwerf, E.J., Lysley, A.: The BRIDGE Project Assistive technology against social exclusion. In: Assistive Technology: Shaping the Future: AAATE 2003, vol. 11, p. 207 (2003)
5. Castro, A.G., Normann, I., Hois, J., Kutz, O.: Ontologizing Metadata for Assistive Technologies-The OASIS Repository. In: First International Workshop on Ontologies in Interactive Systems, ONTORACT 2008, pp. 57–62. IEEE (2008)
6. Deloitte & AbilityNet: Internal market for inclusive and assistive ICT, targeted market analysis and legislative aspects. European Commission, Information Society and Media, Bruxelles (2011)
7. Deloitte & Touche: Access to Assistive Technology in the European Union. Bruxelles. European Commission, DG Employment (2003)
8. Ehrig, M.: Ontology alignment: bridging the semantic gap, vol. 4. Springer (2007)

9. Gower, V., Vanderheiden, G., Andrich, R.: Federating Databases of ICT-based Assistive Technology Products. In: Encarnação, P., Azevedo, L., Gelderblom, G.J., Newell, A., Mathiassen, N.-E. (eds.) Assistive Technology: From Research to Practice, pp. 1345–1351. IOS Press, Amsterdam (2013)
10. Hartmann, J., Sure, Y., Haase, P., Palma, R., Suárez-Figueroa, M.D.C.: OMV–ontology metadata vocabulary. In: ISWC 2005 Workshop on Ontology Patterns for the Semantic Web (2005)
11. Koutkias, V., Kaklanis, N., Votis, K., Tzovaras, D., Maglaveras, N.: An Integrated Semantic Framework Supporting Universal Accessibility to ICT. In: Universal Access in the Information Society, Special Issue: 3rd Generation Accessibility: Information and Communication Technologies Towards Universal Access. Springer (2013)
12. Lagoze, C., Hunter, J.: The ABC ontology and model. J. of Digit. Information 2(2) (2006)
13. Lundälv, M., Derbring, S.: AAC Vocabulary Standardisation and Harmonisation. In: Miesenberger, K., Karshmer, A., Penaz, P., Zagler, W. (eds.) ICCHP 2012, Part II. LNCS, vol. 7383, pp. 303–310. Springer, Heidelberg (2012)
14. Miñón, R., Aizpurua, A., Cearreta, I., Garay, N., Abascal, J.: Ontology-Driven Adaptive Accessible Interfaces in the INREDIS project. In: Procs. of the Int. Workshop on Architectures and Building Blocks of Web-Based User-Adaptive Systems, Haway, pp. 37–39 (2010)
15. Stack, J., Zarate, L., Pastor, C., Mathiassen, N.E., Barberà, R., Knops, H., Kornsten, H.: Analysing and federating the European assistive technology ICT industry. European Commission Information Society and Media (2009)
16. Stenberg, L. (ed.): Project catalogue NUH 1998-2006, The Nordic Development Centre for Rehabilitation Technology. NUH, Helsinki (2007)
17. Vanderheiden, G., Treviranus, J.: Creating a global public inclusive infrastructure. In: Stephanidis, C. (ed.) Universal Access in HCI, Part I, HCII 2011. LNCS, vol. 6765, pp. 517–526. Springer, Heidelberg (2011)
18. Vanderheiden, G.C., Treviranus, J., Chourasia, A.: The global public inclusive infrastructure (GPII). In: Proceedings of the 15th International ACM SIGACCESS Conference on Computers and Accessibility, p. 70. ACM (October 2013)
19. Votis, K., Lopes, R., Tzovaras, D., Carriço, L., Likothanassis, S.: A Semantic Accessibility Assessment Environment for Design and Development for the Web. In: Stephanidis, C. (ed.) Universal Access in HCI, Part III, HCII 2009. LNCS, vol. 5616, pp. 803–813. Springer, Heidelberg (2009)

Results from Using Automatic Speech Recognition in Cleft Speech Therapy with Children

Zachary Rubin[1], Sri Kurniawan[1], and Travis Tollefson[2]

[1] University of California Santa Cruz, Santa Cruz CA 95060, USA
{zarubin,skurnia}@ucsc.edu

[2] UC Davis Medical Center, 2315 Stockton Blvd, Sacramento, CA 95817
tttollefson@gmail.com

Abstract. Most children with cleft are required to undertake speech therapy after undergoing surgery to repair their craniofacial defect. However, the untrained ear of a parent can lead to incorrect practice resulting in the development of compensatory structures. Even worse, the boring nature of the cleft speech therapy often causes children to abandon home exercises and therapy altogether. We have developed a simple recognition system capable of detecting impairments on the phoneme level with high accuracy. We embed this into a game environment and provide it to a cleft palate specialist team for pilot testing with children 2 to 5 years of age being evaluated for speech therapy. The system consistently detected cleft speech in high-pressure consonants in 3 out of our 5 sentences. Doctors agreed that this would improve the quality of therapy outside of the office. Children enjoyed the game overall, but grew bored due to the delays of phrase-based speech recognition.

Keywords: Therapeutic Games, Child Speech Therapy.

1 Introduction

The first two years of a newborns life are a crucial period of time in the development of speech and language. Within the first year, a child is using his or her mouth to form a variety of phonetic structures and is saying their first words. The second year, toddlers are forming basic sentences [1]. Children born with craniofacial defects such as cleft palate are unable to form a variety of structures, using substitutions and compensations that result in speech problems [2]. These can take years to correct and can lag speech development.

Approximately 1 in 700 children are born with cleft lip or palate with wide variability across geographic origin, racial and ethnic groups, as well as environmental exposures and socioeconomic status [3]. Surgery to repair the cleft can be performed within the first year of birth. However, speech therapy to correct impairments often continues until the child is five or six [4]. Both therapists and parents have complained of the difficulty in getting two year-olds to perform speech exercises at home. Developing a tool that can automatically evaluate a

K. Miesenberger et al. (Eds.): ICCHP 2014, Part II, LNCS 8548, pp. 283–286, 2014.

child's speech underneath a motivating game-like environment performing these exercises would drastically improve recovery time. However, very little has been done in this aspect. We begin with a discussion of systems related to our own. Next we provide an explanation of our system. Finally we describe our experiment involving children being evaluated for cleft speech therapy and discuss the results.

2 Speech Adventure

2.1 Speech Recognition Engine

We chose OpenEars, an open-source speech recognition API for iOS devices based on Carnegie-Mellon University's PocketSPHINX, as our recognition engine. OpenEars performs all speech recognition on the device, and does not need to offload any data to an external server. We developed dictionaries with sentences containing target words. Target words have correct pronunciations as well as phonetic equivalents of impairments. The recognition system was provided a 5 megabyte version of the HUB4 acoustical model trained on the Wall Street Journal.

Table 1. Sample High-Pressure Consonant Dictionary

Sentence	Target Word	Correct Phonemes	Impaired Phonemes
Put on Boots	Put	P UH T	HH UH T
Put on Boots	Boots	B UW T S	HH UW T S
Wear a Hat	Hat	HH AE T	HH AA
Open the Door	Open	OW P AH N	OW AH N
Open the Door	Door	D AO R	HH AO ER
Pop a Balloon	Pop	P AA P	HH AA
Pop a Balloon	Balloon	B AH L UW N	HH AE L UW N
Cross the Bridge	Cross	K R AO S	HH R AA S
Cross the Bridge	Bridge	B R IH JH	HH R IH JH

2.2 Game Design

We observed, behind a one-way mirror, children without cleft used an iPad to play virtual games within a larger study conducted by a developmental psychologist that aims at understanding various executive functioning tasks and attention of young children when playing virtual games on an iPad. We observed that children of the target age range are capable of responding to simple prompts and solving simple puzzles on the iPad within 2 minutes of introduction.

This combined with the phrase-based speech recognition engine led us to the solution of a speech-activated storybook. In the game, a narrator talks to the player and guides him or her through the environment. Periodically, a prompt appears for the child to say. Prompts are presented on screen as well as said by the narrator for those too young to read. Using Cocos2D as the base engine, we developed three levels: A tutorial level, a level at home, and a level in a forest.

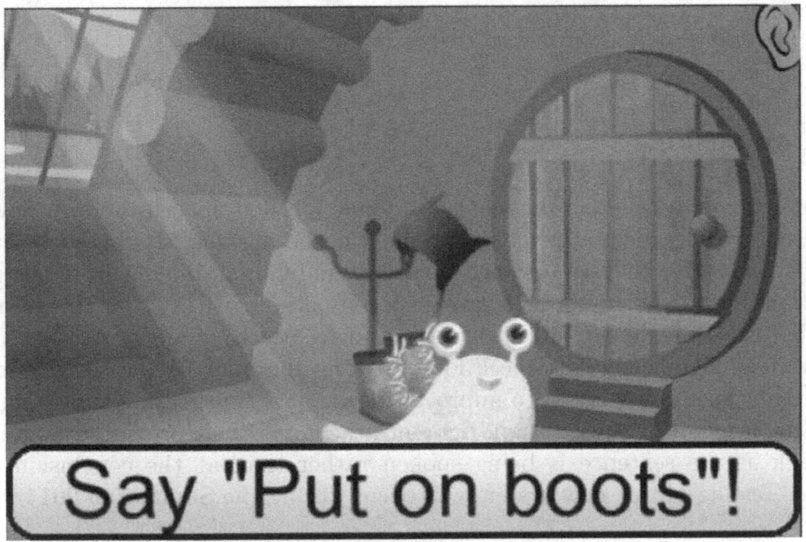

Fig. 1. The home level from the game

3 Cleft Palate Pilot Test

The pilot test included 9 children being evaluated for speech therapy at the UC Davis Medical Center. During the pilot test, doctors handed out the game on an iPad to children under evaluation for services. Doctors recorded the systems evaluation of the childs speech, and compared it against their own as a control. An agreement indicates that the system and therapist's evaluation matched. 3 out of 5 sentences chosen had an extremely high rate of evaluation agreement.

The primary criticism was the game 'took too long'. Doctors informed us that a playthrough should only take two or three minutes. Average playtime was 164.3 seconds with a standard deviation of 50.5 seconds. However, the data shows that most sessions took between two and three minutes, the same length the doctors desire. This means that the environment does not provide enough interaction within those 2-3 minutes to keep a child engaged. The primary cause of this was the phrase-based speech recognition having difficulty a short period of silence that concluded the sentence. In quiet rooms soft noises could reset the timer, leading to singificant periods of 'lag' before the sentence is processed.

Table 2. Evaluation Agreements between System and Pathologist

Phrase	Agreements
Put on Boots	8/9
Wear a Hat	8/9
Open the Door	4/9
Pop a Balloon	4/9
Cross the Bridge	8/9

4 Conclusions

This paper reports the development of a game for cleft speech therapy. Several lessons that we learned from the requirement gathering was, at a high level, that there is a need for the game to accommodate individual differences in the cleft speech problems and to act as a proxy speech pathologist (i.e., for the game to be able to reliably detect subtle changes in cleft speech).

The most significant bottleneck found during the pilot test was the amount of idle time spent on a level. To improve this we have finished implementing the real-time recognition plugin RapidEars into the game. This provides recognition feedback as the sentence is being spoken rather than at the conclusion of a phrase. Testing of this new system will occur during the Summer of 2014.

References

1. How Does Your Child Hear and Talk? American Speech-Language-Hearing Association (2012)
2. Kummer, A.W.: Cleft Palate and Craniofacial Anomalies: The Effects on Speech and Resonance, 2nd edn. Delmar Cengage Learning, New Albany (2008)
3. Dixon, M., Marazita, M., Beaty, T., Murray, J.: Cleft Lip and Palate: Synthesizing Genetic and Environmental Influences. Nature Reviews Genetics, 167–178 (2001)
4. Speech Development. Cleft Palate Foundation (2012), http://www.cleftline.org/parents-individuals/publications/speech-development/

Do-It-Yourself (DIY) Assistive Technology: A Communication Board Case Study

Foad Hamidi[1], Melanie Baljko[1], Toni Kunic[1], and Ray Feraday[2]

[1] GaMaY Lab, Lassonde School of Engineering, York University, Toronto, Canada
{fhamidi,mb,tkunic}@cse.yorku.ca
[2] Toronto Catholic District School Board, Toronto, Ontario, Canada
feradar@tcdsb.org

Abstract. Do-It-Yourself (DIY) and open design approaches allow for the development of customized, affordable assistive technologies. Freely shared designs and software components open doors for new ways to create and to share technology, representing an approach that has the potential to be more efficient, affordable, and effective than commercial approaches to Assistive Technology development and deployment. In this paper, we present a case study of how these methods have been used to develop a DIY, open-source Speech-Generating Device.

Keywords: Do-It-Yourself (DIY), Open-Source Hardware, Open Design, Communication Boards, SGDs, Assistive Technology.

1 Introduction

In this paper, we present a case study that demonstrates the application of DIY and open design methodologies to the creation of TalkBox, an open-source, customizable Speech Generating Device (SGD). TalkBox is intended to be an alternative to commercial SGDs that is more affordable and more easily obtainable. Two prototypes were developed. The first prototype made use of a Makey Makey board for input actions, whereas the second used capacitive touch sensors. A collaborative design methodology was utilized, and our interdisciplinary team consists of a "citizen designer" who is a special education specialist, and students and faculty from an academic research lab.

2 Background

Electronic components and microcontrollers are becoming more readily available and increasingly more affordable; online support communities are flourishing; open-source software and hardware design is increasingly available. All of these trends are converging together, ushering in a new era of open design and subtending a new wave of technology creation that some pundits have called a "new industrial revolution" [1].

The idea of interdisciplinary teams customizing or developing new assistive technologies (AT) for specific users, as opposed to the purchase of commercial

K. Miesenberger et al. (Eds.): ICCHP 2014, Part II, LNCS 8548, pp. 287–294, 2014.

AT that has been designed more generally, is slowly becoming more common. There are several reasons why commercial modes of deploying AT solutions have shortcomings (e.g., high expense, poor fit leading to abandonment [12]). As an alternative, development teams may elect to work under an *open design* ethos — i.e., to deploy the AT through the use of publicly shared design information. Such teams can bring together diverse experiences and knowledge bases — for instance, subject domain knowledge (e.g., engineering and computer science, speech language pathology, occupational therapy, special education teaching, critical disability studies), and life experiences (e.g., as an assistive technology user, as a frequent interaction partner with individuals with disabilities). Our conjecture is that this *open design* approach, when combined with the requisite supportive infrastructure, will be nothing short of transformative for the deployment and uptake of effective AT interventions.

Elements of this approach can be seen in several examples. For example, organizations such as CanAssist[1] and the Tetra Society of North America[2] bring together diverse groups, comprising of individuals with disabilities, engineers and software developers, co-op and graduate students, and volunteers, to develop technological solutions for community-identified problems, oftentimes by customizing and modifying existing computer hardware and software. Other examples can be found in academia, such as in the TAIS research lab[3], which spearheads an initiative whereby final year computer science students develop games and other interactive applications through co-design with children with cerebral palsy [5] and the GaMaY Lab at York[4]. There have been a small number of prior initiatives involving open-source software such as the ITHACA framework [13] and projects COMSPEC [10] and ULYSSES [9], as well as the OATSoft open-source software repository [8]. The open-source hardware approach is relatively new to assistive technology, but is beginning to make inroads. For instance, the specialized Hackcess user forum was created within the Makey Makey on-line discussion board[5], with a stated focus on assistive technology applications.

Two modes of empirical research — exploratory and confirmatory – together are essential to the progress of a discipline [4]. Over time, the field of Open Design for Assistive Technology will shift to a mode of confirmatory research, meaning that its primary objective will be to verify or falsify hypotheses. However, as of this moment, the field is in the mode of exploration and hypothesis generation. Thus, the research methodology of the case study is an appropriate one. In this vein, Hurst and Tobias [7] presented two case studies of projects that involved DIY assistive technology hardware development, both triggered by unsatisfactory experiences with extant (and relatively expensive) consumer solutions. The first case study concerned the development of customized drawing tools, for use by instructors and students in an adaptive art class (so that students could paint

---

[1] See: `http://www.canassist.ca`
[2] See: `http://www.tetrasociety.org`
[3] See: `http://matrix.dte.us.es/grupotais`
[4] See: `http://gamay.eecs.yorku.ca`
[5] See: `http://www.makeymakey.com/forums.`

without using their hands). The second case study concerned a maker (a retired finance professional with an engineering degree) who employed an open design ethos[6] in order to independently adapt or design over 170 different pieces of AT. Our objective is to promote and to support Open Design for AT.

3 An Open-Source, Customizable Communication Board

The authors came together as collaborators on this design project. Feraday is a special education teacher, working for many years with students with various (and often multiple) types of disabilities. Feraday became interested in using maker tools and methodologies to develop custom assistive devices for his students, leading him to develop the first prototype of a speech generating device (SGD). The other team members (Hamidi, Kunić, Baljko; York students and faculty) met Feraday during a visit to the 2013 Toronto MakerFaire[7] and developed a collaborative team in order to develop the next iteration of the SGD.

Design Objectives. At the outset, the team members identified the design priorities of Open Source, Customizability, Low Cost, Durability, and Low Cost.

As per the principles of the open source movement, it is important that all design information is free and openly available, including the hardware design information (i.e., the schematics, circuit layout, etc) and any required software components. Uptake of the SGD is envisioned to be varied and would include the SGD user (the end-user) and other stakeholders, such as parents and teachers, as well as Speech Language Pathologists and other clinical professionals (who would be intermediaries).

The population of potential users is expected to be highly heterogeneous, so it is important that the design be highly configurable and that its components be easy and inexpensive to modify. However, highly configurable systems make use of system abstraction in order to articulate configuration choices. This can be challenging for some end-users, particularly those who are not technology specialists, thereby creating knowledge barriers. Thus, there can be a tension between customizability and ease-of-use.

The cost of the open-source SGD needs to be very low, so that it enters into the category of a consumable (and thus, can be used in very low-stakes experimentation and trial uses). School boards (among the targeted stakeholders) are often subject to highly-constrained budgets.

Although many commercial SGDs are intended to be durable, hardware component failure (due to heavy use) does occur, and replacement can be difficult and expensive. It is important that it is easy and inexpensive to replace or modify the switches or other components of the SGD.

It has become common for devices to hide their functionality. However, design visibility provides the potential for the user or other stakeholders to understand

[6] See: `http://workshopsolutions.com`

[7] See: `http://makerfairetoronto.com`

how the system works, to be empowered to customize or to make repairs, and to learn about interfaces and electronics through hands-on use [11]. We prioritized the design goal to make the underlying components as visible as possible, in order to create the potential for the SGD to be used as an educational tool, for teaching digital design to students with disabilities.

First Prototype. The first target group was a set of specific students in a classroom setting, who who were either non-verbal or used verbal communication rarely. Although some of these students owned commercial AAC systems (which had been provided through extant social services), they were not effective, since they did not provide a good fit with their user's needs and capabilities (for various reasons that, regrettably, cannot be described here due to space limitations).

For the first prototype (Figure 1, top left), all documentation and instructions for fabrication were posted online[8]. The design made use of the Makey Makey Human Interface Device (HID) (JoyLabz, Santa Cruz, CA), which is a circuit board with 18 input ports that can be connected, via alligator clips, to any conductive object (e.g., aluminum foil, metal objects, even fruit and vegetables!) [2]. The conductive object, in the first prototype, was a communication board that was fabricated from polystyrene foam and self-adhesive aluminum duct tape (creating a set of 6 pads which serve as "activation switches"). When any of the activation switches is touched by the user, a closed circuit is formed (provided the user is in contact with a ground). When this happens, the Makey Makey dispatches a signal to the output USB port which emulates either a keyboard key press or a mouse click. The cost of the Makey Makey is ≈$50 CAD and the communication board materials are ≈$10 CAD. The Makey Makey was connected to a consumer off-the-shelf (COTS) computer via USB. The computer was running the SoundPlant software[9], a shareware tool that allows the keys on the keyboard to be mapped to sound files. Through this mapping, each of the switch activations triggered the playback of the associated sound file, implementing, in effect, a basic Speech Generating Device (SGD).

A evaluation session was conducted with one of the target users. The student, who is non-verbal, had difficulty with providing the pressure and precision needed to activate the switches of her commercial AAC system (as arising from multiple disabilities, including cerebral palsy, scoliosis, and spina bifida). She was able to successfully use the prototype to engage in multiple communication exchanges. However, these exchanges revealed several issues. One issue was the inconvenience of grounding (an unfortunate requirement of Makey Makey). Another issue was the requirement of a computer, making the prototype relatively large and inconvenient for placement on the student's wheelchair tray. A third issue was cost: the component costs for the prototype is ≈$60 CAD, plus the (varied but nonetheless significant) cost of a computer.

---

[8] See: `a-role-for-the-makey-makey-in-augmentative-communication` `a-role-for-the-makey-makey-in-augmentative-communication`

[9] See: `http://soundplant.org`

Fig. 1. The first prototype (upper left, computer not shown) and TalkBox, the second iteration (bottom left). On the right, TalkBox in use by a student.

Second Prototype: To address the issues with the first prototype, the design was shifted in several ways. This work unfolded over 6 weeks, with weekly design meetings. The collaborative team employed an iterative design methodology, with frequent, repeated user evaluation and design modifications. GitHub and project websites were created[10], which provided software versioning, issue tracking, open-source deployment, and additional design infrastructure. The first objective was to replace the COTS computer with a Raspberry Pi[11] single-board computer (cost: ≈$40 CAD), connected to a COTS power supply and speaker (≈$20 CAD and ≈$10 CAD, resp'y). Although small (credit-card sized), Raspberry Pi is a fully-fledged computer with processing power sufficient to perform speech synthesis and even high-definition video processing. Because of its size and small power consumption, it is used extensively for embedded and physical computing projects; a vibrant community has already formed around its use[12].

In another shift, we replaced the SoundPlant software with an open-source module, written in the the Scratch programming language. The Raspberry Pi comes pre-loaded with the Scratch interpreter. (Raspberry Pi runs the Linux operating system, which is not compatible with the SoundPlant software.) This software module allows a user to configure one or more *selection sets.* Each *selection set* defines a mapping between the different input actions and a set of user-specified sound files. If multiple selection sets are specified, then TalkBox must be augmented with a "switch" function (e.g., via one of the activation switches or a *mouse button up* input action from a USB-connected mouse). This expanded the available repertoire of words and phrases. Each selection set has its own foam-core strip that has the images labels for the switches (one for each word or phrase), which can be placed on the chassis of the interface by the teacher when the selection set is changed (Figure 1, bottom left). The future addition of a dynamic display would eliminate the need for switching the foam-core strips.

[10] See: `http://hrairhlessil.github.io/TalkBox`, `http://talkbox.eecs.yorku.ca`
[11] See: `http://www.raspberrypi.org`
[12] See: `http://www.computerweekly.com/blogs/open-source-insider/2012/03/`

Another shift in the design concerned the activation switches. We developed an alternative to the Makey Makey using the MPR121 sensor controller (Freescale, Austin, TX). This reduced the cost further (from ≈$50 CAD for Makey Makey to ≈$10 CAD for the MPR121). The MPR121 sensor controller senses human body capacitance and is activated when a body part touches a connected conductive component. The MPR121 does not require a simultaneous connection to a ground wire and provides 12 pins (for up to 12 different switches). Some minor modifications were made to the polystyrene chassis and aluminum tape switch assembly. The TalkBox prototype is shown in Figure 1 (bottom left). All instructions are freely available[12] (e.g., schematics of the electronic components, the developed software code, instructions on how to assemble the hardware and load the software, as well as, small libraries of original voice samples that can be used free of charge for the speech synthesizer). The fabrication cost of the entire TalkBox is ≈$80 CAD.

Further evaluation session were conducted with the same student from the first prototype. She was able to successfully use the TalkBox prototype to engage in multiple communication exchanges, this time without the inconvenience of the grounding and with the benefit of a smaller, more compact unit that could be placed on her wheelchair tray. An initiative has been undertaken in her school board to explore the possibility of a larger-scale use of TalkBox, for a larger group of students, now that the cost is only ≈$80 CAD per unit.

4 Discussion and Future Work

At the outset, the collaborative team set out five design objectives: **open source**, **customizability**, **low cost**, **functional visibility**, and **durability**.

The TalkBox design affords **customizability** in several ways. First, the selection set is entirely customizable by the user. The repository offers a basic selection set, in both a male and female young adult voices, and includes a basic vocabulary for use in the classroom setting and for specific classroom activities (originally designed specifically for our target user). Second, the number of switches is customizable (1-18 switches for Makey Makey and 1-12 switches for the MPR121). The size of the switches is also customizable, albeit within certain constraints for the MPR121 version (the reliability of the touch detection is negatively affected once the size of the pads is made larger than the size currently specified; this issue is not applicable for the Makey Makey version). The TalkBox design also affords **durability**, since it is easy and inexpensive to replace any of the components of TalkBox (e.g., foam board chassis, aluminum foil switches, connector assemblies). Other types of materials can easily be substituted. The objective of **low cost** was achieved, with total fabrication cost of ≈$80 CAD.

This case study also provide concrete illustration of some of the principles of the **open source** development model. First, there is the aspect of participant motivation and co-ordination. As a system of innovation and production, open source relies on the convergence of goal-oriented participants, who come together with concurrent yet different (non-monetary) agendas. In this case study, diverse participants were brought together: an non-verbal individual who is an AT user, her special education teacher, students (undergraduate and graduate), and a faculty researcher. These participants brought together: key insights, rooted in concrete experience and domain expertise, technical and critical analysis skills, and design ideas. Critical analysis can increase awareness and critical reflection on the hidden assumptions, ideologies, values and potentialities of novel artifacts and designs. The participants also had different agendas and motivations. For the students, this project was an excellent learning experience. Projects such as these can offer students experiential education, through meaningful work on socially-relevant projects. For the community partner, the collaboration provided (and continues to provide) on-going access to a stable repository of programming and analysis skills. It also provides a point of entry into the body of scholarly AT research. For academic researchers, collaborations such as this provide valuable community contact and a meaningful application of academic knowledge outputs, via the mode of *knowledge mobilization*, which offers benefits over the more-typical *technology transfer* [5,6],[14].

The aspect of **functional visibility** is on-going work. Our goal is for AT users to be exposed to the designs of their technologies, rather than have them hidden away in black boxes. We feel the SGD has potential for teaching programming and digital design to students with disabilities (the Raspberry Pi, pre-loaded with Scratch, provides access to low-barrier programming). Our objective is to create new ways for people with disabilities to design and to make the technologies that they themselves and other people with disabilities would use, an approach rooted in Participatory Design that has many benefits [3]. To this end, we are developing three modes for obtaining TalkBox: (i) through open design; (ii) through the purchase of an affordable, easy-to-assemble, and customizable kit (possibly with some 3D printed components), and (iii) through the purchase of a ready-made system. We see modes (ii) and (iii) as complementary to (i); even though we have provided detailed instructions and open source components on the project website, there will be those who are not able or inclined to build TalkBox themselves and who will require an alternative means of obtainment. To address this, we are designing the kit under (ii) so that it can be assembled by youth with mild cognitive disabilities, thereby setting up (iii) as a potential opportunity for paid employment (we are currently developing a partnership with a not-for-profit organization that provides skills development for individuals with disabilities). This approach can promote empowerment and agency, in order to further break down the "provider" and "receiver" roles.

5 Conclusion

In this paper, we have described the principles of *open design*, as applied to digital assistive technology. We have presented two prototypes of an Speech Generating Device (SGD), developed under these principles. We have articulated a vision in which *open design* provides an alternative to commercial AT development and deployment. Although each development and deployment route offers its own advantages and disadvantages, we feel that the *open design* approach affords one of the most compelling advantages: open innovation via the power and utility of interdisciplinary collaborations that can bridge academia and the community. We have described and discussed ways in which similar projects might be fostered.

Acknowledgements. We express our sincere thanks to Max and Christine Feraday for the digitized voice recordings and to the Toronto Catholic District School Board and TSU/OECTA for their support, especially Frank Piddisi, Peter Stachiw, Susan Menary and Thérèse MacNeil. The authors gratefully acknowledge funding support from the NSERC Discovery Grant Program.

References

1. Anderson, C.: Makers: The New Industrial Revolution. Crown Business (2012)
2. Collective, B.S.M., Shaw, D.: Makey makey: improvising tangible and nature-based user interfaces. In: Proc. of TEI 2012, pp. 367–370 (2012)
3. Dawe, M.: Let me show you what I want: engaging individuals with cognitive disabilities and their families in design. In: Proc. of CHI 2007 (2007)
4. Gerring, J.: What is a case study and what is it good for? American Political Science Review 98(2) (May 2004)
5. Gómez, I.M., Cabrera, R., Ojeda, J., García, P., Molina, A.J., Rivera, O., Esteban, A.M.: One way of bringing final year computer science student world to the world of children with cerebral palsy: a case study. In: Miesenberger, K., Karshmer, A., Penaz, P., Zagler, W. (eds.) ICCHP 2012, Part I. LNCS, vol. 7382, pp. 436–442. Springer, Heidelberg (2012)
6. Hamidi, F., Baljko, M., Livingston, N., Spalteholz, L.: Canspeak: A customizable speech interface for people with dysarthric speech. In: Miesenberger, K., Klaus, J., Zagler, W., Karshmer, A. (eds.) ICCHP 2010, Part 1. LNCS, vol. 6179, pp. 605–612. Springer, Heidelberg (2010)
7. Hurst, A., Tobias, J.: Empowering individuals with Do-It-Yourself assistive technology. In: Proc. of Assets 2011, pp. 11–18 (2011)
8. Judge, S., Lysley, A., Walsh, J., Judson, A., Druce, S.: OATS–open source assistive technology software—a way forward. In: Proc. of AAC 2006. ISAAC Press (2006)
9. Kouroupetroglou, G., Pino, A.: ULYSSES: A framework for incorporating multi-vendor components in interpersonal communication applications. In: Proc. of AAATE 2001, pp. 55–59 (2001)
10. Mats Lundälv, A., Lysley, P., Head, P., Hekstra, D.: Comlink, an open and component based development environment for communication aids. In: Proc. of AAATE 1999, pp. 174–179 (1999)
11. Perner-Wilson, H., Buechley, L., Satomi, M.: Handcrafting textile interfaces from a kit-of-no-parts. In: Proc. of TEI 2011, pp. 61–68 (2011)
12. Phillips, B., Zhao, H.: Predictors of assistive technology abandonment. Assistive Technology 5(1), 36–45 (1993)
13. Pino, A., Kouroupetroglou, G.: ITHACA: An open source framework for building component-based augmentative and alternative communication applications. TACCESS 2(4), article 14 (2010)
14. van de Ven, A.H., Johnson, P.: Knowledge for theory and practice. Academy of Management Review 31(4), 802–821 (2006)

A Decision-Tree Approach for the Applicability of the Accessibility Standard EN 301 549

Loïc Martínez-Normand[1] and Michael Pluke[2]

[1] School of Computing, Technical University of Madrid, Boadilla del Monte, Madrid, Spain
loic@fi.upm.es
[2] Castle Consulting Ltd. 76 Cowper Street, Ipswich, England
mike.pluke@castle-consult.com

Abstract. Public procurement is one way for public administrations to promote accessibility. By procuring accessible products and services, they raise the awareness about accessibility and they have an impact on industry. In Europe, the European Commission's Mandate M 376 has resulted in a European Standard, EN 301 549, containing accessibility requirements for ICT products and services that are suitable for use in public procurement. EN 301 549 has been drafted using a feature-based approach and can be applied to any ICT product and service. The users of the standard will need guidance to decide which re-quirements of the EN apply to a given product or service. This paper presents a decision-tree approach for that problem. This approach is being validated during the design of the user interface of a support tool for the assessment of the accessibility of ICT products and services.

Keywords: ICT Accessibility, Standards, Accessibility Requirements, European Policy.

1 Introduction

Public procurement is one way for public administrations to promote accessibility. By procuring accessible products and services, they raise the awareness about accessibility and they have an impact on industry, which has to develop accessible solutions to participate in procurements. A well-known example of the application of public procurement in the Information and Communication Technology (ICT) field was the 1998 amendment of Section 508 of the US Rehabilitation Act, and the associated standards, first published in 2000 [1].

In Europe there is an equivalent effort, under the European Commission's Mandate M 376 [2], which has resulted in a European Standard, EN 301 549, containing accessibility requirements that apply to any type of ICT product and service.

Given the current convergence of ICT products and services, where the boundaries between product categories are being constantly blurred, EN 301 549 has been drafted using a feature-based approach, instead of being based on product categories. The result is a standard that can be applied to any ICT product and service, but the users of

K. Miesenberger et al. (Eds.): ICCHP 2014, Part II, LNCS 8548, pp. 295–302, 2014.

the standard (public procurers, suppliers…) will probably need additional guidance to easily decide which requirements of the EN apply to a given product or service.

This paper presents a decision-tree approach for that problem, based on a series of questions that enable people to identify the features of a given ICT product or service and, as a consequence, to identify requirements that apply. This approach is being validated during the design of the user interface of a support tool for the assessment of the accessibility of ICT products and services.

The paper is structured as follows. Sections 2 and 3 describe the Mandate M 376 and the structure of EN 301 549. Section 4 describes the proposed decision-tree approach and section 5 explains how this approach has been implemented and evaluated in a low fidelity prototype of an evaluation tool. Section 6 draws some conclusions and outlines recommendations for refining the decision tree and the design of the user interface of the evaluation tool.

2 Mandate M 376

The European Mandate M 376 [2] was issued with the primary goal of creating a set of functional accessibility requirements that could be applied in the public procurement of any type of ICT product or service. This Mandate was issued in 2005 and technical work started in 2007, with its first phase, focused on field research performed by two expert teams: one under the supervision of ETSI and a second one under the joint supervision of CEN and CENELEC.

The results were two reports published in 2009. The first report, ETSI TR 102 612 [3], collected information about existing ICT accessibility standards and other ICT accessibility requirements. The second report, by CEN and CENELEC [4], collected information about different types of conformity assessment systems and schemes and their application in the context of public procurement of ICT in Europe.

These two reports were analyzed by the European Commission and the three European Standards Organizations to refine the detailed goals of phase 2 of the Mandate. Work on phase 2 started in 2011, having as a goal the following six deliverables [5]:

- A European Standard, EN 301 549 "Accessibility requirements for public procurement of ICT products and services in Europe".
- Three technical reports providing additional material about the development process of the EN, guidelines for contract award criteria and guidelines for conformity assessment.
- An Online Procurement Toolkit for accessible ICT products and services.
- Additional guidance and support material for the procurement of accessible ICT products and services, which will be provided as part of the online procurement toolkit.

The EN and the technical reports were published in February 2014. The toolkit was delivered to the European Commission on the same date and will be published in the future. Feedback on usage of the toolkit will be collected.

3 The Standard: EN 301 549

EN 301 549 [6] has been approved by CEN, CENELEC and ETSI and was published in February 2014. The table of contents of the EN is:

- Introductory clauses: intellectual property rights, foreword and introduction.
- Clause 1: Scope. It explains that the EN contains functional accessibility requirements for ICT products and services and also contains test procedures for each requirement. The Scope also describes situations where the requirements of the EN are not applicable.
- Clause 2: References. This section contains normative and informative references to other standards and documents.
- Clause 3: Definitions and abbreviations. Here relevant terms are defined to clarify their meaning in the requirements of the EN. Some especially relevant terms are "content", "document", "platform software" and "user agent", as they are used to clarify the applicability of requirements.
- Clause 4: Functional performance. This clause describes the needs of persons with disabilities to enable them to locate, identify, and operate ICT functions; and to access the information provided when a physical, cognitive or sensory ability is not available or cannot be used. The conformance with these user needs can be demonstrated by meeting the detailed requirements in clauses 5 to 13.
- Clauses 5 to 13: the requirements. These clauses contain generic requirements (5) and requirement that are specific for ICT that provide two-way voice communication (6), for ICT with video capabilities (7), for the hardware of the ICT (8), for web content (9), for non-web documents (10), for software (11) for documentation and support services (12) and for relay and emergency services (13)
- Annexes. The draft EN contains three annexes. Annex A contains the full text of WCAG 2.0 as an electronic attachment. Annex B explains the relationships between the requirements in clauses 5 to 13 and the functional performance statements of clause 4. Annex C defines the procedures necessary to determine compliance with the individual requirements defined in clauses 5 to 13.

This structure follows a feature-based approach. This implies that most sections of the EN apply to most types of ICT products and services.

4 Feature-Based Applicability of the EN Requirements

In the past there was an expectation that all ICT products or services in a particular product category would share similar user interface features and that these features would quite often be distinct from those of ICT from a different product category. For example, at one time the photocopier user interfaces consisted of a set of dedicated hardware function buttons, a range of lights and a limited functionality visual display. In contrast, computers had general purpose graphical displays and alphanumeric keyboards. Most mobile telephones had small non-graphical displays and a numeric keyboard. Today a graphical touch-screen display could be the primary means of interacting with ICT from any of these diverse product categories.

Because of this convergence, it was necessary to organize the requirements of the EN according to categories of user interface features rather than to ICT product categories (as had been tried in the past). As well as grouping together requirements that applied to the same or related features, each requirement was written so that it was "self-scoping". This was achieved by starting the requirement with text that defined its precise scope of applicability, in the form "Where ICT <pre-condition>". Examples of these pre-conditions include:

- "has operable parts";
- "provides two-way voice communication";
- "displays video with synchronized audio".

Building the self-scoping text into each requirement provides the following benefits:

1. Each requirement is meaningful in its own right. Requirements in some similar standards are only meaningful in a context that is defined outside the requirement itself.
2. The self-scoping text forms the pre-condition of the test of that requirement that are in Annex C of the EN. The remainder of the requirement can be simply parsed into a description of the test method and pass criteria for the test.
3. Compliance with any requirement in the EN can always be assessed by checking both the self-scoping text (the test pre-condition) and, if applicable, by performing the remainder of the test. When the pre-condition is not applicable the requirement is judged to have been satisfied.

The self-scoping text ensures that no ICT will fail a requirement because it does not have a feature to which a requirement relates. If an ICT product has nothing to do with two-way voice communication then anyone attempting to apply a requirement that starts with the self-scoping text "Where the ICT provides two-way voice communication .." will find that the ICT will not fail the test for that requirement as the test's pre-condition will not be met. Although this is a fail-safe mechanism, it would be grossly inefficient to apply every requirement in the EN to each ICT product or service.

Providing the person evaluating an ICT product or service with a set of questions, in the form of a decision-tree, will allow them to identify whether a requirement is applicable to the ICT product or service.

5 A Prototype Implementation of the Decision Tree

The research group CETTICO of the Technical University of Madrid has started designing a workgroup-based support tool where teams of people can annotate the result of performing a conformity assessment of a given ICT product or service according to the requirements of the EN.

The tool will have three user's roles. The administrators will manage users of the systems. The project manager will create and manage evaluation projects, where a project represents the evaluation of one ICT product or service, and will assign evaluators to the project. The evaluators will annotate the individual results for each of the requirements.

The project manager is the user who creates new evaluation projects and has to define the features of the corresponding ICT product or service by answering questions presented by the tool.

The first stage of the development of this tool is focused on the interaction design. A low fidelity prototype (paper-based) has been produced. One of the prototyped tasks is the creation of a new evaluation project, including answering the feature-related questions, as shown in Fig.1. The initial approach was to include one question per existing "self-scoping text" in the requirements, taking into account that some of these texts where shared by several requirements.

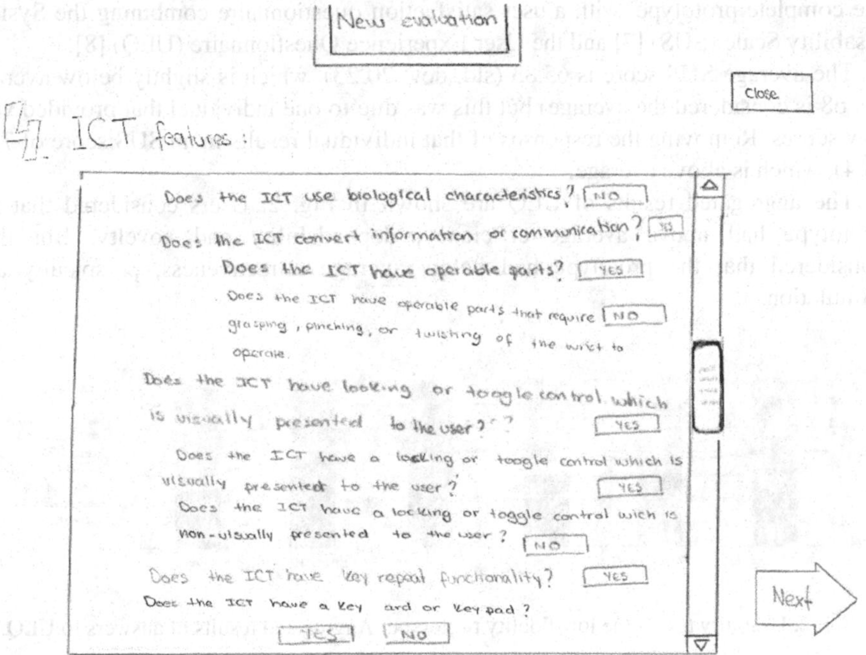

Fig. 1. Creation of a new evaluation project in the low-fidelity prototype. Some of the questions of the feature-based decision tree.

A usability test has been performed on this prototype, with 6 participants that have different levels of knowledge about accessibility and the EN. The participants had to perform 8 tasks associated with the three user's roles (3 tasks for administrator, 2 tasks for project manager and 3 tasks for evaluator). The roles that the users had to perform were selected in a random order.

Table 1 shows the most relevant objective data about the users' performance: number of tasks, number of individual actions per task, percentage of mistakes related to individual actions, percentage of help requests related to individual actions and percentage of completed tasks. Averages and standard deviations are shown.

Table 1. Objective data collected in the usability test of the low fidelity prototype

	Administrator	Project manager	Evaluator
No. of tasks	3	2	3
Actions per task	11.61 (1.06)	18.83 (2.38)	11.77 (1.61)
% of mistakes	1.37% (1.51)	7.75 % (4.79)	6.17% (4.32)
% of help requests	0.94% (1.45)	4.04% (2.84)	0.94% (1.47)
% of completed tasks	88.88% (17.21)	75% (38.18)	55.55% (17.21)

The usability evaluation also collected information about the users' perceptions of the complete prototype, with a user satisfaction questionnaire combining the System Usability Scale (SUS) [7] and the User Experience Questionnaire (UEQ) [8].

The average SUS score is 65.83 (std. dev. 20.23), which is slightly below average (as 68 is considered the average) but this was due to one individual that provided very low scores. Removing the responses of that individual results in an SUS score of 73.5 (8.4), which is above average.

The aggregated results of UEQ are shown in Fig. 2. Users considered that the prototype had above average efficiency, dependability and novelty. But they considered that the prototype had below average attractiveness, perspicuity and stimulation.

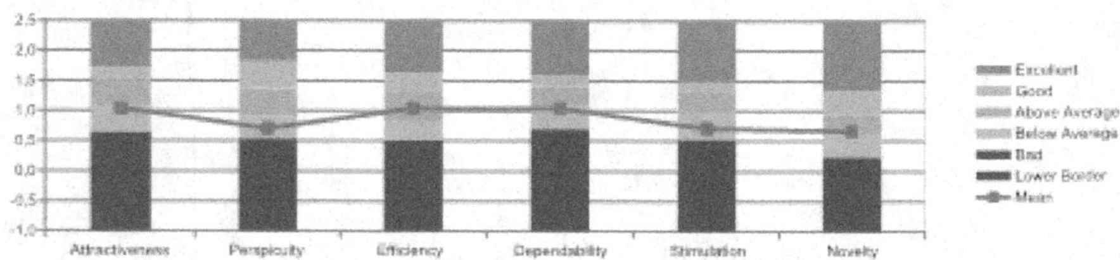

Fig. 2. Usability test of the low fidelity prototype. Aggregated results of answers to UEQ.

The results indicate that the most complex task was the creation of a new evaluation project, where participants needed more user actions, made more mistakes and needed more help. The satisfaction questionnaires show that the prototype seems to have an almost average degree of usability, which leaves room for improvement. Finally, the notes taken during the usability evaluation also suggest some troubles with the number of feature-related questions and how to interpret them.

We believe that this was due to the approach used in the prototype, where a question was asked for each of the individual requirements of the EN that were selected for the prototype.

6 Conclusions and Future Work

EN 301 549 is a European Standard that contains accessibility requirements that apply to ICT products and services. The EN is structured using a feature-based approach due to the increasing convergence of user interface features in the ICT field. The result is that every individual requirement has an applicability condition. These conditions can be used to create a decision tree that would enable the users of the standard to define which requirements apply to a given ICT product or service.

This decision tree has been implemented in a low fidelity prototype of an evaluation tool. The usability test has made clear that the straightforward approach of having all the applicability conditions of the EN converted into questions is not a good one.

In the next iteration of the development of the tool the approach will change to reduce the number of questions. An analysis of the questions based on the applicability conditions is being performed to determine the impact of each question, that is, the number of requirements that apply or don't apply after the question is answered. The underlying idea is to only include questions that impact more than one requirement, because the usability test indicates that if one question only impacts one requirement it will be easier and more efficient if the question is answered as part of the evaluation of the individual requirement.

The first results of this process are shown in table 2, where the candidate first-level questions of the tree are listed, alongside their impact, that is, the number of clauses (requirements or recommendations) affected by the answer to the question. Table 2 shows that there are 6 clauses that, in principle, apply to any ICT product or service. In addition, some of those questions (the ones with more impact) will probably have second- or even third-level questions to better address the complexity of the set of clauses of EN 301 549.

Table 2. First level of a refined decision tree based on feature impact (initial proposal)

Question	Impact
-	6
Does the ICT have closed functionality?	25
Does the ICT have operable parts?	2
Does the ICT have a locking or toggle control?	2
Does the ICT provide two-way voice communication?	15
Does the ICT have video capabilities?	7
Is the ICT hardware or does the ICT have hardware?	30
Is the ICT a web page or does the ICT have web pages?	39
Is the ICT a non-web document or does the ICT have non-web documents?	36
Is the ICT software or does the ICT have software?	70
Does the ICT have product documentation?	2
Does the ICT have support services?	3
Is the ICT intended to provide relay services?	5

This refined decision tree, once completed, will be implemented in a high-fidelity prototype of the tool, and will be evaluated to assess its quality.

References

1. US Access Board. Section 508 standards (2000), `http://www.section508.gov/index.cfm?fuseAction=stdsdoc`
2. European Commission. M 376. Standardisation mandate to CEN, CENELEC and ETSI in support of European accessibility requirements for public procurement of products and services in the ICT domain. Enterprise and Industry Directorate-General (December 2005)
3. ETSI TR 102 612 V1.1.1 (2009-03). Technical Report. Human Factors (HF); European accessibility requirements for public procurement of products and services in the ICT domain (European Commission Mandate M 376, Phase 1) (2009)
4. CEN/BT WG 185 & CLC/BT WG 101-5. Conformity assessment systems and schemes for accessibility requirements. CEN/BT WG 185 Project Team Report. European accessibility requirements for public procurement of products and services in the ICT domain (European Commission Mandate M 376, Phase 1) (2009)
5. European Accessibility Requirements for Public Procurement of Products and Services in the ICT Domain (European Commission Standardization Mandate M 376, Phase 2). Web page (2014), `http://www.mandate376.eu/`
6. EN 301 549 V1.1.1 (2014-02). Accessibility requirements for public procurement of ICT products and services in Europe (2014)
7. Brooke, J.: SUS: a 'quick and dirty' usability scale. In: Jordan, P.W., Thomas, B., McClelland, I.L., Weerdmeester, B. (eds.) Usability Evaluation in Industry. CRC Press (1996)
8. Laugwitz, B., Held, T., Schrepp, M.: Construction and evaluation of a user experience questionnaire. In: Holzinger, A. (ed.) USAB 2008. LNCS, vol. 5298, pp. 63–76. Springer, Heidelberg (2008)

ADAPTAEMPLEO: Interactive Advisor to Adapt Workplaces for Persons with Disabilities and Promote Employment in the Retail Sector

Alberto Ferreras[1], Andrés Soler[1], Rakel Poveda[1], Alfonso Oltra[1], Carlos García[1], Purificación Castelló[1], Juan-Manuel Belda-Lois [1], and José Crespo[2]

[1] Instituto de Biomecánica de Valencia, Universitat Politècnica de València, Valencia, Spain
{alberto.ferreras,andres.soler,rakel.poveda,alfonso.oltra, carlos.garcia,puri.castello,juanma.belda}@ibv.upv.es
[2] AECEMCO: Asociación Empresarial de Centros Especiales de Empleo de COCEMFE, Madrid, Spain
info@aecemco.es

Abstract. An interactive advisor for ergonomic assessment and fitting of workplaces to person with disabilities (physical, sensorial, and/or psychological) is presented. It has been designed to identify areas of mismatching between workplace demands and worker functional capabilities, in order to promote the access to employment, and labor integration for people with disabilities in the retail sector. The methodology includes the process of incorporation as well as the adaptive measures of workplaces by using reasonable adjustments.

Keywords: Ergonomics, Persons with Disabilities, Work Demands, Functional Capacities, Workplace Adaptation, Computer Aided System.

1 Introduction

The incorporation of people with disabilities to the workplace is very important in the entire process of social integration in the community. Although a great effort has been made over the last few years, there are still numerous gaps that cause a very high rate of unemployment among people with disabilities.

The problems that can arise at the time of integration into a workplace for a person with disabilities, usually occur during the selection process or in the adaptation of the workplaces. Some of these problems are the following:

- Knowing what is the real productive capabilities of a person with disabilities,
- Knowing which job is the most suitable for a person with particular capabilities,
- Detecting the problems that exist both in the selection process and in the performance of the job,
- Knowing what type of help exists to adapt the workplace, and how to carry out the adaptation without incurring in high costs to the company.

K. Miesenberger et al. (Eds.): ICCHP 2014, Part II, LNCS 8548, pp. 303–306, 2014.

To resolve these problems there are resources that offer information (associations, government, web pages), and tools and methods that try to facilitate the process of incorporation and adaptation.

Some of these methods (like IMBA [1], JOBFIT [2], or ErgoDis/IBV [3]) raise some issues, such as:

- In many cases, they are complex methodologies that require much specialised training to use them properly.
- They tackle specific aspects, with a very high level of detail.
- They are not easily accessible for the users.

We have carried out a project whose main goal was to develop a web application to promote the access to employment, and labour integration for people with disabilities in the retail sector, by the creation of a methodology that makes it easier for professionals and users to manage the accessibility in the workplace (Fig. 1). The scope of the methodology includes the process of incorporation as well as the adaptation of workplaces by using reasonable adjustments.

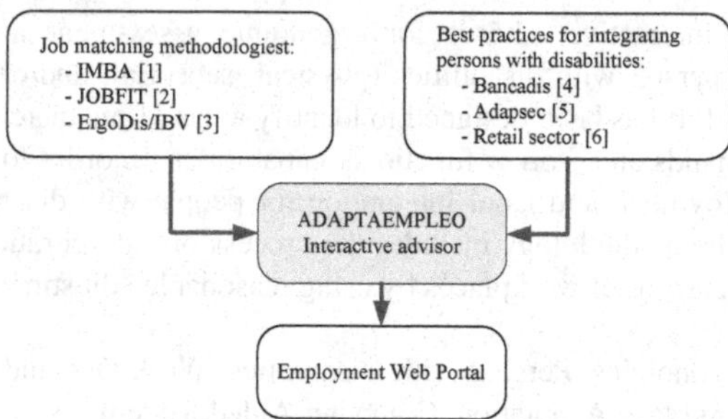

Fig. 1. General overview

2 Methodology

To develop this application, a work plan (6 stages) was followed:

1. Characterization of job seekers (problems, needs, abilities), and workplaces (tasks, environment). It was carried out by means of standardized form, and expert panels in order to obtain the integration map, where it is reflected the adaptation or mismatch between the characteristics (demands) of workplaces, and capabilities of people with disabilities.
2. Definition of web applications requirements. All features, functionality, usability, and accessibility requirements were described in this phase.
3. Design and development. This phase included all tasks related to modules programming, and web environment development.
4. Pilot experimentation. With the participation of 3 retail sector companies, and 19 workers of sheltered employment centers. The tool was explained by means of manuals and video demonstrations. Firstly, participants visited the site, and they car-

ried out a number of tasks, such as, registration, free navigation, adaptation consult, workplace creation, etc.). Then, their impressions were gathered through forms and questionnaires with questions related to task performance (errors), difficulty, satisfaction, usability, functionality, accessibility and open questions.
5. Tool redesign. New functionalities and improvements were added from the results of pilot experimentation.
6. Dissemination of the results.

3 Results: Adaptaempleo Web Portal

The method used is showed in Figure 2. Three different steps can be distinguished. First, "job", and "job seekers" information is gathered. This requires direct observation of workers performing their jobs, and interviews to workers, supervisors, and other people involved in the process. Afterwards, data are processed and, finally, a decision is made depending on results.

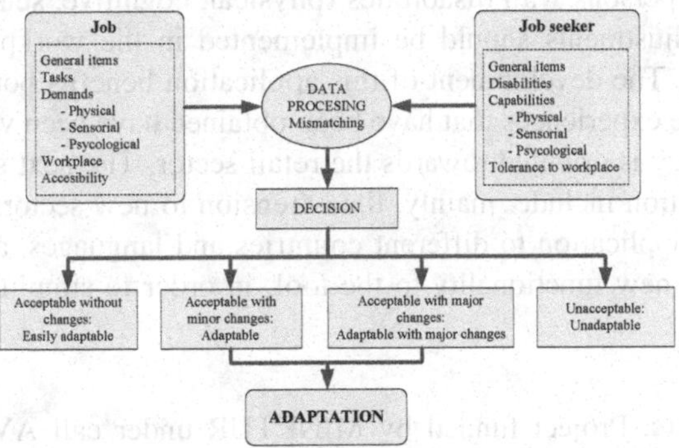

Fig. 2. Method employed to take decisions

The results obtained during this project were compiled in a web portal that can be found at: `http://www.adaptaempleo.es`. The contents of the portal are grouped in two areas:

- Private area. This area implements the interactive advisory modules, and companies or applicants will need to register to access them. These modules include:
  - Advices to people with disabilities for finding employment in the "retail sector": possible posts to be filled, necessary adjustments according to capabilities of the person, etc.
  - Advices to companies to employ people with disabilities: workplaces of the sector that can be filled by persons with disabilities, adaptations according to post and profile of disabilities, etc.
- Public area: This area includes the tutorials, and resources that might be useful to people with disabilities, agencies, employers (government) among others, such as, reference materials, regulations (legislation and guidelines), web pages, etc. Also, there are examples of the most common types of jobs, and best practices.

4 Impact of the Results

The application is aimed at different types of users (individuals, labor integration services, employment web sites, and large companies). At present, the way to reach them is through the employment web site of AECEMCO (business association of sheltered employment centers of COCEMFE). So far, the interest of the application has been validated by user experiences with companies and people with disabilities, who reported a positive experience. For this reason, they are exploring partnerships with the identified agents to achieve greater impact and dissemination. Nowadays, more than 122 registered users (from both companies and particulars) have used the ADAPTAEMPLEO advisor, since its launch in January 2014.

5 Conclusions and Further Work

The tool provides an overview to companies about the adaptation of workplaces, and lets them know if persons with disabilities (physical, cognitive, sensory) can do such jobs, and what adjustments should be implemented in the workplace for adequate performance on it. The development of this application benefits both individuals and companies, and the experiences that have been obtained have been very satisfactory.

The methodology is oriented towards the retail sector. The next steps in the evolution of the application include, mainly, the extension to new sectors or activities, the adaptation of the application to different countries and languages, and the incorporation generation of new functionality to the tool, in order to simplify the information management.

Acknowledgements. Project funded by MINETUR under call AVANZA 2 (action TSI-040202-2011-13).

References

1. Dieckmann, H., Kaiser, H., Kleffmann, A., Schian, H.M., Weinmann, S., Ramsauer, F., Rexrodt, C., Sturtz, A.: IMBA, Integration von Menschen mit Behinderungen in die Arbeitswelt (2007), http://www.imba.de/
2. Legge, J., Burgess-Limerick, R.: Reliability of the JobFit System Pre-Employment Functional Assessment Tool. Work 28(4), 299–312 (2007)
3. Tortosa, L., Ferreras, A., García-Molina, C., Page, A.: The ErgoDis/IBV method - A computer aided system for ergonomic assessment and fitting of workplaces to disabled workers. In: Landau, K. (ed.) Ergonomic Software Tools in Product and Workplace Design, pp. 261–270. IfAO Institut für Arbeitsorganisation, Stuttgart (2000)
4. BANCADIS Project web page, http://bancadis.ibv.org/
5. ADAPSEC Project web page, http://www.ibv.org/adapsec/
6. Piedrabuena, A., Ferreras, A., Oltra, A., García, C., García, A.C., Gimeno, C.: Integración laboral de personas con discapacidad en el sector Comercio-Alimentación. Instituto de Biomecánica de Valencia (2007)

ICT-Based Learning Technologies for Disabled and Non-disabled People

Introduction to the Special Thematic Session

Marion Hersh

Biomedical Engineering, University of Glasgow, Glasgow G12 8LT, Scotland, UK
marion.hersh@glasgow.ac.uk

Abstract. The central section of the paper provides a brief overview of the six papers to be presented in the session and an introduction to the Enable Network Project on which the session is based. It is introduced by a short discussion of technology as both an enabler and barrier to disabled people accessing learning and recommendations to ensure it acts as an enabler rather than a barrier.

Keywords: Education, Learning Technologies, Accessibility, Usability, Overview.

1 Introduction

Education should be considered a basic right. It is essential for both self-development and obtaining qualifications and the possibility of a well-paid and interesting job. However, inequalities in access to education tend to both follow and perpetuate other inequalities in society. In particular, disabled people are one of the social groups who experience barriers in accessing education.

Enablers to changing this include the use of technology, legislation and changes in attitudes and the focus here will be the use of technology to support learning. Developments in ICT have led to a number of exciting possibilities for the use of ICT in education, including mobile learning e.g. [1-2], microlearning [3] and games based learning e.g. [4]. There are also learning technologies designed specifically for disabled people and in many cases they are multi-functional with additional applications or act as combined assistive and learning technologies. The importance of assistive technologies in removing the barriers that disabled learners would otherwise experience to engaging in learning tasks and completing (post-secondary) education has been recognised [5-6].

However, in addition to being an enabler, learning and other technologies can also act as a barrier if not designed appropriately. This may result in them not being fully accessible and usable or otherwise not meeting (disabled) people's needs. In many cases accessibility will mean compatibility with assistive devices. Although it is difficult to predict the future, it seems likely that the use of mobile technologies, including to support learning, will become increasingly important and there may be a proliferation of smaller, lighter devices with increased functionality, memory

K. Miesenberger et al. (Eds.): ICCHP 2014, Part II, LNCS 8548, pp. 307–310, 2014.

and processing speed. However, the very factors, namely very small size and multi-functionality, that make mobile devices attractive by making them easily portable and enabling them to be used at any time and place, are potentially a source of accessibility and usability barriers, particularly to disabled and elderly people. Mobility and small size result in reduced memory and processing speed, and the need for batteries to be regularly recharged [7], as well as small, relatively difficult to see or feel screens, keyboards and pointers. Mobile devices are used in non-ideal physical environments where there are likely to be frequent interruptions [7], further contributing to accessibility and usability barriers. The importance of screen size has been considered in a disciplinary context [7], but not as a wider accessibility issue with implications for the participation of disabled people in mobile learning.

Recognition of the importance of user-centred design and awareness of the context of use [8-9] may be particularly relevant in avoiding accessibility and usability problems for disabled people and promoting successful and enjoyable mobile learning. A study of a number of mobile learning projects [7] identified four main categories of usability issues: physical attributes (e.g. size, weight, memory, battery life), content and software applications, network speed and reliability, and the physical environment. The perception of usability issues frequently depended on the context. In addition, mobile devices were found to be often used in unpredictable real-world circumstances to which people responded constructively, but not in ways that could easily be fed back to inform the technology design [10].

Contextual factors related to the ways in which learning (and other) technologies are used also affect their impact and whether they become an important enabler or yet another barrier. For instance, the increasing use of mobile technology also increases pressures to speed up work and learning and to use all available time. This can have negative impacts on disabled people who may require more structured and calmer environments or longer time periods to engage in learning and other activities, as well as additional rest time. The development of future learning and assistive technologies, for instance the use of brain computer interaction to support learning, also raises issue of appropriate design to ensure these technologies act as enablers rather than barriers to disabled people. This leads to the following recommendations:

1. Following guidelines & standards on accessibility & usability for disabled people.
2. Consultation with and involvement of disabled people in the development, testing and implementation of all learning technologies.
3. The use of design for all to try to ensure that learning technologies are suitable for and take account of the needs of all users regardless of disability or other personal characteristics.
4. The use of human-centred design philosophies which aim to design and implement learning technologies to meet human needs rather than organisational aspirations.
5. Further research to better understand the role of learning technologies as barriers and enablers for disabled people.

2 Session Overview

This session was inspired by the Enable Network for ICT Learning for Disabled People which is investigating the use of information and communication technologies (ICT) to support lifelong learning by disabled adults in order to overcome barriers and increase opportunities. Its work is divided into three main stages. The first stage involved data collection in the 17 partner countries on the current state of the art with regards to ICT learning technologies for disabled learners, relevant legislation and regulations, methodological and pedagogical and end-user issues and the identification of good practice. The second stage drew on this data to obtain frameworks for the categorisation and evaluation of ICT to support learning by disabled adults. These frameworks were then validated through application to previously identified technologies. Ongoing work is analysing the data to compare the situations across the different partner countries and to identify good practice in the use of ICT to support learning by disabled adults, including methodological, pedagogical and end-user issues. Evaluating ICT based learning technologies for disabled people by Marion Hersh presents an overview of the evaluation framework developed by the project and discusses its wide range of applications. The framework comprises sets of principles and three separate methodologies. The paper also discusses the need for an evaluation framework specifically for ICT learning technologies for disabled learners.

The third stage has drawn on the results of the two previous stages to develop on-line in-service training materials on ICT to support disabled learners. These materials will be evaluated and updated in pilot training sessions and the project results will be analysed to produce recommendations for the future research agenda. The development of training modules on ICT to support disabled learners by Simon Ball discusses the production of six training modules and an overarching module with supporting information. The modules cover a number of important topics, including working with disabled people, standardisation and frameworks for accessible learning and free and built-in ICT to support disabled learners, Accessibility in virtual learning environments: an experience of staff training in Latin America by Hector Amado-Salvatierra et al. also discusses training, in this case in accessibility of e-learning systems in higher education. The paper presents the training materials used in blended learning workshops in seven countries in Latin America.

The three other papers focus on learning technologies for particular groups of learners, namely print-disabled, blind and elderly. Supporting senior citizen using tablet computers by Ingo Dahn et al. presents recommendations for the design of user interfaces for older people. These recommendations were obtained through end-user testing of two different interfaces. Development of multimodal textbooks with invisible 2-dimensional codes for students with print disabilities by A. Fujiyoshi et al. discusses the use of multidimensional textbooks. Two-dimensional codes and digital audio players with code scanners are used to enable students to both read the text and listen to it being read out. EduCards – virtual reality and universal learning design application by Marijan Jurešić et al. discusses the use of a system for supporting Braille learning and introducing Braille and sign language to all children at an early age to reduce discrimination. The system comprises cards with Latin and Braille letters and symbolic images. When held in front of a computer the computer recognises the symbol and reads the letter and image name. The session has an international flavour with authors from Croatia, England, Germany, Japan, Scotland and Spain and reports of studies from Japan, and several countries in Latin America.

3 Conclusions

This paper has two main components. The introduction considers the potential roles of technology as both an enabler and barrier to disabled people accessing learning and the conditions to be met to ensure that it acts as an enabler. The central section provides a brief overview of the six papers in the session and thereby illustrates the positive ways in which learning technologies can be used to overcome some of the barriers that disabled people would otherwise face in accessing education. It also provides a short introduction to the work of the Enable Network for ICT Learning for Disabled People.

Acknowledgements. I would like to thank Simon Ball for his very useful comments.

References

1. Kukulska-Hulme, A., Traxler, J. (eds.): Mobile Learning: A Handbook for Educators and Trainers. Routledge (2008)
2. Motiwalla, L.F.: Mobile Learning: a Framework and Evaluation. Computers and Education 49(3), 581–596 (2007)
3. Hug, T.: Didactics of Microlearning: Concepts, Discourses and Examples. WaxmannVerlag (2007)
4. Hersh, M.A., Leporini, B.: Accessibility and Usability of Educational Games for Disabled students. In: Gonzalez, C. (ed.) Student Usability in Educational Software and Games: Improving Experiences, pp. 1–40. IGI Global, Hershey (2012)
5. Day, S.L., Edwards, B.D.: Assistive technology for Postsecondary Students With Learning Disabilities. J. Learning Disability 29(5), 486–492 (1996)
6. Edyburn, D.L.: Assistive Technology and Mild Disabilities. Special Education Technology Practice 8(4), 18–28 (2006)
7. Kukulska-Hulme, A.: Mobile Usability in Educational Contexts: What Have We Learnt! The Int. Review of Research in Open and Distance Learning 8(2) (2007)
8. Evans, D., Taylor, J.: The Role of User Scenarios as the Central Piece of the Development Jigsaw Puzzle. In: Attewell, J., Savill-Smith, C. (eds.) Mobile Learning Anytime Everywhere: Papers from Mlearn 2004 (2005)
9. Malliou, E., Miliarakis, A.: The MOTFAL Project. Mobile Technologies for Ad Hoc Learning. In: Attewell, J., Savill-Smith, C. (eds.) Mobile Learning Anytime Everywhere: Papers from Mlearn 2004 (2005)
10. Kukulska-Hulme, A.: Human Factors and Innovation with Mobile Devices. In: Hansson, T. (ed.) Handbook of Research on Digital Information Technologies: Innovations, Methods and Ethical Issues, pp. 392–403. IGI Global, Hershey (2008)

The Development of Training Modules on ICT to Support Disabled Lifelong Learners

Simon Ball

Jisc TechDis, U.K.
simon@techdis.ac.uk

Abstract. A global consortium has come together under the Enable project to create a suite of freely available, accessible, online, self-paced training modules for tutors working in adult education, who may be supporting disabled students. Topics covered include working with disabled people; pedagogical principles of using ICT to support disabled learners; making online teaching content accessible; free and built-in ICT to support disabled adult learners; end-user issues including accessibility and usability; and standardisation.

Keywords: Training, Online, Education, Lifelong Learning, Adult Education, Disability, Accessibility, Inclusion.

1 Introduction

A consortium of partners from around the world has come together to create the ENABLE project (www.i-enable.eu). This project, funded by the European Commission Lifelong Learning Programme, has several objectives, amongst which is to deliver a suite of training modules for people working in, or supporting, lifelong learning. These modules cover various aspects of ICT supporting disabled lifelong learners, and are freely available for anyone to use (find them here: http://vle.jisctechdis.ac.uk/xerte/play_649). The consortium is also working on getting the modules accredited in the UK, Germany and Poland.

2 Methodology and Module Contents

It was decided to deliver six core modules with a further overarching module covering the introductory principles, background, glossary of terms and so on. The modules cover both assistive and learning technologies. The topics covered are: Working with disabled people; Pedagogical principles of using ICT to support disabled learners; Making online teaching content accessible; Free and built-in ICT to support disabled learners; End-user issues, including accessibility and usability; Standardisation and frameworks for accessible learning; and an Overarching introductory module. The creation of each module was led by a different project partner, with a team of three or four other partners in support. Each of the partner organisations was involved in the

K. Miesenberger et al. (Eds.): ICCHP 2014, Part II, LNCS 8548, pp. 311–314, 2014.

development of at least two modules. Each module title was suggested and iterated by negotiation between the partners. Subtopics were agreed, and partners started to gather and produce content. Finally the modules were built using a free tool for creating accessible e-learning content: Xerte (www.xerte.org.uk). A screenshot of one of the modules is shown in Figure 1, illustrating the clear layout and the feature (bottom left) enabling users to select colour schemes and seek further guidance on how to use their browser to achieve their preferred accessibility settings. As well as being susceptible to the user's browser settings, the modules delivered as Xerte objects are also fully keyboard accessible [1].

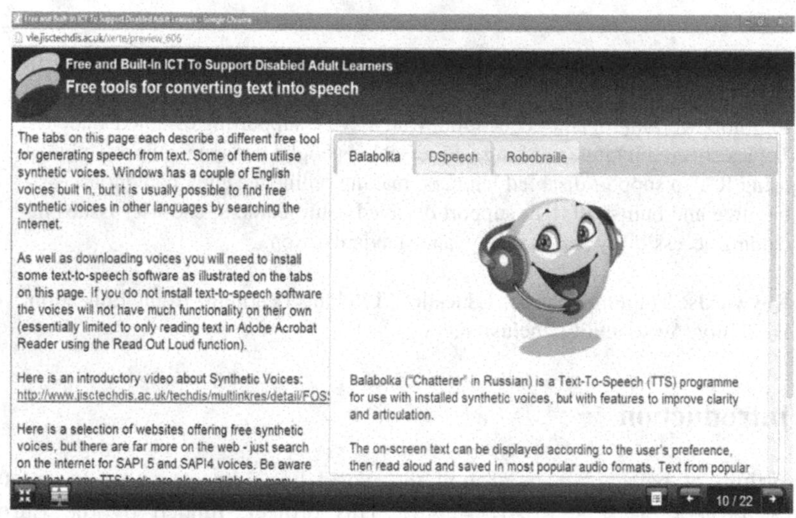

Fig. 1. Sample page from one of the online training modules, delivered using Xerte

Even though Xerte objects are accessible to most disabled people, including screen reader users, and Xerte objects follow a user's browser accessibility settings, we decided to also ensure that each module is accompanied by a text-only version with no colour and no images. The full suite of modules is also being translated into German and into Polish by consortium partners (the Creative Commons licensing permits other translations, subject to clearly referencing the original version).

3 Piloting and Accreditation

At the time this paper was submitted for printing, the consortium was just embarking upon a 12-week phase of user testing and piloting of the modules, initially in the UK and subsequently in Germany and Poland after the translations are complete. Feedback from the pilots will be used to modify and improve the modules where appropriate. The modules will not only be piloted with the intended audience, adult education tutors, but also with disabled students themselves. These pilots will be complete by the time of the ICCHP conference.

Consortium members are also working on possible accreditation avenues for the modules in the UK, Germany and Poland. This is due to take place in the final phase of activity for the Enable project, in the summer and autumn of 2014.

4 Discussion

Disabled people can experience significant barriers to accessing learning. Often failings at an earlier stage in their education lead disabled people to engage in lifelong learning programmes to develop their skills and education further. Many of them already use ICT to overcome some of the barriers they would otherwise face in undertaking education. However, ICT can be both an enabler which increases access and participation (opportunities) and a source of additional barriers, depending on the way in which it is used, and the awareness and knowledge of the educators and those supporting the learner (often families and care workers) about what is possible [2]. Without adequate information the 'wrong' technologies can be employed and disabled learners can fail to successfully achieve their objectives [3]. However, technology should never be the driver for pedagogy, but rather a means to facilitate it, and in particular a means to facilitate inclusive pedagogy [4]. There is a vast variety of types of technology that can be added to the educator's palette of tools, with many purposes and myriad audiences [5]. In addition to aiding inclusivity, technology can also aid productivity, both on the part of the learner and the teacher [6].

There exists already generic guidance for making learning and teaching more accessible (for example [7]). However what we could not find already in existence was training for adult and lifelong educators focusing on the use of ICT to support disabled learners in adult and lifelong learning. Hence the production of these modules. There exist already some freely available resources on disability etiquette (such as [8] and [9] but they are quite concise and not oriented specifically to adult education, nor do they tend to place disability within the wider spectrum of needs and requirements, so we decided this should be our entry point for these resources.

We included a module providing the underpinning pedagogical principles of using ICT to support disabled learners to set the academic framework for this work. This module looks at students as active learners, the role of technology in student-centred learning, and the relation of this to disability. This module draws heavily on the work of Koehler and Mishra [10] and their TPCK framework (Technological Pedagogical Content Knowledge). The next module follows directly on from this pedagogical background in providing tips on making teaching content accessible. This work focuses on the use of common tools in teaching such as MS Word, PowerPoint etc to highlight ways in which simple tweaks to practice can make a huge difference to the accessibility of the resources. Following the positive reception to the author's step-by-step guide to FOSS accessibility tools for libraries [11] this work was revisited for a module on free and built-in (to operating systems, for example) technologies to support disabled adult learners. This then leads naturally into a module on end-user issues, chiefly accessibility and usability. Often these topics are discussed in relation to websites, but not in terms of e-learning and multimedia, and especially not in relation to adult learning. This module links directly back to principles from earlier in the series, referencing accessible documents and pedagogy, for example.

Finally the module series is rounded off with a module on frameworks and tools that can be used in developing accessible online materials for adult education. This draws upon the work of Kerr and Bainbridge [12] in re-presenting the MQAS Orange and MQAS Green frameworks with an adult education audience in mind.

By the time of the ICCHP conference the modules will be available to the public, having been piloted and user-tested, and will be available in German and Polish. Hopefully the author will be able to report some early usage statistics and feedback.

References

1. Ball, S., Tenney, J.: Xerte - a user-friendly tool for creating Accessible Learning Objects. In: Miesenberger, K., Klaus, J., Zagler, W., Karshmer, A. (eds.) ICCHP 2008. LNCS, vol. 5105, pp. 291–294. Springer, Heidelberg (2008)
2. Pepper, D.: Adult Novice Learners of Technology and Their Helpers. School of Information Arts and Technologies, University of Baltimore (2010), http://bit.ly/1gbBoNJ
3. Dawe, M.: Desperately seeking simplicity: how young adults with cognitive disabilities and their families adopt assistive technologies. In: Proceedings of the SIGCHI Conference on Human Factors in Computing Systems, pp. 1143–1152 (2006)
4. Ball, S.: 12 steps towards Embedding Inclusive Practice with Technology as a Whole Institution Culture in UK Higher Education. Jisc TechDis (2009), http://bit.ly/1sEIi3f
5. Hart, J.: The emerging Top 100 Tools for Learning 2010 (2010), http://www.c4lpt.co.uk/recommended/top100-2010.html (retrieved)
6. Ball, S., McNaught, A.: Round Peg, Square Hole: Supporting via the Web Staff and Learners who do not fit into traditional learner-teacher-institution scenarios. In: Miesenberger, K., Klaus, J., Zagler, W.L., Karshmer, A.I. (eds.) ICCHP 2008. LNCS, vol. 5105, pp. 215–218. Springer, Heidelberg (2008)
7. Ball, S.: The Art of the Possible: Using Technology to Make Teaching More Inclusive. In: Moore, D., Gorra, A., Adams, M., Reaney, J., Smith, H. (eds.) Disabled Students in Education: Technology, Transition, and Inclusivity, Hershey, USA, pp. 1–20 (2012)
8. SCIPS, Disability Etiquette. Strategies for Creating Inclusive Programmes of Study (2011), http://www.scips.worc.ac.uk/etiquette.html (accessed March 26, 2014)
9. ABIL. Disability Etiquette Tips. Arizona Bridge to Independent Living (2014), http://bit.ly/1sEIxvp (accessed March 26, 2014)
10. Koehler, M.J., Mishra, P.: Introducing TPCK. In: AACTE Committee on Innovation and Technology (ed.) Handbook of Technological Pedagogical Content Knowledge (TPCK) for Educators, pp. 3–29. Routledge / Taylor and Francis (2008)
11. Ball, S.J.: FOSS Accessibility Tools for Libraries. EIFL (2012), http://bit.ly/OHN2oF
12. Kerr, S., Bainbridge, J.: OUA Let's Get Accessible! Inclusive Curriculum Design (2011), http://bit.ly/1izJCO8 (accessed March 26, 2014)

Evaluating ICT Based Learning Technologies for Disabled People

Marion Hersh

Biomedical Engineering, University of Glasgow, Glasgow G12 8LT, Scotland
marion.hersh@glasgow.ac.uk

Abstract. This paper discusses the need for an evaluation framework specifically for (ICT-based) learning technologies for disabled learners and demonstrates the limitations of existing approaches based on the evaluation of assistive technology or learning technologies for non-disabled learners. It presents elements of the first full such evaluation framework comprising a set of evaluation principles and aims and three evaluation methodologies. It has a wide range of applications including (i) stand-alone and comparative evaluations of ICT-based learning technologies for disabled people; (ii) identifying gaps in provision or the need for modifications; (iii) supporting the design and development of new technologies; (iv) supporting learners in making informed choices about appropriate learning technologies; and (v) supporting the policy process and determination of the future research agenda, including by evaluating the impact of various measures on the effective implementation and use of ICT learning technologies for disabled learners.

Keywords: Evaluation, ICT, learning technologies, aims, principles.

1 Introduction

The importance of education both for personal development and as a means of accessing employment and other opportunities cannot be overemphasised. Although education should be considered a basic right, many disabled people experience barriers in accessing it. Enablers to changing this include the use of technology, legislation and changes in attitudes, but the focus here is on the use of technology.

There have been a number of important developments in the use of ICT in education, including mobile learning e.g.[1,2], microlearning [3] and games based learning e.g. [4]. The use of ICT has a number of potential advantages for disabled learners, but there are also issues of the accessibility and usability of these technologies [4] and their match to the particular needs and learning styles of specific groups of disabled people.

This gives rise to the need for a framework for the evaluation of ICT-based learning technologies for disabled people to ensure best use can be made of them and that learning technology design takes account of the accessibility, usability and other needs of disabled learners.

K. Miesenberger et al. (Eds.): ICCHP 2014, Part II, LNCS 8548, pp. 315–322, 2014.

2 Literature Review and Limitations of Existing Approaches

There are two relevant areas of evaluation literature: (i) learning technologies for non-disabled people; and (ii) assistive technology outcomes. However, as will be discussed later, neither of these areas really covers the evaluation of ICT learning technologies for disabled people.

There is a body of literature on the evaluation of learning technologies, though not a generally accepted methodology or even a set of generally accepted principles. Ongoing debates [5] include the relative merits of quantitative and qualitative approaches, the move from expert to practitioner based evaluation and the role of checklists. The importance of evaluation in context has been recognised [6]. Little attention has been paid to the evaluation of inclusive learning technologies or learning technologies for disabled people.

Four main types of evaluation have been identified [7], of which (i) formative evaluation to improve tool or technology design during development; and (ii) summative evaluation to help users make decisions about what tools or technologies to use and for what applications are the most commonly used. Three main approaches to deciding the types of factors evaluated have been identified [8]: (i) the ICT approach focusing on the technology or system; (ii) the individual differences approach focusing on individuals' attitudes, experiences and abilities; and (iii) the relational approach focusing on users' relationships. Checklists [5] are frequently used in evaluation, relatively easy to use and can provide a comprehensive approach [9]. However, they have also been extensively criticised, for instance [9,10,11].

Support materials for implementing evaluations include the Evaluation and Development Review Unity [12,13]; The Evaluation Cookbook [14]; the ELT toolkit [15] and the Flashlight approach [16,17], which has produced the Current Student Inventory. This is a toolkit of nearly 500 indexed questions which can be used to produce surveys, questionnaires and focus group and interview protocols about technology use, its impact on learning, access to education, teacher-learner and learner-learner interactions. Of these approaches only the Evaluation and Development Review Unity considers accessibility. However, this just appears in one of the suggested approaches rather than being a major feature.

Assistive technology evaluation has generally focused on outcomes rather than technology design and features. Many of the approaches have been influenced [18] by quality of life approaches. Matching Persons and Technology (MPT) comprises a six-step procedure for determining outcomes and the appropriate assistive technology for a particular person in a given environment [19,20]. Related approaches include the Quebec user evaluation of satisfaction with assistive technology (QUEST 2.0) [21], the psychosocial impacts of assistive devices scale (PIADS) [22,23], and Life-H [24]. Taxonomies for assistive technology outcomes are being developed by the Consortium for Assistive Technology Outcomes Research (CATOR) [25] and the Assistive Technology Outcomes Measurement System (ATOMS) project [26].

Outcomes evaluation of assistive technology has also been considered. The educational technology version of MPT considers attitudes, preferences and approaches to learning and technology. The School Function Assessment [27] uses judgement based criterion referenced assessment to provide a detailed picture of the extent to which students with different impairments are carrying out school activities.

As indicated above, the evaluation of learning technologies for non-disabled students very rarely takes account of accessibility issues and, when it does, this is just accessibility with regards to the technology and not also accessibility of the evaluation process. In addition, learning technology is understood in a very limited sense in these evaluation approaches, and does not cover the assistive access technologies and combination of assistive and learning technologies required by disabled students.

The outcomes based approaches generally used for evaluating assistive technology are also not suitable, since not all learning technologies used by disabled people are assistive technologies. The quality of life approach frequently used in evaluating assistive technology outcomes is also too narrow and more relevant to learning technologies which are also assistive technologies. It may also evaluate how important having a particular type of technology is for the person's lifestyle rather than the design of the particular technology or how well it functions. Thus, quality of life approaches may evaluate how useful blind and dyslexic people or a particular blind or dyslexic person finds having a screen reader rather than what they think of a particular screen reader. The importance of learning (and any other applications they are using the technology for) to the particular disabled individual will also make a significant contribution to quality of life based evaluations. While there are general principles that hold for all types of evaluation, this is not the case for the details of evaluation. Thus, different approaches are required for, for instance, a manual wheelchair or long-handled gardening tool and a screen-reader accessible foreign language dictionary or online vocational training tests designed for unemployed physically disabled adults.

3 Development of the Framework

The evaluation framework was developed as part of the work of the Enable Network project and involved a multi-stage process under the leadership of the author. It was developed in parallel with a classification framework, but work on it was initiated after the completion of the first four stages of the development of the classification framework. This had resulted in the author developing draft detailed and six-criterion simple classification methodologies, as well as validation of these methodologies by application to technologies in use in the sixteen project partner countries.

The first stage of development of the evaluation framework involved development of a simple evaluation methodology based on the six criteria of the simple classification methodology [28] plus a further three criteria obtained from examination of the detailed classification methodology. The second stage was validation by application to a number of technologies in use in the partner countries.

The third stage comprised small group discussions by partners at a project meeting. However the meeting comments generally focused on the classification rather than the evaluation methodology. Therefore, to develop the framework further in the fourth stage a short questionnaire (see appendix) about the aims, participants and process of evaluation was drawn up and distributed to partners, members of the End-User Advisory Committees and other contacts and an extensive literature survey was carried out. A synthesis of the replies to the questionnaire, information from the literature, particularly that cited in Section 2, and her own knowledge and expertise was used by the author to produce a list of principles and aims for evaluating inclusive ICT based learning technologies and ICT based learning technologies for disabled people. These principles and aims were then used to produce three different evaluation methodologies.

The fifth stage involved the partners commenting on the evaluation methodologies, aims and principles. In general they were satisfied with the approach and their comments resulted in only small changes being made. The sixth stage was validation of the evaluation methodologies by application to nine technologies with very varied characteristics, as recorded in project deliverable D3.3 [28]. A small number of changes were made as a result of this validation process. Overall, it showed that the methodologies performed well on technologies with very varied characteristics, thereby validating the approach. In the final stage the resulting framework was sent to the partners for any final comments and changes.

4 Results: The Evaluation Framework

The framework [28] comprises sets of principles and aims and three methodologies. The evaluation methodologies comprise:

1. A six-question largely qualitative evaluation particularly for disabled learners and which can be completed in a few minutes;
2. A simple evaluation methodology with the version for experts based on a list of topics and that for disabled learners supported by specific questions; and
3. A detailed evaluation methodology with both quantitative and qualitative options and intended mainly for experts.

Due to space limitations these methodologies will not be described in detail and only a subset of the aims will be stated here. The aims not presented cover confidentiality, treatment of information, the evaluation process and the evaluators (participants completing evaluation questionnaires).

1. The aims of the evaluation
   (a) Clarity about the aims.
   (b) Design of the evaluation to meet these aims.
   (c) Trade-offs between evaluating everything and available resources, including the time and cognitive demands on evaluators, including disabled learners.
2. The underlying philosophy
   (a) Evaluation approaches based on the social rather than the medical model of disability i.e. disability is considered the result of social, infrastructural,

attitudinal and other barriers rather than an individual limitation arising from the person's impairment(s).

(b) Respect for all participants.

(c) Awareness of the four factors of the disabled learner or end-user, the context, the activities and the technology, though it is not necessarily to always consider all of them.

(d) The importance of ethical issues, including provision of full information on the aims and process of evaluation and use of the results, the right not to participate or to withdraw, confidentiality and safeguarding of personal data.

(e) Following good practice in all aspects of evaluation, including confidentiality, ethical issues and health and safety.

3. Accessibility and participation of disabled evaluators

(a) Full accessibility and appropriateness of all aspects of the evaluation process for all participants.

(b) Asking all participants for their requirements in advance and ensuring they are met.

(c) 'Normalising' the concept of having accessibility requirements.

(d) Evaluation room: on ground level or choice of lift or stairs; close to wheelchair accessible toilet; wide door; no clutter; space to move around; any pictures, mirrors or clocks can be removed; windows with heavy blinds or curtains; away from sources of noise such as roads, lifts, stairs, coffee machines, boilers and machinery; calm décor with colour contrasts.

(e) Communication: facing the person to allow lipreading, but not forcing eye contact; interpreters may be necessary and should be briefed in advance on the topics and any special vocabulary; use of direct, unambiguous language; the level of language used should be tailored to the participants.

(f) Documents: availability in alternative formats, which could include electronic, large print, black and white, easy read, and sign language. The particular formats required will depend on the participants.

(g) Length and breaks: the evaluation should be kept as short as possible. Longer evaluations should be divided into sections with short breaks between them. Shorter sessions and longer breaks or evaluation over more than one day may be necessary .

(h) Anxiety: all evaluators should have full information and know exactly what to expect; frequent short breaks can reduce stress; investigators need to be alert to signs of anxiety and to provide support or end the session if necessary.

4.1 Evaluating Learning Outcomes

There is a body of literature on assessing learning outcomes and the associated problems and uncertainties, for instance [29,30,31]. However, there has been less work on assessing learning outcomes for disabled students, though examples include [32,33]. A number of principles for evaluating learning outcomes using a particular technology have been obtained, but only the accessibility principles will be presented here. The general principles and technology specific principles can be found in [28].

4. Accessibility of learning outcomes
   (a) Full accessibility of the assessment location, documents provided, information and communication, including through the use of alternative formats and interpreters.
   (b) Avoidance of unnecessarily restrictive pedagogical or other assumptions or requirements which lead to demands which some disabled learners cannot meet by reason of their impairment(s).
   (c) Where possible, making the assessment procedure for all students accessible to disabled students rather than having different assessment procedures for disabled students.

5 Conclusions

This paper has discussed the need for an evaluation framework specifically for (ICT-based) learning technologies for disabled learners. The limitations of existing approaches based on the evaluation of assistive technology or learning technologies for non-disabled learners have been demonstrated. The full evaluation framework includes sets of principles and aims and three evaluation methodologies for evaluating learning technologies for disabled learners, but due to space limitations only some elements of the framework have been presented.

The evaluation framework has a wide range of applications, including carrying out both stand-alone and comparative evaluations of ICT-based learning technologies for disabled people on the basis of either specific factors or the technology as a whole. It can be used to identify gaps in provision or the need for modifications and support the design and development of new technologies. Its results can support learners in making informed choices about appropriate learning technologies. It can also provide support for the evaluation stage of technology development projects and lifetime evaluation. The framework can be used to identify the characteristics of the (groups of) students particular learning technologies are most suited to, as well as enabling better use to be made of existing technologies and the best choice of technologies for a given disabled learner or group of disabled learners.

It could also have a role in the policy process, including evaluating the impact of various policy measures and other factors on the effective implementation and use of ICT learning technologies for disabled learners, and supporting determination of the future research agenda. There are potentially also wider applications, including to learning technologies for non-disabled students and other uses of ICT.

Acknowledgements. I would like to thank the Lifelong Learning Programme of the European Commission for funding this work (and note that it is not responsible for the content), the Enable project partners for completing an evaluation questionnaire and providing comments and examples to support development of the methodology and the End-User Advisory Committees and other people from outside the project who completed questionnaires or provided information.

References

1. Kukulska-Hulme, A., Traxler, J. (eds.): Mobile Learning: A Handbook for Educators and Trainers. Routledge (2008)
2. Motiwalla, L.F.: Mobile Learning: A Framework and Evaluation. Computers and Education 49(3), 581–596 (2007)
3. Hug, T.: Didactics of Microlearning: Concepts, Discourses and Examples. Waxmann Verlag (2007)
4. Hersh, M.A., Leporini, B.: Accessibility and Usability of Educational Games for Disabled students. In: Gonzalez, C. (ed.) Student Usability in Educational Software and Games: Improving Experiences, pp. 1–40. IGI Global, Hershey (2012)
5. Oliver, M.: An Introduction to the Evaluation of Learning Technology. Educational Technology and Society 3(4), 20–30 (2000)
6. Jackson, B.: Evaluation of Learning Technology Implementation. In: Evaluation Studies, pp. 22–25 (1998)
7. Davidson, K., Goldfinch, J.: How to Add-Value. In: Evaluation Studies. Learning Technology Dissemination Initiative, pp. 4–12. Herriot-Watt University, Edinburgh (1998)
8. Tolmie, A., Boyle, J., Stobie, I.: Evaluating the Use of Computer Mediated Communication Resources by Trainee Educational Psychologists. In: Mogey, N. (ed.) LDTI Evaluation Studies, pp. 31–38. Learning Technology Dissemination Initiative (1998)
9. Tergan, S.-O.: Checklists for the Evaluation of Educational Software: Critical Review And Prospects. Innovations in Education and Training International 35(1), 9–20 (1998)
10. Power on! New Tools for Teaching and Learning, Office of Technology Assessment Government Printing Office, Washington DC (1988)
11. Squires, D., McDougall, A.: Choosing and Using Educational Software: A Teacher's Guide. Falmer Press, London (1994)
12. A Guide to Local Evaluation, Report no. HE/L61, London: Evaluation Development and Review Unit, Tavistock Institute of Human Relations and the Employment Department (1992)
13. Sommerlad, E.: A Guide to Local Evaluation, Report no. HE/L62/1186, London: Evaluation Development and Review Unit, Tavistock Institute of Human Relations and the Employment Department (1992)
14. Harvey, J.: The LTDI Evaluation Cookbook. Learning Technology Dissemination Initiative, Glasgow (1998)
15. Oliver, M., Conole, G., Kewell, B.: An Overview of an Evaluation Toolkit for Learning Technology Use. In: Dooner, M. (ed.) Proceedings of the IEE Colloquium, Exploiting Learning Technology: Issues for Learners and Educators, London (1998)
16. Ehrmann, S.: The Flashlight Project: Spotting an Elephant in the Dark (1997), `http://www.technologysource.org/article/flashlight_project__spotting_an_elephant_in_the_dark/` (accessed November 6, 2013)
17. Ehrmann, S.: Studying Teaching, Learning and Technology: A Tool Kit from the Flashlight Programme. Active Learning 9, 36–39 (1999)
18. Hersh, M.A., Johnson, M.A.: On Modelling Assistive Technology Systems Part I: Modelling Framework Technology and Disability 20(3), 193–215 (2008)
19. Fuhrer, M.J., Jutai, J.W., Scherer, M.J., Deruyter, F.: A framework for the Conceptual Modelling of Assistive Technology Device Outcomes. Disability and Rehabilitation 25(22), 1243–1251 (2003)
20. Scherer, M.J., Craddock, G.: Matching Person and Technology (MPT) Assessment Process. Technology and Disability 14, 125–131 (2002)

21. Demers, L., Weiss-Lambrou, R., Ska, B.: The Quebec User Evaluation of Satisfaction with Assistive Technology (QUEST 2.0): An Overview and Recent Progress. Technology and Disability 14, 101–105 (2002)
22. Day, H., Jutai, J.: Measuring the Psychosocial Impact of Assistive Devices; the PIADS. Canadian J. Rehabilitation 9(2), 159–168 (1996)
23. Jutai, J., Day, H.: Psychosocial Impact Of Assistive Devices Scale (PIADS). Technology and Disability 14, 107–111 (2002)
24. Noreau, L., Fougeyrollas, P., Vincent, C.: The LIFE-H: Assessment of the Quality of Social Participation. Technology and Disability 14, 113–118 (2002)
25. Jutai, J.W., Fuhrer, M.J., Demers, L., Scherer, M.J., DeRuyter, F.: Towards a Taxonomy of Assistive Device Outcomes. Am. J. Phys. Med. Rehab. 84(4), 294–302 (2005)
26. Edyburn, D.L., Smith, R.O.: Creating an Assistive Technology Outcomes Measurement System: Validating the Components. Assistive Technology Outcomes and Benefits 1(1), 8–15 (2004)
27. Coster, W.J., Mancini, M.C., Ludlow, L.H.: Factor Structure of the School Function Assessment. Educational and Psychological Measurement 59(4), 655–677 (1999)
28. Hersh, M.A.: Methodologies for the Categorisation and Evaluation of ICT-Based Lifelong Learning for Disabled People (2013), http://web.eng.gla.ac.uk/assistive/pages/inclusive-learning-conference/enable-deliverables.php
29. Black, P., William, D.: Assessment and Classroom Learning. Assessment in Education 5(1), 7–74 (1998)
30. Boud, D., Falchikov, N. (eds.): Rethinking Assessment in Higher Education: Learning For the Longer Term. Routledge (2007)
31. Boud, D., Cohen, R., Sampson, J.: Peer Learning and Assessment. Assessment & Evaluation in Higher Education 24(4), 413–426 (1999)
32. Fuller, M., Healey, M., Bradley, A., Hall, T.: Barriers to Learning: A Systematic Study of the Experience of Disabled Students in One University. Studies in Higher Education 29(3), 303–318 (2004)
33. Ysseldyke, J.E., Algozzine, B.: Assessment Perspectives: Perspectives on Assessment of Learning Disabled Students. Learning Disability Quarterly, 3–13 (1979)

Appendix: Questionnaire

1. What do you think the main aims of evaluating inclusive learning technologies should be?
2. What do you think are the main factors that should be evaluated?
3. How do you think the evaluation process should be carried out?
4. How do your answers relate to the theories of evaluation?[1]

[1] For partners with knowledge of evaluation theories.

Supporting Senior Citizen Using Tablet Computers

Ingo Dahn, Peter Ferdinand, and Pablo Lachmann

University Koblenz-Landau, Knowledge Media Institute, Koblenz, Germany
{dahn,ferdinand,palmann}@uni-koblenz.de

Abstract. It seems widely accepted that senior citizen need special assistance for using IT technology and that tablet computers are more easy for them to use than PC. The project "Tablets for Seniors" challenged these preconceptions. It evaluated over three months the use of Android tablet computers by a group of 19 seniors, aged between 53 and 82. The group of participants was divided into a subgroup using an interface specifically designed to support seniors and another group working with the native Android user interface. Support requests from both groups, in face-to-face meetings or through a dedicated phone hotline, have been recorded and qualitatively analyzed. As results of this qualitative study we present in this paper recommendations for the design of user interface and accompanying support measures.

Keywords: Tablet Computer, Seniors, User Interface.

1 Tablet Computer for Senior Citizen

Tablet computers have been rapidly taken up after the introduction of the first iPad in 2010. Their gesture based user interface offers new, apparently more intuitive, ways of human-computer interaction. This makes tablet computers attractive as computing devices for people with special needs. It also offers new ways to further adapt the user interface to these needs.

In this paper we explore the promises of this line of development, in particular for the needs of senior citizen.

The project is partially funded by the Ministry of Interior of the German Land Rhineland-Palatinate. It has been supported by a group of industry partners, in particular Deutsche Telekom AG, Samsung AG, Doro Group and mObserve as well as by the Landesseniorenvertretung Rheinland-Pfalz, an organization that coordinates at the level of the German federal state Rhineland-Palatinate several organizations representing senior citizen.

2 Related Research

A lot of publications and literature for the design of educational programs for elderly people in general come from adult, further and vocational education research (for an overview s. ESREA webpage[1]).

---

[1] European Society for Research on the Education of Adults (ESREA): Online `http://www.esrea.org/?l=en`

K. Miesenberger et al. (Eds.): ICCHP 2014, Part II, LNCS 8548, pp. 323–330, 2014.

In the last years a large variety of publications on the design of IT device interfaces, webpages and IT trainings for senior citizens and the adoption by seniors were released (c.p. [1,2,3,4]). In addition, initiatives are undertaken by public authorities to support digital inclusion of their senior citizens (e.g. Silver Surfers' Day in Northern Ireland, UK or the Silver Surfer initiative in the German federal state of Rhineland-Palatinate), offering guidelines for local senior support activities[2].

In contrast, only a few scientific publications on analysis of structures and requirements of successful support measures for senior citizens dealing with IT can be found.

3 Project Setup

Senior participants of the project have been recruited on a voluntary base through the Landesseniorenvertretung Rheinland-Pfalz. Being restricted by the number of available devices for the project, 19 seniors aged between 53 and 82, with a majority of 11 between 63 and 72, have been selected for participation.

The participants did not have experience with using tablet PCs before. Samsung AG provided the participants with tablets from their Galaxy S2 series. These tablets were equipped with WLAN but had no 3G communication capabilities.

Within the study, participants were assigned to two groups, named "Doro Group" and "Android Group". Within Doro Group, seniors received tablets equipped with the Doro user interface, which had been specifically designed to support senior citizens, while the tablets for the Android Group came just with the native Android user interface of these Samsung devices.

The Doro user interface used in the project had been implemented as an overlay over the native Android interface. The Doro interface appears by default during the device's boot process. Escape from the Doro interface to the native Android was possible, though not in an obvious way. The Doro interface contained a fixed selection of apps, accessible through enlarged buttons.

4 Project Methodology

For the participants, the project started June 25th 2013 with the introduction to the project and the tablets with their respective interfaces (Doro/Android), and with accompanying information on the organization of the scientific study, including information on the data protection and privacy policy of the project. Prior to any further activity, the participants filled in a questionnaire to capture their interests and prior experiences. This questionnaire contained the Computer User Self-Efficacy Scale (CUSE) of [5], which proved to be a good predictor for an individual's capability to deal with (future) computer problems. Due to the results of the questionnaire, the project team assigned each of the participating seniors alternately to the Doro and Android Group, taking care that prior CUSE and IT experience was equally distributed among both groups.

---

[2] Silver Surfers' Day Training Guide 2013: Online `http://www.dfpni.gov.uk/silver-surfers-day-2013-training-guide.pdf`

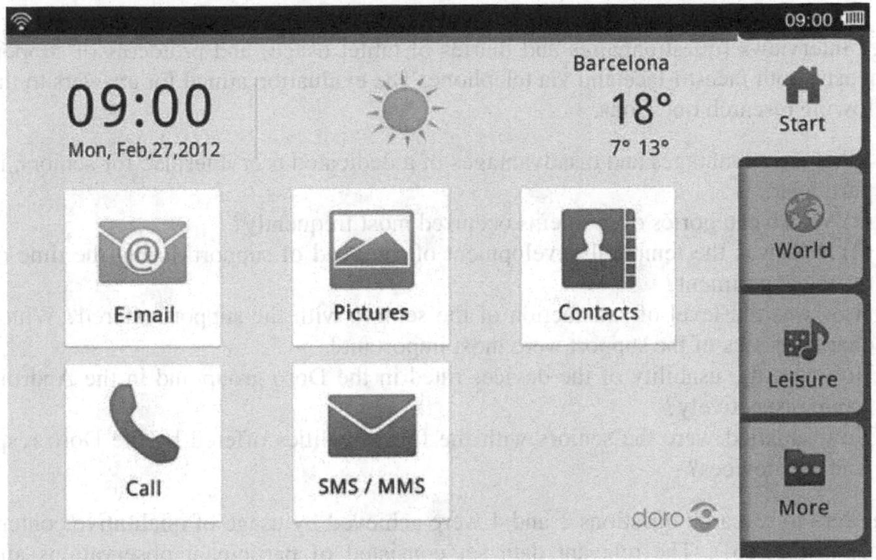

Fig. 1. The Doro User Interface

Throughout the evaluation period, each of the two groups enjoyed its own support measures to minimize interference between the groups, and all measures were run by the same support personnel to grant comparable conditions for both groups in terms of teaching style and social competencies. Overall, three face-to-face support meetings took place for each Group, with separate timeslots for the Groups. Intentionally, participation in these support meetings was non-mandatory. All meetings followed a similar procedure. At the beginning the support personnel collected seniors' questions which came up since the last meeting. The questions then were answered and explained in detail. Also important questions or topics of general interest were introduced by the support personnel proactively (e.g. usage of Skype or video apps). For these topics, participants received detailed step by step guidelines as a handout. Near the end of the meetings, seniors often joined small groups of 2-4 participants discussing and working on upcoming questions cooperatively. All the support meetings have been video-recorded with two cameras.

A dedicated telephone hotline for the project participants was provided by Deutsche Telekom AG from the start until August 20th, when it was replaced by an FAQ website for the last month of the evaluation period. The phone support was designed as a supplement and a fallback for the participants when experiencing - especially blocking - problems between the support meetings. The hotline was run by the same person who led the face-to-face meetings. Thus a continuous personal relationship between the seniors and the personnel was given to encourage usage of support measures. The FAQ website presented questions and answers that have been collected through the telephone support and through the face-to-face support meetings. Communications of the telephone support was noted by the supporting person and classified according to a common set of problem categories developed in the project.

Methodologically, the study is based on participant observation (videography), user interviews (questionnaires and diaries of tablet usage) and protocols of support requests, both face-to-face and via telephone. The evaluation aimed for answers to the following research questions.

1. What are advantages and disadvantages of a dedicated user interface for seniors, in particular:
   (a) Which categories of problems occurred most frequently?
   (b) How was the temporal development of the need of support during the time of the experiment?
2. How was the level of satisfaction of the seniors with the support offered? Which characteristics of the support were most important?
3. How was the usability of the devices rated in the Doro group and in the Android group respectively?
4. How satisfied were the seniors with the functionalities offered by the Doro resp. Android devices?

Answers to research questions 1 and 4 were achieved by usage of qualitative content analysis (cp. [6]). The relevant data set consisted of participant observations and support protocols and had to be preprocessed for further analysis.

In order to enable this analysis, a system of categories was developed to identify individual communication episodes and to classify these episodes w.r.t. the problems and support issues they deal with. Further on, for classifying the episodes, every passage in the protocols was coded with the same set of codes for the

- involved individuals (except support personnel),
- affected components (both hard- or software),
- date of occurrence and
- discussed subject (problem, solution, criticism).

Finally after coding all episodes typical problem categories were identified in an iterative process due to similarity of the discussed subjects and support issues. The resulting data set of participant observation and support protocols was analyzed and visualized using Atlas.ti, software for the qualitative analysis of large bodies of textual, graphical, audio and video data. Additionally, the frequency of appearance was used as an indicator for the importance of the problem categories.

For the evaluation, also descriptive statistics of data from standardized question pools were evaluated. For answering research question 2 a self-designed Likert-type scale was used to aggregate rated responses on the seniors' level of satisfaction with the offered support measures. Additionally, participants were asked to justify their ratings in free text answers, which were categorized by the problems and support issues they deal with. Research question 3 was mainly answered based on descriptive evaluation of standardized usability items adapted from the ISO (International Organization for Standardization) standard 9241-110, covering ergonomic principles for the design of dialogues between humans and information systems. The questionnaire contained items of the subscales self descriptiveness, controllability, conformity with user expectations, error tolerance, suitability for learning and suitability for individualization ([7]).

5 Project Findings

Evaluation of the first research question revealed the following findings. It was observed that web browsing and eMail were the apps which were most relevant to all seniors. This was also reflected in the requests for support. In comparison, the dedicated interface was not better rated (by frequency of the problem categories and their appearance) than the native Android interface. To the contrary seniors using the adapted interface required slightly more support than the others. Seniors experienced problems both in the handling of the devices and the navigation by gestures. Especially, users of the dedicated interface more often missed certain basic functionalities (e.g. configuration of the user interface, setup of background images) among the preconfigured set of apps and sometimes felt patronized in the possibilities of using their device. Thus, a significant difference between both groups, affecting satisfaction with the user interface, resulted from limitations of the apps of the adapted interface.

Since the limited set of apps of the adapted interface could neither be extended nor was it possible to extend the power of the apps, several members of the Doro Group soon requested access to the native Android user interface. Therefore, support for accessing the Android interface was provided, though there was continuous encouragement to use the Doro interface whenever possible.

On the other hand users of the Android interface had problems with the sometimes confusing diversity of apps and its unused control features. Comparing both interfaces, the Doro group members preferred the larger symbols of the Doro interface and the use of tabs over the gesture based control of the native Android interface.

The amount of support request reached its maximum in the first two weeks of the evaluation period and then declined continuously in its further course. This was observed both for support meetings and for telephone support.

To answer research question 2, the participants were asked to express their satisfaction with the offered support measures. Especially this aimed to identify important requirements for successful senior support. The face-to-face support meetings have been rated positively in most cases. Seniors appreciated both the domain competence and the social competence (in terms of friendliness, helpfulness, patience and empathy) of the support. Besides performance and commitment of the support personnel, comprehensibility of the given explanations played an important role. Furthermore the participants liked the combination of individual support both in meetings and via telephone, and personal discussion of support issues in groups during the meetings.

As could be expected from prior research, analysis of the answers in the preliminary questionnaire revealed that there was a differing degree of CUSE and acquaintance of the seniors with IT devices and software, in particular with PCs, often related to their previous work. Thus the requirements for support differed, too, and a few participants would have liked more group work or longer workshops. The same holds for the information content of workshops and explanations. Phone support was judged favorably by most seniors. Again, the high social competence of the support personnel and the availability of the phone support as a fallback were positively emphasized.

The combination of face-to-face support meetings with personal support and with the support hotline with individual support in the meantime has proved to be successful and was appreciated by the seniors. Analyzing the number of support questions revealed the high importance of the four face-to-face meetings. This is where the majority of questions were discussed.

Phone support was most intense during the initial phase of the test and faded out more or less after two weeks. Yet the relevance of the phone hotline showed up, since in the first two weeks seniors requested support on a daily basis. Seniors emphasized that the mere availability of the phone support reinforced their self-confidence when learning to work with the tablet. Interestingly, some participants liked the 'professional' support more than support from relatives (e.g. from children or grandchildren), because some seniors don't like to ask 'impatient' family members for help or feel shy to articulate their problems. In general the feedbacks showed a need for comprehensive and printable manuals and guidelines in the seniors' first language, without too many Anglicism.

Usability of devices (research question 3) achieved only medium rates in total. Ratings of the Android interface came off slightly better than of the adapted interface, but still only averagely. Especially controllability and suitability for individualization of the Android interface was rated higher than for the dedicated interface. This was in line with the lacking possibilities to configure and extend the dedicated apps and interface as already stated in the context of research question 1. Concerning self-descriptiveness, evaluation showed a need of users in both groups for comprehensive manuals and context-sensitive help.

In total seniors gave various feedbacks on the devices and their functionalities (research question 4). Members of both groups liked the devices in particular for allowing mobile internet, photographing and playing games in a fast and easy manner. Comparing the tablet experience with their previous PC experience, the usability of the onscreen keyboard was subject to major criticism.

Thus, and because appropriate apps are missing, the tablets' suitability for office work was widely doubted. On the other hand, fast start-up and quality of the tablet screens were highly appreciated. In general seniors disliked devices (both operating system and apps) for the non-transparency and lacking protection of privacy and user data. Being used from the PC to having control over the file system, the app-centered user interface of the tablets, as compared to the file-centered PC user interface, seniors felt an additional cognitive load when using the tablets. Not being able to control where data are stored on the tablet reinforced existing concerns about the privacy of the seniors' data.

Interestingly it showed that seniors' feedback on the tablet usage was often related to their prior PC experiences. Especially users with PC experiences had problems to control the user interface by gestures and were disappointed by missing functionalities in the user interface of the tablets.

6 Recommendations

Though the number of participants involved in the test does not allow for definite conclusions, the findings suggest the following recommendations for facilitating the use of tablet computers by senior citizen.

- The user interface should be built using widgets or larger buttons instead of standard apps. Moving between screens should be possible also using tabs or buttons in addition to gestures.
- A dedicated user interface for seniors is in danger to fall short of the user needs and to provide an additional barrier for access to requested functionalities. Instead, it is recommended to populate the standard tablet interface with apps with a reduced user interface which can be gradually extended by the seniors themselves when needed.
- The user interface should offer a PC-like mode where a file explorer is prominent, in order to ease transition from the PC world.
- It is recommended to offer seniors a keyboard and access to comprehensive and printable manuals in the seniors' first language.
- Device vendors should take serious users' privacy and implement transparent and trustworthy privacy protection mechanisms in their operating systems, which offer the users full control over their data. These mechanisms should control data usage of apps, too.
- Seniors should be offered personal support when acquiring a tablet. Such support needs to be highly personal. Personnel need to have good domain and especially social competences. Support may be provided by dedicated support personnel or by organizations working already with seniors. Telephone support with a callback-service in a friendly, patient and comprehensive way is recommended for a limited time of at least two weeks.
- In order to be successful, support measures need to be prepared to handle the heterogeneity of the group of seniors. Seniors should have the individual choice to select between a more comprehensive or more restricted initial training with regard to its information content. Especially at the beginning of device usage the need for support is highest and declines as the seniors make learning progress in controlling their device and its features. This should be addressed by a scaffold-like support concept. Since prior knowledge and learning capabilities are differing from senior to senior, the support concept must not be stiff, but should be flexible to offer appropriate starting points.

7 Outlook

The results of the project have been taken up by the project partners Deutsche Telekom and Doro Group. In order to obtain more reliable data, a similar test with a larger user group and different devices, possibly also including smart phones, would be highly desirable.

Since technology underlies a rapid change, especially the requirements analysis for the design of successful support measures for senior IT users would be welcome. It promises a sustainable contribution to the improvement of seniors' IT usage, independent from current technologies. Therefore, existing support concepts for seniors should be analyzed on a wider scale in order to get more representative data.

References

1. Loureiro, B., Rodrigues, R.: Design Guidelines and Design Recommendations of Multi-Touch Interfaces for Elders. In: Proceedings of the ACHI 2014, The Seventh International Conference on Advances in Computer-Human Interactions, Barcelona, Spain, pp. 41–47 (2014)
2. Robier, J., Majcen, K., Prattes, T., Stroisser, M.: Jung und Alt - gemeinsam spielend lernen. In: Boll, S., Maaß, S., Malaka, R. (hrsg.): Workshopband Mensch & Computer 2013. Oldenbourg Verlag, München (2013)
3. Motti, L.G., Vigouroux, N., Gorce, P.: Interaction techniques for older adults using touchscreen devices: A literature review. In: Proceedings of the 25ième Conférence Francophone on l'Interaction Homme-Machine (IHM 2013), pp. 125–134. ACM, New York (2013)
4. Hill, R., Beynon-Davies, P., Williams, M.D.: Older people and internet engagement: Acknowledging social moderators of internet adoption, access and use. Information Technology & People 21(3), 244–266 (2008)
5. Cassidy, S., Eachus, P.: Developing the computer user self-efficacy (CUSE) scale: Investigating the relationship between computer self-efficacy, gender and experience with computers. Journal of Educational Computing Research 26(2), 169–189 (2002)
6. Mayring, P.: Qualitative Inhaltsanalyse. Grundlagen und Techniken (10., neu ausgestattete Auflage). Beltz, Weinheim (2008)
7. Prümper, J., Anft, M.: Beurteilung von Software auf Grundlage der Internationalen Ergonomie-Norm ISO 9241/10, Berlin (1993)

Development of Multimodal Textbooks with Invisible 2-Dimensional Codes for Students with Print Disabilities

Akio Fujiyoshi[1], Mamoru Fujiyoshi[2], Akiko Ohsawa[2], and Yuko Ota[3]

[1] Ibaraki University, Hitachi, Ibaraki
fujiyosi@mx.ibaraki.ac.jp
[2] National Center for University Entrance Examinations, Meguro, Tokyo
{fujiyosi,ohsawa}@rd.dnc.ac.jp
[3] Dai-ni Enzan Elementary School, Shinagawa, Tokyo
ota-y@city.shinagawa.tokyo.jp

Abstract. Utilizing invisible 2-dimensional codes and digital audio players with a 2-dimensional code scanner, we developed a new type of textbooks for students with print disabilities, called "multimodal textbooks." Multimodal textbooks can be read with the combination of the two modes: "reading printed text" and "listening to the speech of the text from a digital audio player with a 2-dimensional code scanner." Since a multimodal textbook looks the same as a regular textbook and the price of a digital audio player is reasonable (about 30 euro), we think multimodal textbooks are suitable for students with print disabilities in ordinary classrooms.

1 Introduction

In 2012, Japanese Ministry of Education, Culture, Sports, Science and Technology published a report about students with developmental disorder in ordinary classrooms in compulsory education. According to the report, 2.4% of students in ordinary classrooms have remarkable difficulties in reading or writing without intellectual retardation. This means that most students with print disabilities are in ordinary classrooms and they use regular textbooks.

Utilizing invisible 2-dimensional codes and digital audio players with a 2-dimensional code scanner, we developed a new type of textbooks for students with print disabilities (Fig. 1). We can read these new textbooks with the combination of the two modes: "reading printed text" and "listening to the speech of the text from a digital audio player with a 2-dimensional code scanner." So we call them "multimodal textbooks." Since sight and hearing help each other, we can read them easily and correctly. Authors have developed auditory testing media for test-takers with print disabilities [1, 2, 3]. To create multimodal textbooks, we took advantage of the experience and technique gained during the development of auditory testing media.

For students with print disabilities, large print textbooks and DAISY textbooks have been available in Japan. Recently, textbook publishing companies

K. Miesenberger et al. (Eds.): ICCHP 2014, Part II, LNCS 8548, pp. 331–337, 2014.

Fig. 1. Multimodal Textbooks

started producing large print textbooks by themselves at their expense. The quality of large print textbooks is very improved. DAISY (Digital Audio Accessible Information System) is a world standard of accessible books for people with print disabilities [4]. A number of textbooks are translated into DAISY by the efforts of volunteers. Many students with print disabilities in special supported classrooms use either large print textbooks or DAISY textbooks. However, the number of students in ordinary classrooms who use these textbooks is very few.

A multimodal textbook consists only of a paper textbook and a digital audio player with a 2-dimensional code scanner. Since the paper textbook looks the same as a regular textbook and the digital audio player is small and can be used with a headphone, multimodal textbooks can be easily used in ordinary classrooms. Multimodal textbooks have the following other features:

- They are easy to carry.
- The price of a digital audio player is reasonable (about 30 euro).
- Students can write memo on the paper textbooks with a pencil or a fluorescent marker.
- Students can study by themselves.
- Teachers can easily get to know positions where students are reading.

In 2011, the first trial version of multimodal textbooks was made. With the trial version, multimodal textbooks were demonstrated to teachers, researchers and editors of textbooks. From October 2012, a practical evaluation started with 8 elementary school students with print disabilities in Shinagawa, Tokyo. From April 2013, the practical evaluation was continued with 30 elementary school students in Shinagawa, Tokyo.

A semiautomatic production system for multimodal textbooks was developed in order to ease the production process of multimodal textbooks. From a PDF file of a textbook, the semiautomatic production system automatically recognize the layout of the textbook, arrange 2-dimensional code on each page of the textbook and produce a manuscript of the speech of the text. The system also has an editor for corrections.

Currently, all 10 titles of elementary school textbooks in Japanese language published by Mitsumura Tosho Publishing Co.,Ltd., all 3 titles of junior high school textbooks in Japanese language published by Mitsumura Tosho Publishing Co.,Ltd., all 12 titles of elementary school textbooks in Japanese language published by GAKKO TOSHO Co.,Ltd, and 2 titles of junior high school textbooks in English language published by SANSEIDO Co.,Ltd. are available as multimodal textbooks.

2 Development of Multimodal Textbook

2.1 Invisible 2-Dimensional Codes and a Digital Audio Player

The introduction of invisible 2-dimensional codes and digital audio players with a 2-dimensional code scanner enable us to develop multimodal textbooks.

We employ 'screen code', an invisible 2-dimensional code system developed by Apollo Japan Co., Ltd. Screen code consists of dots in 2 mm square (Fig. 2). Since the intervals are large enough for the size of dots themselves, dots are almost invisible. If we use invisible ink, which absorbs only infrared light, instead of black ink, dots become totally invisible.

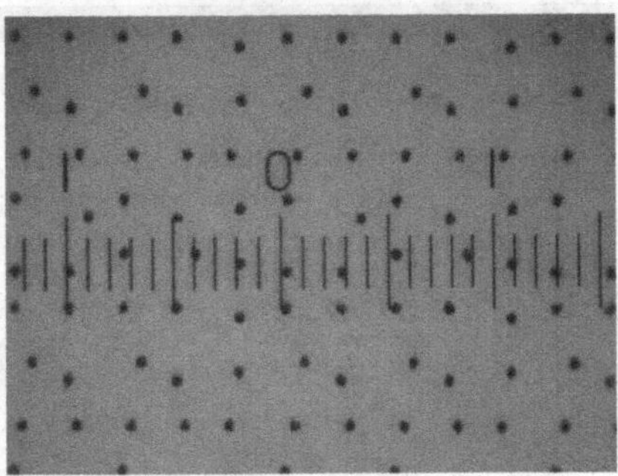

Fig. 2. Dots of 'screen code'

As a reading device for multimodal textbooks, we employ 'Speakun' developed by Apollo Japan Co., Ltd (Fig. 3). Speakun has a 2-dimensional code scanner at its top. When a 2-dimensional code is scanned with Speakun, the corresponding speech sound is reproduced. We can listen to the sound through a headphone or built-in speaker. The sound volume and speed can be adjusted with its buttons mounted at the front side. The sound data is stored in a micro SD card. 2G byte is enough to store all sound data of all textbooks of a student.

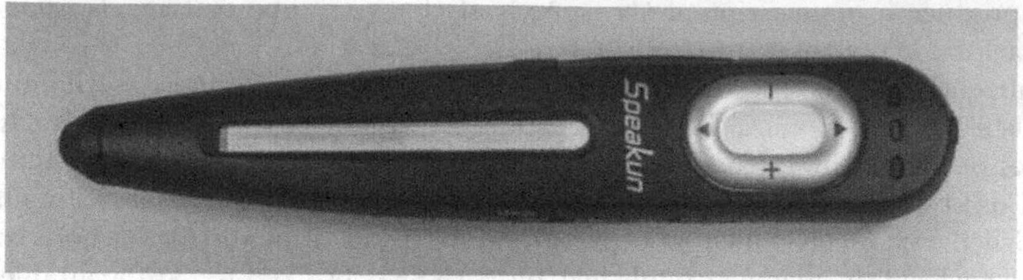

Fig. 3. Speakun

2.2 Semiautomatic Production System for Multimodal Textbooks

Currently, multimodal textbooks are produced by a small number of staffs. In order to ease the production process of multimodal textbooks, a semiautomatic production system for multimodal textbooks was developed (Fig. 4). The system is written in Java, and takes advantage of software packages Ghostscript [5] and PDFMiner [6]. From a PDF file of a textbook, the semiautomatic production system automatically recognize the layout of the textbook, arrange 2-dimensional code on each page of the textbook and produce a manuscript of speech sound. The system also has an editor for corrections.

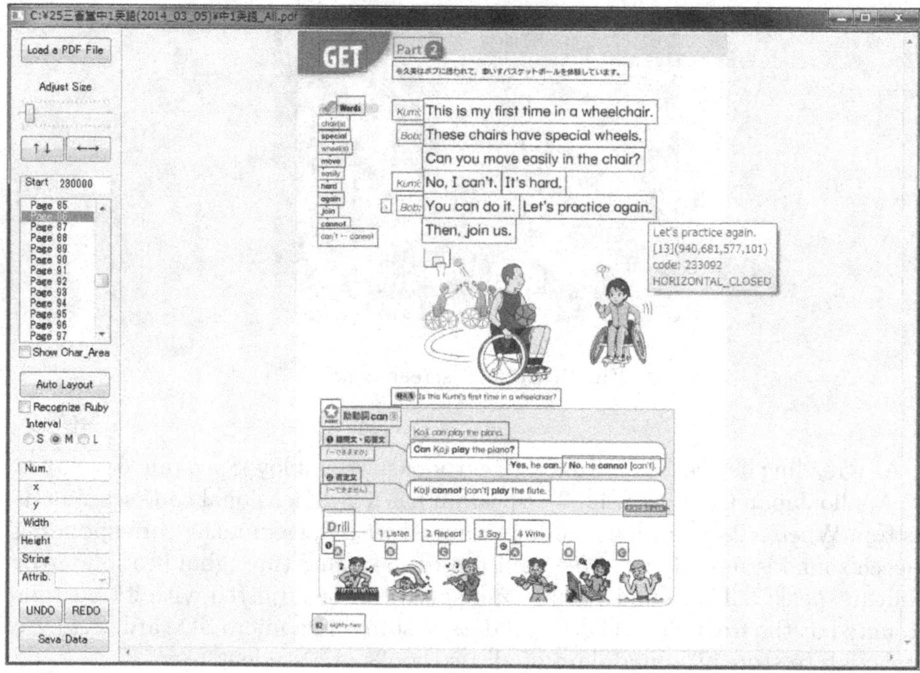

Fig. 4. Semiautomatic production system for multimodal textbooks

The assignment of speech sound files to 2-dimensional codes can also be done with the system. A sound file can be assigned to a set of rectangular areas to print the same 2-dimensional code by a drag-and-drop operation.

With this system, arranging 2-dimensional code on a textbook of 300 pages can be done in 20 hours by a person, which is 5 times faster than without the system. 27 titles of multimodal textbooks have been made so far.

3 Design of Multimodal Textbooks

Multimodal textbooks were designed so that they help to improve users' ability of reading. Thus the "reading printed text" mode should take precedence over the "listening to the speech of the text" mode. In other words, while users are listening to speech sound, we want them to read the corresponding printed text by their sight. Therefore, we put a different 2-dimensional code to each sentences and cut speech sound files into small pieces so that only corresponding speech sound is reproduced by one scan.

Fig. 5 shows a page of a multimodal textbook in English language for junior high schools (New Crown 1, SANSEIDO Co.,Ltd.). Every rectangle is assigned to a different 2-dimensional code except rectangles connected by brown lines. A set of rectangles connected by brown lines is assigned to the same 2-dimensional code.

Users have to scan a 2-dimensional code every time they want to read the next sentence. In order to scan the 2-dimensional code of the next sentence smoothly, users have to trace printed characters of the current sentence.

4 Results of a Preliminary Investigation on Multimodal Textbooks

In August 2013, we made a preliminary investigation in order to check how multimodal textbooks had been used in class and at home. We delivered questionnaires to the users of multimodal textbooks in a practical evaluation in Shinagawa, Tokyo. Since the most users are elementary school students, the questionnaires were entered by a parent or a teacher of them. We have received 15 answered questionnaires from the users of multimodal textbooks. They were from 8 elementary school students in lower grade, 6 elementary school students in higher grades, and 1 junior high school student. The percentage of reply for the questionnaires was 50%. The results are as follows:

4.1 Usage of Multimodal Textbooks

Among the 15 users, 13 persons (87%) mostly use multimodal textbooks at home for preparation and review. Only 2 persons regularly use multimodal textbooks in class.

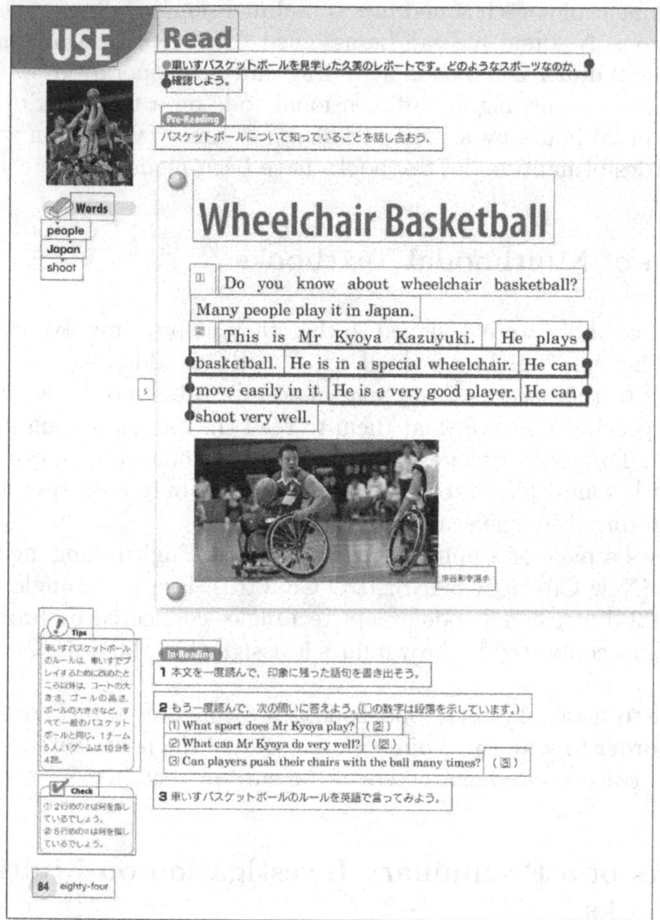

USE Read

●車いすバスケットボールを見学した久美のレポートです。どのようなスポーツなのか，確認しよう。

Pre-Reading

バスケットボールについて知っていることを話し合おう。

Words

people

Japan

shoot

Wheelchair Basketball

1 Do you know about wheelchair basketball? Many people play it in Japan.

2 This is Mr Kyoya Kazuyuki. He plays basketball. He is in a special wheelchair. He can move easily in it. He is a very good player. He can shoot very well.

京谷和幸選手

Tips

車いすバスケットボールのルールは，車いすでプレイするために改めたところ以外は，コートの大きさ，ゴールの高さ，ボールの大きさなど，すべて一般のバスケットボールと同じ。1チーム5人。1ゲームは10分を4回。

Check

① 2行めのitは何を指しているでしょう。
② 5行めのitは何を指しているでしょう。

In-Reading

1 本文を一度読んで，印象に残った語句を書き出そう。

2 もう一度読んで，次の問いに答えよう。(□の数字は段落を示しています。)

(1) What sport does Mr Kyoya play? (2)
(2) What can Mr Kyoya do very well? (2)
(3) Can players push their chairs with the ball many times? (3)

3 車いすバスケットボールのルールを英語で言ってみよう。

84 eighty-four

Fig. 5. A page of a multimodal textbook in English language for junior high schools (New Crown 1, SANSEIDO Co.,Ltd.)

4.2 Impressions from Students

The following impressions were received from students: “It is convenient to read because Chinese characters (kanji) are read by the machine.” “It is easy to study intonation and punctuation of a sentence.” “I can freely choose a sentence to read.” “Because of sound, a lot of sentences can be read.” “The speech speed control is convenient.” and “It is good because we can write the reading of a Chinese character in kana at its side.”

The following requests were also received from students: “Please make any other books be like multimodal textbooks.” and “I want to take tests with sound.” We think they are our big future works.

4.3 Impressions from Parents and Teachers

The following impressions were received from parents and teachers: "A multimodal textbook is easy to use. My child can use it by himself." "My child can study at her own pace with a multimodal textbook." "Children are very interested in mechanism of digital audio players with a 2-dimensional code scanner." and "A multimodal textbook is a pleasant tool since students can use it by themselves for preparation and review."

5 Conclusion

Utilizing invisible 2-dimensional codes and digital audio players with a 2-dimensional code scanner, we developed a new type of textbooks for students with print disabilities, called "multimodal textbooks." Since we can read multimodal textbooks with the combination of "reading printed text" and "listening correspondent speech sound to the text", we can read them easily and correctly.

We want to study other designs of multimodal textbooks. Since the current version of multimodal textbooks was designed so that they help to improve users' ability of reading, it might be suitable for students with print disabilities whose disorder is relatively mild. We plans to make multimodal textbooks with document structure diagrams for students with print disabilities whose disorder is relatively severe. The usage of document structure diagrams has been studied in the development of auditory testing media for test-takers with print disabilities [3].

There are 27 titles of multimodal textbooks available for students with print disabilities. From April 2014, we plan to deliver multimodal textbooks nationwide in Japan.

References

1. Fujiyoshi, M., Fujiyoshi, A.: A new audio testing system for the newly blind and the learning disabled to take the National Center Test for University Admissions. In: Miesenberger, K., Klaus, J., Zagler, W., Karshmer, A. (eds.) ICCHP 2006. LNCS, vol. 4061, pp. 801–808. Springer, Heidelberg (2006)
2. Fujiyoshi, M., Fujiyoshi, A., Aomatsu, T.: New Testing Method for the Dyslexic and the Newly Blind with a Digital Audio Player and Document Structure Diagrams. In: Miesenberger, K., Klaus, J., Zagler, W., Karshmer, A. (eds.) ICCHP 2010, Part 1. LNCS, vol. 6179, pp. 116–123. Springer, Heidelberg (2010)
3. Fujiyoshi, M., Fujiyoshi, A., Ohsawa, A., Aomatsu, T., Sawazaki, H.: Development of New Auditory Testing Media with Invisible 2-Dimensional Codes for Test-Takers with Print Disabilities. In: Miesenberger, K., Karshmer, A., Penaz, P., Zagler, W. (eds.) ICCHP 2012, Part I. LNCS, vol. 7382, pp. 116–123. Springer, Heidelberg (2012)
4. DAISY, `http://www.daisy.org/`
5. Ghostscript, `http://www.ghostscript.com/`
6. PDFMiner, `http://www.unixuser.org/~euske/python/pdfminer/`

Towards a Methodology for Curriculum Development within an Accessible Virtual Campus

Hector R. Amado-Salvatierra[1], Rocael Hernández[1], Antonio García-Cabot[2], Eva García-López[2], Concha Batanero[3], and Salvador Otón[2]

[1] GES Department, Galileo University, Guatemala
{hr_amado,roc}@galileo.edu
[2] Computer Science Department, University of Alcalá, Spain
{a.garciac,eva.garcial,salvador.oton}@uah.es
[3] Automatics Department, University of Alcalá, Spain
concha.batanero@uah.es

Abstract. The constant evolution of assistive technologies helps users with disabilities to have a myriad of choices to access digital content, and the application of accessibility standards and their relationship with assistive technologies enable and potentiate user interaction with web based systems for everyday activities. In the context of education through Virtual Learning Environments, a basic stone of the web accessibility initiative is the content prepared and provided by teachers, but they need to be instructed on how to generate accessible documents and how to provide truly accessible curriculum developments. In this sense, E-Learning solutions adopted by several institutions, including Higher Education Institutions need to be encouraged to validate and promote accessibility within a Virtual Campus. This article presents an initiative promoted by ESVI-AL project, looking to improve accessibility in virtual higher education through the definition of systematic and replicable methodological processes for the design and implementation of accessible virtual curriculum developments.

Keywords: Accessibility, Training, e-Learning, Curriculum Design.

1 Introduction

An evolutionary process of innovation is evident in education enhanced with technology, but this evolution could represent a barrier to people with disabilities (PWD) [1], so accessibility guidelines promoted by different initiatives (e.g. WAI [2] or EU Digital Agenda [3]) and international standards (e.g. WCAG2.0-ISO/IEC 40500 [4]) should be followed. International legislation in terms of technological evolution is reflected on the Convention on the Rights of Persons with Disabilities (CRPD) in Article 9 (points 2.g an 2.h) [5]. The CRPD highlights the importance of promoting access to Information and Communications Technology (ICT) for People with Disabilities (PWD) and specially producing accessible content in early stages at minimum costs. The CRPD and different legislation in several countries, and

K. Miesenberger et al. (Eds.): ICCHP 2014, Part II, LNCS 8548, pp. 338–341, 2014.

particularly in countries for Latin-America (LA), show the importance to fulfill web accessibility standards at all levels in the e-Learning production cycle [6]. In this sense, a methodology that establishes the processes, activities and tasks to be carried out in a virtual education project is proposed. The methodology aims to make the curriculum development accessible and inclusive, covering the entire life cycle, from conception of the educational project, to the delivery of training, also including activities related to the evaluation and optimization of the processes involved in all phases in a virtual campus. The remainder of the paper is structured as follows: Section 2 gives an outline of the foundations that have led to a proposed methodology for accessible curriculum development. Finally, conclusions and future work are presented in Section 3.

2 ESVI-AL Methodology for Curriculum Development

In the context of ESVI-AL project (`www.esvial.org`), with the participation of ten Higher Education Institutions (HEIs) from Europe and Latin-America, a work in cooperation was prepared to develop a holistic proposal to generate a methodology for curriculum development within an accessible virtual campus [7]. To achieve this proposal, four international associations, including the Disabled Peoples' International Organization (DPI) and Latin-American Blind Union (ULAC) were invited to test and validate the generated approach.

Nowadays it is possible to identify more than a hundred standards related to quality and accessibility of virtual training [8]. For the development of the proposed methodology, the most important standards involved in a virtual educational project [9] have been taken into account. In order to provide a universal useful solution in an international context, the Reference Framework for the Description of Quality Approaches (RFDQ) defined in ISO/IEC 19796 [10] was selected. The RFDQ is described in [10] as follows: "a proposed framework used to describe, compare, analyze, and implement quality management and quality assurance approaches" and was prepared to support stakeholders, especially regarding e-Learning, on how to document and redefine their daily activities and processes, as detailed in [11]. It has been used to compare different existing approaches and to harmonize them towards a common quality model, but taking into consideration accessibility in the involved stages in the e-Learning cycle. With this proposal, institutions will be able to define their processes based on RFDQ and then compare them with proposed tasks and results, providing reference criteria for the analysis and evaluation of accessibility in administrative tasks, learning resources and scenarios based on standards related to accessibility.

Related to the RFDQ, which provides a generic framework, an extension in [12] provides a description of the methods and metrics required by stakeholders in an e-Learning project (e.g. administrative staff, teachers, students, etc.). The reference process model covers the whole life cycle of learning and serves as an open descriptive framework, a basic starting point that needs the adaptation to the educational institution, the learning context, and the specific learning situation. RFDQ defines seven processes for the e-Learning cycle [10], which were adapted by the ESVI-AL methodology including accessibility guidelines in each stage:

1. Needs Analysis (NA): The aim of the process is to identify and describe the requirements, demands, and constraints of an accessible virtual educational project.
2. Framework Analysis (FA): This stage involves the identification of the context of an educational project, especially considering accessibility aspects.
3. Conception/Design (CD): This process is prepared to define and design the learning resources in an accessible virtual educational project.
4. Development/Production (DP): This step involves the production and adaptation of the learning resources to meet accessibility requirements.
5. Implementation (IM): Involves the activation and test of accessible learning resources in a virtual campus and its related assistive technologies.
6. Learning Process (PA): This stage is related to the learning-teaching process, looking for a truly inclusive experience using the implemented resources.
7. Evaluation/Optimization (EO): This is a transversal process, describing the evaluation methods for quality assurance for each stage in the cycle.

In this approach, decomposition at two levels of the identified processes was performed, adopting naming convention of "Activities", representing each of the subprocesses, and "Tasks", naming each of the elements in an "Activity". A total of 79 Tasks were identified. For each of the tasks, the methodology identifies four basic elements (results, techniques, metrics and participants). The results or products to be achieved at the end of the performance of the tasks are identified. Techniques or methods to be applied to produce the proposed results are described, as well as the metrics or quality criteria that will verify the correct execution of the task and relevance of the results. Finally the participants involved in performing the tasks are presented. Accessibility issues have a primarily focus on techniques or methods, proposing to the reader the use of standards for specific tasks and providing practical examples. A total of 168 results, 215 techniques and 334 metrics are defined in the revised edition of the proposed approach [7]. These elements are available online as a reference in `http://www.esvial.org/guia`.

3 Conclusions and Future Work

The proposed approach of the ESVI-AL methodology aims to establish a working model for standards and accessibility requirements compliance in the context of virtual education, proposing a generic reference framework, providing stakeholders with hints and best practices. The proposed model will facilitate the development of audits that will allow the diagnosis of quality and accessibility for curriculum developments.

A stakeholder training, especially for teachers, is essential and was tackled by this proposal. An intense training phase with more than 100 participants was prepared; teachers and members from Disabled Peoples' Organizations participating in the experience provided feedback about the proposed ESVI-AL methodology.

This experience has detected that HEIs in Latin-America are not aware of accessibility issues in e-Learning, because they are not enforced by laws as the ones in developed countries (e.g. USA, UK, Spain, etc.), giving a great opportunity to disseminate and train staff with the proposed methodology with the aim to provide the most generic solution as possible, enabling institutions to adapt it to their own processes.

Acknowledgments. This work is supported partially by the European Commission through the project ESVI-AL "Educación Superior Virtual Inclusiva" (ALFA III) (DCI-ALA/19.09.01/11/21526/279-146/ALFA 111(2011)-11) (www.esvial.org)

References

1. Power, C., Petrie, H., Sakharov, V., Swallow, D.: Virtual Learning Environments: Another Barrier to Blended and E-Learning. In: Miesenberger, K., Klaus, J., Zagler, W., Karshmer, A. (eds.) ICCHP 2010, Part 1. LNCS, vol. 6179, pp. 519–526. Springer, Heidelberg (2010)
2. W3C, Web Accessibility Initiative (WAI), http://www.w3.org/WAI/
3. European Comission, Europe's Digital Agenda, Web Accessibility, http://ec.europa.eu/ipg/standards/accessibility/eu_policy/index_en.htm
4. ISO, ISO/IEC 40500:2012. W3C Web Content Accessibility Guidelines 2.0, http://www.iso.org/iso/iso_catalogue/catalogue_tc/catalogue_detail.htm?csnumber=58625
5. United Nations, Convention on the Rights of Persons with Disabilities, http://www.un.org/disabilities/default.asp?id=150
6. Amado-Salvatierra, H., Hernández, R., Hilera, J.R.: Implementation of Accessibility Standards in the Process of Course Design in Virtual Learning Environments. In: Hadjileontiadis, L., Martins, P., Todd, R., Paredes, H. (eds.) DSAI 2012. Procedia CS (Procedia), vol. 14, pp. 363–370. Elsevier B.V., Amsterdam (2012)
7. Hilera, J.R. (ed.): Guía Metodológica para la Implantación de Desarrollos Curriculares Virtuales Accesibles. Servicios de Publicaciones Universidad de Alcalá, Spain (2013)
8. Hilera, J.R., Hoya, R., Vilar, E.T.: Organizing E-learning Standards and Specifications. In: Arabnia, H., Bahrami, A. (eds.) EEE 2011, pp. 99–104. CSREA Press, Las Vegas (2011)
9. Pons, D., Hilera, J.R., Pagés, C.: Standards and specifications to manage accessibility issues in e-learning. In: Graf, S., Karagiannidis, C. (eds.) IEEE Learning Technology Newsletter, TCLT, vol. 13(3), pp. 20–23 (2011)
10. ISO, ISO/IEC 19796-1:2005. ITLET Quality management, assurance and metrics, Part 1: General approach, http://www.iso.org/iso/catalogue_detail?csnumber=33934
11. Stracke, C.M.: Quality Development and Standards in e-Learning: Benefits and Guidelines for Implementations. In: Proceedings of the ASEM LL Conference: e-Learning and Workplace Learning, Bangkok (2009)
12. ISO, ISO/IEC 19796-3:2009. ITLET Quality management, assurance and metrics – Part 3: Reference methods and metrics, http://www.iso.org/iso/catalogue_detail?csnumber=46159

The Use of Assistive Technologies as Learning Technologies to Facilitate Flexible Learning in Higher Education

Michael Goldrick[1], Tanja Stevns[2], and Lars Ballieu Christensen[2]

[1] National College of Ireland, Dublin, Ireland
michael.goldrick@ncirl.ie
[2] Synscenter Refsnæs and Sensus ApS, Hillerød, Denmark
{tanja,lbc}@robobraille.org

Abstract. This paper presents the argument that some assistive technologies have in recent times become more widely used in education to support all students. Building on research gathered as part of a European funded project, the authors present findings that indicate that students are becoming more aware and sensitive to their own learning preferences and their own styles. More importantly however, the paper suggests that through the evolution of technology, students can now choose how to study, where to study and when to study. Underpinning this change, the paper explores how some assistive technologies have evolved into learning technologies by taking into consideration three factors: European social policy, universal design theory and learning preference theories.

Keywords: Flexible Learning, Assistive Technology, Learning Technology, Higher Education, RoboBraille, European Social Policy, Universal Design Theory and Learning Preference Theories.

1 Introduction

The distinction between assistive technologies and learning technologies is one which is becoming much more blurred as learning technologists and educators move towards more universally applicable technologies [1, 2].

Whilst the argument can be made that for sensory and motor disabilities, the term assistive technology is accurate, this paper will illustrate that a great deal of technologies which natural speech outputs, voice recognition and other multimedia functions are beneficial to all students [2, 3]. For example, many free online technologies such as RoboBraille [4], which were designed to facilitate the assistance of blind and visually impaired students, have now become more widely used by teachers as well as students.

RoboBraille is an email- and web based service for converting documents into a variety of alternate formats, including digital Braille, audio books in mp3 and Daisy format, and eBooks. The service may also be used to convert otherwise inaccessible

K. Miesenberger et al. (Eds.): ICCHP 2014, Part II, LNCS 8548, pp. 342–349, 2014.

documents such as image-only pdf files, scanned documents and PowerPoint documents into more accessible formats or formats that are easier to use in terms of orientation and navigation. RoboBraille uses a range of conversion technologies to provide its service, including text-to-speech, text-to-Braille, optical character recognition as well as eBook and Daisy authoring technology. Users of the service include students with special needs, foreign students, foreign language students, mainstream students, faculty and alternate media professionals. The service is free to use for non-commercial, individual users [5, 6].

2 How Have Assistive Technologies Become Learning Technologies?

Amidst key inclusive phrases such as equity of access and equality, it is important to consider firstly how the evolution of support for students with disabilities has become so sophisticated and supported and recognised at a European level.

For centuries, one question has been the source of much dispute for educators and philosophers: How do we learn [7, 8, 9]? Yet in recent times the nature of learning has received new interest, not from the academic community, but from political domains [10, 11, 12]. Within the last decade, the European Council and European Parliament have attempted to redefine what key skills are important and how educators can help produce workers that are self-aware, critical thinkers and problem solvers [12, 13]. In short, Europe has aimed to produce an economy that is based on knowledge and supports learning as a life-long activity.

As a focal point for this increased interest and investment, it is important to highlight the 2001 Organisation for Economic Co-operation and Development (OECD) report entitled 'The new economy beyond the hype' [14]. This report stands out as a landmark of social inclusion as it clarifies how education itself is key to generating a European 'knowledge economy' and argued why each European member needed to fully embrace Information Communication Technology (ICT). Listing two segments, 'things that cannot be done without technology' and 'things that can be done with technology' the report highlighted that the future of learning is located within the de-materialisation of time and space, where learning could take place anytime, anywhere.

Coupled with this, the report also suggested that students could become more reflective, engage in peer supports as well as self-assess their learning needs. As a final point, the report outlined the principles of mass education, where every person could potentially access education [14]. More recent studies from the OECD [15] have continued this reliance on technology, emphasising that higher-order thinking and competencies, referred to as "21st Century skills" are reliant on each student's connectedness, not only with learning media, but also with peers and facilitators.

To achieve this emancipated vision of education, key stakeholders across Europe have drawn upon many pivotal educational theories and philosophies of learning. One of these factors is universal design theory [16].

3 Universal Design Theory

Universal design theory, as the name implies, is a standard through which all learning content can be made accessible and flexible to all potential students, including those students with disabilities [1][17, 18]. Originating from the field of architecture [16], universal design is based on the belief that architectural and technological innovations that were once used solely to help people with disabilities could be used effectively by any person [19].

Through the dissemination of universal design theory, learning technologists have become aware of the potential wider application of assistive technologies and have begun to market these technologies to all students in order to facilitate learning that can take place anytime, anywhere. From a pedagogic perspective, the use of technologies such as text-to-speech software, mind maps, audio recording software and note-taking technology can be used to adapt to an individual's own learning preferences.

As a conversion technology that addresses the universal needs for document conversion amongst mainstream students as well as students with special needs, RoboBraille is an example of a non-stigmatising assistive technology built on the principles of universal design [6].

4 Learning Styles and Preferences

Some modern learning styles and preference tests attempt to identify the stimulus or input of information most favoured, such as visual, aural, reading and writing and kinaesthetic [20]. Other tests tend to focus on the types of activities that the person may work best in [21, 22], or even what attitude to learning will take place [23]. The usage of learning styles and preferences in education has become increasingly popular [24, 25, 26], especially when used to help students to create their own individualised system of learning [27, 28]. Through an appreciation of their individual styles of learning, students can now choose to incorporate technologies such as RoboBraille into their studies, bringing learning away from standalone traditional learning strategies and into a mobile, flexible learning strategy. To present an insight into these processes, the next section summarises the findings and future implications from a 2013 Leonardo da Vinci Project, RoboBraille in Education (LdV RoboBraille in Education).

5 Case Study: Findings from RoboBraille in Education

Conducted over a 24 months period from 2011 to 2013, the goal of the LdV RoboBraille in Education project was to collect and develop new knowledge about how an open source text-to-speech system RoboBraille could be used to support students with specific learning difficulties or disabilities. The European research team involved representatives from Ireland, Denmark, Cyprus, The United Kingdom, Italy and Hungary.

As part of this project, the research team carried out a series of surveys to identify the types of uses, benefits (if any) and the future needs of RoboBraille users. The survey also asked each student to provide a personal statement about their experiences of using the Service. In total, there were 158 respondents to the survey from RoboBraille users across Europe:

Table 1. Respondents, RoboBraille in Education

Respondents	Number
Overall respondents	158
- Educators	83
- Students	75

Of the 158 users who responded to the online survey, 145 opted to answer what sector of education they belonged to, either as a student or as an educator. As can be seen from figure 1 below, the most frequent answer chosen was Further education (44 per cent), followed by Higher education (29 per cent), Secondary education (19 per cent) and other (8 per cent).

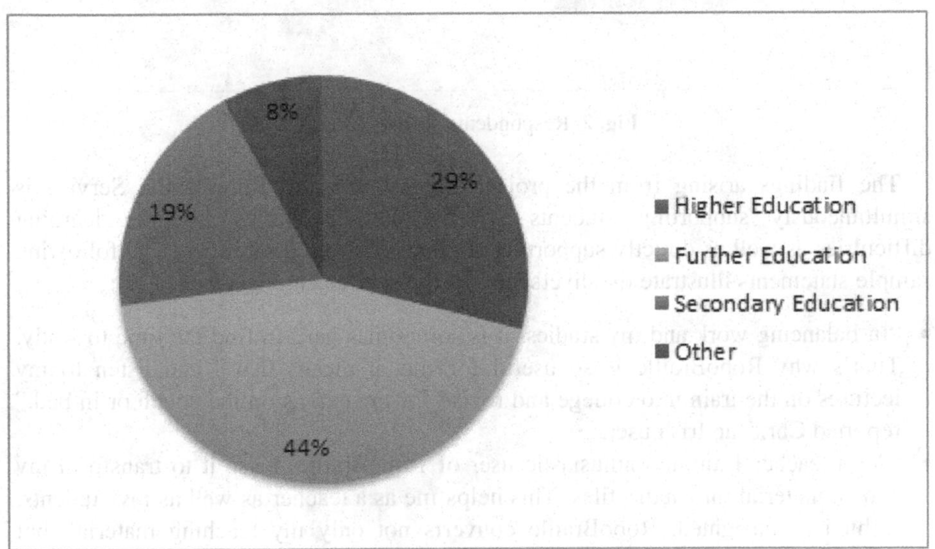

Fig. 1. Respondents split by sector

Whilst all relevant levels of education are represented, it is expected that usage within Higher Education will increase as good practices are disseminated and the growing need for flexible learning opportunities becomes more widely recognised.

Similarly, of the 158 respondents, 144 identified through their personal statements how RoboBraille has positively affected their lives. As expected, a high percentage of these users (69 per cent) are blind or visually impaired. A further 20 per cent of respondents indicated that they have Dyslexia and that the Service is beneficial in supporting their attainment of books and other academic materials. Lastly, a small number of users (11 per cent) claimed that the RoboBraille service has helped them in language learning activities. The usage split is summarised in figure 2 below:

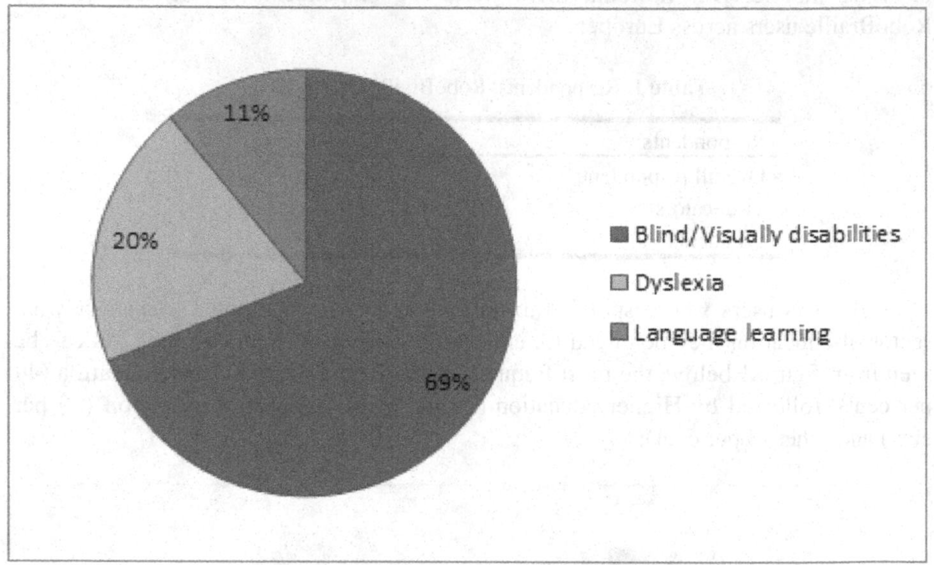

Fig. 2. Respondents split by usage

The findings arising from the project suggest that the RoboBraille Service is simultaneously supporting students with visual disabilities, specific learning difficulties as well as directly supporting students with no disabilities. The following sample statements illustrate the diverse use of the service amongst users [29]:

- "In balancing work and my studies, it is sometimes hard to find the time to study. That's why RoboBraille is so useful for me, it means that I can listen to my lectures on the train into college and revise for my exams on the couch or in bed," reported Chris, an Irish user.
- "As a teacher I am an enthusiastic user of RoboBraille, I use it to transform my course material into audio files. This helps me as a teacher as well as my students, sighted or unsighted. RoboBraille converts not only my teaching material, but converts also my idle time in pleasant "reading" time (articles, essays, magazines)," reported Giorgio, an Italian user.

The above first quote gives an insight into how free technologies like RoboBraille are becoming crucial for individuals who want to learn at their own pace, their own time and in their own environments. Equally, the second quote illustrates that these technologies are not just limited for formal education purposes, but for life-long learning. This realisation has led some researchers to call for a need for hybrid learning environments where learning opportunities are not contained in silos, but are adaptable and flexible: Students are expected to integrate different types of knowledge, for example, formal knowledge, work process knowledge and practical knowledge. Developing an integrated knowledge base is a lifelong learning process across different situations, such as school, hobbies and part-time jobs, in both formal and informal settings [12].

This need for adaptability and flexibility is made possible through the growing acceptance that educators and institutes of education need to embrace technology more in order to increase the personalisation of learning.

6 Conclusions

This paper has outlined how, through the evolution of technology, learning theories and universal design, learning is becoming more flexible and adaptable. Underpinning these advances, the growing importance placed on 21st century skills development allow us to see that the traditional conception of a student is gone. Society has dictated a need for increased cognitive agility, where students have a combination of academic knowledge and transferable skills that need to be nurtured from a young age at school and at home.

However, although the needs and means of flexible and adaptable learning have been uncovered, a huge task of adapting current educational practices and disseminating information amongst students, faculty and relatives remain.

In support of this, the RoboBraille research team has undertaken a new EU funded project, RoboBraille SMART, which aims to create a technology training course for families, students and teachers. This short course will subsequently be promoted as an initiative that supports students with disabilities and students with no disabilities together, using free technologies.

References

1. EDUCAUSE: Learning Technologies, `http://www.educause.edu/ELI/EDUCAUSELearningInitiative/LearningTechnologies/5672`
2. Cook, A.M., Polgar: Cook and Hussey's Assistive Technologies: Principles and Practice. Mosby Elsevier, St. Louis Missouri (2008)
3. Goldrick, M.: Effective Learning Support in Higher Education: My living theory of student-centred learning support in National College of Ireland. Ph.D. Thesis, Dublin City University, Dublin (2010)
4. Christensen, L.B.: RoboBraille – Automated Braille Translation by Means of an E-Mail Robot. In: Miesenberger, K., Klaus, J., Zagler, W.L., Karshmer, A.I. (eds.) ICCHP 2006. LNCS, vol. 4061, pp. 1102–1109. Springer, Heidelberg (2006)
5. Christensen, L.B., Keegan, S.J., Stevns, T.: SCRIBE: A Model for Implementing Robobraille in a Higher Education Institution. In: Miesenberger, K., Karshmer, A., Penaz, P., Zagler, W. (eds.) ICCHP 2012, Part I. LNCS, vol. 7382, pp. 77–83. Springer, Heidelberg (2012)
6. Christensen, L.B.: RoboBraille – Braille Unlimited. The Educator XXI(2), 32–37 (2009); ICEVI 2009

7. Illeris, K.: Towards a Contemporary and Comprehensive Theory of Learning. International Journal of Lifelong Education 22(4), 411–421 (2003)
8. Illeris, K.: Transfer of learning in the learning society: How can the barriers between different learning spaces be surmounted, and how can the gap between learning inside and outside schools be bridged? International Journal of Lifelong Education 28(2), 137–148 (2009)
9. Shim, S.H.A.: A philosophical investigation of the role of teachers: A synthesis of Plato, Confucius, Buber, and Freire. Teaching and Teacher Education 24(3) (2007)
10. Eurydice Key competencies: A developing concept in general compulsory education. Eurydice/European Commission, Brussels (2002)
11. DeSeCo: Definition and Selection of Key Competencies: Executive Summary (June 30, 2005), Web document: `http://www.portal-stat.admin.ch/deseco/news.htm`
12. Zitter, I., Hoeve, A.: Hybrid Learning Environments: Merging Learning and Work Processes to Facilitate Knowledge Integration and Transitions, OECD Education Working Papers, No. 81. OECD Publishing (2012), `http://dx.doi.org/10.1787/5k97785xwdvf-en`
13. Hoskins, B., Fredriksson, U.: Learning to learn: What is it and can it be measured? European Commission, Joint Research Centre, Institute for the Protection and Security of the CitizenCentre for Research on Lifelong Learning (CRELL), Italy (2008)
14. OECD: The new economy beyond the hype. The OCED growth project. Organisation for economic Co-operation and development, Paris (2001)
15. OECD: Inspired by Technology, Driven by Pedagogy: A systemic approach to technology-based school innovations. OECD, Paris (2010)
16. Mace, R.L., Hardie, G.L., Place, J.P.: Accessible environments: Towards Universal Design. In: Presier, W.E., Vischer, J.C., White, E.T. (eds.) Innovation by Design. Van Nostrand Reinhold, New York (1991)
17. Pliner, S., Johnson, J.: Historical, theoretical, and foundational principles of universal design in higher education. Equity of Excellence in Education 37, 105–113 (2004)
18. Scott, S., McGuire, J., Shaw, S.: Universal design for instruction: A new paradigm for adult instruction in postsecondary education. Remedial and Special Education 24(6), 369–379 (2003)
19. Thirunarayanan, O., Pérez-Prado, A.: Integrating technology in higher education. University Press of America (2005)
20. Fleming, N.D.: Teaching and Learning Styles: VARK Strategies. Honolulu Community College (2001)
21. Kolb, A., Kolb, D.: Learning Styles and Learning Spaces: Enhancing Experiential Learning in Higher Education. Acad. Manag. Learn. Edu. 4(2), 193–212 (2005)
22. Kolb, D.: Experiential learning: Experience as the source of learning and development. Prentice-Hall, Englewood Cliffs (1984)
23. Entwistle, N.: Styles of learning and teaching. John Wiley, New York (1981)
24. Bull, S.: Supporting Learning with Open Learner Models. In: 4th Hellenic Conference with International Participation: Information and Communication Technologies in Education, Athens (2004)
25. Felder, R.M., Spurlin, J.E.: A validation study of the Index of Learning Styles. Applications, Reliability, and Validity of the Index of Learning Styles. Intl. Journal of Engineering Education 21(1), 103–112 (2005)

26. Robotham, D.: The application of learning style theory in higher education (1999), http://www2.glos.ac.uk/gdn/discuss/kolb2.htm
27. Dunn, R.S., Griggs, S.A.: Practical approaches to using learning styles in higher education. Greenwood Publishing Group, Westport (2000)
28. Hersh, M.: Classification of ICT-based learning technologies for disabled people: Outcomes of Enable Network Project. In: Encarnação, P., Azevedo, L., Gelderblom, G.J. (eds.) Assistive Technology: From Research to Practice: AAATE 2013. IOS Press (2013)
29. Refsnæs, S., et al.: RoboBraille in education. Catalogue of good practice (2013), http://www.robobraille.org/sites/default/files/resourcefiles/The%20Robobraille%20Service%20in%20Education%20Catalogue%20Long%20Version%20August%202013%20FINAL.pdf

The Literacy of Integrating Assistive Technology into Classroom Instruction for Special Education Teachers in Taiwan

Ming-Chung Chen[1], Chi Nung Chu[2], and Chien-Chuan Ko[1]

[1] National Chiayi University, Chiayi, Taiwan
[2] China University of Technology, Wenshan Chiu, Taipei, Taiwan
nung@cute.edu.tw

Abstract. This study surveyed the special education teachers' literacy for integrating assistive technology into the instruction in Taiwan. At first, a scale for literacy of assistive technology integration for special education teachers was developed through Delphi technique. 391 special education teachers completed the web-based questionnaire. The results reveal that the teachers' AT literacy were inadequate. Though the teachers are aware of the importance of assistive technology, they lack essential skills and knowledge. The results of the analysis also indicated that participation in AT training programs and experiencing with students who used AT devices benefited their AT literacy.

Keywords: Special Education Teacher, Assistive Technology, Literacy.

1 Introduction

Assistive technology (AT) plays an important role in ensuring that students with disabilities can participate in the learning activities equally and effectively and live up to their academic potential. For example, students with dyslexia could acquire knowledge of social study by using talking word processor to read textbooks. Stu-dents with complex communication disorder could respond to teachers' questions by using their augmentative and alternative communication devices. Providing proper AT device and service could assist students with disabilities in achieving the functional performances necessary to become independent and successful learners in academic settings [6], [8], [13].

Realizing that assistive technology is vital to special education, Taiwan education authorities took steps toward incorporating AT device and service into teacher training programs and classroom activities. Efforts included The new Special Education Act of 1997 which stated that the school should provide the students with disabilities necessary assistive technology for them to participate in the learning activities as well as significant funding in purchasing AT devices, conducting many workshops, and seminars related to AT application [11]. More importantly, assistive technology or special education technology was also mandated as core courses for the pre-service

K. Miesenberger et al. (Eds.): ICCHP 2014, Part II, LNCS 8548, pp. 350–357, 2014.

program of special education teacher. Meanwhile, the National Science Council in Taiwan also set up AT as an important research topic to encourage researchers to engage in related studies. In addition, there are many AT resource centers created by the Ministry of Education and local educational units to provide proper AT services for teachers, parents, and the students with disabilities.

As for attitudes, special educators also demonstrated positive attitudes toward applying assistive technology to enhance learning ability for those children with disabilities [15]. Wu and Chen [15] investigated 220 special educators, including administrators, special education teachers, parents, and researchers in special education, to explore their opinions toward issues of applying assistive technology in the special education. The results indicated that most agreed that the AT could assist the students with disabilities to participate in learning; the investment of AT funding is of great worth; and education authorities in Taiwan should provide AT to students with disabilities. However, Wu and Chen's investigation also indicated that lacking enough funding, public awareness, and teacher literacy were the major barriers that prohibited providing proper assistive technology to students with disabilities. And meanwhile, only less than one tenth of the participants thought the special education teachers and the related professionals possessed adequate literacy to utilize technology to assist the students with disabilities to participate in learning at that time.

Teachers' literacy about incorporating AT into classroom activities should be seen as one of the key factors that affect the purposed AT effect since teachers are the ones that administered classroom instructions to students. Due to inadequate training of special education, teachers was regarded as one the most important obstructions [16], education authorities actually conducted many in-services AT related training programs for special education teachers after 1997. The past studies also demonstrated the effects of training program [4]. Chen and Lai [4] conducted a project-based AT in-service training program for 19 special education teachers. The program focused on training the participants to step by step integrate AT into teaching activities. After completing the project, most of them stated that they would commit to integrating AT into their instruction in the future.

2 Methodology

2.1 Participants

Special education teachers from self-contained class and resource program at regular elementary and middle schools in Taiwan were sampled to participate in this investigation. The authors selected the participants based on the list of special education class created by the Ministry of Education. Finally, 400 teachers from elementary schools, 200 for each type of class, and 300 teachers from middle schools, 150 for each type of class. The selected teachers were informed about participation information. However, only 501 teachers participated in filling the questionnaire and 391 of them were valid.

The amount of the participants in each education stage and type of special education class were similar. However, major of the participants (n = 311, 79.53%) were female. Most of them were qualified special education teacher (82.9%), graduated from Departments of Special Education or completed the Special Education teachers pre-service programs in the universities (90.5%), taught students who used AT devices before (77.7%) and in the current class (67.8%), and gained some types of AT training (70.5%).

Besides, the teachers were around thirty years old on average. In middle school, the average age of the teachers in self-contained class were 34.22 (SD=9.53) and 33.78 in resource program (SD=8.87). In elementary school, the average age of teachers in self-contained class was 34.41 (SD=9.13) and 32.0 in resource program (SD=6.5). The teachers in self-contained class taught special education class (middle school: M=5.67, SD=4.98; elementary school: M=4.84. SD=3.77) slightly longer than the teachers in resource program (middle school: M=4.84, SD=3.77; elementary school: M=4.14, SD=3.00). The total seniority of teaching for the teachers in middle school (self-contained: M=9.07, SD=8.78; resource program=8.68, SD=8.12) was slightly longer then the teachers in elementary school (self-contained: M=8.51, SD=8.95; resource program=5.93, SD=5.54). That means that many of them had taught in regular special education class before they taught in special education class.

2.2 Survey Tool

The online survey system is a growing trend to replace conventional paper-and-pencil survey due to lower cost and great speed response for large sample in a short space of time [4]. The questionnaire contains two parts, personal information and Indicators of AT Integration Literacy. The items in personal information part comprise with gender, types of certification, year of teaching, teaching class types, AT related training, pre-service training, and the experience of teaching students who use AT in classroom.

The Indicators of AT Integration Literacy was developed based on the past related literature [3,4,5], [9], [13]. The framework of Indicators of AT Integration Literacy in this study include 10 categories, 1) philosophy and law, 2) AT devices, 3) AT service, 4) concepts of AT integration 5) evaluation 6) selection and acquisition, 7) training, 8) instruction accommodation, 9) implementation and management, 10) resources and support. These categories could be grouped into three subscales: Knowledge, Skill, and Attitude.

The Delphi technique was employed to collect different views and derive consensus from a panel of 14 experts, including experts in assistive technology, special education, and rehabilitation field. The Delphi process involved three review rounds. The panel members were required to rate the importance of each item using a 5-point Likert scale: 1) Not important, 2) Somewhat Important, 3) Moderately Important, 4) Important, and 5) Very important. After three rounds of Delphi process, 51 competencies show concurrence of all panel participants with a rating mean of 4) Important or higher. The final Indicators of AT literacy contains 51 competencies under three subscales: 1) Attitudes with 4 items, (2) Knowledge with 17 items, and (3) Skills with 30 items.

The Indicators of AT literacy has good validity and reliability. The results of Pearson' product-moment correlation test demonstrated the middle relationship among three subscales (coefficients were between .46 to .76, $p<.01$) and high relationship between subscales and total scale (coefficients were between .81 to .91, $p<.01$). The inter consistence of the subscales are high (Cronbach's α coefficients were .95 in Attitude, .96 in Knowledge, .98 in Skill, and .98 for total scale). The test-retest reliability with a week interval was also good (Pearson' product-moment correlation coefficients were .60 for Attitude, .94 for Knowledge, .86 for Skill, and .90 for total scale with $p<.01$).

2.3 Data Analysis

Multivariate Analysis of Variance (MANOVA) was used to test if the AT literacy was different among different education stage, special education class and other related variables. However, the related variables were determined based on the results of Pearson' product-moment correlation coefficient and multiple regression before MANOVA test. The significant level was $p<.05$ in this study. Cohen's d with the pooled standard deviation was used to calculate the effect size if the statistic test was significant. The effect sizes was defined as "small, $d <.5$," "medium, $d< .8$," and "large, $d > .8$".

3 Results

The average rating of AT literacy for 391 teachers is 4.11, (SD = .78), the average rating of Attitude is 4.98 (SD = .95), the average of Skills scale is 3.89(SD = .91), the means of the Knowledge is 3.45 (SD = .87). Based on the rating rule used in the investigation, the range of the score distributes from 1 to 6. We adopted 4 points as the basic requirement for judging the literacy of integrating AT. The results indicated that the teachers only demonstrated the positive attitude for integrating AT into instruction. Their skills and knowledge competencies did not reach the requirement.

Two factors MANOVA was used to examine if teachers' AT literacy was different among the education stages and special education class types (2x2). The result indicated that there was no significant in the interaction between class types and education stage ($\Lambda = 1.00$, df = 1, $p>.05$) neither in the main effect of type of class ($\Lambda = 1.00$, df = 1, $p>.05$). However, the main effect of education stage ($\Lambda = .95$, df = 1, $p<.01$) was significant. In addition, a one-way ANOVA was applied to explore the specific difference among the three scales. The results of ANOVA shown that the significant difference in both attitudes (M = 5.06, SD = .87 for junior high school group; mean = 4.91, SD = 1.00 for elementary school; F = 5.06, $p<.05$, d = .16)and skills scales (mean = 3.78, SD = .90 for junior high school group; mean = 3.99, SD = .92 for elementary school; F = 6.30, $p<.05$, d = .23), but not in knowledge (mean = 3.34, SD = .87 for junior high school; mean = 3.56, SD = .86 for elementary school; F = 2.61, $p>.05$). As mention above, special education teachers in junior high school did have higher level in attitudes scale, however, elementary school teachers got higher level in skills scale. But the effect sizes were small.

The results of multiple steps regression analysis found that: (1) only the regression coefficient of AT training experience shown significant with the score of attitude ($\beta = .15$, $t = 2.84$, $p<.01$), (2) the regression coefficients of AT training experience ($\beta = .26$, $t = 5.37$, $p<.01$ for knowledge, $\beta = .26$, $t = 5.44$, $p<.01$ for skills), pre-service program type ($\beta = .17$, $t = 3.20$, $p<.01$ for knowledge, $\beta = .22$, $t = 4.12$, $p<.01$ for skills), and experience of teaching students who used AT in the past($\beta = .16$, $t = 3.14$, $p<.01$ for knowledge, $\beta = .14$, $t = 2.73$, $p<.01$for skills) shown significant with score of knowledge and skill. Therefore these three variables were used to explore if the teachers' AT literacy were different because of their AT training experience, pre-service program type, and experience of teaching students who used AT in the past.

The results of the three factors MANOVA indicated that only the interaction between experience of teaching students who used AT in the past and pre-service program type were significant ($\Lambda = .98$, df = 1, $p<.05$). The simple main effect shows that for those teachers not graduated from the Department of Special Education, their AT literacy were different between their AT training experience ($\Lambda = .84$, df = 1, $p<.01$, Eta square = .16), however, there was no significant difference among the teachers graduated from the Department of Special Education ($\Lambda = .98$, df = 1, $p>.05$). Furthermore, the results of ANOVA indicated that the major difference existed in Knowledge ($F = 20.20$, $p<.01$, Eta square = .10) and Skill ($F = 26.01$, $p<.01$, Eta square = .13). The mean shows that those teachers who possessed experience (Knowledge: mean = 3.79, SD = .83; Skill: mean = 3.44, SD = .82) performed better than those did not (Knowledge: mean = 3.05, SD = .75; Skill: mean = 2.80, SD = .77) in both Knowledge ($d = .93$) and Skill ($d = .80$) with large effect size. The results illustrated that the effect of teacher's experience of teaching students who used AT devices in the past only displayed when the teachers did not graduate from the Department of Special Education.

When controlling the experience of teachers, the score of AT literacy was different between teachers who graduated from Department of Special Education and teachers who did not (when possessed experience: $\Lambda = .96$, df = 1, $p<.01$, Eta square = .04 ; when no experience: $\Lambda = .71$, df = 1, $p<.01$, Eta square = .30). The results of ANOVA demonstrated that when the teachers possessed experience, the difference happened in Attitude($F = 4.24$, $p<.05$, Eta square = .01), Knowledge(($F = 4.48$, $p<.05$, Eta square = .02), and Skill ($F = 12.24$, $p<.01$, Eta square = .04). the mean shows that the teachers graduated from Department of Special Education reported (Attitude: mean = 5.11, SD = 1.01; Knowledge: mean = 4.14, SD = .90; Skill: mean = 3.65, SD = .87) better than those did not (Attitude: mean = 4.82, SD = .82; Knowledge: mean = 3.79, SD = .83; Skill: mean = 3.44, SD = .82) in subscale of Attitude ($d = .32$), Knowledge ($d = .40$) and Skill ($d = .25$) with small effect size. On the other hand, the results of ANOVA demonstrated that when the teachers did not possess experience in teaching students who used AT devices, the difference happened in Knowledge ($F = 11.14$, $p<.01$, $d=1.19$) and Skill($F = 29.82$, $p<.0$, $d=1.61$). The mean shows that the teachers graduated from Department of Special Education performed (Knowledge: mean = 4.02, SD = .88; Skill: mean = 3.38, SD = .84) better than those did not (Knowledge: mean = 3.05, SD = .75; Skill: mean = 2.08, SD = .77) in subscale of knowledge and skill with large effect size. The results mean that when special education teachers graduated from Department of Special Education possessed better literacy especially when they did not teach students how use AT device before.

Besides, the results of main effect analysis of AT related training indicated that the AT literacy is different among the teachers with different AT related training experience ($\Lambda = .88$, df = 3, $p < .01$, Eta square = .04). The results of ANOVA released the major difference happened in Attitude (F = 4.07, df = 3, $p < .01$, Eta square = .03), Knowledge (F = 13.59, df = 3, $p < .01$, Eta square = .10), and Skill (F = 15.41, df = 3, $p < .01$, Eta square = .11). Based on the results of the multiple post hoc LSD tests, the difference only demonstrated between group A (Credit courses + in-service training group) and group D (no experience) in subscale of Attitude($p < .05$, d = .41). The mean shows that group A (mean = 5.14, SD = 1.00) reported more positive attitude than group D (mean = 4.73, SD = .98), However, the effect size was small. In the subscale of Knowledge, the scores of the group A is different from group B ($p < .05$, d = .51), C ($p < .05$, d = .57), and D ($p < .01$, d = .93). The group B is different from group D($p < .05$, d = .47), but there is no difference between Group B and C, and Group C and D. the mean of the four groups shows that group A (mean = 3.91, SD = .88) is the highest, then group B(mean = 3.48, SD=.78) and C (mean = 3.44, SD = .78). The group D (mean = 3.10, SD = .85) is lowest. In the subscale of Skill, group A (d = .81, effect), B (d = .58), C (d = .56) are different from group D ($p < .01$), but there is no different among these three groups. The mean of group A (4.22, SD = .91), group B (mean = 3.97, SD = .80), group C (mean = 3.96, SD = .81) are higher than group D (mean = 3.46, SD = .96). The results mean that teachers who took AT related courses in pre-service program and AT training program in-service reported the best literacy. The results also indicated lack of training performed worst, especially in the knowledge and skills scales.

4 Discussion

The results of the current study imply that AT literacy of special education teachers is not inadequate. The ratings in the questionnaire shows participants only acquired the basic requirement level. Especially, their essential knowledge and skills were below the basic requirement. However, in comparison with the study of Li. et al., the special education teachers' AT literacy are better in this study. Such superiority was attributed to some efforts done in Taiwan, including lots of in-service AT related training workshops and seminars by Taiwan education authorities that required AT be one of the core courses in Department of special education.

However, the degree of AT literacy was still not satisfactory enough except in the category of attitude. The results released that the teachers possessed positive attitude on AT implement but still need more such knowledge and skills. The authors reviewed the score on each indicator. The results of each indicator's score indicated that those higher than 4 points might regarded basic knowledge and skills, such like understanding the benefits of providing AT, managing proper classroom environment, assessing students' basic abilities. On the other hand, those lower than 4 might be regarded advanced knowledge and skills, such like understanding related regulations for AT and the AT assessment procedure.

The results of difference analysis between school stage and type of special education class demonstrated that the difference only existed between school stages. How-ever, the effect size was very small. The results of related important factors examination also illustrated that AT training experience, experience with teaching students who used AT device, and background of special education training show significant relationship with their AT literacy. Among them, the effect of AT training experience contributes to the teacher education more significantly. In fact, those who did not gain any training got the worst score. It is similar to the past studies conducted in USA [1,2,3], [14], [16]. They indicated training increased AT integration in the classroom for teachers. Furthermore, this study found out those teachers who took AT related courses in pre-service program and attended AT training in-service gained the best score. However, the teachers who took AT related courses only or attended AT training in-service only did not have significant distinction from those who did not gain any experience. The results mean that the special education teachers, in order to posses better AT literacy, should take AT related courses in pre-service teacher preparation program and continue to attend AT training program in in-service.

The results also shed light on some issues needed to be investigated for providing AT related training program. As mentioned previously, providing training and experience could increase the possibility of integrating AT into the classroom [1,2,3], [14], [16]. However, effectiveness of integration depends on the content of the training. Given the distinction between basic and more advanced knowledge and skills, the authors wondered if the in-service and pre-service AT related programs in Taiwan focused on basic part more? Basic knowledge and skills are good initial focus for AT training. But the advanced literacy should also be improved if the teachers are reluctant to integrate AT into their instruction activities. Chen and Lai's [4] study also supported that providing long term workshop with continual supports could assist the teachers to improve their competence of integrating AT into the classroom. Therefore, the advanced knowledge and skill should be included into the in-service AT program in the future.

5 Conclusions

The AT related training program should be considered on all fronts. As mentioned in discussion, teacher with AT training experience both in pre-service and in-service reported better AT literacy. Meanwhile the result of the AT literacy also indicated that the teachers possess higher scores in those basic literacy, for example, the positive attitude, hands on experience; but lower in those advanced knowledge and skills, such like designing proper material for AT users. Therefore the pre-service AT course could still focus on the basic literacy. The special teacher continued education program should extend to advanced knowledge and skills to make sure the teachers could learn from basic AT literacy to advance.

References

1. Bauder, D.K.: The use of assistive technology and the assistive technology training needs of special education teachers in Kentucky schools. Unpublished Doctor Dissertation, University of Kentucky, USA (1999)
2. Behrmann, M.M.: Assistive technology issues in Virginia schools: A five year follow-up study. Unpublished Doctor Dissertation, University of North Carolina, USA (1999)
3. Campbell, D.M.: Views on assistive technology. Unpublished Doctoral Dissertation, University of Massachusetts Amherst, USA (2000)
4. Chen, M.C., Lai, T.Y.: Outcomes of a project-based assistive technology in-service training program. Bulletin of Eastern-Taiwan Special Education 7, 19–34 (2005)
5. Gardner, J.E., Edyburn, D.L.: Integrating technology to support effective instruction. In: Lindsey, J. (ed.) Technology and Exceptional Individuals, 3rd edn., pp. 191–240. PRO-ED Austin, TX (2000)
6. Kirk, A., Gallagher, J.J., Anastasiow, N.J.: Educating exceptional children, 8th edn. Houghton Miffin Company, Boston (2000)
7. Lahm, E.A., Nickels, B.L.: Assistive technology competencies for special educators. Teaching Exceptional Children 32(1), 56–63 (1999)
8. Lewis, R.B., Doorlag, D.H.: Teaching special students in the mainstream. Prentice-Hall Inc., Columbus (1995)
9. Lewis, R.B.: Special education technology classroom applications. Pacific Grove, Brooks Cole (1993)
10. Michigan's Assistive Technology Resource: Michigan's assistive technology checklist for self-assessment, `http://www.matr.org/PDFs/Forms/`
11. Ministry of Education in Taiwan Statics report for special education (2006), `http://www.set.edu.tw/tlearn/book/BookRead.asp?BookID=886`
12. National Association of Station Directors of Special Education, Recommended competencies for professional staff members in the area of assistive technology, `http://www.cde.ca.gov/sp/se/sr/atstaff.asp`
13. Purcell, S., Grant, L.D.: Using assistive technology to meet literacy standards for grades 4-6: A IEP guide. Attainment Company Inc., Verona (2004)
14. Riemer-Reiss, M.L., Wacker, R.R.: Factors associated with assistive technology discontinuance among individuals with disabilities. Journal of Rehabilitation 66(3), 44–50 (2000)
15. Wu, T.F., Chen, M.C.: Policy of assistive technology for special education in Taiwan. Bulletin of Special Education 20, 47–68 (2000)
16. York, M.A.: Assistive technology as viewed by special education teachers in Kansas. Unpublished Doctoral Dissertation, Kansas State University, USA (1999)

University Examination System for Students with Visual Impairments

Konstantinos Papadopoulos, Zisis Simaioforidis, Konstantinos Charitakis, and Marialena Barouti

University of Macedonia, Thessaloniki, Greece
{kpapado,zsimaiof}@uom.gr,
{kcharitakis,ekpmet129}@uom.edu.gr

Abstract. This paper presents the development of a web based, platform independent system for university examination purposes that can be easily accessed and used by students with visual impairments, with minimum effort required to learn its use. The developed examination system allows students with visual impairments to take suitably adapted online written examinations according to their individual and personalized special characteristics and preferences for reading digital text. Those special parameters and characteristics can be applied as predefined user options to the examination platform. The user interface for individuals with low vision is based on the selection of effective color contrast and the principle of legible texts that students need in order to read and write during examinations. Based on the above, it was considered necessary that special parameters and characteristics had to be tested and determined by the end users themselves with N Print tests.

Keywords: Visual Impairment, Examination System, Computer Based Assessment.

1 Introduction

Several studies have focused on the structural and attitudinal barriers that hinder students with visual impairments from participating in higher education [1,2,3,4,5]. Students with visual impairments are less likely to complete their studies in comparison to their sighted colleagues [6]. However, there is no robust evidence to indicate whether this fact reveals an academic failure or a withdrawal which may be due to insufficient support and guidance offered to the students [6]. A reason might be the numerous difficulties experienced by students with visual impairments in their daily academic activities. Such difficulties may include accessing textbooks, attending lecturers, taking notes, sitting examinations and getting the reading lists on time [4].

The way university examinations for students with visual impairments should be conducted is one of a whole range of issues that need to be reconsidered, and requires changes and improvements. University examinations are important because they play a direct role in the assessment of students and the measurement of their progress. Thus, the intention should always be to administer the examinations using

K. Miesenberger et al. (Eds.): ICCHP 2014, Part II, LNCS 8548, pp. 358–365, 2014.

appropriately modified methods so that the results will be as unaffected as possible by the inherent disadvantages of the testing procedure [7].

The available methods for examining students with visual impairments can be classified in two categories. The first comprises the traditional methods while the second comprises contemporary methods that exploit the latest technological advances. Most methods in the first category are based on oral examination (questions asked in first person by the examiners or recorded on tapes and answered by the same means). Among the traditional methods we can also number the use of braille, yet it is usually impossible to establish reciprocal communication in this format, since it would require knowledge of braille from the examiner's part. Contemporary methods include those which use a computer and appropriate software, such as screen reading software, magnification software, as well as peripheral devices like braille displays, CCTV and so on. In both cases examiners must be familiar with the special characteristics of each individual student and hence either the use of braille or the use of special technical equipment and software, adding administrative burden on the examination process itself.

Nowadays the method that is used systematically for the assessment of students with visual impairments in higher education is that of oral examinations. It is well known that this method has disadvantages compared to the traditional method of written examinations [7-8], used for the assessment of the sighted students. Oral examination does not allow equal participation of students with visual impairments, it discriminates them from the sighted students and does not allow their inclusion since they are treated as a different group. In their previous research Papadopoulos and Goudiras [4] examined the possibility of devising suitable written examinations suitable to be taken by students with visual impairments. A stand alone software application was developed in Visual Basic programming language, which allowed computer based written examinations for students with visual impairment. The application was fully compatible with screen reading software and included two different input forms for the two types of users, examiners and students respectively, as well as a central database where all data was stored. The examiners' form allowed examiners to enter examination information (course, date etc.), upload a text file containing all exam questions (.doc file), set the type of questions (multiple choice or ask for full written answers) and set possible answers in case of the former.

Junying & Baiwen [9] developed an exam platform for students with visual impairments which was implemented mainly to be used with keyboard providing guide and feedback by voice. It includes features for management of papers, students, examinations and score reports as well as functions for sending papers, carrying on the examination and adjudicating the papers. Papers can be automatically made by the system once the users set the types of questions, count, scope, difficulty rate and so on. Existing papers with respective answers can also be imported into the system while different exam papers can be sent to different students but papers can also be sent randomly.

2 The University Examination System

The aim was the development of a web based, platform independent system for university examination purposes that can be easily accessed and used by students with visual impairments, with minimum effort required to learn its use. The developed examination system allows students with visual impairments, to take suitably adapted online written examinations according to their individual and personalized special characteristics and preferences for reading digital text.

In order to best manage and control the provided features to its users, it was decided that the architecture of the examination platform should consist of three layers: a) the examination administration layer b) the question answering layer and c) the data management layer, each one of which implemented through a respective subsystem with all necessary modules.

The developed examination system is web based, platform independent, and it can be easily used from any computer with internet connection and screen reading software installed. The system architecture consists of the following subsystems.

2.1 Examination Administration Subsystem

For the implementation of the examination administration subsystem, open interviews with the university's administrative personnel were organized, in order to define user requirements from the administrative personnel perspective regarding the university examination procedure and the administrative information required.

Therefore, the first subsystem includes all the modules that facilitate exams administration and is used mainly from university's administrative personnel in order to manage information regarding administrative parts of the exams (e.g. departments, courses, exam date time and venue, users, exam questions etc.).

Different user roles and groups can be created in order to restrict or allow access to specific information and data according to corresponding credentials (e.g. exam questions only visible and editable by specific examiners).

Special attention was given in the creation of user accounts for students with visual impairments and the information regarding their individual and personalized special preferences for digital text reading. Each student's account was linked to a user profile with Pre-configured settings for color contrast, font, font size, font weight, character and line spacing that would allow them better reading speeds during exams.

2.2 Question-Answering Subsystem

The second subsystem includes all the modules for question and answering during the examination.

The module for entering examination questions uses self explanatory templates that guide the academic staff through the whole process and allows them to enter questions in a simplified manner. The academic staff can enter different types of questions that can be multiple choice, matching questions or ask for full written answers.

Special attention was given in the design and implementation of the user interface of the question answering subsystem, which will be used by students with visual impairments.

Efforts were made to ensure that the frontend student answer forms and templates are compatible with the most widely used screen reading software. Specifically, the same internet browser keyboard shortcuts were chosen as the market leader screen reading software uses, for navigating through each question on a single Question-Answer examination manner. Thus, fast learning rates and the lowest possible confusion during the question answering process were achieved.

For the display of Question-Answer forms, and examination content, the system uses Javascript and jQuery routines in order to achieve cross-browser compatibility and automatic adjustment at any screen resolution, always considering the predefined student profile that was loaded according to corresponding user credentials.

However, Javascript keyboard shortcuts were also used in order to trigger some key features of the frontend such as the integrated audio guide option during the examination at real time. The audio guide option feature provides verbal guidance to students with low vision for changing display styles and prompts them to type single key shortcuts (e.g. 1 for changing font size, 2 for changing line spacing etc. and then Shift+I or Shift+D to increase or decrease respective value).

Presentation of Question-Answer Form. The Question-Answer form is part of the question answering subsystem and it is mainly used by the students with visual impairments during the examination. The students can answer different types of questions either by selecting the correct one in case of multiple choice, match the correct pairs in case of matching questions or typing their answers in case of a full written answer, through a user interface with suitably adopted answer forms.

The user interface was carefully designed in a way that every feature was accompanied by sound readings. Students with visual impairments can "read" the examination questions and the answers they give via synthetic speech. The subsystem is de-signed in order to be fully compatible with screen reading and Text-to-Speech soft-ware. An audio guide option is available to users at any time by pressing the Esc key on their keyboard and it is providing sound guiding for digital text presentation preferences (e.g. contrast, font size etc.) during the answering process.

The subsystem for question answering was continuously tested by the students with visual impairment based on appropriately designed tests. The selection of key-board shortcut keys for navigation through the system's menus and features was not arbitrary. The functions linked to the shortcut keys selected, are similar to those most commonly used by popular commercial software and by special software individuals with visual impairments use in their everyday computer use (e.g. Enter, Tab, Esc, etc.) in order to ensure usability of the solution.

Each student is assigned certain digital text presentation preferences by the time he logs in to the system with his credentials. Special considerations had to be taken for the design of the user interface for answering examination questions not only for the blind but also for students with low vision. Appropriate options were provided to students with low vision in order to be able to receive information by reading, by listening or by combining both ways. Although the system allows students with low vision to use preconfigured settings and preferences entered in their individual user profile, it also provides them with options to change these settings by themselves at any time. In this way issues directly related to their ability of reading digital texts (e.g. color contrast, font, font size, font weight, line and character spacing), are controlled by the students themselves.

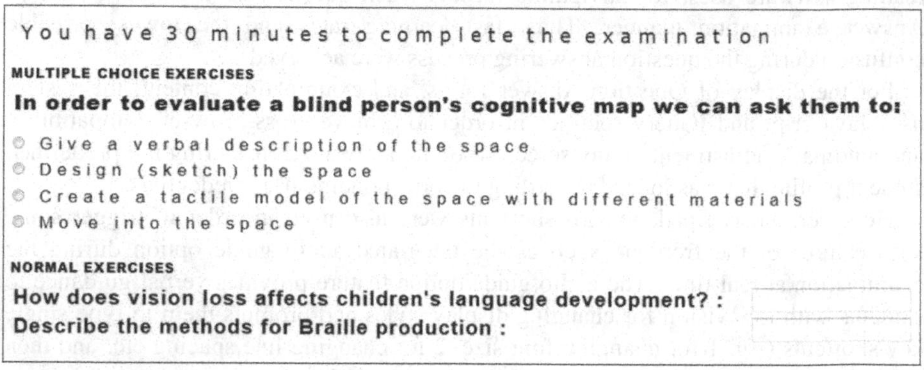

You have 30 minutes to complete the examination

MULTIPLE CHOICE EXERCISES

In order to evaluate a blind person's cognitive map we can ask them to:

- Give a verbal description of the space
- Design (sketch) the space
- Create a tactile model of the space with different materials
- Move into the space

NORMAL EXERCISES

How does vision loss affects children's language development? :

Describe the methods for Braille production :

Fig. 1. User interface of the Question-Answer form showing different digital text preferences

The function of screen panning mode was also integrated in the answering subsystem. The panning mode is very important since it is extensively used by individuals with low vision while reading electronically magnified texts displayed on a limited resolution screen. This feature is integrated to most commercial screen magnification software (e.g. SuperNova).

Digital Text Presentation. Special considerations had to be taken for the design of the user interface for answering examination questions not only by the blind but also by students with low vision. The user interface for individuals with low vision is based on the selection of effective color contrast and the principle of legible texts [10] that the students will need to read and write during examinations. Based on the above it was considered necessary that special parameters and characteristics had to be tested and determined by the end users themselves.

In order to determine the most appropriate digital text presentation settings and achieve optimized functionality of the question answering system for students with low vision, special tests were conducted. Those digital text presentation settings were defined based on evaluation of each student with low vision with the use of special N Print Test [11]. These tests determined the most appropriate contrasts, font type, font size, character and line spacing to be used.

For each one of the above mentioned parameters an N Print test was created. The N Print test created in order to test contrasts, font type and font size consisted of 24 lower case letters of the Greek alphabet and the numbers 1 to 9 printed randomly on the computer screen. The N Print test created in order to test character and line spacing consisted of sentences 3 to 4 lines long. All N Print tests projected to the participants at a distance of 30 cm from the computer screen, using a special construction that keeps the participant's head stable. Before the test, each participant was asked to fill in a form with demographic information about their visual impairment status. N Print tests were conducted two times during the user requirement specification phase.

The first time N Print Tests were conducted with 12 individuals with low vision who were not university students, in order to define which options will be available in the Question-Answering system. Their visual acuity ranged from 1/20 to 8/20. The sample consisted of 9 men and 3 women aged from 18 to 22 years old. The basic values of contrasts, font type, font size, character and line spacing to be included as options in the system were decided based on the values that, when used, resulted with the smaller number of errors and the maximum promptness during the N Print tests. Therefore, regarding the appropriate contrast of color combinations 4 options are included in the Question-Answer form. Regarding the fond size character and line spacing of the text, a wide range of values are included as options for the Question-Answer form.

The second time N Print tests were conducted with 6 university students with low vision, to define their individual preferences in order to enter them as Pre-configured settings in their user account profile. Their visual acuity ranged from 3/10 to 1/20 and one of the participants had reduced visual field. The sample consisted of 3 men and 3 women aged from 20 to 24 years old.

2.3 Data Management Subsystem

The third subsystem of the developed examination system for students with visual impairments is the central database where all entered data is stored and basically connects the other two subsystems and modules. The database holds information concerning the administrative part of the examinations (e.g. departments, courses, semesters, examinations etc.), demographic data of the users (academic staff and students), imported examination questions and records of answers given by students during the exams. All examination questions entered are stored and can be reused later in different examinations.

Moreover each student's individual and personalized special characteristics and preferences for reading digital text is stored including their screen displaying preferences such as contrast, font, font size, font weight, character and line.

3 Conclusion

The developed university examination system is web based, platform independent and it can be easily used by students with visual impairments from any computer with internet connection and minimum requirements of additional software. Blind users only need screen reading software while students with low vision receive information either by reading or listening (with screen reading software) or by combining both modalities.

However, its main advantage is that it provides a selection of preconfigured digital text presentation settings that students with visual impairments can choose by themselves according to their individual preferences, prior to or during the examination. Moreover, the developed examination system allows university students with visual impairments to take exams in the examination venues, together with their sighted classmates and provides them the opportunity to exploit all advantages of written examinations.

The system allows academic staff to select different types of questions (multiple choice, matching questions or ask for full written answers) without considering the special characteristics and preferences of each student individually, and take their burden off for preparing various examination material (recorded tapes, large prints, braille, etc.) saving them time and effort.

The developed examination system contributes significantly to the fair and Non-discriminatory participation of students with visual impairment to university examinations. It allows equal participation of students with visual impairments at university examinations and promotes their inclusion since they are not treated as a different group. Although the examination system was designed for university examinations with specific modifications it can also be used in examinations organized by other organizations as well.

The developed system prints a list of all given answers of every student for each examination. The examiner would have to mark the printed answers and provide the results to the administrative personnel who will announce the results to the students. As future work it is considered that the integration of a feature for automated marking and reporting would reduce the time and effort required for marking and reporting from the examiner's part but also reduce the administrative burden of the administrative personnel.

Acknowledgements. The work presented in this paper was supported by the Operational Programme for Information Society (OPIS, see www.digitalplan.gov.gr) of the Greek Ministry of Economy & Finance, as part of the project titled "Support Services for Individuals and Students with Disabilities at the University of Macedonia". The opinions expressed in this paper do not necessarily reflect views of the OPIS.

References

1. Cole-Hamilton, I., Vale, D.: Shaping the future: The experiences of blind and partially sighted children and young people in the UK (summary report). Royal National Institute for the Blind, London (2000)
2. Gray, G., Wilkins, S.M.: A 'psychology core graphics resource pack' for HE: The development of a resource to support blind and visually impaired students in higher education. The British Journal of Visual Impairment 23, 31–37 (2005)
3. Owen-Hutchinson, J., Atkinson, K., Orpwood, J.: Breaking down barriers: Access to further and higher education for visually impaired students. Stanley Thomas, Cheltenham (1998)

4. Reindal, S.M.: Some problems encountered by disabled students at the University of Oslo – whose responsibility? European Journal of Special Needs Education 10, 227–241 (1995)
5. Roy, A.W.N., Dimigen, G., Taylor, M.: Types of supportive intervention sought by visually impaired graduates to assist their transition from education to employment. British Journal of Visual Impairment 14, 66–70 (1996)
6. Richardson, J.T., Roy, A.W.N.: The representation and attainment of students with a visual impairment in higher education. The British Journal of Visual Impairment 20(1), 37–48 (2002)
7. Papadopoulos, K., Goudiras, D.: Visually Impaired Students and University Examinations. British Journal of Visual Impairment 22(2), 66–70 (2004)
8. Ingenkamp, K.: Lehrbuch ber Padagogischen Diagnostik. Karlheinz Ingenkamp, Weinheim (1985)
9. Junying, A., Baiwen, F.: The application and efficiency analysis of exam platform for people with visual impairments. In: Proceedings of 2012 IEEE Symposium on Robotics and Applications (ISRA), Malaysia, Kuala Lumpur, June 3-5, pp. 1–4 (2012)
10. Papadopoulos, K., Goudiras, D.: Accessibility Assistance for Visually Impaired People in Digital Texts. British Journal of Visual Impairment 23, 75–83 (2005)
11. Mason, H.: Assessment of Vision. In: Mason, H., McCall, S. (eds.) Visual Impairment – Access to Education for Children and Young People, pp. 51–63. David Fulton, London (1997)

"Planet School": Blended Learning for Inclusive Classrooms

Ingo Karl Bosse

University of Dortmund, Faculty of Rehabilitation Research, Dortmund, Germany
ingo.bosse@tu-dortmund.de

Abstract. "Planet School" is currently the most important blended learning platform in Germany. The multimedia content of the popular website is developed especially for teachers by the public service broadcasters WDR and SWR. However, as it stands today, "Planet School" is neither accessible by all students, nor does it meet the needs of the entire student population. This paper presents both the results of the evaluation of the learning platform in inclusive classrooms and first recommendations on how to offer variable content for students with special needs. The revised version of "Planet School" shall address different types of learners and offer accessible and usable materials, including movies, television broadcasts, interactive and multimedia content for students with very different prerequisites for learning. The paper has implications for application-oriented research in the field of e-inclusion and blended learning, for the development of multimedia content by broadcasters and others as well as for the use of multimedia in inclusive classrooms.

Keywords: E-inclusion, Blended Learning, Broadcasters, Inclusive Classrooms, Inclusive Multimedia Learning Materials.

1 Introduction

As almost all European countries, Germany has a dual broadcasting system. Beside a whole range of private networks, there are two public broadcasters: ZDF and ARD. The ARD is a joint television network of nine state broadcasting organizations. It is the world‘s second largest public broadcaster after the BBC. The public service broadcasters' mission is to speak to all groups of society, providing them with information, education and entertainment as well as with innovative and alternative programs, especially for minority groups. WDR and SWR belong to the ARD network. As members of the European Broadcasting Union (EBU), WDR and SWR cooperate with the educational producers of other public broadcasters both in Europe and around the world. Their editorial boards for science and education produce entertainment and learning programs for children. One of these is "Planet School", a combination of school TV and an internet platform with additional information. It hosts specifically produced movies, television broadcasts, interactive learning and multimedia content. Teachers can access "Planet School" anytime and from wherever they choose, thereby broadening their scope for independent living

K. Miesenberger et al. (Eds.): ICCHP 2014, Part II, LNCS 8548, pp. 366–373, 2014.

(www.planet-schule.de. The website is only available in German. Many schools already use the platform for a wide range of subjects. The platform, however, is not specifically designed for students with special needs. In view of the high level of attention currently accorded to inclusive learning in Germany, the idea of remedying this shortcoming by creating a revised version of the website addressing the special needs for students with disabilities, impairments and disadvantages came to the fore. The increased focus on inclusive education in Germany at the moment can be largely explained by the government's ratification of the UN Convention on the rights of persons with disabilities (UNCRPD) in 2009. Article 24 calls upon "States Parties [to] recognize the right of persons with disabilities to education. With a view to realizing this right without discrimination and on the basis of equal opportunity, States Parties shall ensure an inclusive education system at all levels and lifelong learning." [1]. Ever since the ratification of this document, the educational system has been undergoing rapid change. Germany still has a high percentage of students with special needs who visit special schools. However, in the course of last years, there has been a strong tendency towards inclusive education. Since 2009 the percentage of students who go to regular schools increased from 18.4% in 2009 to 25% in 2012. But at the same time the total number of students with special needs increased as well [3]. Within the last time, there is a strong tendency for mainstream media to care about inclusive education. It is expected that "Planet School" can play an important role in this process, because it is very popular at schools.

1.1 Aim of the Project

A hardly addressed characteristic of inclusive learning environments is the accessibility and usability of blended-learning tools. While there is consensus that media education offers special opportunities for inclusive classrooms [2], most of the blended-learning platforms currently on offer are not accessible by and thus not usable for, students with special needs. The website itself is intended for teachers, some parts are produced for students. The project "Planet School: blended-learning content for inclusive classrooms" thus sets out to evaluate and further advance the blended learning platform in favor of teachers who work with students with special needs and the students themselves.

The purpose of this descriptive-exploratory study is to collect qualitative data on the didactical requirements for inclusive education from a teacher's and student's perspective. Valid statements and genuine information are expected. A study about the possibilities of blended learning without involving the students seems incapacitating and paradox. Therefore the study includes cooperative work of people with and without the experience of being regarded as disabled. The data thus gathered lay the foundation for the development of further research modules within the project.

The final aim of this research is to develop universal accessible materials, modules and activities enabling self-directed and independent learning for students with and without handicaps. This article presents the research of the second of five research modules. These data build the basis for the development of the further research modules.

1.2 Research Questions

These considerations led to the two central research questions:

1. How can „Planet School become a universal accessible and barrier-free tool for inclusive education?
2. Is it enough to achieve technical accessibility? How can we design teaching and learning experience that allow full participation?

2 State of the Art in This Area

The acceptance of computers as instrument for people with disabilities has reached a high level. Nonetheless, the European Commission still characterizes the accessibility of learning materials as the most critical issue in the area of education it its disability strategy 2010- 2020 [4]. However, as it stands today blended learning has not yet been widely established in Germany's educational institutions. With regard to the use of information and communication technologies (ICT) for students with special needs, the main focus still remains on assistive technologies [5,6]. However, in an international context, many studies and reports show how ICT can support students with disabilities' inclusion in mainstream schools. As far as the United Kingdom is concerned, Rahamin points out that access to technology is a prerequisite for inclusive education, but, but, besides the necessity for a non-restrictive design, a key question is how information is to be presented. This includes choosing the content. It must be appropriate for the learner (2004: 45). The literature review indicates a lack of attention on the application of ICT for people with (severe) learning difficulties as compared to other groups of disabled people [7]. Research focusing especially on the learning needs of students with (severe) learning difficulties shows that "[i]t may be useful to explore teaching and learning around alternative media such as still and moving images, live theatre and storytelling, digital technology and the arts. Although some teachers are making good use of these media, the potential of these media for providing inclusive literacy experiences could be further developed." [7: 149]. Due to this reason that most of the students with special needs are students with learning difficulties this study has a special focus on this group.

International research has moreover found that there are several indispensable factors that contribute to the successful use of media education in inclusive classrooms. The problem of accessibility, for instance, is frequently noted in this context (Alliance for Digital Inclusion 2006). More recent results show that another decisive factor is the teachers' awareness of the possibilities of implementation in their classes [8]. In addition, results from Portugal show that teachers first have to develop a set of basic digital media skills in order to benefit fully from special knowledge on pupils with special educational needs. Their level of education [8] and their ability to cope with heterogeneous lifestyles are further important factors for success [9].

Together, the review of the relevant literature and reports on evidence-based best practice provide the theoretical framework within which the advancement of "Planet

School" as a non-restrictive blended learning portal is best analyzed. In order for "Planet School" to become a suitable platform for inclusive education, seven decisive factors need to be addressed: 1. accessible web design and universal design, 2. text and language, 3. individualized curricula, 4. differentiated learning arrangements within the same topic, 5. account taken of the complexity of life-realities, 6. cooperative/ collaborative learning, 7. action-oriented instruction [10].

The accessibility of websites is regulated in Germany by the BITV – the accessible information technology enactment, which, in its current version, is based on the WCAG 1. At the time of writing, the BITV is undergoing a complete revision and, once reenacted, will be based on the WCAG 2. Under these laws, the notion of "universal design" is introduced in order to enable people with disabilities to access websites without assistance. Universal design has a special significance, because it can be used as umbrella term for all other dimensions of the theoretical framework. After all, universal design does not only mean developing the content, but also considering the context for which it is produced. It aims to change the way in which all adolescents learn, regardless of whether they have a disability or not. Creating products and environments following a universal design constitutes an attempt to "design products and environments to be usable by all people, to the greatest extent possible, without the need for adaptation or specialized design" [11]. However, producing learning content in accordance with the approach of universal design remains a challenge. Three principles of universal design are essential: First, to provide multiple means of representation (perception, language and symbols, comprehension); second, to provide multiple means of action and expression (physical action, expressive skills and fluency, executive function); and third, to provide multiple means of engagement (recruiting interest, sustaining effort and persistence, self-regulation) [12].

3 Methodology

The project consists of five modules that overlap and lead into each other:

1. Desk-based research (including research for inclusive schools);
2. Testing of "Planet School" in inclusive classes: classroom observations and semi-structured interviews with teachers for special and for mainstream education;
3. Focus groups with teachers in special and mainstream education, as well as with television professionals and with students (with and without special needs);
4. Revising and complementing "Planet School" with respect to the needs of inclusive instruction;
5. Testing of the revised platform.

This paper presents the results obtained by the end of module two. It addresses the current learning practice in inclusive classrooms using "Planet School", drawing on data collected through the observation of lessons and semi-structured interviews with teachers in inclusive schools. In 2013 and 2014, eleven teachers at inclusive schools (primary and secondary) worked with different topics covered by „Planet School". All of the participants had previous experience in inclusive education. The research sample was made up of students with learning, intellectual, physical, emotional and behavioral disorders, with dyslexia, dyscalculia as well as with special needs in language and communication. Fifteen of the thirty students with special needs require special support, due to learning difficulties. As mentioned above, desk research identified seven decisive factors for inclusive teaching. Together they formed the core of the interview guidelines. The main focus, was placed on the practical experiences with the learning materials provided by "Planet School". A pretest was carried out in order to validate the interview guidelines. The audio recordings of the talks were transcribed in full and evaluated by means of summarizing content analysis in MAXQDA. The results were evaluated on the basis of combination of a deductively developed category system and inductively oriented procedure [13: 67ff]. Finally, the coding of all categories was analyzed, compared and interpreted.

4 Results: Inclusive Teaching and Learning with Planet School

The results of the summarizing content analysis underline the teachers' relative satisfaction with the usability of "Planet School" for inclusive classrooms. In general, the teachers deemed "Planet School" to be very attractive and easy to understand for children. The most quoted statement was that the website fits really well with the life-realities of the students. In their opinion, the platform offered a diverse range of materials, highlighting in particular the availability of appealing films. With regard to the platform's future development, however, they noted that they would greatly appreciate the possibility of being able to exert direct influence over the further development of the learning platform.

Not all parts of the website are meant for students. Some sections are produced exclusively for teachers in which materials like films and worksheets are made available for download. With regard to the parts dedicated to students such as, for example, the learning games, the teachers called attention to the following issues concerning accessibility and universal design: the possibility to use the tab key instead of a mouse throughout the platform; the possibility to jump forward and backward; the possibility to convert all text to speech; the need for more possibilities to repeat exercises, the possibility to obtain better contrasts on screen; and, finally, the possibility to improve scalability for all kind of contents. Concerning the worksheets, the teachers stated that they would like to work with word documents that can be adapted to the individual needs of their students, or at least barrier-free PDFs. The teachers also expressed a request for more clearly structured worksheets. In their opinion, the design should be simpler and exclude logos and captions or any visual clutter that are not absolutely necessary. One recurrent wish was for the teaching materials to be kept simple, since especially the overwhelming number of elements for interaction can be confusing for students. Indeed, a similar statement can be made with regard to the entire platform: the at times unclear structure of the interface runs the risk of confusing and overstraining many students with special needs. It is currently possible to find countless topics on every site whilst headings are frequently mixed. A navigator could be helpful to return to the starting point and an improved search function could show all materials on similar topics.

Furthermore, the summarizing content analysis shows that, from the teacher's point of view, text and language are considered to be of high importance for inclusive education. The font type selected for the platform thus has to be a sans serif font such as Arial or Helvetica. It should also be possible to choose different fonts and font sizes. The platform should moreover offer short text with action-oriented tasks for weak readers or alternative texts with visualizations. For complex topics like politics or history, it would be helpful to have a version making use of more simple language.

Many statements addressed the issue of accommodating differentiated learning arrangements. The teachers identified a strong need for materials to be provided for different levels of learning concerning complexity, time frame and speed. There seems to be a need for the different levels to be labeled more clearly. Some of the expressions currently used for all of the different levels available (for all, for experts, for professionals) have stigmatizing effects. Neutral terms or the use of different colors would be more appropriate for inclusive education. Furthermore, didactical instructions for teachers and working tasks for students on every worksheet are indispensable. The didactical instructions should be categorized in terms of action-oriented learning, game, worksheet, etc. The structure of all materials ought to be less overloaded and clearer. There is also a strong need for alternative methodological approaches to be offered for a given topic (e.g. visual learning, experiments, etc.). Alternatives for saving the results obtained should be offered action and product oriented. There are already some materials for cooperative learning available. The teachers would moreover like to see a greater variety of methods for cooperative learning and a greater variety of methods available for use within one lesson.

Another decisive factor is to offer more movies with persons with special needs. The teachers appreciated that there were several clips on the topic of disability, but noted that adults with special needs hardly appear in any of the visual material on offer. The presence of persons with disabilities should rather be the norm as opposed to the exception on "Planet School". Many of the teachers interviewed produced their own materials. Some expressed to share their work and ideas with others, not least through the use of social media.

The teachers stressed that most of their students with special needs belong to the group of adolescents with learning difficulties – a group which needs action and product-oriented instructions. Thus, if writing is the main aspect, alternative tasks such as, for example, playful or physical exercises should also be on offer. Practical activities that allow basic experiences like some of the experiments already include. These action-oriented exercises ought to be clearly labeled as such.

The results presented here already outline a number of first recommendations that can be used to develop a revised version of "Planet School" that takes better account of the needs of inclusive education. Focus groups with teachers for special and for mainstream education, television professionals and students with and without special needs will discuss these recommendations. Finally "Planet School" ought to address different types of learners and offer accessible and usable learning materials for a greater variety of students with special needs. The data collected from the schools participating in this research shall be used for technology-related and content-related decisions.

5 Conclusion and Planned Activities

In following their mission to provide basic service for all groups of society, and especially for minority groups, public broadcasters like WDR and SWR have a responsibility to offer learning content suitable for all students, including those with special needs. Learning platforms like "Planet School" have the advantage of being able to meet the flexible needs of diverse 21st-century learners [14]. This advantage becomes especially clear for inclusive classrooms in which students with a wide range of prerequisites learn together. The research presented in this article focused on a problem at the interface of technology and inclusive (media) education.

This study focuses on the evaluation and development from the point of view of specialists on inclusive education: experienced teachers. Furthermore the perspective of the users that means teachers as well as students is indispensable. Desk research identified seven decisive factors to be addressed in order for "Planet School" to become a suitable platform for the purpose of inclusive education: accessible web-design and universal design, text and language, individualized curricula, differentiated learning arrangements within the same topic, account taken of the complexity of life-realities, cooperative/ collaborative learning, action-oriented instruction. The qualitative interviews carried out with teachers show that the material is attractive and multifaceted. The films were deemed meaningful, exciting, usable and not too abstract. There is, however, no special version available for students with hearing or seeing impairments. The topics correspond to the daily lives of students, by, for example, broaching issues such as conflicts on the bus or the creation of Facebook profiles. All in all, the current version of "Planet School" is suitable for most students, yet still restricts those with special needs on different levels. The results show that the text and language as well as differentiated learning arrangements are especially important. The deliberate and purposeful use of individualized instructional materials is essential for successful inclusive schooling. The materials should allow active and student directed learning. "Planet School" ought to cover different levels that meet the needs of all children in order to avoid any kind of obvious differentiation for particular groups. There is a strong demand for more active exercises: practical partner- and group work that lead to concrete actions. Departing from the teachers' views, we share the view that "[a] five-level model of school learning is proposed that is realistic, because it covers individuals' prerequisites reaching from learning difficulties to special interests and giftedness" [15: 387].

All the recommendations provided for the revision of the platform will be discussed in focus groups with teachers working in special mainstream education, television professionals as well as with students. Finally, each topic covered in "Planet School" is to be revised one by one before the blended learning platform is presented to the public in the framework of a big campaign for inclusive learning run by the two broadcasters, WDR and SWR. The campaign includes teacher trainings, because they are a decisive factor to implement blended learning in inclusive classrooms.

The move of the popular mainstream website "Planet School" towards inclusion is an important step towards the empowerment of persons with disabilities as part of the knowledge-based society. This study promises to be a big step towards firmly establishing blended learning as a practical means for education in inclusive classrooms.

References

1. United Nations: Convention on the Rights of Persons with Disabilities and Optional Protocol. United Nations, New York, USA (2006)
2. Rahamin, L.: From integration to Inclusion: Using ICT to Support Learners with Special Educational Needs in the Ordinary Classroom. In: Florian, L., Hegarty, J. (eds.) ICT and Special Educational Needs. A Tool for Inclusion, pp. 35–45. Open University Press, McGraw Hill Education, Maidenhead (2010)
3. KMK – Kultusministerkonferenz: Sonderpädagogische Förderung in allgemeinen Schulen (ohne Förderschulen) 2011/12. KMK Berlin (October 15, 2012)
4. European Commission. Employment, Social Affairs and Equal Opportunities: EU Disability Strategy 2010-2020. Summary of the main outcomes of the public consultation, Brussels (2010)
5. Bosse, I.: Inklusion in der Mediengesellschaft. In: Gapski, H. (ed.) Informationskompetenz und inklusive Mediengesellschaft. Schriftenreihe Medienkompetenz des Landes Nordrhein-Westfalen, pp. 11–28. Kopaed, Düsseldorf (2012)
6. Bosse, I.: Keine Bildung ohne Medien! Perspektiven der Geistigbehindertenpädagogik. Teilhabe 52(1), 26–32 (2013)
7. Lacey, P., Layton, L., Miller, C., Goldbart, J., Lawson, H.: What is literacy for students with severe learning difficulties? Exploring conventional and inclusive literacy. Journal of Research in Special Educational Needs 7(3), 149–160 (2007)
8. Pietrass, M.: Leeres Wissen durch E-Learning? Zeitschrift für Pädagogik 51, 61–74 (2005)
9. Riberio, J., Moreira, A., Pisco Almeida, A.M.: Preparing special education frontline for a new teaching experience. eLearning Papers No. 16 (September 2009)
10. Booth, T., Ainscow, M. (eds.): Index for Inclusion. Developing Learning and Participation in Schools. CSIE, Bristol (2011)
11. Trace Center: General Concepts, Universal Design Principles and Guidelines, `http://trace.wisc.edu/world/gen_ud.html`
12. CAST: Cast, `http://www.cast.org/udl/index.html`
13. Mayring, P.: Qualitative Inhaltsanalyse. Grundlagen und Techniken. Beltz Pädagogik, Weinheim und Basel (2010)
14. Edyburn, D.L., Edyburn, K.D.: Tools for Creating Accessible, Tiered, and Multilingual Web-Based Curricula. Intervention in School and Clinic XX(X), 1–7 (2011)
15. Wember, F.: Herausforderung Inklusion: Ein präventiv orientiertes Modell schulischen Lernens und vier zentrale Bedingungen inklusiver Unterrichtsentwicklung. Zeitschrift für Heilpädagogik 10, 380–387 (2013)

Ensuring Sustainable Development of Simultaneous Online Transcription Services for People with Hearing Impairment in the Czech Republic

Zdenek Bumbalek[1] and Jan Zelenka[2]

[1] The Masaryk Institute of Advanced Studies, Czech Technical University in Prague
Kolejní 2637/2a, 160 00 Prague 6, Czech Republic
zdenek.bumbalek@muvs.cvut.cz
[2] Transkript Online s.r.o., Dlouhá 37, 110 00 Prague 1, Czech Republic
zelenka@transkript.cz

Abstract. Real-time speech transcription is a service of potentially tremendous positive impact on quality of life of the hearing-impaired. Nevertheless there is a total lack of government funding for these assistive services in the Czech Republic. In the article, we present such a business model of a socially orientated service that enables its long term sustainable development and provides online transcription services for personal use of the target group for free.

Keywords: eScribe, Online Transcription, Speech to Text Services, Business Model, Social Entrepreneurship, and Hearing Impaired People.

1 Introduction

The presented project Transkript responds to the communication needs of people with hearing disabilities, particularly people deafened and hard of hearing people, who are unable to use sign language. These people, because of their handicap, prefer Czech language in its written form as their means of communication. Although this group constitutes 1% of the total population of the Czech Republic, its communication needs are still neglected. The project helps to ensure the legal right of the people to a choice of communication means, among other possibilities of "simultaneous transcription." Even though this means of communication is formally enshrined in the Czech legislation – Act no. 384/2008 coll., so far, there have not been any systematic provisions from the state that would financially and organizationally ensure this right to be fulfilled.

The aim of the project is to help create a better financial, organizational, technical, and in the long run even cultural, political and socio-economic environment for improving the quality of life for hearing impaired people. The presented solution is to build a social enterprise, whose main activity would be operation of the online transcription for the hearing impaired and whose clients will be socially responsible companies that will gain a significant competitive advantage in communication with

K. Miesenberger et al. (Eds.): ICCHP 2014, Part II, LNCS 8548, pp. 374–381, 2014.

hearing impaired clients. The project aims to design and implement such a business model of a socially orientated service that enables its long term sustainable development and provides online transcription for personal use of the target group for free. From technical perspective, the aim is to develop and subsequently improve the system for providing an online transcription service, which will be supported by a wide range of devices with internet access. The development will also include technologies of speech synthesis and recognition.

2 Historical Overview of Text Based Services for Hearing Impaired People

From the historical point of view, the long-distance transmission of text without a physical transport of letters, known as telegraphy, is older than telephony. Telegraphy was the first telecommunication service which could have been used by the hearing-impaired users for communication in real time. In the period of analog telephony (until the 1990s), hearing-impaired users could benefit from analog facsimile messaging (fax). In that time, the first service designed for the hearing-impaired, known as TTY (Teletypewriter for the deaf) [1], was established and operated. In the nineties, analog telecommunication services were replaced by digital communication (telephone exchanges of the 4th generation). From the wide variety of digital telecommunication services, hearing impaired people could use the TELETEX [2] service for text transmission and TELEWRITING [2] for transmission of hand-written texts in real time. Special digital text phones – TDDs (Telecommunications Devices for the Deaf) [1] – were operated in Western Europe and USA. The expansion of the Internet had high impact on communication of the hearing-impaired. E-mail and instant messaging were services helping to the hearing-impaired to overcome communication barriers. One of the most used services by the hearing-impaired is the Short Message Service (SMS) [2], which was introduced as part of the Global System for Mobile Communications (GSM) [2] series of standards in 1985. Hearing-impaired people often label SMS as the most important discovery after the invention of handwriting. Rapid development of the Internet enabled creation of a large number of multimedia services, some of them focused on the specific needs of the hearing-impaired people. Projects and services known as total communication have appeared. A well-known software platform for total communication is Skype, which was enhanced with videoconferencing in 2006. Special attention of the ITU resulted in the ITU T.140 [3] standard, dedicated to communication of the hearing impaired. ITU T.140 was standardized in 1998 and brings transmission of real-time text (RTT) [4] to Internet telephony and Next Generation Networks (NGN) [5]. With rapid growth of computing abilities systems that can synthesize speech from text (Text-To-Speech (TTS)) or recognize speech from voice (Automated Speech Recognition (ASR)) have recently achieved remarkable progress.

3 Current Situation and Contemporary Research

Today's speech-to-text services (STTS) are generally provided by one of the following methods: 1. physically present transcribers [6]; 2. remote-transcription carried out by human transcribers [1][7][8]; 3. concepts based on ASR [9][10]; 4. ASR combined with human error-correction [11].

Physically present transcribers are highly limiting because there is great shortage of educated transcribers, costs of these services are high and they are restricted to particular locations. An alternative is using ASR. Yet, ASR is limited in recognition accuracy, especially of colloquial speech and of difficult national languages such as Czech. Today, ASR systems are largely trained on literary texts. ASR techniques are very sensitive to many miscellaneous characteristics of the input signal. From fundamental signal attributes (signal input level, sample frequency) across disturbing influences (background noise, other voices, music) to the culture of idea formulation (fluent speech with minimal unfinished sentence fragments). Remote transcription and ASR combined with human error-correctors is limited by costs and human resources too.

Assistive STTS, based on ASR technologies, are described in many studies [12]. Google Voice Search [13] is an application for searching the web using human voice. A leader in using ASR in assistive technologies is the Liberated Learning Project (LLP) [14]. In cooperation with LLP, IBM develops the ViaScribe [15] software, designed for real-time captioning. Synote [16], a web application for disabled students, captioning lectures and multimedia content on the Internet, was developed by University of Southampton. ASR of minor languages such as Czech attract less commercial interest and are developed mainly in the academic domain (e.g. in the Czech Republic at the Technical University of Liberec [17], University of West Bohemia [18], CTU [19], etc.). An interesting enhancement in using ASR is the so-called shadow speaker [9], a person who re-pronounces the speech to be transcribed. This results in a more intelligible and less noisy input for the ASR system.

In 2010, the EU ratified the Convention on the Rights of Persons with Disabilities [20]. Three articles of the Convention have direct impact on the hearing impaired (Article 9, 21, 24). In many EU states this Convention has helped to support creation of social enterprises providing assistive STTS funded by government or state associations, for example VerbaVoice [21] in Germany or Bee-Communications [22] in the UK.

Although the Czech Republic adopted a law [23] in 2008 guaranteeing the hearing-impaired the right to choose a communication system that matches their needs (STTS including), no conditions were created or funds dedicated to fulfill this law. Because of lack of government funding for assistive STTS, we have proposed an innovative approach and business model to socially oriented services such as simultaneous online transcription services for people with hearing impairment and we have established a social enterprise providing these services. We have confirmed in our research, that assistive STTS has high potential as a commercial product too for companies with frequent client interaction (banks, shops, …) to help decrease costs and increase efficiency in communication with hearing-impaired clients.

4 Business Model and Marketing Concept

From the commercial perspective, the project is based on offering an effective service for communicating with hearing impaired people to companies. This leads to shortening the service time and especially it prevents any possible misunderstanding.

4.1 Service

It is a service of transcription of speech into text, based on modern communication and voice technologies in cooperation with trained transcribers and stenographers. The service was initially offered through a web application and via main lines, mobile phones and internet calls. Since March 2013, the service is also available through an integrated mobile application for smart phones and tablets. The service is offered in three main versions:

- **Tablet transcription for face to face communication** – this mode is used for transcription of the immediate communication between the hearing impaired and hearing person. Mediation of the voice and real time transcription is provided by a tablet with the eScribeDroid application. Ongoing transcription is available only to the person with a hearing disability. Connection to such a transcription by a third party is prohibited due to security reasons.
- **Mass transcripts** – this mode is used to transcribe collective events such are lectures or conferences. This transcript can be viewed either through the eSribeDroid application or through a website. Voice channel is separated from the transfer of the transcribed text.
- **ASR based transcription** – this mode uses automatic speech recognition engine provided by Google. The accuracy and quality of this service could not be guaranteed by Transkript. On the other hand it is available always and anywhere independently on the office hours of the transcription centre. It could be used especially for short transcriptions with lower requirements on accuracy.

4.2 Target Group and Customers

Customers of this service can be divided into two groups:

1. **People with hearing impairment:** The main motivation of the project is to be able to provide transcription services free of charge to hearing impaired people who will form the majority of the customers – respectively the service users. The financial provision of this service is paid from the sales for commercial and public sector.
2. **Commercial and public sector:** The service is offered to multinational companies with significant number of clients with hearing disabilities. Online transcription considerably increases the prestige of the brand in the community of people with hearing disabilities and their families.

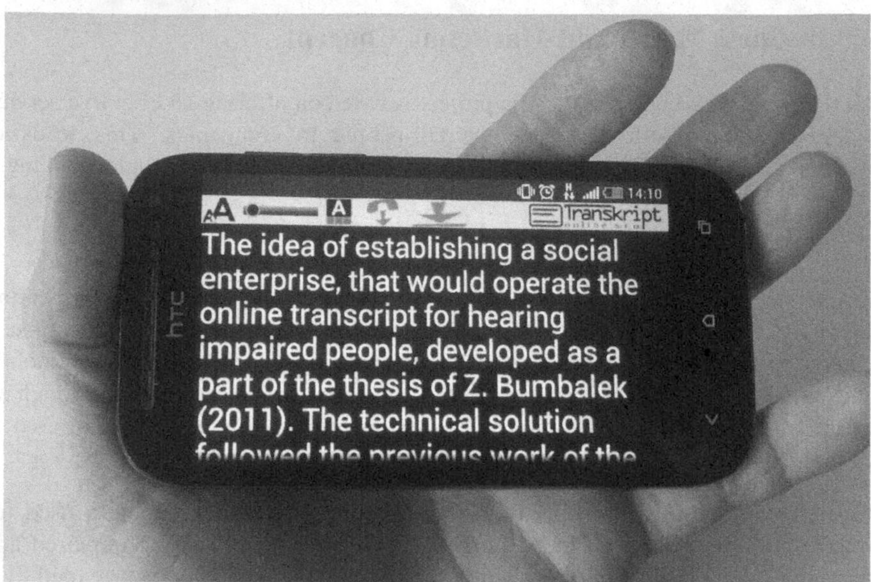

Fig. 1. Online transcription services available at Android Smartphone. The application is available for free at Google play market under the name eScribeDroid.

5 Market Analysis

According to the estimate of the Czech Union of the Deaf there are about 300 to 500 ths. people with hearing disabilities, of which up to 100 ths. people are deafened or with a severe hearing problem, who are not able to use the sign language. This high number of people, together with the fact, that they form a specific community that could be approached this way, is the major reason of the interest of companies to introduce online transcription within their contact points.

Currently there is no social enterprise registered in the Czech Republic that would deal with similar activities. The main competitive advantage of this project is continuing the existing prototype of the system of online transcription called eScribe [7]. This prototype is further developed and improved within the project. This unique technology of online transcription significantly reduces the costs of operating the service as compared to physically present transcribers and also considerably increases the potential capacity of the available transcripts. The Centre for Mediating Simultaneous Transcription (CMST) [6] also deals with the simultaneous transcript in the Czech Republic, this centre provides services of physically present transcribers. The Masaryk University in Brno is working on developing a Polygraf system [24], which allows a local provision of a transcription by using a physically presented transcriber in the same room. The equivalent of this service is offered by Telefonica O2 in “Call for people with hearing disability” [25]. However this service does not allow remote transcription in a real-time communication between a deaf person and the hearing person – which is the most common communication scenario.

Fig. 2. Overview of all contact points with online transcription in the Czech Republic

On the European scale, there is a similar service offered by a German company VerbaVoice [21] and a British company BeeCommunication [22]. Both of these companies are using a completely different business model.

6 Existing Results

During the first two years of running the project, we were able to design a long term, sustainable model of providing online transcription services to people with hearing disabilities. In October 2012 the Transkript social enterprise was founded. Online transcription service is currently available at 127 contact points of three corporate clients throughout the Czech Republic. The mobile application eScribeDroid, which allows providing online transcription for personal use of hearing impaired people across the whole Czech Republic, has been developed. There was a total number of 1,627 units of transcriptions provided in 2013, of which 67% were provided free of charge to deaf users for personal purposes. The upward trend of this service is confirmed by the fact that 37% of all transcripts were realized in Q4 2013. The service is available 8 hours a day, 5 days a week and it is provided by two transcribers working in parallel. We also managed to implement several community events of which the most important were guided tours of the Botanical gardens with online transcription during the Impaired Hearing Awareness Week (IHAW) in September 2013. In December 2013 a non-profit pilot was launched in collaboration with the Department of Social Affairs in Prague 12. Transcript is used by social workers during visits of deaf clients in their homes or in hospitals.

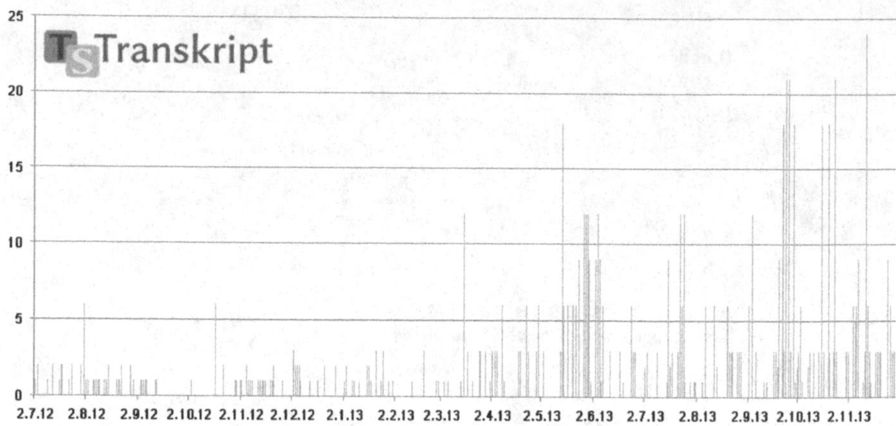

Fig. 3. Number of provided online transcriptions in 2013

7 Future Perspectives

In 2014, we expect an increase of more than 300% of the commercial points of contact with the transcription. Expected revenues have the potential to offer a total of 18,000 units of the transcripts for personal use by hearing impaired people for free. We intend to extend the project to Slovakia, where we have already entered into a partnership with organizations of hearing impaired people ANEPS. A major difficulty of the project is the lack of professionally trained transcribers. Respond to this shortage, we prepare an activity, which aims to select and train suitable candidates for online transcribers from the target group of people with visual disabilities. These people have significantly better short-term memory and concentration, due to their handicap. These abilities are the main prerequisites of professional transcribers. Due to the orientation barriers and difficulties to travel to unknown places, this profession was not available to people with visual impairments. Online solution of the service allows to work from home and opens career opportunities to this group of people. Such an approach has a significant potential to multiply the social impact of the project.

Acknowledgements. Research described in the paper was supported by Student Grant Contest (SGS) No. SGS13/162/OHK5/2T/32.

References

1. Lang, H.,, G.: A phone of our own: the deaf insurrection against Ma Bell. Gallaudet University Press (2000)
2. Vickrey Van Cleve, J.: Deaf history unveiled: interpretations from the new scholarship. Gallaudet University Press (1999)

3. ITU-T recommendation T.140: Protocol for multimedia application text conversation, ITU-T (1998)
4. Proposal R1 for Implementation of Real-Time Text Across Platforms, http://trace.wisc.edu/docs/2008-RTT-Proposal/ (cited December 01, 2009)
5. http://www.itu.int/en/ITU-T/gsi/ngn/Pages/default.aspx
6. Czech Union of Deaf, http://prepis.cun.cz/
7. Bumbalek, Z., Zelenka, J., Kencl, L.: Cloud-based Assistive Speech-Transcription Services. In: Miesenberger, K., Karshmer, A., Penaz, P., Zagler, W. (eds.) ICCHP 2012, Part II. LNCS, vol. 7383, pp. 113–116. Springer, Heidelberg (2012)
8. Bumbalek, Z., Zelenka, J., Kencl, L.: E-Scribe: Ubiquitous Real-Time Speech Transcription for the Hearing-Impaired. In: Miesenberger, K., Klaus, J., Zagler, W., Karshmer, A. (eds.) ICCHP 2010, Part II. LNCS, vol. 6180, pp. 160–168. Springer, Heidelberg (2010)
9. Forman, I., Brunet, T., Luther, P., Wilson, A.: Using ASR for Transcription of Teleconferences in IM Systems. In: Stephanidis, C. (ed.) Universal Access in HCI, Part III, HCII 2009. LNCS, vol. 5616, pp. 521–529. Springer, Heidelberg (2009)
10. Kheir, R., Way, T.: Inclusion of Deaf Students in Computer Science Classes Using Real-Time Speech Transcription. In: Proceedings of the 12th Annual SIGCSE Conference on Innovation & Technology in computer Science Education, ITiCSE 2007, Dundee, Scotland, June 25-27, pp. 192–196. ACM, New York (2007)
11. Wald, M.: Captioning for Deaf and Hard of Hearing People by Editing Automatic Speech Recognition in Real Time. In: Miesenberger, K., Klaus, J., Zagler, W.L., Karshmer, A.I. (eds.) ICCHP 2006. LNCS, vol. 4061, pp. 683–690. Springer, Heidelberg (2006)
12. Borodin, Y., Dausch, G., Ramakrishnan, I.V.: TeleWeb: Accessible Service for Web Browsing via Phone. In: W4A2009 Collocated with WWW 2009, Madrid, Spain, April 20-21 (2009)
13. http://www.google.com/mobile/voice-search/
14. The Liberated Learning Consortium, http://www.liberatedlearning.com/
15. IBM ViaScribe, http://www-03.ibm.com/able/accessibility_services/ViaScribe-accessible.pdf
16. Wald, M.: Synote: Accessible and Assistive Technology Enhancing Learning for All Students. In: Miesenberger, K., Klaus, J., Zagler, W., Karshmer, A. (eds.) ICCHP 2010, Part II. LNCS, vol. 6180, pp. 177–184. Springer, Heidelberg (2010)
17. Laboratory of Computer Speech Processing, Institute of Information Technology and Electronics, Faculty of mechatronics, Infotmatics and Interdisciplinary Studies, Technical University of Liberec
18. The Department of Cybernetics of the Faculty of Applied Sciences, University of West Bohemia in Pilsen
19. Speech Processing and Signal Analysis Group, Department of Circuit Theory, FEE CTU Prague
20. http://www.un.org/disabilities/convention/conventionfull.shtml
21. http://www.verbavoice.de/
22. http://www.bee-communications.com
23. Czech law no. 155/1998: Communications systems for the hearing-impaired as amended by Act no. 384/2008
24. http://www.teiresias.muni.cz/?chapter=8-4
25. http://www.telefonica.cz/tiskove-zpravy/169468-Sluzby_pro_neslysici_zdarma.html

User Interface Design of Sound Tactile

Tatsuya Honda[1] and Makoto Okamoto[2]

[1] Future University Hakodate, Graduate School of Systems Information Science
[2] Future University Hakodate,
116-2 Kamedanakano, Hakodate 041-8655, Japan
{g2113030,maq}@fun.ac.jp
http://www.fun.ac.jp/

Abstract. We have developed a device that allows sounds to be perceived via hair vibrations by deaf people; the concept is similar to cat whiskers, which can detect air currents. The device converts the loudness of a sound into a vibration with a certain power, and the users wear the device in their hair in much the same way as a hair slide. When the device detects a sound, it relays the information to the user by both shaking the hair and activating a light-emitting diode. This allows other users of the device to gain information about the sound, and facilitates sharing. The results of an assessment experiment showed that deaf people could understand animal-call patterns and car-engine sounds.

1 Introduction

People with hearing loss or those who are deaf and communicate using sign language are unable to distinguish or hear sounds such as animal calls, vehicles, and alarms. Although a number of tools have been designed to solve such problems, these tools still have some shortcomings [1,2,3]. We have developed a device that allows sounds to be perceived via hair vibrations using a concept similar to cat whiskers, which can detect air currents. The loudness of a sound is converted into a vibration with a certain power by the device, and the users wear the device in their hair, similar to a hair slide. When sound is detected by the device, information is relayed to the user by both shaking the hair and activating a light-emitting diode (LED) (Fig. 1).

The present study is part of the Future Body Project. This project aims to create new interpretations of the human senses through the use of technology. Akita et al. (2005) have also developed a new type of sensing device, especially for the visually impaired [4].

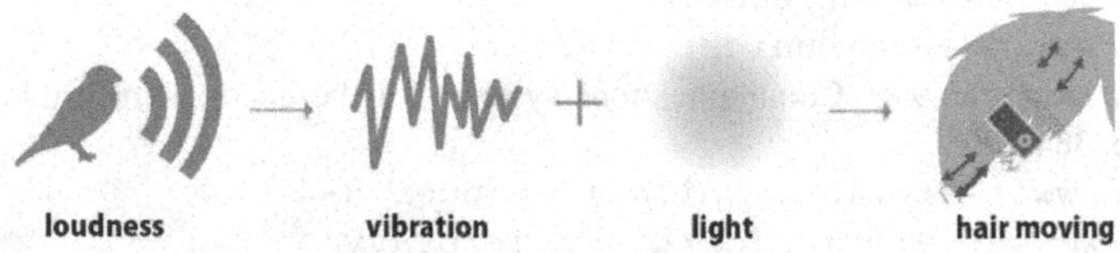

Fig. 1. Illustration of the device operation

K. Miesenberger et al. (Eds.): ICCHP 2014, Part II, LNCS 8548, pp. 382–385, 2014.

2 ONTENA

Our sound-feedback tool (Figs. 2 and 3) is named ONTENA, and it converts sound with a loudness of 30 to 90 dB into vibrations and brightness on a scale of 0 to 255. The device is worn in the hair to transfer the vibrations to the scalp. As the device is not worn as a wristwatch-type device, both hands of the user are as free as possible. The device relies on the fact that the mechanoreceptors in the scalp are extremely sensitive to small changes in the hair strands. If the amplitude of the vibration applied by ONTENA changes slightly, the user can then detect this small change in the vibration and will be able to perceive the loudness and pattern of the incoming sound.

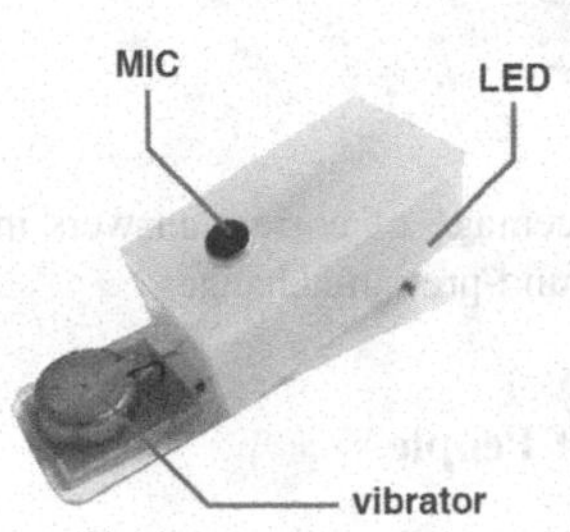

Fig. 2. ONTENA device

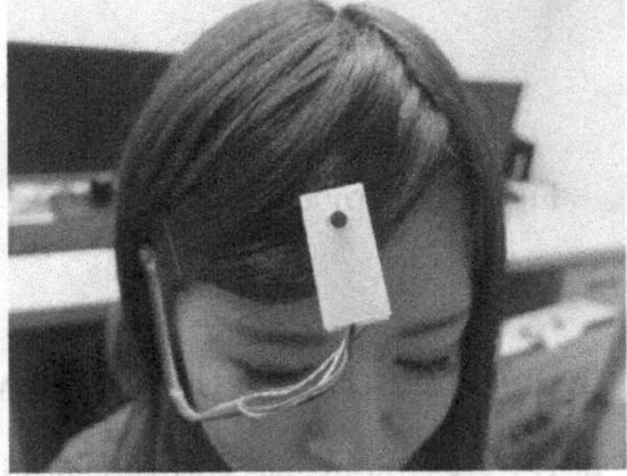

Fig. 3. Overview of the device in use

3 Sound Recognition by ONTENA

3.1 Experiment 1: Sound-Pressure-Change Distinction

We conducted experiments to demonstrate the effectiveness of ONTENA. Experiments were carried out with three examinees, ages 19–23, and all examinees have normal hearing without a handicap. First, we placed ONTENA in their hair, and the examinees wore headphones that played white noise to block out their hearing function. Second, we subjected the examinees to six types of acoustic stimuli (Table 1) by using a speaker (Fig. 4). The sound pressure of the stimulus was changed every 4 s. Examinees were subjected to each stimuli three times, for a total of 18 times. After the sound stimuli, we asked the examinees if the loudness was becoming louder or softer. The examinees were given only a 10-s break between each stimuli. Finally, this process defined one trial, and this trial was repeated three times.

Table 1. Sound stimuli

Loud → soft	**Soft → loud**
90 dB→70 dB	30 dB→90 dB
90 dB→50 dB	30 dB→70 dB
90 dB→30 dB	30 dB→50 dB

From the experimental results, every examinee could properly discern each change in sound pressure (Fig. 5). The percentage of questions answered correctly was nearly 100%, implying that changes in sound pressure may be detected by using our hair. We performed the same experiment on deaf subjects, and the results were almost the same.

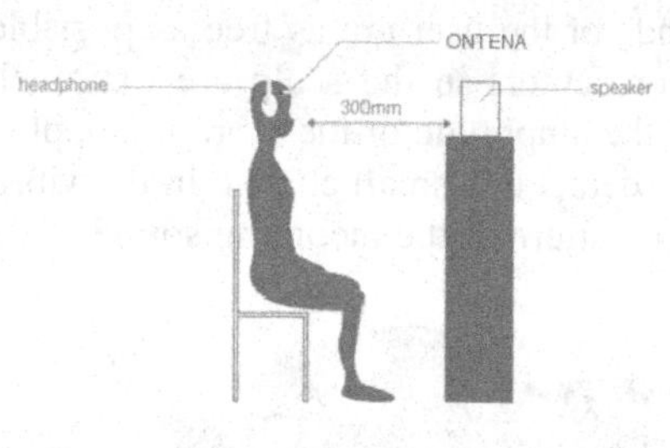

Fig. 4. Experimental setup

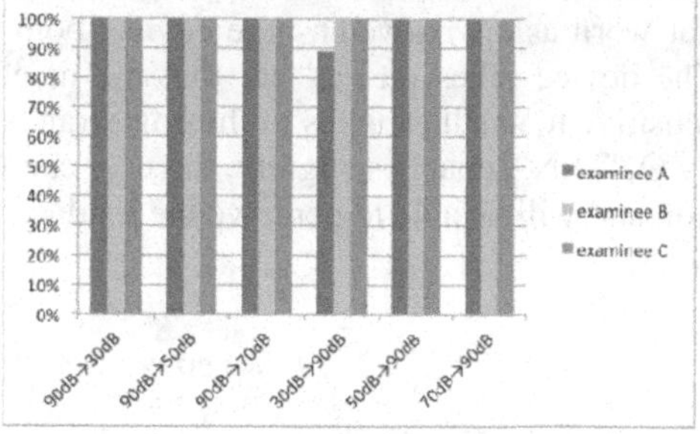

Fig. 5. Percentage of correct answers in discriminating sound-pressure changes

3.2 Experiment 2: Reactions to Movies by Deaf People

In the next experiment, we showed movies to deaf examinees using ONTENA. Three types of movies were used: a car race, the buzz of a cicada, and the song of a bird. We monitored the reactions of the examinees and conducted interviews about their change in impression after viewing the movies.

During this experiment, the device allowed the deaf people to correlate changes in the sound pressure to music patterns, animal calls, and engine sounds (Fig. 6). One deaf examinee said "I could understand the bird call and the buzzing of cicadas for the first time in my life. I could feel the pattern and loudness. I also understood the car closing in on me; the engine sounds also became bigger and bigger. I never knew."

Fig. 6. Screenshot of the vision experiment

4 Conclusions

We have developed a device named ONTENA to perceive sound via hair vibrations. ONTENA is not only a sensory device but also a communication tool; however, it is not limited to the hearing impaired or deaf. In the future, we may be able to use this device to listen to dolphin and bat calls.

Finally, to our surprise, the deaf people who were using ONTENA used their voices when reacting to the sounds (Fig. 7). In general, deaf people communicate with each other using sign language, but they used both sign language and their voice when using ONTENA. When they became excited after perceiving a sound, they conveyed their emotions by using their voice; thus, ONTENA would be a valuable communication tool for deaf people.

Fig. 7. In an instant, the deaf people used their voice

References

1. Orita, S., Mizushima, M., Furuya, K., Haneda, Y., Kataoka, A.: A Method and Efficiency of Transforming Auditory Signals into Vibrations for Perception by Hearing-impaired people. IEICE, WIT 104(388), 41–46 (2004)
2. Mizuno, T., Uchida, M., Ide, H.: Evaluation of Cognition of Navigated Information evoked Vibratory Stimulus. IEICE, MBE 106(592), 41–44 (2007)
3. Orita, S., Aoki, M., Furuya, K., Kataoka, A.: System and Efficiency of Transforming Auditory Signals into Vibrations under Noisy Environment for Hearing-Impaired People. The IEICE Transactions J90-D(10), 2765–2774 (2007); Kawashima, M.: Information Science and Electronics, Tsukuba College of Technology (2004)
4. Akita, J., Ito, K., Komatsu, T., Ono, T., Okamoto, M.: CyARM: Direct Prevention Device by Dynamic Touch. In: Proceedings of the International Conference on Perception and Action, ICPA13 (2005)

Enhancing Storytelling Ability with Virtual Environment among Deaf and Hard-of-Hearing Children

Sigal Eden[1] and Sara Ingber[2]

[1] School of education, Bar-Ilan University, Ramat Gan, Israel
ueden@upp.co.il
[2] School of education, Tel-Aviv University, Tel Aviv, Israel

Abstract. The study conducted a 3-month intervention to improve deaf and hard-of-hearing children's storytelling ability through training in arranging episodes of temporal scripts, and telling the stories they created. We examined 65 D/HH children aged four to seven years who were divided into two groups: virtual reality (VR) technological intervention and pictorial non-technological intervention. Participants completed pretest and posttest measures and demonstrated significant improvement in storytelling achievements following intervention. In the VR group the improvement was much more significant. In addition, participants at an early age at onset of treatment correlated with children's better achievements in storytelling.

Keywords: Deaf, Hard-of-Hearing, Virtual Reality, Storytelling, Sequential, Language.

1 Introduction

Assessment of children's oral narratives is of significant interest to researchers and practitioners, as being a proficient narrator is an important skill in the life of young children. Oral narrative skills are a key component of most school curricula [10]. Whereas hearing children naturally acquire language by exposure and interaction with the environment, deaf and hard-of-hearing (D/HH) children need early intervention programs to enhance their ability to acquire language and speech [17]. Over the years, many studies have investigated language development in this population, documenting various difficulties in language acquisition [11].

The present study aimed to examine the effect of an intervention program—virtual reality (VR) intervention versus pictorial intervention—on the storytelling ability of D/HH children. The basis of our study was the concept that language performance is one of the biggest hurdles in the education and development of D/HH children [13].

1.1 Storytelling Ability and Deaf and HH Children

Storytelling is an imperative and innovative pathway to enhance learning due to the fact that such activity prompts learners to reflect to construct meaning based on their observations and knowledge. Therefore, to develop and enhance students' storytelling

K. Miesenberger et al. (Eds.): ICCHP 2014, Part II, LNCS 8548, pp. 386–392, 2014.

ability has become an important issue for both educators and researchers [16]. Telling a story is a complex task requiring mastery of linguistic means that could connect units of text and the ability to reflect the order of events and arrange them chronologically. In addition, it requires the ability to arrange a guiding perception and thought around a certain idea, and ultimately it leads to the formation of a textual construction to highlight the point of the story [11]. Studies suggest that there are positive effects in academic, intellectual, social and emotional development of children who are encouraged to use storytelling [3]. As regards the cognitive-lingual aspect of storytelling that directly relate to the current research, it can be considered an important factor in terms of cognitive development [14]. LaMontagne, Morey and Walk (2004) suggest that storytelling is a successful strategy to increase pragmatic oral skills, the ability to use language in specific contexts for specific purposes, leading to greater ability to write [2].

Hearing children acquire discourse competencies like storytelling through everyday interactions, and are systematically supported in this process by adults [1]. D/HH children appear to have considerable difficulty producing an organized narrative. Their stories are less complete than narratives of hearing children; often lack a core story; include little/no description of the characters and environment; omit events; altogether provide an unclear image of the protagonist and poor development of the characters, actions, and reactions [19], [23], [30].

1.2 Virtual Reality and Children with Special Needs

VR is defined as the use of interactive simulations created with computer hardware and software to present users with opportunities to engage in environments that appear to be and feel similar to real world objects and events [29]. The innovative concept of this platform lies in the use of VR technology for the development of the working display environment that also provides navigation, immersion and interaction capabilities for all collaborative users in real time. The current intervention program used VR, a computer-simulated environment that can simulate places in the real or imaginary world. VR enables the user to be an active part of the environment. VR does not limit the presentation of information or the movements of the user. Consequently, abstract concepts can be presented in a creative way by making them more concrete, and by presenting a special viewpoint of processes which the real world cannot provide [6], [21].

VR has emerged as a promising tool in many domains of therapy and rehabilitation [25]. The use of this technology in the areas has shown encouraging results being reported for applications that address children's physical, cognitive, and psychological functioning [24]. Various researchers have investigated VR and its impact on populations with special needs such as physical disabilities, intellectual disability, sensory deficits, learning disabilities, attention deficits, and so forth [5], [9], [20], [26,27].

VR technology also focused on D/HH children. In previous research [4], [6] the findings demonstrate that the VR representation and the signed representation enabled the best perception of sequential time. Another research with D/HH participants was an exploratory study [12]. Young D/HH children experienced an intervention program to improve their temporal sequence and storytelling ability using pictorial scripts. [12] found an improvement in those abilities after the intervention. The current study, expands the pictorial intervention developed at [12], and adds a unique technological intervention using VR. We compared a pictorial intervention to a VR technological intervention, assuming that children's storytelling ability of a script that contains a temporal order will benefit from the advantages of the technology.

2 Method

2.1 Participants

Participants were 65 Israeli kindergartners (25 boys, 40 girls) aged 4:0 to 6:6 (M = 63.91; SD=10.05) whose HL was identified early in life and who had no additional problems. At the time of the study, the participants with HL comprised two groups: 42 children attending inclusive kindergartens and 23 attending special co-enrollment kindergarten settings.

In our study, according to language and communication assessments, the vast majority of the children in the inclusive group (16 out of 17, 94%) revealed spoken language delays of less than 1 year compared to the norms for their age group, whereas 15 of the 17 children in the co-enrollment group (88%) revealed spoken language delays greater than 1 year compared to their age norms. For the purpose of this study, the sample was therefore divided into two groups according to spoken language delay: those lagging behind their age by less than a 1-year gap, and those lagging behind their age by more than a 1-year gap.

2.2 Intervention Design and Procedure

The 65 participants were divided into two intervention groups:

1. Pictorial mode—three temporally logical scenarios each consisted of four illustrated pictures. The three scenarios were taken from the daily life of a child who is baking a cake, planting a tree and making a chocolate milk drink. The pictures were presented randomly and the child had to arrange them according to the sequence of their occurrence and tell the story he created.
2. VR mode—the same scenarios were adapted to the technology. Each of the episodes had its own opening screen represented by a picture. Four small separate pictures in random order appeared in a column on the right side of the screen, representing different episodes of the scenario. When any of the pictures was pressed, the participant was brought into a specific VR episode in which s/he could move around in the environment, using the mouse to manipulate the objects and interact with them. After experiencing the VR world, the participants entered a multimedia program designed to arrange the episodes in the correct sequence for the scenario.

   The participants were asked to drag the pictures of the specific scenario using a mouse and arrange them in the appropriate place according to the logical time-sequence that they had worked out, and then tell the story they created. After the participants had finished, they pressed a button that allowed them to generate and watch a video clip (consisting of the four episodes) reflecting the time-sequence that they had created. They also received feedback from the multimedia program informing them if they were correct or not.

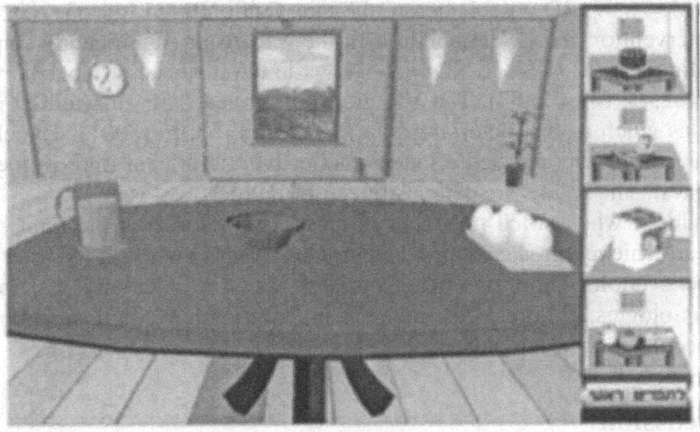

Fig. 1. Episodes in a Virtual World

Before and after a 3-month intervention, in 20 minutes' individual weekly meetings, the children were tested in the storytelling subtest of language screening test [8].

3 Results

In order to examine participants' progress in storytelling ability due to the intervention, we conducted t-tests for dependent variable comparing the pretest and posttest scores on the storytelling measures. The results were normally distributed. No significant difference was found between the pictorial group (M = 7.94, SD = 6.13) and the

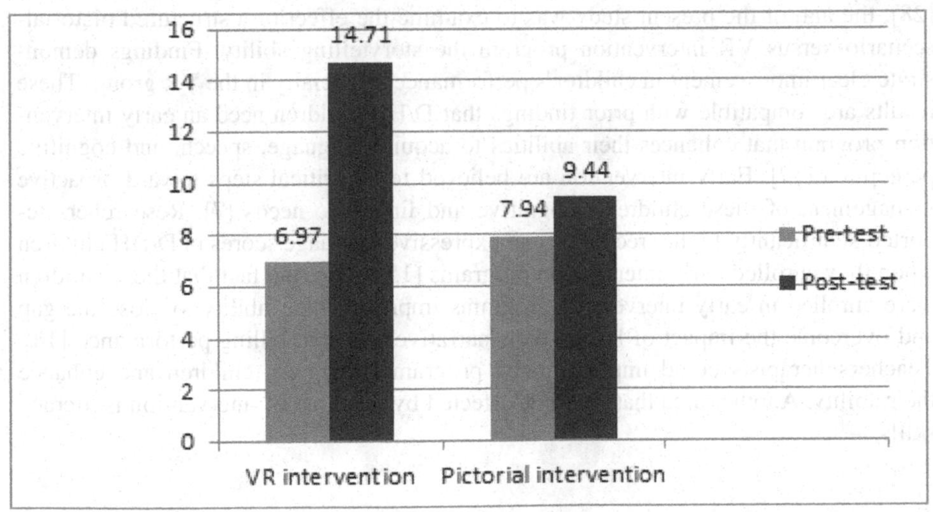

Fig. 2. Participants' Progress in Storytelling Ability Due to the Intervention

VR group (M = 6.97, SD = 4.74) before the intervention, t-.71, df=63, NS. However, after the intervention the D/HH children in the VR group significantly improved in the storytelling test (M = 14.71, SD = 5.44), while the pictorial group achieved lower scores (M = 9.44, SD = 6.57). The VR group improved their storytelling ability almost twice as much as the pictorial group (f=3.50, df=63, $p < .001$). The children in the pictorial group demonstrated a much smaller but significant improvement on the storytelling test. The results are demonstrated in Figure 2.

Also, children who started treatment in an early intervention program before the age of 1 year achieved greater improvement than children who started after; children with a genetic etiology did significantly better after the intervention than children with other etiologies; children with cochlear implant(s) showed greater improvement than their peers with hearing-aids.

4 Discussion

Deaf children need an early intervention program that enhances their abilities to acquire language, speech, and cognitive perception. This is critical toward proactive management of these children's cognitive and linguistic needs [7], [17]. The narrative abilities of the children progressed following an intervention program [18], but the technological mode is much more effective.

A few advantages of VR may be key attributes for those findings– the sense of immersion, the high level of interactivity and the active learning process. The ability of VR to make the abstract more concrete, thereby making it easier to perceive time, was mentioned by several researchers [20], [22].

Also, the participant become an active part of the virtual environment, and not a passive observer. It may suggest that children need a more active representation and expression mode in order to attain a higher level of abstraction.

In light of the difficulties in storytelling that D/HH children experience [19], [23], [28], the aim of the present study was to examine the effect of a structured pictorial-scenario versus VR intervention program the storytelling ability. Findings demonstrate clear improvement in children's performance, especially in the VR group. These results are compatible with prior findings that D/HH children need an early intervention program that enhances their abilities to acquire language, speech, and cognitive perception [17]. Early intervention are believed to be critical steps toward proactive management of these children's cognitive and linguistic needs [7]. Researchers reported significantly higher receptive and expressive language scores in D/HH children when they enrolled early intervention programs [15]. Also, the fact that these children were enrolled in early intervention programs improved their ability to close the gap and overcome the impact of HL on their narrative and storytelling performance [18]. Teachers/therapists could implement the program among the children and enhance their ability. Another area that could be affected by this kind of intervention is literacy skills.

References

1. Becker, C.: Narrative competences of deaf children in German sign language. Sign Language & Linguistics 12(2), 113–160 (2009)
2. Brice, R.G.: Connecting oral and written language through applied writing strategies. Intervention in School and Clinic 40(1), 38–47 (2004)
3. Chen, C.-H., Wang, S.-Y., Lee, Y.-C.N.: Developing story performing system for children. In: Stephanidis, C., Antona, M. (eds.) UAHCI 2013, Part III. LNCS, vol. 8011, pp. 143–152. Springer, Heidelberg (2013)
4. Eden, S.: The effect of 3D virtual reality on sequential time perception among deaf and hard-of-hearing children. European Journal of Special Needs Education 23(4), 349–363 (2008)
5. Eden, S., Betzer, M.: Three-dimensions vs. two-dimensions intervention programs: the effect on the mediation level and behavioral aspects of children with intellectual disability. European Journal of Special Needs Education 26(3), 337–353 (2011)
6. Eden, S., Passig, D.: Three-dimensionality as an effective mode of representation for expressing sequential time perception. Journal of Educational Computing Research 36(1), 51–63 (2007)
7. Eisenberg, L.S., Widen, J.E., Yoshinaga-Itano, C., Norton, S., Thal, D., Niparko, J.K., Vohr, B.: Current state of knowledge: Implications for developmental research–key issues. Ear & Hearing 28(6), 773–777 (2007)
8. Guralnik, E., Room, A.: A screening test for preschool Hebrew speaking children. Environmental Education: Teachers College Yearbook - Seminar HaKibbutzim 19, 105–124 (1993) (Hebrew)
9. Harris, K., Reid, D.: The influence of virtual reality play on children's motivation. Can. J. Occup. Ther. 72, 21–29 (2005)
10. Heilmann, J., Miller, J., Nockerts, A.: Sensitivity of narrative organization measures using narrative retells produced by young school-age children. Language Testing 27(4), 603–626 (2010)
11. Hogan, A., Shipley, M., Strazdins, L., Purcell, A., Baker, E.: Communication and behavioural disorders among children with HL increases risk of mental health disorders. Australian & NZ Journal of Public Health 35(4), 377–383 (2011)
12. Ingber, S., Eden, S.: Enhancing sequential time perception and storytelling ability among deaf and hard-of-hearing children. American Annals of the Deaf 156(4), 391–401 (2011)
13. Joseph, G.: A study on certain factors influencing language performance of the hearing impaired students. Asia Pacific Disability Rehabilitation Journal 14(2), 201–208 (2003)
14. Kara, N., Aydin, C.C., Cagiltay, K.: Investigating the activities of children toward a smart storytelling toy. Educational Technology & Society 16(1), 28–43 (2013)
15. Kennedy, C., McCann, D.C., Campbell, M.J., et al.: Language ability after early detection of permanent childhood hearing impairment. The New England Journal of Medicine 354, 2132–2141 (2006)
16. Liu, C.-C., Chen, H.S.L., Shih, J.-L., Huang, G.-T., Liu, B.-J.: An enhanced conceptmap approach to improving children's storytelling ability. Computers & Education 56, 873–884 (2011)
17. Moeller, M.P.: Early intervention and language development in children who are deaf and hard of hearing. Pediatrics 106, E43 (2000)
18. Nikolopoulos, T.P., Lloyd, H., Starczewski, H., Gallaway, C.: Using SNAP dragons to monitor narrative abilities in young deaf children following cochlear implantation. International Journal of Pediatric Otorhinolaryngology 67(5), 535–541 (2003)

19. Pakulski, L.A., Kaderavek, J.N.: Narratives production by children who are deaf or hard-of-hearing: The effect of role-play. Volta Review 103(3), 127–139 (2001)
20. Passig, D., Eden, S.: Enhancing the induction skill of deaf and hard-of-hearing children with virtual reality technology. Journal of Deaf Studies and Deaf Education 5(3), 277–285 (2000)
21. Passig, D., Eden, S.: Cognitive intervention through virtual environments among deaf and hard-of-hearing children. European Journal of Special Needs in Education 18(2), 1–10 (2003)
22. Passig, D., Eden, S.: Enhancing time-connectives with 3D Immersive Virtual Reality (IVR). Journal of Educational Computing Research 42(3) (2010)
23. Paul, P.V.: Literacy and deafness: The development of reading, writing, and literate thought. Allyn & Bacon, Needham Heights (1998)
24. Rizzo, A.A., Kim, G.: A SWOT analysis of the field of Virtual Rehabilitation and Therapy. Presence: Teleoperators and Virtual Environments 14(2), 1–28 (2005)
25. Rizzo, A.A., Schultheis, M.T., Kerns, K., Mateer, C.: Analysis of assets for Virtual Reality applications in neuropsychology. Neuropsychological Rehabilitation 14(1/2), 207–239 (2004)
26. Rizzo, A.A., Strickland, D., Bouchard, S.: Issues and Challenges for Using Virtual Environments in Telerehabilitation. Telemedicine Journal and e-Health 10(2), 184–195 (2004)
27. Standen, P.J., Brown, D.J., Cromby, J.: The effective use of Virtual Environments in the education and rehabilitation of students with Intellectual Disabilities. British Journal of Educational Technology 32(3), 289–299 (2001)
28. Walker, L., Munro, J., Rickards, F.W.: Teaching inferential reading comprehension of students who are deaf or hard-of-hearing. Volta Review 100(2), 87–103 (1998)
29. Weiss, P.L., Rand, D., Katz, N., Kizony, R.: Video capture virtual reality as a flexible and effective rehabilitation tool. Journal of Neuro Enginneering and Rehabilitation (2004), http://www.jneuroengrehab.com/content/1/1/12
30. Yoshinaga-Itano, C.: Beyond the sentence level: What's in a hearing impaired child's stories? Topics in Language Disorders 6, 71–83 (1986)

Teaching Morse Language to a Deaf-Blind Person for Reading and Writing SMS on an Ordinary Vibrating Smartphone

Andras Arato[1], Norbert Markus[1], and Zoltan Juhasz[2]

[1] Wigner Research Centre for Physics, Hungarian Academy of Sciences Budapest, Hungary
[2] Pannon University, Veszprem, Hungary

Abstract. Deaf-blind people have a very small window to the world. New technology can help, but portable Braille lines are expensive. We developed and tested a very low cost method for reading and writing SMS messages with a Hungarian deaf-blind person using Android smartphone with vibrating motor built in. Words and characters were converted to vibrating Braille dots and Morse words. Morse was taught as code for recognizing characters and also as language for recognizing words.

Keywords: Deaf-blind, Morse language, Language teaching.

1 Introduction

PG was born deaf and became blind when he was 45. He learned reading and writing Braille and also to send SMS messages on his simple phone with no feedback. Until recently he was able to read messages only with the help of his deaf wife.

A straightforward solution would be a haptic touch screen but this is not yet available [3]. PG knows several languages such as spoken Hungarian, Hungarian sign language, writing block letters in the hand, Lorn and Braille.

2 The Extended Definition of Language

From the point of view of learning we can give the definition of language as follows: It is for communication among people. The community speaking the given language has an identity. The perception is accomplished with some of the human sensory organs. The reproduction is done by a motoric program. The perception and the reproduction are controlled by a common, hierarchically structured mental dictionary. [1]

In spoken language, the perception is accomplished with hearing and the reproduction with speaking organs. In sign language perception is haptic in the case of a deaf-blind person. The difference between the spoken language and the Morse language is minor. The speech has three main characteristics: the rhythm, the energy and the frequency, the Morse is characterized only with rhythm. We can interpret Morse as extreme speech. Deaf-blind persons can percept vibrating Morse with their hand.

Hearing people perceive Morse language with their ears. Before they have to learn the "phonetics" of Morse characters, but they also have to learn whole words and

K. Miesenberger et al. (Eds.): ICCHP 2014, Part II, LNCS 8548, pp. 393–396, 2014.

phrases too. Hearing people learn spoken languages in a similar way. We have to build our mental dictionary which is a hierarchical structure. Deaf-blind people do the same with vibrating Morse.

Teaching Morse language we found, that different speeds must be learned separately. If somebody learns fast rhythm he or she has to learn slow rhythm too. PG had similar difficulties with vibrating Morse. See later the problem with "m" /--/ and "i" /../ in the next chapter.

3 The Process of Learning Morse Language

The most difficult part of creating the assistive device for PG seemed to be the task of teaching him the Morse language. We embossed for him the Hungarian Morse codes in Braille. We introduced a new code for the Space = AS /.-.../ (the code for wait in international Morse code), since the usual pause cannot be used in single-character cursoring mode. For simplicity we only have two levels of cursoring, the character-by-character and the word-by-word level.

PG learned the codes in a few weeks, but it was only a theoretical or "dry" knowledge. Learning language is effective in live practice, so we modified our Mobile SlateTalker (MOST for Android) program's text entry mode [2]. Text entering is done in Braille dot by dot. A single vibration indicates successful dot entry. A double vibration indicates clearing the Braille dot. Our deaf-blind learner could enter characters in Braille accurately after a few minutes of practising. He was motivated with this success very much.

Recognising Morse characters by the phone's vibration proved more difficult for him. Facilitating this process we introduced a control for changing the code speed. We suggested him to learn at a relatively high speed [4] and finally we found 15 characters/minute adequate as a general speed. Now he uses 10 characters/minute for unknown texts and 15 for known ones e.g. reading menu words. He also asked us to help him distinguish Dit-s from Dah-s, so we changed the weight from 1:3 to 1:4.

As a last resort, he has a haptic Braille support when reading in character-by-character mode: he can check every letter dot-by-dot in Braille mode. Touching any one of the dots of the Braille cell it vibrates if it is „raised".

It was an interesting experience when he first changed from a relatively high Morse code speed (15 characters/minute) to a low one (10 characters/minute). He recognized the code for "i" /../ as "m" /--/ several times. It underlines the correctness of our research about the necessity of building the mental dictionaries for different speeds [1]. We strengthened the motoric-control side of PG's Morse language knowledge using a relay buzzer and Morse key. The relay buzzer was not found satisfying, so we finally used vibrating motor with the Morse key.

In this video [7] you can see the learning process with PG using a Morse straight key and a vibrating motor. PG has problems understanding unknown Morse words. He asked to slow down and increase pause between characters sent. He recognizes his name sent by the first author, and answered sending his name. The communication between the two persons is done by speech and writing block letters in PG's hand, arm or shoulder. Sending with correct rhythm is always emphasized.

4 Developing the Special Version of the Mobile SlateTalker Program

- We chose an ordinary Android phone, installed MObile Slate-Talker on it and placed a special Braille mask over its touch screen.
- We decided to enable MOST to give haptic Morse feedback in the menus and for reading texts by character, word, sentence, etc.
- A special haptic feedback has been added to facilitate entering Braille cells dot by dot accurately.
- A so-called haptic Braille touch exploration mode has been developed to allow checking each individual Braille dot of the currently cursored character.
- The Morse code speed may be changed any time on the Braille mask.
- The Morse code weigh can be changed at compile time.

As a useful side-product, the new features may also be beneficial for the hearing blind users in extremely noisy or very quiet environments.

The entire MOST program with a fully-fledged haptic support seemed to be too high as an entry level for PG. We decided to create a special restricted program environment for him within MOST. In this environment, he only finds things he has acquainted with and he only has to use the skills he has already acquired during the weekly Morse sessions. As he learns something new, that particular feature is added very soon to this deaf-blind mode.

In this restricted environment, PG cannot get lost, and cannot activate functions unusable for deaf-blind (e.g., answering or placing phone calls, starting audio playback, etc.). He is prevented from venturing out to the uncharted waters of the MOST program and the Android system. Currently, incoming calls are immediately rejected and alert dialogs that happen to pop up accidentally are immediately dismissed programmatically.

The main turning point came in late December 2013. He was allowed to take home the specially programmed Android phone and could read and send SMS text messages all by his own. We witnessed (and still do) numerous occasions of his pleasure over his newly gained autonomy, as he gradually realizes how much he can achieve with an ordinary, off-the-shelf Android smartphone without the need of constantly relying on others' assistance.

Each week, PG comes up with a new demand for a feature he wants to be added. This is how just recently an intuitive method of easily replying text messages got built in the special environment for deaf-blind, and his ideas and demands keep coming. For instance, his latest assignment for us is a haptic alarm clock. A recently introduced new feature includes reporting the current time, date and battery charge level by haptic Morse digits and delimiters when a dedicated Info button is pressed.

In this video [5] PG is looking for the requested name (A András) in his phonebook. He can read the known names in Morse with a reasonable speed (15 characters/minute). You can hear the buzzing of the vibrating motor of the smartphone. The text-to-speech output is only used for debugging purpose. After he finds the requested name, he switches the program to text entering mode, where he enters characters in braille with vibrating feedback. After escaping from text entry, he instructs the program to send an SMS.

In the next video [6] PG demonstrates how he perceives Morse output pressing the Info key of the program. First he finds the time output, second he finds the date, and finally he finds the battery charging level 90 percent, which he says is enough.

5 Future Goals

PG uses his morse-braille vibrating phone every day. He has a reliable feedback and his phonebook is increasing. He asked to add full phonebook handling possibilities including searching functions. His second priority request was the alarm clock application.

In this final video [8] PG asks us to add a possibility to our program to send longer messages to his computer to be able to read them in braille. We can do that, but we warned him that he has to pay more to the mobile operator for the Internet traffic. We have to thank our deaf-blind interpreter Ildikó for her work in this project.

6 Conclusion

Dual Tactile Morse-Braille output is a very low cost and usable method for writing and reading SMS messages by a deaf-blind person. He could learn Morse characters and words in a relatively short period of time (3 months). Teaching Morse must be treated as teaching a language. Teaching the recognition of whole words is necessary as early as possible.

References

1. Arató, A., Markus, N., Juhasz, Z.: Speaking and understanding Morse language, speech technology and autism. In: Miesenberger, K., Karshmer, A., Penaz, P., Zagler, W. (eds.) ICCHP 2012, Part II. LNCS, vol. 7383, pp. 311–314. Springer, Heidelberg (2012)
2. Markus, N., Malik, S., Juhasz, Z., Arató, A.: Accessibility for the Blind on an Open-Source Mobile Platform. In: Miesenberger, K., Karshmer, A., Penaz, P., Zagler, W. (eds.) ICCHP 2012, Part II. LNCS, vol. 7383, pp. 599–606. Springer, Heidelberg (2012)
3. `http://www.tacmon.eu/new/`
4. `http://www.justlearnmorsecode.com/farnsworth.html`
5. `http://www.kfki.hu/~ha4aa/PG/SMS-sending.MOV`
6. `http://www.kfki.hu/~ha4aa/PG/Info-in-Morse.MOV`
7. `http://www.kfki.hu/~ha4aa/PG/TrainingMorse.MOV`
8. `http://www.kfki.hu/~ha4aa/PG/Requests.MOV`

Urgent Communication Method for Deaf, Language Dysfunction and Foreigners

Naotsune Hosono[1], Hiromitsu Inoue[2], Miwa Nakanishi[3], and Yutaka Tomita[4]

[1] Oki Consulting Solutions Co., Ltd., Shibaura, Minato-ku, Tokyo, Japan
keiolab@gmail.com
[2] Chiba Prefectural University of Health Sciences, Chiba, Japan
[3] Kogakuin University, Shinjuku, Tokyo, Japan
[4] Fujita Health University, Toyoake, Aichi, Japan

Abstract. This paper discusses a communication method with smart phones for deaf or language dysfunction people as well as foreigners at the urgent time of sudden sickness or fire in order to report to the nearest fire station. Such method is originally proposed by a hearing impaired person. Their appearances are the same in the daily life. However at the unexpected situation, they will be suddenly in trouble at such the occasion of disasters or accidents. The previous research, which was introduced at ICCHP 2010, proposed a method to create pictograms or icons referring to multiplex local sign languages with Multivariate Analysis (MVA). Those outcomes are drawn on a booklet to be held a dialogue between deaf and hearing people. This time they are implemented on a smart phone. Normally the usability is measured by the effectiveness, efficiency and satisfaction. Then this time the outcome is measured by the efficiency, that how quickly to report the fire station nearby. The evaluation gathering deaf people and a foreigner found that this method is about three times quicker to do the first report to the station comparing with text messaging on a smart phone.

Keywords: Inclusive Media, Context of Use, Computer Human Interface, Human Centred Design, Sensory Evaluation, Tablet Terminal.

1 Introduction

At the disaster of East Japan Earthquakes and Tsunami on 11 March 2011, there were nearly 15,000 victims including disabled people. In such a situation even phlegmatic person may upset and be lost cognitive and behave like dementia. Looking at the disaster the important information could not reach to the residents on the spot. This must be particularly serious problems for disabled people such as deaf, language dysfunction or foreigners who are difficult in bi-directional communication [1].

To solve such issues a booklet titled "SOS card" was produced and about 6,000 copies were distributed to the public facilities including local fire stations. The booklet is gathering pictograms and icons just menu like. Hearing impaired people have simply to point them at the time of communication [2,3]. There are about 790 fire stations in Japan and once equipped FAX machines for such people. Recently

K. Miesenberger et al. (Eds.): ICCHP 2014, Part II, LNCS 8548, pp. 397–403, 2014.

introducing a tablet terminal such as a typical smart phone is quite useful and improves their daily life. Considering such background, the "SOS card" is to be implemented on the smart phones such Android terminals [4].

Recently modern Information and Communication Technology (ICT) expands opportunities to implement accessible applications used by disabled people as inclusive media such as a tablet terminal with full functions; high speed processing, large memory size and remote communication. Previously those applications were rarely existential or quite expensive, however nowadays they are accessible with less expensive or sometimes free of charge.

2 Survey of the Previous Work

This paper is a successive research of "Context Analysis of Universal Communication through Local Sign Languages applying Multivariate Analysis" which was presented at ICCHP 2010 in Vienna [5]. The previous paper discussed a method to create pictograms or icons referring to multiplex local sign languages with the concept of context of use on dialogue with Multivariate Analysis (MVA). Since pictograms or icons are universal communication tools, Human Centred Design (HCD) [6] and context analysis by Persona model by Alan Cooper [7] are applied in the research. HCD is based on the context of use which is organized by four factors as user, product, task and environment in use [8]. The purpose of the previous research was to figure out a method to create meaningful pictograms or icons referring to several local sign languages (SL). The sign language is basically a communication method from one person to the other for hearing impaired persons.

The first step is to create two Personas with applying the Persona Model under HCD. A created Persona is a deaf person in a situation where he suffers a sudden illness while commuting in the morning, and is carried to the hospital by an ambulance. The next step is to extract words that are fundamentally essential to the dialogues of the scenarios [9]. The research is initially focused upon creating pictograms or icons to make dialogues since the fundamentals of sign language are hand shape, location and movement. This research references to a collection of animation figures consists of seven local sign languages of American (ASL), British (BSL), Chinese (CSL), French (FSL), Korean (KSL), Japanese (JSL), and Spanish (ESL).

Then the Correspondence Analysis of Multivariate Analysis (MVA) by statistic software; Statistical Package for Social Science (SPSS) is applied [10,11]. They are plotted that such as similar local sign languages are to be plotted closely on a plane [12]. In the characteristics of Correspondence Analysis, the subjects who have general and standard ideas are positioned in the centre, whereas those who have extreme or specialized ideas are positioned away from the centre. Following to the cycle process of HCD, the original designer is asked to summarize and design an animation like pictogram showing a few exclusive local sign languages by referring to the outcome by the sensory evaluation mentioned above.

The final step was validation of the outcome by the same manner as the first sensory evaluation step 4 above, and MVA is once again performed. The outcome including the newly designed pictogram is plotted with other seven local sign languages in order to prove and measure whether the newly created pictogram represents of the cluster.

The newly designed one will have represented related sign languages since it is plotted close to those sign languages. Whereas the other sign languages were plotted further down. In order to prove the outcome, Supplementary Treatment of MVA by SPSS is applied with adding newly designed one to the seven sign languages. These deployments of the plots are similar in seven and eight sign languages experiments.

In the previous research the followings are concluded:

- Newly designed animation pictograms are all positioned in the centre of the related local sign languages cluster.
- Even though almost of the subjects are different at the first and second experiment, the general outcome plot patterns hold similar patterns in space.
- In oriental sign languages of Japanese, Chinese, and Korean tend to be plotted closely together.

Through the proposed method, the relationship between selected words and local sign languages are initially explained by sensory evaluation of the subjects.

3 Implementation over the Tablet Terminal

The previous research outcomes are drawn by pictograms and icons with help of MVA. For instance ache portions are drawn in two dimensions. Ache depth and severe pain are in the third dimension. The hearing impaired and people will simply touch the designated pictogram or icons to communicate the remote support people in such urgent situation by ubiquitously carrying the tablet terminal with touch panel. The modern tablet terminals are equipped inclusive media with the following functions; Tap to select, Double tap to do scaling, Drag to jump, Flick or Swipe to move next page, Pinch in/out with double fingers, accelerate sensor to position upright, Photo browsing to display icons or pictograms, Backlight for dark place usage, GPS and Wi-Fi function to download the new contents.

Following to the human centred design process, the first approach is to observe the activities of telephone exchanges at command console in a fire station and analyzed the dialogue process at urgent situations in Figure 1 [13]. In general most of telephone reports are either fire conflagration or sudden illness. Then the following five processes to implement on the tablet terminal were extracted for the communication between a reporter in trouble and a lifesaver.

1. Registration of the face information of the reporter on the tablet terminal before urgent situation.
   There are plenty of preparation time to register such information; Name, Address, Age, Gender, Classification of the Disability, e-mail Address, Date of Birth, Anamnesis, Primary Care Hospital, and the Relatives Information, etc.
2. At the exact moment of urgent report.
   The most important matter at this moment is to report promptly to the nearest fire station. Applying the previous research result, selected words are drawn with pictograms or icons excluded time consuming text input to be easily used by hearing impaired people by simply to click them. The report includes exact GPS data of the location in order to find the reporter promptly by the lifesavers.

3. At the time of fire engine or ambulance dispatching to the location
   Since the hearing impaired people often complain this dispatch time without any communication. To ease their worries, bi-directional devising is prepared.
4. At the time to find the reporter location
   Many injured people are under the rubble in East Japan Earthquakes in 2011 and lifesavers were difficult to find out them. Since deaf people must face much more difficulties, a torch and whistle functions to let notice are implemented on the smart phone.
5. Dialogue on the spot
   Even at face to face communications with the lifesavers after reaching at the spot, such pictograms and icons will be useful since normally a few lifesaver understand sign language.

The product is referring to the user experience of usability by elderly people on Automated Teller Machine (ATM) considering the similarity in low cognitive at emergency situation and elderly people behavior [14,15]. There are three points in the guidance to design a tablet with a touch panel:

1. Make limited choice referring to "Magic Number" by G.A. Miller [16]
2. Change the screen explicitly
3. Make confirmation with step by step operation

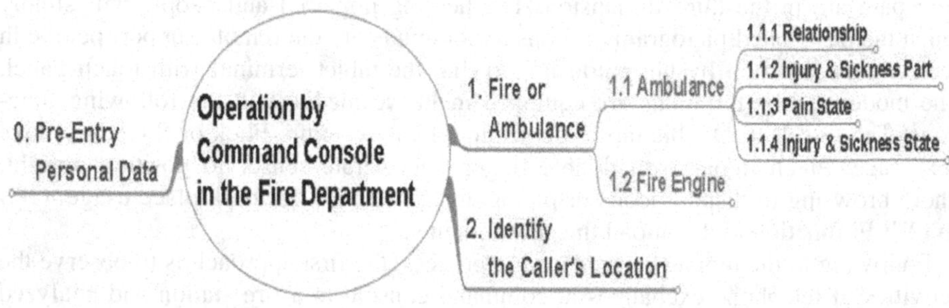

Fig. 1. Telephone exchanges at command console in a fire station and analyzed the dialogue process

4 Evaluation of the Produced Contents over the Tablet Terminal

A proposed application on the tablet terminal was evaluated by hearing impaired people in the manner of the usability test based on working hypothesis. The following six tasks were prepared to compare with applications between on the tablet terminal and on personal computer (PC). Those tasks requested the subjects virtually to call ambulance and fire brigades. The evaluation test was performed by seven hearing impaired participants and a foreigner (subjects) in total. All experiment instructions were informed to hearing impaired subjects by a sign interpreter. Subjects were allowed to use memo notes.

- Task-1: Filling out the pre-entry personal data
  A trial to fill out the personal data sheet such as name, address, age and one's history of disease, etc.
- Task-2: Fire report by the tablet terminal.
  This scenario is that "The forest is on fire. The reporter recognizes a flame but no fume. The one is safe since the one is away from the fire spot. There is no injury. Please help".
- Task-3: Fire report by text of e-mail with PC
  The scenario is "This building is on fire. My floor is different from the fire spot. The reporter cannot recognize flame but fume. There are some injuries. Please help".
- Task-4: Ambulance request by text of e-mail with PC
  The scenario is "Please call ambulance since the reporter was run over by a car. One is middle aged male. The reporter is conscious but the leg is broken with blooding. It is quite painful. One have once experienced fracture and took to surgery. Please deliver an ambulance soon".
- Task-5: Ambulance request by the tablet terminal
  The scenario is "The reporter's daughter is urgent sick. She is grown up and pregnant. She might be preterm birth. She is conscious but appeals her savior pain in the belly. She was once suffering from gallstones. Please deliver an ambulance soon".
- Task-6: Interview with filling out questionnaires
  After the evaluation the subjects are asked about usability of the tablet terminal with Semantic Differential (SD) Method.

The results must be analyzed under "the Context of Use" whose result is measured by the effectiveness, efficiency and satisfaction. This evaluation opportunity focused particularly on the efficiency with comparing two options between applying the tablet terminal and without it by text messaging. The efficiency result found that the first report time to reach the nearest fire station is three times quicker by using the terminal. The interview after the evaluation, many hearing impaired people pointed out that this tablet terminal service will ease their predicted mental concern at the urgent situation. This relates the basic concept of Satisfaction in the Context of Use or User Experience (UX).

5 Conclusion and Future Work

Currently about 20 screen contents on the tablet terminal are prepared by the Software Development Kit (SDK) of MIT APP Innovator and distributed onto Android touch panel terminal through DeployGete for the evaluation. The hearing impaired users are simply tapping the pictograms or icons on the sequences on the screen. The screen transition processes are based on the telephone dialogues of the command console of the Kasuga Onojo Nakagawa Fire Department in Kyushu Prefecture in Japan. Then the process is analyzed and drawn by MindMap software. The tablet terminal includes the cognitive design experience on ATM for elderly people since under such an urgent situation people would be upset and hard to communicate and behave a cognitive decline.

The research development of the tablet terminal is once started from the basis of standalone and now it is possible to connect to the remote lifesavers at fire station by Internet technology. The remaining issues are that currently it is implemented solely on the Android mobile terminals but it is necessary to support Apple-iOS users. The political issue is that the tablet terminal must be delivered free of charge for everybody. A day will come that this tablet terminal as accessible media will replace the commonly used FAX machines for particularly hearing impaired people, dysfunction, elderly people and foreign people.

Acknowledgements. This research is supported and funded by the Project organized by Fire and Disaster Management Agency under Ministry of Internal Affairs and Communications (MIC) of Japan. The basic idea comes from Mr. M. Suzuki of Architectural Association of Japanese DEAF (AAJD). Dr. H. Akatsu of Oki Electric Ind. Co., Ltd. introduced the cognitive design method on ATM for elderly people. Special thanks to Mr. T. Yamashita of Cosmocity who programmed software on the tablet terminal, as well as Mr. T. Inaba and Mr. F. Miyajima of Kasuga Onojo Nakagawa Fire Department in Fukuoka Prefecture in JAPAN and Mr. M. Nishijima of Oki Consulting Solutions Co., Ltd. at the system design and evaluation of the tablet terminal throughout this research.

References

1. Miki, H., Hosono, N.: Universal Design with Information Technology (Japanese version). Maruzen, Tokyo (2005)
2. Hosono, N., Inoue, H., Nagashima, Y., Tomita, Y.: Sensory Evaluation Method to Create Pictograms Based on Multiplex Sign Languages. In: ACHI 2013, Nice (2013)
3. Hosono, N., Miyajima, F., Inaba, T., Nishijima, M., Suzuki, M., Miki, H., Tomita, Y.: The Urgent Communication System for Deaf and Language Dysfunction People. In: Yamamoto, S. (ed.) HIMI/HCII 2013, Part II. LNCS, vol. 8017, pp. 269–274. Springer, Heidelberg (2013)
4. Hosono, N., Inoue, H., Miyajima, F., Inaba, T., Nishijima, M., Nakanishi, M., Tomita, Y.: Emergency Communication Tool for Deaf, Language Dysfunction and Foreigners. In: Encarnação, P., Azevedo, L., Gelderblom, G.J., Newell, A., Mathiassen, N.E. (eds.) Assistive Technology: From Research to Practice. Assistive Technologies Research Series, vol. 33, pp. 1096–1100. IOS Press, Amsterdam (2013)
5. Hosono, N., Inoue, H., Nagashima, Y.: Context Analysis of Universal Communication through Local Sign Languages Applying Multivariate Analysis. In: Miesenberger, K., Klaus, J., Zagler, W., Karshmer, A. (eds.) ICCHP 2010, Part II. LNCS, vol. 6180, pp. 200–204. Springer, Heidelberg (2010)
6. International Organization for Standardization: ISO9241-210 (former 13407:1999), Ergonomics Human-centered design processes for interactive systems (2010)
7. Cooper, A.: About Face 3. Wiley, Indianapolis (2007)
8. International Organization for Standardization: ISO9241-11, Ergonomic requirements for office work with visual display terminals (VDTs), Guidance on usability (1998)
9. International Organization for Standardization: ISO9241-110, Ergonomic requirements for office work with visual display terminals (VDTs), Dialogue principles (2006)
10. Field, A.: Discovering Statistics Using SPSS, 3rd edn. Sage Publications, Thousand Oaks (2009)

11. SPSS: Categories in Statistical Package for Social Science ver.18, SPSS (2009)
12. Hosono, N., Inoue, H., Tomita, Y.: Sensory analysis method applied to develop initial machine specification. Measurement 32, 7–13 (2002)
13. Endsley, M.: Towards a Theory of Situation Awareness in Dynamic Systems. Human Factors 37(1), 32–64 (1995)
14. Akatsu, H., Miki, H., Hosono, N.: Designing 'Adaptive' ATM based on universal design. In: Proceedings of 2nd Int. Conf. for Universal Design in Kyoto 2006, pp. 793–800 (2006)
15. Akatsu, H., Miki, H., Hosono, N.: Design principles based on cognitive aging. In: Jacko, J.A. (ed.) Human-Computer Interaction, Part I, HCII 2007. LNCS, vol. 4550, pp. 3–10. Springer, Heidelberg (2007)
16. Miller, G.A.: The Magical Number Seven, Plus or Minus Two: Some Limits on our Capacity for Processing Information. Psychological Review 63, 81–97 (1956)
17. Hartson, R., Pyla, P.S.: The UX Book: Process and Guidelines for Ensuring a Quality User Experience. Morgan Kaufmann Publishers, Waltham (2012)

Building an Application for Learning the Finger Alphabet of Swiss German Sign Language through Use of the Kinect

Phuoc Loc Nguyen, Vivienne Falk, and Sarah Ebling

Institute of Computational Linguistics, Zurich, Switzerland
{phuocloc.nguyen,vivienne.falk}@uzh.ch,
ebling@cl.uzh.ch

Abstract. We developed an application for learning the finger alphabet of Swiss German Sign Language. It consists of a user interface and a recognition algorithm including the Kinect sensor. The official Kinect Software Development Kit (SDK) does not recognize fingertips. We extended it with an existing algorithm.

Keywords: Sign language, Swiss German Sign Language, Finger Alphabet, Kinect, Learning Environment.

1 Introduction

Swiss German Sign Language (*Deutschschweizerische Gebärdensprache*, DSGS) is the sign language of the German-speaking area of Switzerland. We developed an application for learning the finger alphabet of this language. It consists of a user interface and a recognition algorithm including the Kinect sensor. The official Kinect Software Development Kit (SDK) does not recognize fingers. We extended it with an existing algorithm to recognize the palm of the hand, the contour of the hand, and the fingertips.

2 Automatic Sign Language Recognition through the Kinect: Related Work

The aim of the DictaSign project [2] was to make online communication easier for Deaf people by means of sign language avatars. During the project, three prototypes were developed: a search-by-example application, a sign language translator, and a sign language wiki. For the search-by-example application, the user signs a phrase in front of the Kinect, the sign sequence is recognized, and possible matches to the input are presented. The user can select the appropriate phrase or add a new phrase. This application was trained for German Sign Language and Greek Sign Language. The sign language translator works similarly: The user signs a phrase which is recognized by the computer with the help of the Kinect. Subsequently, the recognized phrase is shown in four other sign languages. The sign language wiki has the same functionality as a spoken language

K. Miesenberger et al. (Eds.): ICCHP 2014, Part II, LNCS 8548, pp. 404–407, 2014.

wiki, with the difference that here, an avatar presents the content. [1] used the Kinect to recognize Chinese Sign Language.

3 User Interface

To create the learning interface for our application, we used Microsoft's Visual Studio Express 2010. The interface consists of four windows: a main window named *Gebärdensprach-Lernumgebung* ('Sign language learning environment') and three subwindows named *Wissenswertes* ('Useful to know'), *Dein Name* ('Your name'), and *Fingeralphabet* ('Finger alphabet'). The subwindow *Wissenswertes* conveys general information about sign languages, in particular, about Swiss German Sign Language. In the subwindow *Dein Name* ('Your name'), the user can enter a name or word. Upon pressing a button, the corresponding finger signs in Swiss German Sign Language appear. For images of the hand shapes, we relied on a freeware font package[1].

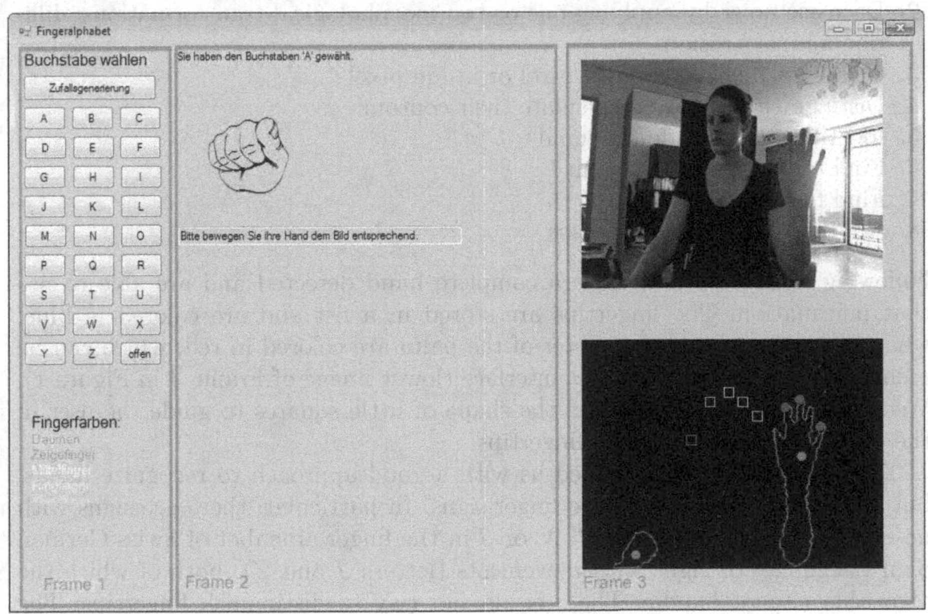

Fig. 1. Window *Fingeralphabet* ('Finger alphabet')

The subwindow *Fingeralphabet* ('Finger alphabet', Figure 1) is where the recognition through the Kinect takes place. In Frame 1, the user can choose a letter by pressing the appropriate button. Alternatively, he or she can generate a random letter. Following the selection of a letter, the appropriate finger sign and a text field appear in Frame 2. In this frame, instructions on how to perform

[1] http://www.fontspace.com/tanja-schulz/zoefingerabc-regular

the sign are also given. The Kinect camera creates two images in Frame 3: The upper image shows the user in 2D (color view), the lower is a live tracker of the hand (depth view).

4 Automatic Recognition of Swiss German Sign Language Using the Kinect

The fact that the Kinect is able to provide depth and color data simultaneously made it one of the most important milestones in sign language recognition. The Kinect is capable of obtaining information in a resolution of 640x480 with 30 frames per second. We used the Xbox version without near mode.[2] The Kinect itself can recognize up to six skeletons, but not in detail. The official SDK has no function to recognize fingers. We therefore extended it with the algorithm of [3] to recognize the palm of the hand, the contour of the hand, and the fingertips.[3] The algorithm is divided into eight steps:

1. Define the nearest and farthest point for the Kinect to recognize
2. Decrease noise by applying one or two morphological transformations: dilation and/or erosion
3. Classify a pixel as contour pixel or inside pixel
4. Distinguish hands and calculate their contour
5. Identify pixels inside the hand
6. Find the center of the palm
7. Find the fingertips
8. Allocate points in a 3D space

Following these steps, we have a complete hand detected and are able to use that information: The fingertips are stored in a list and are colored in blue, while the contours and the center of the palm are colored in red, which can be seen in the depth stream in our interface (lower image of Frame 3 in Figure 1). We introduced anchor points in the shape of little squares to guide the user in the process of positioning the fingertips.

The algorithm of [3] provided us with a good approach to recognize hands, but it does not easily recognize finger signs. In particular, there are signs with no extended fingers (e.g., *E*, *M*, *N*, or *S* in the finger alphabet of Swiss German Sign Language) or signs with movements (letters *J* and *Z*), both of which the algorithm cannot handle. There is also no way to distinguish fingertips: The algorithm generates a list of fingertips from left to right. In cases where one or more fingers are not spread out, the list is not complete and the indices for the fingers would not be correct anymore. In other words, we cannot determine whether a finger is in its designated square. Therefore, we just tested whether a fingertip was inside a square at all. If this was the case, the color of the fingertip changed from blue to green.

---

[2] The near mode allows the device to get reasonable values in a short distance of 40 to 300cm instead of 80 to 400cm.

[3] `http://frantracerkinectft.codeplex.com/`

5 Outlook

The steps to recognize the hand and its fingertips outlined in Section 3 are quite performance-heavy. As our next step, we will improve this part. After that, we will work on improving the actual recognition. The algorithm we applied looks for a specific angle to identify fingertips; if the fingertips are inside the palm, the situation is as if there were no fingers. We plan to include a second camera to provide information from an additional angle. At the same time, we will try to better exploit the 3D information provided by the Kinect. We will perform our experiments with the new version of the Kinect that was recently released.

A more distant goal is to extend our application so that full signed sentences may be recognized. For this, it will be necessary to combine hand/finger recognition with face and body recognition.

References

1. Chai, X., Li, G., Chen, X., Zhou, M., Wu, G., Li, H.: VisualComm: A tool to support communication between deaf and hearing persons with the Kinect. In: Proceedings of the 15th International ACM SIGACCESS Conference on Computers and Accessibility, ASSETS 2013, pp. 76:1–76:2. ACM, New York (2013), http://doi.acm.org/10.1145/2513383.2513398
2. Efthimiou, E., Fotinea, S.E., Hanke, T., Glauert, J., Bowden, R., Braffort, A., Collet, C., Maragos, P., Lefebvre-Albaret, F.: Sign language technologies and resources of the Dicta-Sign project. In: Proceedings of the 5th Workshop on the Representation and Processing of Sign Languages: Interactions between Corpus and Lexicon, LREC 2012, Istanbul, Turkey, pp. 37–45 (2012)
3. Trapero Cerezo, F.: 3D Hand and Finger Recognition using Kinect. Tech. rep., Universidad de Granada (UGR), Spain (2012)

TerpTube: A Signed Language Mentoring Management System

Deborah I. Fels[1], Daniel Roush[2], Paul Church[1], Martin Gerdzhev[1], Tara Stevens[2], and Ellen Hibbard[1]

[1] Ryerson University, Toronto, Ontario, Canada
{dfels,pchurch,ehibbard,mgerdzhe}@ryerson.ca
[2] Eastern Kentucky University, USA
{daniel.roush,tara.stevens}@eku.edu

Abstract. Signed language interpreter training programs are necessary to support the training of professional signed language interpreters who facilitate the communication between Deaf and hearing people. However, these programs have few tools that provide asynchronous or non-face-to-face means of giving feedback to or communication with learners in the signed language by peers, instructors or mentors. TerpTube has been designed to support these asynchronous activities through the use of video and signlinking within a computerized mentoring management system. Initial user studies show that mentors and mentees/students found TerpTube easy to use to create and post video material and provide commentary on that video in American Sign Language without the use of text. Having the ability to provide comments to comments was thought to be a good idea but made the user interface confusing.

1 Introduction

In order to facilitate communication between Deaf and hearing interlocutors, professional signed language interpreters are commonly used and often legally required as intermediaries [1,2,3]. Preparing interpreters for professional service requires that they develop high-levels of fluency in their working languages. Examples of these language pairs include American Sign Language (ASL) and Spoken English or Quebec Sign Language (LSQ) and Spoken French [1]. Signed languages are visual/gestural/spatial languages that typically do not have a standard written system and are not easily represented in writing systems developed for spoken languages [4,5]. Learning a signed language requires a student to use the visual, gestural and spatial modalities rather than written, aural, or spoken ones. This usually means that signed language interpreter training programs rely on face-to-face language instruction and make extensive use of video language materials instead of written texts.

[1] Signed languages are natural languages that are not based on the surrounding spoken language and are not universal. For example, British Sign Language and American Sign Language are mutually unintelligible despite the fact that they are both surrounded by spoken English in their respective countries.

K. Miesenberger et al. (Eds.): ICCHP 2014, Part II, LNCS 8548, pp. 408–414, 2014.

People who are interested in becoming professional interpreters are typically not yet native or fluent signers and therefore must become proficient in a signed language as well as develop the ability to interpret between their working languages. In order to meet the growing demand for interpreters, academic programs exist in universities and colleges to educate and train students in language, Deaf culture, and interpretation practices. As is common at these institutions, students must complete assignments, receive feedback from instructors and peers, practice, be evaluated and have access to learning materials [6]. However, because students are still developing fluency in their second language, preparing them for professional-level service by the end of their academic training is challenging. Developing appropriate language teaching methods and materials is also challenging. For signed language learning using written text (where the written text is a different language such as English) for these activities is less desirable [7]. Rather, using video, which can record signed languages, is optimal due to the visual nature of the language. Learning management systems such as Blackboard are not designed to support video in this way and, as a result, interpreting instructors often turn to online public services such as YouTube or Deafvideo.TV. However, these public video services are not designed to support educational or language mentoring tasks such as turning in assignments, uploading and downloading content, grading and providing feedback for a specific class. Managing access for students and instructors in specific courses, or for informal language mentoring through these services are also difficult.

In this paper a system called TerpTube that has been designed as a signed language mentoring management system is described. TerpTube provides the functionality to support instructors, mentors, and students in sign language interpreting programs and in the wider language community, to upload video content, make comments on that content and associate those comments with specific moments in the video, reply to comments and organize groups into mentors/instructors and mentees. Mentors/instructors and mentees have different roles and as such have access to different functionality. Preliminary qualitative results are also presented from an initial usability study involving nine mentors and mentees.

2 System Design

The main purpose of TerpTube is to provide software tools for supporting American Sign Language (ASL) and English-ASL interpreter education (although it could easily accommodate other language pairs such as French-LSQ, French-LSF, English-BSL, etc.). An important issue in interpreter training is finding ways to asynchronously provide feedback in ASL on submitted ASL assignments. In addition, having opportunities for Deaf community members, students in different cohorts, teaching assistants and (hearing or Deaf) instructors to act as ASL mentors is essential in interpreter training. Presently these activities are accomplished using a variety of techniques and technologies ranging from synchronous (face-to-face) in class or tutorial sessions to attempting to use tools such as YouTube to providing text-based feedback. Most of these techniques are not easily doable in ASL and are not accessible by Deaf community members who have a vested interest in interpreter training. For instance, there are no standard language tags for signed languages[2] in the YouTube language filter [8]. TerpTube is specifically designed using inclusive design concepts that preference visual media to meet the linguistic and instructional needs of teachers and students of ASL. It is being developed and designed by a team of ASL and interpretation teachers in partnership with inclusive design software engineers.

The dominant technologies for the TerpTube interface are video, graphics and signlinking (for an explanation of signlinking see [7], [9]. All components of TerpTube are available as video and/or graphics instead of text although text can optionally be used for titles or names, or for feedback/comments if necessary. Target users for TerpTube are students in interpreter education, instructors, Deaf community members participating in the education as mentors, and teaching assistants. Users are classified as either mentees or mentors and will have different options available to them depending on these roles; mentors are the users who will be providing feedback to mentees. A person can also occupy both roles, for example, a student in her third year of a program can be a mentor to first year students and can be mentored (take on a mentee role) by fourth year students.

Once a user has logged into TerpTube they have a number of options: 1) create and access Forums; 2) create and join Groups; 3) create and access video logs; and 4) access member's directory to change user profile, add/delete members to friends list. Forums allow content to be organized into general categories, while Groups connect users with similar interests or goals and allow mass communication. A vlog is a personal video blog where users create content and share with friends. Members have access to a directory that allows them to search for other mentors or mentees, add other members to their friend list, and edit their user profile to highlight their ASL expertise and specialties.

Figure 1 shows the opening page of TerpTube once a user has logged in. One of the most important features of TerpTube is the ability of mentees and mentors carry out the training activities using ASL. As seen in Figure 2, a mentee can post an ASL assignment in his Forum. Mentors that are members of the mentee group, can then view the assignment, video record comments in ASL and insert them at the applicable location/time in the assignment. The location of the comment is notated on the density bar of the original ASL assignment video and the video comment appears beside it. The mentee can then add video comments in response to the first comment and so on. Comments can also be text-based or can be uploaded as a separate file and will still appear in conjunction with the original assignment video.

3 User Evaluation

The research questions for the user evaluation component of the TerpTube project are:

1. What are the usability issues of the TerpTube interface and is there a difference between mentor and mentee perspectives?
2. What supports are expected from mentors/mentees for providing feedback on video-based ASL content generated as part of interpreter training?

---

[2] "Signed languages" is an emerging term to refer to different visual/gestural languages such as American Sign Language and to dispel the misperceptions that there is one universal sign language.

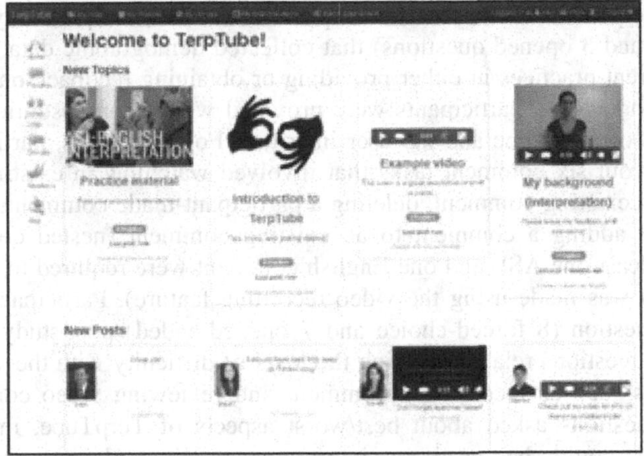

Fig. 1. Opening page of TerpTube after user logged in

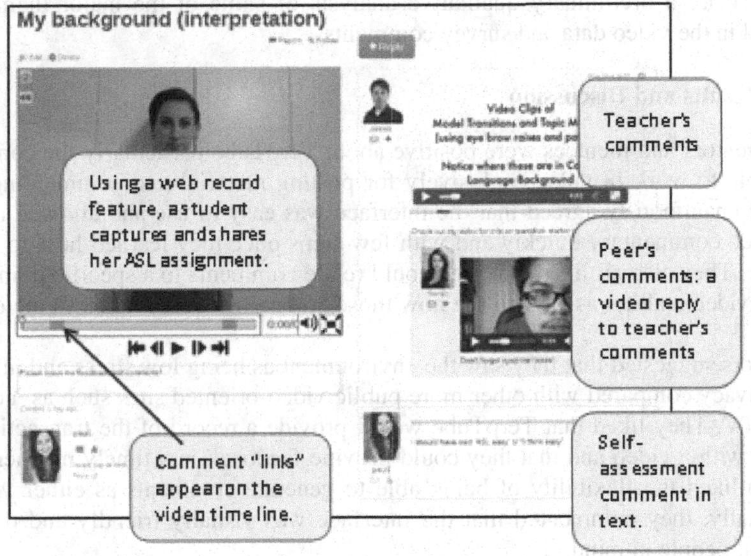

Fig. 2. Example of student assignment video with instructor comments

3.1 Methodology

Four Deaf mentors/instructors and five hearing mentees/students (five female, four male) from two signed language interpreter training programs were recruited to evaluate the usability of TerpTube. Participants ranged in age between 18 and 60+ years. Self-rated computer skills ranged from intermediate to advanced where advanced meant having some programming skills. Social media or video based technology use ranged from once a month to weekly for mentors to daily for most mentees.

Study participants were asked to complete a 24 question pre-study survey (21 forced-choice and 3 opened questions) that collected demographic data and information about current practices in either providing or obtaining feedback on assignments and student work. Next, participants were provided with a demonstration of the different features of TerpTube and the user interface. Following this, participants were asked to carry out six comment tasks that involved watching an existing video and then editing an existing comment, deleting a participant-made comment, making new comments and adding a comment to an existing comment (nested comment). For comments, at least one ASL and one English comment were required to be made (the ASL comment was made using the video recording feature). Participants then completed a 15 question (8 forced-choice and 7 opened-ended) post-study survey. The forced-choice questions related to rating the level of difficulty with the various TerpTube functions such as recording a comment and reviewing video comments. The open-ended questions asked about best/worst aspects of TerpTube, improvements, how the tool could be used in interpreter training classes and advantages/disadvantages of using TerpTube for video assignments. All sessions were video recorded all keystrokes and mouse movements were logged. The data presented in this paper are a preliminary qualitative analysis of some of the major themes that appeared in the video data and survey comments.

3.2 Results and Discussion

All of mentors and mentees were positive about TerpTube particularly the concept of being able to work in video exclusively for posting material and commenting on it. They all unanimously agreed that the interface was easy to use and allowed users to post video commentary quickly and with few steps once they learned how to use the interface. They also all liked that they could relate comments to a specific point in the original video and it was easy to see how those comments were related to the original video.

Mentors suggested that they saw the environment as being low stress and affording more privacy compared with other more public video-oriented sites such as YouTube or DeafTV. They liked that TerpTube would provide a record of the transactions associated with a video and that they could provide feedback in a timely manner. Mentors also liked the flexibility of being able to generate comments as either video or text. Finally, they commented that the interface was visually friendly and designed with Deaf people in mind.

Mentees said that they liked being able to submit their work from any Internet-enabled computer and that they did not need to use an on-campus server. They also suggested that TerpTube may be advantageous to students who were shy in class as they would not be put on the spot to perform but could take the time to make a high-quality video. Wang [10] suggests that video enables online learners to be more confident and expressive. In addition, he suggests that having facial expressions and body language available through video provides a more personal method of communicating with online students compared with text or audio communication. Signed languages are visual languages and interlocutors must use the visual channel in order to send and receive communication messages. There would appear to be similarities regarding the benefits of video between sign language interpreting learners and online learners.

Mentors and mentees found different aspects of TerpTube that needed improvement. Specifically, mentors were concerned about the cost of the system and implementing it at their institutions. Cost was not discussed during the study and perhaps they thought that a complicated video-based system would require more computing hardware that was available at their institutions. They also suggested that teaching students how to use TerpTube may be cumbersome and time consuming. Mentees said that it seemed to take a long time to learn how to use it and that might be difficult for some students. Learning to use any new computer-based educational application requires the development of proper learning materials. As such, the unique visually-oriented interface provided for TerpTube may need extra training materials so students can understand the meaning of its visual elements and novel functionality such as the signlinking feature. While efforts have been made to reduce the cognitive load for using the interface as recommended by [11], it does not follow the conventions of text-based interface designs. For example as seen in Figure 1, there are few text descriptions unless added by the user (e.g., titles, optional text comments, etc.), commenting and comment placement is accomplished via a time-line based interface and visual signed language oriented, icons provide most of the button or function labels.

As most of the students in interpreter training programs would likely be more accustom to text oriented interfaces such as those available for common web browsers and office productivity software, specific training materials that address these differences must be developed. However, mentors and mentees did not require excessive amounts of time to become familiar with the TerpTube interface and functionality, and were able to successfully carry out the main tasks within the 45 minute time allocated to this part of the study. To deploy TerpTube in any organization would require proper documentation and demonstration material to be developed. Particular attention should be paid to the functions of signlinking and the nesting of comments capability. Finally, they wanted all bugs to be worked out before deploying it in their institutions.

Mentees suggested that the nested commenting interface (comment on a comment) was confusing. As a result of this concern, TerpTube has made formatting modifications to make the comment hierarchy easier to see. An important comment made by mentees was that they thought that students should be required to post comments in ASL (as video) and not be allowed to use text. Mentors, however, liked the option of using either text or video. Restricting the use of text on TerpTube could be a course management function rather than a software function. Allowing an instructor to customize TerpTube as video only for his/her course could be a future development for the software.

4 Conclusion

The basic functionality of TerpTube of being able to use video to post, comment on and provide feedback to either the posts or comments seems to be a highly desirable tool for students/mentees and instructors/mentors in the signed language training programs participating in our user study. In addition, it would seem that being able to use either video or text to provide feedback is acceptable to instructors or mentors but that students/mentees prefer video commentary. Finally, mentors and mentees all suggested the appropriate training materials would be required in order to take full advantage of TerpTube. Future work on TerpTube involves ensuring that all bugs are removed from the software tool, ensuring that all functionality is completed and that training materials in ASL are generated. Further user testing and longitudinal evaluation within actual courses are required before TerpTube can be made widely available to interpreter training programs.

Acknowledgements. Funding is generously provided by US Department of Education, National Institute on Disability and Rehabilitation Research, the Social Sciences Humanities Council of Canada, and the Graphics, Animation and New Media (GRAND) Centre of Excellence. We also gratefully acknowledge the interpreter training programs and participants from Eastern Kentucky University, and George Brown College in Toronto, Canada.

References

1. Canadian Association for the Deaf (CAD). Interpreting. Canadian Association of the Deaf, `http://cad.ca/interpreting.php` [Cited: January 31, 2014]
2. National Association of the Deaf (NAD). Public accomodations. National Association of the Deaf, `http://nad.org/issues/civil-rights/ada/public-accommodations` [Cited: January 31, 2014]
3. Napier, J.: Sign language interpreter training, testing, and accreditation: An international comparison. American Annals of the Deaf 149, 350–359 (2004)
4. Lucas, C.: Methods for studying sign languages. In: Bayley, R., Cameron, R., Lucas, C. (eds.) The Oxford Handbook of Sociolinguistics, pp. 280–298. Oxford University Press, Oxford (2013)
5. Metzger, M., Roy, C.B.: The first three years of a three-year grant: When a research plan doesn't go as planned. In: Nicodemus, B., Swabey, L. (eds.) Advances in Interpreting Research Inquiry in Action, pp. 59–84. John Benjamins, Amsterdam (2011)
6. Sawyer, D.: Fundamental aspects of interpreter education: Curriculum and assessment. John Benjamins, Amsterdam (2004)
7. Roush, D.: Universal Design in technology used in interpreter education. International Journal of Interpreter Education 2, 25–40 (2010)
8. Hibbard, E., Fels, D.I.: The vlogging phenomena: A Deaf perspective. In: Dundee: ASSETS 2011, pp. 59–66 (2011)
9. Fels, D.I., Richards, J., Hardman, J., Lee, D.G.: Sign language web pages. American Annals of the Deaf 151, 423–433 (2006)
10. Wang, Y.: Supporting synchronous distance language learning with desktop videoconferencing. Language Learning & Technology 8, 90–121 (2004)
11. Oviatt, S.: Human-centred design meets cognitive load theory. In: Multimedia 2006, Santa Barbara, pp. 871–880 (2006)

Collaborative Gaze Cues and Replay for Deaf and Hard of Hearing Students

Raja Kushalnagar and Poorna Kushalnagar

Rochester Institute of Technology,
Rochester, New York, USA
http://www.rit.edu/avd

Abstract. Deaf and Hard of Hearing students who use visual accommodations face difficulties in following multimedia lectures due to the delay in visual translation and dividing attention between simultaneous visuals. As a result, deaf students miss information. We address these difficulties with two approaches: visual cues and live replay in recorded lectures. Our analysis found that when deaf students view the lecture videos with cues, they show less delay in switching to the active visual information source and report high satisfaction with the cues. The students who liked the cues were more likely to demonstrate reduction in delay time associated with shifting visual attention. Similarly, when deaf students used gaze controlled replay with lecture videos, they miss less information and report high satisfaction with live replay.

Keywords: Accessible Technology, Educational Technology, DHH Users.

1 Introduction

Deaf and hard of hearing (deaf) students usually require visual accommodations to follow lectures. Although accommodation services such as interpreters and captions improve access to spoken information for deaf students, significant but subtle barriers remain. First, there is a *delay* issue where as the accommodations provider has to listen, understand and rapidly present the information to the student. Second, there a *split attention* issue where the student is forced to choose and switch between interpreter/captions and the lecture visual (e.g., slides). Third, there is an excessive *cognitive load* issue when students spend extra effort putting together the split and delayed information.

These issues are especially acute in some fields like mathematics, science and engineering, which make heavy use of detailed visuals and explain via sequential steps. Hearing viewers do not face these issues, as they are able to look at their screens and listen to the simultaneous spoken explanation. Deaf viewers, on the other hand, in addition to the delay and split attention issues, have to look away from the visual translation of speech to search and observe details in the lecture visual. This puts them at risk of losing information, as the failure to understand a single sentence can be enough to slow down or even derail learning. Deaf students spend less time watching the course materials and ultimately gained less information in class, than their hearing peers [7],[5].

K. Miesenberger et al. (Eds.): ICCHP 2014, Part II, LNCS 8548, pp. 415–422, 2014.

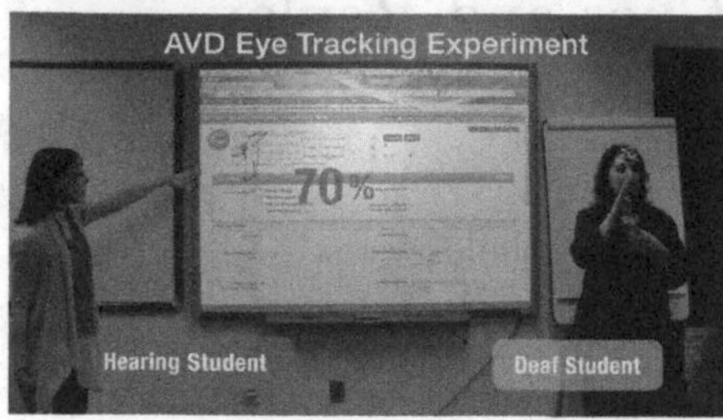

(a) The hearing viewer spends the majority of time (in this video, around 70%) watching the demonstration on the screen while listening. The hearing student has sufficient time to understand the demonstration on the screen.

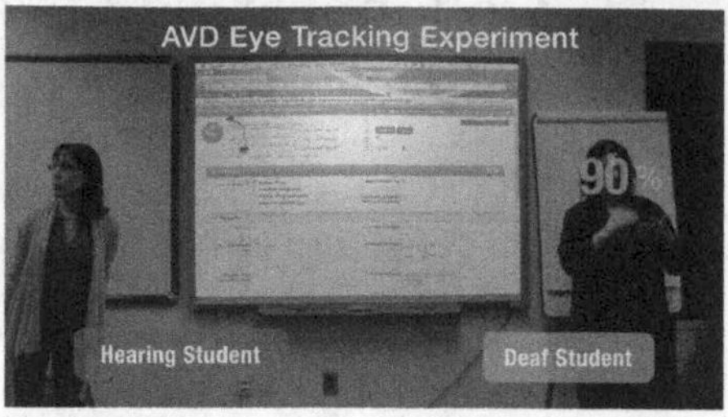

(b) The deaf viewer spends majority of the time (in this video, around 90%) watching the interpreter and occasionally shifts gaze to the demonstration. The deaf student lacks time to understand the demonstration screen.

Fig. 1. Differences in eye-gaze patterns between hearing and deaf students during the process of viewing multimedia lectures

2 Related Work

Deaf students spend less time watching the slides or teacher, than their hearing counterparts as shown in Figure 1. Previous studies have shown that deaf students look at the instructor 10% of the time as shown in Figure 1b and on the slides 14% of the time [3], as compared to hearing students who looked at the slides for 63% of the time and 29% of the time on the instructor as shown in Figure 1a. Other studies have reported similar numbers for deaf students' viewing percentages on the instructor and slides respectively: 15% and 22% reported by Marschark [8], and 12% and 18% reported by Cavender et al [1].

3 Accessible Computing Aids

The delay, split attention and cognitive load barriers are difficult to address without accessible technology aids. The flexibility of accessible computing leads to multiple approaches that can be combined to address these barriers. We explore the efficacy of two technical aids: visual cues and replay.

3.1 Visual Accessibility of Audiovisual Information

Audiovisual information with visual accessibility (i.e., sign language interpreters or captions) may result in cognitive overload, especially in information-dense contexts. This overload is a major reason why deaf students get less out of classroom lectures than their hearing peers [8]. Therefore, accessible multimedia that includes visual representation of the audio stream must be presented in a way that reduces the effects of visual dispersion and cognitive overload [2],[4]. Prior research shows that hearing students benefit from combined visual and auditory

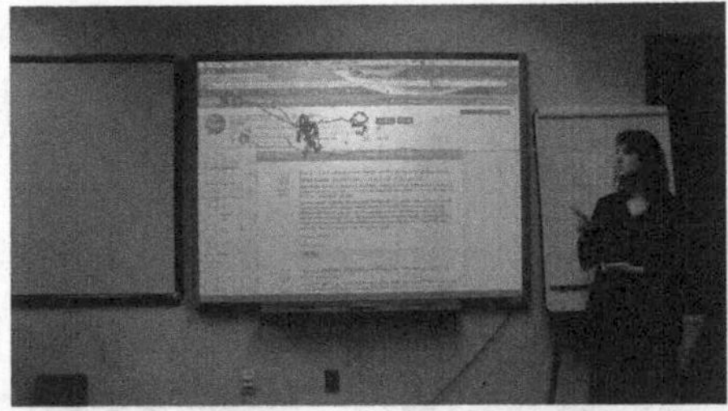

(a) The hearing viewer (red) follows the demonstration on the screen while listening; the deaf viewer (pink) follows the interpreter and then shifts gaze to the demonstration

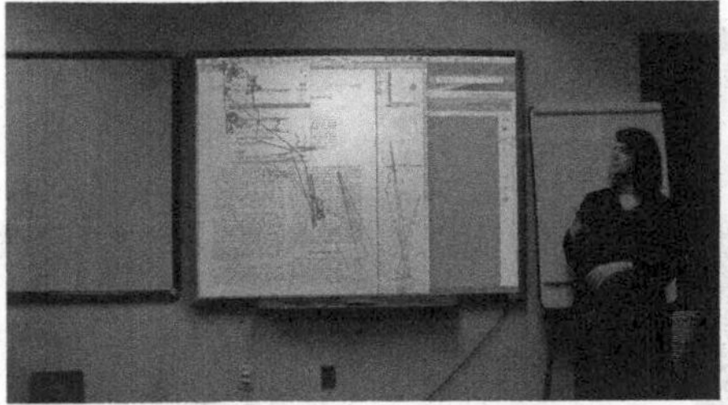

(b) The hearing viewer (red) tracks what the teacher is saying. The deaf viewer (pink) is not able to track and searches the screen for the current focus of the demonstration.

Fig. 2. Differences in eye-gaze patterns between hearing and deaf students during the process of viewing multimedia lectures

materials [1] and multi-modal classrooms are now becoming the norm. The information in many lectures is not presented in a way that corresponds to deaf viewers' cognitive abilities. True accessibility provides equal access to information, which would be true only if attention resources and speed of information processing remained constant across individuals and situations. In addition, students often encounter visual noise, such as line of sight interference, obstruction or poor lighting. Visual noise can be a mere annoyance for hearing students, but is rarely so for deaf students.

Figure 2 illustrates both problems: delay and search. In Figure 2a, the teacher is demonstrating the steps needed to search for a library resource. In the three-second time-lapse snap shot of the deaf and hearing students' eye gaze paths, there is a clear difference between their eye gaze path. In Figure 2a, the hearing student's eye-gaze is closely following a demonstration step along with the teacher's auditory explanation. On the other hand, the deaf student's eye-gaze is initially focused on the interpreter. A couple of seconds later the deaf student realizes the next demonstration step has occurred and belatedly switches gaze to the screen as shown. Then, the student has to deal with a search problem: as shown in Figure 2b, the student spends extra time searching for the mouse pointer and obtaining for contextual information.

3.2 Nonverbal Cues

Nonverbal cues can be critical for comprehension. Suppose the slide has multiple lines as shown in Figure 3a. Here, the teacher points at a specific line and simultaneously states "This sequence will be on the test", and then immediately flips to the next slide. A deaf student who is watching the interpreter and not the teacher, will catch the fact that a sequence will be asked on the test. But the student will not know which sequence is being discussed. On the other hand, a hearing student who is looking at the teacher will be able to determine which line

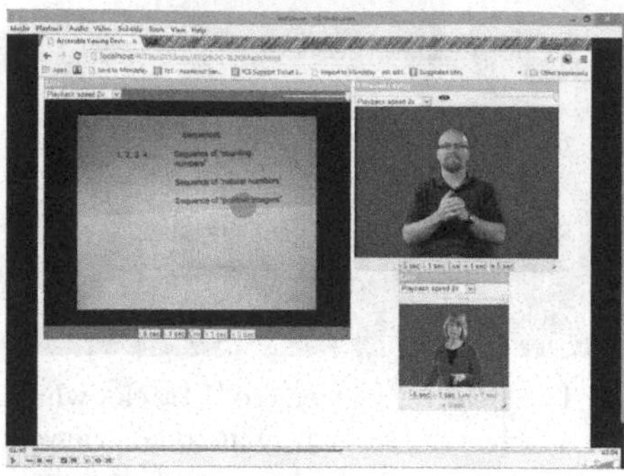

(a) A pre-recorded large transparent cue becomes visible when the viewer looks at the lecture visuals window

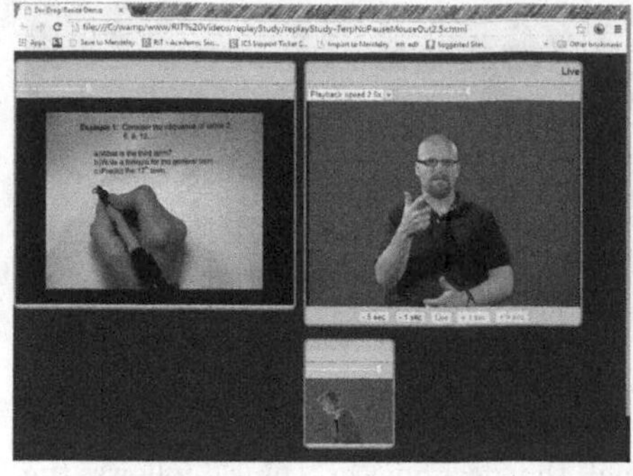

(b) The interpreter video pauses when the viewer gaze no longer is in the window, and resumes at a fast rate when the viewer's gaze returns to that window

Fig. 3. Gaze Cue and Replay Interface

is being referenced. If the teacher follows universal design principles, the teacher would avoid vague references and be more specific in each modality. For example, the teacher could say: "The sequence of positive integers will be on the test", but many teachers either do not know, or continue to use nonverbal references out of habit. As such, the prevalence of nonverbal cues in lectures imposes an additional barrier for deaf students in managing information-rich lectures with audio-visual cues. They have to rely on scanning their environment for visual information.

3.3 Visual Cues

We explore whether visual cues can mimic the functionality of non-verbal cues and guide the viewers' attention. Visual cues have been shown to quickly show who is talking, or to highlight the active part of the visual (slides or demonstration) as shown in Figure 3.

3.4 Live Replay

Students must orient to see, but do not need to do so to listen. One implication is that interpreters know students miss information when not looking. They tend to pause when students look away and summarize the missed information when they resume looking at the interpreter. However, if there is more than one deaf student in the class, the interpreter cannot pause unless all students look away at the same time, which is unlikely. By providing real-time replay, a student could look at the slide and then go to the interpreter screen and back up a few seconds to catch any auditory information that they missed and fast-forward to the current time.

4 Evaluation

We implemented a collaborative gaze interface, AVD-Gaze. The AVD-Gaze interface has two components: a gaze recorder and a gaze displayer. The gaze recorder uses a Mirametrix S2 eye-tracker to capture and write a viewer's gaze coordinates in a specific window to an XML file in real-time. The gaze displayer reads the XML file's gaze coordinates and overlays a cue on the video as shown in Figure 3a. We also implemented a live-replay interface, in which the window video stops if the viewer's gaze goes out of the window as shown in Figure 3b. We investigated whether AVD-Gaze's visual cues and live-replay improved attention and outcomes for deaf students watching a lecture with auditory-to-visual accommodations.

4.1 Stimuli

For the study, we recorded an hour long lecture on pre-algebra. We chose this topic and content because most college students are familiar with it. Although though the prerecorded nature of the course eliminated interaction with the lecturer or the other students, we chose an actual lecture in order to test the relevance of our techniques in a natural setting. The material was neither very dense nor technical, yet was presented in a highly visual and engaging fashion. We divided the lecture into two segments so that the visual cues could be shown exactly twice in a balanced, repeated measures design.

For the gaze recording component, we recruited an interpreter student to view the lecture video, and recorded their raw eye tracking data so as to reduce lag when the viewer quickly changes their gaze. The eye-tracker used in this study is a Mirametrix S2 Eye-Tracking Device operating at 60 Hz with gaze position accuracy $< 0.5°$.

For the cue, we generated two kinds of cues: 1) a 2 second time-averaged fixed-circle cue with an 100 pixel diameter, and 2) a time-averaged variable-size circle cue that changed size according to fixation duration, with 90% transparency.

4.2 Participants

Twelve deaf participants ages 18-27 (5 female, 7 male) were recruited. All participants typically requested accommodations. We recruited through email and word of mouth on campus. For all respondents, scheduling and follow up was done through email. All participants were reimbursed for their participation.

When participants came in for the study, they were directed read a description of the study and provide informed consent. Next, the students were asked to complete a short demographic questionnaire in order to determine eligibility for the test.

Next, the participants completed a calibration procedure to match up gaze with the size of the display. Then the participants watched the video lectures which consisted of four video segments, each four minutes long. Half of the participants watched the lecture without a visual cue and then with it; the other half watched it with the order reversed. Similarly, half of them watched the lecture with live playback and then with no live play back, and the other half watched it with the order reversed. The total time for the study was about 20 minutes. We measured user preferences using Likert scale and open-ended questions. After each segment, and evaluated whether students perceived the cues or live replay as helpful.

After the participant completed watching the sequence of segments, they were asked to complete a questionnaire. Then they were asked to answer in their own words in response to the questions that asked for their thoughts about following the lecture with cues.

5 Results

For the participants' eye gaze patterns, we focused on fixations, rather than all gaze points, because a pause is required for information absorption. We defined a fixation as 100 milliseconds within a 30-pixel radius.

We observed that students adopted very different strategies of where the students chose to distribute their visual attention during class. As expected, the majority of time was spent on either the interpreter or the captions and rarely on the teacher or slides. This supports prior research: our participants spent on average 12.2% on the teacher and 18.1% on the slides compared to 16% and 22% reported by Marschark et al [8].

Subjects had positive reactions to the averaged cue, but much more positive reactions to the variable size and transparency cue. When presented with the time-averaged cue, subjects rated the statement"Did you like the visual cues?" with answer choices rating from"1-I didnt like it at all" to "5-I like it a lot," with an average rating of 3.9 ($SD = 0.9, \chi = 10.07, p < .05$). When presented with a variable size cue with 90% transparency that showed the extent of the gaze view over the past 2 seconds, students gave a higher rating of 4.5 ($SD = 0.5, \chi = 12.19, p < .05$). The cues appear to aid deaf student's decision-making process on where to shift and focus attention on an active source. One participant commented, "The cues significantly reduced my worry that I would miss noticing a new slide". There was a trend in preference for large and subtle visual cues.

Subjects had positive reactions to live-replay. Live-replay helps participants review visual information that they had just missed. In response to the question "Did you like live-replay?", the average rating was 4.4 ($SD = 0.4, \chi = 11.39, p < .05$). Students tended to use live replay when there was both spoken and visual information presented at the same time. One participant commented: "I am a slow reader and cannot fully understand the slides in class. Live replay really gives me enough time to read the information on the slides."

6 Conclusion

Reactions to both the collaborative cue and live-replay features of AVD-Gaze were very positive. The statement "AVD-Gaze would be a valuable tool in the classroom" received an average rating of 4.7 (SD = 0.5) between 4-Agree and 5-Strongly Agree. The statement "AVD-Gaze would be a valuable study tool after class" received an average rating of 4.4 (SD = 0.8). All participants liked the flexibility of changing the size and position of windows.

Regardless of whether the visual accommodation was presented as a sign language interpreter or captions, the preponderance of eye gaze on the accommodation was still dominant, with or without cues or live replay. The visual accommodation transforms the viewing experience into a visually focused task on sign or text comprehension. Moreover, the viewers spend much less time examining the picture.

Most students liked the real-time rewind feature and commented that they would like to use it in their classes to aid in content capture and recall. Students also noted that they preferred to "live playback" captions at their fastest comfort level so that they could always strive to watch the information "live."

We found that students who liked the cues were more likely to look at the active current source and rated lectures more positively. Furthermore, the use of cues resulted in a more balanced distribution between focus on the visual representation of audio and other classroom visual information sources. It appears that eye-tracking cues helps subjects better distribute their visual attention.

Eye gaze tracking resulted in improved student performance in terms of switching delay to the active source. However, simply presenting the actual eye-tracking center of focus was not enough. The visual and cognitive resources required in following the interpreter or captioner appeared to induce tunnel vision. This made it difficult for students to notice changes in other information sources. Participants wanted sufficiently large cues to be visible with peripheral vision, yet subtle enough to not interfere with the visual source. Students who made use of the cues also liked them and found them helpful. These comments were supported by their subjective ratings.

Since deafness is low incidence, deaf students tend to be thinly spread and often the only deaf student in their school. There tends not to be much institutional memory and though the accommodations are individualized not only according to the student but also to available resources at the school. As a result, deaf students tend to have a much more diverse set of learning strategies [6], compared to their hearing peers. It seems deaf students are be best served by enabling them to choose from a variety of pre-tested and configurable reference cues. Collaborative eye gaze with visual cues and live-replay are just two important aspects of the larger project to improve access to mainstream classes for deaf students. These study findings highlight the fact that visibility and cognitive load is a key factor in evaluating a device's usability by deaf consumers.

7 Future Work

After seeing their eye-gaze patterns, many participants commented that they did not realize the extent of their "tunnel vision" in locking in on interpreters or captions. They expressed interest in distributing their focus more evenly between classroom information sources, and to become more aware of source shifts. This feedback could be used as a habilitation tool to enable deaf students to better manage their attention in classrooms.

Acknowledgements. We thank our participants for their time and comments in evaluating the captions. This work is supported by a grant from the National Science Foundation IIS-1218056.

References

1. Cavender, A.C., Bigham, J.P., Ladner, R.E.: ClassInFocus. In: Proceedings of the 11th International ACM SIGACCESS Conference on Computers and Accessibility - ASSETS 2009, pp. 67–74. ACM Press, New York (2009), http://portal.acm.org/citation.cfm?doid=1639642.1639656
2. Kushalnagar, R.S., Cavender, A.C., Pâris, J.F.: Multiple view perspectives: improving inclusiveness and video compression in mainstream classroom recordings. In: Proceedings of the 12th International ACM SIGACCESS Conference on Computers and Accessibility - ASSETS 2010, pp. 123–130. ACM Press, New York (2010), http://portal.acm.org/citation.cfm?doid=1878803.1878827
3. Kushalnagar, R.S., Kushalnagar, P., Manganelli, G.: Collaborative Gaze Cues for Deaf Students. In: Proceedings of the Dual Eye Tracking Workshop at the Computer Supported Cooperative Work and Social Computing Conference. ACM Press, Seattle (2012)
4. Kushalnagar, R.S., Lasecki, W.S., Bigham, J.P.: Captions Versus Transcripts for Online Video Content. In: ACM (ed.) 10th International Cross-Disclipinary Conference on Web Accessibility (W4A), pp. 32:1–32:4. ACM Press, Rio De Janerio (2013), http://dl.acm.org/citation.cfm?id=2461142
5. Lang, H., Pagliaro, C.: Factors predicting recall of mathematics terms by deaf students: implications for teaching. Journal of Deaf Studies and Deaf Education 12(4), 449–460 (2007), http://www.ncbi.nlm.nih.gov/pubmed/17548804
6. Lang, H.G.: Higher education for deaf students: Research priorities in the new millennium. Journal of Deaf Studies and Deaf Education 7(4), 267–280 (2002), http://www.ncbi.nlm.nih.gov/pubmed/15451865
7. Marschark, M., Leigh, G., Sapere, P., Burnham, D., Convertino, C., Stinson, M., Knoors, H., Vervloed, M.P.J., Noble, W.: Benefits of sign language interpreting and text alternatives for deaf students' classroom learning. Journal of Deaf Studies and Deaf Education 11(4), 421–437 (2006), http://www.ncbi.nlm.nih.gov/pubmed/16928778
8. Marschark, M., Sapere, P., Convertino, C., Seewagen, R.: Access to postsecondary education through sign language interpreting. Journal of Deaf Studies and Deaf Education 10(1), 38–50 (2005), http://www.ncbi.nlm.nih.gov/pubmed/15585747

Toward a Reversed Dictionary of French Sign Language (FSL) on the Web

Mohammed Zbakh, Zehira Haddad, and Jaime Lopez Krahe

Thim Chart, Université Paris8, St Denis, France
{mohammed.zbakh,zhaddad-bousseksou,jlk}@univ-paris8.fr

Abstract. On the web, we can find dictionaries for viewing a sign of French Sign Language (FSL), from a word. However, finding a word from a sign is much more complicated. For this purpose, we propose to design a web application to find the meaning of a FSL sign in the French language from the sign's features. In order to do this, we have developed an intelligent system capable of learning and self-improving by feeding off the information presented to it during its use. We have managed to find a middle ground between the reliability of the results and the ergonomics of Human-Machine Interfaces (HMI).

Keywords: Human Machine Interface, Classification Algorithms, French Sign Language, Learning Algorithm.

1 Introduction

The Sign Languages (SL) are based on the visual-gestural channel, which means, it is the gesture that takes the role the phoneme has in the spoken language [1]. This specificity of SL to be transmitted in a space creates difficulties in its modeling. Research in this field has changed considerably with the advance of technologies such as image processing and the emergence of technical devices such as motion sensors.

Within the existing literature, we can find some works on automatic processing of video sign language [2, 3] and others on LSF sings categorization and classification [4]. Additionally, IVT (International Visual Theatre) proposes a bilingual dictionary divided in three parts [5]: The first describes the evolution of communication in the deaf community, it is particularly focused on linguistic and cultural evolution. The two other parts show a set of 4500 signs classified by theme. The dictionary offers the possibility to search through two indexes: an alphabetical one, corresponding to the French translations of signs, and a second one in which signs are sorted by configuration. Note, however, that t the search can be quite tedious if we are looking for the meaning of a specific sign as the dictionary does not offer a quick and easy way to access this sign. On top of that, paper dictionaries have certain limits related to their format.

With this project, we propose to develop a web application in the form of a reversed dictionary: French Sign Language (FSL) French. This free web accessible application provides a wider visibility to the general public. In fact, sign language

K. Miesenberger et al. (Eds.): ICCHP 2014, Part II, LNCS 8548, pp. 423–430, 2014.

(SL) has long suffered from a considerable lack of mediation which has been identified as one of the main reasons of the great instability and heterogeneity of this language. Unfortunately, setting up an accessible diffusion system for SL has been proved difficult. This is mainly due to the absence of a language identification protocol and the poor mediation inside this language. SL are also subject to local and cultural diversity, which often lead to different dialects. The reference dictionaries that we propose to diffuse on the net can provide a wider mediation and thus offer a greater stability.

The main objective of this work is to exploit the advantage computers and web networks offer to build a database that can contribute to the stabilization of the FSL. To do this, we will rely on the FSL dictionary developed within our team:
`http://www2.univ-paris8.fr/ingenierie-cognition/masterhandi/etudiant/projets/site_lsf/dico_lsf/recherche.php`

Here, we present the design of a web platform that offers a compromise between the quickness of the algorithms and the reliability of the result. This compromise has been carefully crafted to offer a system that is both simple (few fields to fill), fast (in computation and response time) and reliable accurate results).To achieve that, we began our analysis by applying some clustering algorithms such as neural networks, decision trees and support vector machines. The results led us to propose a machine learning system based on certain coefficients.

2 French Sign Language : Parameters and Modeling

The definition of a sign in FSL is based on different gestural and emotional parameters [5]. The sign is characterized by one or more hand shapes, the position of the hand in space, its movement, its orientation and the facial expressions that accompany it. As part of this work, we use a database of 3000 signs indexed and stored in a format usable by a web technology. In a first phase, we limit ourselves to the 500 most used signs in FSL. Then, once the system is implemented, it will be able to expand and learn from the other signs. The first step of this research is to model signs. In order to provide a simple and ergonomic sign modeling, we considered the following parameters:

As the first parameter we choose the hand shape. Note that there isn't a universally used and accepted number of hand shapes, even the identification of each sign has not been standardized [6]. Indeed, scholars don't agree on the matter since their classification of hand shaped ranges from 39 to 139 [3], [5], [7, 8]. Consequently, given the absence of agreement on a specific number of hand shapes used in the FSL [5], we selected 59 hand shapes. In order to present to the user a simple and easily accessible interface, we present the list of hand shapes in a catalog of 12 classes according to their similarity (Figure 1). Each class contains at most 6 configurations. The goal of this organization is to facilitate the access to the signs database.

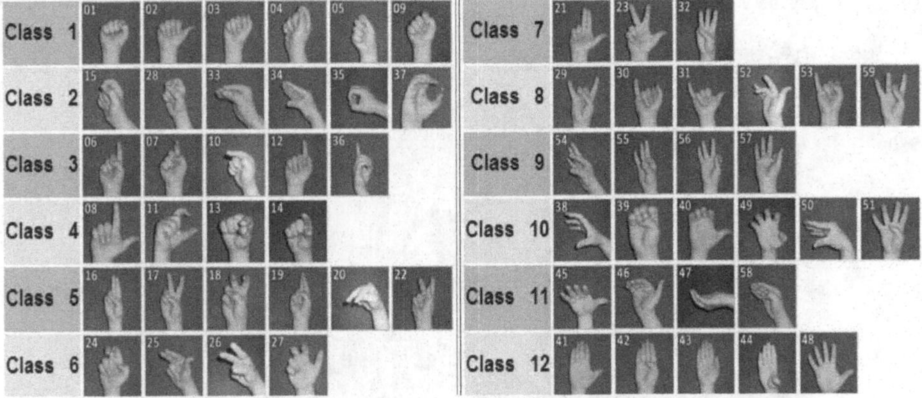

Fig. 1. The 59 hand shapes used

The second parameter is the hand position. Generally, the proposed positions are quite numerous and complex. Ergonomic constraints guided us towards selecting a simpler model than the model presented in the IVT [5] which cites different detailed positions. We have worked (Figure 2) on five front spaces (Head, Chest, Abdomen, Left arm and Right arm) and three lateral positions (contact with the body, close contact and distant contact). In total, our model manages 15 sites by combining the frontal plane and lateral plane.

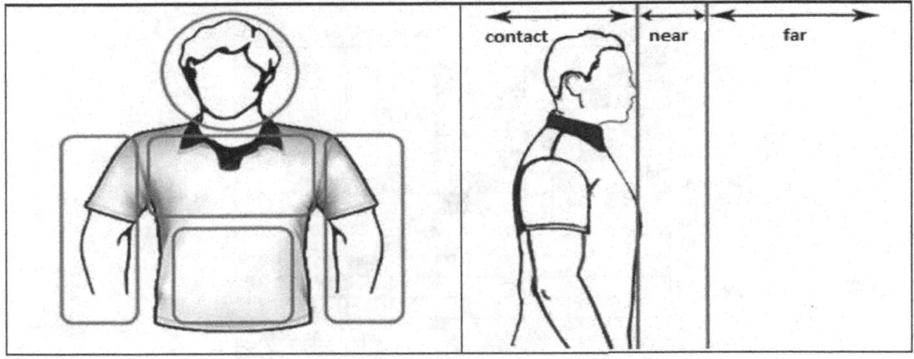

Fig. 2. The different hand positions in space

Thereafter, we proceeded to the creation of similarity matrices for hand shapes (Figure 3) and the position in space (Figure 4). These matrices are used to initialize our classification system. It was seized by practitioners of the FSL.

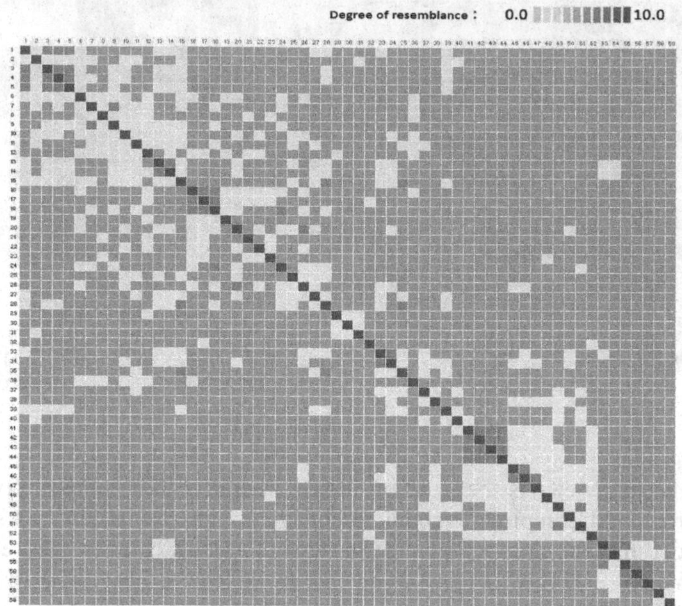

Fig. 3. Similarity matrix corresponding to the hand shapes

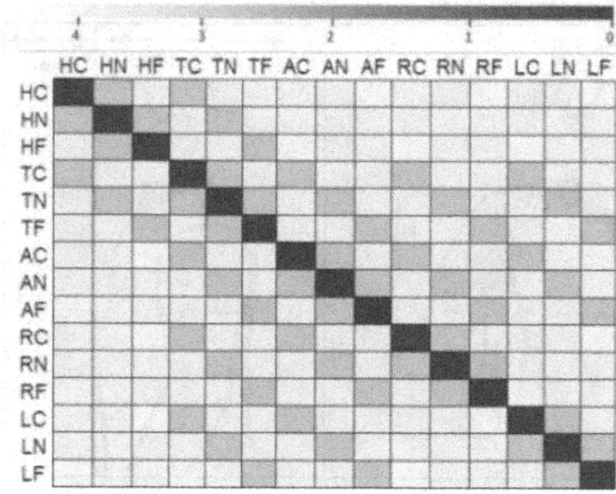

Fig. 4. Similarity matrix corresponding to the hand positions

During the first phase of our experiments, we conducted preliminary tests in order to define an experimental protocol on the signs. We have implemented a web interface that allows the selection of a hand shape and assigns to it a position in space. Next, we investigated the validity of the results with respect to the input data and the corresponding signs proposed. The first results of this experiment showed that two parameters are insufficient to find a particular sign. We found a success rate of 55 % which is rather low.

The second stage of this research was, hence, to add a third parameter: the movement of the hand. Thus, we defined 10 hand movements that encompass all possible movements in the FSL. Figure 5 shows the distribution of these movements into two categories. The first one corresponds to the movements which can be performed by a single hand, while the second one corresponds to those that require the use of both hands simultaneously or alternately. Note also that some movements can be described through the combination of movements of the first class exercised simultaneously by two hands (Example: iteration with two hands).

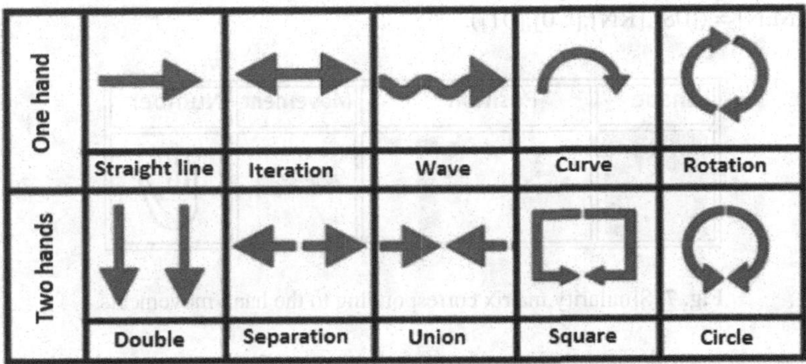

Fig. 5. The movement of hand during the sign

We have also taken into account the signs that occur without movement. In total, we used eleven elements to represent all the possible hand movements. The similarity matrix corresponding to this parameter is shown in figure 6.

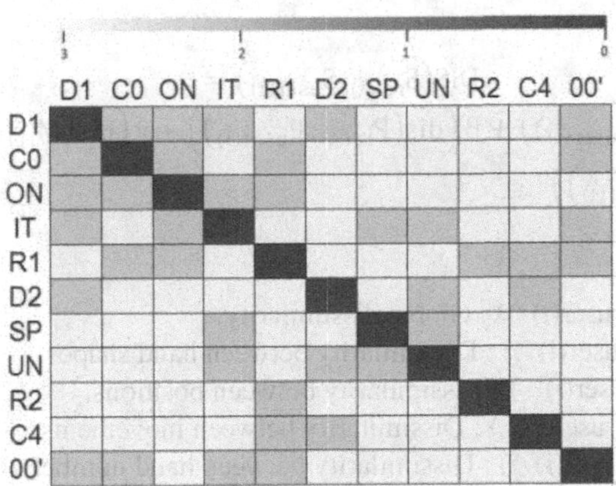

Fig. 6. Similarity matrix corresponding to the hand movements

In order to better filter our results, we decided to add another element in the coding. This element is related to the number of hands employed. This addition allows us to better discriminate the different signs when the database becomes larger.

Finally, each sign can be represented by the four parameters: [C, P, M, N], with:

C: Hand shape.
P: Position.
M: Movement.
N: the number of hands used.

To illustrate this encoding, consider the example of the sign "Lundi" ("Monday" in French). This sign, which corresponds to the graphical representation shown in figure 7, is encoded by the following parameters:
[C,P,M,N] = ([08],[RN],[C0],[01]).

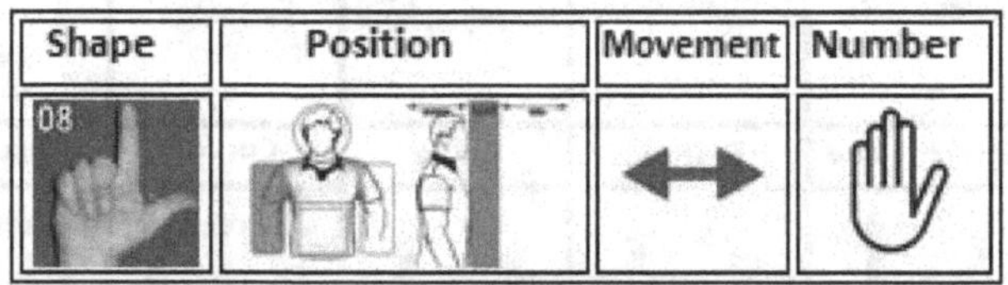

Fig. 7. Similarity matrix corresponding to the hand movements

3 Classification and Results

Using the previous parameters, we preceded to the normalization of the different similarity matrices. We propose to use the following function, which takes into account the global reference symbols and the encodings of the users. The latter is based on the values of the three similarity matrices which correspond to the correct result. To do that, we decided to operate with the matrices initialized and normalized by the following formula:

$$DIS\left(S_{ref(i)}, S_{user(i)}\right) = \sum_i \alpha\left(dis\left(C_{ref(i)}, C_{user(i)}\right)\right) + \beta\left(dis\left(P_{ref(i)}, P_{user(i)}\right)\right) + \gamma\left(dis\left(M_{ref(i)}, M_{user(i)}\right)\right) + \delta\left(dis\left(N_{ref(i)}, N_{user(i)}\right)\right) \quad (1)$$

Where :

DIS(S_ref(i) ,S_user(i)) : Global dissimilarity.
dis(C_ref(i) ,C_user(i)) : Dissimilarity between hand shapes.
dis(P_ref(i) ,P_user(i)) : Dissimilarity between positions.
dis(M_ref(i) ,M_user(i)) : Dissimilarity between movements.
dis(N_ref(i) ,N_user(i)) : Dissimilarity between hand numbers.
$\alpha,\beta,\gamma,\delta$: Learning coefficients with $\alpha+\beta+\gamma+\delta=1$.

We introduced this formula with four learning coefficients assigned to the four used parameters. These coefficients are estimated to fit the experiments. Before starting the experiments, we generated the confusion matrix signs using the previous formula (with $\alpha= \beta= \gamma= \delta$). The measure of dissimilarity between all signs gives a symmetric diagonal matrix zero M [i,j]. However, if the matrix M [i ,j] is null when i $\neq$ j, this indicates a confusion of the two signs i and j in the representation space. This means similar coding of the signs i and j despite their visual difference. Such difference can exist in other settings (facial expressions), which we have not used in this study due to the ergonomic constraints.

After defining our calculation function, we launched our system for experimental tests. Twenty participants contributed to this experiment. These participants have different levels in the practice of FSL. Throughout this step, participants made a total of 6348 observations, which we subsequently filtered in the analysis phase by removing answers too far from reality. Note that the experiments were carried out with static and equal coefficients. The main objective is to define the coefficients values that can fully optimize the results.

Finally, we fixed the more appropriate formula for our system by sorting the classification results. This formula is the following:

$$[(0.41*C) + (0.27*P) + (0.23*M) + (0.09*N)] \tag{2}$$

The obtained coefficients optimize the maximum number of replies and the success rate for our system. By analyzing these learning coefficients, we observe that the fourth coefficient (number of hands) plays a minimal role. We believe that such parameter can be used at the end to filter the results by redirect the responses to the correct class of signs.

The developed application allows the user to model easily and quickly the sign that he wants to know the meaning of. Once the various parameters are entered, the sign is coded. The results of this coding are presented to the user in the form of a wall of words (Figure 8). The system sorts the signs according to their degree of similarity. The display is based on the results: the font size of the words displayed is related to the level of correspondence to the coding signs.

Fig. 8. Wall of words according to the degree of resemblance

4 Conclusion

The presented model has allowed us to build a flexible and adaptive architecture to search for a sign. The platform collects user queries by adjusting the learning coefficients and coding signs in the database.

Currently we only consider the observations of the subjects that participated in our experiments. That has allowed us to control the coding and avoid possible interference consultations. However, in the future, we propose to work on the generalization of the system so that, with time, it can self-manage and expand by itself.

The system is available to the public on our website to perform sign searches: `http://www2.univ-paris8.fr/ingenierie-cognition/master-handi/di/`

References

1. Cuxac, C.: La Langue des Signes Française: les Voies de l'Iconicité, Faits de Langues, Ophrys, vol. 15-16 (2000)
2. Lefebvre-Albaret, F., Dalle, P.: Body posture estimation in sign language videos. In: Kopp, S., Wachsmuth, I. (eds.) GW 2009. LNCS, vol. 5934, pp. 289–300. Springer, Heidelberg (2010)
3. Braffort, A.: ARGo: An architecture for sign language recognition and interpretation. In: Harling, P., Edwards, A. (eds.) "Progress in Gestural Interaction", International Gesture Workshop (GW 1996). Springer (1997)
4. Aznar, G.: Informatisation d'une forme écrite de la langue des Signes Française, Phd thesis, Université de Toulouse (2008)
5. La langue des Signes 1, 2 et 3. International Visual Theatre Edition (1998)
6. Boutora, L.: Vers un inventaire ordonné des configurations manuelles de la Langue des Signes Française. JEP, Dinard (2006)
7. Bonnal, F.: Sémiogenèse de la langue des signes française: étude critique des signes attestés sur support papier depuis le XVIIIe siècle et nouvelles perspectives de dictionnaires, Thèse de doctorat, Université Toulouse le Mirail (2005)
8. Cuxac, C.: La Langue des Signes Française: les Voies de l'Iconicité, Faits de Langues, Ophrys, vol. 15-16, pp. 97–130 (2000)

A Novel Approach for Translating English Statements to American Sign Language Gloss

Achraf Othman and Mohamed Jemni

Research Laboratory LaTICE-GE, University of Tunis 5,
Av. Taha Hussein, B.P. 56, Bab Mnara, 1008 Tunis, Tunisia
achraf.othman@ieee.org,
mohamed.jemni@fst.rnu.tn

Abstract. In this paper, we present a study on the relationship between American Sign Language (ASL) statements and English written texts toward building a statistical machine translation (SMT) using 3D avatar for interpretation. The process included a novel algorithm which transforms an English part-of-speech sentence to ASL-Gloss. The algorithm uses a rule-based approach for building big parallel corpus from English to ASL-Gloss using dependency rules of grammatical parts of the sentence. The parallel corpus will be the input of the translation model of the SMT for ASL. The results we obtained are highly consistent, reproducible, with fairly high precision and accuracy.

Keywords: Sign Language Processing, Hybrid Machine Translation, Artificial Corpus, Gloss Annotation System.

1 Introduction

Machine translation for Sign language (SL), although has been explored for many years, are still a challenging problem for real practice. In fact, Sign Languages (SL) are very specific; they are actually very close to spoken language in the structural aspect and expression. Also, they use the same cognitive schema in their structure [2]. The need to go through an abstract level of structural representation languages is essential. And a main initial part of the project WebSign [6] that aims to design an avatar interpreter of an input text to sign language using statistical machine translation approach [11]. WebSign is the main framework of many other applications as MMSSign [7] for accessibility of Deaf to mobile technology and the tool described in [5] for sign language recognition. In this work, we propose an improved approach for generating the American Sign Language Gloss (ASL-gloss) from dependency grammar rules [12].

In fact, we will present a new approach for generating statements of American Sign Language toward translating an English text and at the same time build a parallel corpus between these two languages. In a previous paper presented in ViSiCAST project [1] [16] authors presented the the syntactic level of their approach. In this paper, we include more than 52 grammatical relations when generating dependencies. This has also allowed us to generate non-manual

K. Miesenberger et al. (Eds.): ICCHP 2014, Part II, LNCS 8548, pp. 431–438, 2014.

components. Research on lexical analysis, syntactic, morphological and semantic English text is very advanced, and there are several tools that deliver results with accuracy rates close to 98% and a recall (recall) close to 90%. Our approach is divided into two main parts: the first is the full automatic text processing of input data and its representation in the form of a semantic graph. The second step is the generation of transcription-Gloss using XML API.

In section 1, we detail the grammatical components of American Sign Language. Section 2 provides the details of our approach to generate ASL statements from an English sentence. Section 3 briefly discusses the evaluation method. We conclude the paper with an overview of the work.

2 Grammatical Components of ASL

2.1 Verbal Core

The main grammatical component [9] in American Sign Language (ASL) is the verbal core. The verb in ASL is the primary entity for the construction of the statement taking into account the dependencies with other signs of speech. Using the example shown in Figure 1, the word 'ASK' has two different signs, the first configuration of the hand facing the person who is in front of the signer. For the second, the index of the dominant hand is facing the signer.

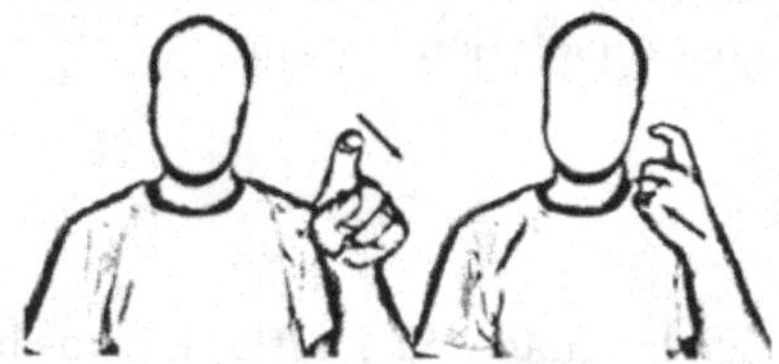

Fig. 1. Two forms of the verb 'ASK' in ASL. The left corresponds to the phrase 'I ASK YOU' and the right is the phrase 'YOU ASK ME'.

The phenomenon shown in Figure 1 has been observed in several languages like ASL [13], the Australian sign language [8], Brazilian Sign Language [14], British Sign Language [17], Dutch Sign Language [15], Japanese Sign Language [4] and others. The verb agreement generally refers to some systematic covariance between a formal or semantic property of an element and a formal property of another, for example between the object and the subject. Corbett [3] extends this definition stating that there are four main elements of the systematic covariance: Controller and target and Domain and Functions. A fundamental question concerning the phenomenon shown in Figure 1 is how to achieve the consent of the subject-verb and object, and if that is the case, what are the relevant characteristics to achieve. Several approaches have been proposed in the linguistic research of American Sign Language. We can cite for example the R-locus analysis proposed by Lillo and Klima in 1990 [10].

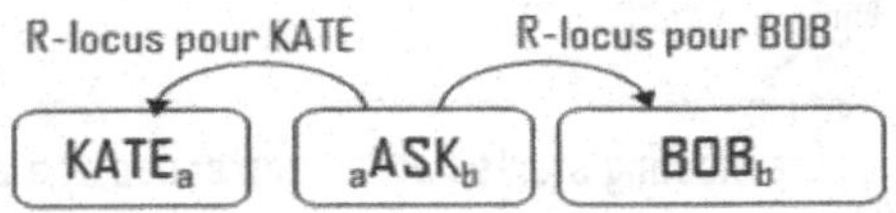

Fig. 2. R-locus relation in the sentence 'Kate asked Bob a question'

2.2 Other Components of ASL

In the example of Figure 2, the R-locus relationship is made to specify agreements with the word 'ASK'. According to this analysis, the relationship is described as an agreement between a noun phrase and a verb in the sense that they share a repository index, which is constructed as an open R-locus. In ASL, we have many components like:

- The time component (see Figure 3) is used when signing events and time, ASL uses Time-Topic-Comment structure. Signs with time indications or time periods are found in the beginning of the sentence ;
- Classifiers or Modifiers: are signs that use handshapes that are associated with specific categories (classes) of size, shape, or usage. They are used to express position, stative description, and how objects are handled manually. For example, the '1-Handshape' is used for individuals standing or long thin objects ;
- Pronouns : the index or forefinger handshape is used to indicate the pronouns "me," "you," "he-she-it," "we," "you-all," and "they". Using pronouns in ASL is the same as in English but we need to refer to a noun before using a pronoun ;
- Construction of a statement or word order: there exist three aspects of word order: a functional aspect, where the order of items provides information about the combination of words and which, in turn, provides guidance on how to interpret the sentence. And, an articulatory aspect which arises because generally, it is impossible to articulate more than one sign at a time. And, the presumption of the existence of a basic word order;
- Sentence types in ASL : are used to make an assertion, ask a question, to give an order, to express an emotion, etc. Sentence types develop grammaticalized forms associated to these conversational uses ;
- Negation : the expression of sentential negation in ASL features many of the morphological and syntactic properties attested for spoken languages. However, non-manual markers of negation such as headshake or facial expression have been shown to play a central role and they interact in various interesting ways with manual negatives and with syntactic structure of negative clauses ;
- Coordination and subordination : involves the combining of at least two constituents which are basically interpreted with non-manual signs ;
- Coreference (see Figure 4) : occurs when two or more expressions in a text refer to the same person or thing.

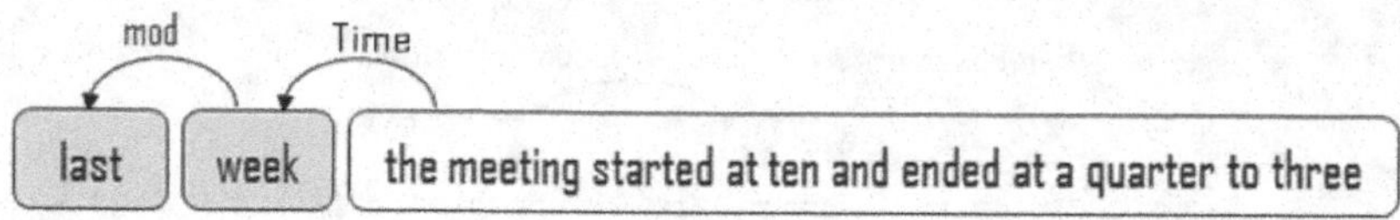

Fig. 3. Temporal dependence in 'Last week, the meeting started at ten and ended at a quarter to three'

Fig. 4. The relationship of coreference in the sentence 'Mary said she would help me'

2.3 Relationships between ASL Components

The study of relations between grammatical dependencies between the words in a sentence in English, shows that from these relationships, we can generate structures in ASL. Therefore, given a sentence as input, can we build a statement in ASL? To answer this question the deaf use their cognition for the interpretation of a fast and implicit way. First of all, the brain directs the signs (for example: *tense* → *subject* → *verb* → *object*). Then, the deaf created its space of designation by placing the different subjects and objects taking account semantic relationships between the objects. In the previous section, we show that syntactic, morphological and semantic analysis are very important and will be our starting point in our automatic translation system into sign language from from the dependencies rules between the extracted signs of grammatical relations.

3 Our Approach

The organization levels of linguistic processing of our system is similar to the triangle model of Vauquois. Thus, as shown in Figure 5, the system is organized in three main levels: lexical, syntactic and semantic levels which are a chain of linguistic processing

The set is built around several modules supervised by a control module. These modules contain the various data on which the analysis and the generation of the message will be made:

- Data for segmentation: Sentence boundaries detection and tokenization ;
- Monolingual lexicons with morphological information ;
- Word-to-word translation from a dictionary ;
- Chunking grammar to separate grammatical components like nominal group, prepositional phrases, verb groups, etc. ;
- Dependency grammar for syntactic relationships between words ;
- Translation based on grammatical function ;

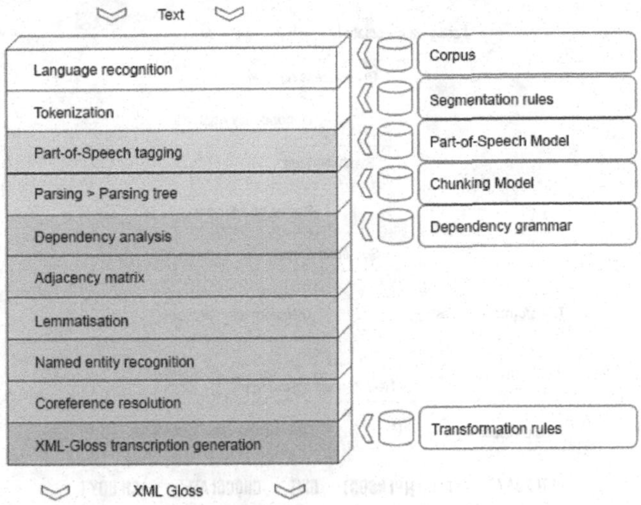

Fig. 5. Architecture of the proposed system

- Semantic construction rules, to refine the relevance of syntactic relations and retain only those emitting a sense ;
- Graph transformation rules for the reformulation.

The main stages of the analysis is done in a conventional manner according to the scheme shown in Figure 5. Thus, after a segmentation step, morphological, syntactic and semantic information retrieval of each word of the source statement are sought in a lexicon. A dependency grammar is then used to build the tree representing the syntactic structure of the utterance. The tree obtained for the analysis of a sentence like "Kate gave chocolate for each boy, yesterday" is given by Figure 6. Indeed, the structure of the target sentence in ASL is $Tense \rightarrow Subject \rightarrow Verb \rightarrow Object$. The first step is applied directly to the input sentence pretreatment followed by an analysis of dependence between words which will be described in the following sections. After this step, the system analyzes the semantic structures between words. Following this analysis, the system generates a specific ASL syntactic structure. Then, we proceed to the linearization and formatting according to the transcription system XML-Gloss.

As mentioned earlier, our approach is based on the dependency relationships of grammatical parts of the English input sentence (see Figure 7). From the dependency relationships, we define a finite graph G with n vertex, which n is the number of words of the input sentence. The edge between two vertex i and j is noted (Vi, Vj). The set of edges is V. In our example, figure 6 is an illustration of the dependency graph. After that, we generate the adjacency matrix A which is determined from G.

Thereafter, to build the ASL statement, we define the output rule. For example, in our case, we follow the TSOV rule $tense \rightarrow subject \rightarrow verb \rightarrow object$. This rule will be useful to extract word from adjacency matrix.

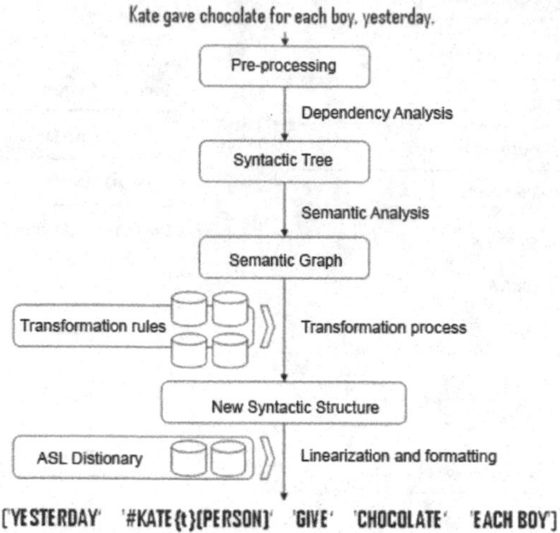

Fig. 6. Overview of how the proposed translation system

At the end, we implement the existing tool to recognize named-entity and to detect coreference in the input sentence toward adding sematinc information to the ASL statement like classifier and pronouns references.

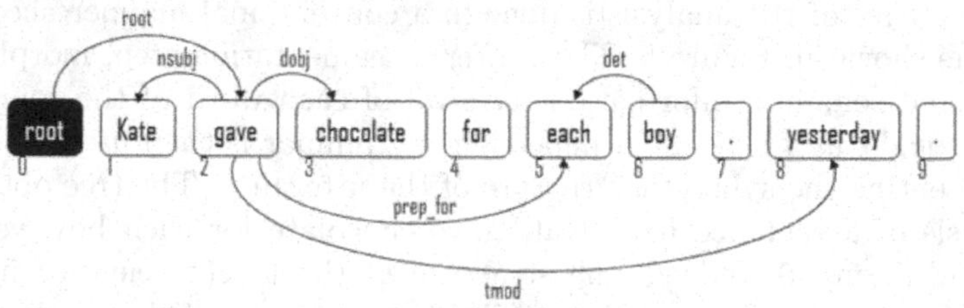

Fig. 7. Dependency links for the sentence 'Kate gave chocolate for each boy, yesterday'

4 XML-Gloss Transcription Generation Process

Generating the XML-Gloss transcription is a simple task, just browse entities resulting from algorithms to build ASL statement and make a call of specific methods from API-XML-Gloss. For example for the sentence "YESTERDAY #KATE{t} GIVE CHOCOLATE EACH-BOY", the output is shown in Figure 9.

5 Evaluation

To evaluate our system, we began by comparing manually each sentence to its transcription and the generated transcript. However, this task is a huge time

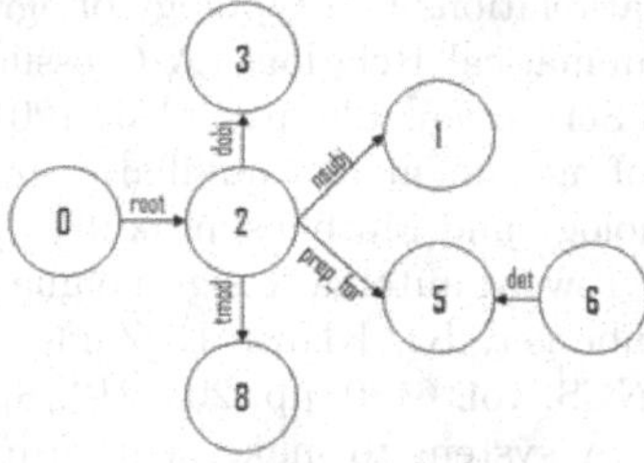

Fig. 8. Dependency graph of the sentence 'Kate gave chocolate for each boy, yesterday'

t

YESTERDAY #KATE GIVE CHOCOLATE EACH-BOY

Fig. 9. Gloss annotation of the sentence 'Kate gave chocolate for each boy, yesterday'

consuming since that the number of sentences exceeds $100k$. Our solution is to evaluate only the transfer between the two languages (English and ASL) rules such that, we reduced significantly the time and cost of the evaluation. Otherwise, we take one sentence e in English and its matrix of adjacency M. We define a transfer rule $R(i \Rightarrow j)$ as:

For our system, we evaluate 820 transfers rules extracted from the books of learning ASL. The accuracy rate is equal to 82% for 6720 phrases calculated from the formula:

$$T(precision) = \frac{count(validsentences)}{count(sentences)} \quad (1)$$

6 Conclusion

The approach of generating speech in ASL from dependency grammatical rules presents an interesting solution for automatic translation of text to sign language transcript. The overall architecture of the generation system has been described as well as its main modules. The experimental results are very promising and currently we are integrating this system in the WebSign framework in order to improve its translation efficiency.

References

1. Bangham, J., Cox, S., Elliott, R., Glauert, J., Marshall, I., Rankov, S., Wells, M.: Virtual signing: Capture, animation, storage and transmission - an overview of the visicast project. In: IEEE Seminar on Speech and Language Processing for Disabled and Elderly People, pp. 6/1–6/7 (2000)
2. Bellugi, U., Poizner, H., Klima, E.S.: Brain organization for language: Clues from sign aphasia. Human Neurobiology 2, 155–170 (1983)

3. Corbett, G.: Grammatical relations in a typology of agreement systems. In: Argument Structure and Grammatical Relations: A Crosslinguistic Typology. Studies in Language Companion Series, vol. 126, pp. 37–54 (2012)
4. Fischer, S.D.: The role of agreement and auxiliaries in sign languages. Sign Linguistics Phonetics, Phonology and Morphosyntax 98(3), 103–119 (1996)
5. Jaballah, K., Jemni, M.: Toward automatic sign language recognition from web3D based scenes. In: Miesenberger, K., Klaus, J., Zagler, W., Karshmer, A. (eds.) ICCHP 2010, Part II. LNCS, vol. 6180, pp. 205–212. Springer, Heidelberg (2010)
6. Jemni, M., Elghoul, O.: A system to make signs using collaborative approach. In: Miesenberger, K., Klaus, J., Zagler, W.L., Karshmer, A.I. (eds.) ICCHP 2008. LNCS, vol. 5105, pp. 670–677. Springer, Heidelberg (2008)
7. Jemni, M., Ghoul, O.E., Yahya, N.B., Boulares, M.: Sign language mms to make cell phones accessible to deaf and hard-of-hearing community. In: CVHI 2007 Euro-Assist Conference and Workshop on Assistive Technology for People with Vision and Hearing Impairments (2007)
8. Johnston, T., Schembri, A.: Australian Sign Language: An Introduction to Sign Language Linguistics. Cambridge University Press (2007)
9. Liddell, S.K.: Grammar, gesture, and meaning in American Sign Language. Cambridge University Press (2003)
10. Lillo-Martin, D., Klima, E.S.: Pointing out differences: Asl pronouns in syntactic theory. Theoretical Issues in Sign Language Research 1, 191–210 (1990)
11. Othman, A., Jemni, M.: Statistical sign language machine translation: from English written text to american sign language gloss. International Journal of Computer Science Issues 8, 65–73 (2011)
12. Othman, A., Tmar, Z., Jemni, M.: Toward developing a very big sign language parallel corpus. In: Miesenberger, K., Karshmer, A., Penaz, P., Zagler, W. (eds.) ICCHP 2012, Part II. LNCS, vol. 7383, pp. 192–199. Springer, Heidelberg (2012)
13. Padden, C.: Interaction of morphology and syntax in american sign language. Doctoral thesis, University of California (1983)
14. de Quadros, R.M., Quer, J.: Back to back(wards) and moving on: On agreement, auxiliaries and verb classes. In: The 9th Theoretical Issues in Sign Language Research Conference (2008)
15. Rathmann, C.: The optionality of agreement phrase: Evidence from signed languages. Doctoral thesis, The University of Texas at Austin (2000)
16. Sáfár, É., Marshall, I.: The architecture of an English-text-to-sign-languages translation system. In: Recent Advances in Natural Language Processing (RANLP), pp. 223–228 (2001)
17. Sutton-Spence, R., Woll, B.: The Linguistics of British Sign Language: An Introduction. Cambridge University Press (1999)

Hand Location Classification from 3D Signing Virtual Avatars Using Neural Networks

Kabil Jaballah and Mohamed Jemni

LaTICE Research Laboratory, University of Tunis, Tunis, Tunisia
Kabil.jaballah@utic.rnu.tn,
Mohamed.jemni@fst.rnu.tn

Abstract. 3D sign language data is actively being generated and exchanged. Sign language recognition from 3D data is then a promising research axis aiming to build new understanding and efficient indexing of this type of content. Model-based recognition strategies are commonly based on recognizing sign language features separately. Those features are: the handshape, the hand position, the orientation and movement. In this paper, we propose a novel approach for hand position classification in the space. The approach is based on a two-layer feed-forward network and generates classifications which are very close to human perception. Evaluations have been made by 10 PhD students and 2 sign language experts. The evaluation of the results shows the superiority of our approach compared with classic methods based on the calculation of the distance between the hand and the face as well as the method of K nearest neighbors. In fact, the misclassification average of our methods was the lowest with 4.58%.

Keywords: Virtual Signers, Sign Language Recognition, Hand Position, 3D Classification, Neural Networks.

1 Introduction

3D sign language has been investigated since several years. This promising research axis is getting more interest from the community of deaf. It allows people to create sign language in its visual/dynamic form through a virtual signer. Many systems have been proposed so far. Although the naturalness and comprehensibility [1] of these virtual signers have to be ameliorated, many systems proposed in the literature have been actively used. H-animator [2] , WebSign [3], eSign [4] and VSigns [5] are able to generate 3D signing avatars which are compliant with H-anim[1] and Web3D[2]. The recognition of 3D sign language is subsequently important in the context of building new understandings of the structure of SL (Sign Language). It also aims to efficiently index and catalog the generated 3D signed scenes. In this context, most of the surveyed approaches try to recognize the sign language parameters separately, and then

[1] http://www.h-anim.org
[2] http://www.web3d.org

K. Miesenberger et al. (Eds.): ICCHP 2014, Part II, LNCS 8548, pp. 439–445, 2014.

implement a Hidden Markov Model [6] based on the movement-hold model [7]. The recognized parameters are the handshape, the hand location, orientation and movement. In this paper, we focus on the hand location in the signing space. The hand location is used by the signers in order to construct the discourse universe and to express spatial relationship between objects. The location could be used, in some cases, as a morphological component of the sign itself. For example, the only difference between the sign "FATHER" and "MOTHER" in American Sign Language (ASL) is the location of the hand (lower face for "MOTHER" and upper face for "FATHER"). A study showing the importance of including an efficient spatial referencing for 3D sign language animations has been presented in [8]. In the literature, the hand location is commonly recognized by calculating its distance to the face or by classifying it using K nearest neighbors. In this paper we modeled the signing space in order to support absolute spatial referencing as well as body parts-relative referencing. We designed a neural network and trained it to recognize hand locations from 3D sign language data. Our method generated results which are much closer to human perceptions then the surveyed methods. The evaluations involved 10 Phd students and 2 sign language experts and the average classification rate of our approach reached 4.58% which is considered as satisfactory.

2 Related Work

Sign language recognition approaches are basically divided into appearance-based methods and model-based methods. In our case, dealing with 3D sign language conducted us to focus in model-based sign language recognition parameters where hand location is mostly tracked using distance measures. There are two ways to reference objects and concepts in the signing space [9]. The first way is relative referencing according to signer's body parts. The second way is the absolute referencing which is important since a signer could target specific points to place/look to objects. In the litterature, R.H Liang and M.Ouhyoung [10] modeled 22 positions of the space according to the Stokoe's [11] notation system and matched those positions in 3D sign language data using dynamic programming. Vogler and Metaxas used colored gloves to track about 20 positions of the hand [6] by using the movement-hold model [7] and Hidden Markov Models. Recently, J.Han and al [12] used dynamic time warping DTW to track sign language subunits. The location was fetched by calculating Euclidean distance between hand and head. However, the space location was not encoded through semantic annotation and was used only to implement the low level features vector for DTW tracking. The head distance based method was also used in [13]. In [14] the authors fetched the positions of the hand to construct a feature vector that will be sent to a global neural network which gathers all sign features (location, orientation, handshape, movement). In this last study, the space was modeled as a rectangular prism including 14 regions. None of the linguistic models for signing space has been used.

Most of the studied approaches in the literature use head-to-hand distance and Nearest Neighbors classification in order to recognize the hand location in the signing space. In our work, distance based methods didn't generate good results. The correlation between the automatically recognized locations and human perceptions was not satisfactory.

3 Signing Space Modeling

3D signing space in front of the signer could be used to locate the sign itself as well as pointing (indexing) objects or concepts in particular locations. The importance of a good 3D model to express spatial relationships between objects has been shown in [15]. During the VisiCAST [16] project a 3D signing space model based on the liddell & Johnson phonology and relative referencing has been proposed. However, it is dedicated to HSPG grammar that has been designed for the project. Generally, the granularity of the space locations is the main issue. In our work we segmented the 3D space into 20 regions to allow efficient 3D body-proximity referencing as specified in [7]. Moreover, thanks to forward kinematics. The absolute space locations can be computed in order to recognize pointed (indexed) objects as well as their spatial relationships.

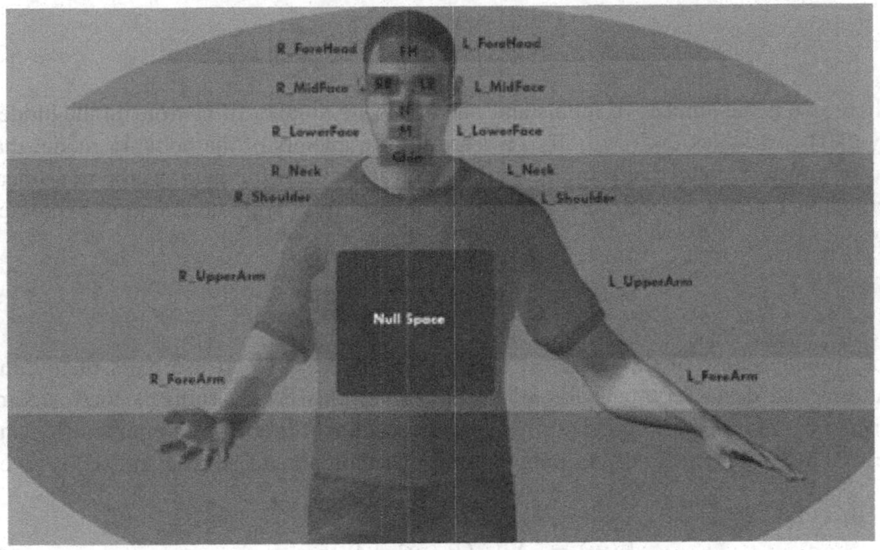

Fig. 1. Signing space modeling and segmentation

4 Neural Network Classification

In our study, we deal with 3D sign language data that is generated through dedicated signing avatars systems, through 3D devices like data-gloves and through manual methods using H-anim[3] compliant software. The first step we designed consists of extracting relevant 3D-keyframes from the continuous sign language data by following the method described in [17]. Then we extract the 3D rotation angles of the "collar", the "shoulder" and the "elbow". We use forward kinematics to compute and normalize the position in the 3D global signing space of the hand. We also include the rotation angles of the head in the input feature vector of our neural network. As shown in the following figure, we designed a two-layer feed-forward network where the input vector is composed of 6 values which correspond to head rotation angles (X_L,Y_L,Z_L) around the skullbase's in the local coordinate system and the hand position(X_G,Y_G,Z_G) in the global coordinate system.

Multilayer feedforward ANNs (MFNN) has been successfully used as classifiers [18]. The hidden layers were used to investigate the effects of the algorithms on the hyper plane and the output units are used to represent classes for possible outputs (Space regions). Mathematically the functionality of a hidden neuron is described by:

$$(j=1nwjxj+bj)\ . \tag{1}$$

Where the weights { w_j,b_j } are symbolized with the arrows feeding into the neuron.

The network output layer contains 20 neurons which is equal to the outputs of the approximation problem of 20 regions-of-space classification. The output of the network is given by:

$$\gamma(\theta) = g(\theta, x) = \sum_{i=1}^{nh} w_i^2 \sigma\left(\sum_{i=1}^{n} w_{i,j}^1 x_j + b_{j,i}^1\right) + b^2\ . \tag{2}$$

where n=6 is the number of inputs and nh=10 is the number of neurons in the hidden layer. The variables {w_i^2, $w_{i,j}^1$, $b_{j,i}^1$, b^2} are the parameters of the network model that are represented collectively by the parameter vector θ. In the neuron, the non-linear activation function we selected was the commonly used sigmoid function expressed by

$$Sigmoid[x] = \frac{1}{1+e^{-x}}\ . \tag{3}$$

The training phase of the designed network has two steps and use pairs of training patterns and desired outputs for all the 20 target classes. Learning is then accomplished by minimizing the Least Mean Square of the difference of computed (R_j) and desired response (D_j) for all training patterns. The computed Energy Error (E) is given by

$$E(w) = \frac{1}{2}\sum_{j=1}^{N}(R_j(w) - D_j)^2\ . \tag{4}$$

[3] http://www.h-anim.org/

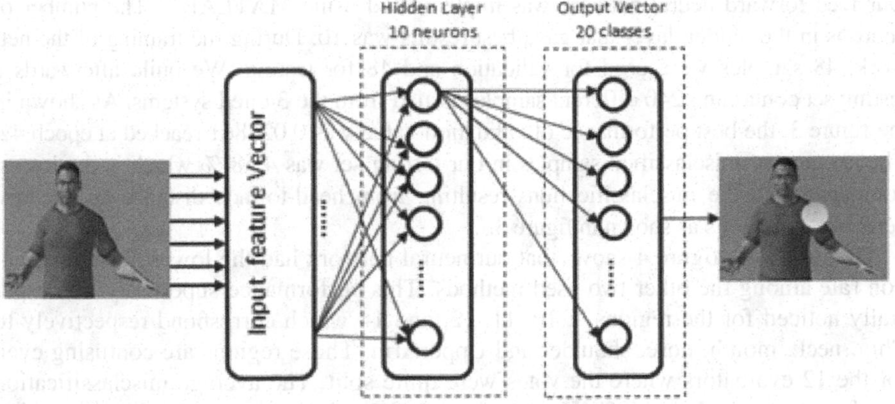

Fig. 2. Two-Layer Feed-forward neural network for hand location classification

5 Experimentations

During the experimentations, we collected a set of data composed of examples of signing avatars targeting each of the 20 signing space regions. We used WebSign [3], H-animator [2] and Poser[4]. Each of those systems was used to generate 8 differents sign pointing each of the 20 regions which give as 480 of total training data. The target output classes for this dataset were made by 10 Phd students and 2 sign language experts who were asked to give the output class for every sign, and the class with best voting was selected.

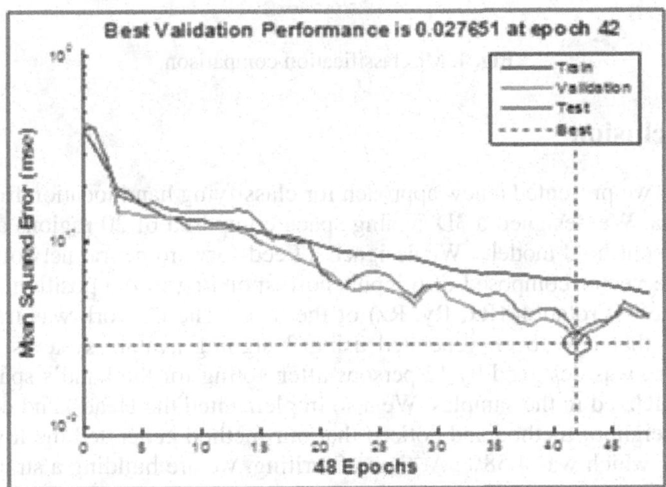

Fig. 3. Best validation performance of the neural network training

[4] http://poser.smithmicro.com/poser.html

Our feed-forward neural network was implemented using MATLAB[5] . The number of neurons in the hidden layer that gave best results was 10. During the training of the network, 48 samples were used for validation and 48 for testing. We build afterwards a testing set containing 240 different samples issued from the 3 cited systems. As shown in the figure 3, the best performance of validation value was 0.027861 reached at epoch 42. The average of misclassified samples in our testing set was 4.58 % which is the lowest compared with the misclassifications resulting from head-to-face distance and nearest neighbor's methods as shown in figure 3.

The following figure 4 shows that our neural network had the lowest misclassification rate among the other two used methods. This performance superiority was especially noticed for the regions 9, 10, 11, 12, and 14 which correspond respectively to Chin, neck, mouth, nose, shoulder and UpperArm. Those regions are confusing even for the 12 evaluators where the votes were quite split. The average misclassification rate for our method is 4.58%. However, using the neighbor method, after optimizing the K parameter for each class center, the average was 6.25%. Regarding the head-to-hand distance, misclassification reached 7.5% which is the highest rate.

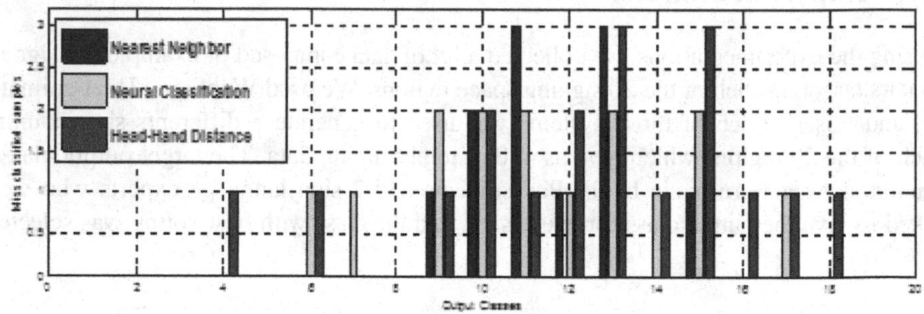

Fig. 4. Misclassification comparison

6 Conclusion

In this paper, we presented a new approach for classifying hand location from 3D sign language data. We designed a 3D signing space composed of 20 regions as specified in the movement-hold model. We designed a Feed-forward neural network that receives a feature vector composed of 6 inputs corresponding to the position of the hand as well as the 3D rotation (Rx, Ry, Rz) of the head. The network was trained using 480 samples that have been generated using 3 signing avatars systems. The target outputs matrix was designed by 12 persons after voting for the hand's space location that they visualized in the samples. We also implemented the Head-hand distance and the nearest neighbor method and noticed that our method generated the lowest classification error which was 4.58%. At time of writing, we are building a strategy to recognize another parameter which is the handshape. In the feature, hand orientation and hand movement will be studied in order to build a full framework for 3D sign language classification.

[5] http://www.mathworks.com/

References

1. Huenerfauth, M., et al.: Evaluating American Sign Language generation through the participation of native ASL signers. In: ACM SIGACCESS Conference on Computers and Accessibilit. ACM, New York (2007)
2. Buttussi, F., Chittaro, L., Nadalutti, D.: H-Animator: A Visual Tool for Modeling, Reuse and Sharing of X3D Humanoid Animations. In: International Conference on 3D Web Technology, New York (2006)
3. Jemni, M., Elghoul, O.: A System to Make Signs Using Collaborative Approach. In: Miesenberger, K., Klaus, J., Zagler, W.L., Karshmer, A.I. (eds.) ICCHP 2008. LNCS, vol. 5105, pp. 670–677. Springer, Heidelberg (2008)
4. Zwiterslood, I., Verlinden, M., Ros, J., van der Schoot, S.: Synthetic Signing for the Deaf: eSIGN. In: Conference and Workshop on Assistive Technologies for Vision and Hearing Impairment, Granada (2004)
5. Papadogiorgaki, M., Grammalidis, N., Sarris, N., Strintzis, M.G.: Synthesis of Virtual Reality Animations from SWML using MPEG-4 Body Animation Parameters. In: Sign Processing Workshop, Lisbon (2004)
6. Vogler, C., Metaxas, D.: ASL recognition based on a coupling between HMMs and 3D motion analysis. In: Sixth International Conference on Computer Vision (1998)
7. Liddell, S., Johnson, R.: American Sign Language: The Phonological Base. Sign Language Studies (164)
8. Huenerfauth, M.: Improving Spatial Reference in American Sign Language Animation through Data Collection from Native ASL Signers. In: Stephanidis, C. (ed.) Universal Access in HCI, Part III, HCII 2009. LNCS, vol. 5616, pp. 530–539. Springer, Heidelberg (2009)
9. Perniss, P.M.: Achieving spatial coherence in German Sign Language narratives: The use of classifiers and perspective. Lingua 117(17), 1315–1338 (2007)
10. Liang, R., Ouhyoung, M.: A real-time continuous gesture recognition system for sign language, In: International Conference on Automatic Face and Gesture Recognition, Nara, Japan (1998)
11. Stokoe, W.C.: Sign Language Structure: An Outline of the Visual Communication Systems of the American Deaf. Studies in Linguistics: Occasional Papers (18) (1960)
12. Han, J., Awad, G., Sutherland, A.: Modelling and segmenting subunits for sign language recognition based on hand motion analysis. Pattern Recognition Letters 30(16), 623–633 (2009)
13. Ding, L., Martinez, A.M.: Modelling and recognition of the linguistic components in American Sign Language. Image and Vision Computing 27(112), 1826–1844 (2009)
14. Oz, C., Leu, M.: American Sign Language word recognition with a sensory glove using artificial neural networks. Engineering Applications of Artificial Intelligence 24(17), 1204–1213 (2011)
15. Braffot, A., Dalle, P.: Sign language applications: preliminary modeling. Universal Access in the Information Society 4 (2008)
16. Bangham, J., Cox, S., Elliott, R., Glauert, J., Marshall, I., Rankov, S., Wells, M.: Virtual Signing: Capture, Animation, Storage and Transmission - An Overview of the ViSiCAST Project. In: IEEE Seminar on Speech and Language Processing for Disabled and Elderly People (2000)
17. Jaballah, K., Jemni, M.: Toward Automatic Sign Language Recognition from Web3D Based Scenes. In: Miesenberger, K., Klaus, J., Zagler, W., Karshmer, A. (eds.) ICCHP 2010, Part II. LNCS, vol. 6180, pp. 205–212. Springer, Heidelberg (2010)
18. Masters, T.: Advanced algorithms for neural networks: a C++ sourcebook. John Wiley & Sons, NY (1995)

Towards a Phonological Construction of Classifier Handshapes in 3D Sign Language

Kabil Jaballah and Mohamed Jemni

LaTICE Research Laboratory, University of Tunis, Tunis, Tunisia
Kabil.jaballah@utic.rnu.tn,
Mohamed.jemni@fst.rnu.tn

Abstract. 3D sign language generation has showed real performances since several years. Many systems have been proposed aiming to generate animated sign language through avatars, however, the technology still young and many fundamental parameters of sign language like facial expressions and other iconic features have been ignored in the proposed systems. In this paper, we focus on the generation and analysis of descriptive classifiers also called Size and Shape Specifiers (SASSes) in 3D sign language data. We propose a new adaptation of the phonological structure of handshapes that have been given by Brentari. Our adapted framework is able to encode 3D descriptive classifiers that can express different amounts or sizes of shapes. We describe the way our model has been implemented through an XML framework. Our model is a way to link the phonological level with the 3D physical animation level since it is compliant with sign language phonology as described by Brentari as well as Liddel & Johnson and compliant with the 3D animation standards.

Keywords: 3D Sign Language, Classifiers, phonology.

1 Introduction

In sign language, handshape is considered as the core parameter and has been widely studied in last years. Handshapes occur to describe many parts of any signed lexicon. It is used to describe a classifier, to construct a fixed form, to sign manual alphabets and words derived from it. The construction of a handshape has been considered for a long time as a core single unit where the hand is represented with a symbol [1,2]. This phonologic approach was proposed by Stokoe [1] who assigned a symbol to describe the hand as a core form. The approaches involved later to come with a new vision of handshape phonology because of articulatory similarities that have been noticed across different handshapes. A new representation of the phonology of a handshape has been subsequently proposed. The latter representation assumes that there are some basic handshapes from what we can derive more handshapes by changing the behavior of some features. This approach focuses on the "selected fingers" which are the active fingers that the signer changes the aperture (open-close) and "unselected fingers" which are the non-active fingers that remain in the background.

K. Miesenberger et al. (Eds.): ICCHP 2014, Part II, LNCS 8548, pp. 446–453, 2014.

The phonological representation of a handshape as proposed by Brentari [3] is well detailed and able to illustrate almost all handshapes in a given signed lexicon. In this context, special kinds of handshapes are classifiers. Classifiers have been studied and their iconic aspect has been demonstrated by Willcox [4] as they can convey metaphors, spatial relationships between object as well as description of sizes, shapes and amounts. Actually, classifier predicates, as they are called, are very important and not much considered in 3D sign language. Matt Huenerfauth showed in [5] the importance of designing a system able to generate spatially complex articulation like classifier predicates.

In this paper, we present the handshape structure as described by most researchers and we explain the advantages of the model given by Brentari [3]. We outline the different classifiers that exist in the literature and the importance of the iconic concepts that they can convey, we put a special focus on the descriptive classifiers and the fact that classic phonological approaches are enable to encode the non-discrete parameters like graduation in size and shape and we give our methodology to encode 3D classifier handshapes. We show the way we implemented the model we came up with using XML by instantiating several examples.

2 Classifiers in Sign Language

Classifiers in sign language are specific handshapes or body postures designed to convey additional information regarding nouns and verbs (predicates), such as, location, shape, size, manner or kind of action. They are for sign language what adjectives are for spoken languages. In ASL, there are many classifier handshapes used to represent specific "classes" or "categories" of objects. It is obvious that many handshape classifiers require additional non-manual signs to convey the right meaning. Whereas, there are commonly recognized handshapes typically used to show various categories or classes of objects.

2.1 Descriptive Classifiers

Descriptive classifiers (DCLs) are also known as size and shape specifiers (SASSes) are used to describe a person or an object. SASSes describe are able to describe physical properties like size, shape, depth and texture. They are subsequently considered as adjectives. The following figure shows 5 examples of DCL's as described below:

- CL-F: represents small round flat objects.
- CL-O: can represent a paper, a book or a pie.
- CL-B: describes smooth, flat surfaces
- CL-C-(claw): represents small spherical objects (with fingers closer together).
- CL-L-curved: describes circular or oval shaped objects dish, rug, and platter.

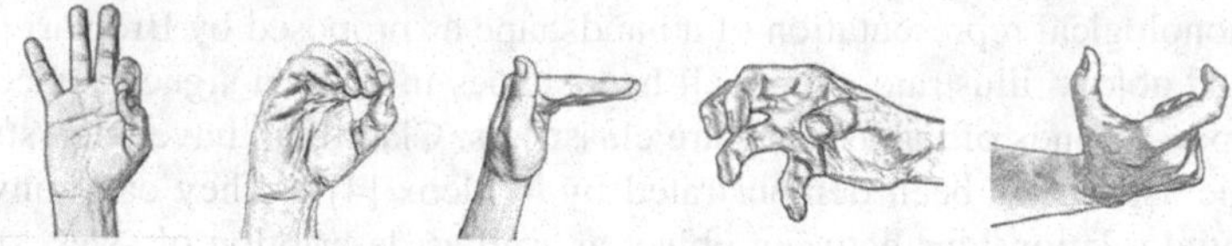

Fig. 1. Examples of descriptive classifiers from left to right: CL-F, CL-O, CL-B, CL-C (claw)[1]

Phonologically, the variation of the size, shape of an objected is conveyed through the alteration of the selected fingers and joints. The selected fingers and joints features are then contrastive even though it seems that joints configuration are more contrastive then selected fingers feature like showed in [6] and [3]. Actually, this kind of classifiers embeds a high level of iconicity since it imitates the physical aspect of the described object (size, shape, depth, etc.). Moreover, it can be used in many cases to express gradient variation in the physical aspects. This ability to use DCLs gradiently is the result of the gradient alteration of the joints configuration.

2.2 Gradient Variation in Descriptive Classifiers

The ability of descriptive classifiers to express gradient variation in size and shape shows its high level of iconicity. For example, the classifier CL-F can be used within many variations in the joints configuration to express variation in the perimeter of round objects like coins or discs like illustrated in figure 8. The same figure 8 shows also the example of classifier CL-G which expresses different variations in the thinness of a flat object like a strip of paper or the variation of the amount of water in a cup. In the example below, we expose the ability of classifiers CL-F and CL-G to go through four gradient variations that result on "small" towards "very big" amounts or perimeters.

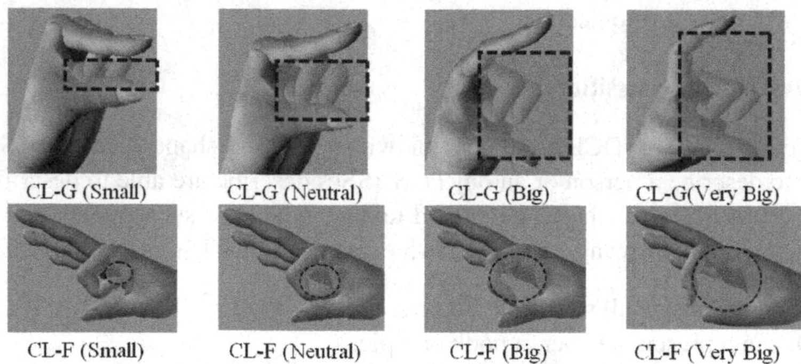

Fig. 2. Examples of gradient variation in CL-G and CL-F classifiers

[1] http://www.lifeprint.com/asl101/pages-signs/classifiers/classifiers-frame.htm

There is however another issue related to this property which resides on the uncertainty of the graduation conveyed through the classifier's handshape. By analogy with spoken languages, the gradient variation in classifiers can be considered like the variation in vowel length to express variation in length or duration. Indeed, the perception of the signed size or shape might differ slightly from one person to another. This behavior is difficult to model using the proposed approaches. Phonologically, gradient feature is a non-discrete parameter which is difficult to represent through the "selected fingers" and the "joints" features since the latter feature embed a final set of states and rules that don't handle gradient classifier. Recently, researchers suggested using at least four joints configurations in order to represent the gradient variation in DCLs, especially for round objects; it was the case in [6].

In some cases, joints of the handshape are not contrastive. In fact, some descriptive classifiers like the CL-claw and CL-L which are two-handed classifiers. The gradient variation expressed through those classifiers are conveyed by the alteration of the joints configuration of external articulations especially the shoulder. The selected fingers feature remains unchanged during the construction of the CL-L and the CL-claw, the joints configuration remain also the same. In our work, we adapted the phonological description proposed by Brentari to make it able to represent two-handed classifier handshapes as well as to encode non-discrete features like the gradient variation conveyed by Size and Shape Specifiers (SaSSes).

2.3 Phonological Structure of DCL

The main objectives of the phonological representation are the following:

- Present a common phonological description towards representing both classic handshapes as well as classifiers.
- Include a new feature able to encode the non-discrete properties of the handshape such as iconic behavior
- Handle the gradient variation conveyed through descriptive classifiers also called size and shape specifiers (SaSSes).
- Handle specific two-handed classifiers where extra-hand joints are contrastive.

The following figure shows the phonological structure that we came up with. The model is borrowed from what has been proposed in the literature with adding the nodes "quantity, "joints1" and "amplitude" under the node "hands" and the node "amplitude" under the node "fingers1". The given structure is able to encode classic handshapes and classifiers as well specific descriptive classifiers that convey non-discrete behavior like gradient sizes or amounts.

The phonological structure above is adapted from the models given by most of the researchers like what has been proposed in the most recognized studies [6,7] and [2]. We propose a new structure by adding some features that aim to handle the two-handed classifiers and describe better the iconic property conveyed by size and shape specifiers. The added nodes are:

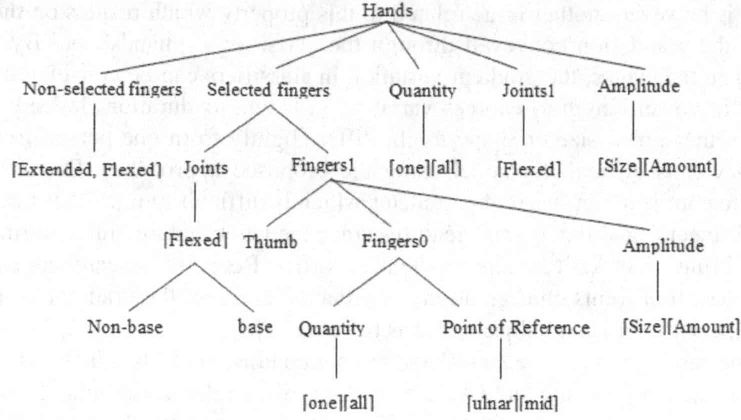

Fig. 3. Phonological structure of 3D handshapes and classifiers

- Quantity: This node has been introduced under the hands node in order to specify whether the classifier is two-handed or not. In this context, the value "one" means that the handshape (or classifier) is signed using one hand. The right or left hand is not specified since it depends on whether the signer is left-handed or right-handed. If the classifier or handshape is two-handed, the value of quantity is "all". This is actually the case of some classifiers like CL-L and CL-C classifiers where a symmetric flexure of shoulders joints is contrastive towards expressing the size of the signed object. In case where "all" is specified, two other nodes must be specified as well; the "joints1" and the "amplitude".
- Joints1: this node is specified when the value of "Quantity is set to "all". The node joints aims to specify the symmetry that links the posture of the arms by specifying their flexion/extension behavior. Actually, the feature "flexed" attribute values are the same as the feature flexed that belongs to the " joints" node.
- Amplitude: New node "amplitude" has been added for each of the nodes "hands" and "fingers0". In fact, in two-handed classifiers, the shoulder joints of both arms are those which affect the gradient size of the signed object. However, in one handed classifiers, the node amplitude will encode the gradient degree expressed by the joints configurations of the selected fingers. This node aims to encode the iconic property expressed by descriptive classifiers like size, perimeters of round objects, amount of water in a cup etc. What makes this kind of handshape difficult to model is the information conveyed is uncertain and can be evaluated differently from one person to another. The perception of human is subsequently primordial to evaluate a size or an amount expressed by such a classifier.

In this context, we introduce a new methodology for encoding this kind of information. In fact, the size or amount of an object is modeled through fuzzy logic. 12 participants were involved in the evaluation of different sizes and amount in order to set the closest membership functions that will encode the gradient degree that expresses size or amount. The methodology is detailed in [8]. The aim of the new methodology is based on the prediction of a crisp value that expresses the size of an object. This crisp value is obtained through a fuzzy inference system that takes as input the joints configurations and calculates the degree of membership of each configuration in one of the four categories of size "Very Small", "Small", "Neutral", "Big", "Very Big". Finally a crisp value going from 0 to 10 will be calculated to express the size.

3 Implementation of the Proposed Model

The visual (real) classifier is encoded through the phonological model that we adapted. Then, the features of the handshape are encoded using the XML based structure so we can store templates and reuse them later in different context. The XML based tagging is also important towards the portability of the proposed approach. In fact, it will allow us to be independent of the 3D animation language that will be used for animating the 3D handshape.

3.1 Overview of the XML Scheme

The figure below shows a portion of the XML schema that we designed in order to instantiate samples of new 3D handshape classifiers. The full schema code can be found in the appendix. As we can see in the figure, some nodes attribute values are restricted to a range of data. This is the case of the node "joints" values are restricted to a textual content using the tag <xs: restriction base="xs:string">. The range of data used is set using the tag <xs:enumeration> for each option. Regarding the nodes where the attribute range of values is restricted to an interval [0,1] which is actually the case of the node "Amplitude", we use the tag <xs:restriction base="xs:integer"> to specify that the possible values type and then we adjust the tags <xs:minInclusive value="0"/> and <xs:maxInclusive value="10"/> in order to set the interval. The full schema code can be found by following the link.[2]

3.2 Instantiation of the Proposed Structure

The previous XML schema is used to validate the instances of 3D handshape classifiers that will be generated through various ways. In the context of our research, we instantiated more than 20 classifiers and approximately 40 core handshapes that have been used for generating animated virtual signers as part of the WebSign project [9]. The following table 1 illustrates the new nodes added in the phonological structure of classifier handshapes and the way they add more clearness to the conveyed visual/spatial behavior. In fact, the classic structure, there is no specification on the size or amount intensity. The joints of selected fingers are specified by using one of the predefined ranges of possible values. In the model we came up with, the feature "amplitude" brings more accuracy and precision on how the joints configuration should be. When generating the 3D handshape, the specified amplitude will be converted into a precise angle of rotation of the selected fingers. The classic representation has another drawback since we need to describe each hand separately. Then, the given description doesn't contain any information on the other hand's posture. In the new structure, we can notice the presence of a new feature called "joints1" which allows us to know

[2] https://www.dropbox.com/s/ne9aqpt2j5la3cw/phono.xsd

more about the posture of the other hand's configuration. Thus, in the case of one handed classifier, the feature "quantity" is to "one" and subsequently, the feature "amplitude" of the node "hands" is not implemented.

Table 1. Example of implementation of a classifier

<table>
<tr><th>Classifier</th><th colspan="2">Phonological description</th><th>XML instantiation</th></tr>
<tr><td rowspan="2">CL-G (small)</td><td>Classic representation</td><td>Hands:
Non-selected fingers: "Flexed"
Selected-fingers:
Joints: "bent"
Fingers1:
Thumb
Fingers0:
Quantity: "one"</td><td rowspan="2"><hands xsi:noNamespaceSchemaLocation="phono.xsd" xmlns:xsi="http://www.w3.org/2001/XMLSchema-instance">
<non-slected-fingers>flexed</non-slected-fingers>
<selected-fingers>
<joints>Bent</joints>
<fingers1>
<Thumb>
</Thumb>
<fingers0>
<Quantity>One</Quantity>
</fingers0>
<amplitude>3</amplitude>
</fingers1>
</selected-fingers>
<quantity>One</quantity>
<joints1>Flat-closed</joints1>
</hands></td></tr>
<tr><td>New representation</td><td>Hands:
Non-selected fingers: "Flexed"
Quantity: "One"
Joints1: "Flat-closed"
Selected-fingers:
Joints: "bent"
Fingers1:
Thumb
Amplitude: 3
Fingers0:
Quantity: "one"</td></tr>
</table>

4 Conclusion

In this paper, we showed the need of handling handshapes phonology in the generation of 3D sign language. We focused on the classifier predicates which bring iconicity to the signed discourse. We studied the most common phonological structures of handshapes and came up with a new model able to convey gradient size/amount within SASSes as well as handling two-handed DCLs. We implemented our model trough an XML framework and generated more than 20 examples as part of the Websign project. We showed the clearness that our structure brings to the studied handshapes compared to the classic description methods. At time of writing we are investigating new ways to handle the iconicity conveyed by other classifiers especially handling classifiers where tools and objects are manipulated.

References

1. Stokoe, W.C.: Sign Language Structure: An Outline of the Visual Communication Systems of the American Deaf. Studies in Linguistics: Occasional Papers (18) (1960)
2. Liddell, S., Johnson, R.: American sign language, the phonological base. Sign Language Studies 64 (1988)
3. Brentari, D.: Handshape in sign language phonology. In: Companion to Phonology. Wiley-Blackwells, New York (2011)
4. Willcox, S.: Cognitive iconicity: Conceptual spaces, meaning, and gesture in signed language. University of New Mexico, New Mexico (2003)

5. Huenerfauth, M.: Spatial representation of classifier predicates for machine translation into American sign language. In: 4th Internationnal Conference on Language Ressources and Evaluation, pp. 24–31 (2004)
6. Eccarius, P.: Finding common ground: A comparison of handshape across multiple sign languages. Prude university (2002)
7. van der Hulst, H.: Acquisitional evidence for the phonological composition of handshape. In: GALA (1996)
8. Jaballah, K., Jemni, M.: Fuzzy Analysis of Classifier Handshapes from 3D Sign Language Data. In: Petrosino, A. (ed.) ICIAP 2013, Part II. LNCS, vol. 8157, pp. 621–630. Springer, Heidelberg (2013)

Efficient Tracking Method to Make a Real Time Sign Language Recognition System

Maher Jebali[1], Patrice Dalle[2], and Mohamed Jemni[1]

[1] Research Lab. LaTICE, ESSTT University of Tunis, Tunisia
maher.jbeli@gmail.com,
mohamed.jemni@fst.rnu.tn
[2] Research Lab. IRIT Univ. of Toulouse3, France
patrice.dalle@irit.fr

Abstract. In the field of automatic treatment of natural languages, the analysis and the exploitation of each statement in sign language (SL) have a great importance. In fact, the own specificities of SL such as the simultaneity of many parameters, the significant role of the facial expression, the use of space to structure the statement, as well as the technical specificities, such as the change lightening and the presence of occlusion in the space of one-sighted-capture, have a deep effect on tracking the different parts of the body. In this paper, we propose an empiric method of tracking adapted to the specificities of SL that we use to elaborate a real time recognition system based on a prediction approach.

Keywords: Sign Language Recognition, Object Tracking, Sign Language Modeling.

1 Introduction

SL is used by the deaf and hearing-impaired communities, in order to establish communication. It can be described as a visual language which characterized by the motion of certain parts of the body such as, the face, the mouth, eyes, trunck and hands. At the present time, we can admit that several researchers are meant to put the stress on the automatic analysis and recognition of signs, particularly automatic SL interpretation [4]. This may help SL users to communicate without referring to human interpreter. To succeed in this achievement, video treatments and linguistic models are developped. Several tasks use special markers [2] to overcome occlusions problems, but this do not allow us to put in practice the real application used by all deaf people, due to the difficulty in using these devices. To overcome these obstacles, many tracking algorithim have been suggested. The particle filter (PF) algorithm has become very common for non-linear or non-Gaussian problems. Popularly, colur features and contours are used by PF tracking algorithm [7]. The inconvenience of the colour based algorithms, is that it is impossible to handle occlusions between similarly coloured target because it disregards the spatial information. the authors of [3] Suggested a PF based

K. Miesenberger et al. (Eds.): ICCHP 2014, Part II, LNCS 8548, pp. 454–457, 2014.

tracker using color cue. However, the position of each object can not be precisely determined during occlusion, since the filters share the same skin blob. In the few last years, scalability was addressed by turning to sign linguistics to help classification and recognition. to overcome the problem of the vocabulary size or the complexity of modeling, many researchers shaped signs using sub-units, such as cooper and all. [1] who linked the subunits resulted from 2D and 3D information simultaneously, and they showed the efficiency of this approach with an independant signers (76%). We must highlight that the majority of works do not contain a real time SLR system, although it is primordial aim. So that, the applications can be used by deaf community. In this work, we are exhibiting an orginal approach which allows us to recognize signs in a real timing and in a particular context. The proposed method of recognition is based on prediction, in a context of dialogue between interlocutors and the system. At this level, the recognition stage requires a tracking stage of different body parts. Our tracking method is in fact an emperic method and the recognition is adapted dynamically to different levels of dialogue.

2 Multiple Components Tracking

Some approaches tend to make a training step and create a model which depends on the colour of skin, lightening and conditions related to the environement in the training set. This work presents an explicit definition of skin regions for initialisation suggested by Kovac and all. [6]. The main obstacle to achieve high recognition rate are the chrominance and luminance components which are not decoupled , which result in an inaccurate detection in the shadow area. However, the advantage side of this approach is that can ignore the training stage, in addition, it is easy to be applied. In the YCrCb color space, the skin colour is shaped as a bivariate normal distribution. Y component indicates the luminance and is rejected to find solutions to shadow problems, we note that the regions are much better detected. After that, we treat the issue of head and hands tracking. It is consisting of A) for each frame, we assign one or multiple labels for different bodyparts. B) the estimation of rectangles at region with multiple occluded labels. In this context, two cases are manifested. One or two objects in the occlusion case and three objects in the case of non-occlusion. The position of the face is determined by using the skin segmetation before occlusion (first frame). We consider that the connected region with the most significant area which is situated in the upper part of the frame corresponds to the face.

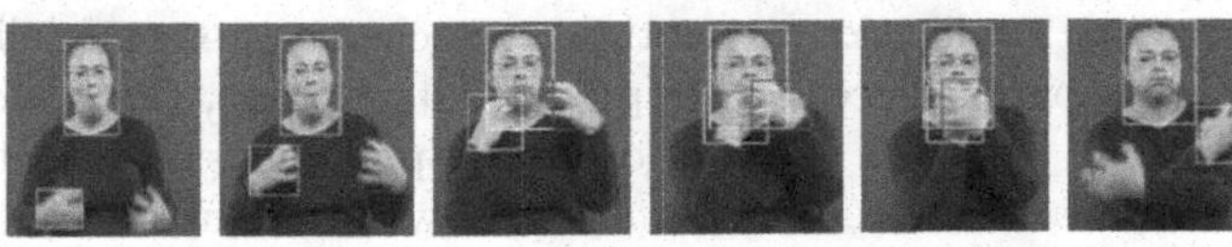

Fig. 1. Multiple components tracking

Not Occluded Objects: concerning hand labeling, we applied a linear prediction of centroid position of each hand; considering the preceding frames; the predictor coefficient match to the model of constant velocity. Afterwards, we attribute the labels based on the minimum distances between the centroids of the objects and the predicted positions. On each object, we also adapt one rectangle assuming that it can rougly approximate the head or hand blob. We intend to use the suitable rectangles in case of occlusions.

Occluded Objects: Similarly to the previous case, we refer the linear prediction for all parameters of rectangles of the current frame. When a number of consecutive occluded images is important, it can results in cases of ambiguity in the exit of occlusion. To overcome the uncertainty of two hypothesis (is the right hand on the right or on the left, and the same for the left one), we estimate the interim centroid of each party of the body corresponding to the skin model between consecutive frames. Add to this, we are repeating the prediction and the estimation of the correspondant model reculing faster through the sequence of the opposit frame, which is based on hand holding the ordinary position which is either the left or the right one of upper part of the body. Figure 1 illustrates the tracking result of the image sequences with and without occlusion. We notice that the system provides a precise tracking even during occlusions. Our tracking experiments were based on more than 20 videos and reach 80% of accuracy.

3 Sign Language Recognition Modeling

We are using the previous described algorithm to generate models of recognition. The signs are pre-analysed before being added to the basis which can be enriched in an incremental manner. there is no complilation of the whole basis ; it will be done during the interpretation, only on small groups of condidates signs. In fact, aiming to put in practice a fast and robust SLR system, we tend to exploit an approach of prediction-verification when possible. In an ascending classical approach, detection-tracking-measure-characterization-recognition, the presence of errors in the first levels will cause errors of recognition. Or, for the mentioned reasons, will risk to have frequent errors or inaccurance in these levels of image analaysis. At this stage, we can palliate this default through static approaches which directly link the signal aspect to the decision, as it has been used in vocal language treatement, but this fact can suppose important size corpus which are not available in SL, however the characteristics of SL need opposingly more important corpus than vocal languages. We are studying a generic system of interaction in SL with a computing system in the context of scenario which can be changed from one application to another. the scheme of our modeling system is detailed in [5]. Apart a necessarily upward initial phase, the system exploit the scenario and the acquired information in the previous stages to predict the content and the form in different levels. This allows it through a compilation in a real time of the predicted sign characteristic to substitue the signs description, least robust, regarding its labeling by checking the estimated characteristics which are not meant to be numerous and precise, and therefore, much more reliable. This coupling understanding-recognition also exploit the specifity of SL, the narrow imbrication between the shape and meaning from the earlier stages, the given morphological data which are presented in the phonological component of the basis. Knowing that, the limit of this approach is presented in the possibility of being well predicted, but this can not be denied it allows to achieve real applications, request system, pedagogical or playful application, where such scenario exist.

4 Conclusion

We suggested an integrated framework for head and hand tracking in videos of SL, it is in fact employed in prediction based SLR. Concerning the detection of different components, a simple skin colour modeling is defined having results on fast and reliable segmentation. Additionally, the tracking result on occlusion disambiguation in order to facilate feature extraction. The experiments were based on more than 20 videos and reach 80% of accuracy. The suggested prediction based recognition framework analyzed temporal visual signal obtained from the tracker which is changing dynamically in each level of dialogue, showing a system that allows a compilation in real time to be used by all the deaf with no exception.

References

1. Cooper, H., Ong, E.J., Pugeault, N., Bowden, R.: Sign Language Recognition using Sub-Units. Journal of Machine Learning Research 13, 2205–2231 (2012)
2. Cem, K., Furkan, K., Yunus, E.K.: Real time hand pose estimation using depth sensors. In: IEEE International Conference on Computer Vision Workshops (ICCV Workshops), pp. 1228–1234 (2011)
3. Gianni, F., Collet, C., Dalle, P.: Robust tracking for processing of videos of communication's gestures. In: Sales Dias, M., Gibet, S., Wanderley, M.M., Bastos, R. (eds.) GW 2007. LNCS (LNAI), vol. 5085, pp. 93–101. Springer, Heidelberg (2009)
4. Habili, N., Lim, C., Moini, A.: Segmentation of the face and hands in sign language video sequences using color and motion cues. IEEE Transactions on Circuits and Systems for Video Technology 14, 1086–1097 (2004)
5. Jebali, M., Dalle, P., Jemni, M.: Towards Sign language recognition system in Human-Computer interactions. In: Fourth International Conference on Information and Communication Technology and Accessibility. Hammamet (2013)
6. Kovac, J., Peer, P., Solina, F.: Human skin color clustering for face detection. In: EUROCON International Conference on Computer as a Tool, vol. 2, pp. 144–148 (2003)
7. Lefebvre-Albaret, F.: Traitement automatique de vidos en LSF, modlisation et exploitation des contraintes phonologiques du mouvement. Phd thesis, University of Toulouse (2010)

A Virtual Signer to Interpret SignWriting

Yosra Bouzid and Mohamed Jemni

Research Laboratory of Technologies of Information
and Communication & Electrical Engineering LaTICE, University of Tunis, Tunisia
yosrabouzid@hotmail.fr,
Mohamed.jemni@fst.rnu.tn

Abstract. In the absence of a standardized writing system to transcribe their native sign language, deaf signers cannot communicate between each other in their own language except face-to-face. They can't leave messages, read books take class notes and send email in sign language. Certainly, being able to read and write their own language would bring to these signers the same advantage that writing systems for spoken languages bring to speakers. SignWriting system seems at present the most appropriate method that could meet the deaf needs than other existing notations, as it was intended as an everyday tool for reading and writing. However, such script requires a training to learn to interpret the proposed transcriptions. In this paper, we present an avatar-based system named, tuniSigner, able to display and interpret automatically sign language transcriptions, in the well known SignWriting system. Showing how the actual gestures should be performed in virtual reality would be very useful to signers.

Keywords: Deaf, Hearing Impaired, Virtual Avatar, Signwriting, Sign Language.

1 Introduction

Given their inability to hear sounds, Deaf and Hard of Hearing people depend on visual and gestural faculties to communicate, express themselves and make sense of the world around them. The natural language for these persons is the Sign Language which has its own linguistic features, grammatical rules and syntax, but does not have, until now, a widely established writing system. Indeed, the lack of a standardized writing form for their primary language limits the possibility of the hearing impaired to provide information in a form equivalent to the signing gestures. Therefore, they are often required to access documentation or communicate in a language that is not natural to them [1], and this can pose a serious accessibility flaw in their daily lives especially for those who have low literacy skills. As is well known deaf signers experience dramatic difficulties in acquiring and using written Vocal Languages. The global survey report of the World Federation of the Deaf and the Swedish National Association of the Deaf for 2008 indicates that only five percent (5%) of the world's Deaf people can read and write, while, 90% are totally illiterate or semi-literate.

To date, the most attempts that have been proposed to write sign language have confined themselves to the notation of the base form of the sign, such as one would

K. Miesenberger et al. (Eds.): ICCHP 2014, Part II, LNCS 8548, pp. 458–465, 2014.

find in a dictionary or in short sentences [2], and this make them impractical for general users. SignWriting is another writing formalism based on the transcription of manual and also non-manual elements of non-standard signs and complex units through symbols. It depicts actually a promising alternative to provide documents in an easy to grasp written form of any sign language. Nevertheless, a training to learn to interpret the static transcriptions is needed for deaf signers who are accustomed to the use of their preferred language in a visual-gestural modality. In this paper, we present an avatar based system called, tuniSigner, to synthesize sign language animations from SignWriting notations. The virtual interpreter can make the notation content completely accessible to deaf learners who do not know how it read.

2 Related Work

Thanks to their flexibility and cost effectiveness, virtual avatars have become increasingly common elements of user interfaces for a wide range of applications dedicated for the Deaf. We present in this section a brief background of the relevant works that have been proposed to render an animated avatar from sign language notations.

2.1 Stokoe Notation

William Stokoe was the leading pioneer of Sign Language research. He invented the first notation system to record American Sign Language (ASL) using combinations of a limited number of smaller units called cheremes. The development of the Stokoe system advanced the field of sign linguistics significantly, but it is now outdated [3]. This system is seen actually as inadequate to represent sign language for regular use, because it has no way of indicating non manual features such as facial expressions. It was created essentially as a tool for linguists to describe singular signs in a dictionary.

SignSynth is a sign language synthesis application developed at the University of New Mexico to generate many signs using Stokoe parameters. It takes as input a sign language text in ASCII-Stokoe notation and converts it to an internal feature tree. This underlying linguistic representation is converted then into 3D animation sequences using VRML in order to be rendered automatically by Web3D browser [4].

2.2 HamNoSys Notation

Hamburg Notation System is a well established phonetic transcription system which has been in widespread use since its original version in the tradition of Stokoe-based system. It includes over 210 iconic characters to represent the SL phonemes including non manual features and information about the signing space. The purpose of HamNoSys has never been a usage in everyday communication. It was designed essentially to comply with research requirements, including corpus annotation, sign generation, machine translation and dictionary construction [5].

ViSiCAST [6] and eSign [7], two EU-funded projects, have achieved significant result in creating animations from HamNoSys. The eSignEditor is the main component of the avatar-based system, which is used to turn a HamNoSys representation of a sign into SiGML, an XML based-language, and sent it to the animation synthesiser, Animgen. The major task of Animgen is to enrich the SiGML data with the avatar geometry data such as vertex coordinates and rotation values. This combined data is fed into the avatar rendering engine which will animate a virtual agnet in real-time.

2.3 SignWriting Notation

SignWriting (SW) is a practical writing system for deaf sign languages. Although it can surely be used in linguistic tasks, the SW system is essentially designed to be used by common deaf people. It is conceived to be used in writing sign languages for the same purposes hearing people commonly use written oral languages [8][12], such as taking notes, reading books, writing emails, learning at school, etc.

The International SignWriting Alphabet ISWA comprises 639 base symbols to represent the different phonological aspects of SL like movements, mimics and timing aspects (sequentiality and simultaneity) in terms of highly iconic glyphs. By combining these, signs can be written in a full body form using a stick person, a 'stacked' form which removes the stick figure for placing the iconic symbols above and below each other, or in a short hand form [9]. Despite SW is closely visually resembles the concrete signs, a deaf user requires a training to master the different symbols and characteristics governing the notation for becoming a proficient reader or writer.

VSign [10] and SASL [11] provide two examples of avatar-based systems which use SignWriting notation as input. Both approaches interpret and convert the SWML (SignWriting Markup Language) format [13], as an XML encoding of SignWriting, to a sequence of body animation parameters (BAPs) of the MPEG-4 standard for driving a VRML avatar in real time. However, it should be noted here that VSigns has been fairly successful but has experienced a number of problems when contacts and complex movements are involved in the notation; they were not accurate enough in the output. On the other hand, SASL's method has achieved an average recognition rate of 82% over 8 tested notations.

3 System Description

The proposed system forms a part of the WebSign project which is concerned with developing web-based applications and services to improve the accessibility of people with hearing impairments to spoken and written information using avatar technology. The main purpose of the present tool is to provide additional support for these individuals to learn and use a written form of their mother tongue, by offering them a visual-gestural language alternative to its content. It takes a SignWriting notation provided in an XML-based variant (SWML) as input and generates the equivalent signing gestures performed by a humanoid in a virtual space. Fig. 1 gives an overview of the system architecture which consists of three main modules.

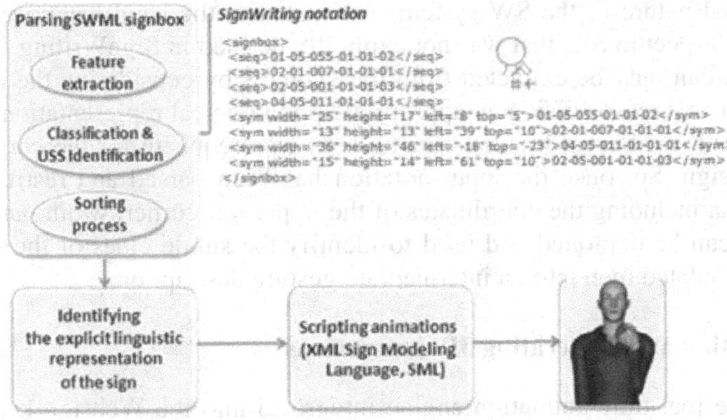

Fig. 1. An overview of the system architecture

3.1 Parsing SWML Sign-Box

An SWML sign-box can include two types of elements: "sym" as spatial symbol and "seq" as sequential symbol. The spatial symbols include 2-dimensional positioning and are considered unordered, while sequential ones form an optional ordered list of symbols IDs organized by the SignSpelling Sequence rules.

For parsing and processing the SWML sign-box, the following steps must be performed: first, extract the associated information with each spatial symbol that can capture an articulator or some aspect of its movement. Second, define the set of spatial tokens representing hands, directional movement, finger movement and contact as an underlying structure of the sign (USS). The USS is used to identify the type of the written sign which may be static or dynamic, produced with one-hand or with both hands, symmetrical (in which both hands have the same shape, the same location and make the same movement) or not symmetrical, in unit (both hands move as a group to the same direction) or not in unit, simple or compound. We assume here that a compound sign comprises at least two hand symbols and two movement symbols for each articulator (right or left).

According to the type and the underlying structure of the sign, a set of precedence rules will be applied appropriately to arrange the list of symbols. For example, the sign "broke" presented in Fig. 1, is a simple sign articulated with one hand where its USS includes one hand shape, a symbol movement and a touch contact. In this case, a precedence rule based on the direction of the movement arrow is used to determine if the touch contact occurs before or after the motion. This kind of rules serves essentially to identify the predecessors of a directional movement that are located at the tail of the arrow, and its successors that are located at the arrow head.

3.2 Identifying the Explicit Linguistic Representation of the Sign

SWML is not complete enough and phonologically-based enough to be used for the underlying linguistic representation of a sign. It is merely an XML adaptation of SignWriting which can provide information about the relative position of each basic symbol in the notation. However, some implicit information may be omitted given the bi-dimensional nature of the SW system. For instance, the hand location is a salient phonological aspect in SLs that was not explicitly defined in SignWriting and thereby in SWML. It can only be extracted from the symbols by considering the most likely positions. For this reason, using an appropriate phonological representation that explicitly specifies the different linguistic features is a prerequisite for the correct performance of a sign. So, once the input notation has been parsed and restructured, the collected data, including the coordinates of the upper left corner, width, and height of each glyph, can be exploited and used to identify the subtle clues of the sign which will be reformulated then into an intermediate gesture description.

3.3 Scripting and Generating 3D Animations

Thanks to the real time animation engine integrated into the Websign kernel, an H-Anim compliant avatar can be used to render any sign language gestures annotated with a scripting language named SML [14]. The Sign Modeling Language provides an extra layer around X3D for facilitating the control and manipulation of the virtual agent. It can describe the signed utterance in terms of translation or Euler rotation of a group of joints, such as the neck, wrist, eyebrows, eyelids and so on. Therefore, the main goal of the present phase is to achieve the automatic conversion of the linguistic representation of the SignWriting notation into SML before sending it to the WebSign player and generating the corresponding animations (Fig. 2).

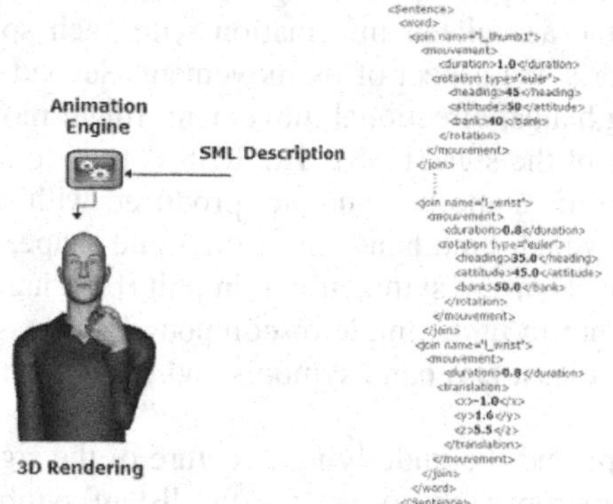

Fig. 2. Rendering 3D animation from SML script

For example, the hand movement is defined in SML as a translation of the wrist joint toward a specific position in the signing space or on the body signer in case of contact. Fig. 3 illustrates some examples of face and body contact. Basing on the initial position of the hand, the trajectory form of the movement symbol (straight, curved, circular, etc) and the size of articulation (short, medium, large), the intermediate positions can be calculated automatically. It is important to know that an animation solver based on inverse kinematics [15] is employed to perform the analytic computation in the real time: rotations for shoulder, elbow, and wrist joints are commutated by inverse kinematics in accordance with 3D positions of wrist joint in the space.

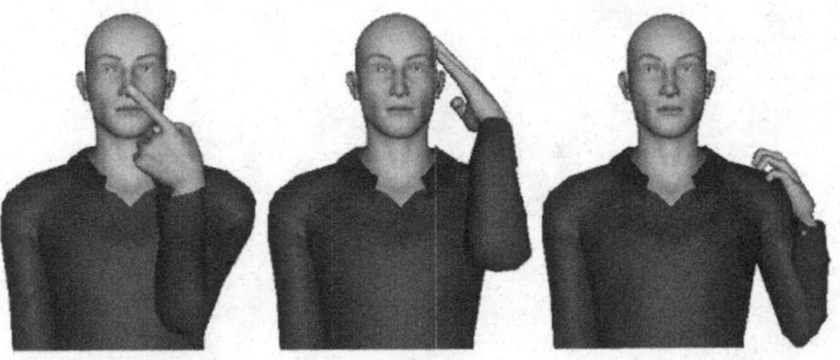

Fig. 3. Examples of face and body contact

For the non manual gestures which present a key component in all sign languages, WebSign avatar can produce the important facial expressions and body postures basing on two different techniques: a Rigging method [16] to simulate the head swinging, gaze changes, tongue movement, and a physics based muscle method [17] for emulating facial mimics like eyebrows, cheeks and mouth motions (Fig. 4). The control of such articulators is done via SML.

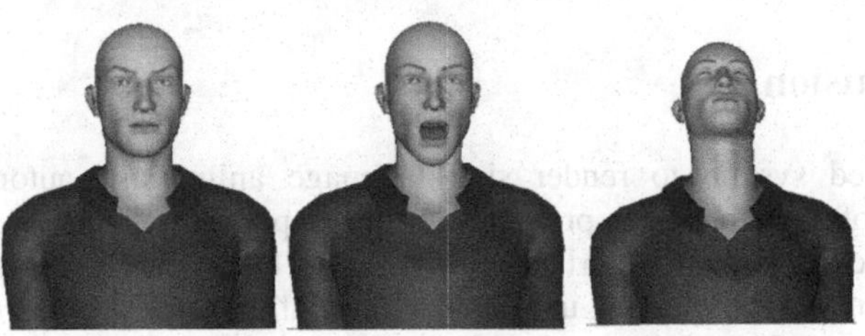

Fig. 4. Examples of non manual gestures

4 Preliminary Results

The proposed system has been evaluated with more than 1000 SignWriting notations, from different sign languages (Tunisian Sign Language, French Sign Language and American Sign Language). The XML-encoded corresponding to each notation is obtained from SignPuddle website (www.signbank.org/signpuddle).

The results we have obtained, so far, are valuable and very promising. However, in order to achieve an objective evaluation, we have provided a simple web user interface for our system (Fig. 5). The user can search the sign he want to learn, click and the virtual agent will demonstrate the 3D signing animation that corresponds to its SignWriting notation. The user can also evaluate the accuracy of signing animations and give feedback. tuniSigner is accessible online at http://www.tunisigner.com/

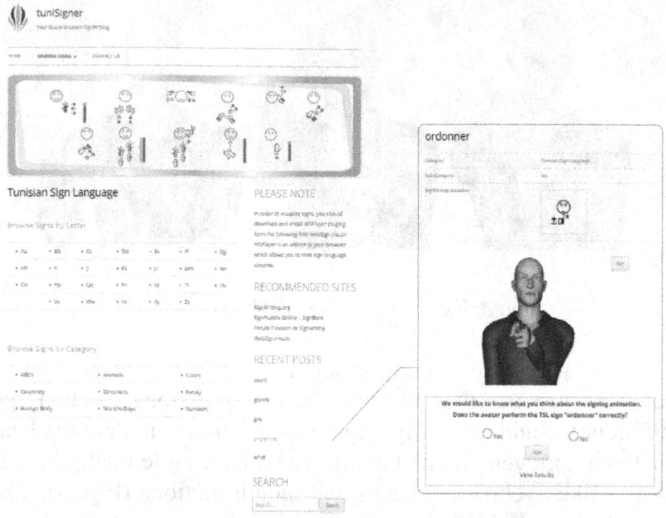

Fig. 5. tuniSigner interface

5 Conclusion

An avatar-based system to render sign language animations automatically from SignWriting notations has been presented in this paper. Showing how the actual gestures should be performed in virtual reality would be of paramount importance not only for deaf and hard of hearing users but also for all interested in learning SW.

In our future works, we plan to extend our multilingual dictionary to include more individual signs and sentences from different sign languages. Besides, we aim to provide online multimedia courses and games for deaf children to motivate them to learn SignWriting.

References

1. Borgia, F., Bianchini, C.S., Dalle, P., Marsico, M.D.: Resource Production of Written Forms of Sign Languages by a User-Centered Editor, Swift (SignWriting improved fast transcriber). In: Proceedings of the International Conference on Language Resources and Evaluation (LREC), Istanbul, Turky (2012)
2. Braem, P.B.: SignWriting and Swiss German Sign Language (November 2002)
3. Stokoe, W.C.: Sign language structure: An outline of the visual communication systems of the American deaf. Studies in Linguistics: Occasional Papers (8) (1960)
4. Grieve-Smith, A.B.: SignSynth: A Sign Language Synthesis Application Using Web3D and Perl. In: Wachsmuth, I., Sowa, T. (eds.) GW 2001. LNCS (LNAI), vol. 2298, pp. 134–145. Springer, Heidelberg (2002)
5. Hanke, T.: HamNoSys—Representing sign language data in language resources and language processing contexts. In: Workshop Proceedings: Representation and Processing of Sign Languages (LREC), Paris, pp. 1–6 (2004)

6. Bangham, J., Cox, S., Elliott, R., Glauert, J., Marshall, I., Rankov, S., Wells, M.: Virtual signing: Capture, animation, storage and transmission - An overview of the ViSiCAST project. In: Proceedings of the IEEE Seminar on Speech and Language Processing for Disabled and Elderly People, London, UK (2000)
7. Smith, R., Morrissey, S., Somers, H.: HCI for the deaf community: developing human-like avatars for sign language synthesis. In: Proceedings of the 4th Irish Human Computer Interaction Conference (IHCI), Dublin, Ireland (September 2010)
8. Sutton, V.: International Movement Writing Alphabet, Center for Sutton Movement Writing, L, La Jolla
9. Smith, K.J.W.C.: Sign Language – are we making information accessible? Deafax, UK
10. Papadogiorgaki, M., Grammalidis, N., Sarris, N.: VSigns – A Virtual Sign Synthesis Web Tool. In: Workshop on Information and Knowledge Management for Integrated Media Communication, Greece, pp. 25–31 (2004)
11. Moemedi, K., Connan, J.: Rendering an animated avatar from SignWriting notation. In: Proceedings of the Southern Africa Telecommunication Networks and Applications Conference, Western Cape (2010)
12. da Rocha Costa, A.C., Dimuro, G.P.: *SignWriting*-Based Sign Language Processing. In: Wachsmuth, I., Sowa, T. (eds.) GW 2001. LNCS (LNAI), vol. 2298, pp. 202–205. Springer, Heidelberg (2002)
13. Costa, A.C.R., Dimuro, G.P.: SignWriting and SWML: Paving the way to sign language processing. In: TALN Workshop, Batz-sur-Mer (June 2003)
14. Jemni, M., Elghoul, O.: A system to make signs using collaborative approach. In: Miesenberger, K., Klaus, J., Zagler, W.L., Karshmer, A.I. (eds.) ICCHP 2008. LNCS, vol. 5105, pp. 670–677. Springer, Heidelberg (2008)
15. Yahia, N.B., Jemni, M.: A Greedy Inverse Kinematics Algorithm for Animating 3D Signing Avatars. In: Proceedings of the 4th International Conference on Information and Communication Technology & Accessibility (ICTA), Tunisia (2013)
16. ElGhoul, O., Jemni, M.: WebSign: A system to make and interpret signs using 3D Avatars. In: Proceedings of the Second International Workshop on Sign Language Translation and Avatar Technology (SLTAT), Dundee, UK (2011)
17. Bouzid, Y., ElGhoul, O., Jemni, M.: Synthesizing Facial Expressions for Signing Avatars using MPEG-4 Feature Points. In: Proceeding of the 4th International Conference on Information and Communication Technology & Accessibility (ICTA), Tunisia (2013)

A Multi-layer Model for Sign Language's Non-Manual Gestures Generation

Oussama El Ghoul and Mohamed Jemni

Research Laboratory LaTICE National High Engineering School of Tunis University of Tunis, Tunis, Tunesia
oussama.elghoul@utic.rnu.tn,
mohamed.jemni@fst.rnu.tn
http://www.latice.rnu.tn

Abstract. Contrary to the popular believes, the structure of signs exceeds the simple combination of hands movements and shapes. Furthermore, sign significance resides, not in the hand shape, the position, the movement, the orientation or facial expression but in the combination of all five. In this context, our aim is to propose a model for non-manual gesture generation for sign language machine translation. We developed in previous works a new gesture generator that does not support facial animation. We propose a multi-layer model to be used for the development of new software for generating non-manual gestures NMG. Three layers compose the system. The first layer represents the interface between the system and external programs. Its role is to do the linguistic treatment in order to compute all linguistic information, such as the grammatical structure of the sentence. The second layer contains two modules (the manual gesture generator and the non-manual gesture generator). In first module the non-manual gestures generator uses three dimension facial modeling and animation techniques to produce facial expression in sign language.

Keywords: Multi-layer Model, Non-Manual Gesture, Sign Language, Machine Translation.

1 Introduction

Despite the variety of the representation forms of the information, it remains dedicated to hearing people. In this context we are working on the automatic generation of sign languages using virtual signers. Our aim is to provide to the community an easy way to transform textual information to 3D animations in sign languages. In previous works, we proposed an approach to produce automatically manual gestures for sign languages machine translation and we obtained an interesting result. However, the system that we developed still unachieved because we omitted a primordial part of sign languages (the non-manual gestures). The real challenge is to produce linguistically correct sentences. It is for this reason that we started by studying the structure of sign languages before proposing a linguistically based model for automatic sign generators. Many

K. Miesenberger et al. (Eds.): ICCHP 2014, Part II, LNCS 8548, pp. 466–473, 2014.

studies have been done by linguistics and psychologists, which aim to specify the structure of signs and to determine the visual alternatives of some phonological parameters of spoken languages. It is appeared that non-manual gestures play a primordial role in the sign language communication. In fact, facial expression is used on various grammatical levels: lexical, morphological, syntactic and pragmatic functions. Furthermore, recent linguistic studies have proved that facial expressions are used in the prosodic feature.

2 Non-Manual Gestures and Highly Iconic Structures

Cuxac is a French researcher who began his research on sign languages in the 80s. It is thanks to him that the study of sign languages is deflected to a new aspect that distinguishes them from other languages. According to Cuxac, a sign can be expressed in two different ways. The first mode of expression is to use a standard vocabulary. Unlike the first, the second mode focuses on a visual description of the situation. It uses so-called highly iconic structures.

The highly iconic structures are more used than standard signs, except in the dialogues. Some sign languages use both modes at the same time and even allow their combination. The highly iconic structures can describe the situation through a kind of staging that facilitates understanding. Cuxac call it transfers. He counts the transfer of shape/size, situational and personal.[1,2] [5]

2.1 The Transfer of Shape and Size

The transfer of size and shape is used to specify the size and/or the shape of an object, a place or a character partially or globally. During a transfer of shape and/or size the hands of the signer will have the form or/and the size of the signed object. For example, when the signer speaks of a balloon, he uses a round hand shape to suggest the shape of the ball.

This transfer can be expressed using configurations, orientation and movement of the hands. In addition to the manual gestures, it can be conveyed using facial expression.[1,2]

2.2 The Transfer of Situation

The transfer of situation allows the signer to describe in his signing space, movement or action of the situation. It can reproduce scenes that illustrate the movements of an actor relative to another. For example, in the case of a person riding in a car, the signer will first choose a location for the car, and then he will set a landmark through his dominated hand, which represents the car. After that, with his other hand (the dominant hand), the signer will represent the movement of the person.[1,2]

Situational transfers occur in three phases:

- Configuration of the rental by the dominated hand;
- Configuration of the actor by the dominant hand;
- Movement of the dominant hand;

The phrase "the plane takes off" will be translated into sign language by staging visually the takeoff of the aircraft. Transferring the situation performs this staging. Indeed, the dominated hand takes the form of the runway while the right hand will take the shape of the aircraft. Then, the dominant hand, which is initially placed on the dominated hand, makes a motion simulating that of takeoff.[1,2]

2.3 Transfers of Person

The transfer of person is the act of playing the role of the character transferred. Structures of transfer involve the whole body of the speaker. An entire story can be told. Similarly, its facial expressions define the state of mind of the character, or the relationship established between it and the action that it performs.

While the transfer is not completed, the gaze direction of the eye can not cross that of the listener. Indeed, the transfer stops at the first crossing of the eyes of the speaker and the listener. Person transfers are varied, there are those who are highly iconic and those who are reduced with an incursion of standard signs iconicity.[1,2]

3 Grammatical Functions of Non-Manual Gestures

3.1 Phonological Function

From a phonological point of view, we distinguish 4 classes of non-manual gestures: Head and body movements, facial expressions, mouth gestures and the echo phonological gestures. The first class includes signs which consist of both hand gestures and movements of the head and body. As an example, we quote the sign sleep that is to tilt the head to the right (or left) and place hands below as if they support it. Head movements can also accompany the negative particles NOT or NO. In American Sign Language, the two signs NOT and NO, are signed with a single sideward head movement accompanying the movement of the hand.

Facial expressions are also part of the lexicon of several words. Sometimes, they represent the only difference between two signs that are formed by the same hand gestures.

Studying thoroughly facial signals, linguistics approved that mouth gestures have an essential functionalities in sign languages phonology. They can serves to disambiguate hand gestures. In the literature, we identified two types of mouth signals: mouthing and mouth gestures. Mouthings are derived from spoken languages. They are a silent articulations of spoken words (or a part of spoken work) accompanied by hand gestures. Mouthing serves to the disambiguation of signs, where the manual part is identical. As example, in British sign language, the signs UNCLE and BATTERY differs only by the mouth articulation. Contrary to mouthing, mouth gestures are not derived from spoken languages. They are among the phonological signals of sign languages. In other term, they are the set of any mouth activity which does not derive from the spoken language. Similarly to mouthing the mouth gestures can serves to disambiguate hand gestures. In the literature, we distinguish three functions for mouth gestures and mouthing: disambiguation of similar hand gestures, specification of meaning, and carrying meaning when there are no manual gestures.

Recent linguistic research on mouth gestures in SL, have discovered an interesting relation between hand and mouth gestures. They revealed that manual and oral actions are coordinated. So, this dependence is not derived from spoken languages. The mouth gestures produced thanks to this relation are called "echo phonological gestures" which means the mouth activities that are in correlation with hand gestures. In BSL, the sign WIN is produced by rotating the hand at the wrist repeatedly at the same time the mouth articulation resembles to a rounded vowel.[3]

3.2 Morphological Functions

There are two types of Non-manual gesture that have a morphological role. The first one may fulfill an adjectival function and the second may fulfill an adverbial function. Non-manuals may be a part of the lexical specification of an adjectival sign. They can also serve to the realization of adjectival meanings when it is synchronized with the manual sign that it modifies. This functionality allows, for example, to express that an object is smaller or bigger than the normal. In the example below, the signer blows his cheeks when he articulates the sign CAR to express that the car is small. The last facial activity is represented by)(. When the Non-manual accompanies manual adjective it plays the role of intensifier. In (1) the adjective small is signed by the facial action)(synchronized with the manual sign of the nominal car. In (2) the adjective small is signed by a manual gesture which follows the nominal gesture. In order to express that the car is very small, the adjective will be accompanied by the gesture)(. [3]

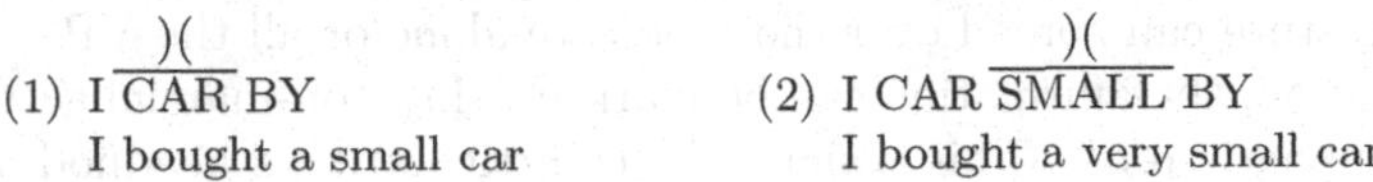

)(
(1) I CAR BY
I bought a small car
)(
(2) I CAR SMALL BY
I bought a very small car

Fig. 1. Morphological function of NMG

Mouthing can play an adjectival function. As example in Norwegian sign language, the sign Red car is produced by a simultaneous manual articulation of the word car and mouthing the word red.

Further than nouns mouth gestures may modify verbs. In this instance, the adverbial function of the non-manual describes how the action is done. As example, the facial expression 'lips pressed together and protruded' signifies an action done effortlessly. However, the facial expression noted 'th', which consists to protrude the tongue between the teeth, signifies an action done carelessly. In 1998, John Benjamins identifies ten different facial gestures that can be used as adverbs; they will be detailed in next sections.

3.3 Syntactic Functions

Negation and Affirmation. In sign languages, both manual and non-manual gestures can express the negation. In the literature we identified three different non-manual negators. The first one is the lexically marked head turn (described in the section 3.1), the second consists to the headshake *hs*, the third is a backward or forward head tilt *bht* or *fht* and finally a negative facial expression. In many sign languages non-manual negators are essentials. However, in some sign languages, non-manual gestures are not enough to sign negative sentences. In fact, manual gestures are required to negate sentences.

For example, in American Sign Language, in the sentence *"I didn't buy a car"*, the particle NOT is optional. In this case the sign can be expressed using hand or headshake. If the particle NOT is used, the headshake can accompany only it or spread over it and the entire verb phrase VP Otherwise, it should spread the VP . [3]

Manual negator can precede or exceed the VP depending on Sign languages. For example, the last sentence will be signed as indicated in 3. It can occur on its own to negate a sentence. In this case, it appears on the predicate or after the sentence.

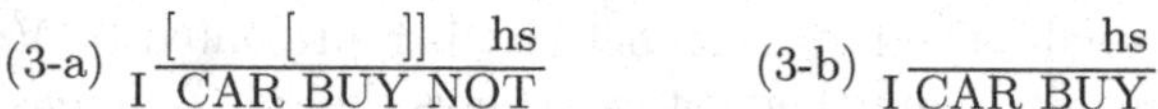

Fig. 2. MG and NMG synchronization in negative sentences

The last example illustrate that in the negation the synchronization between manual and non-manual gestures differs from sign language to another. The non-manual gesture can spread over the predicate alone or all the VP.

As the negation, the affirmation can be marked using non-manual gestures to express the emphatic tense. This is signed by co-articulating a headnod *hn* with the manual gestures of the sentence.

Interrogation. NMG are essential in the production of interrogative sentences for the majority of sign languages. Furthermore, it represents the only mark of the interrogation in most sign languages. This does not mean that non-manual gestures are not used in interrogative sentences. Indeed, in some sign languages, particles are used as optional markers.

The eyebrows represent the main marker of the question. Different types of questions (Yes/No, Wh) are indicated by different shapes of eyebrows. Take the case of Yes/No Questions in ASL, any clause will be accompanied by the non-manual gestures. In this case, the eyebrows are raised *re* and the head and shoulders will be moved forward. [3]

Unlike the Yes/No questions, the Wh-questions are usually accompanied by a lowering of the eyebrows *le*. Depending on the sign language, the nom-manual can spread over the entire clause or accompany the particle of the wh-question.

For example , in ASL, in the sentence *'Who buy a car?"*, the non manual marker can spread over the sentence. It can also appear only with the particle WHO when it is in the end position.

Topics. Reinhart and Gundel, confirmed that the topic is by default the subject of the sentence. But, it may play others grammatical roles. The topic is marked, mainly, by raising eyebrows. However, many other non-manuals are combined in order to mark the sentences topic. More than one topic can be in a sentence. However there are a restriction concerning their number. For example, in ASL and NGL, the maximum number of topics per sentence can not exceed two. [4]

Generally it appears at the beginning of the sentence. It precedes interrogative and imperatives phrases. Reversing the order is ungrammatical. When the topic preceeds a wh-question, it co-occur with the non-manual that marks the question. In such case, the non-manual that marks the wh-question cannot spread over the topic.

As mentioned in the beginning of this section, raising eyebrows and chin generally marks the topic. Moreover, the head is frequently lowered with the end of the sign. The non-manual marker of the topic should be always co-articulated with a manual gestures and starts slightly before it. The topic is separated from the rest of the sentence by a pause that can be co-occured by an eye blink.

4 Proposed Model

We propose in this paper a conceptual model to be used for the development of facial animation generators. The proposed module can be used to develop animation generators to be integrated within machine translation systems. As shown on Figure 3, the system is composed by three layers. The first layer represents the interface between the system and external programs. It provides the linguistic treatment. The second layer contains two modules (the manual gesture generator and the non-manual gesture generator). The NMG generator uses three dimension facial modeling and animation techniques to produce facial expression in sign language.

In previous sections we have demonstrated that a sign can be expressed in two different ways. The first manner of expression is to use a standard vocabulary. The second one, focuses on a visual description of the situation. Furthermore a sign can be produced by combining the two modes. It is in this context that we propose two sub-modules which undertake the non-manual gestures' production. The two sub-modules communcate together in order to allow the passage from one mode to another.

Finally, NMG and MG are synchronized by a special module which generates the final animation description playable by the avatar.

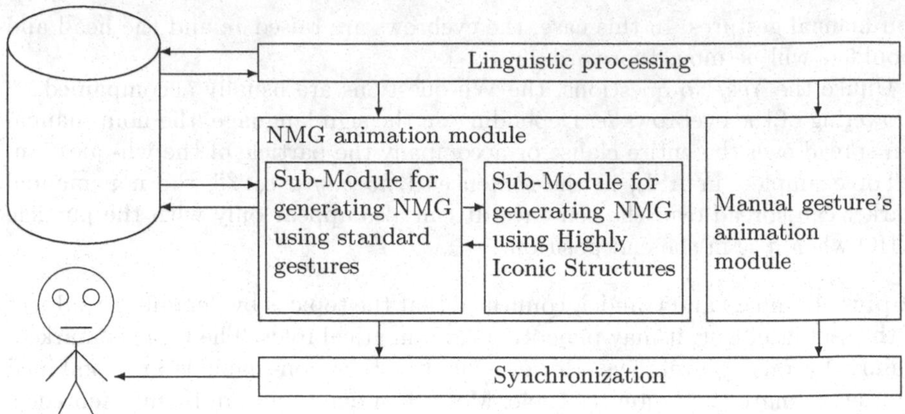

Fig. 3. General architecture of the proposed model

From grammatical point of view (Figure 4), synthesized expression differs from word to another (phonological level): with some words appropriate expressions are used and with others visual speech is done. Furthermore, facial expressions are influenced by the emotion of signer. In this context, we have designed the NMG module that generates standard signs with specific sub-modules which interact together. In fact, if the sign needs a particular expression then the treatment starts by the sub-module Phonological level and if the sign needs a visual speech then the treatment starts by the corresponded sub-module. After that, results can be modified by the emotion sub-module with the goal to add a realistic emotion to the generated expression.

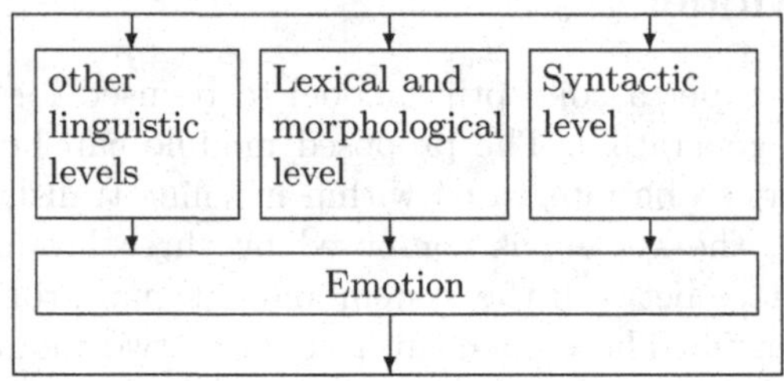

Fig. 4. Module for generating NMG using standard gestures

From visual point of view, the sign is described thanks to the highly iconic structures. We propose a sub-module dedicated to generate signs using iconic description. Three sub-modules compose the proposed module. Each one is devoted to generate a specific transfer of the highly iconic structures.

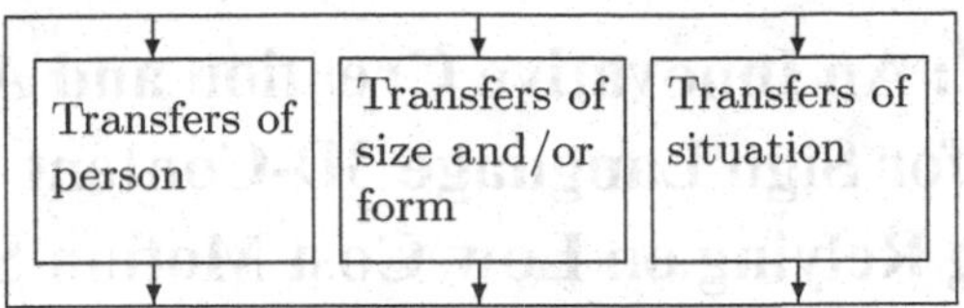

Fig. 5. Module for generating NMG using Highly Iconic Structures

The model is implemented and tested in WebSign project. The system is based on Web Services and each sub-module is developed undependably which facilitates the update of services and the use of implementation of new functionalities. We implemented only standard gestures. The Highly Iconic Structure module is planned to be developed in the future.

The proposed model facilitates the development and the update of sign languages generation systems. It offers more readable implemented codes. It allows the development of the system using an incremental approach. The localization of errors become easy, just we need to debug the concerned module (the web service in our case). It guarantees the generation of linguistically correct signs.

5 Conclusion

In this paper we proposed a conceptual model that aims to simplify and organize the development of sign language generation. We focused our interest to the non-manual gesture generation. An elaborated study is done in order to understand how non-manual gestures are used on sign language communication and assure the generation of grammatically correct signs.

References

1. Sallandre, M.-A., Cuxac, C.: Iconicity in sign language: A theoretical and methodological point of view. In: Wachsmuth, I., Sowa, T. (eds.) GW 2001. LNCS (LNAI), vol. 2298, pp. 173–180. Springer, Heidelberg (2002)
2. Cuxac, C., Sallandre, M.-A.: Iconicity and arbitrariness in French Sign Language. In: International Colloquium Verbal and Signed Languages: Comparing Structures, Constructs and Methodologies, Rome, Universit Roma Tre, October 3-4 (2004)
3. Pfau, R., Quer, J.: Nonmanuals: Their grammatical and prosodic roles. In: Brentari (ed.), pp. 381–402 (2010)
4. Pfau, R.: Topics and Conditionals in Sign Languages. In: DGfS 2008 Workshop on Topicality Bamberg, February 28 (2008)
5. Émilie, C.: Les gestes non manuels en langue des signes francaise, annotation, analyse et formation, Thesis mars (2010)
6. Stokoe, W.C.: Sign Language Structure: An Outline of the Visual Communication System of the American Deaf. Studies in Linguistics: Occasional Papers 8 (1960)

SIGN^{MOTION}: An Innovative Creation and Annotation Platform for Sign Language 3D-Content Corpora Building Relying on Low Cost Motion Sensors

Mehrez Boulares and Mohamed Jemni

Research Laboratory of Technologies of Information and Communication & Electrical Engineering (LaTICE)
Ecole Supérieure des Sciences et Techniques de Tunis, Tunisia
mehrez.boulares@gmail.com,
Mohamed.jemni@fst.rnu.tn

Abstract. The manual transcription process of Sign Language is a work-intensive step which requires considerable effort to create Signs. Even, often the result of this step misses the natural aspect of motion to be conform to the natural human interpretation. In other words, the lack of the sign language annotated corpora is closely related to the difficulty of the sign creation task. In this paper, we propose a novel tool Sign^{motion} for creating an annotated sign language corpus based on Natural Human Gestures: By overlaying a real signer motion onto an articulated 3D skeleton using Microsoft Kinect and Leap motion sensors. Sign^{motion} is created to support the natural 3D facial expression, the natural 3D body posture and gives the possibility to annotate and analyze each sign and motion in the recorded animation. The resulting data and structure are precise enough to create and to store signs to be used for Sign Language data analysis or Machine Translation using virtual signer.

Keywords: Transcription, Sign Language, Kinect, Leap Motion, Virtual Agent, Facial Expression, Motion Analysis, Machine Translation, Corpus.

1 Introduction

The human gesture transcription process is a crucial step in the sign language data analysis and machine translation field based on 3D-content. However, the majority of existing Sign Language annotation tools such as ELAN [12] or [11] work or ANVIL [9] were created to annotate videos. Otherwise, these tools are not able to produce enough of structured and precise data to create a 3D content based Sign language corpora. While the utility of existing tools, formats and structures is unquestionable, their variety and the lack of annotated corpus based on 3D content able to improve the sign language data analysis (SL Machine translation, SL recognition, etc) fields is becoming a critical problem.

In order to create a structured and annotated sign language corpora based on 3D content, we built a tool Sign^{motion} with the purpose to create our own sign language animation framework using a low cost motion capture device such as Microsoft

K. Miesenberger et al. (Eds.): ICCHP 2014, Part II, LNCS 8548, pp. 474–481, 2014.

Kinect and Leap motion. Sign^{motion} allows users to create and annotate their animations in easy way by making the animation more structured through matching each sign in the phrase to his appropriate 3D content. Our tool enables also the real time tracking of face expressions through the Kinect sensor to be combined with motion to obtain a natural sign. Moreover, we adopted the movement and hold [5] model combined with our declarative transcription language [6] to produce the second version of our sign modeling language SML version 2 (SML_{v2} [4]) which contains the necessary description tags to animate any 3D virtual signer.

Our methodology relies on the 3D motion analysis to extract the motion curve parameters of each sign produced by Kinect sensor. The obtained motion curve will be used with inverse or direct kinematic solver to animate the virtual signer based on left and right hand movements and locations. We used the Leap Motion sensor to detect and to match automatically the user hand shape configuration to our virtual signer. Sign^{motion} offers also the possibility to store the created and annotated sign language phrase in SML_{v2}(shown in figure 4 (A)) format with the original sentence.

The remainder of this paper is organized as follows. In section 2, we present some related works. Section 3 is devoted to describe our approach. Finally, we give a conclusion and some perspectives.

2 Previous Works

Up today, we have deduced that there is a lack related to existing tools that offer the ability to create and annotate sign language animations in order to be used in the sign language data analysis fields. However, the sign language animation can be video recordings, manually animated characters or motion capture data. We can introduce ELAN project as video-based framework which is devoted to annotate sign language videos without producing any information related to the animation processing using 3D contents. Moreover, motion data can also be acquired by manually annotating the video with symbolic labels on time intervals in a tool like ANVIL [8,9]. Consequently, this kind of annotation tools cannot produce sufficient information to animate 3D virtual signer.

We can also mention the work of [10] as a manually animated characters tool. Their method of gesture annotation is based on the idea that a human coder can reconstruct the pose of a speaker from a simple 2D image (e.g. a frame in a movie). For this purpose they provide a solution to match single poses of the original speaker with the 3D skeleton. Therefore, this kind of works still proprietary and neglects the motion accuracy, the natural aspect of movement and the textual annotation parameter.

The majorities of existing animation creation software are based mainly on pre-synthesized animation or generated animation. There are some works that rely on pre-synthesized animation such as Mathsigner or DIVA framework [2] that uses higher cost motion capture pre-recorded animation. Concerning motion capture process is very precise but requires the human subject to act in a highly controlled lab environment (special suit, markers, and cameras), the equipment is very expensive and significant post-processing is necessary to clean the resulting data [1]. Therefore, the generated animations are proprietary, can't be used by other systems and they lack of structured annotation which cannot be used in the sign language machine translation field or in the sign language recognition field. In generated animation field, there are

SignSmith studio, Tessa ViSiCAST, eSIGN, Dicta-Sign [3] works. However, SignSmith studio provides a gesture builder to create signs with elementary movement and allows users to script an ASL performance (using a dictionary of signs), eSIGN is based on synthetic signing works by sending motion commands in the form of written codes for the Avatar to be animated. In other words, there are many different transcription systems used by animation generation software to codify gestures but textual annotation of sign language 3D content is still rare.

3 SIGN^{MOTION} Tool

Sign^{motion} is a supplement layer developed around WebSign project [4]. This tool relies on virtual agent technology integrated into WebSign plugin to animate the avatar through sending motion commands in the form of written codes. The motion commands are based on data related to real time bones rotations provided by Kinect sensor. These data are converted in order to be supported by our animation engine which is based on x3d technology.

Sign^{motion} allows mainly the sign creation process in a natural way using a low cost motion capture sensors (Microsoft Kinect& Leap Motion). In fact, our tool enables the real time reconstruction of the signer pose to match the natural poses and hand shape of the human signer with our 3D avatar .Additionally, Sign^{motion} supports the real time facial expression tracking and emotion detection in the animation creation processing.

3.1 The Sign Creation Processing

The sign creation interface shown in figure 1(B), gives an overview of how user can activate Kinect sensor to track his movement in real time through our 3D virtual signer. However, this interface allows to the user to record, play, replay, make a pause and stop the created animation in easy way. As mentioned in figure 1(B), user has the possibility to browse frame by frame his recorded animation through a simple track bar. Furthermore, he can edit his sign language animation in order to adjust the Leap Motion parameters such as palm orientation and hand shape configuration of both right and left hand.

The sign creation interface integrates the Kinect& Leap Motion posture configuration tab which gives also the possibility to readjust the rotation values of 6 articulations (Left Shoulder, Left Elbow, Left Wrist, Right Shoulder, Right Elbow and Right Wrist) or to choose the appropriate hand shape of the 3D virtual signer in order to obtain an accurate sign language animation.

As mentioned in figure 1(A), the ASL phrase "The dog bites the cat" is composed of three principal signs. The first one is devoted to animate the sign "dog" using the right hand classifier predicate and using the left hand to place this sign on a left location in the signing space to indicate that "DOG-INDEX$_a$" sign will be referenced at this place. The second part of this ASL phrase describes the sign of "cat" using the right hand classifier predicate and using the left hand to place this sign on a right location in the signing space to indicate that "CAT-INDEX$_b$" sign will be referenced at this place also. The third part describes the sign "dog bites cat" by pointing to the right and left position respectively using right and left hand in order to make a reference to "dog" and "cat" signs already mentioned. In this part, the verb (sign) bites defines the action from left hand using classifier of "bites" to the right hand location.

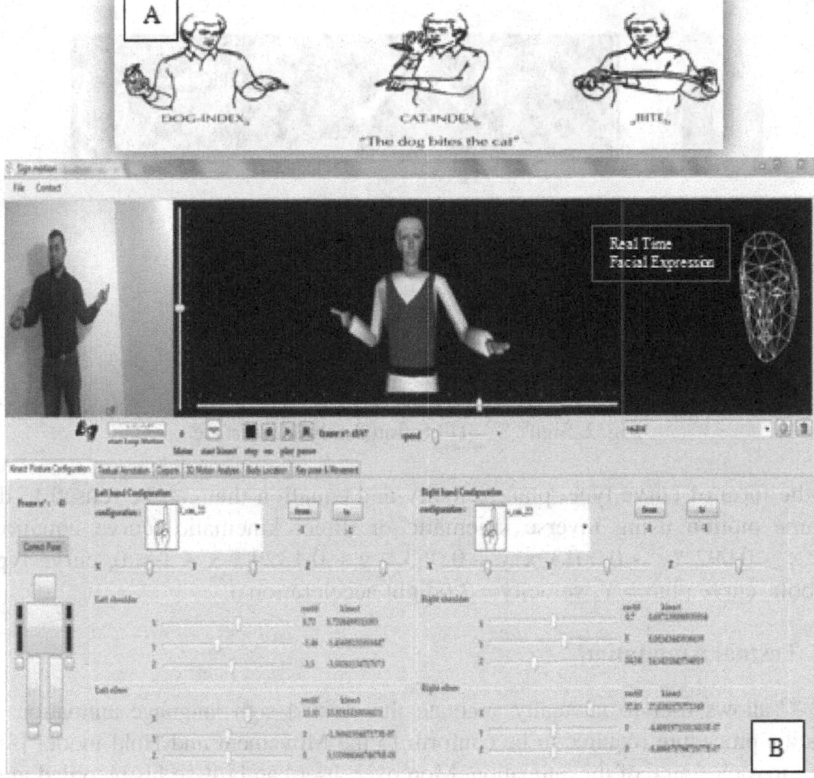

Fig. 1. An overview of the Sign^{motion} principal interface

Although, using Sign^{motion} user can create his SL phrase in easy way. This tool allows the automatic human poses and hand shapes tracking by activating the Kinect and Leap Motion sensors through start Kinect and start Leap Motion buttons. Furthermore, the signer can record, play, replay, stop, make a pause and edit the created sign language animation to adjust recorded parameters if necessary.

3.2 The 3D Motion Analysis

Sign^{motion} was created to build signs easily and precisely in order to be used by other sign language animation engine in the form of annotated 3D content corpora. However, to reach this goal, we choose to analyze human motion in order to recognize motion type and curve equation. These extracted parameters will be used by animation engines based on direct or inverse kinematic solver. Furthermore, we propose to analyze the 3D motion trajectory by using our approximation technique based on 3D nonlinear regression [7] of motion data matrices provided by Microsoft Kinect. In other words, user chooses the frames "from" "to" from the recorded animation and clicks on "Analyze Motion" button. Moreover, figure 2 gives an idea about the motion analysis result applied to our ASL phrase "The dog bites the cat" precisely to describe the motion related to the "bites" action using the left hand. The result of this step will

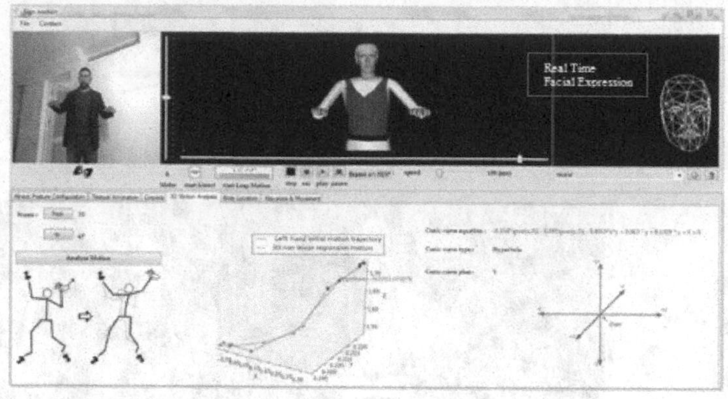

Fig. 2. Sign^{motion} 3D Motion Analysis interface

be in the form of curve type, plan, velocity and equation that can be reused to draw the same motion using inverse kinematic or direct kinematic (curve equation: $-0.154*x^2 - 0.092*y^2 - 0.0013*x*y + 0.063*y + 0.1329*x + 1 = 0$, curve type = hyperbola, curve plan = Y, velocity = 2 (slight acceleration)).

3.3 Textual Annotation

Sign^{motion} allows user to manually annotate the created sign language animation. The annotation procedure requires to be conform to the Movement and Hold model [5] according to each frame of the animation. Moreover, user can browse his recorded animation in easy way through the Sign^{motion} track bar and he can choose which frame will be annotated as a Movement or as a Hold frame. The fields shown is figure 3 represent the sign language parameters related to hold or movement frame in the recorded animation. However, the content of the majority of these fields are loaded automatically according to recorded and treated animation respectively in the Kinect & Leap motion poses recording module and in the motion analysis module. Certainly, user can manually adjust the annotation parameters by choosing itself the right specificity.

Sign^{motion} gives the possibility also to generate two different annotation format according to the textual annotation information. The first annotation format (shown in figure 4 (A)) which is based on XML structure and it's composed of a principal tag "Sentence" and "Sign" tags to describe the animation in a textual form. Moreover, each "Sign" tag has multiple tags composed of "Hold" and "Movement" tags. The "Hold" tag integrates hand shape location and palm orientation for both left and right hand. The "Movement" tag is composed of left hand and right hand tags which describe the movement type, the curve equation, the curve plan and the motion velocity extracted from Kinect & Leap motion analysis module. The right or left hand tags integrate also sign language parameters to indicate the hand shape configuration, the spatial location "from" "to" and the palm orientation in order to reproduce precisely the annotated 3D animation. In fact, hold and movement tags include faces and body tags. As shown in figure 4 (A)(after zoom), Faces tag includes face points, face triangles (polygons), face expression values such as BrowLower, BrowRaiser, JawLower,

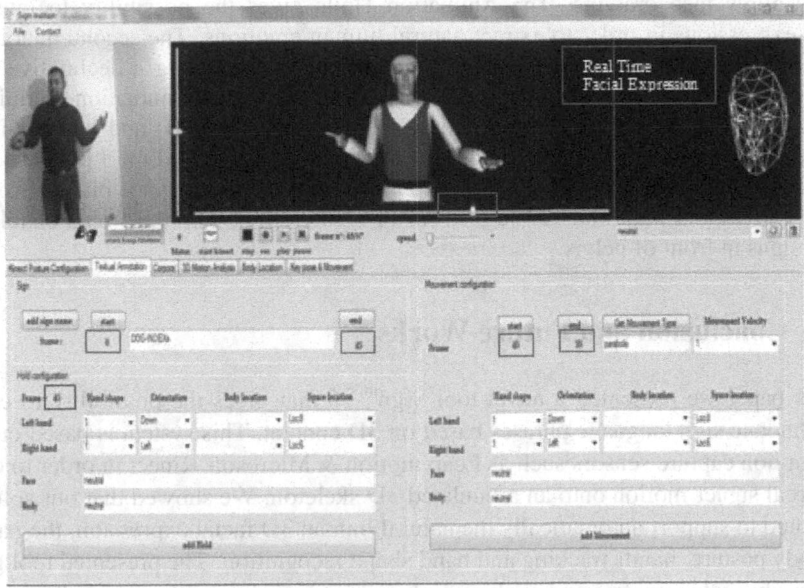

Fig. 3. An overview of the Sign^{motion} textual annotation tab

Fig. 4. (A) An overview of the Sign^{motion} textual annotation format (SML_{v2}) of the created 3D content. (B) Sign^{motion} Space location (C) Sign^{motion} Body location POC (Point of Contact)

etc...., and Animation Unit AU such as AU_BrowLower, AU_JawLower, AU_LipCornerDepressor. However, face points, face triangles and face expression values allow face drawing. The Animation Units gives the possibility to interpret facial expressions in order to extract natural human emotions. The second annotation format is devoted to describe the sign language animation using a declarative transcription system elaborated in [6] work. Indeed, in our textual annotation module we are based on space location specification shown in figure 4 (B) and body point of contact POC shown in figure 4 (C). The Sign space is composed on 3 plans such as the plan shown in figure 4 (B). The first plan is devoted to use space plan in front of head. The second plan aims to be in front of signer chest. The third plan enables to place signs in front of pelvis.

4 Conclusion and Future Works

In this paper we presented a novel tool Sign^{motion} that gives the possibility to create and annotate sign language phrases based on 3D content. This system is based on low cost motion capture sensors such as Leap motion & Microsoft Kinect in order to overlay a real signer motion onto an articulated 3D skeleton. We showed that our solution is created to support automatically the natural human 3D facial expression, the natural 3D body posture, hands tracking and hand shape recognition. The presented tool gives the possibility to annotate and analyze each sign and motion in the recorded animation in order to store and to generate an accurate and reusable structure SMLv2that can be used in Sign Language data analysis fields (such as Machine translation and SL recognition based on 3D-content). We have tested this system in our laboratory and we have succeeded to create a parallel American Sign Language (ASL) corpora which contains 100 English phrases and there corresponding ASL SMLv2 phrases. During the evaluation of our work, we have seen that we can ameliorate the poses accuracy and the annotation interface to be more interactive and easy to use.

References

1. Heloir, A., Neff, M., Kipp, M.: Exploiting motion capture for virtual human animation: Data collection and annotation visualization. In: Proc. of the LREC Workshop on "Multimodal Corpora: Advances in Capturing, Coding and Analyzing Multimodality", ELDA (2010)
2. Braffort, A., Sansonnet, J.P., Martin, J.C., Verrecchia, C.: Diva, une architecture pour le support des agents gestuels interactifs sur internet. Technique et Science Informatiques 29(7), 777–806 (2010)
3. Efthimiou, E., Fotinea, S., et al.: DICTA-SIGN: Sign Language Recognition, Generation and Modelling with application in Deaf Communication. In: Proceedings of CSLT 2010 (LREC 2010), pp. 80–83 (2010)
4. Jemni, M., Elghoul, O.: A system to make signs using collaborative approach. In: Miesenberger, K., Klaus, J., Zagler, W., Karshmer, A. (eds.) ICCHP 2008. LNCS, vol. 5105, pp. 670–677. Springer, Heidelberg (2008)
5. Liddell, S.K., Johnson, R.E.: An analysis of spatial locative predicates in American Sign Language. In: Edmondson, W.H., Karlsson, F. (eds.) Papers from SLR 1987 - Fourth International Symposium on Sign Language Research. Signum-Verlag, Seedorf (1990)

6. Boulares, M., Jemni, M.: Declarative Transcription System for Sign Language Dictionaries Creation. In: Assistive Technology: From Research to Practice. Assistive Technology Research Series, vol. 33, pp. 1151–1157 (2013), doi:10.3233/978-1-61499-304-9-1151
7. Boulares, M., Jemni, M.: 3D Motion Trajectory Analysis Approach to Improve Sign Language 3D-based Content Recognition. In: Proceedings of the Intl' Neural Network Society Winter Conference (INNS-WC 2012), Procedia Computer Science, vol. 13, pp. 97–107. Elsevier (2012)
8. Kipp, M., Neff, M., Albrecht, I.: An Annotation Scheme for Conversational Gestures: How to economically capture timing and form. J. on Language Resources and Evaluation - Special Issue on Multimodal Corpora 41(3-4), 325–339 (2007)
9. Kipp, M.: Anvil: The video annotation research tool. In: Durand, J., Gut, U., Kristofferson, G. (eds.) Oxford Handbook of Corpus Phonology. Oxford University Press, Oxford (2014)
10. Nguyen, Q., Kipp, M.: Annotation of Human Gesture using 3D Skeleton Controls. In: Proceedings of the 7th International Conference on Language Resources and Evaluation, LREC 2010, ELDA (2010)
11. Crasborn, O., Sloetjes, H., Auer, E., Wittenburg, P.: Combining video and numeric data in the analysis of sign languages with ELAN annotation software. In: Vetoori, C. (ed.) Proceedings of the 2nd Workshop on the Representation and Processing of Sign Languages: Lexicographic Matters and Didactic Scenarios, pp. 82–87. ELRA, Paris (2006)
12. Wittenburg, P., Brugman, H., Russel, A., Klassmann, A., Sloetjes, H.: ELAN: a professional framework for multimodality research. 2006. In: Proceedings of LREC, pp. 1556–1559. ELRA, Paris (2006)

Gestures in Sign Language: Animation and Generation in Real-Time

Nour Ben Yahia and Mohamed Jemni

University of Tunis Research Laboratory on Technologies of Information and Communication & Electrical Engineering (Latice), Tunis, Tunisia
benyahia.nour@gmail.com,
mohamed.jemni@fst.rnu.tn
http://www.latice.rnu.tn

Abstract. Many statistics have confirmed that many deaf are enabled to access to written information. As a solution, computer applications designed for deaf person, have been created. Therefore, to facilitate access to information, new methods improving the dialogue between human and machine are required. The signs generation is based on different parameters such as manual configuration, orientation of hands, the location where the sign is made, the movement made by hand and the facial expression accompanying the realization of the sign. We take into account all these parameters and the system presented in this paper is based also on avatars which have many degrees of freedom. The challenge of this project is to find the tradeoff between computational time and realistic representation that must be closer to real-time generation signs.

Keywords: Sign language, Animation, Avatar.

1 Introduction

The new technologies of information and communication invest more and more our daily space. We observe the emergence of new services that tend to facilitate the generation, the propagation and the consultation of information. However, such technical progress is not accessible to everyone. An individual may encounter difficulties in accessing information for varieties of reasons that may be economic, cultural, linguistic or physical. Moreover, many statistics have confirmed that many deaf are enabled to access to written information. As a solution, computer applications [1] designed for deaf person, in particular who are illiterate, have been created. Therefore, to facilitate access to information, new methods improving the dialogue between human and machine are required. The development of virtual characters (avatar) able to generate postures in Sign Language (SL), is a response to this request. These applications are based on an automatic gestures generation [2], [3]. Generally, within the set of admissible postures, the user is free to manipulate the avatar rather than specifying the value of each individual degree of freedom. The Inverse Kinematics (IK) method automatically computes these values in order to satisfy a given task usually expressed

K. Miesenberger et al. (Eds.): ICCHP 2014, Part II, LNCS 8548, pp. 482–489, 2014.

in Cartesian coordinates [4]. In this context, our work consists in developing an animation solver [5] [6]. This system permits to animate automatically different body parts of an avatar in order to improve realistic animation of virtual character gesture [7] and allow deaf person to visualize realistic gestures [8].

2 Description of the Problem

The IK method automatically computes these values in order to satisfy a given task usually expressed in cartesian coordinates [4]. This technique requires the resolution of nonlinear complex equations and is usually expressed as a constraint-satisfaction problem. However, this is a laborious task because of the high number of degrees of freedom present in the model i.e. fifty for a human model without considering the fingers [9]. Building a system for animating SL requires highly complex and intuitive controls for human model based on positioning and animation of joints with multiple degrees of freedom in real time. In addition, the signing avatar model is comprised of several kinematic chains (Figure 1) and each chain generally has different end effectors. The control of

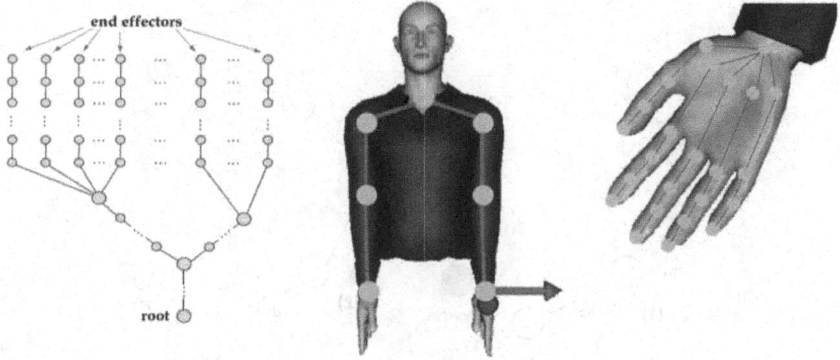

Fig. 1. Several kinematics chains

a human model in 3D by means of IK requires a simultaneous multitasks application. For example, we may consider tasks that control the position of left hand and another of right hand. The balance of human model will be controlled by another task which provides some information concerning forces and mass distribution. Therefore, it is essential for an IK solver to be able to solve problems with multiple end effectors and targets. The control of multiple kinematics chains improve the introduction of the SL constraints such as symmetry and anti symmetry. To solve the IK problem, the most popular approaches use the numerical Jacobian matrix to find a linear approximation [10]. Solutions based on the Jacobian matrix produce realistic postures [11], but most of these approaches suffer from high computational cost given that the matrix calculations are very complex and singularity problems. Also, the Cyclic Coordinate Descent (CCD) algorithm [12] is a heuristic iterative method with low computational cost for each joint per iteration, which can solve the IK problem without matrix manipulations; consequently it formulates a solution very quickly. This method can be applied to solve problems with only one target that can be manipulated by the user; kinematic chains with multiple end effectors can not be resolved, then this method can not be used to animate virtual characters based on SL constraints.

3 Our Solution

The used IK method here [13], involve the previously calculated positions of the joints to find the solution to achieve the target. This method minimizes the error of the system by adjusting each joint angle. The proposed method starts from the last joint of the IK chain, iterate and adjust each joint along the chain. Thereafter, it iterate in the reverse way, in order to complete the adjustment. This method, instead of calculating directly the angle rotations, try to find the joint locations. Hence, the time dedicated to compute and resolve the constraints can be saved. So, we can generate realistic and human animation in real time.

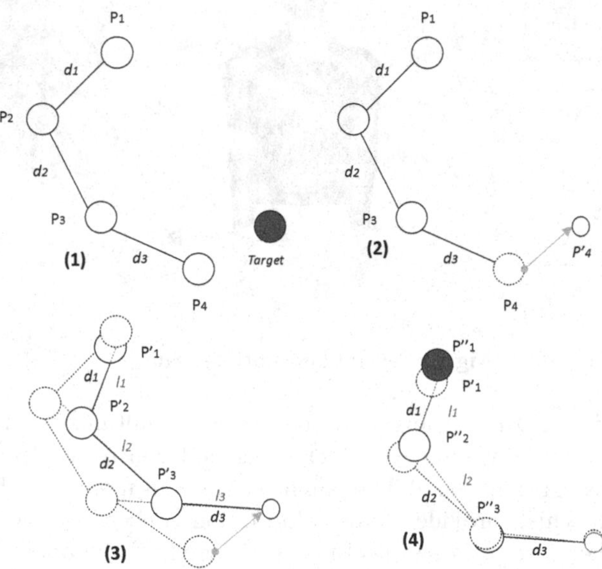

Fig. 2. Inverse kinematics method. (1) The initial position of the manipulator with 4 joints and the target. (2) move the end effector p_4 to the target. (3) find the joint p_3' which lies on the line l_3 that passes through the points p_4' and p_3, and has distance d_3 from the joint p_4' .(4) repeat the same procedure but this time start from the base and move outwards to the end effector.

If we consider (Figure 2) p_1, ..., p_n the joints of the avatar. Note that p_1 is the root joint and p_n is the end effector. The target is symbolized by a red point. The method used is illustrated with a single target and 4 joints (Figure 2). First we calculate the distances between each joint $di = |p_{i+1}\text{-}p_i|$, for $i = 1, ..., n-1$. Assuming that the new position of the end effector be the target position, $p'_n = t$, we find the line, l_{n-1}, which passes through the joint p_{n-1} and p'_n. The new position of the p'_{n-1} joint, lies on that line with distance d_{n-1} from p'_n. Similarly, the new position of the p'_{n-2} joint, can be calculated using the line l_{n-2}, which passes through the p_{n-2} and p'_{n-1}, and has distance d_{n-2} from p'_{n-1}. The algorithm continues until all new joint positions are calculated. The new position of the root joint, p'_1, should not be different from its initial position. Another iteration is completed when the same procedure is repeated but this time starting from the root joint and moving outwards to the end effector. Thus, let the new position p''_n, then find the line l_1 that passes through the points p''_1 and p'_2, we define the new position of the joint p''_2 as the point on that line with distance d_1 from p''_n. This procedure is repeated for all the joints, including the end effector. After one complete iteration, the solution is often not just, means that the end effector doesn't coincide with the target. The procedure is then repeated, as many time as needed, until the end effector is the same or achieve to the desired target.

4 Applying the Technique

We tested several approaches like Newton methods and the family of Jacobian matrix. But, we noticed that these algorithms don't obey in real-time and this logical due to the matrix size used and the operations performed on it. The IK method converges to any given goal positions , seeing that the target is reachable. However, if the target is not within the reachable area, there is a termination condition that compares the previous and the current position of the end effector, if this distance is less than an indicated tolerance. The method gives very good results and converges quickly to the desired position because (Table 1) it's based only on the position computing and avoids the tedious rotations computing.

Table 1. Results for a single kinematic chain with reachable and unreachable target

Method	**Reachable target**		**Unreachable target**	
	Number of iterations	Execution time (sec)	Number of iterations	Execution time (sec)
our IK method	15	0.014	67	0.06
CDD	26	0.13	400	3.9
Jacobian method	1000	11	4000	40

5 Automatic Gestures Generation

Our system relies on several inputs and on interactive avatar with X3D [14]. We can from a web interface create the sign by selecting the desired joint and move along different axis (x, y, z) to the target position. The system, based on IK, calculate automatically in a real-time the angles of rotation of each joint that are required to generate the posture. From a biomechanical study [15], we identify the degrees of freedom of each joint. This study has allowed us to generate real time and natural postures of the virtual character. We can from a SML description [16], containing the position of the desired joint as shown (Figure 3), generate the animation of the avatar in real time.

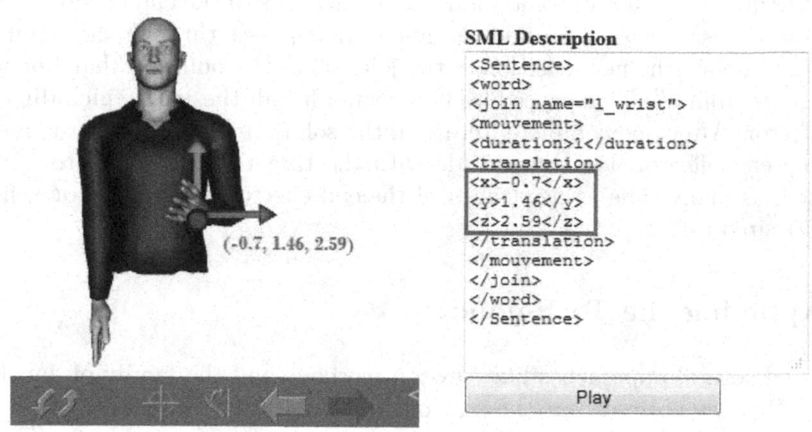

Fig. 3. The Avatar's animation with a SML description

5.1 Animation with SL Constraints

The animation engine is integrated into the project Websign [16] to facilitate the task of creating signs. Our approach is based on a thorough study of SL and gestures classification [17,18]. We have identified the constraints that need to be used for automatic SL generation postures i.e. symmetry relations, that facilitate the specification of movement of the non-dominant hand knowledge of those dominant articulator and various types of repetition in sign [19]. We extended to process models with multiple end effectors and achieve the different targets positions (Figure 4). We tested the animation engine by adding constraints of SL [20] as the notion of symmetry either total or anti-symmetry and of course along different axis x, y and z. The figure 5 shows the use of this notion. We can through the created interface, apply a symmetry or antisymmetry constraints on different axes to the selected joint. The system automatically calculates the solutions and generate animation in real-time. The solver have several kinematic chains to solve; the first chain $left$: $shoulder, elbow, wrist$ the second $right$: $shoulder, elbow, wrist$.

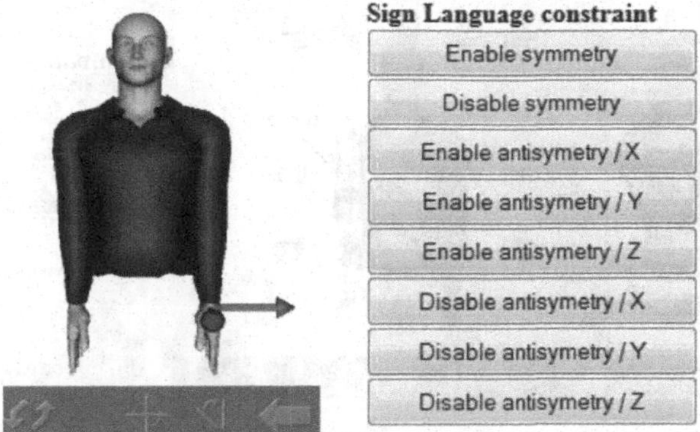

Fig. 4. Gesture builder with SL constraints

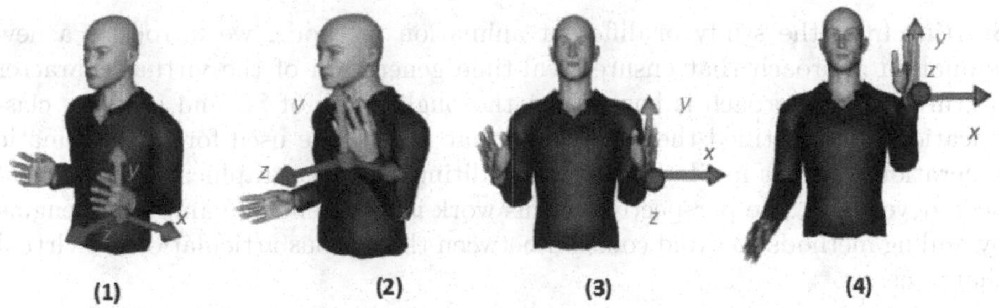

Fig. 5. Signing avatar using Inverse kinematics method: (1) activate symmetry for different axis. (2),(3),(4) activate antisymmetry for x,y,z axis

5.2 Animation with SL Space Location

Since the first descriptions of Stokoe [21], there is agreement that the signs are formed by a set of parameters: configuration (shape of the hands); location (the location where the sign will be executed), the orientation (orientation of the palms of the hand relative to the signer) and movement with various characteristics. The use of space is one of the characteristics of SL. It is possible to place concepts in space or make reference. Signs may also be produced at locations in the signing space surrounding the avatar [22]. We currently distinguish three levels offset A, B, C and fifteen degrees of forward distance for spatial locations (for example $B_1, B_2, B_3 ... B_{15}$). According to these, we extend our system to manage these constraints. We decompose the signing space by adding cubes in the X3D scene (level A in green color, level B in red and C in blue).From a description SML the avatar access to different locations in the signing space by adding the title of the position location (for example B_2 in Figure 6) to translation tag to the SML code. Therefore, the system generate the animation and different gestures in real time.

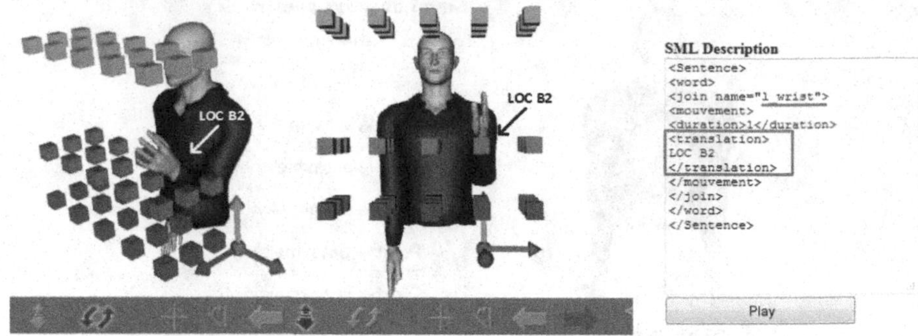

Fig. 6. The Avatar's animation with SL location

6 Conclusion and Future Work

Starting from the study of different animation methods, we introduce a new animation approach that ensures real-time generation of the virtual character postures. Our approach is based on a thorough study of SL and gestures classification. We identified the constraints that need to be used for the automatic generation postures in SL. To facilitate editing signs , a graphical interface had been developed. The perspective of this work is to extend the animation engine by adding methods to avoid collision between the various articulations of virtual character.

References

1. Lebourque, T., Gibet, S.: Synthesis of hand-arm gestures. In: Proceedings of Gesture Workshop on Progress in Gestural Interaction, London, UK, March 19, pp. 217–225. Springer (1996)
2. Boulares, M., Jemni, M.: A route planner interpretation service for hard of hearing people. In: Miesenberger, K., Karshmer, A., Penaz, P., Zagler, W. (eds.) ICCHP 2012, Part II. LNCS, vol. 7383, pp. 52–58. Springer, Heidelberg (2012)
3. Jemni, M., Ghoul, O., Ben Yahia, N., Boulares, M.: Sign language mms to make cell phones accessible to the deaf and hard-of-hearing community. In: Conference and Workshop on Assistive Technology for People with Vision and Hearing Impairments (CVHI), Granada, Spain, August 28-31 (2007)
4. Welman, C.: Inverse kinematics and geometric constraints for articulated figure manipulation. PhD thesis, Simon Fraser University (1993)
5. Ben Yahia, N., Jemni, M.: An inverse kinematics based approach for animating 3D signing avatars. J. Mobile Multimedia 9(1&2), 1–14 (2013)
6. Jemni, M., Elghoul, O.: An avatar based approach for automatic interpretation of text to sign language. In: 9th European Conference for the Advancement of the Assistive Technologies in Europe, San Sebastin, Spain, October 3-5, pp. 260–270 (2007)
7. Liddell, S.: Structures for representing handshape and local movement at the phonemic level. In: Theoretical Issues in Sign Language Research, vol. 1, pp. 37–66. University of Chicago Press, Chicago (1990)

8. Kendon, A.: How gestures can become like words. In: Cross-Cultural Perspectives in Nonverbal Communication, pp. 131–141 (1988)
9. Baerlocher, P.: Inverse kinematics techniques for the interactive posture control of articulated figures. PhD thesis, Ecole Polytechnique Federale de Lausanne (2001)
10. Wolovich, W., Elliott, H.: A computational technique for inverse kinematics. In: The 23rd IEEE Conference Decision and Control, Las Vegas, USA, vol. 23, pp. 1359–1363. IEEE Institute of Electrical and Electronics Engineers (December 1984)
11. Buss, S.R.: Introduction to inverse kinematics with jacobian transpose, pseudoinverse and damped least squares methods. IEEE Journal of Robotics and Automation 17 (April 2004)
12. Canutescu, A., Dunbrack Jr., R.: Cyclic coordinate descent: A robotics algorithm for protein loop closure. Protein Science 12(5), 963–972 (2003)
13. Ben Yahia, N., Jemni, M.: A new approach for animating 3D signing avatars. In: Murgante, B., Misra, S., Carlini, M., Torre, C.M., Nguyen, H.-Q., Taniar, D., Apduhan, B.O., Gervasi, O. (eds.) ICCSA 2013, Part I. LNCS, vol. 7971, pp. 683–696. Springer, Heidelberg (2013)
14. Brutzman, D., Daly, L.: X3D: extensible 3D graphics for Web authors. Morgan Kaufmann (2010)
15. Tolani, D., Goswami, A., Badler, N.: Real-time inverse kinematics techniques for anthropomorphic limbs. Graphical Models and Image Processing 62(5), 353–388 (2000)
16. Jemni, M., Elghoul, O.: A system to make signs using collaborative approach. In: Miesenberger, K., Klaus, J., Zagler, W.L., Karshmer, A.I. (eds.) ICCHP 2008. LNCS, vol. 5105, pp. 670–677. Springer, Heidelberg (2008)
17. Wittmann, H.: Classification linguistique des langues signées non vocalement. Revue Québécoise de Linguistique Théorique et Appliquée 10(1), 215–288 (1991)
18. Bellugi, U., Klima, E.S.: Le langage gestuel des sourds. Recherche (La) Paris (95), 1083–1091 (1978)
19. Papadogiorgaki, M., Grammalidis, N., Makris, L., Strintzis, M.G.: Gesture synthesis from sign language notation using mpeg-4 humanoid animation parameters and inverse kinematics. In: 2nd IET International Conference on Intelligent Environments, IE 2006, vol. 1, pp. 151–160. IET (2006)
20. Klima, E.S., Bellugi, U.: The signs of language. Harvard University Press (1979)
21. Stokoe, W., Casterline, D., Croneberg, C.: A dictionary of American Sign Language on linguistic principles. Linstok Press Silver Spring, MD (1976)
22. Valli, C.: Linguistics of American sign language: An introduction. Gallaudet University Press (2000)

Improving Accessibility of Lectures for Deaf and Hard-of-Hearing Students Using a Speech Recognition System and a Real-Time Collaborative Editor

Benoît Lathière and Dominique Archambault

EA 4004 – CHArt-THIM, Université Paris 8, France
benoit.lathiere@gmail.com,
dominique.archambault@univ-paris8.fr

Abstract. The purpose of this study is to experiment the usability of a speech recognition system to help deaf and hard-of-hearing students to understand the lesson inside the classroom by subtitling the speech of the professor in live. The proposed solution is to repeat the professor's speech in a microphone plugged to a notebook with a speech-to-text software and to generate the text inside a collaborative editor displayed in front of the student. The repeater is a valid volunteer listening the professor's speech in the classroom. The software transforms the voice in text. The deaf student could read the text on his own device (a notebook or a mobile device).

Keywords: Deaf and Hard-of-Hearing Students, Speech Recognition, Collaborative Text Editor, Live Transcript.

1 Deaf Students, Lip Reading and Sign Language

In the French educative system, most deaf students use the French Sign Language (LSF) as the primary language [8]. Most of the time, their French writing level is low, or not good enough to write scholar document themselves. During their studies, they can have a note-taker (a volunteer classmate) who take note (handwritten or on a laptop computer) and LSF interpreters during the lesson who translate the professor's speech into sign language. Other deaf or hard-of-hearing students use the lip-reading and/or the cued speech to disambiguate phonemes[5][6]. Some of them do not use any human help, so no alternate solution is searched for them.

The main fail for signing students is to read and write documents in written French, because they do not use enough French writing before their university life (during their education, from primary school to university). Therefore, they have some troubles to choose courses where they need to read and write a lot of documents and where interpreters are not always available during the lessons. That is why the signing students choice is mainly limited to courses with interpreters, most of the time in the department of linguistics. The side effect is that they have a limited choice beyond

K. Miesenberger et al. (Eds.): ICCHP 2014, Part II, LNCS 8548, pp. 490–497, 2014.

courses. Additionally the university proposing proper human help for them (interpreters, cued speech coders) may be far from their home!

Moreover, the interpreters need a good understanding of the lesson to code correctly. In high-level degrees, some courses can be a problem for interpreters and coders. Whether the vocabulary does not exist – the interpreter and the deaf student create a new sign according to a common meaning – or the interpreter does not always have the necessary skills to understand the explanations of the professor [9]. It is a real problem for opening courses to deaf undergraduates – especially in technical and scientist courses. That is why a signing deaf student should also use written French for his university life and his professional future.

2 State-of-the-Art

Generate text from speech to deaf people is not a new solution. For many years, note-takers are used to create written documents from the professor's speech. If they are cheap and easy to recruit, the notes are not still good enough. And the notes are not immediately available.

In conferences or in some universities, some Stenotypists use special keyboards to transcript all the speech, in live. But there is not enough professionals able to perform this task, and it remains expensive. This system is often called "Communication Access Real-Time Translation (or CART)".

Using the speech recognition system to generate text is another solution. Other projects like the Liberated Learning[1], an international consortium focused on advancing speech recognition technologies to improve accessibility. Two prototypes had been developed: ViaScribe[2], an interface over the IBM's ViaVoice speech recognition system (now outdated), and the Caption Editing System[3] over ViaScribe (with ViaVoice and Dragon Naturally Speaking) to share live corrections via a network. The global project seems to be still active, according to their website.

The National Technology Institute for the Deaf[4], part of the Rochester Institute of Technology in the U.S.A., use several systems of captioning, in live or differed. But no automatic speech recognition system is used for now.

3 A Good Transcription in a Very Short Time

The system we describe here aims at opening more lessons to deaf students by having a high-fidelity text version of the speech of the professor as a lesson support in live and on the desk of the student – in addition to the classic handouts.

---

[1] More details on `http://liberatedlearning.com`

[2] ViaScribe:`http://liberatedlearningtechnology.com/?page_id=509`

[3] Caption Editing System:
`http://liberatedlearningtechnology.com/?page_id=514`

[4] More details on: `http://www.ntid.rit.edu`

A note-taker does not cost a lot of money and is easy to recruit. His task is to take written notes during the lesson because the deaf student cannot understand the lesson (via himself or interpreters) and writes notes at the same time.

The main drawback with a usual note-taker is that these notes are only available after the lesson (one or two days after, if notes are at first handwritten). Sometimes, the student sits near the laptop computer of the volunteer, therefore the notes are directly available for reading. But this is not always possible and often the volunteer in the back while the deaf student is installed on the first row in front of the professor.

Secondly, the quality of notes is not equal according to volunteers, and misspelled words, errors or lack of understanding may occur. The professor usually misses time to review.

In addition, this current system will not help deaf students improving their language level [2]. On the opposite, our proposal aims to use live reading and therefore to help the student improving their level in written language, using a high-fidelity transcript. If the student does not understand what the professor says, he can quickly switch between its lips and the transcription to read the missed idea.

4 The Repeater in Action

The first element of our system is the repeater role. A volunteer student (in the same course is preferred – or a former note-taker) repeats word-to-word the professor's speech in a microphone connected to a notebook equipped with a speech recognition software [7]. For that, we use Dragon Naturally Speaking by Nuance – which is powerful and cheap – in a dictation mode to obtain a plain text version of the speech. The latency time is about 3-5 seconds with a recent computer. Additionally we use a micro-mask – a microphone that covers the mouth of the speaker. This has 2 important advantages: on the first hand it avoids that the voice of the repeater disturbs the other students of the professor, and on the other hand it limitates background noise.

For performance reasons, we do not format by voice (bold, italic, underline, titling, …). Because Dragon listens to the entire phrase to detect the context and accords the verbs, the transcription can take a long time (something more than 10 seconds). To accelerate the text rendering, a tip is to truncate the phrase in small parts, by using comas and points. It is useful when the professor's speech has blanks or he is thinking about his ideas. The student does not wait for the full generated sentence to understand the main idea. A small part be recognised and displayed in less than 3 seconds.

5 The Quality of the Generated Text

The generated text is immediately and automatically put into a text editor, displayed in front of the deaf student, on his/her own laptop. But the speech recognition system is not perfect, up to now, even with lots of training hours on Dragon. And some special words (like family names) may be misspelled.

At this point we can notice two mean errors:

1. Missed phrases by the repeater (possible causes: background noise from the room, too fast speech, tiredness of the repeater...). In this case, an ellipsis sign is pronounced and added to indicate a lack of text,
2. Nonsense phrases due to a bad recognition, this situation grows up with the voice rate.

These errors can disrupt the deaf student reading whereas he/she is supposed to use text captioning to avoid misunderstanding! So, the high-fidelity text recognition is a major element of our method. The repeater can not easily correct it himself – repeating the speech of the professor in a microphone has a high-level cognitive charge and the repeater has to hold the micro-mask with the hand – and has no time for that. If the repeater focuses on the generated text to check it, he cannot hear the speaker and loses these words. A lack of text is then created and we fall down in a loop!

6 Correct Misspellings by a Collaborative Work – One Repeater, Many Correctors

We will now see how to fix the errors and improve the quality of the displayed text to the deaf student. The main idea here is to use a human help (called the "reviser" further in the text) to do the necessary corrections and changes directly in the generated text.

During the last decade, popular public projects and Web applications using collaborative editing via Internet grew up [3]. Now students are used to participate to a collaborative project (academic or not) with just a personal computer (a classical laptop or even a mobile device – a tablet or a smartphone).

To give the reviser the ability to correct the generated text, we have chosen a web-based open-source real-time collaborative text-editor, called Etherpad[5]. This is an autonomous product which works as a client-server architecture. The client is just a modern Web browser.

The text produced by Dragon is directly displayed in this tool. With this shared document, if a word is misspelled or missing, the reviser can quickly correct it. And we can have several revisers in same time to do the corrections. One repeater, many correctors – each of them with a different device.

The deaf student can see in real time the generated text and its corrections. If he/she does not understand an idea, he/she can add a note or a question directly linked to a paragraph. Then a reviser can ask details to the professor.

The reviser can even add some special notes like books references, small formulas, emails or URLs. All the things that the repeater cannot add by voice with Dragon.

7 Extending the Tool to our Needs

In the idea to have a unique tool, we have implemented some additional modules to extend functionalities.

[5] More details on: `http://www.etherpad.org`

If the professor shows an important object for the lesson (ex: an old piece of pottery), a reviser can take a shot of it with a regular webcam in two clicks. The picture will be automatically added to the shared document. Obviously, the created document and all these elements can be exported in various formats (MS Word, Open Document, PDF) with one of our additional modules.

After a while, the generated document can be long (more than two screen-pages). To avoid the laborious task to scroll frequently to the bottom to see the new text appears, the deaf student can activate an option to keep view at the bottom of the window, in order to follow the text. Each time a text is added, the window scrolls down slowly.

Another function is the subtitling-style window. A frame can be displayed at the bottom of the browser and displays only the newest phrases in white on a dark background (without graphic elements). After 5 seconds, the text disappears slowly with a fade-out effect. This frame reproduce what we can see in conferences when the speech in displayed on a large screen. The main document is still available.

8 Not All the Courses Can Easily Be Transcript

Despite the speech-to-text system allows improving accessibility of lessons, not all of these can benefit from this system [4].

By our tests, we can classify lessons in three main categories:

1. "Lecture": this is a regular lesson (in an amphitheatre by example). The professor speaks out the lesson with few interactions with students. We can display notes or shows slides on the board. The special vocabulary can be prepared by the repeater before the lesson with the supports of the professor.
2. "Technical lesson": in this scenario, the repeater task is more complex. The vocabulary is very technical. The professor can even use lot of tables, charts and illustrations on the board. The repeater must transcripts formulas, diagrams and examples, but he cannot describe all the elements displayed on the board. The task of the reviser is more important and can sorely help to construct an efficient document.
3. "Tutorials and group works": the main problem here is the dialogues between group members. It is a hard situation to an interpretor or a cued-speech coder. This is the same problem for the repeater, even more complex, due to the speech-to-text latency. A reviser is not a god help here, because the problem comes from the generated text itself.

Obviously, contexts with these mixed scenarios can be met. The problem will be mostly the same: several speakers talking together, quickly, with uncompleted phrases. In this case, the repeater cannot transcript the ideas with fidelity. And using several repeaters could be as complex as just one.

9 Prerequisites and Recommendations for the Best Results

To be sure that our speech-to-text solution with a repeater works at best, there are some prerequisites to apply before the lesson and recommendations during this one.

Firstly, it is important that the software Dragon knows the specific vocabulary (new words, abbreviations, names, ...). The repeater should obtain the course materials before the lesson to find the new words and pre-record them of his own voice in Dragon. The live recognition will be better. The repeater also has the possibility to train oneself to pronounce correctly the more complicated. During our tests, the prepared lessons (based on previous documents written from note-takers) gave better recognition results.

Unfortunately, some professors do not provide the texts of their speech before the lesson, with or without giving a reason (usually they prepare it lately, or they do not write it down). That is a real problem for lesson accessibility, globally for the impaired students and despite the help of the support centre for students with disabilities.

Secondly. With the preparation, the most important recommendation is the classroom environment. The place must be quiet. By example, avoid opening windows and doors when the outdoor is noisy. Obviously, the classmates must respect the repeater and deaf students!

The repeater must listen to the professor's speech clearly. The professor must be aware to the deafness and his behaviour during the lesson is very important. His speech must be normal, not fast, with a strong voice and frequently small pauses. Probably the most difficult problem is to pronounce not finished or unstructured phrases. Otherwise, the software will generate weird text, unusable for the deaf student!

If the professor has a guest, they should not speak at the same time. They should wait a couple of seconds before switching speaker. This small break allows the repeater to indicate the change of the speaker in the generated document. In this context, we could imagine two repeaters, but even in that case, a break between each speaker is very important to avoid blended texts in the document.

10 Time Is Everything

The latency time between each part of our system is a problem. The elapsed time between the professor's speech and the generated text must be the shortest to be useful for the deaf student. On each step of the process, several precious seconds are lost. Therefore, at the end of the transcription process, the global elapsed time can be longer than five seconds, sometimes even more. Dragon can be set up to increase speed generation or to improve quality.

When the repeater discovers Dragon for the first time, the recognition is not good and the training sessions are very important. At the beginning, the quality option is preferred to the speed. With time and progress, the cursor can be put on the speed option if the results are still good. The expert repeater needs to find the good balance.

The text synchronization in the real-time text editor takes about one second – test passed with five actors (repeater/revisers/readers) on a local network. So, the limiting factor is the repeater mechanism and the speech-to-text recognition software. To gain in time, a good solution could be to drop the repeater and to ask the professor to directly speak in a microphone. But, he/she would need to perform annoying training sessions and, first of all, to speak with a special utterance. A similar test had been done by a mathematical professor[6] some years ago but the results was not good (not only because the numerous formulas).

---

[6] In 2008, Mister Mohamed Amamou, professor of mathematical at school of Lecanuet in Rouen, tested using of Dragon Naturally Speaking to transcript his maths lesson in live to deaf students. Students used PC with speech synthesis to ask details.

11 Tests Protocols

We did several test sessions during real lessons with volunteer deaf students and professors. We chose different lesson types to test benefits and limits. The duration was approximately half an hour each. After each test, a survey was completed by the deaf student to collect his/her opinion and study profile.

In a second phase, the solution with a human reviser to correct misspelled phrases using the collaborative editor, has been tested during remote conferences. It is not necessary that the repeater and the reviser are in the same place. But the listening must be very clear. The repeater used earphones with high volume to cut off his own voice and can focus on the speaker's voice. After the test, a survey is filled by the reviser to know if the system is efficient for him/her (Web interface, text speed, audio quality, ...).

The duration of the conferences were exceeding an hour, which is very tiring for the repeater because the cognitive charge is important and also because a continuous speech dehydrate! Some breaks (each half-an-hour by example) are necessary. As for sign language interpretors, two repeaters could work in relay in a long session.

In this situation, the main problem is the latency between the speech and the generated text. If the elapsed time is too large, the reviser does not remember the speech and cannot locate misspelled phrases. It is important to generate the text as quick as possible. The text is displayed to the audience in live, with errors and corrections.

12 Cost Saving

Beyond the technical aspect and the usability, the cost of the system is a real concern for a public university. Despite the French law for disabled people (applied since 2005) and the donation from Ministry of Education, the budget of the university is not extensible.

In the current system, the most expensive resources are the sign language interpreters. They are expensive and not always available (a French national problem : there is a very limited number of LSF interpreters in the whole country). In a quick analyze, if we use actual note-takers as repeaters and revisers (for similarity compensation), and despite the cost of the computing infrastructure (notebooks, microphones, servers, network bandwidth, ...), this solution can be a good replacement for cases where interpreters are not available or inefficient (within scientific courses for instance).

The perfect scenario might be a mixed solution within the courses. The cost should not be the unique guide for making a choice. The good solution is still the one which help the deaf student to improve their skills (languages and others) and pass their degrees.

13 Conclusions

Our first results show that the speech recognition system can help deaf students to both access to more lectures and improve their French skills, which is the main goal. But the generated document can help any impaired people who cannot take notes or want more details than light notes from classmates.

With the collaborative real-time editor system, classmates are involved in the construction of a final document for everyone. The disabled student is no more a passive listener but a full actor of the lesson. Everybody wins to participate to the process. We can say that the system brings closer all the classmates, impaired students together with their mainstream peers. That is the illustration to the inclusive school [1].

Furthermore, in a conference, not only the deaf or hard-of-hearing people can be interested by a live transcription. Anybody can lose the thread of the discussion at any moment. Thereby, the text can help anyone to understand the missed ideas.

References

1. Antia, S.D., Jones, P.B., Reed, S., Kreimeyer, K.H.: Academic Status and Progress of Deaf and Hard-of-Hearing Students in General Education Classrooms. Journal of Deaf Studies and Deaf Education 14(3), 293–311 (2009)
2. Bochner, J.H., Walter, G.G.: Evaluating Deaf Students' Readiness to Meet the English Language and Literacy Demands of Postsecondary Educational Programs. Journal of Deaf Studies and Deaf Education 10(3), 323–343 (2004)
3. Bouquillion, P., Matthews, J.T.: Le web collaboratif. In: Mutations des Industries de la Culture et de la Communication, p. 150, Presses Universitaires de Grenoble, Grenoble (2010)
4. Dell, N., Hutchin, J.: How and why Remote Captioning works for me. The Limping Chicken (May 9, 2013)
5. Dunlap, B.: Alternate methods of communication for the deaf & hearing impaired. Livestrong (October 6, 2010)
6. Long, G.L., Vignare, K., Rappold, R.P., Mallory, J.: Access to Communication for Deaf, Hard-of-Hearing and ESL Students in Blended Learning Courses. IRR ODL 8(3) (2007)
7. Luff, J.: Realtime speech translation will revolutionise how we communicate. WIRED (April 16, 2013)
8. Richardson, J.T.E., Marschark, M., Sarchet, T., Sapere, P.: Deaf and Hard-of-Hearing Students' Experiences in Mainstream and Separate Postsecondary Education. Journal of Deaf Studies and Deaf Education 15(4), 358–382 (2010)
9. Schick, B., Williams, K., Kupermintz, H.: Look Who's Being Left Behind: Educational Interpreters and Access to Education for Deaf and Hard-of-Hearing Students. Journal of Deaf Studies and Deaf Education 11, 3–18 (2006)

Examining the Characteristics of Deaf and Hard of Hearing Users of Social Networking Sites

Ines Kožuh[1], Manfred Hintermair[2], and Matjaž Debevc[1]

[1] University of Maribor, Faculty of Electrical Engineering and Computer Science, Smetanova ulica 17, SI-2000 Maribor, Slovenia
{ines.kozuh,matjaz.debevc}um.si

[2] University of Education Heidelberg, Keplerstraße 87, D-69120 Heidelberg, Germany
hintermair@ph-heidelberg.de

Abstract. In this study we examined whether the level of hearing loss is related to the frequency of communication within different situations and performance activities on social networking sites. It was also investigated as to how the frequency of activities were related to the perceived accessibility of these sites. Firstly, the findings revealed that users with lower levels of hearing loss communicated more frequently with hearing persons in the written language than users at higher levels. In contrast, they communicated less frequently with deaf users in sign language than those with higher levels of hearing loss. Secondly, users with lower levels of hearing loss posted videos more frequently than those with higher levels. Thirdly, the more frequently the deaf and hard of hearing users actualized their profiles, posted photos, videos, commented and liked the content, the higher the perceived accessibility of those sites they reported.

Keywords: Deaf, Hard of Hearing, Social Networking Sites, Communication, Evaluation.

1 Introduction

Over the past decade social networking sites (SNSs) have become extremely popular and an almost ubiquitous technology of everyday life. In 2013, each month more than 1.9 billion users accessed the most popular SNS Facebook across all devices. The use has been intensive with 874 million users accessing monthly and 507 million users accessing daily across mobile phone [1].

These high percentage user rates indicate how important it is to know the users' various characteristics, like gender, age, language skills, technology use skills and/or types of disability that may affect using SNSs. Deaf and hard of hearing (D/HH) people have some communication specificities compared to hearing people and people with other types of disabilities. They can face difficulties when using written language. For instance, it can take three years for the deaf to progress one level in reading compared to hearing people [2]. Thence, it is very important to examine the situation of D/HH people on SNSs in relation to their communication situations offline. In particular, it is important to investigate how D/HH people use SNSs, how

K. Miesenberger et al. (Eds.): ICCHP 2014, Part II, LNCS 8548, pp. 498–505, 2014.

accessible these users perceive SNSs to be, how they communicate online and how it relates to their communication situations offline.

In previous research, to the best of our knowledge, there has been a lack of research into investigating those activities of D/HH users on SNSs in relation to their characteristics and communication. Existing studies have mostly addressed the use of these platforms among hearing users by considering their gender, ethnicity and race [3,4]. When it comes to D/HH users, previous studies have mostly focused on online interactions and online communities [5,6]. In particular, Shoham & Heber [5] found that D/HH internet users' interactions mostly deal with social support and providing informational support for online peers, whereas Valentine & Skelton [6] substantiated in their study that the Internet liberated Deaf communities from fixed time and spaces typical for Deaf clubs, as new forms of communities emerged on the internet. It is advantageous that previous studies addressed interactions online; however, the experiences of D/HH users of SNSs have not been comprehensively examined, although a theoretical model for examining such experiences has been proposed [7].

The main purpose of the study presented in this paper is to meet this deficiency, as it extends previous research by including a sample of D/HH people to examine how the level of hearing loss is associated with using SNSs and any communication within these environments. Thus, the following research questions were examined:

- *RQ1:* Are there statistically significant differences between groups with different levels of hearing loss in frequency of communication using different modes of communication and with persons with different levels of hearing loss?
- *RQ2:* Are there statistically significant differences between groups with different levels of hearing loss in frequency of performing activities on SNSs?
- *RQ3:* Is there a statistically significant relationship between perceived accessibility and frequency of performing activities on SNSs?

Firstly, it is expected to find differences between groups with different levels of hearing loss in frequency of communication on SNSs. In particular, it is hypothesized that users with higher levels of hearing loss will communicate more often with deaf persons in sign language than users with lower levels of hearing loss. Secondly, finding differences is to be expected between both the aforementioned groups in frequency of performing activities on SNSs. Users with lower levels of hearing loss are expected to perform activities more frequently than users with higher levels of hearing loss, as the content of SNSs seems to be based on written rather than sign language. Thirdly, it is anticipated that the more accessible D/HH people perceive SNSs to be, the more active users they will be.

The paper is organized as follows. We start by presenting the research methods; participants, measures, and data analyses are presented. Next, the results are presented and described. Discussion and conclusion with study limitations follow.

2 Methods

2.1 Participants

The sample for this study was recruited from the D/HH population in Germany. Specifically, 245 D/HH persons were surveyed. Out of these, 199 respondents were users of SNSs and were included in the study as the main subjects of the research. The survey was put online and was hosted at SurveyGizmo.com a commercial survey-hosting website. Participants were invited to participate through e-mail messages sent to the representatives of major German web portals for the deaf and their clubs. An invitation with was also published in online communities of D/HH people.

2.2 Measures

The instructions and the questionnaire were presented in both German written and sign language. Before the participants were able to start completing the questionnaire, they had to read the instructions and consent to participating in the study. A questionnaire survey is available on the following address: `http://medijske.um.si/doc/Questionnaire_Kozuh_et_al.pdf`.

The measuring instrument was a questionnaire comprising sections classified into two parts: (a) an offline context and (b) an online context. First, within the offline context we investigated the following sections: (i) demographic characteristics, (ii) communication situation offline, and (iii) use of technology. Second, within the online context we investigated the use of SNSs.

The Offline Context. The first section contained questions capturing data on gender, age, level of education, level of hearing loss and parents' hearing status.

The second section comprised questions capturing data on the communication forms used during their educational processes, modes of communication with family members in the early years and the preferred mode of communication now. In addition, three sets of three questions measured their skills in sign, spoken, and written language. The alpha reliability coefficients [8] of three questions measuring each type of skill were as follows: sign language skills .97, spoken language skills .89 and written language skills .89. Participants estimated their skills administered with 5-point Likert-type response categories ranging from 1 (very poor) to 5 (excellent).

The third section contained questions capturing technology use skills and perceived availability of technology. The users reported how skilled they were in using computers, smart phones and tablets, and which devices were available to them for using SNSs.

The Online Context. This section contained questions capturing data on reasons and purposes for using SNSs, frequency of using, activities on these online platforms, communication situation online, perceived usefulness, and accessibility of SNSs.

More precisely, to define the reasons for using SNSs participants were asked to estimate to what extent they used SNSs in regard to enjoyment, helpfulness, and learnability. In order to define the purposes they were asked to what extent they used SNSs for (a) fun and (b) school or work. They responded using answer options ranging from 1 (I totally disagree) to 5 (I totally agree).

In order to estimate the frequency with which SNSs were used, participants responded on answer options ranging from 1 (barely – once or less per month) to 4 (very often – once or more per day). In order to examine those activities performed on SNSs, participants were asked how often they actualized their profiles, posted photos and videos, liked, commented and shared various posts, such as photos and videos. They responded using answer options ranging from 1 (never) to 5 (very often – once or more per day).

The communication situation online was examined by measuring the frequency of communicating with recipients having different hearing status (hearing, hard of hearing, and deaf) and modes of communication (sign and written language). They responded using answer options ranging from 1 (never) to 5 (very often – once or more per day).

Perceived usefulness and perceived accessibility of SNSs were measured by two questions where the participants were asked as to what extent they agreed that SNSs were easy to use and that SNSs were suitable for D/HH people as users with hearing loss. They responded using answer options ranging from 1 (I totally disagree) to 5 (I totally agree).

2.3 Data Analyses

Cronbach's Alpha coefficient [8] was used to check the internal consistency reliability of a set of items for one variable. Parametric correlation (Pearson's correlation coefficient) was used to inspect any statistical associations between variables. A One-way Analysis of Variance (One-way ANOVA) statistical model was used to check statistically significant differences between independent samples [10]. All the analyses were performed using SPSS version 21.

3 Results

3.1 Descriptive Statistics

Table 1 shows participants' basic characteristics. 62.31% of users of SNSs were female. The mean age of the participants was 37 years (age range: 12 – 72, SD = 12.60). According to the definition of hearing loss released by ANSI [8], the majority had profound hearing loss (more than 90 dB). For the purposes of this study we classified them into three groups. The first group contained users with mild to moderately-severe hearing loss (27 – 70dB), the second comprised users with severe (71 – 90 dB) and the third group consisted of users with profound hearing loss (more than 90dB).

Table 1. Basic characteristics of the sample

Characteristics	n	%
Level of hearing loss		
Group 1 (mild, moderate and moderately-severe hearing loss)	20	10.1
Group 2 (severe hearing loss)	46	23.1
Group 3 (profound hearing loss)	126	63.3
unclassified (unknown hearing loss)	7	3.5
Preferred mode of communication		
German spoken language	41	20.6
German spoken language with signing	50	25.1
German sign language	69	34.7
total communication	39	19.6
Frequency of using SNSs		
rarely (once a month or less)	12	6
sometimes (twice to three times a month)	14	7
often (once to six times a week)	64	32.2
very often (once or more times a day)	109	54.8

The majority had hearing mothers (69.80%) and hearing fathers (70.35%). Forty-nine per cent of participants completed middle school; those who graduated and finished elementary school followed (31.18%). The majority used Facebook (91.5%) and Google Plus followed (18.6%). Other SNSs, like HearZone, Deaf-Point, LinkedIn, Xing and Stayfriends were used to a lesser extent.

On average, the participants reported good written language skills (M = 4.15, SD = .72), sign (M = 3.80, SD = 1.28) and spoken language skills followed (M = 3.30, SD = 1.02). During the educational process, the majority used German spoken language (41.21%); those who used spoken language in combination with sign language (26.63%) and those who used total communication (18.09%) followed. Similarly, spoken language prevailed when communication with the family at home (59.8%). Intriguingly, the majority preferred a combination of sign and spoken language in everyday communication.

Participants estimated their technology use skills as--personal computer (M = 4.09, SD = 1.09), smartphone (M = 3.38, SD = 1.68) and tablet (M = 2.13, SD = 1.58). On average, SNSs were available and accessed the more frequently from a computer (M = 4.09, SD = 1.09) and the least frequently from a tablet (M = 2.13, SD = 1).

The majority used SNSs very frequently (54.8%). Those with lower levels of hearing loss reported the highest score (M = 3.55, SD = .83), whereas those with the lowest level of hearing loss reported the lowest score (M = 3.32, SD = .86).

With regard to the purposes for using, D/HH tended to use SNSs for fun (M = 3.92, SD = 1.1) and for school or work (M = 3.18, SD = 1.46). Regarding the reasons for using SNSs, participants reported that they used SNSs due to fun (M = 3.80, SD = 1.14), helpfulness (M = 4.15, SD = .88) and learnability (M = 3.75, SD = 1.1).

In regard to reporting the frequency of performing activities on SNSs, users most frequently liked posts (M = 3.27, SD = 1.17), whereas posting comments followed (M = 3.09, SD = 1.12). The least frequent was the posting of videos (M = 1.84, SD = .97). The perceived usefulness of SNSs was reported with a mean score 3.90 (SD = 1.06), whereas perceived accessibility was similarly estimated (M = 3.90, SD = 1.17).

3.2 Correlational Analyses

In order to answer the first two research questions, statistical differences were checked by conducting a one-way ANOVA. The first research question asked whether there were differences between groups with different levels of hearing loss in frequency of communication with different modes of communication and with persons with different levels of hearing loss. Statistically significant differences between the groups were found in frequency of communication with different modes of communication and recipients with different levels of hearing loss in the following situations (see Fig. 1):

- frequency of communication with deaf persons in sign language ($F(2, 189) = 4.8$, $p < .01$),
- frequency of communication with hard of hearing persons in written language ($F(2, 189) = 3.45$, $p < .05$),
- frequency of communication with hearing persons in written language ($F(2, 189) = 8.22$, $p < .01$),

With regard to the abovementioned results, first regarding the frequency of communication with deaf persons in sign language, those with the lowest level of hearing loss communicated the least frequently (M = 1.6, SD = 1.05) compared to other groups. The most frequent communication in sign language with deaf persons was reported by those with the highest level of hearing loss (M = 2.39, SD = 1.38). Second, those with the middle level of hearing loss communicated the most frequently with hard of hearing persons in written language (M = 3.43, SD = 1.24). Those with the highest level of hearing loss communicated less (M = 2.83, SD = 1.40) than those with the lowest level (M = 2.90, SD = 1.17). Third, those with the lowest level of hearing loss communicated the most frequently with hearing persons in written language compared to other groups (M = 3.60, SD = 2.68).

The second research question asked whether there were statistically significant differences between groups with different levels of hearing loss in frequency of performing activities on SNSs. Analysis showed statistically significant differences between groups with different levels of hearing loss only in posting videos on SNSs, $F(2, 189) = 3.87, p < .05$. Users with the lowest level of hearing loss posted videos the least frequently (M = 1.35, SD = .67), whereas a group of users with the middle level of hearing loss posted them the most frequently (M = 2.07, SD = 1.08).

The third research question asked whether there was a statistically significant relationship between perceived accessibility and frequency of performing activities on SNSs. In order to find an answer, a bivariate analysis was conducted. The results revealed a positive statistically significant relationship between perceived accessibility and actualizing profiles ($r = .26, p < .01$), posting photos ($r = .23, p < .01$), videos ($r = .22, p < .01$), liking the content ($r = .22, p < .01$) and posting comments ($r = .18$, $p < .05$). It indicated that the more often these activities on SNSs were performed, the more accessible these sites were perceived.

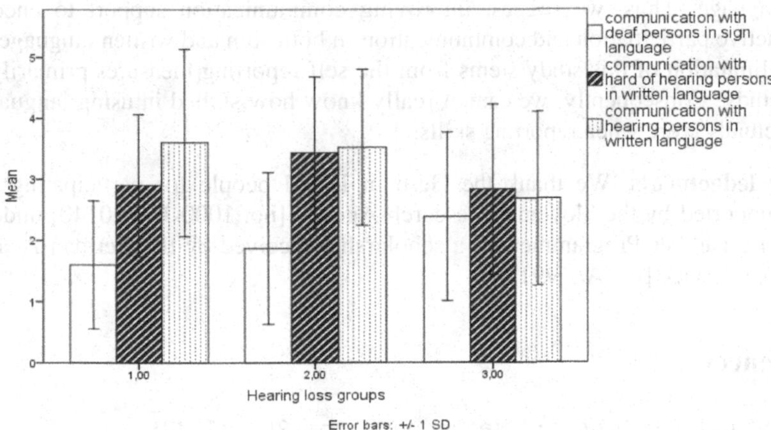

Fig. 1. Frequency of communication on SNSs

4 Discussion

In this study we found that users with higher levels of hearing loss communicated more often with deaf persons in sign language on SNSs than users with lower levels. In contrast, those with low levels of hearing loss communicated more often with hearing persons in written language than other groups. Intriguingly, a group of users with the middle level of hearing loss communicated the most frequently with the hard of hearing in written language. Those with the lowest level of hearing loss followed.

The results also showed that a group of users with the lowest level of hearing loss posted videos the least frequently. The most frequent posting was reported by those with the middle level of hearing loss. It may indicate that videos represent content popular to a lesser extent among the profoundly deaf. Moreover, the results revealed that the more often D/HH users actualized profiles, posted photos, videos, liked and commented posts, the more accessible they perceived these sites. It may indicate that these activities contribute the most to perceived accessibility of SNSs.

5 Conclusion

The findings suggest that hearing loss is an important aspect in using SNSs and communication between D/HH users. They can also contribute to better awareness of these users' needs. Intriguingly, deaf users reported slightly more frequent communication on SNSs than those with hearing loss within the range from mild to moderately-severe. However, communication in written language was among the profoundly deaf users the least frequent compared to all groups. It can indicate a need for support in communication in written language for these users. Similarly, posting videos was the least frequent activity on SNSs, although it has a potential for communication in sign language. Thus, we suggest improving communication support to encourage users' active participation and communication in both sign and written language.

The limitation of this study stems from the self-reporting measures primarily used in the study. Consequently, we cannot really know how skilled in using language the users actually were when reporting skills.

Acknowledgements. We thank the German D/HH people for participating in the study supported by the Slovenian Research Agency [no. 1000-11-310140] under The Young Researcher Programme and a scholarship received by the German Academic Exchange Service [no. A/13/91743].

References

1. Constine, J.: (2013), http://techcrunch.com/2013/12/29/facebook-international-user-growth/
2. Schirmer, B.R.: Dimensions of deafness: Psychological, social and educational. Allyn & Bacon, Boston (2001)
3. Hargittai, E.: Whose Space? Differences among Users and Non-Users of Social Network Sites. Journal of Computer-Mediated Communication 13(1), 276–297 (2007)

4. Junco, R., Merson, D., Salter, D.W.: The effect of gender, ethnicity, and income on college students' use of communication technologies. Cyberpsychology, Behavior, and Social Networking 13(6), 619–627 (2010)
5. Shoham, S., Heber, M.: Characteristics of a Virtual Community for Individuals Who Are d/Deaf and Hard of Hearing. American Annuals of the Deaf 157(3), 251–263 (2012)
6. Valentine, G., Skelton, T.: An umbilical cord to the world: The role of the Internet in D/deaf people's information and communication practices. Information, Communication & Society 12(1), 44–65 (2009)
7. Kožuh, I., Hintermair, M., Ivanišin, M., Debevc, M.: The Concept of Examining the Experiences of Deaf and Hard of Hearing Online Users. In: Pérez Cota, M. (ed.) 5th International Conference on Software Development and Technologies for Enhancing Accessibility and Fighting Info-exclusion: DSAI 2013, Procedia Computer Science, vol. 27, pp. 148–157. Elsevier, Oxford (2014)
8. Cronbach, L.J.: Coefficient alpha and the internal structure of tests. Psychometrika 16(3), 297–334 (1951)
9. American National Standards Institute: Specifications for Audiometers. ANSI publication ANSI/ASA S3.6-2010, American National Standards Institute, New York, USA (2010)
10. Howell, D.: Statistical Methods for Psychology. Duxbury/Thomson Learning, USA (2002)

A Smart-Phone Based System to Detect Warning Sound for Hearing Impaired People

Koichiro Takeuchi[1], Tetsuya Matsumoto[1], Yoshinori Takeuchi[2], Hiroaki Kudo[1], and Noboru Ohnishi[1]

[1] Graduate School of Information Science, Nagoya University, Japan
takeuchi.kouichirou@a.mbox.nagoya-u.ac.jp,
{matumoto,kudo,ohnishi}@is.nagoya-u.ac.jp
[2] Department of Information Systems, School of Informatics, Daido University, Japan
ytake@daido-it.ac.jp

Abstract. We propose a simple system for detecting warning sound. The system processes a signal captured by a microphone by an IIR band pass filter with a pass band covering warning sound spectrum and then applies an IIR comb filter corresponding to the fundamental frequency of warning sounds. The system calculates the ratio of the mean of the absolute values of the input signal to the output signal of the comb filter. If the ratio is smaller than a threshold, the system judges that warning sounds exist. As an experiment result, the proposed system can detect the ambulance sirens with accuracy above of 94% under noisy environments of SNR 0 dB, while over-detection rate is less than 3%. In an experiment using five real sounds recording approaching siren on the road, its accuracy ranges from 30 to 82%.

Keywords: Sound Source Recognition, Warning Sound, IIR Comb Filter, Real Time.

1 Introduction

Auditory sense plays an important role in communication, entertainment and perceiving the situation of the surrounding environment. For example, people walking on road hear several sounds such as moving cars, horns of cars, sirens of emergency vehicles and alarms of railroad crossings, and they behave well to avoid dangers. The hearing impaired people, however, cannot perceive such sounds and may meet accidents [1-3]. Therefore they need a system for detecting sounds relating to dangers. Such systems are useful for elder persons with low ability of hearing and people with a headphone, and will support car drivers if microphones are appropriately set to cars.

We propose a simple system for detecting warning sounds such as horn and siren by using a smart phone which has become very popular. The features of our system compared with the related work described in the next section is that the system needs very low computation cost without calculation of Fourier spectrum and correlation functions, and its portability.

K. Miesenberger et al. (Eds.): ICCHP 2014, Part II, LNCS 8548, pp. 506–511, 2014.

2 Related Work

There are some studies relating to detection of warning sounds. Shimada et al. [4] proposed a system for estimating the direction of multiple horns. The system estimates the fundamental frequency of horns using a comb filter, and the number of horns based on the harmonic structure of horns, and determines the direction of horns based on the arrival time difference between microphones obtained by cross-correlation functions. This system has a problem of the low estimation accuracy of the fundamental frequency in a case of low SNR. Itagaki et al. [5-6] detected the siren of emergency vehicles such as ambulances, police cars and fire engines, and the horns of cars by using harmonic structure and peak emphasis. They conducted experiments, in which a single source or two mixed sources were inputted to their system. As a result, their system can recognize warning sounds in the noisy environment of SNR 0 dB.

Meucci et al. [7] reported a system to detect emergency sirens using the measurement of Module Difference Function (MDF). MDF is a kind of comb filter. They calculated the fundamental frequency of a siren based on the peak of MDF and detected it. In that study, the various parameters of siren detection are discussed.

Iwasa et al. [8] proposed a system to detect an approaching sound source and to recognize a sound source using the pulse neuron model. This system recognizes the sirens of ambulances and police cars, and the engine sound of scooters. The input signal of this system is divided to 11 frequency bands. The detection of approaching sound is done based on the difference of the sound pressure of current and past input signals. The recognition is done based on a competitive learning network using pulse neurons. This network learns the difference in the sound pressure of divided frequency bands. This system was simulated on computer and implemented on FPGA (field programmable gate array) and tested. This system has the problems that noisy warning sound is not considered and that the computer processing time of the system is long.

Ohtsuka et al. [9] developed a method using past 60 analysis frames to judge the existence of a siren. In this method, the frequency of appearance of the fundamental frequency obtained based on the peak of the spectrum is counted. When the frequency of appearance exceeds a threshold, this method judges the existence of a siren.

3 Detection System

3.1 Basic Idea

The characteristic of warning sounds such as horn and siren is that the sounds consist of the fundamental frequency (f0) component and its harmonic components. Figure 1 shows amplitude spectrum of Japanese ambulance sirens, which consist of low frequency (f0=770 Hz) and high frequency sections (f0=960 Hz).

Such harmonic structure can be detected by a comb filter, which removes harmonic components from an input signal. As a result, the power of filter output becomes smaller than that of the filter input. Then we can judge the existence of warning sound based on the ratio of comb filter output power to its input power.

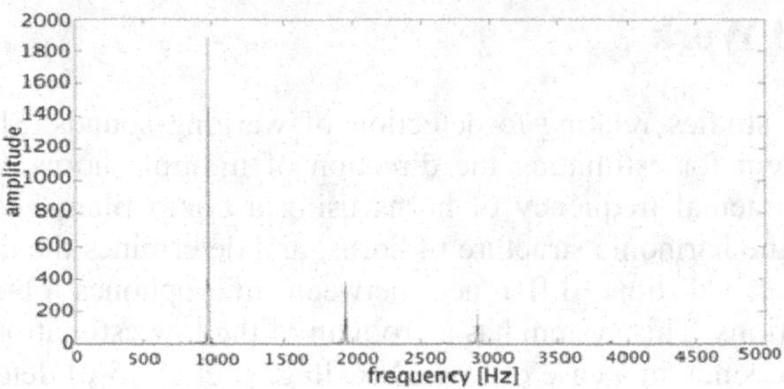

Fig. 1. Spectrum of ambulance sirens (high frequency)

Because the comb filter deletes very low frequency components including DC, which is major in environment noises, the system uses a band-pass filter to delete DC and to emphasize frequency components relating to warning sounds.

3.2 Detection Method

We explain how to detect warning sounds in a case of ambulance sirens. The siren has two fundamental frequencies of 770 Hz and 960 Hz, which are repeated alternately. Figure 2 shows the flowchart of detection processing.

1. Input a signal *i(n)* consisting of 1024 samples (a frame) to the system (f_s=44.1KHz).
2. Apply an IIR (Infinite Impulse Response) band-pass filter to the input signal and obtain the filter output *y(n)*. The Butterworth filter is used and its cutoff frequencies of the band-pass filter is set to 220Hz and 4410Hz.
3. Apply IIR comb filters for high and low frequency sections of ambulance sirens to the output of the band-pass filter, respectively. The outputs of two comb filters are calculated as follows:

$$o_{770}(n) = \frac{1.9}{2}\{y(n) - y(n-57)\} + 0.9 * o_{770}(n-57) \quad (1)$$

$$o_{960}(n) = \frac{1.9}{2}\{y(n) - y(n-57)\} + 0.9 * o_{960}(n-57) \quad (2)$$

4. Calculate the means of the absolute values of the three signals over a frame: the band pass filtered signal and the output signal which filtered with comb filters for high and low frequency sections.
5. Calculate the amplitude ratios, R_{770} and R_{960}, of two comb filter outputs for the high and low frequency to the band-pass filter output.

$$R_{770} = \frac{\sum_{n=1}^{1024}|o_{770}(n)|}{\sum_{n=1}^{1024}|y(n)|}, \; R_{960} = \frac{\sum_{n=1}^{1024}|o_{960}(n)|}{\sum_{n=1}^{1024}|y(n)|} \quad (3)$$

6. Select lower amplitude ratio of the two amplitude ratios.
7. If the value of the selected amplitude ratio is below a pre-determined threshold Th_R, the system judges that a siren exists in the corresponding frame.

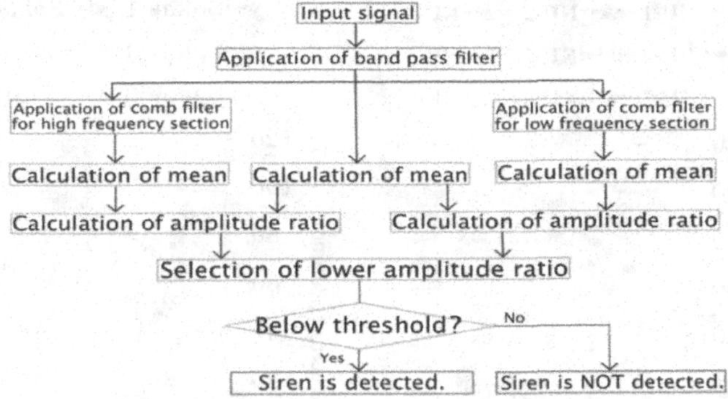

Fig. 2. Flowchart of detection processing for detecting ambulance sirens

4 Experiment and Result

We conducted three experiments. Experiment 1 evaluates how well the system detects the warning sound by changing noise level, and experiment 2 the performance of the system when the siren doesn't exist. Experiment 3 evaluates the performance by using real sound.

In experiments 1 and 2, we used three kinds of noise; two environment noises and white noise. One environment noise was recorded near Nagoya University on a rainy day (nine recordings; called as NU-#) and the other on a busy street on a sunny day (five recordings; called as Sakae-#).

Experiments were done on a PC emulating Android smart phone environment. Sampling frequency (f_s) is 44.1 kHz and quantization level is 16 bits. The threshold of the amplitude ratio Th_R was set to 0.9. The detection accuracy was calculated as follows:

Acc =100*(# of frames detected as warning sound)/(the number of total frames) [%]

In experiment 1, we used ambulance siren sound in a CD. Changing SNR (10 dB, 0 dB, -10dB), we synthesized siren signals corrupted by the noises. The time duration of synthesized signals is about 20 seconds (800 frames). Figure 3 shows the accuracy rate in detecting siren corrupted by NU and Sakae/white noise, respectively. The detection accuracy is more than 94% for SNR 0 and 10 dB, although the mean accuracy for -10 dB is 62%.

As a result of experiment 2 to evaluate the performance of the system when the siren doesn't exist, the rate of over-detection of warning sound is 0.6 % for NU noise, 1.6 % for Sakae noise and 0 % for white noise. Therefore, the system is less likely to do over-detection.

In experiment 3, we recorded sirens of ambulance cars approaching to a hospital on the road. Table 1 shows the detection accuracy for five recordings. The rate ranges from 30% to 82% and its average is 48% (SD 22%).

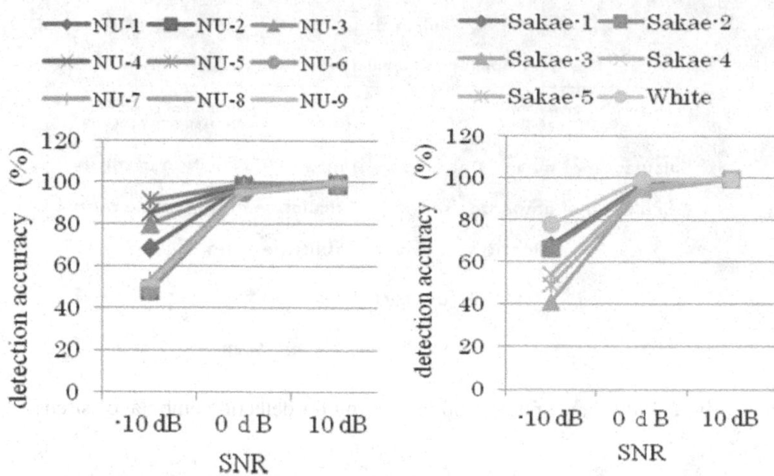

Fig. 3. Accuracy of detecting the ambulance siren corrupted by noises, left part: NU noise, right part: Sakae noise / white noise

Table 1. Detection accuracy of sirens recorded in the real environment

	Rec. 1 (30 s.)	Rec. 2 (15 s.)	Rec. 3 (21 s.)	Rec. 4 (25 s.)	Rec. 5 (49 s.)
Acc (%)	30	82	31	39	58

5 Discussion

Computation complexity of the proposed method is O(N), where N is the number of data points in one frame. This is less than that of the conventional methods using Fourier transform and autocorrelation, whose complexity is O(NlogN). Furthermore the proposed method can realize real-time processing because the processing is done in time domain whenever a new data is sampled and can output the result immediately after the last data is sampled.

The results of experiments 1 and 2 demonstrate that the proposed method accurately detects sirens under SNR 0 dB with very few over-detection. Low accuracy for SNR -10dB and real sounds should be improved by introducing a comb filter with fractional delay [10] to cope with the Doppler shift and by judging based on multiple frames.

6 Conclusion

This paper has proposed the simple system to detect warning sounds for the safety of pedestrians. Because of low computation cost and real-time processing, it will be easily realized by a smart phone. The experiment results show the effectiveness of the system.

Future subjects are to implement programs for detecting other warning sounds, and to conduct a field test by using a smart phone.

References

1. Miyazaki, S., Ishida, A.: Traffic-alarm sound monitor for aurally handicapped drivers. Medical and Biological Engineering and Computing 25(1), 68–74 (1987)
2. Baba, H., Ebata, M.: Study on detection of the electronic siren from an ambulance. Acoustical Society of Japan 52(4), 244–252 (1996)
3. Goo, B., Itoh, K.: A study on living sound identification system for the hearing impaired person. IEICE Technical Report WIT2002-69 (2002)
4. Shimada, Y., Takeuchi, Y., Matsumoto, T., Kudo, H., Ohnishi, N.: Simultaneous Direction Estimation of Horns by a Microphone Array. IEICE Technical Report EA 105(555), 45–50 (2006)
5. Morishita, R., Takeuchi, Y., Matsumoto, T., Kudo, H., Ohnishi, N.: Detecting the sirens of emergency vehicles for safe driving. IEICE Technical Report WIT 109(467), 15–20 (2010)
6. Itagaki, T., Matsumoto, T.Y., Takeuchi, Y., Matsumoto, T., Kudo, H., Ohnishi, N.: Recognizing warning sounds using the harmonic structure and peak emphasis. IEICE Technical Report WIT 111(472), 13–18 (2012)
7. Meucci, F., Pierucci, L., Del Re, E., Lastrucci, L., Desii, P.: A Real-Time Siren Detector to Improve Safety of Guide in Traffic Environment. In: 16th European Signal Processing Conference (EUSIPCO 2008), Lausanne, Switzerland, August 25-29 (2008)
8. Iwase, K., Fujisumi, T., Kugler, M., Kuroyanagi, S., Iwata, A., Danno, M., Miyaji, M.: A Detection System of Approaching and Recognition Sound Source by Pulsed Neuron Model for On-Vehicle Safety Driving Support Device. Electronics and Communications in Japan D J91-D(4), 1130–1141 (2008)
9. Otsuka, S., Hara, H., Ozawa, S.: Emergency Vehicle Detection System Using a Microphone on-Vehicle, IPSJ ITS 12-5 (2003)
10. Singh, A., Dhillon, D.N., Bains, S.S.: A Review on Fractional Delay FIR Digital Filters Design and Optimization Techniques. International Journal of Computer & Organization Trends 3(10) (November 2013)

A Support System for Teaching Practical Skills to Students with Hearing Impairment

SynchroniZed TAbletop Projection System: SZTAP

Takuya Suzuki[1] and Makoto Kobayashi[2]

[1] National University Corporation Tsukuba University of Technology, Amakubo 4-3-15, Tsukuba City, Ibaraki, Japan
[2] National University Corporation Tsukuba University of Technology, Kasuga 4-12-7, Tsukuba City, Ibaraki, Japan
suzukit@a.tsukuba-tech.ac.jp, koba@cs.k.tsukuba-tech.ac.jp

Abstract. In the class of practical lesson such as painting or modeling to hearing impaired students, conventional translation services do not make enough effects because students cannot see a signer or captioning texts and teacher's operation simultaneously. To solve the problem, we propose a tabletop projection system with special software which displays synchronized explanation texts which is prepared in advance. With this system, the teacher can project text information just besides operation area on the table. To control the timing of changing those texts, the teacher use foot pedals. Hearing impaired students' answers for questionnaires after a practical lesson of Manga drawing with proposed system showed that it was useful for such a lesson.

Keywords: Hearing Impaired Student, Practical Lesson, Tabletop Projection.

1 Introduction

Division of industrial technology in Tsukuba University of Technology is unique one in Japan, which is only for students with hearing impairment. This division is composed of a department of industrial information and a department of synthetic design and we are focusing on a problem in the class of teaching practical skills in the department of synthetic design. Teachers of this department usually use sign language with various visual materials for education and this combination is effective in most of lectures. However, they do not bring out enough advantages when students study practical skills like painting a picture, making a sculpture, and drawing a Manga. In those cases, teachers must show how to do it with making a model to the students in real time and it is difficult to explain these operations using sign language at a same time. Of course sign language translator is helpful though, hearing impaired students should move their eyes between the signer and the teacher's operation. This situation is shown in the left side of Fig. 1. Moving their eyes back and forth, left and right makes them be tired and lose concentration. Additionally, the time-lag of translation causes confusing and makes them to have frustration. Synchronization between the real operation and translation text is important in the practical skill lesson. Captioning

K. Miesenberger et al. (Eds.): ICCHP 2014, Part II, LNCS 8548, pp. 512–515, 2014.

services has also the same problems. There is a translation system which displays texts to the handy tablet device and it is really helpful and the speed of captioning is fast enough in these days[1]. However, even with such a system, hearing impaired students should move their eyes in the practical lesson and there still is time-lag, especially in the case of Japanese language since it has very complicate writing system[2].

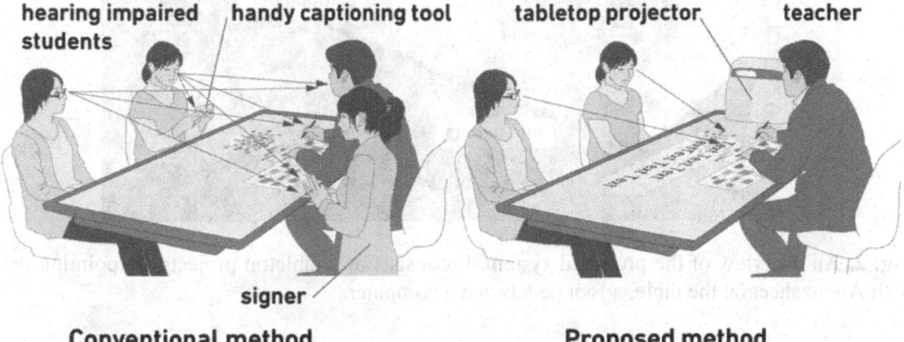

Fig. 1. Comparison between a conventional method and a proposed method in the lesson of practical skill. HI students have to move their eyes in conventional method. They do not have to do it in the case of using proposed method.

To solve the problem, we thought that putting text information around the operation area might be one of the solutions. It is shown in right side of Fig. 1. Concern about projection system for hearing impaired people, Takahashi, et al had a same idea and they developed a handy laser projection device which can show text information to the object in museum[3]. This device is an appropriate tool for explaining object, it is not fit for the situation of teaching practical skills in the lecture room.

2 Synchronized Tabletop Projection System: SZTAP

Fig.2 shows proposed system named Synchronized Tabletop Projection System, SZTAP. It is composed of a tabletop projector, a pointing pen device, a set of foot pedals, and a computer to which a special software based on SZKIT[4] is installed. This software needs an explanation text file that is composed of several text blocks. Each text blocks should be separated by a brank line and of course it is prepared previously. The software displays one text block and it allows the teacher to change the text by the foot pedals. Stepping on the right pedal forwards the text block, and stepping on the left pedal backwards it. Addition to it, the center pedal has the function of hiding the text. Because of this simple operation, teachers can synchronize the explanation texts and their operations. About the position of the text block on the table, it is controlled by the pen device of Anoto technology.

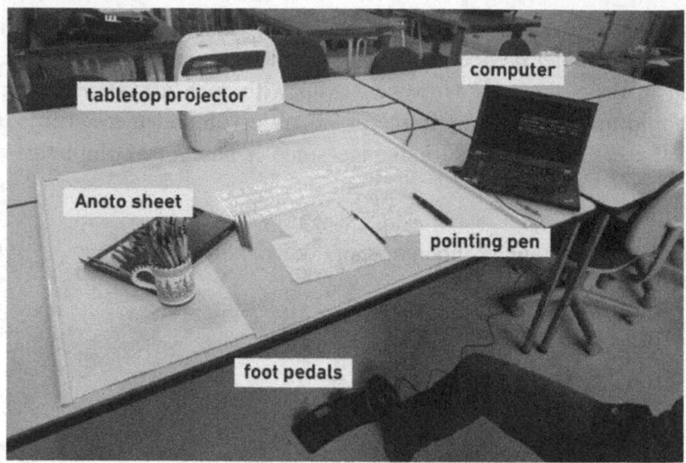

Fig. 2. An overview of the proposed system. It consists of a tabletop projector, a pointing pen with Anoto sheet on the table, a foot pedals and a computer.

3 Evaluation of SZTAP in Manga Lesson

We conducted pretesting of SZTAP in mock lesson and it was clear that SZTAP works properly. After the pretesting, we tried to use it in the practical lesson of Manga drawing. We invited a professional Manga artist as a visiting teacher and ten hearing impaired students took part in the special lesson. The teacher had no experience to teach something to hearing impaired students. The duration of the lecture is about ninety minutes. Fig. 3 shows a scene of the lesson. In this lesson, we prepared web camera to capture the teacher's face and display it on the table because hearing impaired students commented they couldn't see the teacher's face in the pretesting session.

Fig. 3. Visiting teacher shows how to draw Manga to students with hearing impaired with SZTAP

After the lesson, these hearing impaired students were required to answer questionnaires of understanding levels and to make comments of advantages and disadvantages of SZTAP compare with conventional sign language translation and captioning service. They made various answers though, the tendency of the answers can be summarize as follows.

- Advantage of SZTAP: "It is easy to get information because we don't have to move our eyes," "We can concentrate on what is going on during the lesson," "We can understand technical terms exactly compare with sign language," "It has enough speed compare with captioning service and it has good synchronization. We can follow the teacher's operation."
- Disadvantage of SZTAP: "The teacher cannot change text information during the lesson," "Even if the teacher hit on an extra idea during the lesson, she cannot add it."

In general, as shown in that half of those students commented there was not significant disadvantage on SZTAP, they seemed to accept it as effective support system. Addition to it, the Manga artist commented that she had been able to operate the system without any trouble and to draw same as usual.

4 Summary

To support to teach practical skills to hearing impaired students in department of design, tabletop projection system was proposed and evaluated. The evaluation with ten hearing impaired students showed that the system was useful for practical lesson and it was cleared that teacher could operate the system properly even if she was beginner.

Acknowledgement. This research was supported by JSPS KAKENHI Grant Number 25350280.

References

1. Damm, C., Ondra, S.: Polygraf-Universal Access to Presentations. CSUN2013 (2013)
2. Miyoshi, S., Kuroki, H., Kawano, S., Shirasawa, M., Ishihara, Y., Kobayashi, M.: Support Technique for Real-Time Captionist to Use Speech Recognition Software. In: Miesenberger, K., Klaus, J., Zagler, W.L., Karshmer, A.I. (eds.) ICCHP 2008. LNCS, vol. 5105, pp. 647–650. Springer, Heidelberg (2008)
3. Takahashi, T., Namatame, M., Kusunoki, F., et al.: A Laser Show Device Works in An Open Space for Hearing-Impaired Students. In: Second Asia International Conference on Modelling & Simulation (AMS 2008), pp. 385–389 (2008)
4. Kobayashi, M., Suzuki, T., Wakatsuki, D.: Teaching Support Software for Hearing Impaired Students Who Study Computer Operation. In: Miesenberger, K., Karshmer, A., Penaz, P., Zagler, W. (eds.) ICCHP 2012, Part I. LNCS, vol. 7382, pp. 10–17. Springer, Heidelberg (2012)

Differentiation, Individualization and Influencing Factors in ICT Assisted Learning for People with Special Needs

Introduction to the Special Thematic Session

Andreja Istenic Starcic[1,2,3]

[1] University of Primorska, Faculty of Education, Koper, Slovenia
[2] University of Ljubljana, Faculty of Civil and Geodetic Engineering, Ljubljana
[3] Macquarie University, Learning and Teaching Center, Sydney, Australia
andreja.starcic@siol.net

Abstract. The differentiated and individualized instruction in ICT assisted learning environments enhances accessibility and promotes the equal participation of individual learners with a variety of needs, preferences and accessibility requirements. ICT has the potential to provide assistance, compensation and to enable potential, but if the interventions are not adequately designed they can present additional obstacles. Influencing factors in learning in general and in ICT assisted learning are considered to accommodate diverse learners in multicultural environments. Directions and potential topics of research and development in this field are: factors which influence ICT assisted teaching and learning of people with special needs; providing differentiation and individualization of learning resources, instructional methods and modes of delivery, teaching and learning approaches and strategies; design, implementation and evaluation of ICT assisted learning environments accommodating diverse learners; the competence of teachers and learners; the competence of organizations for providing ICT for diverse audiences.

Keywords: Differentiated Instruction, Individualized Instruction, ICT Assisted Learning, People with Special Needs.

1 Introduction

The equitable accessibility of lifelong education and lifelong learning for people with special needs in mainstream settings is examined. ICT has the potential to provide assistance, compensation and to enable potential, but if the interventions are not adequately designed they can present additional obstacles. The research and development has to focus on the potential of differentiation and individualization in ICT assisted learning environments to enhance accessibility and promote the equal participation of individual learners with a variety of needs, preferences and accessibility requirements. Differentiated instruction is based on grouping of learners, while individualization tailors instruction for the individual needs of each learner. It includes learning resources, instructional methods and modes of delivery. The factors which influence

K. Miesenberger et al. (Eds.): ICCHP 2014, Part II, LNCS 8548, pp. 516–519, 2014.

ICT assisted learning of people with special needs need to be considered from different perspectives to explore teaching and learning as personal processes, environmental processes and behavioral processes. Influential models, such as the Technology Acceptance Model (TAM), have been widely applied to mainstream populations (and widely published in literature) but insufficiently examined with regard to the learning of people with special needs.

The study of various learning environments, technological solutions and tools, ICT assisted teaching and learning practices within pre-school, primary, secondary, tertiary level, lifelong learning including career development, and work-place learning of people with special needs - with regard to facilitating learners with various attributes.

When diverse groups that include both students with special needs and students who do not have special needs, then the following need to be taken into consideration:

- Factors which influence ICT assisted teaching and learning of people with special needs both in specialized and in mainstream education and learning;
- Providing differentiation and individualization of learning resources, instructional methods and modes of delivery, teaching and learning approaches and strategies;
- Design, implementation and evaluation of ICT assisted learning environments and/or technological solutions, applications and tools accommodating diverse learners to support differentiated and individualized instruction;
- The competence of teachers and learners for ICT assisted learning and teaching for diverse learners; the competence of organizations for providing ICT for diverse audiences.

2 Factors Influencing Teaching and Learning Supported by Information Communication Technology

Efforts at different levels of education to accommodate students with disabilities have traditionally been made after a student's disability or access need has been identified which caused a segregation of students from and within mainstream learning environments. Studies of computer and internet usage and engagement have traditionally took place separately for mainstream population and/or with regards to particular disability groups. The research studies have to adopt universal design and examine engagement of diverse user groups [1]. The directions could be the following:

- Studies of learning environments and learning environments universally designed supporting differentiated and individualized instruction
- The deployment of ICT assisted learning solutions for special needs among mainstream population
- Evaluation and quality assurance in ICT assisted learning for diverse learners groups
- Focusing on end-user participation in research, design, development and evaluation process (for example: research based design, real-life usability testing, contribution analysis, experimental design, theory driven evaluation)

3 Differentiated and Individualized Instruction

In inclusive learning environments all students can participate in all learning activities and their individual needs, capabilities, learning styles and approaches are addressed. Within internal differentiated instruction in a classroom, small group learning is introduced. Organizational mode of group learning facilitates heterogeneous groups of students heading towards learning objectives. Group learning supports individual's learning outcomes as also group outcomes. Socio-cultural theories of learning and instruction highlight the social and cultural context in cognition and learning. Cognition and knowledge are shared and distributed. Collaborative learning provides a natural learning environment where knowledge is shared, distributed, and co-constructed [2]. Learners interact, share, exchange and co-construct the knowledge. Knowledge is socially negotiated [3]. The outcomes of the individual and the group are interrelated. Computer supported collaborative learning is an influential pedagogical strategy facilitating differentiated instruction on the level of learning contents, learning methods and approaches, assessment and learning outcomes. Students with special needs tend to use computer and internet even more than their students without special needs. It reduces their isolation and facilitates sociability.

Individualized instruction doesn't refer to individualized learning where individual learner has tailored learning environment for independent learning. Individualized instruction takes place in the classroom or any forms of formal, informal or non-formal learning. It takes into account individual differences as for example capabilities, motivation, interests, achievements, learning styles or approaches. Teaching approaches and teaching environment provides personalized and individualized learning experiences for all learners.

4 Design, Implementation and Evaluation of ICT Assisted Learning Environments

Research of ICT assisted learning and/ or technological solutions, applications and tools accommodating diverse learners including people with special needs and people who do not have special needs has not received sufficient attention. Solutions designed for particular disability groups could be beneficial for all improving effectiveness and quality of user experiences. The role of ICT to facilitate accessibility for students with special needs to normal curriculum, to participation in classroom activities gradually transforms from assistive and compensatory function to participatory and creative function [1]. The project ENABLE Network of ICT Supported Learning for Disabled People 2011-2014, funded with support from the Lifelong Learning Program of the European Commission, is gathering data and good practices of ICT assisted learning environments, applications and tools, providing the portal for end-users (people with special needs, teachers, parents, organizations) [4].

5 The Competence of Teachers and Learners for ICT Assisted Learning

Participation in network society and autonomous usage of digital environments involve skills, attitudes, capabilities, competences, and literacies for social, cultural and professional engagement. It consists of creativity, problem solving, and multimodal design. The gap in participation is caused by lack of competences [5].Teachers consequently inform learners and develop their literacies needed for social engagement. Teacher education curriculum includes ICT and educational technology but until recently hasn't involved notions of ICT supporting people with special needs. The expansion of ICT solutions, applications and tools provides potentials for diverse learners including learners with special needs. The ICT usability and web accessibility [6] in teaching and learning for diverse learners has to be integrated in teacher's higher education curriculum and continuous professional development.

6 Conclusion

Contributions within the highlighted topics could inform design, implementation, evaluation and quality assurance of ICT assisted learning environments for diverse learners. This could introduce a powerful way for institutions and end-uses in organizations and the delivery of education and training to implement new approaches in ICT supported learning.

References

1. Istenic Starcic, A., Bagon, S.: ICT supported learning for people with special needs: Review of seven educational technology journals 1970-2011. British Journal of Educational Technology 45(2), 202–230 (2014)
2. Resnick, L.B.: Shared Cognition: Thinking as Social Practice. In: Resnick, L.B., Levine, J.M., Teasley, S.D. (eds.) Perspectives on Socially Shared Cognition. American Psychological Association, Washington (1996)
3. Vygotsky, L.S.: Mind and society. Harward University Press, Cambridge (1978)
4. The project ENABLE Network of ICT Supported Learning for Disabled People, http://i-enable.eu/ (retrieved April 2, 2014)
5. Jenkins, H., Purushotoma, R., Clinton, K., Weigel, M., Robison, A.J.: Confronting the challenges of participatory culture: Media education for the 21st century. The MacArthur Foundation, Chicago (2009) (Jenkins, H. (ed.)
6. Miesenberger, K., Hengstberger, B., Batusic, M.: Web_Access: Education on Accessible Web Design. In: Miesenberger, K., Klaus, J., Zagler, W., Karshmer, A. (eds.) ICCHP 2010, Part 1. LNCS, vol. 6179, pp. 404–407. Springer, Heidelberg (2010)

Learning Environments – Not Just Smart for Some!

Andreja Istenic Starcic[1,2,3] and Sharon Kerr[3]

[1] University of Primorska, Faculty of Education, Koper, Slovenia
andreja.starcic@siol.net
[2] University of Ljubljana, Faculty of Civil and Geodetic Engineering, Ljubljana, Slovenia
[3] Macquarie University, MQAS-Learning and Teaching Center, Sydney, Australia
sharon.kerr@mq.edu.au

Abstract. This paper is discussing Universal Curriculum Design in Higher Education for curriculum delivered on and using the facilities of Smart Devices. The case study in Australia (2012-2013) was focused on universal design and pedagogical approach involving a literature review and an analysis of the university context with a placement orientation module design in the spirit of inclusive practice for delivery via smart devices. Through legislative requirements the majority of Smart Devices are developed with inbuilt accessibility features. Developing curriculum using Universal Design Principals ensures that students and faculty have the opportunity to maximize the capability and facilities of their Smart Devices. Contemporary working and learning environments depend on ICT integration. Smart environments such as smart phones are facilitating ubiquitous engagement. University education has to prepare graduates to take proactive roles in engaging with ICT providing them with learning environments that both model and demonstrate best practice.

Keywords: Universal Curriculum Design, Learning Environment, Disability, Higher Education, Smart Devices, Sensory Independent Learning.

1 Introduction

In recent discussions about facilitating students' capabilities and competences more attention is given to work integrated learning and work placement. Work integrated learning provides an overview of current professional development, real life settings where knowledge and competencies can be applied and developed. Professional identity development starts during college and university education and is supported by placements where organizational cultures are met. Career aspirations and planning processes depend on a student's capabilities for reflection and self-direction. Universities and colleges need to prepare students to be ready to meet the challenges associated with searching for and negotiating their employment. Globally government policies are focusing on facilitating employability for all citizens [1], [19]. In response to these Government's actions there is a need created for competences for contemporary technology driven work environments, universities to recognize this in academic learning environments and organizations providing placements to have a legal and ethical commitment to creating diverse and inclusive work integrated learning.

K. Miesenberger et al. (Eds.): ICCHP 2014, Part II, LNCS 8548, pp. 520–527, 2014.

Contemporary working and learning environments depend on ICT integration. Smart environments such as smart phones are facilitating ubiquitous working and learning. University education has to prepare graduates to take a proactive role in engaging with ICT by providing them with this type of learning environments. Universities need to support all students in developing capabilities and competences for engaging in ICT supported learning and working in a manner that accommodates diversity. For students with disabilities the way in which an ICT learning experience is designed can determine whether or not they have access, can fully participate and be engaged.

In 2012 the case study was launched supporting the design and implementation of an orientation module Pace Yourself, for students about to undertake placement and community participation activities. The module was designed in the spirit of inclusive practice, to meet the requirements of ensuring universal design or barrier free design. An online placement orientation module is designed for delivery through smart devices.

2 Innovative Uses of Emerging Didactical and Pedagogical Approaches

Efforts at the postsecondary level to accommodate students with disabilities have traditionally been made after a student's disability or access need has been made known to faculty (e.g. participating in the lecture or tutorial, taking an examination, participating in collaborative activities, engaging in interaction in organized activities and those outside lecture rooms). This approach has had the non-intended consequence of segregation of students from mainstream learning environments and the provision of an often inferior learning experience.

Learning environments consist of physically defined and virtually defined spaces providing learning for individuals and groups. Universal curriculum design fosters inclusion of students with disabilities supporting individualization and differentiated instruction within existing learning environments. It aims at facilitating all students within the same environment responding to particular disability needs and abilities without any special accommodations. Here we focus on the initial design of learning environments to be suitable for all students and not the adaptation of individual students to an inaccessible environment. During the earlier stage of integration policies of people with special needs the approach was adaptation of individuals to the environments, while now inclusion policies have at their underpinning the adaptation of environment to the needs of people with special needs. Inclusive agenda in Australia supported by federal and states legislation [6,7,8] and the United Nations' Convention on the rights of persons with disabilities [27].

Differentiated curriculum in response to differentiated learning needs require universal instructional design, delivery and classroom management. In provision of solutions for differentiated curriculum that enable all students the opportunity to engage with their normal curriculum, curriculum authoring tools [2], learning management systems [14] and accessibility of ICT based resources to facilitate engagement within education and social participation have been investigated. Web based education [5], [20], [29] foster pedagogical and technological inclusion providing innovative use of didactical and pedagogical approaches. *"From the assistive, compensational and enabling function of ICT, the focus has moved towards equal engagement of students with disabilities and quality of teaching and learning methods providing differentiated instruction, competences for ICT use and creative expression"* [11]. The Universal design movement recognized the benefits for everyone in the building of a more functional environment. Universal instructional design facilitate a more flexible and adaptable approach to teaching and learning in higher education for all students. In order to achieve inclusion of people with disability, higher education needs to meet challenges associated with curriculum, learning environments, processes, and study outcomes all which need to be transparent and open for employers and the community. Work integrated learning and placements provide this transparency of the curriculum and outcomes in terms of capabilities and competencies which are on display. Student with disability meeting learning objectives, engaging in learning activities and assessment, using learning resources, taking part in collaboration and networking, interacting with fellow students and teachers, engaging in work integrate learning and community participation are all major components of equal participation in the mainstream curriculum.

3 Method

A case study has been undertaken starting in 2012 to 2013 to support universal curriculum design and its implementation. The orientation module *Pace Yourself* was design involving (1) The review of related research articles to identify learning and teaching aiming for inclusion of students with disabilities applying universal design. (2) Document analysis of Macquarie University policy documents, learning environments and resources with special focus on *PACE – participation and community engagement of the course FOBE 201- Working with an employing people with disabilities* and official reports on students' engagement is conducted.

The review and document analysis has followed the research question: How is universal design examined and applied in higher education? The review of related research articles was conducted in Web of Science (WOS) database and a manual search of the seven educational technology journals (BJET, CE, JCAL, ETR&D, ETS, AJET, TOJET). A manual search of all volumes from 1970 to 2013 was undertaken. Searches were conducted from November 2012 to February 2013 and updated in December 2013. In the inclusion and exclusion process for related studies the condition of inclusion applied was *universal design in ICT supported learning in higher education* as a topic of the article. The qualitative data analysis applied design of coding categories based on analysis data process searching for topics and patterns. Identified five topics are presented in the finings section. The case study is strongly informed by researcher's perspectives with their experience in conducting and evaluating courses applying universal design.

4 Results – The Orientation Module Pace Yourself

To support universal curriculum design a review of the literature with identified topics was utilized. Little research has been undertaken to investigate ICT in learning of disabled students in higher education [11], [24]. Reviewed articles focus on: (1) universal design principles discussed within different topics of teaching and learning in higher education and (2) universal instructional design discussed at the system level to supporting inclusion of students with disabilities (3) the universal curriculum design in higher education (4) the professional development and teacher's competences for universal instructional design and (5) the universal design principles for web based environments and ICT.

The nine UD principles for instruction are: equity, flexibility, intuitive use, perceptible information, tolerance for error, low physical effort, size and space for, community promoting communication and collaboration, inclusive instructional climate [23]. UD instructional design is discussed at the system level considering developmental and implementation strategies following the legislation providing multicultural and social justice in education [24]. Universal design curriculum provision is in multiple means of representation, multiple means of expression and multiple means of engagement [3]. Universally designed teaching and learning considering particular disability needs such as visual aids, accessible class notes, assessment formats, and multimodal representations may be considered as effective instructional practices for all students [23]. University teachers' awareness and professional development is discussed [9], [15] highlighting also professional learning of mentors at work placements [26].

Digital inclusion in higher education was articulated around accessibility predominantly on technical accessibility and only in recent years pedagogical and institutional factors in addition to the technical have been investigated [4] in order to provide best or "smart" use of technology [25]. Web based environments and ICT are considered from different perspectives of operability, standards and delivery [5].

At Macquarie University the inclusion of students with disabilities is a central priority as evidenced by the launching the Disability Action Plan (DAP) 2012-2017 [17]. The University currently delivers many hundreds of courses to its 30,000 students using an online facility iLearn which utilizes the Moodle learning management system, chosen for its accessibility. As part of the commitment to implementing the DAP, guidelines have been developed to assist staff in material design for their iLearn units. This DAP highlights a focus on the placement and community participation program to accommodate students with disability according to their needs [6]. Participation and community engagement at Macquarie University has a strong international dimension placing students in companies and community organizations across the globe. The course "FOBE 201 – Working with and employing people with disabilities" was first offered in 2012. Guidelines for inclusive learning design [13] are based on online auditing tools developed by MQAS in 2010 MQAS Orange [18] and MQAS Green [17] tool.

Macquarie University Accessibility Services, based on the experience gained from running the course FOBE201 through 2 semesters in 2012, identified that there was a necessity to develop an orientation unit that would assist students with disability prior to commencement of placement. A variety of factors has been reported through internal documentation from the two course leaders and an assistant in supporting disabled students when engaging placement. The university PACE hub has also reported the need to identify appropriate placements for students with disabilities and prepare them for their placements. In reporting documents the need for all students to be familiarized with the workplace and ensure that they have adequately prepared themselves for their placement and reflected honestly on their own cognitive, emotions, social, physical and/ or sensory strengths and limitations was noted. Further students who rely on assistive technologies for communication or may need accommodations for access in the workplace feel confident to disclose this with both the university and work placement to ensure that satisfactory arrangements can be made prior to the commencement of the placement.

As already highlighted earlier in this paper, through replying to the need of students with disability, better solutions can be provided for all students. Applying universal design in facilitating a stimulating learning environment is beneficial for all students, including those with disability when preparing them personally and professionally for their field placement. The *Pace yourself* module curriculum design is aiming for all students to be engaged in all contexts connecting academic, organizational and home environments. Generations of students are engaged in ubiquitous interactions with their peers, gaming and other free time activities. As unit designers we need to capitalize on their attitudes and habits in ICT usage in building productive online learning environments. Curriculum has to provide the bridges between formal and informal learning, and personal and academic life to enable professional engagement. The *Pace yourself* module is designed to be applied through various web tools which students use on a daily basis for their free time activities. In order to connect to students' habits and interests, this orientation unit was designed to be delivered to all students on their smart devices.

The curriculum facilitates knowledge sharing, focusing on personal needs supported by reflection activities. Module content is designed in HTML5 to allow access from various mobile devices. Web 2.0 tools are used to provide authentic and flexible learning spaces which students can use in their free time. Students are encouraged to use podcasts or video recording in their reflection tasks through the module and also to design a podcast resume for employers. Collaboration among students while taking placement at different locations is facilitated through social media networks.

5 Discussion

The top down and bottom up approaches leads to systemic change and support for professional development and collaboration with experts for teachers and supporting service providers at universities. The multiple dimensions are explored as our institutions shift from exclusive to inclusive environments: scholarly teaching and learning with research based improvements for inclusion; faculty research on a daily basis as for example adopting an action research cycle to their practice; professional development of teaching staff, quality assurance with institutional evaluation based on participation of all stakeholders, risk management and strategy adapted for inclusion, building inclusive organizational culture and promoting participatory planning and evaluation. Awareness of inclusive environments need to be promoted among all students preparing them for proactive engagement in smart and inclusive work environments.

Teaching has to be aligned at all times to all students and to consider students with special needs only when they present for support for their particular requirements for assignments or assessment is missing the opportunity for a more flexible study environment for all students.

Universal curriculum design supports students learning providing multiple modes and methods of representations in concept development an understanding as also multiple modes and methods of engagement. Accessible web based environments and ICT and resources are considered among facilitators of inclusion. Together with the universal design in ICT are also related approaches which have to be considered. The capability approach looks at designing technology in such a manner that all users are provided with the opportunity to engage with the ICT device or application. This may mean however that users access these devices in different manners according to their personal preferences and capabilities. If we design using the capability approach, as faculty we are recognizing "well-being freedom" and "agency freedom" as the capability sensitive design is embodying the value of justice. Design constituencies include moral considerations concerning autonomy, privacy, sustainability, and accountability, responsibility need to be at the core of all we do and teach. Diversity in terms of social and environmental diversity bridges the articulation of resources into capability and functioning [22]. To achieve this Johnstone identifies: particular groups or individuals, particular capabilities, particular situations or context, and particular interventions (technologies, artifacts) [12].

6 Conclusion

Summarizing again the title of this article: "Learning environments - not just smart for some", is highlighting the opportunity for us to develop a better experience for all. When designers face the challenge of developing ICT platforms and applications in such a manner that solutions for end users with disabilities are inbuilt, the result is innovations which provide better user experiences for all. An important added value of universally designed solutions is in higher specter of all individuals' needs and consequently higher level of usability for all. Universal design more than just bringing solutions for those with disability. It is a holistic approach that brings flexibility and smart solutions to smart environments. It is not about adaptation of environment for particular disability requirements, but it is developing better solutions for all through thinking about particular special needs requirements. Investment in research and development for special needs facilitate knowledge and has transferability of solutions for society in general.

Acknowledgments. We would like to acknowledge the work of students in FOBE201 and Sharon Kerr and Michaela Baker as authors of the FOBE201 course. This research and the design of the orientation module Pace Yourself was conducted during the period of visit by Andreja Istenic Starcic as a Visiting fellow to Macquarie University Learning and Teaching Centre. This research is a part of the project ENABLE Network of ICT Supported Learning for Disabled People 2011-2014. The ENABLE project is funded with support from the Lifelong Learning Programme of the European Commission.

References

1. Australian Government. Department of Families, Housing, Community Services and Indigenous Affairs. Disability & Careers, http://www.fahcsia.gov.au/our-responsibilities/disability-and-carers/publications-articles/for-employers
2. Bain, A., Parkes, J.R.: Curriculum authoring tools and inclusive classroom teaching practice: a longitudinal study. British Journal of Educational Technology 37(2), 177–189 (2006)
3. Center for Applied Special Technology. Universal design for learning, http://www.cast.org/udl
4. Draffan, E.A., Rainger, P.: A model for the identification of challenges to blended learning. ALT-J 14(1), 55–67 (2006)
5. Di Iorio, A., Feliziani, A.A., Mirri, S., Salomoni, P., Vitali, F.: Automatically Producing Accessible Learning Objects. Educational Technology & Society 9(4), 3–16 (2006)
6. Disability Discrimination Act. Act No. 135 (1992), http://www.comlaw.gov.au/Series/C2004A04426
7. Disability Standards for Education 2005 Section 6.2, http://www.comlaw.gov.au/Details/F2005L00767
8. Fair Work Act. Act No. 28 (2009), http://www.comlaw.gov.au/Details/C2011C00580
9. Fichten, C.S., Asuncion, J.V., Barile, M., Généreux, C., Fossey, M., Judd, D., Robillard, C., De Simone, C., Wells, D.: Technology Integration for Students with Disabilities: Empirically Based Recommendations for Faculty. Educational Research and Evaluation 7(2-3), 185–221 (2001)
10. Hellman, R.: Universal Design and Mobile Devices. In: Stephanidis, C. (ed.) Universal Acess in HCI, Part I, HCII 2007. LNCS, vol. 4554, pp. 147–156. Springer, Heidelberg (2007)
11. Istenic Starcic, A., Bagon, S.: ICT supported learning for people with special needs: Review of seven educational technology journals 1970-2011. British Journal of Educational Technology 45(2), 202–230 (2014)
12. Johnstone, J.: Technology as Empowerment: A Capability Approach to Computer Ethics. Ethics and Information Technology 9(1), 73–87 (2007)
13. Kerr, S., Baker, M.: Six practical principles for inclusive curriculum design. In: Tynan, B., Willems, J., James, R. (eds.) Outlooks and Opportunities in Blended and Distance Learning. Advances in mobile and distance learning (AMDL) book series, pp. 74–88. IGI Global: Information Science Reference, Hershey
14. Luke, R.: AccessAbility: Enabling Technology for Life Long Learning Inclusion in an Electronic Classroom – 2000. Educational Technology & Society 5(1), 148–153 (2002)
15. Lombardi, A.R., Murray, C.: Measuring university faculty attitudes toward disability: Willingness to accommodate and adopt Universal Design principles. Journal of Vocational Rehabilitation 34, 43–56 (2011)
16. Macquarie University Disability Action Plan 2012-2017, http://www.humanrights.gov.au/disability_rights/action_plans/Register/MQU_Action_Plan_2012_ACCESSIBLE%29.pdf
17. MQAS. Green tool, http://www.mq.edu.au/ltc/mqas/green.htm
18. MQAS. Orange tool, http://www.mq.edu.au/ltc/mqas/orange.htm

19. National People with Disabilities and Career Council (2009) Shut out: The Experiences of People with Disabilities and their Families in Australia. National Disability Strategy Consultation Report, http://www.fahcsia.gov.au/sites/default/files/documents/05_2012/nds_report.pdf
20. Nevile, L., Treviranus, J.: Interoperability for Individual Learner Centred Accessibilty for Web-based Educational Systems. Educational Technology & Society 9(4), 215–227 (2006)
21. NSW Anti-Discrimination Act 1977 No. 48 (2012), http://www.legislation.nsw.gov.au/maintop/view/inforce/act+48+1977+cd+0+N
22. Oosterlaken, I.: Design for Development: A Capability Approach. Design Issues 25(4), 91–102 (2009)
23. Pliner, M.S., Johnson, J.R.: Historical, Theoretical, and Foundational Principles of Universal Instructional Design in Higher Education. Equity & Excellence in Education 37, 105–113 (2004)
24. Scott, S.S., McGuire, J.M., Shaw, S.F.: Principles of Universal Design for Instruction. University of Connecticut, Center on Postsecondary Education and Disability, Storrs, CT (2001)
25. Seale, J., Draffan, E.A., Wald, M.: Digital agility and digital decision-making: conceptuaising digital inclusion in the context of disabled learners in higher education. Studies in Higher Education 35(4), 445–461 (2010)
26. Tee, S., Cowen, M.: Supporting students with disabilities - Promoting understanding amongst mentors in practice. Nurse Education in Practice 12, 6–10 (2012)
27. The United Nations' Convention on the rights of persons with disabilities (2008), http://www.un.org/disabilities/convention/conventionfull.shtml

Different ICT Competency but Similar Pattern between Students with/without Learning Disabilities?

Results from Structural Equation Modeling Testing

Ming-Chung Chen[1], Chen-Ming Chen[1], Ya-Ping Wu[1], Chien-Chuan Ko[2], and Yao-Ming Yeh[3]

[1] Department of Special Education, National Chiayi University, Chiayi, Taiwan
tomson2@ms18.hinet.net,
{mtchen,ping78kimo}@mail.ncyu.edu.tw
[2] Department of Computer Science and Information Engineering, National Chiayi University, Chiayi, Taiwan
kocc@mail.ncyu.edu.tw
[3] Department of Computer Science and Information Engineering, National Taiwan Normal University, Taiwan
ymyeh@ice.ntnu.edu.tw

Abstract. This paper explored if the ICT skills is different between students with/without learning disabilities across the grades. Meanwhile the current paper also explored if the structural equation modeling (SEM) is different between the students with/without learning abilities. 547 students with LD and 2298 students without LD from grade 3 to grade 9 participated in this survey. The results indicated that although the ICT skill is different between the students with/without LD, the structure of model is similar between the two groups.

Keywords: ICT skills, Structural Equation Modeling, Students with Learning Disabilities.

1 Introduction

Regardless of the purposes of use, the information and communication technology (ICT) has become ubiquitous. The skills needed to use ICT are becoming one of the most important life skills. However not all students have equal opportunities to access information technology. Unequal access to ICT for some students has created a digital divide. The issue of the digital divide has been explored since the 1990s in relation to several factors including: demography, gender, social economic status (SES), disabilities, and age [1,2,3,4,5].

Although many factors have been explored, no study explored if the factors related to digital divide is different between students with/without disabilities? Students with specific learning disabilities (LD) are the major population of the students with disabilities in the school. They are regarded to be familiar with the ICT skills required by the National curriculum. However, they might meet difficulties when participating in e-learning activities [6]. But do they gain required ICT skills? What factors relate to

K. Miesenberger et al. (Eds.): ICCHP 2014, Part II, LNCS 8548, pp. 528–531, 2014.

their ICT skills? Do the relationship among the related factors and ICT skills differ between the students with/ without learning disabilities? Therefore, there are two concrete questions for this study: 1). Is the ICT skill different between students with/without learning disabilities across the grades? 2). Is the structural equation modeling (SEM) different between the students with/without learning abilities?

2 Methodology

547 students with LD and 2298 students without LD from grade 3 to grade 9 participated in this study. The self-report questionnaire was use to investigate the participants' ICT skills.

2.1 Instrument

A questionnaire, Scale of Digital Participation of Elementary School Students, was designed to collect the data. The questionnaire consists of two major subscales: ICT skills and ICT attitude. The subscale of ICT skills consisted of 3 computer skills, which were basic computer operation skill (10 items), Microsoft office use skill (27 items), and Internet usage skill (10 items). It is a yes/no question. If the student can perform this task, then he/she can earn one point for this item. The average point was used to represent ICT competencies for each category. Higher points indicated better competency. The subscale of attitude incudes two concepts, they are motivation (4 items,), and perceived confidence of using ICT (2 items).

Content validity of the questionnaire was established by a panel of experts from the fields of special education and computer education. The internal consistency of each type of ICT skill, represented by Cronach's α, were reliable (Basic = .80, Office=.95, Internet= .89, motivation=.42; perceived confidence=.39) which were established by recruiting 178 typical developing children from grades 3 to 8 in Taiwan.

2.2 Data Analysis

Winsteps 3.66, kind of item response theory (IRT) software was used to calculating the ICT skills, then t-test was conducted to exam if the ICT skills were different between students with/without LD across grades. On the other hand, Structural Equation Modeling (SEM) is considered an appropriate statistics procedure as it enables exam predictive effects of demographic information and ICT attitude on ICT skills.

3 Results

3.1 ICT Skills

This study adopted average scores, calculated by Winsteps 3.66, of Office, Basic, and Web to represent the participants' ICT skills. As results of t-test on the table one indicated, the ICT skills are significantly different between the students with/ without LD in all grades except grade 3.

Table 1. The ICT skills of students with/without LD

Grade	Group	N	Mean	SD	T	df	p
3	NLD	336	-0.310	0.999	2.027	23.632	.054
	LD	20	-0.653	0.716			
4	NLD	344	0.173	1.081	4.797***	57.396	.000
	LD	41	-0.511	0.833			
5	NLD	341	0.737	0.903	7.261***	379	.000
	LD	40	-0.373	1.007			
6	NLD	368	0.957	0.757	5.076***	36.926	.000
	LD	35	-0.038	1.137			
7	NLD	486	0.912	0.792	3.048**	24.254	.005
	LD	24	0.236	1.073			
8	NLD	386	0.966	0.739	2.476*	39.750	.018
	LD	37	0.543	1.014			
9	NLD	350	1.032	0.723	3.239**	45.052	.002
	LD	41	0.512	0.998			

3.2 SEM Testing

This study used location of living, gender, grade, and ICT attitude as the predictors for ICT skills. The fitness whole model was good (GFI=.981, AGFI=.957, SRMR=.0328, RMSEA=.068. Therefore, disability (with/without LD) was added as moderator to test if the structure of each model is similar.

Coefficients of paths were compared for each model after normalized. Critical ratio was used to exam if the coefficient of each path for the two groups is significantly different by z-test. The direct and indirect effects of ICT attitude, gender, grade, and location of living on ICT Skills for two groups are shown in Table 2. As the table 2 shown, the coefficient of path for the four predicts factors on the ICT skills are similar. Meanwhile the critical ratios of each path are smaller than 1.96, means that the factor of disability did not moderate the relationship of each path.

4 Discussion

The results of this study figure out that the ICT skill is different between the students with/without LD. However, the structure of model is similar between the two groups. The results indicated that relationship of the four essential predictors and ICT skill are same between the two groups. Furthermore, the ICT attitude and grade demonstrated the powerful prediction on ICT skill. It means that although the ICT skill of students with LD is worse than the students without LD, they still can possess the ICT skills if they can have better motivation and confidence of IC using. Providing the students with LD proper ICT learning program might improve their attitude of ICT using.

Table 2. The coefficient of paths and critical ratios for students with/without LD

Independent Variable		Outcome Variable	Coefficient of path		Critical ratios	Explanation of variance	
			NLD	LD		NLD	LD
attitude	→	computer skills	.66***	.61***	1.588	67%	65%
gender	→		.06***	.08	.565		
grade	→		.47***	.51***	1.487		
citylevel	→		-.09***	-.13*	-1.318		

* p<.05 ***p<.001

References

1. Lebens, M., Graff, M., Mayer, P.: Access, attitudes and the digital divide: children's attitudes towards computers in a technology-rich environment. Educational Media International 46(3), 255–266 (2009)
2. Martin, S.P.: Is the digital divide really closing? A critique of inequality measurement in a nation online. IT & Society 1(4), 1–13 (2003)
3. Mckenzie, K.: Digital divide: The implications for social inclusion. Learning Disability Practice 10(6), 16–21 (2007)
4. Vicente, M.R., López, A.J.: A multidimensional analysis of the disability digital divide: Some evidence for internet use. Information Society: An International Journal 26(1), 48–64 (2010)
5. Yael, E., Zeev, S.: Age, gender, ethnicity and the digital divide: University students' use of web-based instruction. Open Learning 21(2), 99–110 (2006)
6. Fichten, C.S., Ferraro, V., Asuncion, J.V., Chwojka, C., Barile, M., Nguyen, M.N., Klomp, R., Wolforth, J.: Disabilities and e-Learning Problems and Solutions: An Exploratory Study. Educational Technology & Society 12(4), 241–256 (2009)

The Application of Computer-Based Chinese Handwriting Assessment System to Children with Dysgraphia

Ting-Fang Wu[1], Guey-Shya Chen[2], and Hui-Shan Lo[3]

[1] Graduate Institute of Rehabilitation Counseling,
National Taiwan Normal University, Taipei, Taiwan
tfwu@ntnu.edu.tw

[2] National TaiChung University of Education, Taichung, Taiwan
grace@mail.ntcu.edu.tw

[3] Department of Special Education, National Taiwan Normal University, Taipei, Taiwan
80209003e@ntnu.edu.tw

Abstract. The purpose of this study is to develop a computer–based Chinese handwriting assessing system. This on-line evaluation system consist two kinds of input modules, one is copying Chinese characters and the other is memory writing. This system can provide immediate information about students' handwriting process and products. The parameters of process record the spatial and temporal characteristics of handwriting, which including the total time of writing, on paper time, in air time, the ratio of in-air time/ on-paper time, and the speed. The parameter of production is accuracy of handwriting. 25 children aged between 8 and 10 years with dysgraphia and 50 typically developing children of similar age participated in this study. The results indicated that children with dysgraphia had significantly lower accuracy rate in both copy and memory writing tasks. Children with dysgraphia also demonstrated grater the ratio of in-air time/ on-paper time in both copy and memory writing complex characters. The system proposed in this study is able to record the real time handwriting performance of pupil with and without writing difficulties. The kinematic and kinetic indicators provide more information about how children control their motion when writing. Further studies can include more writing forms, such as copying, writing in memory, dictation, and free writing in the assessment system to comprehensively understand the writing problems of the children with dysgraphia.

Keywords: Children with Dysgraphia, Handwriting, Computer-Based Assessment.

1 Introduction

Handwriting is an essential means of communication, which enables the expression, recording, and transmission of ideas of students throughout their educational career [1,2,3]. Handwriting difficulty or dysgraphia was defined as a disturbance or difficulty

K. Miesenberger et al. (Eds.): ICCHP 2014, Part II, LNCS 8548, pp. 532–539, 2014.

in the production of writ-ten language that is related to the mechanics of writing [1]. Children with dysgraphia usually spend more effort to write legibly compared to their peers. Difficulty in the mastery of the mechanical aspects of handwriting may interfere with the higher order writing, such as composition of text [4]. It may due to when handwriting is not automatically, the act of handwriting needs increased demands on memory and attention resources, therefore, constrain the performance of composition which required high cognitive process [4].

Researchers have suggested that handwriting difficulties may have serious consequences for the student's academic progress, emotional well-being and social functions [5]. The difficulty of handwriting will not be remediated if untreated even when those children growing up [6]. Hence, in order to remediate the difficulties of handwriting as early as possible, the accurately identifying handwriting problems have been a challenge for primary educators. Traditionally, standardized handwriting scales have been used to evaluate hand writing performance [7]. The objective of these scales was to determine how best to define the 'quality', ' readability' or ' legibility' of the handwriting in writing samples [5]. Those evaluation scales mainly focus analysis of the final writing product. The substantive information about writing process of children with poor handwriting was lack due to the limitations of the assessment tools. However, the real time, dynamic characteristics about handwriting process will sever important basis to understand the underline problems of handwriting difficulties.

Many educational tools for Chinese characters writing have been developed [8, 9] [10], however, most of them did not provide sufficient information for diagnosing students' writing skills at the spatial and temporal characteristics. Researchers have suggested our pencil 'traveled' above the writing surface before we write character segments, letters and words successively [11]. If we spent more in-air time, it may imply that some underlying difficulties during the process of writing and that are manifested in the quality of their written products. [11]

A stand-alone computer-based assessment for Chinese handwriting was developed [12, 13]. This on-line evaluation system provides immediate information children's performance about stroke orders and global structures in writing Chinese characters. The system could accurately identify children's writing problems such as wrong stroke orders or incorrect strokes. Based on the previous system, the new version is developed to assess the spatial and temporal characteristics of children's Chinese handwriting.

2 Development of Evaluation System

The architecture of this computer-based evaluation system is shown in Figure 1. There are different kinds of digital equipment can be connected to this system through Internet. Instead of typing on a keyboard, the learner inputs the characters through a hand writing input device.

As Figure 1 depicts, this computer-based evaluation system is implemented with PHP and MySQL on an Apachie web server. Several major interfaces of system modules are described in the following subsections.

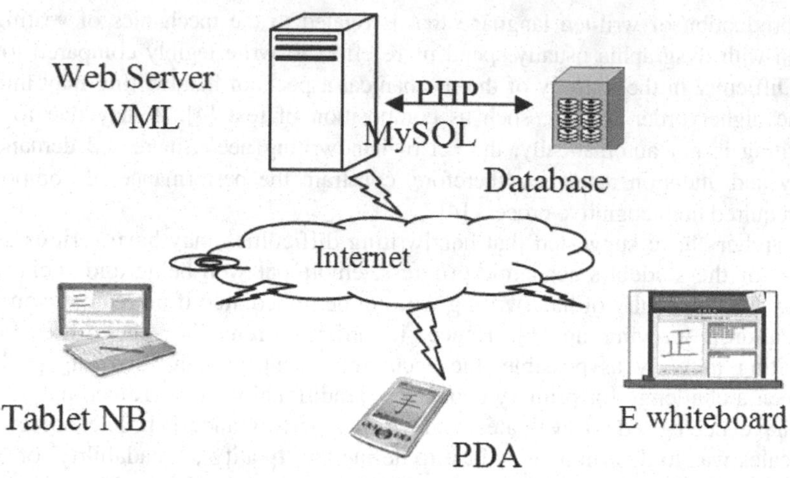

Fig. 1. Architecture of computer-based evaluation system

There are two kinds of input modules in the system, one is copying Chinese characters and the other is memory writing. When children copied the Chinese characters, the target character is displayed at the left-hand side of the screen (shown in Fig 2). Then children copied this Chinese character at the other side of the screen using light pen or mouse. When finished, press the blue button placed at the bottom.

Fig. 2. Input page for copying task

The other input module is memory writing task (shown in Fig 3). In this task, the child was asked to watch the Chinese character and memorize this character. When the child had memorized the target character, he/ or she clicked the red bottom, then the target character would disappeared. The child had to write the character without visual cue.

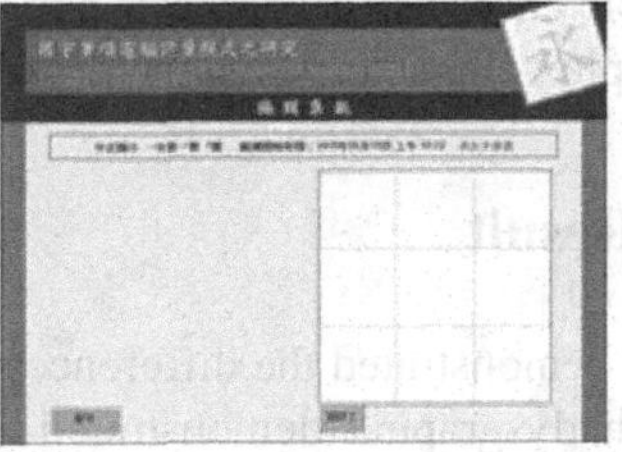

Fig. 3. Input page for memory writing task

3 Experiment Method

3.1 Participants

The study recruited 25 children aged between 8 and 10 years with dysgraphia (18 male, 7 female) and 50 typically developing children of similar age (25 male, 25 female). These children were recruited from public elementary schools from New Taipei City in Taiwan. The dysgraphia children were all identified as handwriting difficulty and received special education services at school. Children with documented neurological deficits, intellectual delay or physical impairments were excluded from this study.

3.2 Procedure

Each child was assessed individually in a quiet evaluation room. The child was instructed how to use this system and 5 minutes practice were allowed for the child to be familiar with the system. In addition, the requirements of copying and memory tasks also were instructed before the formal evaluation.

3.3 Measurement Parameters

In this study, we used six parameters to assess students' handwriting process and products. The parameters of process include the total time of writing, on paper time, in air time, the ratio of in-air time/ on-paper time, and the speed. The total time, in air time and on paper time, were recorded in millisecond (ms). The parameter of production is accuracy. The followings are the definitions of those parameters.

- Accuracy: number of correctly written characters/ number of simple characters (or complex characters)
- Total time: the length of time from the first stroke to end stroke
- On-paper time: the length of time when the pen touches tablet
- In-air time: the total writing minus on-paper time
- Ratio: in-air time/ on-paper time
- Speed: total word length of the character/ on-paper time

- Simple character: a character had less than ten strokes
- Complex character: a character had equal or more than ten strokes

4 Result

Table 1 demonstrated the differences between the two groups in copying tasks. Children with dysgraphia demonstrated significantly lower accuracy rate than typically developing children in both copying simple and complex characters. In copying simple characters, there were no significant differences between children with and without dysgraphia in all parameters except the speed. Children with dysgraphia copying faster than control group when copying simple characters.

In copying complex Chinese characters, there were no significant differences between children with and without dysgraphia in all parameters except accuracy and the ratio of in-air time/ on-paper time. Children with dysgraphia demonstrate greater the ratio of in-air time/ on-paper time than children without dysgraphia, which indicating that children with dysgraphia spent longer time between strokes in copying complex characters.

Table 1. Performance in copying task between Children with dysgraphia and control group

	Control group(N=50) (mean±S.D.)	dysgraphia (N=25) (mean ±S.D.)	*p*
Simple characters			
accuracy	0.9±0.11	0.8±0.18	0.009**
total time	16366.2±4460.9	15090.3±3707.3	0.22
on-paper time	6123.6±2346.9	5194.2±1692.1	0.08
in-air time	10242.7±2538.0	9896.1±2834.8	0.59
ratio	1.91±0.62	2.25±0.79	0.44
speed	0.13±0.03	0.14±0.03	0.03*
Complex characters			
accuracy	0.7±0.26	0.53±0.29	0.046*
total time	20050.3±5296.8	19336.2±35342	0.55
on-paper time	7151.7±2809.3	5975.2±1627.1	0.06
in-air time	12898.6±2900.1	13361.0±2887.6	0.52
ratio	1.88±0.54	2.35±0.75	0.003**
speed	0.12±0.03	0.13±0.03	0.117

*$p<.05$; ** $p<.01$

Table 2. demonstrated the differences between the two groups in memory writing tasks. In memory writing task, there was significant difference in accuracy between children with and without dysgraphia in both simple and complex Chinese characters. There were no significant differences found between children with and without dysgraphia in other parameters in memorizing simple Chinese characters.

Table 2. Performance in memory writing tasks between Children with dysgraphia and control group

	Control group(N=50) (mean±S.D.)	dysgraphia (N=25) (mean±S.D.)	*p*
Simple characters			
accuracy	0.8±0.11	0.7±0.18	<0.001**
total time	17700.4±4395.5	17856.1±5598.1	0.90
on-paper time	5419.0±2354.3	4455.0±1086.2	0.06
in-air time	12585.9±3524.1	13401.1±5074.5	0.42
ratio	2.76±1.19	3.31±1.20	0.62
speed	0.15±0.05	0.17±0.04	0.14
Complex characters			
accuracy	0.7±0.2	0.4±0.23	<0.001**
total time	22607.3±6059.7	24823.2±8184.9	0.2
on-paper time	6563.1±2522.5	5564.0±1277.3	0.07
in-air time	16135.0±4310.3	19259.2±7394.6	0.02*
ratio	2.84±1.15	3.72±1.25	0.004**
speed	0.14±0.05	0.15±0.05	0.05

*p<.05; ** p<.01

In memorizing complex Chinese characters, there were no significant differences between children with and without dysgraphia in total time, on-paper time and speed. However, children with dysgraphia demonstrate greater in-air time and the ratio of in-air time/ on-paper time than children without dysgraphia, which indicating that children with dysgraphia spent longer time between strokes in memorizing complex characters.

5 Discussion

In summary, children with dysgraphia preformed poorer accuracy in both copying and in memory tasks. The major difference between two groups was found in the ratio of in-air time/ on-paper time both copying and memory complex characters. Compared to previous research, that children with dyslexia wrote significantly less accurate than their peers was also shown in Lam's study [14]. The reason may due to that the children with dysgraphia had poor visual perceptual skills and processing skills which result in missing stroke, additional strokes or reversed writing [2,3] [14].

Previous research also indicated that children with handwriting difficulty had more total writing time and in air time in copy task [6], [14]. However, in our study, children with dysgraphia did not spend more in air-time or total time than their peers. The reason may result from the different ways to calculate in-air time and total time in these studies. In Lam's study, the children were asked to write 90 Chinese characters continuously and recorded the total time of writing whole 90 Chinese characters. The children with dyslexia performed longer in air time and total time than control group. In Lam's study, longer in air time and total time may due to that children with dysgraphia pause longer both between the stroke and the next stroke, as well as between the character and the next character [14]. In our study, we record total time, in air time, and on paper time in each character. We only calculate the total time, in air time, and on paper time between the stroke and the next stroke, but not between the character and the next character.

When comparing children's performance in copy tasks and memory tasks, both groups demonstrated lower accuracy rate, higher total time, higher in-air time and the ratio of in-air time/ on-paper time in memory tasks than in copy tasks, especially in memorizing complex characters. The results indicated that memory writing tasks seem to be harder than copy tasks. The memory task we used in this study had never been used in other studies. However, when students doing their homework and other academic works they need to use not only copy but also memory writing tasks.

The system proposed in this study is able to record the real time handwriting performance of pupil with and without writing difficulties. The kinematic and kinetic indicators provide more information about how children control their motion when writing. Further studies can include more writing forms, such as copying, writing in memory, dictation, and free writing should in the assessment system to comprehensively understand the writing problems of children with dysgraphia.

Acknowledgments. The authors would like to thank the National Science Council of the Republic of China for financially supporting this research under Contract No. NSC 98-2511-S-415-011-MY3.

References

1. Hamstra-Bletz, L., Blote, A.: A longitudinal study on dysgraphic hand-writing in primary school. Journal of Learning Disability 26, 689–699 (1993)
2. Tseng, M.H., Cermak, S.H.: The influence of ergonomic factors and perceptual-motor abilities on handwriting performance. American Journal of Occupational Therapy 47, 919–926 (1993)
3. Tseng, M.H., Chow, S.M.K.: Perceptual-motor function of school-age children with slow handwriting speed. American Journal of Occupational Therapy 54, 83–88 (2000)
4. Berninger, V., Graham, S.: Language by hand: A synthesis of decade of research on handwriting. Handwriting Review 12, 11–25 (1998)
5. Rosenblum, S., Weiss, P., Parush, S.: Handwriting evaluation for developmental dysgraphia: Process versus product. Reading and Writing: An Interdisciplinary Journal 17, 433–458 (2004)
6. Rosenblum, S., Weiss, P., Parush, S.: Product and process evaluation of handwriting difficulties. Educational Psychology Review 15, 41–81 (2003a)
7. Graham, S.: The reliability, validity, and utility of three handwriting measurement procedures. Journal of Educational Research 79, 373–380 (1986)
8. Takesue, N., Mochida, K., Kitadai, Nakagawa, A.M.: A handwriting-based Kanji learning system enabling teachers to designate evaluation points. ISPJ SIG Technical Report 15, 15–22 (2005)
9. Huang, P.R.: Front tool for internet Chinese teaching. In: The Fourth International Conference on Internet Chinese Education, Taipei, Taiwan, June 3-5 (2005)

10. Sun, K.T., Wang, C.I.: An intelligent tutoring system for teaching the stroke order of Chinese characters. In: The Sixth International Conference for Advancement of Computing in Education, Beijing, China (1998)
11. Rosenblum, S., Parush, S., Weiss, P.L.: The in air phenomenon: Temporal and spatial correlates of the handwriting process. Perceptual and Motor Skills 96, 933–954 (2003b)
12. Chen, G.-S., Jheng, Y.-D., Lin, L.-F.: Computer-based assessment for the stroke order of Chinese characters writing. In: The Second International Conference on Innovative Computing, Information and Control (ICICIC 2007), Kuma-moto, Japan, September 5-7 (2007)
13. Chen, G.-S., Jheng, Y.-D., Yao, H.C., Liu, H.-C.: Stroke order computer-based assessment with fuzzy measure scoring. WSEAS Trans. on Information and Applications 2(5), 62–68 (2008)
14. Lam, S.S.T., Au, R.K.C., Leung, H.W.H., Li-Tsang, C.W.P.: Chinese handwriting performance of primary school children with dyslexia. Research in Development Disabilities 32, 1745–1756 (2011)

Developing Accessible Teaching and Learning Materials within a User Centred Design Framework

Introduction to the Special Thematic Session

E.A. Draffan

University of Southampton, Southampton, United Kingdom
ead@ecs.soton.ac.uk

Abstract. This special thematic session includes papers discussing a wide range of methodologies for the development of accessible teaching and learning materials based on user centric approaches. They do not just highlight individual needs with regards to skills and abilities, but also take into account localization issues in terms of language and cultural differences. There are also frameworks for strategies to suit particular tasks and the environment in which they are taking place. The latter may be an educational setting, workplace, leisure facility or at home. All these aspects are impacted on by legislation that can be supportive in terms of the user access but may also be a barrier where global standards differ and guidelines are of limited help unless they allow for the development of new media representations and innovative technologies.

Keywords: Accessibility, Teaching and Learning Materials, User Centred Design, Disability, Print Impairment.

1 Introduction

As the use of technology to support those with disabilities has become more widely available across educational establishments, so has the development of teaching and learning materials in formats that can support many more print impaired users whether the difficulties are due to cognitive, sensory and/or physical difficulties. These media formats range from interactive video systems for those with hearing impairments to screen reading or text to speech output with links to tactile devices for the blind. However, there remains the dilemma of producing resources that have been developed using a user centered approach, which may also be required to fit a standardized set of criteria.

Maguire [1] highlights some key elements pertaining to human centered design including involvement of potential users with an understanding of the tasks they are undertaking and how this impacts on software application development. This may be to do with the amount of functionality that can be undertaken by the technology and how much is dependent on the user skills and abilities. There is also the need to constantly check that what is being developed, perhaps as a framework as well as a technology tool, suits those supporting the user. Iterative design methodologies are

K. Miesenberger et al. (Eds.): ICCHP 2014, Part II, LNCS 8548, pp. 540–542, 2014.

essential and a multidisciplinary approach is considered to be beneficial as a way of ensuring that the wider aspects of localization, environmental issues, language and cultural differences are also taken into account. Encouraging close cooperation between educators, linguists, learning technologists, accessibility professionals, assistive technology and mainstream developers can provide improved outcomes, but only if a truly participatory approach is adopted with users at the centre of any developments.

Interface design as an important aspect of accessible digital resource development and this is also mentioned by all the authors in the papers presented. The acceptance of any technology and the content it is presenting to the consumer, needs to be easy to use [2] as well as being perceived as a useful adjunct to the strategies already adopted [3]. It is felt this is particularly important when it is recognized that those with disabilities may take much longer to access digital materials compared to their peers [4].

The practicalities of developing materials for those with intellectual challenges is often overlooked when thinking about online materials, in particular for those with autism and cognitive impairments such as low intellectual abilities. The complexities of navigation and ability to make choices from the amount of information presented by the usual online learning situations may be barriers to equal access [5]. These and other features found in the virtual learning environments developed as containers for teaching and learning materials may not always be as accessible as one would wish. Evaluations have shown that some accessibility checks are overlooked when documents are uploaded or images and videos are included. These checks may also include elements that affect e-reading such as the type of format used and its ability to be read aloud with text to speech or to be used with magnification tools, zoom or color and font changes [6].

One final issue that will be addressed is the fact that technologies and the formats developed to be used by the various devices and software, move forward at a considerable pace. This is not always the case when it comes to the standards, guidelines and legislation in place, which may be several years out of date. There have been recent updates to the Web Content Accessibility Guidelines (WCAG) [7] with ongoing work to include mobile technologies. However, bridging of the gap between standards, guidelines and legislation and the technologies they address can affect all end-users by presenting unnecessary barriers. These barriers may include copyright laws related to different print impairments and where a user is within a country or particular educational system not addressed by the legal frameworks. The barriers may also be related to the access to digitized text or the sharing of materials due to digital rights management issues.

All these aspects of resource design and development will be covered in the following papers that draw further attention to the issues and offer strategies for the development of accessible teaching and learning materials within a user centered design framework.

- Developing a New Framework for Evaluating Arabic Dyslexia Training Tools
- A Fully Accessible Arabic Learning Platform for Assisting Children with Intellectual Challenges
- Electronic Braille Blocks: A Tangible Interface-based Application for Teaching Braille Letter Recognition to Very Young Blind Children

- Fostering Better Deaf/Hearing Communication Through a Novel Mobile App for Fingerspelling
- EBooks, Accessibility and the Catalysts for Culture Change
- Legislation and Standards of Accessibility Versus Intelligent Design

References

1. Maguire, M.: Methods to support human-centred design. Int. J. Hum-Comput. St. 55(4), 587–634 (2001)
2. Davis, F.D., Bagozzi, R.P., Warshaw, P.R.: User acceptance of computer technology: A comparison of two theoretical models. Management Science 35(8), 982–1003 (1989)
3. Davis, F.D.: A technology acceptance model for empirically testing new end-user information systems: Theory and results. Unpublished Doctoral Dissertation. Massachusetts Institute of Technology (1986), http://pubsonline.informs.org/doi/pdf/10.1287/mnsc.35.8.982
4. Nielsen Norman Group Report: Beyond ALT Text: Making the Web Easy to Use for Users With Disabilities, http://www.nngroup.com/reports/accessibility
5. Williams, P.: Exploring the challenges of developing digital literacy in the context of special educational needs communities. Innovation in Teaching and Learning in Information and Computer Sciences 5(1), 1–16 (2006), http://journals.heacademy.ac.uk/doi/abs/10.11120/ital.2006.05010006
6. Web2Access, http://www.web2access.org.uk/
7. Web Content Accessibility Guidelines (WCAG) 2.0 – W3C Recommendation (December 11, 2008), http://www.w3.org/TR/WCAG20/

eBooks, Accessibility and the Catalysts for Culture Change

E.A. Draffan[1], Alistair McNaught[2], and Abi James[1]

[1] WAIS, ECS, University of Southampton, United Kingdom
ead@ecs.soton.ac.uk, A.James@soton.ac.uk
[2] JISC TechDis, York, United Kingdom
alistair@techdis.ac.uk

Abstract. The evolution of any product is usually in response to perceived benefits; either for the workflow, cost-benefit or for the end users. The development of accessible digital print resources at source of publication is uniquely advantageous in many ways. A system with improved accessibility for humans also enables content to be machine read[1]. Although the global publishing and digital distribution industries have not uniformly embraced accessibility, the United Kingdom (UK) has been able to make significant positive progress. The UK has not embraced a specific disability ebook format and distribution system; instead, through a model of cross-industry stakeholder engagement, a cultural shift has begun to embed accessibility at source within the publishing industry. The authors maintain that the cultural change witnessed is not a coincidence and has its roots in a particular set of catalysts being initiated by stakeholders resulting in a model that could be replicated.

Keywords: eBooks, Accessibility, Culture Change, Disability, Print Impairment, ereading.

1 Introduction

Digital books have become known as ebooks or electronic versions of printed books [2]and when developed in an accessible way can offer many people effective access to a wide range of text based materials. They have the potential to remove many of the barriers faced by print impaired or disabled readers. George Kerscher [3] described a print disabled individual as being “A person who cannot effectively read print because of a visual, physical, perceptual, developmental, cognitive, or learning disability.”

The content of an accessible ebook can be identified via key headings with easy navigation and informative detail to support bookmarking and annotations. The text can be made larger or smaller by the user; it can offer users the chance to adjust colours or contrasts and can even be read out using text to speech tools [4]. In the UK, approximately 4% of learners in higher education have a print disability, such as dyslexia or visual impairment [5,6], while those with mobility, dexterity and concentration difficulties can struggle to handle the printed page or read for long periods of time. The market for easy to access digitised leisure reading has been recognised to support and enhance the lives of many more older people with age related sight loss

K. Miesenberger et al. (Eds.): ICCHP 2014, Part II, LNCS 8548, pp. 543–550, 2014.

[7] and those with print impairments [8] while access to small, portable devices capable of distributing and displaying digital text and ebooks (such as Kindle and iPad devices) has created consumer demand and increased expectations for digital reading products. For these reasons accessible digital text should be considered as one of the most important catalysts for culture change and it is clear that the use of ereaders and ebooks is generally on the increase in the United States and in Europe with publishers embracing 'born-digital content' (content that is at the outset digital rather than converted from print materials) [9,10].

However, potential and reality can be very different when it comes to accessibility. The publishing industry is complex and multi-layered involving many partners from those creating digital files to those distributing them or manufacturing devices to consume them. Barriers can include technical and bureaucratic challenges. Publishers may need new skills to understand the opportunities and limitations of accessible publishing technologies. Contracts may need amending to ensure accessibility added in one part of the supply chain is not stripped out in another. Accessibility is a niche field sitting between developers, content authors, publishers, distributors, device manufacturers, educators and disability support provision. Nevertheless there can be significant savings for teaching and learning providers who procure an accessible ebook platform compared to the use of an in-house conversion service [11]. Examples of the way in which early adopters using systems that offer accessibility to their digital books have gained market advantage can be seen below:

- Reduced costs in servicing individual requests from library services. UK publishers serving the FE and HE sector supply between 500 and 1500 files a year in response to disability requests so this is a significant potential saving. [12]
- Improved access to tenders – the Open University has a briefing document for suppliers outlining "Accessibility requirements for database platforms and full text" with more than 3 pages of accessibility requirements. JISC Collections tendering process for suppliers was recently updated to include specific (and demonstrable) accessibility functions for users.

2 Overview of Accessible eBooks Formats and Distribution Systems

The ereader and the ebook have a symbiotic relationship, in that the ebook cannot be read without a device or software application and this may mean that a format is linked to a machine such as the Kindle device and its ebook format (AZW). However, over the years many devices and applications have accepted a broader range of formats such as Portable Document Format (PDF), plain text and ePub. The ePub or electronic publication format is an open ebook standard developed by the International Digital Publishing Forum. It offers increased possibilities for accessibility, with the option to include good navigation of content, reflow of text depending on the screen size or magnification plus font changes. Text to speech or screen reading may be available depending on the Digital Rights management (DRM) or the built-in options available on the ereader device or application.

A recent sample test of ebook accessibility was undertaken by the authors [13] based on the Web2Access testing procedure [14]. This addressed the accessibility of 14 ebook applications across 4 different operating systems (covering smartphones, tablets and desktop computers) for those with dyslexia. Scores for accessibility varied from 100% to 48.5%. However, within the results, it was identified that certain operating systems allow the programs or apps to provide more accessible ebooks with the use of built in text to speech or font and colour changing options. Devices with iOS apps averaged 87.1%, Android 65.5% and Windows desktop apps averaged 56.8%. None of the formats tested included ones specifically designed for print impairment. Whereas a combination of formats developed in Sweden has provided an accessible standard known as the Digital Accessible Information SYstem (Daisy) [15].

There are similarities with the latest versions of ePub 3.0 formats and the Daisy format. The former was the open format that proved to be most accessible on the iOS, Android and Windows devices evaluated. However, it should be noted that some devices that will read ePub format are not as easy to use as the dedicated Daisy book readers, which can be helpful for those who become blind later in life with larger buttons and easy navigation. So there may be a dilemma for those organizations with libraries or repositories of accessible ebooks as to which formats should be offered to users. Across the world, national organizations such as Bookshare in the USA, the Austrian Blind Union, the Belgium Oeuvre Nationale des Aveugles and Nota Danish National Library for persons with Print Disabilities offer Daisy formats with successful electronic and postal delivery services. But these systems are not always able to instantly offer their readers the latest commercially available ebooks. It is felt that "eBooks should enable all readers, using whatever assistive technology they may require, to access new books as they are published in ebook form and at no additional cost." [16]

There is also the issue of sharing accessible ebooks and at present it is only those organizations who have dedicated systems for developing alternative formats that are involved in what have become known as 'Trusted Intermediary Global Accessible Resources' such as the materials on the World Intellectual Property Organisation database, the European Network of Trusted Intermediaries network and Bookshare [17].

3 Modeling a Framework for eBook/etext Accessibility

There are many stakeholders involved with ebook/etext accessibility including the main participants, namely those individuals with print impairments/disabilities. In order to ensure reasonable adjustments can be made there needs to be close collaboration between those developing the online market places, ereader and ebook providers and supporting organizations. The evolving technology developments mean that government bodies and organizations involved in the legal, copyright, policy, procedures and information provision need to continue to cooperate at all levels. In order to look at each area more closely the authors have taken the example of the UK's post- compulsory educational setting to demonstrate a possible framework for ebook/etext accessibility. The follow short paragraphs explain the stakeholder involvement and provide a basis from which to discuss the catalysts for cultural change.

3.1 Disabled Learners – Awareness, Empowerment, Ambition, Rights

The percentage of students entering post-compulsory education in the UK and declaring a disability continues to increase [18]. Due to improved legal entitlement to reasonable adjustments, including alternative formats (Equality Act 2010) throughout education plus financial support for print impaired students in higher education (the Disabled Students Allowances) [19] and growing aspirations fuelled in part by the activities of advocacy groups, this group has higher expectations on the support and provision provided to them within education.

3.2 Learning Providers – Awareness, Responsibilities

Growing awareness and responsibility for accessibility and equality amongst further and higher education providers has led to sector demand to remove barriers to printed material and improved provision of accessible ebooks. Projects such as Load2Learn [20] and JISC TechDis auditing tools [21] have assisted education professionals and staff to become up-skilled in accessibility issues and technology-based study strategies for print impaired learners.

3.3 Technology Evolution in Education

Access to online resources is standard in post 16 education in UK. Digital texts can be found in most institutions [22] and research funded by the CLAUD group of HE libraries (Creating Libraries Accessible for Users with Disabilities) concluded that incorporating ebooks into the Alternative Format service can enable libraries to "provide a more far reaching service at little or no real cost" [23]. Organizations are also exploring opportunities for 'Bring Your Own Device' (BOYD) policies, and many are investing heavily in wireless connectivity and exploring mobile-friendly library systems. Learning providers are increasingly well-placed to maximize their use of accessible digital resources.

3.4 Technology Evolution – Publishing

The market for e-books has developed strongly with a shift in the way people access information online. This has given publishers a strong incentive to publish in a way that maximizes delivery options. The convergence of EPUB3 with the DAISY standard has given a unique opportunity to meet access requirements at the same time as maximizing business needs. E-resources that are flexible and adaptable enough to be accessible to assistive technologies tend to be suitable for use with smart phones, tablets and a range of other devices. This stakeholder involvement is not unique to the UK and as has been mentioned elements can be seen across Europe and in the USA via networks such as eAccess+ [24], but based on the experiences of the authors, it is only when all stakeholders are brought together through a series of catalysts that significant influences on the development of accessible e-books can be achieved.

4 The Catalysts

The following elements are considered to provide a secure basis from which to build the cultural changes required to fulfill equal access to ebooks and etexts for those with print impairments across the world

4.1 Positive Coalitions

Organizations representing disability groups and accessibility professionals have joined forces in groups, such as the 'Right to Read Alliance' and the 'Publishers Accessibility Action Group'. By engaging with the publishing community and learning providers, these coalitions have been able to demonstrate the legal, economic and social benefits of accessible digital texts while disseminating best practice. Continued lobbying and engagement has led to a recent change in the copyright legislation within the UK with a number of exceptions being made for those with print impairment [25].

4.2 Centrally Funded Advice and Guidance on Technology

Through the UK Government funded JISC Legal and JISC TechDis [26] legal, copyright and accessibility information is offered to post-16 learning providers. Involvement with EDItEUR who coordinate development of the "standards infrastructure for electronic commerce in the book, e-book and serials sectors" [27] and WIPO, has provided a platform for online training resources for publishers as well as the facilitation of library and disability staff contributions to publisher training standards.

4.3 User Focused Advice and Guidance

Lack of awareness within learning providers and users as to the gains of using alternative formats has, in the past, helped to limit access to reasonable adjustments, as highlighted in the recent Metadata-enabled Tools for Assistive Living and Learning (METALL) project [28]. Recently UK regional and national groups have been working to disseminate the message about accessible ebooks/etexts directly to learners and educators while developing informative documents for their networks.

4.4 Active Peer Networks

Peer networks are essential for moving theory into practice. In the UK peer review networks [28] have played a significant role in creating a culture of accessible ebooks, allowing regular exchange of ideas and practice. As learning providers become more consistent in their requirements from suppliers, accessibility begins to become a marketable commodity allowing suppliers providing accessible texts to gain a vital competitive edge. Procurement policies are increasingly demanding a high degree of accessibility from suppliers so suppliers with good accessibility enjoy reduced competition. This applies even when a publisher's files are distributed through other platforms over which they have little control. [29]

4.5 Focused Resources and Pragmatic Approaches

Well-defined roles and projects provide a vital bridge between publishers, suppliers and advocacy organizations, allowing each to understand the other more effectively.

Creating a culture of partnership is essential. Taking a pragmatic approach to accessibility and recognizing that partial accessibility is better than none, brings accessibility onto the "radar of possibility" [30] and is a stage that may have to be accepted in the drive for total accessibility.

5 Conclusion

Experiences across the world and in many industries has shown that to retrofit accessibility is difficult and often an afterthought [31]. The UK's approach of working strategically in alliances that try to solve the common problem of accessible ebooks has proved more effective than working independently in silos. Strategic alliances can create the conditions for cultural change, focused resources and collaborative organizations. There is the benefit of accessibility being seen as a spectrum of compliance (where everyone is on the journey) rather than as an "accessible/inaccessible" dichotomy where, if at first there are failures, the only option is to abandon further attempts. A key feature in the cultural change in ebook accessibility in the UK has been the willingness of all the stakeholders to move beyond vested organizational interests and focus on the single purpose for which all the stakeholders exist - maximizing benefits to end users. Training and information resources will need to be continually updated and disseminated through all the stakeholders and directly to the users if the rate of progress in the provision of accessible digital text for all print impaired individuals is to be maintained.

References

1. Dawson, A., Wallis, J.: Twenty issues in e-book creation. Against the Grain 17(1), 18–26 (2005), http://cdlr.strath.ac.uk/pubs/dawsona/ad200501.htm (accessed April 3, 2014), ISSN 1043-2094
2. Oxford Dictionaries. Oxford University Press (2010), http://www.oxforddictionaries.com/us/definition/american_english/e-book (accessed April 3, 2014)
3. Kerscher, G.: Reading Rights Coalition - USA, http://www.readingrights.org/definition-print-disabled
4. Anderson-Inman, L., Horney, M.A.: Supported eText: Assistive technology through text transformations. Reading Research, 153–160 (2007), http://onlinelibrary.wiley.com/doi/10.1598/RRQ.42.1.8/abstract (accessed April 3, 2014)
5. Equality Challenge Unit. Equality in higher education: statistical report 2012 Part 2: students (2012), http://www.ecu.ac.uk/publications/files/equality-in-he-stats-report-2012-students.pdf (accessed April 3, 2014)

6. Further Education and Skills in England: Learner Equality and Diversity (2012), http://data.gov.uk/dataset/further-education-and-skills-in-england-learner-equality-and-diversity (accessed April 3, 2014)
7. Kretzschmar, F., Pleimling, D., Hosemann, J., Füssel, S., Bornkessel-Schlesewsky, I., et al.: Subjective Impressions Do Not Mirror Online Reading Effort: Concurrent EEG-Eyetracking Evidence from the Reading of Books and Digital Media. PLoS ONE 8(2), e56178 (2013), http://www.plosone.org/article/info%3Adoi%2F10.1371%2Fjournal.pone.0056178, doi:10.1371/journal.pone.0056178 (accessed April 3, 2014)
8. Gonzalez, M.R.: The effect of interactive eBooks on the reading comprehension of struggling readers and students with reading disabilities. Ph.D. thesis, Walden University (2010), http://www.editlib.org/p/125628 (accessed April 3, 2014)
9. Zickuhr, K., Rainie, L.: E-reading rises and device ownership jumps - Pew Research Center, USA (2014), http://www.pewinternet.org/files/2014/01/PIP_E-reading_011614.pdf (accessed April 3, 2014)
10. Anscombe, N.: Experimenting with E-books, Research Information (2014), http://www.researchinformation.info/features/feature.php?feature_id=457 (accessed April 3, 2014)
11. McMahon, A.: Accessible Books - who pays Assistive Technology Network presentation (2013), http://www.jisctechdis.ac.uk/assets/Documents/Events/130213ebooks_AMcMahonDundeeUni.ppt (accessed April 3, 2014)
12. McNaught, A.: Phone conversations with production / rights managers. Palgrave MacMillan and Sage (March-April 2014)
13. Mc Naught, A.: Personal correspondence with Nicky Whitsed, Director of Library services Open University (April 2014)
14. James, A., Draffan, E.A.: Accessibility of ebook devices & digital documents. Presented at the 9th BDA International Conference 2014, UK (2014)
15. Web2Access, http://web2access.org.uk/test (accessed April 3, 2014)
16. The Daisy Consortium, http://www.daisy.org/about_us (accessed April 3, 2014)
17. The Publishers Association. Joint statement on accessibility & e-books (2010), http://www.publishers.org.uk/index.php?option=com_content&view=article&id=2207:joint-statement-on-accessibility-a-e-books&Itemid=1655 (accessed April 3, 2014)
18. Beaumon, B.: Bookshare: Making accessible materials available worldwide. In: World Library and Information Congress: 77th IFLA General Conference and Assembly, San Juan, Puerto Rico (2011)
19. Higher Education Statistics Agency (2012/13) UKPIs: Widening participation of students in receipt of DSA (table T7), http://www.hesa.ac.uk/index.php?option=com_content&task=view&id=2062&Itemid=141
20. Disabled Students Allowances, https://www.gov.uk/disabled-students-allowances-dsas/overview (accessed April 3, 2014)
21. Load2Learn - Accessible etexts for schools and organizations - RNIB and Dyslexia Action, https://load2learn.org.uk/ (accessed April 3, 2014)
22. JISC TechDis Online Accessibility Self Evaluation Service (OASES), http://www.jisctechdis.ac.uk/oases (accessed April 3, 2014)
23. e-books for FE project ebooks for Further Education colleges, http://fe.jiscebooks.org/ (accessed April 3, 2014)

24. JISC Techdis, Libraries and Alternative formats research Part 3: Are some disabilities treated less favourably than others? (2013), http://www.jisctechdis.ac.uk/assets/Documents/laafr3.doc
25. Intellectual Property Office, Government takes important step towards modernising copyright: Press Release (2014), https://www.gov.uk/government/news/government-takes-important-step-towards-modernising-copyright (accessed April 3, 2014)
26. eAccess+ Hub - Accessible Documents, http://hub.eaccessplus.eu/wiki/Accessible_documents (accessed April 3, 2014)
27. JISC, http://www.jisc.ac.uk/ (accessed April 3, 2014)
28. EDItEUR, http://www.editeur.org/2/About/#Intro (accessed April 3, 2014)
29. McNaught, A.: Phone conversation with Huw Alexander, Digital Sales manager. Sage (April 2014)
30. METALL project, Final Report Dolphin Consortium (2013), http://metallproject.wordpress.com/final-report/ (accessed April 3, 2014)
31. International Association of Accessibility Professionals (2013), http://download.microsoft.com/download/3/2/F/32F27B21-CF1A-4AD9-972E-F2A692BEB575/Society-of-Accessibility-Professionals.pdf

Electronic Braille Blocks: A Tangible Interface-Based Application for Teaching Braille Letter Recognition to Very Young Blind Children

Rabia Jafri

Department of Information Technology, King Saud University, Riyadh, Saudi Arabia
rabia.ksu@gmail.com

Abstract. A software solution for teaching Braille letter recognition to very young blind children is presented which allows them to interact with the computer by manipulating NFC-tag embedded blocks with Braille letters embossed on their sides. Braille letter recognition is taught and reinforced through various exercises and games and auditory feedback is provided via a speech interface. By embedding interactivity into physical blocks, our system provides the best of both worlds: the manipulation and exploration of physical objects in accordance with the sensory dependence and developmental needs of young children and the exploitation of the power of digital technology to extend and enhance the learning process taking place through traditional exploratory play. Furthermore, this is a cost-effective solution and does not require children to have previous experience with computers. This system can be easily adapted in the future to teach other concepts such as Braille numbers, shape or texture recognition.

Keywords: Tangible User Interfaces, Braille Literacy, Blind, Visually Impaired, Educational Software, Children.

1 Introduction

Braille reading proficiency is an essential skill for blind children that has been shown to be the strongest predictor of higher levels of education and employment in adult life [1,2]. Nevertheless, Braille literacy rates for school age children in the United States have declined from more than 50 percent (40 years ago) [3] to only 12 percent today [4]. This decline is partly attributed to the mainstreaming of blind students to public schools which are not adequately equipped to provide Braille education both in terms of the amount of time that the teachers can afford to expend on Braille instruction as well as the amount of money available for purchasing Braille teaching materials [1].

Educational software for teaching Braille may provide a viable solution to both these problems. Once a lesson has been given, an automated tutor can supplement the teacher's efforts and mitigate the demands on her time by reinforcing the concepts at the student's pace via various exercises and games. With the decreasing cost of technology,

K. Miesenberger et al. (Eds.): ICCHP 2014, Part II, LNCS 8548, pp. 551–558, 2014.

such software solutions can be made available at relatively low expense as compared to traditional Braille materials.

Learning the Braille alphabet is the first step towards attaining Braille literacy and many children who are congenitally blind or become legally blind early in life have to acquire this ability at a young age. Notwithstanding the benefits mentioned above, computer software based educational tools are not considered developmentally appropriate for this age group since these are usually presented exclusively through a screen-based medium and do not afford interaction through the exploration and manipulation of physical objects proven to be so essential for the cognitive and emotional development of young children [5,6]. This issue is even more pertinent for blind children who, being deprived of their sense of sight, depend greatly on their other senses, especially, hearing and touch, to gain an understanding of abstract concepts. Though electronic Braille displays and haptic interfaces (such as vibrotactile touchscreens [7]) are widely available to allow access by the visually impaired to digital information, this kind of interaction has been found to be problematic for very young children due to their fine motor skills not being sufficiently developed [8].

Tangible user interfaces (TUIs), which couple physical objects to digital representations, have been shown to enhance learning for children by enriching their experience, play and development [9,10]. Studies on this topic have reported that interaction with tangibles encourages engagement, excitement and collaboration [11], promotes discovery and participation [12], makes computation immediate and more accessible [13], and offers a resource for action in addition to an alternative form of data representation [14]. As pointed out in several studies (e.g., [15,16]), these interfaces appear particularly suitable for learning in abstract problem domains by relating abstract concepts to physical experiences or concrete examples.

We have, therefore, designed a computer application for teaching the Braille alphabet to very young blind children which allows them to interact with the computer by manipulating physical objects, namely blocks with Braille letters embossed on them. Our system teaches and reinforces Braille letter recognition through various exercises and games and provides feedback to the user via a speech interface. By embedding interactivity into physical blocks, our system provides the best of both worlds: the manipulation and exploration of physical objects in accordance with the sensory dependence and developmental needs of this user group and the exploitation of the power of digital technology to extend and enhance the learning process taking place through traditional exploratory play. This system can be easily adapted in the future to teach other concepts such as Braille numbers, shape or texture recognition.

2 Related Work

The benefits offered by tangible interfaces for learning have fueled research in this area resulting in several educational applications for children being developed in recent years which utilize this form of interaction. To mention just a few: Wyeth and Wyeth [17] have designed Electronic Blocks which young children can physically stack to build computer programs that interact with the physical world. Color Cubes [18] – which are the main inspiration for our system – allow children to see the effect of mixing colors on the computer screen by placing two different colored cubes with

RFID tags embedded in them on a surface with an RFID tag reader. Zuckerman et al. [19] have introduced "Montessori-inspired Manipulatives" (MiMs), technology-enhanced building blocks that enable children to physically explore abstract concepts; an example of MiMs are SystemBlocks, a hands-on simulation tool to explore systems concepts. Hashagen et al. [20] have developed "Der Schwarm", a full-body interaction environment enabling children to learn about swarm or flock behavior. Girouard et al. [21] have created Smart Blocks for exploring the concepts of volume and surface area of 3D objects. Campos and Pessanha [22] have designed an augmented reality tangible interface to help kindergarten children study animals and the environments they live in. Antle et al. [23] have developed "Towards Utopia", a tangible user interface-based tabletop learning environment which allows children to learn about concepts related to sustainable land use planning. Hunter et al. [24] have developed two educational applications on the Siftables platform [25] for children aged 4-7 years: Make a Riddle [25], which provides a word-to-block mapping that allows sentence formation, and TeleStory [25], which enables children to participate in the creation of an animated scene on a television.

However, the benefits of tangible interfaces have yet to be exploited for the education of blind children. Our search for educational applications built specifically for blind children yielded only a handful of games [26] and some Braille literacy coursewares [27] which utilize vibrotactile touchscreens with audio outputs for interaction. Though some tangible interface-based applications for the visually impaired do exist (such as the collaborative music application developed by Omori and Yairi [28] and MICOO (multimodal interactive cubes for object orientation) introduced by Manshad et al. [29]), however, the only such educational solution geared towards young children that we came across was AutOMathic [30], a system to teach arithmetic and beginning algebra using Braille-embossed blocks with barcodes affixed to their bases. The child can pick up a block, pass it over a barcode scanner attached to a computer and then place it within a grid on a touchpad device. In this way, an arithmetic problem, and later, its solution, can be laid out on the grid. Throughout the setup and solution phases, the computer builds, maintains and updates an internal model of the problem's current status, tendering advice via speech whenever appropriate. This solution, however, is cost-prohibitive, requiring expensive components such as a large touchpad device, and involves the extraneous step of passing each block over a barcode scanner – identifying the block automatically when it is placed on the grid would be a more user-friendly alternative. Other than AutOMathic [30], we were unable to find any applications for the education of young blind children in general and the development of Braille alphabet recognition and Braille literacy skills in particular which make use of tangible user interfaces.

The scarcity of TUI-based Braille education applications for young blind children in the state of the art coupled with the huge learning potential of these interfaces, as revealed by several studies [9,10,11,12,13,14,15,16], provided us with the impetus for developing a TUI-based Braille alphabet recognition application for this user group. Our aim is to explore if such a solution would enhance their learning experience and make it more fun and engaging. We proceed to describe the design of our application in detail in the next section.

3 Electronic Braille Blocks: Design and Architecture

Electronic Braille Blocks is a software solution being developed for teaching Braille letter recognition to very young blind children. Children will interact with the system by providing input via a tangible interface and receive auditory feedback via a speech-based interface. The tangible interface will consist of two parts:

1. Blocks with Braille letters embossed on their sides and NFC (Near Field Communication) tags affixed to their bases. The blocks would be small enough to be manipulated by little hands and would be made of durable materials, such as wood or plastic, to withstand rough handling by young children.
2. A groove-based surface, allowing simultaneous placement of multiple blocks (see Fig. 1) and concealing an NFC tag reader connected to a PC.

When the child will place a block on the surface, the software will detect which letter is on the block and will provide appropriate auditory feedback to the child. The system architecture is shown in Fig. 2.

Some usage scenarios for this system are as follows:

- The child feels the Braille letter on a block. He then puts the block on the surface and the program tells him (via speech) what the letter on the block is and provides some examples of words starting with that letter.
- The program asks the child (via speech) to find the letter that begins the word "ball". The child tries to find the block with the letter "B" and places it on the surface. If the correct letter has been chosen, the program congratulates the child; otherwise, it encourages him to try again.
- The program asks the child to put three random blocks on the surface and detects the letters on the blocks. It then asks him to take the blocks off the surface and put them back again in alphabetical order. If the correct order is accomplished, the program congratulates the child; otherwise, it encourages him to try again.

Fig. 1. Groove-based surface allowing for multiple block placement / insertion

We are consulting with Braille instructors from the King Saud University Disability Center in Riyadh, Saudi Arabia as well as from various institutes for the blind in the US to determine what exercises would be most effective in teaching and reinforcing Braille letter recognition if incorporated into our system. Since games have been reported to be more efficacious for teaching concepts than traditional methods of instruction [31], we would prefer to present these exercises in the format of games to create a more engaging and fun learning experience.

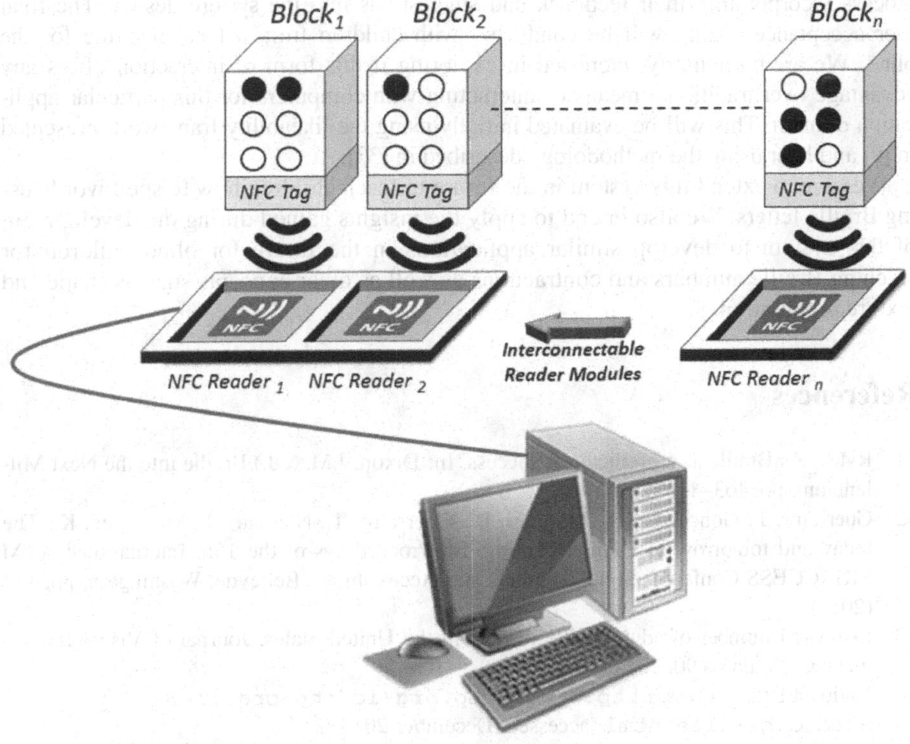

Fig. 2. System architecture

4 Conclusion and Future Work

A TUI-based educational application for teaching Braille letter recognition to very young blind children has been described in this paper. The tangible interaction provided by NFC tag-embedded blocks with Braille letters embossed on them is developmentally appropriate for this user group and in accordance with their sensory dependence. Additional benefits offered by this system include the following: Since the children interact with the system through physical blocks - everyday objects that they are familiar with - they do not need to have previous experience with computers (for example, knowing how to manipulate a mouse or a keyboard) in order to use this system. Moreover, the tangible interaction would add elements of fun, engagement and discovery to the learning process and may even facilitate collaboration if multiple children are using the program at the same time. To keep the cost of the system as low as possible – an important consideration for any educational tool [32] – we have utilized COTS (commercial off-the-shelf) components such as NFC tags and NFC tag readers for the TUI and plan to use readily available inexpensive materials for the blocks.

We are in the process of building a prototype version of this system. We will continue consulting with Braille instructors for young children throughout the development process incorporating their feedback and suggestions into the system design. The final user acceptance testing will be conducted with children from a local institute for the blind. We are particularly interested in exploring if this form of interaction offers any advantage over traditional means of interacting with computers for this particular application domain. This will be evaluated initially using the likeability framework presented in [9] and later using the methodology described in [33].

We plan to extend this system in the future to teach children how to spell words using Braille letters. We also intend to apply the insights gained during the development of this system to develop similar applications in the future for blind children for teaching Braille numbers and contractions as well as other concepts such as shape and texture recognition.

References

1. Ryles, R.: Braille as a predictor of success. In: Dixon, J.M. (ed.) Braille into the Next Millennium, pp. 463–491 (2000)
2. Guerreiro, J., Gonçalves, D., Marques, D., Guerreiro, T., Nicolau, H., Montague, K.: The today and tomorrow of Braille learning. In: Proceedings of the 15th International ACM SIGACCESS Conference on Computers and Accessibility, Bellevue, Washington, pp. 1–2 (2013)
3. Estimated number of adult braille readers in the United States. Journal of Visual Impairment & Blindness 90, 287 (1996)
4. National Braille Press, `http://www.nbp.org/ic/nbp/braille/needforbraille.html` (accessed: December 2013)
5. Yelland, N.: Reconceptualising Schooling With Technology for the 21st Century: Images and Reflections. Information Technology in Childhood Education Annual 1999, 39–59 (1999)
6. Haugland, S.: Early Childhood Classrooms in the 21st Century: Using Computers to Maximise Learning. Young Children 55, 12–18 (2000)
7. Southern, C., Clawson, J., Frey, B., Abowd, G., Romero, M.: Braille Touch: mobile touchscreen text entry for the visually impaired. In: Proceedings of the 14th International Conference on Human-computer Interaction with Mobile Devices and Services Companion, San Francisco, California, USA, pp. 155–156 (2012)
8. Marco, J., Cerezo, E., Baldassarri, S.: Bringing tabletop technology to all: evaluating a tangible farm game with kindergarten and special needs children. Personal and Ubiquitous Computing 17, 1577–1591 (2013)
9. Zaman, B., Abeele, V.: How to measure the likeability of tangible interaction with preschoolers. In: Proc. CHI, Nederland, vol. 5 (2007)
10. Xie, L., Antle, A.N., Motamedi, N.: Are tangibles more fun?: comparing children's enjoyment and engagement using physical, graphical and tangible user interfaces. In: Proceedings of the 2nd International Conference on Tangible and Embedded Interaction, Bonn, Germany, pp. 191–198 (2008)
11. Price, S., Rogers, Y., Scaife, M., Stanton, D., Neale, H.: Using 'tangibles' to promote novel forms of playful learning. Interacting with Computers 15, 169–185 (2003)
12. O'Malley, C., Stanton Fraser, D.: Literature Review in Learning with Tangible Technologies. Discussion Paper (2004)
13. McNerney, T.S.: From turtles to Tangible Programming Bricks: explorations in physical language design. Personal Ubiquitous Comput. 8, 326–337 (2004)

14. Fernaeus, Y., Tholander, J.: Finding design qualities in a tangible programming space. In: Proceedings of the SIGCHI Conference on Human Factors in Computing Systems, Montreal, Quebec, Canada, pp. 447–456 (2006)
15. Antle, A.N.: The CTI framework: informing the design of tangible systems for children. In: Proceedings of the 1st International Conference on Tangible and Embedded Interaction, Rouge, Louisiana, pp. 195–202 (2007)
16. Marshall, P.: Do tangible interfaces enhance learning? In: Proceedings of the 1st International Conference on Tangible and Embedded Interaction, Baton Rouge, Louisiana, pp. 163–170 (2007)
17. Wyeth, P., Wyeth, G.: Electronic blocks: Tangible programming elements for preschoolers. In: Proceedings of the Eighth IFIP TC13 Conference on Human-Computer Interaction, pp. 496–503 (2001)
18. Marshall, P., Price, S., Rogers, Y.: Conceptualising tangibles to support learning. In: Proceedings of the 2003 Conference on Interaction Design and Children, Preston, England, pp. 101–109 (2003)
19. Zuckerman, O., Arida, S., Resnick, M.: Extending tangible interfaces for education: digital montessori-inspired manipulatives. In: Proceedings of the SIGCHI Conference on Human Factors in Computing Systems, Portland, Oregon, USA, pp. 859–868 (2005)
20. Hashagen, A., Büching, C., Schelhowe, H.: Learning abstract concepts through bodily engagement: a comparative, qualitative study. In: Proceedings of the 8th International Conference on Interaction Design and Children, Como, Italy, pp. 234–237 (2009)
21. Girouard, A., Solovey, E.T., Hirshfield, L.M., Ecott, S., Shaer, O., Jacob, R.J.K.: Smart Blocks: a tangible mathematical manipulative. In: Proceedings of the 1st International Conference on Tangible and Embedded Interaction, Baton Rouge, Louisiana, pp. 183–186 (2007)
22. Campos, P., Pessanha, S.: Designing augmented reality tangible interfaces for kindergarten children. In: Shumaker, R. (ed.) Virtual and Mixed Reality, HCII 2011, Part I. LNCS, vol. 6773, pp. 12–19. Springer, Heidelberg (2011)
23. Antle, A.N., Wise, A.F., Nielsen, K.: Towards Utopia: designing tangibles for learning. In: Proceedings of the 10th International Conference on Interaction Design and Children, Ann Arbor, Michigan, pp. 11–20 (2011)
24. Merrill, D., Kalanithi, J., Maes, P.: Siftables: towards sensor network user interfaces. In: Proceedings of the 1st International Conference on Tangible and Embedded Interaction, Baton Rouge, Louisiana, pp. 75–78 (2007)
25. Hunter, S., Kalanithi, J., Merrill, D.: Make a Riddle and TeleStory: designing children's applications for the siftables platform. In: Proceedings of the 9th International Conference on Interaction Design and Children, Barcelona, Spain, pp. 206–209 (2010)
26. Raisamo, R., Patomäki, S., Hasu, M., Pasto, V.: Design and evaluation of a tactile memory game for visually impaired children. Interacting with Computers 19, 196–205 (2007)
27. Meijer, P.B.L.: An Experimental System for Auditory Image Representations. IEEE Transactions on Biomedical Engineering 39, 112–121 (1992)
28. Omori, S., Yairi, I.E.: Collaborative music application for visually impaired people with tangible objects on table. In: Proceedings of the 15th International ACM SIGACCESS Conference on Computers and Accessibility, Bellevue, Washington, pp. 1–2 (2013)
29. Manshad, M.S., Pontelli, E., Manshad, S.J.: MICOO (multimodal interactive cubes for object orientation): a tangible user interface for the blind and visually impaired. In: The Proceedings of the 13th International ACM SIGACCESS Conference on Computers and Accessibility, Dundee, Scotland, UK (2011)

30. Karshmer, A.: AutOMathic Blocks: The Next Step. In: Business Analytics and Information Systems (2008)
31. Mayo, M.J.: Games for science and engineering education. Commun. ACM 50, 30–35 (2007)
32. Horn, M.S., Jacob, R.J.K.: Tangible programming in the classroom: a practical approach. In: CHI 2006 Extended Abstracts on Human Factors in Computing Systems, Montreal, Quebec, Canada, pp. 869–874 (2006)
33. Zuckerman, O., Gal-Oz, A.: To TUI or not to TUI: Evaluating performance and preference in tangible vs. graphical user interfaces. International Journal of Human-Computer Studies 71, 803–820 (2013)

Fostering Better Deaf/Hearing Communication through a Novel Mobile App for Fingerspelling

Jorge Andres Toro[1], John C. McDonald[2], and Rosalee Wolfe[2]

[1] Integrated Computer Solutions, Bedford, MA USA
jtoro@ics.com
[2] School of Computing, DePaul University, Chicago, IL USA
{jmcdonald,wolfe}@cs.depaul.edu

Abstract. Fingerspelling is a critical communication of sign language used not only by deaf children but also by parents, teachers and interpreters who support them. The recognition of fingerspelling is particularly difficult for sign language learners and support software for practice is particularly limited due to the fluid and natural way that signers will spell with their hands. Any software tool that helps people practice reading fingerspelling must be natural enough to represent the fluidity of this motion while at the same time being flexible enough to spell any list of words in the target language in any order.

To address these needs, this paper introduces a novel mobile app called "Fingerspelling Tutor" that produces natural full-motion fingerspelling using a realistic 3D computer animated character. The app can fingerspell any word that the user types in and can provide practice and quizzing opportunities for the user that are not limited to a fixed set of word lists. The software also allows users to post on social media sites to share their progress with fellow students.

1 Application Need

Fingerspelling is a method of signing letters of an alphabet that is used in deaf education and often serves as a bridge between signed and spoken languages. In the United States, fingerspelling is used for proper nouns and for technical terminology for which there is no generally accepted sign. [1]

Fingerspelling recognition is a critical communication skill not just for deaf children, but also for hearing parents, teachers of deaf children and for interpreting students. Deaf children face enormous barriers to education and opportunities, due in large part to difficulties in learning to read. For example, in the United States, deaf students have great difficulty in acquiring English. The average reading skill of deaf high school graduates is at or below the fourth-grade level, which precludes college [2]. To address this problem, many deaf education programs are introducing American Sign Language (ASL) and/or signed communication systems based on English such as Signed English (SE), Signing Exact English (SEE) and Pidgin Signed English (PSE). For all of these, fingerspelling plays an essential role in communication [3]. Studies have shown that increased contact with fingerspelling has a significant positive impact on a deaf child's reading ability [4].

K. Miesenberger et al. (Eds.): ICCHP 2014, Part II, LNCS 8548, pp. 559–564, 2014.

Regardless of the sign language or communication system used, teachers, interpreters and parents, who foster and serve deaf children need to be fluent in fingerspelling, but fluency in fingerspelling is a rare commodity. Many teachers of deaf children are not skilled in fingerspelling, and have to rely on an interpreter for this critical skill [5]. This is often not possible due to the scarcity of qualified educational interpreters [6]. In addition, over 90% of deaf children have two hearing parents [7]. Hearing parents do not have the same means of communication with their deaf children as they do with their hearing children, and must face the challenges of learning a second language.

Unfortunately, fingerspelling is a difficult skill to acquire. In interpreter training programs, it is the first skill taught, but the last skill mastered [8]. This problem is common to all adult learners. Particularly difficult is fingerspelling *recognition*, which involves viewing a person who is fingerspelling and reading the words being spelled.

There are several barriers to fingerspelling fluency. First, fingerspelling is rarely, if ever, perfectly produced [9]. Handshapes corresponding to the letters are heavily influenced by the letters preceding and succeeding them. Second, finger-spelling is not a series of static forms, but a continuous motion where the fingers move constantly, and do not stop after forming each handshape. During finger-spelling, the hand is rarely in a canonical letter form. As Wilcox [9] observes, "If students are trying to perceive unambiguous handshapes – the forms they were probably taught in class – then there is little wonder why they find fingerspelling so difficult. They are looking for something that isn't there".

Other barriers include limited practice opportunities, and lack of materials for self-study. A common suggestion in ASL classes is to practice with a partner [10]. Due to demanding schedules, this is not always possible. Self-study is also difficult due to the lack of supporting media. For learning spoken languages, there are a vast number of free and commercial interactive programs that are available for laptops and mobile devices. This is not the case for fingerspelling.

2 The State of the Art

There are three main alternative technologies for fingerspelling practice, each with its merits. The earliest electronic resources were video recordings which appeared in the 1980s. The 1990s saw the appearance of CDs and DVDs designed for finger-spelling practice [11]. In all of these media, the fingerspelled words were fixed. It was not possible to create / study new words, as this would require more video recordings at an added cost. Since the videos were recorded at low frame rates, motion blur was also a problem, as was lack of variation in the presentation order. As a student viewed the recording repeatedly, it was not clear if the student was improving their recognition skills or merely memorizing the recording.

The rise of the Internet paved the way for several web sites such as [12] that offer fingerspelling practice. On these sites, students can view a word as a succession of snapshots, each showing a single letter. Once the spelling is complete, students can guess the word and receive feedback. The advantage of these sites is their flexibility. A site can spell any word by simply shuffling the snapshots of the letters and can produce new words without incurring costs for additional recordings. However, there is a drawback due to the static nature of the snapshots. Per Wilcox, most of fingers-pelling is comprised of the motion between the letters, not the letters themselves. There is no connective movement in these practice tools.

3D animation is a promising alternative that has the flexibility to shuffle letters to create new words, as well as having the potential for producing the natural transitions between letters, as Wilcox describes. These are the same transitions that occur when a human fingerspells a word. With 3D animation, it is also easy to display finger-spelling without motion blur.

Despite the enormous potential of 3D animation, there are significant challenges to adapting it for fingerspelling. Similar to the requirements for a 3D character in an animated movie, the 3D hand model for fingerspelling must closely resemble a human hand, including a simulation of the behavior of the hand's soft tissue, especially in the webbing between the thumb and palm. The joints of the 3D hand must mimic the articulation of human joints, of which the base of the thumb is particularly problematic [13].

This is where the similarity between animating movie characters and animating fingerspelling ends. In a movie, the motion of a character is created once and is then frozen for all time. Animation for fingerspelling must be flexible enough to accommodate the spelling of any word while maintaining natural motion. The lack of physicality in 3D animation complicates the situation. Unless prevented, the fingers will pass through each other when transitioning between closed handshapes such as in the letters M, N, T, S and A in ASL. This requires a system to prevent finger collisions.

These complexities entail large computational requirements, and require significant CPU/GPU power to render the animation in real time. For this reason, previous efforts have either sacrificed realism to gain real-time speeds by using a simplified 3D model that did not accurately portray a human hand and/or did not prevent collisions [14], [15]. Other systems sacrificed real-time responsiveness to maintain the realism of the model [16].

3 Methodology Used

Our goal was a real-time display that would not severely impact computing resources but would preserve the realism of 3D animation. We achieved this by *pre-rendering* the animation and carefully organizing the renderings as a series of small video clips that each contained a single letter-to-letter transition. Since each clip had a transition between only two letters, the problem of collisions became more tractable. This technique creates any word by combining clips to display the fingerspelled word in real time. We have used this technology in a fingerspelling recognition drill and practice application called "Fingerspelling Tutor", which provides self-study opportunities for improving fingerspelling recognition skills. Users can type any word and see it fingerspelled, or they can quiz themselves. The software tracks user performance, including average fingerspelling speed (letters per second) and recognition accuracy (number of correct responses).

As a desktop application, this software has been in used in interpreter training programs, deaf education programs and for parent support both locally and nationally

[17]. A previous study [18] revealed that the software is easy to use and the avatar's appearance is appealing. Additional feedback from this study indicated a desire for a mobile version of Fingerspelling Tutor that would run on tablets and smart phones.

4 Results

To address this need we have built a completely new version of the software. Figure 1 shows two screen shots from the mobile app. It has adds enhancements to the original desktop software including improved natural motion and a more lifelike avatar.

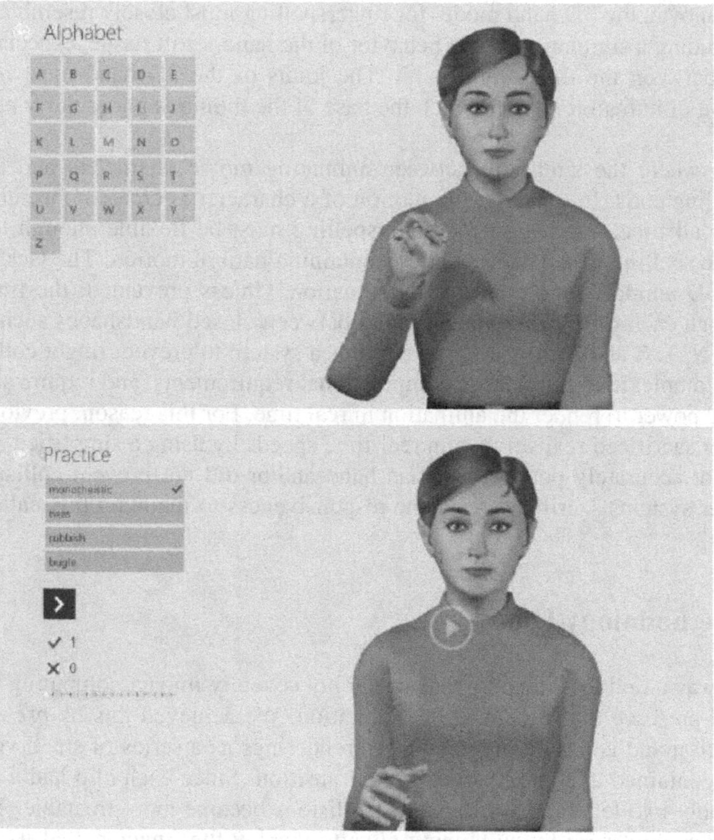

Fig. 1. Screen shots from new mobile Fingerspelling Tutor

Once downloaded, the mobile app can be used without additional Internet resources. However, it will also allow users to share their progress on one of several social media sites, adding a social element to the overall experience and introducing a new layer of engagement with the app.

5 Impact

The introduction of this new mobile app provides practice opportunities to foster a skill that is in great need, where previously no such opportunity existed. Students, teachers and parents are no longer constrained to a desktop for fingerspelling recognition practice. With the mobile app, they can now practice anywhere or at any time.

As more parents and teachers become skilled in fingerspelling, they will be better able to communicate with deaf children. This will in turn give deaf children more language contact which fosters improved literacy skills and better access to higher education, jobs, and social services.

6 Conclusion and Future Work

Our goal is to deploy this app in education programs where the desktop software was used previously and to conduct a study of user preferences and usage. Based on the feedback from this study, we plan to make any necessary changes to the app and freely distribute it to the general public. In addition, we plan to expand the app be-yond ASL. In every country, the national signed language has its own unique fingerspelling system, and people who are learning their country's signed language would benefit from a resource for fingerspelling practice.

References

1. Battison, R.M.: Lexical Borrowing in American Sign Language. Linstok Press, Silver Spring (1978)
2. Gallaudet Research Institute: Stanford Achievement Test, 9th edn., Form S, Norms booklet. Gallaudet University, Washington DC, USA (1996)
3. Strong, M. (ed.): Language Learning and Deafness. Cambridge University Press, Cambridge (1988)
4. Ramsey, C., Padden, C.: Natives and Newcomers: Gaining Access to Literacy in a Classroom for Deaf Children. Anthropology & Education Quarterly 29(1), 5–24 (1998)
5. Jones, T., Ewing, K.: An analysis of teacher preparation in deaf education: Programs approved by the Council on Education of the Deaf. American Annals of the Deaf 147(5), 71–78 (2002)
6. Schick, B., Williams, K., Kupermintz, H.: Look Who's Being Left Behind: Educational Interpreters and Access to Education for Deaf and Hard-of-Hearing Students. Journal of Deaf Studies and Deaf Education 11(1), 3–20 (2006)
7. Meyers, J.E., Bartee, J.W.: Improvements in the Signing Skills of Hearing Parents of Deaf Children. American Annals of the Deaf 137, 257–260 (1992)
8. Grushkin, D.A.: Lexidactylophobia: The irrational fear of fingerspelling. American Annals of the Deaf 143, 404–415 (1998)
9. Wilcox, S.: The Phonetics of Fingerspelling. John Benjamins Publishing, Amsterdam (1992)
10. Smith, C., Lentz, E., Mikos, K.: Signing Naturally - Student Workbook Level 1. Dawn Sign Press, San Diego (1988)

11. Jaklic, A., Vodopivec, D., Komac, V.: Learning sign language through multimedia. In: Proceedings of the International Conference on Multimedia Computing and Systems 1995, pp. 282–285. IEEE, Washington DC (1995)
12. Vicars, B.: Dr. Bill Vicars' American Sign Language (ASL) Fingerspelling Practice Site, http://asl.ms
13. McDonald, J., Alkoby, K., Carter, R., Christopher, J., Davidson, M., Ethridge, D., Wolfe, R.: An improved articulated model of the human hand. The Visual Computer 17(3), 158–166 (2001)
14. Su, A.: VRML-based Representations of ASL fingerspelling on the World-Wide Web. In: Third International ACM SIGCAPH Conference on Assistive Technologies, http://www.csdl.tamu.edu/~su/publications/assets98_.html
15. Dickson, S.: Advanced Animation in Mathematica. The Mathematica Journal 15(2) (2013), doi:dx.doi.org/doi:10.3888/tmj.15-2
16. Adamo-Villani, N., Beni, G.: Automated finger spelling by highly realistic 3D animation. British Journal of Educational Technology 35(3), 345–362 (2004)
17. Jamrozik, D.G., Davidson, M.J., McDonald, J.C., Wolfe, R.: Teaching Students to Decipher Fingerspelling through Context: A New Pedagogical Approach. In: Roberson, L., Shaw, S. (eds.) Putting the Pieces Together: A Collaborative Approach to Educational Excellence - Proceedings of the 17th National Convention of Interpreter Trainers, San Antonio, USA, pp. 35–47 (2010)
18. Jamrozik, D.G., Wolfe, R.: Using Contextual Cues in Deciphering Fingerspelling: New Discoveries and Techniques. Deaf Studies Today! Orem, Utah, USA (2009)

Developing a New Framework for Evaluating Arabic Dyslexia Training Tools

Fadwa AlRowais, Mike Wald, and Gary Wills

School of Electronics and Computer Science, University of Southampton, Southampton, UK
{fmar1v10,mw,gbw}@ecs.soton.ac.uk

Abstract. Compared to numerous studies in dyslexia, there is still a paucity of research exploring dyslexia in Arabic and especially the issues that arise in deciding the success or failure of Arabic dyslexia training tools. The present research attempts to address this gap by developing an Arabic Framework for Dyslexia Training Tools (AFDTT) that can be utilized to support the design and guide the evaluation of such training tools. This paper demonstrates the development, confirmation and refinement of the AFDTT. Drawing upon established theories and prior research findings, the initial version of the proposed framework has been developed. Confirmation and refinement involving feedback from content experts were carried out on the components of the proposed framework.

Keywords: Dyslexia, Arabic, Framework, Training Tool.

1 Relevant Research Literature

Technology can help facilitate the lives of individuals with dyslexia. The range of available technological resources for identifying, training and supporting individuals with dyslexia is steadily growing. However, in order to address the difficulties experienced by this group and achieve the objectives of these resources, all these resources should be based on clear standards and appropriate guidelines developed especially for this population.

Al-Wabil et al. [1] reported the results of a workshop that was conducted to check some published principles supporting accessibility of electronic content for readers with dyslexia and discover issues linked to Arabic script and not mentioned in the reviewed principles. In another study by Al-Wabil et al. [2] a set of guidelines was presented for supporting designing and guiding the evaluation of educational games for children with dyslexia. They synthesized Neilsen's guidelines for evaluating user interfaces [3] and the interactive guidelines toolkit for evaluating software for individuals with disabilities [4] with their experience obtained from a list of development software projects, including educational games for Arabic children with dyslexia.

A notable system called MyLexics was developed by Abdullah et al. [5]. This system is a courseware to support children with dyslexia in learning to read and write in the Malay language. It utilizes multimedia elements to provide interactive and independent learning that can be applied at school or at home. Deibel [6] proposed a computer-based

K. Miesenberger et al. (Eds.): ICCHP 2014, Part II, LNCS 8548, pp. 565–568, 2014.

accommodation project to address the diversity of needs, stigma risks and self-advocacy challenges that are faced by users with reading disabilities. Moreover, a useful study by Beacham [7] investigated how learners with dyslexia can improve their learning when it is based on computer materials. From this, a set of guidelines was created based on some attributes of learners with dyslexia to design "dyslexia friendly learning materials" [7, p.75]. A notable approach was proposed by Hazoury et al. [8] to teach Arabic decoding to students with dyslexia. They highlighted a set of instructional guidelines for teaching Arabic decoding for students with dyslexia resulting from their experience with different teaching techniques.

2 Development of the Arabic Framework for Dyslexia Training Tools

An extensive literature review in different fields helped in formulating significant theoretical findings in dyslexia. The findings from relevant studies were analyzed, synthesized and utilized in developing a set of ninety seven elements, taking into consideration features of the Arabic language and related cultural factors that account for the unique needs of Arabic individuals with dyslexia [9]. These elements are used as the theoretical foundation for the construction of the proposed AFDTT. The illustration of the ninety seven elements is provided at:

`http://eprints.soton.ac.uk/id/eprint/357183`

Sixteen new themes have been created to categorize the elements and to incorporate them within the framework. The themes have been allocated on the basis of having the same objectives for each group of elements and constitute the main components of the AFDTT. The established elements form the description for the components (themes) and could help achieve the objectives identified for each of them. Figure 1 shows the themes and how they were used to group the elements.

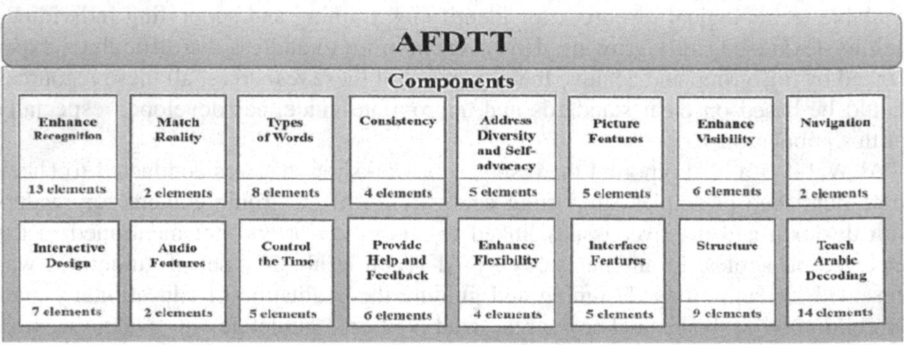

Fig. 1. The structure of the AFDTT

3 Confirmation and Refinement of the AFDTT

3.1 Methodology

Taking into consideration the objectives of this stage, it is clear that both quantitative and qualitative research methods are suitable options. This is because the developed AFDTT needs to be confirmed and refined and this can be done by conducting expert reviews with experts from different content domains and linking these interviews with a questionnaire. The questions were developed using the AFDTT as a guide and reference. They include ninety-seven closed ended questions that utilize a five-point Likert scale to measure the importance of each element in the AFDTT, and to serve as a quantitative research method. This can help to gain confirmation for the content of the AFDTT. In addition, some open ended questions were asked in the expert review, which can be used in a qualitative textual analysis. These open ended questions can help in gaining insight into the comprehensibility and clarification of the content of the AFDTT from expert experience and to find out the reasons behind their decisions regarding the importance of the elements. In addition, these types of questions can produce unanticipated responses which could help to discover new elements not covered by the set presented. The main phase of the survey involved nineteen experts who had completed the questionnaire and sixteen of those were interviewed with an average interview time from one to three hours for each interview. In order to analyze the resulting quantitative data, SPSS was used. QSR Nvivo was used to help in managing and analyzing the resulting qualitative data.

3.2 Results and Findings

The importance of all the elements in the proposed AFDTT, except three, was confirmed through the results and findings of this research including by the production of statistically significant results for all these elements. The findings also revealed a number of reasons for agreement with these elements. The results and the findings were consistent in considering three elements, from three different components; Interactive Design, Picture Features and Teach Arabic Decoding respectively, as unimportant. No statistically significant results were produced from these elements and neither did the findings identify any reason to keep them in the proposed AFDTT, so they were excluded. Further findings of this research provided significant reasons to exclude two other elements from the Teach Arabic Decoding component. Furthermore, thirty one elements in twelve components were improved, including two merging operations. Five new elements emerged from the findings and were incorporated into three different components. One element is added to the Picture Features component, related to avoiding segmentation in the picture. Two elements are constructed to support the Audio Features component, focusing on avoiding the merging of more than one sound at the same time and offering a control for the speed of the speech. Two elements are incorporated into the Provide Help and Feedback component, which support provision of balanced and encouraging feedback and avoiding negative feedback.

4 Conclusions and Future Work

The present research has attempted to address the gap in deciding what are the appropriate dyslexia training tools for Arabic speakers with dyslexia by developing an Arabic Framework for Dyslexia Training Tools (AFDTT). This paper reports of the development, confirmation and refinement of AFDTT. Following the analysis of the results and findings, from the ninety seven elements in the AFDTT, five were excluded, five new elements were added and two were merged with other elements. The final form of the AFDTT consists of sixteen components and ninety three elements. In the current stage, an instrument for applying the AFDTT was developed and an experiment for validating the developed instrument will be designed and conducted. The developed framework is expected to contribute to the development of Arabic teaching technology for individuals with dyslexia. It could be helpful in improving designers' knowledge of the needs of speakers with dyslexia. It could also be used to check the ability of the training tools to take into account the difficulties experienced by Arabic speakers with dyslexia which could prevent them from benefiting from these resources.

References

1. Al-Wabil, A., Zaphiris, P., Wilson, S.: Web Design for Dyslexics: Accessibility of Arabic Content. In: Miesenberger, K., Klaus, J., Zagler, W., Karshmer, A. (eds.) ICCHP 2006. LNCS, vol. 4061, pp. 817–822. Springer, Heidelberg (2006)
2. Al-Wabil, A., ElGibreen, H., Al-Suwaidan, A., Al-Salloom, R.: Heuristics for the Creation and Evaluation of Educational Game Software for Children with Dyslexia. In: International Conference on Information and Multimedia Technology (ICIMT). King Saud University Scientific Repository, Saudi Arabia (2010)
3. Nielsen, J., Molich, R.: Heuristic Evaluation of User Interfaces. In: Carrasco, J.C., Whiteside, J. (eds.) Proceedings ACM CHI 1990, pp. 249–256. ACM, New York (1990)
4. Sharp, H., Rogers, Y., Preece, J.: Interaction Design: Beyond HCI, 2nd edn. Wiley, UK (2007)
5. Abdullah, M., Hisham, S., Parumo, S.: MyLexics: An Assistive Courseware for Dyslexic Children to Learn Basic Malay Language. ACM SIGACCESS Newsletter 95, 3–9 (2009)
6. Deibel, K.: Understanding and Supporting the Use of Accommodating Technologies by Adult Learners with Reading Disabilities. ACM SIGACCESS Newsletter 86, 32–35 (2006)
7. Beacham, N.: Dyslexia-friendly Computer-based Learning Materials. In: Phipps, L., Sutherland, A., Seale, J. (eds.) Access All Areas: Disability, Technology and Learning, pp. 73–77. JISC TechDis Service and ALT, Oxford (2002)
8. Hazoury, K., Oweini, A., Bahous, R.: A Multisensory Approach to Teach Arabic Decoding to Students with Dyslexia. Learning Disabilities: A Contemporary Journal 7(1), 1–20 (2009)
9. AlRowais, F., Wald, M., Wills, G.: An Arabic Framework for Dyslexia Training Tools. In: 1st International Conference on Technology for Helping People with Special Needs (ICTHP), Riyadh, Saudi Arabia, pp. 63–68 (2013)

A Fully Accessible Arabic Learning Platform for Assisting Children with Intellectual Challenges

Moutaz Saleh and Jihad Mohamad Aljaam

Department of Computer Science & Engineering, Qatar University, Doha, Qatar
{moutaz.saleh,jaam}@qu.edu.qa

Abstract. Children with intellectual challenges (IC) are growing up with wide exposure to computer technology. Computer software and assistive devices have the potential to help these children in their education, career development, and independent living. In spite of the current spread of the use of computers in education in the Arab world, complete suites of solutions for children with IC are very scarce. This paper presents a fully accessible Arabic learning platform for assisting IC children in the State of Qatar. The platform provides four main components which are divided into learning management content, multimedia educational tutorials, edutainment games, and ontology-based learning with the aim of enhancing those children skills, understanding, communications, and memorization skills, while overcoming their obesity problems. The effectiveness of the proposed platform has been tested on IC children, and the results show clear advances on such children's learning capabilities and improved largely their performance.

Keywords: Intellectual Challenges, Learning, Assistive Technology, Accessibility, Multimedia Tutorials, Edutainment Games, Ontology.

1 Introduction

Increasing attention has recently been drawn in the Human-Computer Interaction (HCI) community towards the design and development of accessible computer applications for children with intellectual challenges (IC) [1]. Due to better healthcare and education, the quality of life for IC children has been obviously improved especially that these children grow up and live in the community while surrounded by computer applications and software. Compared to children with other types of developmental disabilities, children with IC can be considered fairly unique in that all three major types of capabilities: cognitive, motor, and perceptual are affected but the disability often is mild. Therefore, those children are requiring special computer solutions design to constantly adapt to the their evolving needs. Despite the potential benefit of the usage of assistive computer technology for individuals with IC and the potential that this technology may provide for them, there is a substantial need of baseline information on a number of topics, including the basic computer skills of people with IC, the objectives for using computers, and the difficulties they experience while

K. Miesenberger et al. (Eds.): ICCHP 2014, Part II, LNCS 8548, pp. 569–576, 2014.

using computers. Knowledge on these issues will help researchers and practitioners to form an accurate picture of this unique population, and understand how to help them to make better use of computer technology.

In this paper, we present an Arabic learning platform for assisting IC children with the aim of enhancing their understanding, communications, thinking, memorization skills, and obesity problems. Our proposed platform offers fully accessible learning management content, multimedia educational tutorials, edutainment games, and ontology-based learning components that would maximize the learning process through reducing the administrative and teaching overheads and effectively involving the IC children's parents. The remaining part of this paper is organized as follows: section 2 describes the related work, section 3 introduces the proposed platform services, section 4 presents the evaluation process and collected results, while section 6 concludes the paper and states the future works.

2 Related Work

Researchers in special education are to some extent informed of the potential of computer technology in helping individuals with IC [2]. The claim is that computer technology can help people with IC increase confidence and motivation through creative activities and web browsing. Computer technology also has other benefits, including errorless learning, patient feedback, immediate feedback, self-paced learning, and independence of learning. Though, Lloyd et al. [3] advised that the actual benefits of computer technology may be reduced or not even apparent depending on the quality of the software, examples are the contents of many software programs are not age appropriate, many educational software are unable to reach educational goals and are used as a tool for mere entertainment, and many applications do not promote independent learning.

It is important to examine how assistive technologies could help individuals with IC be more independent, yet remain connected to others and in touch with caregivers, to get assistance when needed. The empirical study conducted by Ortega-Tudela & Gomez-Ariza [4] examined the impact of an educational software program on learning mathematical counting skills. The authors suggested that children who used educational software benefit from the integration of auditory and visual information, personalized task sequences that help to address attention deficit and working memory limitations and the presentation of animated objects that helps overcome deficits in thinking. There have been many efforts in developing edutainment systems with tangible user interface (TUI) aimed at promoting both learning and physical activities for children with IC [5,6]. Such systems either interact with the computer as an input device or as both an input and an output device. Examples of this include Magic Stick [7], ActiveCube [8], Wii Balanced Board and Equilibrator [9]. All of these different types of tools were proposed to involve children into physical activity through edutainment games.

3 Proposed Platform

The main focus of this research paper is to propose a full accessible Arabic-based learning platform to enhance the learning capabilities, understanding, communications, thinking, memorization skills, and obesity problems of Qatari children with IC. Towards this aim, our proposed platform have following objectives:

- Objective-1: To build Arabic-based learning content management system for supporting and monitoring the learning process for the children with IC.
- Objective-2: To develop interactive educational multimedia contents that are linked to the required teaching objectives of children with IC.
- Objective-3: To design physical edutainment games for addressing the need of integrating physical activity into the daily lives of children with IC.
- Objective-4: To propose an Arabic ontology-based learning for online retrieval of multimedia contents that improves the understanding capabilities of children with IC.

The platform is implemented based on the above objectives. Following subsections describe each objective's activities.

3.1 Learning Management Control

The platform supports and monitors the learning process for the children with IC through automating the learning management procedures and involving the teacher, children, and parents in the learning process. As illustrated in Figure 1, four types of users are identified in this platform, those are the administrator, teacher, parent, and student. It is the responsibility of the administrator to manage all settings, user accounts, uploads educational contents plan objectives, and eventually links these contents with their corresponding personalized study plans. The learning process in the class is managed by the teacher who can control the educational contents to be viewed on the smart board as well as the student PC tablets.

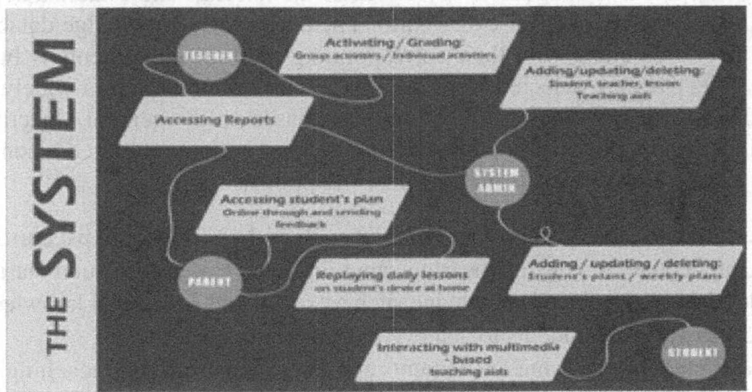

Fig. 1. Platform Users

The platform also effectively contributes in increasing the level of interaction between the parents and their children through: 1) sending periodic short SMS and emails about the children's progress. 2) accessing the paltform to post feedbacks about the children personalized study plan. 3) following up with the children's daily classes since the class materials are daily installed on the children's tablet. 4) reviewing children's daily reports and contact teachers for any inquiries. Of course, student is the main user of the platform who can smoothly interact with the educational multimedia contents available on both class smart board and PC tablet.

During the class, the platform can be used in two ways: First, group activities in which the platform will use a smart board to view contents, i.e. lessons, puzzles, quizzes, etc. The children will then interact with these contents by simply touching the smart board. Second, individual activities where each child in the class has her/his own PC tablet. The teacher controls the class by distributing different multimedia contents to the children's tablets according to their level of abilities and personalized study plan. Accordingly, the platform supports individual learning style as it treats each student independently according to his/her predefined personalized study plan and then monitor the performance individually. It also, accelerates the teaching process by having the parents follow up with their children's daily classes and reduces the administrative overhead on the teachers and save their time and effort in preparing assistive teaching tools.

3.2 Multimedia Tutorials

The platform provides several interactive educational multimedia contents which are designed on the basis of Mayer's cognitive theory of multimedia learning [10] and operant conditioning [11], and linked to the required teaching objectives of each child's personalized study plan. The platform provides dynamicity in offering such multimedia contents when considering children's level of abilities and speed of interaction. Designing multimedia tutorials for children with IC is not an easy task. In fact, children have different ways of understanding words and concepts even though they are classified to be of the same intellectual disability. Hence, our special education instructors set first the general objectives of the tutorials and establish accordingly a personalized study plan for every child. Then, a specific knowledge database that contains the words along with their corresponding multimedia contents is built. The tutorials' objectives are selected from the FACE curriculum which is widely used to teach children with IC. We develop the tutorials based on the general objectives, and we carefully design the scenarios by selecting the appropriate multimedia contents, as shown in Figure 2, with a focus on the following points:

- Inspired from the local Qatari environment such as dress, food, shops, currency.
- Suites intellectual, vision, and hearing capabilities such as color/sound clarity.
- Includes different types of knowledge such as social and functional knowledge.
- Interacts easily with students to achieve their learning objectives
- Motivates students by using excitements contents apart from rigid teaching.
- Varies in teaching styles i.e. multiple choices, match objects, and find similarities
- Features the ability to repeatedly updates, improves, and personalize contents.
- Organized logically i.e. from easy to difficult, and basic to advance.

Fig. 2. Examples of Developed Multimedia Contents

To achieve high quality, every lesson is reviewed iteratively by two special education instructors who work closely with the graphic designer and the multimedia developer. Once the final design is approved, we add the corresponding voices using the standard Arabic language. Final tutorials are stored in a specific database and can be used incrementally according to children's performances.

3.3 Physical Edutainment Games

The platform offers an edutainment tool with tangible user interface (TUI) aimed at promoting both learning and physical activities for children with IC. This tool, as depicted in Figure 3, is a padding system that consists of a custom number of tiles that are used to interact with a number of software games specially designed to suit the mental need of children IC. Three games that focus on enhancing the children understanding and widen their knowledge have been developed so far.

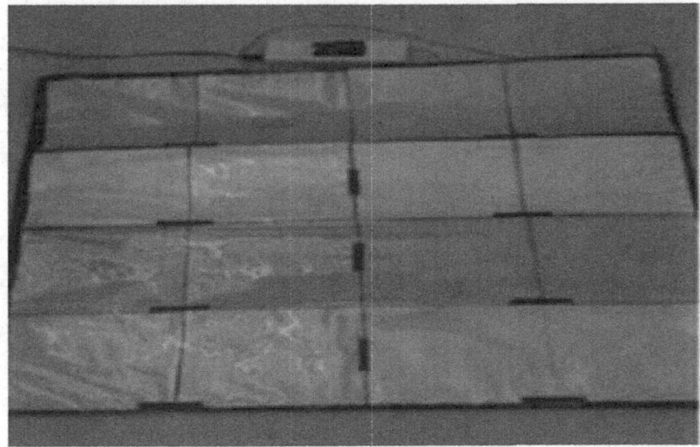

Fig. 3. Proposed Edutainment Gaming System

The games have different difficulty levels that can be customized whenever needed to suit every child in the classroom. The first game targets the children with IC who have some difficulties to identify or recognize objects or numbers. The game is called the "Twin Match", where children have to identify a set of four twin images displayed on the screen. The second game is called "Memory Game", it requires children to remember the location of matching pairs of pictures among set of images from different categories. The third game is the "Math Game", and aims at enhancing the basic arithmetic skills (i.e., add, subtract, organize numbers, etc.) of the children with IC while playing on the mat. Hence, our proposed TUI games not only does help in improving children's cognitive development and skills, but also involves them into physical activities, therefore offering both mental and healthy benefits through promoting children's learning process and overcoming their obesity problems respectively.

3.4 Ontology-Based Learning

The platform features the option of generating the multimedia educational tutorials dynamically. To do so, we adopt the model shown in Figure 4 which consist of: Arabic text processing tool for knowledge extraction (i.e., actors, action, event, location), semantic ontology to retrieve the associated multimedia elements, corpus design provides the functionality of getting most used terms with their corresponding multimedia, and web search engines to offer services for getting additional contents. The instructor can send to the platform the educational text and get the corresponding multimedia tutorials. Also, he/she can customize the tutorials based on the specific needs of each child in the classroom. The dynamic tutorials would become more time efficient due to the automated machine learning process. Therefore, the platform will statistically learn the preferred customization per student and will generate automatically the customized tutorials. This would efficiently result in enhancing the learning capabilities, understanding and communication skills for such children.

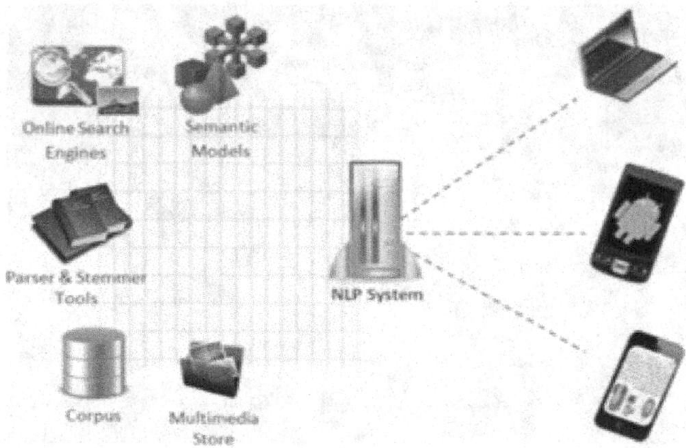

Fig. 4. Ontology-based Learning Model

4 Evaluation and Results

The evaluation process for children with IC takes different aspects compared to those for normal children due to the limited capabilities of the first group. Here, we tested the proposed learning platform on a set of children with IC, with different cognitive disabilities at Qatari Shafallah Center for Children with Special Needs [12]. We consider two main assessment types: individual and curriculum-based. In individual assessment, children performance is monitored independently and differently according to their disability. This tend to help us in determining children weaknesses points and how it is related to their disabilities towards designing their most effective educational contents. In curriculum-based assessment, the children performance is continuously evaluated against a predefined group plan objectives and then collected results are used to make comparisons and update existing teaching methods if necessary. Additionally, to evaluate our edutainment games effectively we adopted three developmental studies which are the trend, coherent, and panel. In trend study, all children participating in the learning process, are surveyed and the collected data are analyzed towards improvement. In coherent study, the students' performance are monitored over specific duration and sampled every 3-4 weeks for analysis of progress and feedback. In panel study, two identical groups of students are followed up through specific period, and their progress is then carefully evaluated.

Figure 5.a shows a chart for five sessions indicating the means and standard deviations for the time required for the children to complete a game. We can conclude that the skills of the children improved with time, and thus predicts a likely opportunity for cognitive enhancement over the long term, provided that the game is practiced regularly. Similarly, Figure 5.b shows that the children effective participation has increased dramatically with the time because they have enjoyed playing and they start to feel more comfortable and confident with learning-pads. Finally, Figure 5.c illustrates the motivation levels with the multimedia lessons for all tested children. We can conclude that children with DS and ID performed equally good with the multimedia lessons, with an average score of 70%. On the other hand, females outperformed the males which indicates motivation levels and effectiveness of the multimedia lessons are higher for females in general.

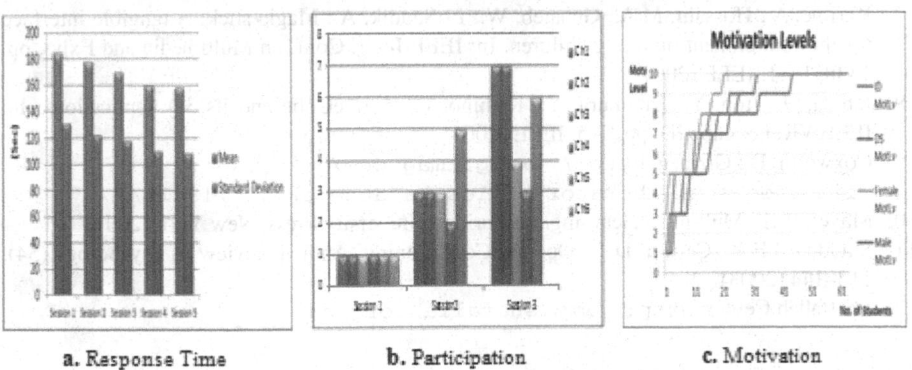

a. Response Time **b.** Participation **c.** Motivation

Fig. 5. Performance Measures used for Platform Evaluation

5 Conclusions

This paper presents a complete accessible Arabic learning platform for assisting Qatari children with IC. The platform provides learning management content, multimedia educational tutorials, edutainment games, and ontology-based learning with the aim of enhancing those children learning capabilities, understanding, communications, thinking, memorization skills, and obesity problems. The effectiveness of the proposed platform has been extensively evaluated, and the collected results showed important improvements on such children's capabilities, while reducing the administrative and teaching overhead and involving the children's parents in the learning process. As future work, more performance studies and analysis will be conducted.

Acknowledgment. This publication was made possible by a grant from the Qatar National Research Fund under its award NPRP 09-052-5-003. Its contents are solely the responsibility of the authors and do not necessarily represent the official views of the Qatar National Research Fund.

References

1. Dawe, M.: Desperately seeking simplicity: How young adults with cognitive disabilities and their families adopt assistive technologies. In: Proceedings of the ACM Conference on Human Factors in Computing Systems (CHI), pp. 1143–1152. ACM (2006)
2. Black, B., Wood, A.: Utilising information communication technology to assist the education of individuals with Down syndrome, Portmouth, UK (2003)
3. Lloyd, J., Moni, K., Jobling, A.: Breaking the hype cycle: Using the computer effectively with learners with intellectual disabilities. Down Synd. Res., 68–74 (2006)
4. Ortega-Tudela, J.M., Gomez-Ariza, C.J.: Computer assisted teaching and mathematical learning in Down syndrome children. Comput. Math. Down Synd. 22, 298–307 (2006)
5. Richardson, B., Leydon, K., Fernström, M., Paradiso, J.A.: Z-Tiles: Building Blocks for Modular, Pressure-Sensing Floorspaces. In: Proceedings of CHI, pp. 1529–1532. ACM (2004)
6. Lund, H.H., Klitbo, T., Jessen, C.: Playware technology for physically activating play. Artificial Life and Robotics 9(4), 165–174 (2005)
7. Karime, A., Hossain, M.A., Gueaieb, W., El Saddik, A.: Magic stick: A tangible interface for the edutainment of young children. In: IEEE Inter. Conf. on Multimedia and Expo, pp. 1338–1341. IEEE (2009)
8. Ichida, H., Itoh, Y., Kitamura, Y., Kishino, F.: ActiveCube and its 3D applications. In: IEEE VR, no. cube ID, pp. 2–5. IEEE (2004)
9. Coxworth, B.: Gizmag, http://www.gizmag.com/wii-based-equiliberator-builds-balance-skills/18414/
10. Mayer, R.E.: Multimedia learning. Cambridge University Press, New York (2001)
11. Staddon, J.E.R., Cerutti, D.T.: Operant Conditioning. Annual Review of Psychology (54), 115–144 (2003)
12. Shaffallah Center: http://www.shafallah.org.qa

Using Mobile Technologies to Support Individuals with Special Needs in Educational Environments

Introduction to the Special Thematic Session

Linda Chmiliar

Athabasca University, Athabasca, Canada
lindac@athabascau.ca

Abstract. The use of mobile devices is on the increase worldwide, and mobile technologies are opening up opportunities for individuals with special needs to easily access supports, information, services, and education. Mobile technologies can provide benefits to individuals with special needs including: increased productivity, improved safety, learning activities, reduced isolation, access to interfaces for communication, text to speech functionality, scanning, voice or video prompting, and so on. This paper provides a brief introduction to a series of papers that explore a number of ways that mobile technologies can benefit individuals with special needs in educational environments across a range of ages from preschool to adult.

Keywords: mobile technology, special needs, education.

1 Introduction

The use of mobile devices is on the increase worldwide, and mobile technologies are opening up opportunities for individuals with special needs to access supports, information, services, and education. Mobile technologies can provide benefits to individuals with special needs including: increased productivity, improved safety, reduced isolation, access to interfaces for communication, text to speech functionality, scanning, voice or video prompting and so on. This paper provides a brief introduction to a series of papers, that explore a number of ways that mobile technologies can benefit individuals with special needs in educational environments across a range of ages from preschool to adult.

2 Background

Mobile devices such as smartphones, e-book readers, and tablets have changed the world of technology in ways that we could not have imagined. Due to the availability of these devices and their affordability, the use of mobile devices has exploded worldwide. These devices are portable and convenient, and are more cost effective than laptops, desktop computers, or traditional assistive technologies. These devices

K. Miesenberger et al. (Eds.): ICCHP 2014, Part II, LNCS 8548, pp. 577–578, 2014.

provide access to a variety of tools such as accessibility options, productivity tools like word prediction, texting, voice recognition, apps for learning, text-to-speech, multimedia capabilities, and much more. Applications loaded onto these devices can help individuals to find, use, and produce content.

Mobile device use has been readily adopted into education and special education environments. These devices can help to address the unique needs of individuals with varying abilities and needs. A number of mobile devices can act as personal computing devices that can be customized through access to a variety of apps, built-in accessibility features, and accessories. Several factors have drawn educators and other professionals who work with individuals who have special needs to mobile devices. Mobile devices are typically more cost effective than traditional assistive technologies. These devices are lightweight and portable making it easier to have access and supports with you all of the time. Many mobile devices have touchscreen interfaces that are intuitive and easy to learn. This makes it easy for individuals with special needs to learn how to use the device. Mobile devices typically have a long battery life, which means that individuals relying on the devices for communication or other essential activities can count on access to their device throughout the day. In addition, these devices have enjoys a high degree of social acceptability with most individuals with special needs no matter what their age. For individuals with special needs, this means that they are using the same technologies as their peers. This is such an important factor that has a significant impact device use.

Mobile technologies offer significant opportunities to help enable individuals with special needs to participate more fully in educational environments. Unfortunately, at this point in time technology development is moving at a faster pace than the research publication cycle, and as such, research on the supports the mobile devices can provide individuals with special needs is just emerging. The following papers report on a range of research that provides some insight at to the possibilities of mobile device use by individuals with special needs.

Learning with the iPad in Early Childhood

Linda Chmiliar

Athabasca University, Athabasca, Canada
lindac@athabascau.ca

Abstract. Young children typically learn skills and knowledge through play and the exploration of their environment. In the last few years, many preschool children have also had the experience of playing on their parent's smart phone and/or tablet. Although, there is some research that indicates that exploration that includes the use of digital technologies can support the development of preschool children, research looking specifically at learning with the iPad for preschool children is just beginning to emerge. The focus of this study was to look at the use of the iPad by preschool children with special needs over a 6 week period of time.

Keywords: Mobile Technology, Special Needs, Preschool, iPad.

1 Introduction

Young children typically learn through skills and knowledge through play activities and active exploration of their environment. In the last few years, many preschool children have also experienced play activities on their parent's smart phone and/or tablet. There is some research that indicates that play exploration that includes the use of digital technologies can support the development of preschool children, but research looking at learning with the iPad for preschool children is just beginning to emerge. The focus of this study was to look at the use of the iPad by preschool children with special needs over a 6 week period time. The study examined the applications the children chose to use, parent perceptions of the use of the iPad by the child, parent/child interactions while using the iPad, and the supports that the parents felt that they needed to use the iPad effectively with their children.

2 Background

The use of the digital technologies for learning with preschool children is an area that has received some attention in the literature. Wang et al [1] looked at the value of interactive games and educational software in early childhood education, and the computer has become a common place learning tool in the education of young children [2]. Roschell, Pea, Hodley, Godin, and Means [3] found that activities on the computer could be stimulating and motivating for young children, and instructional activities on the computer can result in improved skills [4]. In other studies, Johnson, Perry, and Shamir [5] found that preschool and kindergarten children demonstrated

K. Miesenberger et al. (Eds.): ICCHP 2014, Part II, LNCS 8548, pp. 579–582, 2014.

many positive skills changes as the result of computer-assisted instruction, and Li and Atkins [6] reported an association between early computer use and the development of concepts and cognition during the preschool years.

Digital technologies may also be very helpful for preschool children with special needs. Digital activities may provide stimulating activities that interest and motivate children with special needs. They may also support active exploration for young children who might be less able to explore or learning in typical ways because of their disability [7].

Although the research identified above demonstrates that computer assisted instruction can be beneficial for young children, research on the use of the iPad with preschoolers is just beginning to appear. The iPad offers the ability to explore and play in a new way. With its simple touch screen with multi touch finger gesture controls, engaging multimedia capabilities, access to thousands of early learning applications, and reasonable cost, the iPad has great potential as an early learning digital tool. However, little information exists on how this digital tool can be utilized effectively with preschool children with special needs. The focus of this exploratory study was on the use of iPads by preschool children with a range of mild to severe special needs.

3 Methodology

This research project explored the use of iPads by 6 preschool children with special needs over a 6 week period of time. The children demonstrated a range of special needs including: speech and language delays, attention difficulties, poor social skills, fine and gross motor problems, and so on. All the children were enrolled in a community based preschool program that provided educational support in a rural community.

The children received an iPad loaded with a range of early learning applications to play with for 6 weeks. The applications included apps for early math and counting, pre-reading, tracing, learning early concepts, printing, puzzles, coloring, and so on. Prior to beginning the study, a parent of each child was interviewed to determine the current skill level of the child and the child's previous experiences with technology. Each child was provided with an introduction to the iPad to ensure that they were able to figure out how to navigate the device. Several apps were introduced that provided practice with the basic navigation skills of tapping, swiping, and drag and drop. Once the child could demonstrate the skills to a reasonable degree, the child was introduced to a number of apps on the iPad. The parents also received basic information on how to use the iPad if they were not already familiar with the device.

The data collection for this qualitative study primarily included: a pre and post interview with a parent, a journal kept by the parents of the iPad of the apps used by the child, and observations of the child using the iPad at the beginning of, and at the conclusion of the research.

4 Results

At the beginning of this study, none of the children had difficulties learning how to navigate the iPad and use the apps provided. Most of the children picked up on how to tap the screen quite quickly and were able to use the tool within about 20 minutes. Two of the children needed more support and had not quite figured out how to use the iPad without prompting by the end of the first 20 minute session. The parents of these children indicated that they needed an additional 2 o 3 practice sessions to become fully independent. Throughout the remainder of the 6 weeks, the parents indicated that the children used the iPad completely independently, finding and using the apps that they wanted to play with.

Throughout the six weeks of the study the majority of the children participating found the early learning apps on the iPad to be engaging and entertaining. The parents reported that the children were engaged in learning activities for extended periods of time and often practiced skills over and over. Even skills such as tracing and coloring, that many of the children did not normally like to do, seemed to capture the children's interest. All of the children involved in the study evidenced some learning gains throughout the six weeks in 1 or more areas. The majority of the children learned to print their name. Several of the children learned to print a number of letters of the alphabet and were even printing the letters on paper. One little boy had progressed to doing complex puzzles on the iPad. Several parents also reported that they thought that their child's language skills had improved during the 6 week time period. They were able to give examples of words that their child was now using and saying correctly that were directly related to an app that the child was very interested in.

A few issues arose during the course of the study. Some of the children wanted to play on the iPad more than the parents wanted them to. A number of parents indicated that they had to monitor the use of the iPad. One parent indicated that she just let the child play on the iPad because it was better than television in her mind. There were also a couple of children that were not that interested in using the iPad, preferring instead more active play or access to other technologies.

5 Conclusion

Overall, the results of this initial exploratory study of preschool children and the iPad are quite positive. All of the children, regardless of their special needs, learned how to use this device very quickly. The majority of the children learned how to tap and navigate within 15-20 minutes. Throughout the 6 weeks of the study, these children were also able to use this device independently to learn. This result indicates quite a departure from the use of computer assisted learning where children often experienced difficulties learning how to use the technology and required continual supervision to use the technology successfully. This technology provides preschool children with special needs an opportunity to engage in independent play and learning.

All of the parents indicated that their child demonstrated learning gains during the six week period that they attributed directly to specific apps on the iPad. Some of the parents indicated that the skills that their child practiced and learned were skills they had worked on for some time with not success. So why were so many learning gains evidenced during the 6 weeks. Several explanations come to mind. First, the students were interested and motivated to play games on the iPad. They were paying attention to what was happening on the screen and were highly motivated to "win" the game or "earn" a reinforcement. Second, the games provided an environment rich in verbal, visual, and tactile feedback that is very attractive to young children. Finally, the children were motivated to practice skills over and over again because they were fun and reinforcing.

This exploratory study is the first of a number of studies that will be conducted that will look at the use of the iPad with preschool children with special needs. Due to the very limited scope of the study, and the small number of preschool children participating in the study, it is a bit early to make any earth shattering conclusion regarding the use of tool to support preschool students with special needs. However, very positive results were reported by the parents indicating that this device may be an excellent early learning tool. Further research in this area is imperative.

References

1. Wang, F., Kinzie, M., McGuire, P., Pan, E.: Applying Technology to Inquiry-based Learning in Early Childhood Education. Early Childhood Education Journal 37, 381–389 (2009)
2. Nikolopoulou, K.: Early Childhood Educational Software: Specific Features and Issues of Localization. Early Childhood Educational Journal 35, 173–179 (2007)
3. Roschelle, J., Pea, D., Hoadley, C., Gordin, D., Means, B.: Changing How and What Children Learn in School With Compute Based Technologies. Children and Computer Technology 10, 76–101 (2013)
4. Hitchcock, C., Noonan, M.: Computer-assisted Instruction of Early Academic Skills. Topics in Early Childhood Education 20, 159–173 (2000)
5. Johnson, E., Perry, J., Shamir, H.: Variability on Reading Ability Gains as a Function of Computer-Assisted Instruction Method of Presentation. Computers and Education 55, 209–217 (2010)
6. Li, X., Atkins, M.: Early Childhood Computer Experience and Cognitive and Motor Development. Pediatrics 113, 1715–1722 (2004)
7. Primavera, J., Wiedelight, P., DiGiacomo, T.: Technology Access for Low-Income Preschoolers: Bridging the Digital Divide. In: Proceedings of the American Psychological Association, pp. 1–26 (August 2001)

The Influence of Age and Device Orientation on the Performance of Touch Gestures

Linda Wulf[1], Markus Garschall[1,3], Michael Klein[1], and Manfred Tscheligi[2,3]

[1] CURE – Center for Usability Research & Engineering, Vienna, Austria
{wulf,garschall,klein}@cure.at
[2] ICT&S, University of Salzburg, Salzburg, Austria
manfred.tscheligi@sbg.ac.at
[3] AIT Austrian Institute of Technology GmbH, Vienna, Austria
{markus.garschall,manfred.tscheligi}@ait.ac.at

Abstract. Touch interaction has become a popular and widespread interaction technique. Recent studies indicate significant potential for touch interaction with regard to the integration of older adults into the world of ICT. We carried out a study with the goal of gaining deeper insight into performance differences between young and old users as well as the influence of tablet device orientation on performance. We implemented an application for the iPad that measures various performance characteristics when performing six gestural tasks—tap, drag, pinch, pinch-pan, rotate left and rotate right—for both portrait and landscape orientations. Results showed the importance of device orientation as an influencing factor on performance and indicate that age is not the exclusive influencing factor on touch interaction performance.

Keywords: Gesture, Tablet, Touchscreen, Aging, Age-Related Differences, Device Orientation, User Evaluation.

1 Introduction

Recently, touch interactions have been widely applied in public kiosk systems as well as current mobile and tablet devices. Being a direct and therefore more intuitive form of interaction compared to traditional point and click systems [13], touch interaction shows high potential for adoption by novice users in general, and specifically by older adults with little to no ICT experience [4], [10], [1]. Tablet applications in particular have the potential to reach older adults and minimize the digital divide because they meet with a high degree of acceptance [12].

Especially tablet applications have the potential to reach older adults and to minimize the digital divide because they meet with a high degree of acceptance [13]. This conclusion is supported by the growing number of senior specific services (e.g. drug intake reminders – MyMedSchedule[1] , cognitive training games –Lumosity[2] , health

[1] http://www.mymedschedule.com
[2] http://www.lumosity.com

K. Miesenberger et al. (Eds.): ICCHP 2014, Part II, LNCS 8548, pp. 583–590, 2014.

app – WebMD[3] or memory assistance – Park'n'forget[4]) that are mainly provided on touch devices.

However, designing touch interactions for older adults requires special attention and must take age-related changes - e.g. regarding fine motor control, finger size and joint flexibility - into account [7]. Current developments bring new possibilities for advanced gestures on tablet devices into the design space such as drag, pinch and rotate. The focus in this paper is set on the basic gestures that are currently applied in consumer electronic products (e.g. smartphones, tablets) for object manipulation by using one or two fingers.

Although many studies investigate older users specifically, there is a need for more studies that compare touch interactions of older adults and younger users. Additionally, there has been little prior research into the relationship between device orientation and touch interaction behavior.

We conducted a study that aims to aid the future design of interfaces and interactions for virtual object manipulation by comparing older and younger users' performance of six touch gestures under two devices orientations (portrait/landscape), as measured by task completion times, finger lift rates and missed target rates.

Our study is based on the work of Kobayashi et al. [5]. As their results indicate that a larger screen outperforms a smaller screen such as a smartphone, we focused our study on touch interactions on a tablet. We chose a 9.7-inch iPad in order to replicate the setup of Kobayashi et al. Furthermore, in addition to the four touch gestures of Kobayashi (tap, drag, pinch, pinch and panning) [5], we included two rotation gestures (left and right) as commonly found in mobile applications, such as Maps and iPhoto. By the virtue of this setup, we expected better insights about older adults performing complex touch gestures. Quantitative measurements for performance were task completion time and error rates. Data for both measurements were logged by the prototype while users executed object manipulation tasks that compared the six different basic touch gestures. Additionally, a post-interview queried user preferences for device orientation and for the gestures themselves.

Overall, our results indicate that young participants show faster completion times and lower error rates than older participants. Device orientation has no effect on completion time but shows an effect on error rates and furthermore an interaction effect of age and device orientation.

The following sections give an overview of related work, describe the study setup and prototype, illustrate results, discuss the findings and finally provide conclusions and an outlook on future work.

2 Related Work

Touch gestures are a promising focus of current research and industry. Compared to indirect input paradigms such as the mouse, touch inputs are up to twice as fast to perform, easier to interact with and seen as more preferred by most users [4]. Moreover, touch interactions are manageable not only by young but also by older adults [6].

[3] http://www.webmd.com

[4] http://parknforget.topapp.net

Recent studies that have focused on older adults' use of touch gestures indicate that they show a general positive attitude toward multi-touch interactions [1], [10]. Nevertheless, gestures designed for younger users might not be suitable for older ones [10]. Hourcade et al. [3] state that specific age-related limitations may result in decreased accuracy rates and increased movement times. Findlater et al. [2] state that touch interaction can decrease older adults' performance time and the error rates of younger and older users when compared with desktop and mouse interactions. Results from Stößel et al. [11] indicate no significant loss in accuracy but differences in the way older adults perform gestures. Older users are slower, are more likely to use symbolic gestures than gestures for direct manipulation, and are less likely to work with multiple fingers [9]. A similar result from Siek et al. [8] indicates that older and younger participants can physically interact at the same competence level when using PDA applications. However, older persons are more tolerant when it comes to gestures that are slightly more complex [9]. Further, Kobayashi et al. [5] evaluated four basic touch gestures. Results indicate that older users performed most gestures reasonably well. The limit of this study is that it lacks in comparison with younger users. Moreover, Kobayashi et al. [5] state that further studies should focus on the comparison of younger and older users in terms of addressing performance measures, interaction behaviors and preferences.

Our study intends to pick up where the work of Kobayashi et al. and others left off by comparing detailed performance measures from younger and older adults when carrying out six different gestures under two device orientations. Additionally, our inclusion of rotation and pinch-panning gestures, device orientation variations, and detailed error analysis differentiates our work from that of Findlater et al. [2].

3 Experimental Design

For the comparative evaluation a 6x2x2-design was chosen. Each participant executed six gestures with each device orientation (within-subject factors). Age was set as a between-subject factor. The dependent variables are task performance time, missed target rate and finger lift rate. A "missed target" refers to any detection of fingers outside of the target image object. A "finger lift" refers to any time a user lifted one or both fingers after having started a gesture but before completing the task. For instance, if a user needed three separate rotation gestures in order to fully complete a rotation task, the number of finger lifts would be counted as 2.

3.1 Participants

In total 40 participants were invited and divided into two age groups: older and younger participants. 20 younger (10 female, 10 male) between 25 and 45 years old (mn=33.9; sd=6.18) and 20 (11 female, 9 male) older adults between 65 and 85 years old (mn=71.85; sd=5.13) participated in the study. We deliberately omitted participants between 46 and 64 years in order to enhance differentiation of age-related effects. All participants were right-handed and had no self-reported restrictions of hands or fingers. In the younger user group half of the participants had previous experience with touch devices, while in the older user group 12 participants had no experience and 8 some experience.

3.2 Apparatus and Setup

A native iPad application, created using Xcode and taking advantage of the iOS 5 SDK's pre-defined gesture recognizers, was developed for the purpose of the comparative evaluation. The app was run on a 9.7-inch first-generation iPad, with a resolution of 1,024x768 pixels at a density of 132 pixels per inch.

Six gestural tasks were implemented—tap, drag, pinch, pinch with panning, rotate left and rotate right (see Fig. 1, device in portrait mode).

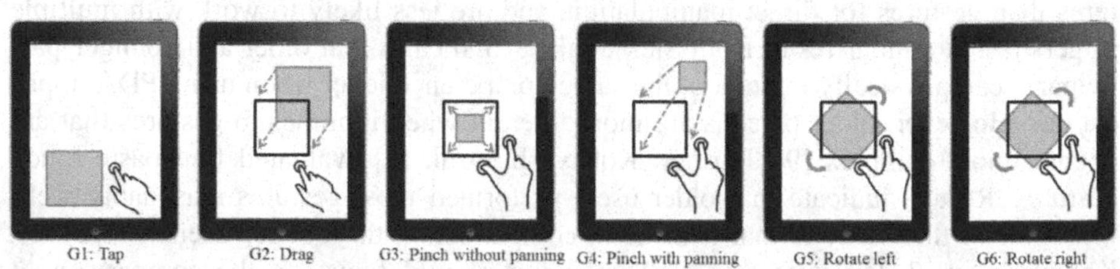

Fig. 1. Basic gestures for object manipulations

The tasks were based on those used by Kobayashi et al. [5], with the addition of the rotation gestures. Two additional gestures (rotate left, rotate right) were added since these gestures require a more complex performance. The following paragraph provides a short description of the six different gestures in focus:

A tap involves quickly placing a finger on a target and then removing it. A drag involves placing a finger on a target, moving it to a new position and then releasing it. A pinch involves placing two fingers within a target's boundaries and increasing or decreasing the space between the fingers in order to resize the target. Pinch with panning is similar to a pinch, except that parallel movement of both fingers can additionally be used to move an object. Rotate left involves placing two fingers within a target's boundaries and turning the two fingers in a counterclockwise direction, as one would turn a dial; rotate right functions similarly but with a clockwise turn.

For all gesture types other than rotation, images were positioned pseudo-randomly (to ensure even distribution) in one of 16 screen areas. For tapping tasks, the test subject had to simply tap the object, while for all other tasks the user had to adjust the position/size/rotation of the image so that its edges fit inside a border frame at the center of the screen which was 200x200px with 20-pixel-wide borders, so that the target size could range from 190x190px to 210x210px. Task repetitions used varying images, image sizes (120px, 180px, 240px, 300px or 360px) positions (16 possibilities) and rotations (30, 60, 90, 120 or 150 degrees); all variations were randomized in a balanced fashion.

Tasks could be performed in training mode, in which no logging was performed, or in timed trial mode, in which data such as initial image position/size/rotation, task com-pletion time, number of finger lifts and number of missed targets was logged. All error types were automatically logged from our prototype. Errors were measured per task, e.g. a task was counted as incomplete if at least one Target miss or Finger lift error occurred.

3.3 Hypotheses

In order to investigate the extent to which device orientation and age influence the performance of touch gestures the following hypotheses were formulated:

- H1: Younger and older users differ from each other in their task completion times, missed target rates and finger lift rates under both device orientations.
- H2: Device orientation has no influence on completion times, missed target rates or finger lift rates for younger or older users.

To compare performance differences of the one-handed single- and multi-touch gestures for the manipulation of objects, the study was divided into four steps: First the participants received the instruction for the study. They were asked to hold the tablet in a manner that was comfortable for them to hold, but not placing it flatly on the table. Secondly, in the training phase the gesture performance was demonstrated to them by the study supervisor. The participants were then asked to complete five training tasks for each gesture (without logging). Afterwards the evaluation phase started where the participants had to perform 16 tasks (with logging) for each of the 6 gestures. For each gesture trial the device orientation (portrait/landscape) was randomized. In the final step the participants were asked to provide feedback regarding their preference for device orientation and the various touch gestures.

4 Results

To test our hypotheses three mixed ANOVA were conducted with age as between-subjects factor, device orientation as within-subjects factor and task completion time, missed target rates and finger lift rates as dependent variables. Considering our hypotheses, this test has the highest statistical power. Table 1 provides an overview about main effects of age on performance measure.

Table 1. Results of the ANOVA - main effect of age on completion time and error rates

	Age (reported in means (Sd))		
Performance measures	**Young**	**Old**	*Sign.*
Completion time	1.684 (0.2089)	3.063 (0.208)	$p \leq 0.5$*
Missed target	3.506 (1.842)	16.887 (1.89)	$p \leq 0.5$*
Finger lift	27.951 (1.894)	42.048 (1.797)	$p \leq 0.5$*

Means reveal faster completion times and lower error rates of both types for younger users than for older users.

For the second hypothesis, the results showed that the effect of device orientation on completion time is not significant (p=.61). For rates of missed targets (see Fig. 2), the effect of device orientation is significant, $F(1.37) = 12.123$, $p < .05$, $\eta 2 = 0.247$. Means show higher values for portrait orientation (mn=11.521, se=1.52) than for landscape orientation (mn=8.872, se=1.208).

Further calculations showed a significant interaction between device orientation and age, F(1.37)= 16.444, p<.05, η2=0.308. Means reveal higher values for older participants for both device orientations ($mn_{portrait}$=19.754, $mn_{landscape}$=14.021) than for younger participants ($mn_{portrait}$=3.288, $mn_{landscap}$e=3.724).

For the finger lift condition (see Figure 2), the results also showed a significant effect of device orientation, F(1,36)=351.163, p<.05, η2=0.907, but with higher mean values for landscape orientation (mn=48.994, se=1.849) than for portrait orientation (mn=21.005, se=1.052).

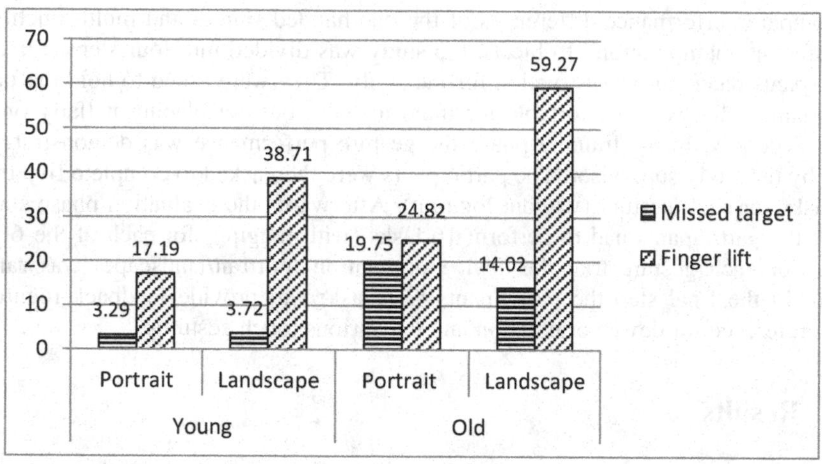

Fig. 2. Rates of Missed targets and Finger lifts

Results from the qualitative analysis partly align with the quantitative results. In particular, a clear preference for landscape format was found for both age groups ($portrait_{old}$= 11.1%, $landscape_{old}$= 62.5%; $portrait_{young}$= 25%, $landscape_{young}$= 40%). In terms of gesture preference, feedback from some older users indicated that performing rotation gestures was exhausting/uncomfortable (6/20), impractical (4/20) or inefficient (2/20). Consistent preferences between left or right rotation were not evident. Half of older users (10/20) had difficulty precisely positioning two fingers within the targets' edges in order to perform the pinch gesture. The tap and drag gestures were both perceived to be very easy and quick to perform (tap: 14/20, drag: 13/20), while pinch with panning was indicated to be "fun" due to its encouragement of dexterity (3/20). Overall, older participants seemed to be quite open to touch gestures, and they appreciated the novelty of device control that they offer.

5 Discussion

This study showed that device orientation is an important influencing factor on touch gesture performance. It can be concluded that chronological age is not an exclusive influencing factor on performance on touch devices. We found that the rates of missed targets and finger lifts are influenced by device orientation as well as by the interaction of age*device orientation.

Our most significant finding regarding device orientation was that landscape orientation resulted in more than twice the number of finger lifts than portrait orientation, across both age groups. Thus, portrait orientation seems to be the better approach for discrete touch gesture performance. The cause of this effect is unclear. One possibility is that it is easier to stabilize the iPad in a second hand in portrait orientation; this points to possibilities for future studies. Despite these performance results, the mentioned preferences in both age groups clearly tended toward landscape orientation. Further research is needed to discover the reasons for this discrepancy.

Younger participants clearly have an advantage regarding hitting the targets on the screen. Our results showed almost five times higher missed target rates for older compared to younger users. This stands in contrast to the findings of Stößel et al. [11]. This difference potentially stems from the different task assignments that the participants from both studies were confronted with, e.g. the lack of multi-touch gestures that points to the need for more research regarding the influence of different device or task characteristics on touch gesture performance.

In order to focus our study on a limited set of research questions, it was necessary to limit it in a number of ways. We focused only on iPad usage; it remains to be seen whether similar results would apply to other devices and form factors. The requirement for participants to hold the tablet in one hand and perform gestures with the other helped ensure the comparability of our results, but at the cost of excluding some modes of real-world tablet usage. Our exclusion of participants between the ages of 46 and 64, while allowing us to draw starker contrasts, prevents us from drawing conclusions about gradual age-related changes.

Future work should further investigate the influence of personal factors such as habits and physiological constraints, as well as device characteristics such as weight and screen size on touch gesture performance.

References

1. Czaja, S.J., Gregor, P., Hanson, V.L.: Introduction to the Special Issue on Aging and Information Technology. ACM Trans. Access. Comput. 2(1), Article 1, 4 pages (2009)
2. Findlater, L., Froehlich, J.E., Fattal, K., Wobbrock, J.O., Dastyar, T.: Age-related differences in performance with touchscreens compared to traditional mouse input. In: Proceedings of the SIGCHI Conference on Human Factors in Computing Systems (CHI 2013), pp. 343–346. ACM, New York (2013), doi:10.1145/2470654.2470703
3. Hourcade, J.P., Nguyen, C.M., Perry, K.B., Denburg, N.L.: PointAssist for Older Adults: Analyzing Sub-Movement Characteristics to Aid in Pointing Tasks. In: Proc. CHI 2010, pp. 1115–1124. ACM, New York (2010)
4. Kin, K., Agrawala, M., DeRose, T.: Determining the benefits of direct-touch, bimanual, and multifinger input on a multitouch workstation. In: Proc. GI 2009, pp. 119–124. Canadian Information Processing Society, Toronto (2009)
5. Kobayashi, M., Hiyama, A., Miura, T., Asakawa, C., Hirose, M., Ifukube, T.: Elderly user evaluation of mobile touchscreen interactions. In: Campos, P., Graham, N., Jorge, J., Nunes, N., Palanque, P., Winckler, M. (eds.) INTERACT 2011, Part I. LNCS, vol. 6946, pp. 83–99. Springer, Heidelberg (2011)
6. Nacenta, M.A., et al.: Separability of spatial manipulations in multi-touch interfaces. In: Proceedings of Graphics Interface 2009. Canadian Information Processing Society (2009)

7. Rogers, W.A., Fisk, A.D.: Technology Design, Usability and Aging: Human Factors Techniques and Considerations. In: Charness, N., Schaie, K.W. (eds.) Impact of Technology on Successful Aging, pp. 1–14. Springer, New York (2003)
8. Siek, K.A., Rogers, Y., Connelly, K.H.: Fat finger worries: How older and younger users physically interact with PDAs. In: Costabile, M.F., Paternó, F. (eds.) INTERACT 2005. LNCS, vol. 3585, pp. 267–280. Springer, Heidelberg (2005)
9. Stößel, C.: Familiarity as a factor in designing finger gestures for elderly users. In: Proc. MobileHCI 2009, Article 78, 2 pages. ACM, New York (2009)
10. Stößel, C., Blessing, L.: Mobile device interaction gestures for older users. In: Proc. NordiCHI 2010, pp. 793–796. ACM, New York (2010)
11. Stößel, C., Wandke, H., Blessing, L.: Gestural interfaces for elderly users: Help or hindrance? In: Kopp, S., Wachsmuth, I. (eds.) GW 2009. LNCS (LNAI), vol. 5934, pp. 269–280. Springer, Heidelberg (2010)
12. Werner, F., Werner, K., Oberzaucher, J.: Tablets for Seniors – An Evaluation of a Current Model (iPad). In: Ambient Assisted Living, Advanced Technologies and Societal Change, Part 4, pp. 177–184 (2012)
13. Wood, E., et al.: Use of computer input devices by older adults. Journal of Applied Gerontology 24(5), 419–438 (2005)

A Tablet-Based Approach to Facilitate the Viewing of Classroom Lecture by Low Vision Students

Stephanie Ludi, Michael Timbrook, and Piper Chester

Department of Software Engineering, Rochester Institute of Technology Rochester, USA
{salvse,mpt2360,pwc1203}@rit.edu

Abstract. In this paper we describe a tablet-based system that is designed to help students with partial sight access math and science lecture material in and out of the classroom. The instructor writes material on the whiteboard, that has a Mimio Capture bar affixed magnetically as well as sleeves for the markers. The lecture material is sent as written strokes that the iOS app displays for the student in real-time. Students can adjust the size and contrast of the material, as well as write notes on the lecture itself for later viewing. The access to lecture provided by the system provides students the ability to follow an active lecture and take more ownership over learning through note taking.

Keywords: Education, Mathematics, Tablet, Visually Impaired.

1 Introduction

In math and science classes, the instructor typically often writes on the board and refers to parts of the equations or diagrams as he/she presents the concepts to the class, who are asking questions and taking notes. Part of the presentation often involves working through examples or homework exercises. Unlike many humanities courses, where discussion and oral presentation are the primary means of conveying material, visual representations of material are critical in math and science courses.

In the United States, many low vision students have note takers, who are usually either another student in the course or a (paid) volunteer who sits in the course and takes notes. The result is that students have to wait to get class notes until after class, when it is too late to ask questions during the course of the lecture. The instructor's oral presentation is then disjoint from the written notes. The student often misses in-class activities that are written on the board or the student may miss written reminders or announcements that are not spoken. The reliance on another student's notes is risky, due to the reliance on the quality and quantity of another student's notes.

If resources allow, some students may use a camera, or CCTV sys-tem. These devices can take up valuable desk space, and can be awkward to follow lecture and take notes at the same time. The use of a handheld camera or monocular makes the task of watching the lecture through a small area and taking notes simultaneously a difficult task. These assistive technologies can be expensive, bulky, and heavy to transport to/from class. Additionally, glare from the board or an obstruction can impede access to material.

K. Miesenberger et al. (Eds.): ICCHP 2014, Part II, LNCS 8548, pp. 591–596, 2014.

Research has shown the importance of involving visually impaired students in the classroom experience beyond contrived, trivial experiences/activities that do not challenge the student or include them in the experiences that the rest of the class experiences [6]. AccessLecture seeks to address this gap, in terms of access to material presented on the board during lecture, enabling the student to ask questions at the time of presentation and participate in class activities that rely on presented material. AccessLecture also presents a single view, reducing the need for the student to shift focus between the board and their written notes.

Via the use of low-cost commercial Mimio hardware, the instructor's written strokes are displayed to the student in class as well as outside of class when the student reviews course material. The iPad is portable and has many accessibility features that already make it a good platform for visually impaired students. The other key aspect of AccessLecture is easy set up for both student and teacher. The student need only start the app and connect to the class and day's lecture shell. Instructor set up of the Mimio Capture hardware simply involves affixing a small bar to the board with a magnet and slipping markers into their respective sleeves, allowing for writing to occur without altering the instructor's style.

2 Related Work

The bulk of research focuses on making math and science more accessible to blind students. Researchers have explored lecture in terms of distance education such as embedding text-to-speech features in slides used in web-based lecture [5], [10], [14]. In terms of science instruction, research has shown the importance of involving visually impaired students in the classroom experience beyond contrived, trivial experiences/activities that do not challenge the student or include them in the experiences that the rest of the class experiences [6]. AccessLecture seeks to address this gap, in terms of access to material presented on the board during lecture, enabling the student to ask questions at the time of presentation and participate in class activities that rely on presented material.

The use of tactile tablets and other assistive technologies are very expensive and require extensive teacher training. A study published in the Journal of Visual Impairment and Blindness studied the use of various assistive technologies used by teachers in the classroom [1]. The study showed that a majority of teachers/staff that support visually impaired students are not prepared to use such technologies and thus students are impacted. The intent is for no training on the teacher's part in terms of presenting material on the whiteboard. Such low overhead will be important for teacher buy-in to use the system.

To make math more accessible, much research has been done on the creation of tactile or audio-based representations of material, including calculators and tablets that can be used for the study of math and science [2], [4,5], [7], [12,13,14]. In addition representations of math in speech, haptics, and Nemeth code are studied [10,11]. The preparation of materials using these techniques can be costly, time consuming and low vision students (who have functional vision) are more focused on visual issues such as magnification.

A recent project, Note Taker, allows a low vision student to view (and record) a lecture as well as take notes [3], [8]. The Note Taker team from Arizona State University designed a camera that enables a student to pan and zoom as needed in order to record lecture material. A PC Tablet-style laptop is used to view the video feed as well as take notes. The student can view notes and lecture material at a later time, or rewind lecture to help with an obstructed view of lecture material. Rather than relying on a camera, AccessLecture receives written material as strokes sent via Mimio hardware. No issues with glare or obstruction exist. Note taker's camera and software adds contrast and color inversion capabilities, while AccessLecture will have these features built into the iPad app with low overhead (as is the case with Zoom).

3 Design

Initial requirements were derived after surveys and interviews with students and teachers [9]. The process involved pre-college and university level math and science students and instructors. Results included technology and features preferences, as well as environmental and domain-specific information to aid the team in the design and testing activities.

The iPad app connects to a server and requests the lecture stream, which is saved locally to the iPad (see Figure 1), enabling the user to zoom in/out with either multi-touch (pinching) or icons, adjust contrast, and take notes on the ongoing lecture (which can be saved). The student navigates the whiteboard by moving the area being focused on with a finger. Notes can be written digitally, with a keyboard or with a stylus or finger. Additional preferences can be set for note taking colors, thickness, along with zoom speed.

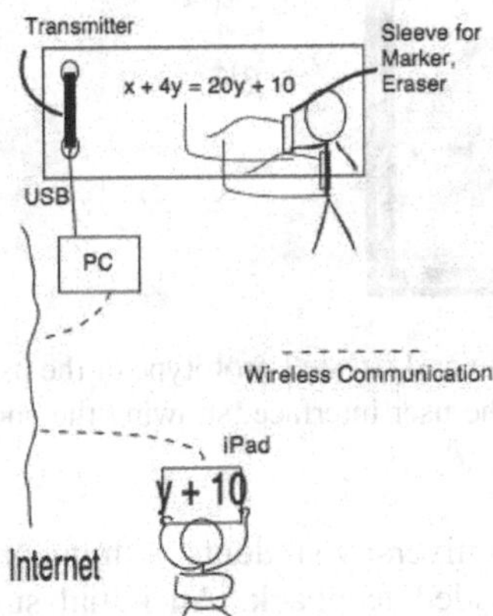

Fig. 1. Overview of the AccessLecture system showing the Mimio hardware sending stroke data to server then onto the student's iPad

The Apple iPad was selected because of its generous 10-inch screen size, native touch/gesture support, accessibility features, and portability. The iPad is a mainstream device that can also be used for other purposes. The Mimio was selected for the proof-of-concept means of capturing written material due to its portability and low cost. In addition, the capture of the strokes in the marker/eraser requires less bandwidth than capturing the entire whiteboard at once (as a camera would do). Such stroke-based capture also mitigates issues with glare, position of the teacher or accommodating obstacles which can impact capture of material with a camera.

The user interface for the iPad AccessLecture app primarily consists of the lecture view (see Figure 2a). In this view, the student views lecture according to their viewing preferences (zoom, inversion) and adds/views their notes. In future, the student can fully navigate lecture as in a similar manner as watching a video such as the use of time indices to locate specific parts of the video. The view has modes for material viewing and for note taking on the lecture itself. Note taking requires support for text, math/ science notation.

4 Methodology

After the real time presentation of the lecture material was validated technically and initial feedback by two visually impaired stake-holders was considered, the team wanted to ensure that the AccessLecture user interface is visually accessible and the tasks of following a short lecture and taking notes on a simulated lecture can be completed to the user's satisfaction.

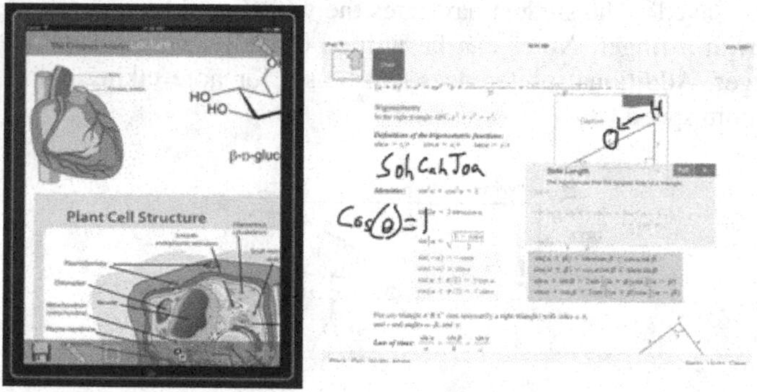

Fig. 2. a - (left) a screenshot of an early, tested prototype of the user interface, b - (right) a more recent version (in progress) of the user interface, showing the addition of a note on top of lecture material

During initial testing, ten university students with uncorrected vision that is considered to be low vision provided feedback. An initial survey gathered background information (e.g. visual acuity, use of accessibility features, use of mobile devices) while a post-survey focused on user preferences regarding the user interface, workflow, and tasks. During each user session, the participants were asked to complete a set of tasks during a 5 minute, simulated lecture that talked about biology and a math problem. Participants were asked to perform a fixed set of tasks (setting interface preferences, identifying the different icons and their purpose, feature navigation, content zooming, and typing notes with both a virtual keyboard or writing directly on the screen). The app captured the participant's notes.

5 Results

The findings present direction for interaction and workflow in the lecture view, and provide feedback for user preferences. At this stage ease of learning and user satisfaction are of particular importance. Table 1 provides a sample of these findings.

Table 1. Initial Feedback for Accessibility

Accessibility Preferences and Satisfaction	
Ability to zoom in to read written material and diagrams	9/10
Pinching gesture to zoom in/out is useful	8/10
Buttons and double tapping to zoom out useful	4/10
The zoom increment settings are useful (tap to zoom)	6/10
The icons are identifiable, size is easy to select and does not obscure content	10/10

All participants expressed interest in using AccessLecture in class and to take notes. They liked the option to use their finger or a stylus to take notes, and 7 out of 10 liked the ability to write on the ongoing lecture. The note-taking interface was strongly disliked. For example, the eraser icon was not clear enough and over time, the teacher's writing clashes with the notes. The result has been the development of a note manager that flags a note that can then be activated, thus removing the clashing between student notes and lecture material. In addition some icons are being changed to better adhere to changes to Apple's UI Guidelines for iOS version 7.

6 Conclusions and Future Work

While the basic accessibility features and settings have been implemented to support the lecture viewing workflow, the recently overhauled note taking user interface remains to be tested to assess improvement over this last prototype. Recent work (renamed AccessMath) also seeks to provide more flexible text and graphic notes that are attached to lecture at a time stamp. Additional customizations to notes and lecture navigation features are also being finalized. In future, improved storage for lectures, time shifting for recordings, and the audio recording of the lecture are planned. The application also needs testing in a classroom. These tasks will provide a more robust solution that can be used by low vision students, as well as other students who need a central means of accessing course material.

References

1. Abner, G., Lahm, E.: Implementation of Assistive Technology with Students Who Are Visually Impaired: Teachers' Readiness. Journal of Visually Impairment and Blindness 96(2), 98–105 (2005)

2. Brown, L.M., Brewster, S.A.: Drawing by ear: interpreting sonified line graphs. In: Proc. International Conference on Auditory Display, ICAD 2003, Boston, MA, pp. 152–156 (2003)
3. Black, J.A., Hayden, D.S.: The Note-Taker: An assistive technology that allows students who are legally blind to take notes in the classroom. In: 2010 IEEE Computer Society Conference on Computer Vision and Pattern Recognition Workshops (CVPRW), June 13-18, pp. 1–8 (2010), doi:10.1109/CVPRW.2010.5543587
4. Bonebright, T.L., Nees, M.A., Connerley, T.T., McCain, G.R.: Testing the effectiveness of sonified graphs for education: A programmatic research project. In: Proc. International Conference on Auditory Display, Espoo, Finland, pp. 62–66 (2001)
5. Davison, B., Walker, B.N.: Sonification Sandbox overhaul: software standard for auditory graphs. In: Proc. Int'l. Conf. Auditory Display (ICAD 2007), pp. 386–390 (2007)
6. Fraser, W.J., Maguvhe: Teaching life sciences to blind and visually impaired learners. Journal of Biological Education 42(2), 84–89 (2008)
7. Gardner, J.A.: The accessible graphing calculator: a self-voicing graphing scientific calculator for windows (1999), `http://dots.physics.orst.edu/calculator/`
8. Hayden, D., Astrauskas, M., Yan, Q., Zhou, L., Black, J.: Note-taker 3.0: an assistive technology enabling students who are legally blind to take notes in class. In: Proceedings of the 13th International ACM SIGACCESS Conference on Computers and Accessibility (Dundee, Scotland, October, 2011), Assets 2011. ACM, New York (2011)
9. Ludi, S., Canter, A., Ellis, L., Shrestha, A.: Requirements Gathering for Assistive Technology that Includes Low Vision and Sighted Users. In: Workshop on Usability and Accessibility Focused Requirements Engineering, as part of the International Conference on Software Engineering (June 2012)
10. Rughooputh, S., Santally, M.: Integrating text-to-speech software into pedagogically sound teaching and learning scenarios. Journal of Educational Technology Research and Development 57(1), 131–145 (2009)
11. Stanley, P.: Assessing the mathematics related communication requirements of the blind in education and career. In: Miesenberger, K., Klaus, J., Zagler, W., Karshmer, A. (eds.) ICCHP 2008. LNCS, vol. 5105, pp. 888–891. Springer, Heidelberg (2008)
12. TouchGraphics, Talking tactile tablet (2011), `http://www.touchgraphics.com/`
13. Walker, B.N., Lindsay, J., Godfrey, J.: The audio abacus: representing a wide range of values with accuracy and precision. In: Proc. 10th International Conference on Auditory Display (ICAD 2004), Sydney, Australia (2004)
14. Walker, B., Mauney: Universal design of auditory graphs: a comparison of sonification mappings for visually impaired and sighted listeners. ACM Transactions on Accessible Computing (TACCESS) 2(3), 16 pages (2010)

The iPad as a Mobile Learning Tool for Post-secondary Students with Disabilities

Linda Chmiliar and Carrie Anton

Athabasca University, Athabasca, Canada
{lindac,carriea}@athabascau.ca

Abstract. The use of the iPad as a mobile learning tool in post-secondary settings with students with disabilities is an area still relatively unstudied. This research study investigates how 2 post-secondary students with disabilities participating in a university course, used iPads in their studies. The study examines: how students used the iPad; if the iPad, the course materials on the iPad, and the apps helped to support students in their course work; what issues arose and how they were addressed; and what kinds of supports the students needed to use this tool effectively in their studies.

Keywords: Mobile Technology, Special Needs, Post-Secondary Students, iPad.

1 Introduction

The use of the iPad as a mobile learning tool in post-secondary settings with students with disabilities is an area still relatively unstudied. This research study investigated how 2 post-secondary students with disabilities, used iPads provided to them for their studies. The study examined: how the students used the iPads; if the iPad, the course materials on the iPad, and the apps helped to support students in their course work; what issues arose and how they were addressed; and what kinds of supports the students needed to use this tool effectively in their studies. This paper reports on results from the initial stages of the study.

2 Background

The iPad is a relatively new learning tool whose use is by and large unstudied in the post-secondary academic environment. The iPad may be able to support students with disabilities by providing access to electronic e-text readers, digital course materials, and apps that can be used for a range of academic activities.

In a survey of post-secondary students, it was found that increasing numbers of students own tablets, and increasingly prefer mobile devices for reading compared to previous results where students clearly indicated that they preferred hard text [1]. Due to the increasing ownership of tablets by students, the academic community has started to explore the use of tablets to deliver academic content as well as examining the use of digital textbooks. Several studies have looked at the use of digital books

K. Miesenberger et al. (Eds.): ICCHP 2014, Part II, LNCS 8548, pp. 597–600, 2014.

and e-readers with varying results. Demski [2] reported the results of a study with three universities, and concluded the e-readers had limitations that made them inadequate for reading textbooks. On the other hand, benefits including a reduction in the amount of paper used and a reduction in textbook costs have been reported [3]. Martinez-Estrada and Conaway [4] in a study of the use of Kindle eBooks found that the ebooks supported student learning and course outcomes. Geist [5] also explored the use of iBooks on iPads with students, and found that students liked using iBooks for course work and appreciated the convenience it afforded.

There has been minimal research on the use of the iPad as a learning tool in the post-secondary environment. Bush and Cameron [6] found that the majority of students perceived electronic course materials on an iPad in the app, iAnnotate, to be as good as or better than printed course materials. In addition, the multi-modal functionality of the iPad supported study and classroom learning. Mang and Wardley [3] found that 96% of student participants in their study felt that the iPad tablet had enhanced their learning, and 92% indicated that they would like to use the tool in future courses. Nee [7] examined the use of e-texts and found that students indicated that the use of e-texts helped to improve their academic work.

Students with disabilities have been enrolling in post-secondary institutions for many years but unfortunately, education success for these students tends to be lower than that of the general student population. The provision a range of supports for students on the iPad may be an important course accommodation for students with disabilities to help them succeed, but there is a lack of research in this area.

3 Method

This research project was structured around a Participatory Action Research (PAR) model that focused on co-developing a research program with people rather than for people [8]. It involved participants in the research process from the beginning of the project, through the data gathering and analysis, to the final conclusions [9]. The participants in this PAR were two students with permanent, diagnosed disabilities who access alternate format course material services from the university. Each student is enrolled in at least one course at the university. The students received an iPad with retinal display to use for a course loaded with the course materials in various accessible file formats including PDF, RTF, DOC, DOCX and EPUB. A range of apps that could be used for learning and studying were also loaded onto the iPads, including apps for reading, writing, reference, planning and organization, study skills, advance organizers, and communication. A third iPad was set up in an identical fashion in order to support the students with technical issues and training. Course material was distributed to the students via Drop Box. Technical support, training and interviews were available via e-mail, telephone, Skype and Face Time.

Once informed consent was obtained from the students volunteering to participate, each student met with the researchers at the beginning of the study to receive information about the course materials and apps on the iPad. The students were able to ask questions and a plan was developed as to how the student was going to use the iPad in the course. Each student met with the researchers once a month to review how the student was using the iPad and to address any issues. Resources and training material were frequently distributed to the students with the intention of prompting them to continue to explore the various categories of apps and tools on the iPad.

The data collection for this qualitative study primarily involved field notes from each meeting with each student. This data was organized topically to look for patterns and trends.

4 Results and Conclusion

The results reported here represent data collected during the first half of the project. Full data collection will likely be complete July 2014.

The first student was a female over 40 years of age. She has a psychiatric disability and has difficulties with reading and writing. This student owns a number of technologies including a Mac computer, an iPhone, and an iPad with Retinal Display, but primarily uses the desk top computer in her studies. During the initial stages of the research this first student found a number of apps that she is now using successfully in her studies. The student indicated that she now uses the iAnnotate app for everything as it is a "wicked" app that works much more like a program than an app. She was using the Voice Dream app to download reading materials and liked the voice in text to speech function. The student had used the Inspiration app for mapping out course content that had to be memorized and was very pleased with the dictionary app that was provided. The student reported that "…if you find something that works for you, you sort of stay with it and don't explore more." She felt that time is very precious when you are a student and the time to explore tools to support learning is very limited.

The second student was a female between the ages of 30 and 40 who has difficulties with writing, idea expression, distractibility and organization. This student owns as a DELL laptop, Apple computer, and a smart phone. At the beginning of the research, the second student found that she was overwhelmed because there were so many apps available and she felt that she did not "have time to fool around with them." She indicated that if she had to spend time to figure out an app, she did not want to use it. Gradually, she found apps that she liked to use including: Pages, Dropbox, Bookshelf, and Dragon Dictation. The student reported that she now takes the iPad everywhere she goes and finds that the size and weight of the iPad convenient. She also reported that she now uses the iPad for almost all of her learning. Her laptop is now only being used to format and submit assignments and that she has "…not touched (her) computer much in the last (month)." The student also indicated that the iPad really help her to "keep…distractions minimal" because her social media was not available.

Despite having very different backgrounds and learning needs, the two students in the initial stages of this study reported similar findings in a number of areas. Both students expressed frustration with trying to find apps, indicating that there are too many choices and not enough time as a student explore, find, and learn effective learning tools. Both students indicated a strong preference for apps on the iPad that were easy to figure out and use, that had the features they required for learning. Once they found apps that met their needs they were happy to incorporate them into their learning routines, and both students reported that when they found what they liked – they were "kind of stuck on what (they) liked." Both students were surprised at what they were able to do on the iPad, and both students had found apps loaded on the iPad that met the majority of their specific learning needs.

For the second student, the mobility that the iPad affords her was a significant factor. The student indicated that she takes the iPad everywhere she goes and "… (does) homework in my truck or at work." Being able to work on her course work anywhere anytime was a huge plus for this student.

A few difficulties with the iPad implementation occurred. Both students reported not having time to figure complex apps out, preferring apps that were simple and easy, but functional. Time challenges were also related to figuring out how to use the device, finding apps they liked, and getting all of their information on the iPad.

Overall, the initial results for this study are very surprising. Within a few short weeks after receiving the iPads for use in this research study, both students indicated that they were now doing almost all their course work on the iPad despite any difficulties they had experienced. The following months will provide additional information regarding how the iPad can support learning for post-secondary students with disabilities.

References

1. Desantis, N.: Tablet ownership triples among college students. Chronicle of Higher Education 58 (2012)
2. Demski, J.: The device versus the book. Campus Technology 23, 26–34 (2010)
3. Mang, C., Wardley, L.: Effective adoption of tablets in post-secondary education: Recommendations based on a trial of iPads in university classes. Journal of Information Technology Education, Innovations in Practice 11, 301–317 (2012)
4. Martinez-Estrada, P., Conaway, R.: E-Books: The next step in educational innovation. Business Communication Quarterly 75, 125–135 (2012)
5. Guist, E.: The game changer: Using iPads in college teacher education classes. College Student Journal 45, 758–768 (2011)
6. Bush, M.H., Cameron, A.H.: Digital Course Materials: A Case Study of the Apple iPad in the Academic Environment. UMI ProQuest Dissertations & Theses (2011)
7. Nee, E.A.: College Students with Learning Disabilities: Experiences Using E-Texts. In: UMI ProQuest Dissertations & Theses (2012)
8. McIntrye, A.: Participatory Action Research. In: SAGE University Paper. SAGE Publications,Thousand Oaks (2007); Google eBook
9. Green, L., George, A., Daniel, M., Frankish, J., Herbert, C., Bowled, W., O-Neill, M.: Appendix C: Guidelines for Participatory Research in health Promotion. In: Minkler, M., Wallerstein, N. (eds.) Community-Based Participator Research for Health. Jossey-Bass, Inc., San Francisco (2003)

Author Index

Ahmad, Muneeb Imtiaz I-513
Ahmetovic, Dragan I-537, I-564
Ahn, Chunghyun I-8, I-53
Akita, Junichi II-65
Ala, Silvia I-297
Alabastro, Nicolò I-564
Alavi, Ali I-214, I-237
Ali, Syed Abid I-356
Aljaam, Jihad Mohamad II-569
Al-Khalifa, Atheer S. I-145
Al-Khalifa, Hend S. I-145
Alm, Norman I-264
Almasri, Bassam I-572
Al-Mouh, Najd A. I-145
AlRowais, Fadwa II-565
Amado-Salvatierra, Hector R. II-338
Andreasson, Kim I-137
Andrich, Renzo II-275
Angkananon, Kewalin II-267
Antener, Gabriela I-157
Anton, Carrie II-597
Aoki, Takamitsu II-238
Aranda, Joan II-152
Arato, Andras II-393
Archambault, Dominique I-606, II-490
Argyropoulos, Vassilios I-77
Argyropoulos, Vassilis I-533
Arteaga, Sonia M. I-634
Ashikawa, Taira I-69
Astell, Arlene I-264
Aupetit, Sébastien I-93
Aussenac-Gilles, Nathalie I-61

Balakrishnan, M. II-34
Balasi, Panagiota I-506
Baljko, Melanie II-287
Ball, Simon II-311
Barouti, Marialena II-108, II-358
Batanero, Concha II-338
Belda-Lois, Juan-Manuel I-256, I-260, II-303
Benavidez, Carlos I-101
Ben Yahia, Nour II-482
Bermúdez i Badia, Sergi I-113
Bernareggi, Cristian I-537, I-564
Bianchetti, Roberto I-181, I-193, I-197
Bier, Michael I-169
Birbaumer, Niels I-248
Bogdan, Martin I-248
Bohnsack, Marco I-141
Bolfing, Anton I-109, I-157
Bolinger, Elaina I-248
Bordegoni, Monica I-289
Bornschein, Jens I-545, I-588, II-26
Bose, Roopa I-121
Bosse, Ingo Karl II-366
Boulares, Mehrez II-474
Bouzid, Yosra II-458
Bramwell-Dicks, Anna I-348
Brayda, Luca II-12
Brimant, Loïc II-210
Brin, Julie II-210
Brzoza, Piotr I-519
Bühler, Christian I-17, II-54
Bumbalek, Zdenek II-374
Burzagli, Laura II-172
Buykx, Lucy I-348

Cabrera, Rafael II-252
Calabrese, Stefania I-157
Campus, Claudio II-12
Cantón, Paloma I-463
Cardoso, Claudia I-101
Cardoso, Francisco I-297
Carrasco, Eduardo II-100
Casals, Alicia II-152
Cassola, Fernando I-297
Castelló, Purificación II-303
Chamonikolaou, Sofia I-77
Chanana, Piyush II-34
Charitakis, Konstantinos II-108, II-358
Chen, Chen-Ming II-528
Chen, Chia-Ling II-203
Chen, Guey-Shya II-532
Chen, Hsieh-Ching II-203
Chen, Ming-Chung II-350, II-528
Chen, Weiqin I-502
Chen, Yong I-642

Chester, Piper I-377, II-591
Chmiliar, Linda II-577, II-579, II-597
Choi, Kup-Sze II-244
Christensen, Lars Ballieu II-342
Chu, Chi Nung I-459, II-350
Church, Paul II-408
Cizdziel, Benjamin I-403
Cockshull, George I-41
Colineau, Joseph II-210
Connor, Joshue O I-348
Constantinescu, Angela II-128
Cottrell, Peter I-634
Coughlan, James M. I-427, I-437
Covarrubias, Mario I-289
Cremers, Anita I-494
Crespo, José II-303
Crombie, David I-45
Csuti, Péter I-272
Cugini, Umberto I-289
Czaja, Sara J. I-455

Dahn, Ingo II-323
Dalle, Patrice II-454
Darvishy, Alireza I-185
Darzentas, Jenny S. I-340, II-260
Das, Supriya II-34
Davidson, Matthew I-129
Debevc, Matjaž II-498
de Carvalho, Fausto I-297
Deligiorgi, Despina I-533
Depta, Tomasz I-301, I-309, I-399
Dias, Roberto I-113
Dietzsch, Nils I-169
Ding, Chaohai II-73
Do, Julie I-403
Doblies, Luchin I-185
Dobosz, Krzysztof I-301, I-309, I-399
Dobosz, Magdalena I-301, I-399
Dorigo, Martin Lukas I-383
Dowland, Paul I-383
Draffan, E.A. II-540, II-543
Dubielzig, Markus II-100
Dye, Richard I-264

Ebling, Sarah II-404
Eden, Sigal II-386
Edler, Cordula I-177
El Bedewy, Shereen I-525
El Ghoul, Oussama II-466
Eljailani, Murtada I-360, I-369
Elkabani, Islam I-572
Ellis, Maggie I-264
El-Safty, Ahmed II-116
Embregts, Petri I-276
Emiliani, Pier Luigi II-172
Erle, Markus I-181, I-193
Ertl, Thomas II-116, II-120
Ervé, Sylvie II-210
Esser, Tyler I-403
Evers, Vanessa I-276

Fajardo-Flores, Silvia I-606
Falk, Vivienne II-404
Farcy, René I-411
Fels, Deborah I. I-1, II-408
Felzer, Torsten II-180
Feraday, Ray II-287
Ferdinand, Peter II-323
Fernandes, Jorge I-101
Ferracuti, Francesco II-156
Ferreras, Alberto II-303
Ferreras Remesal, Alberto I-256, I-260
Fiołka, Tomasz I-301, I-309, I-399
Flores, German I-403
Fonseca, Benjamim I-297
Fösleitner, Claudia II-100
Fritsch, Lothar I-316
Fuertes, José L. I-463
Fujimoto, Yoshiharu II-65
Fujiyoshi, Akio II-18, II-331
Fujiyoshi, Mamoru II-18, II-331
Fume, Kosei I-69
Fusco, Giovanni I-427

Gaisbauer, Gottfried I-231
Gallagher, Blaíthín II-260
Gappa, Henrike I-445
García, Carlos II-303
García-Cabot, Antonio II-338
García-López, Eva II-338
Gardner, John A. I-580
Garrido, Marcelo II-252
Garschall, Markus I-650, II-583
George, Julia I-169
Gerdzhev, Martin II-408
Gerino, Andrea I-537, I-564
Giannoutakis, Konstantinos II-275
Giantomassi, Andrea II-156
Gilbert, Lester II-267
Gill, Carol J. I-471

Goldrick, Michael II-342
Gómez, Isabel María II-252
González, Ángel L. I-463
Goto, Hideaki I-658
Götzelmann, Timo II-1
Gowans, Gary I-264
Gower, Valerio II-275
Gruber, Markus I-231
Guerrero, Luis A. II-164
Guerrier, Yohan I-419
Guillot, Julie II-210
Gutiérrez, Henry I-101
Gutiérrez y Restrepo, Emmanuelle I-101

Haddad, Zehira I-642, II-423
Hafner, Petra I-441
Hajjam, Jawad II-210
Hakkinen, Markku II-8
Hamidi, Foad II-287
Hamřík, Pavel I-85
Harakawa, Tetsumi I-602, I-630
Harriehausen-Mühlbauer, Bettina I-383
Heck, Helmut II-54
Hernández, Rocael II-338
Hersh, Marion II-307, II-315
Hettich, Dirk T. I-248
Heumader, Peter I-231, I-237, II-58, II-234
Heylen, Dirk I-276
Hibbard, Ellen II-408
Hintermair, Manfred II-498
Hobé, Thierry II-210
Hoda, Takuma I-658
Hofer, Samuel I-181, I-193
Honda, Tatsuya II-382
Hong, Ki-Hyung I-49
Horiike, Kazuki I-33
Hosono, Naotsune II-397
Huang, Yu Ting I-459
Hulme, David I-41
Hutter, Hans-Peter I-185

Iarlori, Sabrina II-156
Ikeuchi, Hidetaka II-256
Ingber, Sara II-386
Inoue, Hiromitsu II-397
Inoue, Kaoru I-451
Ishii, Kazuyoshi I-602, I-630
Istenic Starcic, Andreja II-516, II-520
Ito, Kiyohide II-65
Ivanchev, Mihail II-81
Iwabuchi, Mamoru II-238

Jaballah, Kabil II-439, II-446
Jadán-Guerrero, Janio II-164
Jafri, Rabia I-356, II-551
James, Abi II-543
Jang, Inseon I-8, I-53
Jang, Younseon I-8
Jang, Yujin I-49
Jaworek, Gerhard I-662
Jebali, Maher II-454
Jemni, Mohamed II-431, II-439, II-446, II-454, II-458, II-466, II-474, II-482
Jessel, Nadine I-596
Jouffrais, Christophe II-92
Juhasz, Zoltan II-393
Jürgensen, Helmut I-121

Kacorri, Hernisa I-614
Kaklanis, Nikolaos II-275
Kammoun, Slim II-92
Kamollimsakul, Sorachai I-332
Kanahori, Toshihiro I-557
Karshmer, Arthur I. I-517
Kaser, Karl II-234
Kerr, Sharon II-520
Kitamura, Naoya I-360
Klein, Eduard I-109
Klein, Michael II-583
Ko, Chien-Chuan II-350, II-528
Kobayashi, Makoto I-283, II-512
Köble, Josef I-153
Koda, Satoko II-42
Koester, Daniel II-128
Kolski, Christophe I-419
Komatsu, Takanori II-65
Kopeček, Ivan I-85
Kouroupetroglou, Georgios I-77, I-533, I-614
Koutny, Reinhard II-58, II-234
Kožuh, Ines II-498
Kudo, Hiroaki II-506
Kudo, Kazuki I-360
Kulyukin, Vladimir II-50
Kunic, Toni II-287
Kunz, Andreas I-205, I-214, I-237
Kurniawan, Sri I-403, I-634, II-283
Kuroda, Yuka I-69

Kuroda, Yusuke II-18
Kushalnagar, Poorna II-415
Kushalnagar, Raja I-25, II-415
Kuwahara, Noriaki I-433
Kwatra, Kunal II-34

Lachmann, Pablo II-323
Laparra-Hernández, José I-256
Laparra-Herrero, José I-260
Lathière, Benoît II-490
Lee, Heeyeon I-49
Lemariè, Julie I-61
Li, Shujun I-129
Li, Yunjia I-41
Liimatainen, Jukka II-8
Lim, Wootaek I-53
Li-Tzang, Cecilia W.P. II-203
Lo, Hui-Shan II-203, II-532
Lo, King-Hung II-244
Lohmeijer, Andries I-276
Longhi, Sauro II-156
Lopez Krahe, Jaime I-642, II-423
López-Vicente, Amparo I-260
Louis, Nathalie II-210
Loyo, Estíbaliz II-100
Lucke, Ulrike II-81
Ludi, Stephanie I-377, II-591

Macé, Marc J-M. II-92
MacKenzie, I. Scott II-180, II-195
Maćkowski, Michał I-519
Maganheim, Johannes S. I-513
Manduchi, Roberto I-403
Mansutti, Alessandro I-289
Markus, Norbert II-393
Martínez, Loïc I-463
Martinez, Manuel II-128
Martínez-Normand, Loïc I-101, II-295
Martins, Paulo I-297
Martos, Aineias I-77, I-533
Masatani, Akihiro II-65
Mascetti, Sergio I-537, I-564
Mashat, Alaa I-478
Másilko, Lukáš I-549
Matsumoto, Tetsuya II-506
Matsuzaka, Haruo I-360, I-369
Mattheiss, Elke I-650
Matuz, Tamara I-248
McCall, Karen I-202
McDonald, John C. II-559
McNaught, Alistair II-543
Mech, Mrinal II-34
Memeo, Mariacarla II-12
Merlin, Bruno II-195
Mersch, Pierre I-45
Miesenberger, Klaus I-161, I-205, I-220, I-231, I-237, I-324, I-525, II-58, II-234
Minagawa, Hiroki I-33
Minatani, Kazunori I-622, II-42
Mintz, Joseph I-486
Mitobe, Kazutaka I-13
Miura, Atuyoshi II-256
Miura, Masamichi II-226
Miura, Takahiro I-360, I-369
Mizuoka, Yoshiaki I-69
Moder, Thomas I-441
Mohamad, Yehya I-245, I-248, I-445
Mojahid, Mustapha I-61
Molina, Alberto Jesús II-252
Moore, Douglas I-41
Morales, Lourdes M. I-634
Morgado, Leonel I-297
Morimoto, Kazunari I-433
Morita, Masahiro I-69
Mühlhäuser, Max I-209, I-214, I-226, I-237
Murali, Vidya I-427
Muratet, Mathieu II-210
Muskens, Luuk I-391
Mussinelli, Cristina I-4

Nagatoshi, Masuji II-256
Nair, Sankaran N. I-455
Nakajima, Kazuya I-630
Nakajima, Sawako I-13
Nakamura, Kenryu II-238
Nakamura, Mio I-451
Nakanishi, Miwa II-397
Naveteur, Janick I-419
Neerincx, Mark I-494
Nguyen, Phuoc Loc II-404
Nietzio, Annika I-137, II-54
Niiyama, Yuka II-65
Nikolaraizi, Magda I-77
Nordbrock, Gabriele I-445
Nussbaum, Gerhard II-218
Nyéki, Ágnes I-272

Obraczka, Katia I-403
Oh, Tae I-25

Ohnishi, Noboru I-33, II-506
Ohsawa, Akiko II-331
Ohtsuka, Satoshi I-602, I-630
Okada, Maiko I-451
Okamoto, Makoto II-65, II-382
Okochi, Naoyuki I-13
Olmedo, Rafael II-100
Oltra, Alfonso II-303
Onishi, Junji I-360, I-369
Ono, Tetsuo II-65
Ono, Tsukasa I-360, I-369
Oriola, Bernard I-61
Osawa, Akiko II-18
Ošlejšek, Radek I-85
Ostie, Patrick I-214
Ota, Yuko II-331
Otaegui, Oihana II-100
Othman, Achraf II-431
Otón, Salvador II-338
Otsuki, Ryoko II-65

Page, Álvaro I-256
Papadopoulos, Konstantinos II-108, II-358
Paredes, Hugo I-297
Parker, Stefan II-218
Parr, Aidan I-348
Parsons, Sarah I-478
Paul, Rohan II-34
Pavkovic, Aleksander II-1
Pecl, Jiří I-549
Pelka, Bastian I-17
Perdomo, Dolores I-455
Perl, Alexander I-169
Petrie, Helen I-313, I-332, I-340, I-348, II-260
Petz, Andrea I-161, I-324
Pfab, Isabel I-494
Plhák, Jaromír I-85
Pluke, Michael II-295
Poirier, Franck I-419
Pöll, Daniel I-237
Pölzer, Stephan I-220, I-231, I-237
Ponsard, Christophe II-136
Popescu, Cristina II-210
Poppe, Ronald I-276
Poveda, Rakel II-303
Poveda-Puente, Rakel I-260
Power, Christopher I-332, I-340, I-348
Prescher, Denise I-588, II-26
Ptak, Jakub I-309
Puhl, Steffen I-141
Pullmann, Jaroslav I-445
Purdy-Say, Aidan I-41

Radeck-Arneth, Stephan I-226
Radomski, Stefan I-209, I-226
Ramachandran, Vignesh I-25
Rapp, Bastian E. I-662
Rasta, Kamyar I-137
Rath, Matthias I-177
Raynal, Mathieu II-195
Reddy, Thimma II-50
Regal, Georg I-650
Reidsma, Dennis I-276
Reins, Frank II-54
Renaud, Karen I-129
Riesch, Markus I-109, I-197
Riga, Paraskevi I-614
Rinderknecht, Stephan II-180
Rivas Gil, Salvador II-148
Robinson, James I-41
Robra-Bissantz, Susanne I-169
Rosenstiel, Wolfgang I-248
Rouillé, Vincent I-93
Roush, Daniel II-408
Rubin, Zachary II-283

Sahasrabudhe, Shrirang II-8
Sakajiri, Masatsugu I-360, I-369
Sakuma, Naomi I-451
Saleh, Moutaz II-569
Sánchez Martín, Víctor II-148
Sano, Syoudai II-238
Sasaki, Chihiro I-451
Sasaki, Nobuyuki I-602, I-630
Sasaki, Yuta II-18
Sato, Yuji I-33
Sauzin, Damien II-188
Schauerte, Boris II-128
Schmitz, Bernhard II-116, II-120
Schnelle-Walka, Dirk I-209, I-214, I-226, I-237
Schouten, Dylan I-494
Schrammel, Johann I-650
Schulz, Richard I-455
Schulz, Trenton I-316
Schulze, Eva II-144
Schwarz, Thorsten I-662
Shahid, Suleman I-391, I-513

Shen, Huiying I-427
Shen, I-hsuan II-203
Shpigelman, Carmit-Noa I-471
Signore, Alessandro I-506
Sik Lanyi, Cecilia I-272
Simaioforidis, Zisis II-358
Simon, Helen J. I-437
Snaprud, Mikael I-137
Snoeck, Vincent II-136
Soler, Andrés II-303
Sorin, Laurent I-61
Spencer, Adam I-202
Spiller, John II-100
Stengel, Ingo I-383
Stevens, Tara II-408
Stevns, Tanja II-342
Stiefelhagen, Rainer II-128
Stöger, Bernhard I-525
Stolz, David I-185
Suenaga, Takatoshi II-89
Sullivan, Helen II-8
Suzuki, Masakazu I-557
Suzuki, Takuya II-512
Swallow, David I-348
Szabó, Ferenc I-272
Szucs, Veronika I-272

Taibbi, Marzia I-537
Takahashi, Yoshiyuki II-226
Takeuchi, Koichiro II-506
Takeuchi, Yoshinori I-33, II-506
Taniguchi, Kimihiko II-238
Tekin, Ender I-437
Thaller, David II-218
Thelen, Manuela I-445
Timbrook, Michael I-377, II-591
Tollefson, Travis II-283
Tomita, Yutaka II-397
Toro, Jorge Andres II-559
Truillet, Frédéric Philippe II-188
Tscheligi, Manfred I-650, II-583
Tsuji, Airi I-433
Tzovaras, Dimitrios II-275

Uebelbacher, Andreas I-197

Valenzuela, David II-252
van Cann, Paul I-391
van Delden, Robby I-276
van der Vos, Peter I-276
van Dijk, Betsy I-494
van Lent, Rico I-391
van Oorsouw, Wietske I-276
Vaughan, Philip I-264
Velasco, Carlos A. I-348, I-445
Vella, Frédéric II-188, II-210
Vigouroux, Nadine II-188, II-210
Vijfvinkel, Alexander I-391
Vinagre, Manuel II-152
Vlad, Petra II-210
Voegler, Jens I-545
Voigt, Achim I-662
Votis, Konstantinos II-275

Wada, Kazuyoshi I-451
Wakatsuki, Daisuke I-33
Wald, Mike I-41, I-478, II-73, II-267, II-565
Wasserburger, Wolfgang II-100
Watanabe, Tetsuya II-42
Weber, Gerhard I-545, I-588, II-26
Wieser, Manfred I-441
Wilhelm, Elisabeth I-662
Wills, Gary II-73, II-565
Wojaczek, Marcin I-301, I-309, I-399
Wolfe, Rosalee II-559
Wu, Ting-Fang II-532
Wu, Ya-Ping II-528
Wulf, Linda II-583

Yabuno, Naoki I-433
Yamagami, Tetsujiro I-13
Yamaguchi, Katsuhito I-557
Yamaguchi, Toshimitsu II-42
Yang, Guang II-238
Yeh, Yao-Ming II-528
Yuan, Tangming I-506

Zaim, Emre I-231
Zantout, Rached I-572
Zbakh, Mohammed II-423
Zegarra Flores, Jesus I-411
Zelenka, Jan II-374
Zinke, Francis II-81
Zirk, Anna II-144
Zirpel, Hannes I-169